SPOT QUIZ

"They still believe in things like curfews. Imagine a Big Ten school ten years ago . . ."

"Almost equal number of cats and chicks. The mellow art hip style predominates . . ."

"Guys admit that 'we don't really know how to date and are sexually frustrated . . .' "

"BC pills available from student health . . ."

"People are talking about pledging and pinning . . ."

"Lids go for $10 and you can smoke on campus. Acid is prevalent among younger kids . . ."

"Academically excellent but very difficult . . ."

"Cats and chicks are liberated, professors are liberated, secretaries are liberated, everyone is liberated . . ."

What colleges are they talking about? You'll find all—and we do mean *all*—the answers in

THE UNDERGROUND GUIDE TO THE COLLEGE OF YOUR CHOICE

SIGNET and MENTOR Books of Special Interest

The Underground Guide to the College of Your Choice

SUSAN BERMAN

"My real message?
Keep a good head and
always carry a lightbulb."
—BOB DYLAN

A SIGNET BOOK from
NEW AMERICAN LIBRARY
TIMES MIRROR

SIGNET, SIGNET CLASSICS, MENTOR, PLUME AND MERIDIAN BOOKS
are published by The New American Library, Inc.,
1301 Avenue of the Americas, New York, New York 10019

FIRST PRINTING, MARCH, 1971

  4 5 6 7 8 9 10 11 12

PRINTED IN THE UNITED STATES OF AMERICA

Underground Guide to the Staff

Editor-in-Chief: Susan Berman
Editor: Alan Neckritz
Head Researcher: James E. Zane
Assistant Researchers: Stella Nathan, Paul Webb
Typist: Ruth V. Halley

I'd like to thank my agent,
Cyrilly Abels, for all her help.

INTRODUCTION — *In 100 words or less*

This guide will contribute to the generation gap. They used to send you to college to keep you off the streets, now sending you puts you on the streets. Go anyway. This book is the whole truth and nothing but the truth, but once you get to college—don't believe everything you read.

Peace,
THE STAFF
(who live, learn and work in Berkeley).

This book is dedicated to my parents, Dave and Gladys Berman . . . who never had the opportunity to go to college, and to Aunt Marge and Uncle Chickie.

CONTENTS

Contents

ALABAMA

Alabama State College
Montgomery, Alabama

Alabama State was originally founded as a state college for blacks in 1873. It's a straight campus in the middle of Montgomery.

SERGEANT PEPPER SECTION:

C average and average ACTs required. 2,400 students, of which 400 are graduate students. 350 out-of-state students. All black except for 15 whites.

ACADEMIC BULLSHIT:

The best departments are Music (string instruction), Elementary Education and Business. Graduate departments include Education, Music and History. Dr. Otis D. Simmons is the most popular professor—he teaches in the Music department.

There are no student-initiated courses or free U courses. Efforts are under way to establish a Black Studies department. Some independent study, no study abroad. Test bit.

BREAD:

Tuition is $130 a semester in-state, $200 out-of-state. No fraternities. Dorms run about $115 room and board a month. Lots of work-study. Some campus jobs available, especially in the dining hall. A few loans and scholarships. Expensive wardrobes aren't necessary.

BROTHERS AND SISTERS:

Ratio cats : chicks—1 : 1.5.

Well, the answer to the question of drug use reads, "Drugs are not a problem on our campus."

And the reference to chicks, "Girls have been given a great deal of freedom but not to the extent of promiscuity." Cats and chicks are straight. Greeks control the campus. People are into football heroes.

The local hangs for the straights are the "Varsity Inn," the "Regal Cafe" and the Union.

It's hard to score on campus as "students are repulsed by drugs." (But how do the drugs feel?) No political clubs, just "political parties."

17

SURVIVAL:

Well . . . there are no BC pills dispensed, no abortion referrals, no drugs, no health-food store near campus.

ENVIRONMENT:

Mental—Students are reading *The Learning Tree* and *The Campus Power Struggle*.

Physical—It's an urban campus but nice. Green landscape—21 modern type buildings. Alabama climate is hot in summer and rainy in spring and fall. Not much pollution. Students visit the City Park, five blocks from campus, to escape. Some students go home to escape (and where do they go to escape that?).

University of Alabama
University, Alabama

"Almost once a month the student government organization sponsors really good entertainment like Johnny Mathis or Andy Williams."

It's the South, folks, and down at the U of Alabama, the best courses are those in southern history. Alabama is a big state school and fairly cosmopolitan for the area but not exactly unstructured and groovy. They still believe in things like curfews and George Wallace. Imagine a Big Ten school ten years ago and you've got Alabama.

SERGEANT PEPPER SECTION:

State school, semester system.

Any Alabama high-school graduate can get in. Out-of-state students have to be in the upper two-thirds of their graduating class. ACT tests required, medium scores O.K.

25,000 students in U of Alabama system with 18,631 of these at the main campus at Tuscaloosa. Smaller campuses at Huntsville and Montgomery and Medical school at Birmingham.

15,051 undergraduate and 3,580 grad students.

One-third out-of-state students.

ACADEMIC BULLSHIT:

The courses are big theater type old-fashioned knowledge courses but if that's where you're at, some of them are good. History is very heavy on the Old South (I wish I were in the land of cotton . . .). Blacks put heavy pressure on the administration last year and got . . . a course! ("The Negro in 20th century America.")

Business, History and Engineering have good technical graduate schools with abundant facilities—the other graduate schools are poor. Research is very difficult as the library is poorly stocked and the staff isn't helpful.

Grades are still the rule—juniors and seniors with a B average may elect ONE course a semester (not to exceed FOUR overall) on a Pass/Fail basis.

Dr. Robert Mitchell in the history department seems to be a favorite. "Stern, and a tough grader, but all the students I know really respect the man. He's able to inspire hard work." Ugh.

No student-initiated courses, but get this: the Afro-American Association scored a coup when they succeeded in bringing a top NAACP official to speak. (Remember the NAACP?)

There is a new experimental college—like a free U—with courses on witchcraft, sex (it has to go underground) and drugs.

The teacher-student relationship is on an academic level only.

No independent study or study abroad programs to speak of.

BREAD:

In-state is $288 a semester and $588 for out-of-state. All girls under 21 are required to live in dorms—$300 a semester. Half of the men live off campus. Many cheap rooming houses in the $20–$40 a month range. Small two-bedroom apartments go for $100–$140.

Dates consist of fraternity parties or movies—average cost.

Both cars and bikes popular. Tight loans, scholarships and work-study. Campus jobs are terrible.

BROTHERS AND SISTERS:

Ratio of cats : chicks—3 : 1.

"Ninety-five per cent of the chicks are the Southern belle type, dressing in conservative dresses. Black chicks are the most hip with the Afro style—the only blue jeans are on farm kids and they are sneered at. Forty per cent of the cats are Greeks and dress conservatively also—but with moderately longish hair (means one inch sidewalls above ears)." Dating centers around fraternity parties (this campus should bill itself as an historical event). There are three males to every female. No social provisions are made for independents. Greeks run the show.

Pets are not allowed and are impounded. "Any football player is a big hero even when 'Bama loses."

"You even see white girls walking around with black boys and vice versa." Far out! Hardly any lynchings any more.

"The Chukker" is the most popular pub in town. On campus a large cafeteria called the "Super Store" is the meeting place for all. Radicals, blacks, Greeks all have their own corner—no one mixes. Conservatives hang out in—that's it—churches. Meet a nun.

Political action is nonexistent—the SDS chapter folded last year because of apathy. The big group is the Associated Women's Society, which, after a long three-year battle, succeeded in moving up the girls' curfew from 11:00 to midnight.

The first demonstration was this year when Abbie Hoffman was denied the right to speak. "Radicals held a sit-in in the Administration Building to no avail. Right after President Mathews barred Hoffman he allowed George Wallace to deliver a political oration. The police are tough—especially on jaywalking."

SURVIVAL:

Not many smoke but grass is available. "Drugs are played down here. There is supposed to be a local rooming house where every-one knows about where marijuana can be purchased."

No BC pills are given out anywhere or abortion referrals either, but then girls have to be in the dorms by 1 A.M. Friday and Satur-day anyway.

Student health is adequate. There is a clinic run by the Psychol-ogy department that gives out free counseling services, supposedly good. The student government association is staffed by a straight Marine Corps Vietnam vet and a radical—advice depends on who happens to be giving advice on a particular day.

No underground paper; campus paper, *Crimson White*, is fair.

ENVIRONMENT:

Mental—Alabama is a suitcase school—kids go to New Orleans, Atlanta or Florida beaches for a vacation. Read *The Peter Principle* and *Environmental Handbook*.

Physical—The campus is located on the Warrior River, a pol-luted, filthy mess with no recreational park or water facilities within 50 miles. Air pollution from a paper mill. A few plush new build-ings but most of the campus is old brick buildings.

ARIZONA

Arizona State University
Tempe, Arizona

Arizona State is a hot, dry, hedonistic, healthy place to be—for your body. Not too many cerebral students but signs of improvement are imminent.

SERGEANT PEPPER SECTION:

Not too difficult to enter. In-state must rank in upper three-fourths of class, out-of-state in upper two-thirds. ACTs required. 27,000 students, mostly from North Central states. About 10% minorities.

ACADEMIC BULLSHIT:

Best departments include Architecture, Philosophy and Engineering. Morris Starsky is a very popular professor in the Philosophy department. He may not be back next year because of taking part in anti-war demonstrations. Tom Wolfe, in Sociology, is known for being a radical. The Engineering department has very good facilities. Sociology students take part in a lot of community projects like Upward Bound. There is a new Law school which looks good so far.

Some Pass/Fail in the Liberal Arts department. Some class participation, some papers and tests. No student-originated courses or Free U. Classes range in size from 10–400. There is no Third World College although there are a few black history courses called a "shuck" by the blacks. The Indian Studies program run by the Education department is good. Independent study if you are a junior and have a 3.0. Business-type relationship between most students and teachers.

BREAD:

In-state tuition is $165 per semester, out-of-state $605. Loans and scholarships are tight as is work on campus—it pays $1.40 per hour. It's very hard to scrounge in this area. Many students live in dorms. They have regulations, aren't coed, and cost $450 with room and board. Apartments are $100–$175 per month for a one-bedroom. Trailers are becoming more popular at $90 a month. Frats run about $600 a semester. About half the students have expensive threads and cars. Dates can run from a quarter to $10. Some used-book stores, but not good deals.

BROTHERS AND SISTERS:

Ratio cats : chicks—3 : 2.

Anything goes—there are all types from heavy hips to straights. The average is between lukewarm hip and straight. Some chicks are the Villager sorority types and some are hip. Some cats are the frat types with monogrammed T-shirts and flattops. Lukewarm hip chicks wear fancy bell-bottoms, lots of eye makeup and heeled sandals. Everything they wear is brand new and shiny clean. The well-dressed dudes wear fancy shirts and wide bell-bottoms with leather belts. They drive Porsches. The students turn on but are politically apathetic. Hip chicks ball their boyfriends and like acid rock. They know a little about ecology. Most have been in one peace march. The heavy hips wear clean army jackets and drop acid on the weekend.

The conservatives like football, "Sugar, Sugar," Corvettes and Colt 45. Some are studying to be stockbrokers.

But everyone is casual, lots of white pants and colored body shirts.

Lots of dating in the straight and conservative set. The hips live together and keep cool. Some people have been kicked out of apartments for cohabitation. Fraternities still exist but are losing membership.

Radicals meet at "Perry's Bar" in Tempe, straights at "J.D.'s" (bar joint). For general audience, the "Blue Coat," the "Village Inn" and the "Bowling Barrel."

About 1,000 students can be counted on to show up for demonstrations, which are usually peaceful. They had a fair amount of support for the strike against involvement in Cambodia. BLOC (Black Liberation Organizational Committee) has been trying to get a Black Studies program going. The RSU has been active in strikes. The Young Republicans usher at football games and try to break strikes. Outside pigs have only been called in a couple of times. Phoenix city jail is bad news.

SURVIVAL:

If you like the casual hedonistic life Arizona is for you. Lids go for $10, caps for $3. Dark rooms and studios on campus. No BC pills on campus but available in town, likewise for abortion referrals. The Lutheran Center on campus has a very good draft counselor. There's a hippie clinic and suicide prevention center in Phoenix. Pets roam the campus. Many health-food stores in Phoenix, along with fresh air and sunshine. The campus paper is the *State Press*—ugh.

ENVIRONMENT:

Mental—People are talking about the relevant issues and reading Jerry Rubin and Paul Ehrlich.

Physical—ASU is in Tempe, a suburb of Phoenix. It's a hot, dry desert. Some air pollution from copper mines, but rarely bad. Noise pollution is terrible because there is a big military base nearby. The buildings range from the old square type to one designed by Frank Lloyd Wright. Students escape by going camping in the desert.

University of Arizona
Tucson, Arizona

The University of Arizona is a "Fun in the Sun" Beach Blanket Bikini school. Blond, healthy sun-tanned populace, no starving radicals. Barry Goldwater's alma mater.

SERGEANT PEPPER SECTION:

24,066 students attend the University of Arizona. Requirements for entrance: out-of-staters must be in top one-half of high-school graduating class and have an average ACT score of 22; in-state must be in top two-thirds of graduating class and also have an ACT score of 22. There are 2,000 minority students.

ACADEMIC BULLSHIT:

Good undergraduate departments include Journalism, French and English. The graduate school of Medicine is good. Popular professors include Mr. John Lee in Journalism, Dr. Byrd Granger (folklore) and Dr. Don Larson in Journalism.

Some Pass/Fail, some papers instead of tests, no student-originated classes, no Third World College. All the Arizona schools are still somewhat deserving of their reputations as play schools. There's a Free U that offers "Sensitivity Training" and "Drama." Honors students are allowed independent study. Summer school program in Guadalajara.

BREAD:

In-state is $159.50 a semester, out-of-state is $600. Loans and scholarships are pretty available, campus jobs are abundant at $1.45 an hour. Work-study is also available. Most students live in dorms. They cost $130–$180 per room per semester plus $250 for food. This school is one of the largest fraternity schools left in the country—29 fraternities, 15 sororities. Some students are apartment dwellers—this costs from $100–$200 per month. Fraternities cost $600 per semester.

A few students live in trailers. They are hard to get and cost $50 per month. Transportation includes cars, bikes and hitching. An expensive wardrobe is not necessary but many people have them. Straights spend bread on movies, liquor for dates. Hips just buy dope. The ASUA book store has used books. Scrounging is hard unless you get a trailer.

BROTHERS AND SISTERS:

Ratio cats : chicks—1.5 : 1.
Remember madras? Well, it's still happening to a certain extent

at University of Arizona. Cool jocks join fraternities and pinnings are looked upon as the ultimate. The school is about 30% luke-warm hip including those grass-smoking, sideburned football players.

During the strike to protest the involvement in Cambodia, only 150 students showed up at the rally. The school is like a playground and the dating gestalt is set up very well. At the beginning of the year all the names, pictures and addresses of sorority chicks are sent to the fraternities. Pick and choose like a bargain-basement sale. Doris Day land. Blond hair, blue eyes and freckles makes cheerleader, score 10.

In all fairness, some are heavy hip—old clothes, naturals, the whole treatment. But fraternities still control the school, and smoking grass is considered a bit daring for sorority chicks.

So far the school has had two major demonstrations. 400 students took over the ROTC building last year, and the Student Liberator Action Movement organized the strike in May, 1970. The November, 1969, moratorium drew a crowd.

Hips hang out around Park and 6th Avenue. Bands play in the local parks. Straights meet at fraternity houses or at a night club called the "Green Dolphin."

Lids go for $10. Mescaline for $3. Scoring done from friends—frequent busts.

SURVIVAL:

Arizona is a healthy outdoor type place—more thinking going on all the time. BC pills and competent medical advice at student health. Ed Morgan at the Associated Students of the University of Arizona office does good draft counseling. Free hippie clinic for bad trips is called the "Awareness House." Pets are allowed on campus. The *Arizona Daily Wildcat* is good but straight. The underground paper is the *Druid Free Press*. Women's Liberation is embryonic.

ENVIRONMENT:

Mental—People are talking about "the world situation" and Paul Ehrlich's *Population Bomb*.

Physical—Warm *Arizona Highways* weather. The campus is urban—in the center of Tucson. Lots of barren, beautiful mountains around. Not much air pollution but lots of noise from jets. The campus is nearly all red brick, wide lawns and roadways. Escapes include Mexico and ski country. People split on the weekends.

Grand Canyon College
Phoenix, Arizona

Grand Canyon College is a small southern Baptist school with a "Christian Emphasis." Students must be 23 to live off campus by themselves. The school receives no government funds and is poor.

SERGEANT PEPPER SECTION:

Grand Canyon is fairly easy to get into, especially if you are southern Baptist. Nothing is for sure, but they like it if you are in the upper one-half of your class. 759 students, 17 minority students. Undergraduate only.

ACADEMIC BULLSHIT:

The best departments are Speech and Religion, but there is nothing extraordinary about either of them. Dr. Bill Heintze of the Religion department and Mr. Maurice Field of the Business department are the most popular teachers. Traditional academia—no Pass/Fail, tests, student-originated classes, no Free U, one course in "American Minority Peoples." No independent study.

BREAD:

Tuition is $400 a semester. One-third of the students live in the dorm which costs $400 per semester plus food. There were seven cases of food poisoning in the dorm last year. Apartments in Phoenix range from $80–$165 for a one-bedroom. Scholarships and loans are tight, but campus jobs at $1.45 an hour are easy to get. No scrounging if you live on campus. Most students have cars, parking is available. An average date costs $6–$10 for a movie and coffee.

BROTHERS AND SISTERS:

Ratio cats : chicks—1 : 1.
Everyone here is neat-looking and straight. The chicks (ladies would be more applicable) iron all their dresses and wear nylons. Boys look like pre-exec. No sexual activity (or little), dating and kissing goodnight. No fraternities and no politics—just plain old Christianity.

SURVIVAL:

In this world, hard. Maybe they know something we don't. No sinning, no living. No alcohol allowed. No BC pills, no abortion referrals, no shrinks. Student health is fairly competent in the other areas. No draft counseling on campus, but available in Phoenix. As to Women's Liberation—"The last thing in the world we want is to be liberated, we want to get married."

ENVIRONMENT:

Mental—People are reading the Bible and a few have discovered that shocker, *Portnoy's Complaint.*
Physical—The school is on outskirts of Phoenix and has typical Arizona weather. The campus buildings are all one-story red brick with white trim. Lawns with white walkways go through—quaint. Escapes include the Verdi River and skiing at the Sugar Bowl.

Northern Arizona University
Flagstaff, Arizona

"The lights went out in the dorm last week. No, it was two weeks ago. It was so exciting I kind of hate to forget it."

SERGEANT PEPPER SECTION:

8,000 students, 2% minority. Arizona residents must have graduated in upper two-thirds of their high-school class. Out-of-state students must be in upper one-half of their high-school class. Some board scores required.

ACADEMIC BULLSHIT:

The best departments are Forestry, Business and Education. Once a student declares a major, he has little freedom to pick any electives. Good professors are Professor Shutt, Psychology, "he keeps things rolling," and Professor Phil Boroff, English, "talks our language." Traditional academia. Tests, no Pass/Fail. Classes about 30 students and no student-originated courses except for "Black History." No Free U and not much recruitment of black students. Some student-professor dating but not allowed "in your department." Independent study but impossible to qualify for study abroad in Europe.

BREAD:

In-state tuition $152, out-of-state is $332.50 per semester. Loans and scholarships are easy to get. Campus jobs pay $1.45 per hour. Work-study is very available. Students can't scrounge if they live on campus and it's difficult off campus. Most people live in dorms. They cost about $325 per semester for room and board. Chicks get locked up in their rooms at 11 P.M. weeknights and 2 A.M. weekends. No coed dorms. Off-campus studio apartments are about $75. Almost everyone has wheels—hitchhiking is illegal in Flagstaff. Chicks have expensive casual threads, dates are cheap, not much to do in Flagstaff.

BROTHERS AND SISTERS:

Ratio cats : chicks—5 : 3.

Campus populace is evenly divided between lukewarm hip (gringy clothes, long hair, sideburns and apolitical beliefs) and straights (madras shirts, light blue Sta-prest pants, white socks and black loafers, white blouses for the chicks). Some conservatives with flattops and chicks with dyed blond bubbles and tons of makeup. Cats have big cars and panty raids are popular. "You have to get the chicks drunk to ball them." People still ball in motels. (Should we register as Mr. and Mrs.?) From the school paper:

Bucking broncs and nationally famous bulls such as "Cold Taco" and "Spike" will be trying to outperform college rodeo teams at NAU's Intercollegiate Rodeo, May 2 and 3 at Flagstaff's Pow-Wow arena. Rodeo time is set for 1 P.M. on both Saturday and Sunday, with morning go-rounds and slack runs beginning at 8 A.M.

Approximately 25 rodeo teams from Nevada, Southern Oregon, California and Arizona will have both male and female teams at this 14th annual event, according to Art Ray, publicity chairman of Rodeo Club.

The cowboys and cowgirls will be vying for prizes, trophies and important regional points. "Regional points are very important because each year the top three cowboys and cowgirls and the winning regional teams in each event are invited to the College National Finals Rodeo," Ray said.

Hang on to your hats!

Fraternities still exist and in 1970 they opened a Black Fraternity (Kappa Alpha Psi).

Pigs bust students for panty raids. Girls are kicked out of school if they are caught tossing panties out of the windows. The Young Republicans usher at football games. There's a Students for Environmental Education Committee that raps.

To meet a radical, go to the "University Inn"—50¢ for beer and music. Straights go to "Stein's Beer Parlour." Mixed bags go to the "Latin Quarter."

SURVIVAL:

Like all Arizona schools—good for asthmatics.

The school has the facilities for creative arts but not much student interest. Student health is the worst—"they diagnose brain tumors as ulcers." You can get BC pills, but it's a hassle. Religious groups on campus do draft counseling. The campus paper is the *Lumberjack*—good if you like rodeos. Lids go for $10, acid for $3. Lots of narcs and busts. "Ray's Health Food Store" in Flagstaff is nutritious. Women's Liberation is nonexistent. ("Girls cannot go out of the dorm with bare feet.")

ENVIRONMENT:

Mental—People talk about classes and ecology and read *Atlas Shrugged*.

Physical—Flagstaff is a small Arizona city—mountains and trees are all around. The campus is large, lots of lawns and buildings. Little air pollution so far. All the buildings are brick or Arizona flagstone (pinkish-orange rock), modern ranch style.

To escape, people go to Tucson and hit the "big city." They also go skiing at Snow Bowl, five miles away. Everyone splits on the weekend. The college is at 7,000 feet elevation.

Prescott College
Prescott, Arizona

A small new private school, four years old, accredited enough to get you out of the draft but not fully accredited yet. Freshmen have to go through a month of orientation to acquaint them with the outdoors—spent at Lake Powell in Utah (the Glen Canyon Dam). Prescott is a relaxed outdoorsy place to go to school.

SERGEANT PEPPER SECTION:

230 students, most from out-of-state. No set eligibility requirements. Eligibility is determined by whether the school considers you "their type of student." All undergraduate.

ACADEMIC BULLSHIT:

Favorite professors include Tom Kelly, John Barnes and Lyndon Hargrave (a leading ornithologist [birds]). The Anthropology department is considered their best. They just did an extensive study on twig figures in the Grand Canyon.

Pass/Fail ONLY and mostly papers rather than tests. Class participation is very important as most classes are small. Teacher : student ratio is 1 : 8. Many student-originated courses. Tutorial for black studies. Several foreign students and 11 minority students. Just about everything approved for independent study.

BREAD:

Tuition is $2,000 per year for everyone. All but 26 students live on campus in dorms. Dorms house about nine students—are new and are lax in regulations. Things are run on the honor system which says, "If you think it is wrong or will hurt the school, don't do it." Students interpret this as "Don't get the school busted."

Few loans or scholarships—several campus jobs at $1.45 an hour. No work-study and scrounging is impossible. About a third of the students have cars, expensive clothes are nowhere. The average date is a stroll out in the country or a horseback ride which is free.

BROTHERS AND SISTERS:

Ratio cats : chicks—1 : 1.

Lots of heavy hips. People wear old levis and holey sweaters, peasant blouses. Long hair and many beards. Chicks are natural-looking and clean. Only 10% lukewarm hip. There is no formal dating—chicks liberated and couples living together. No off-campus entertainment—the whole scene revolves around the campus. Hip music, dope and the Great Outdoors are the most popular entertainment.

No real politics. People come to this school to get away and enjoy themselves while imbibing a little learning. There is nothing to fight except littering—that is being done. The campus sparkles. You don't even put out a cigarette on the ground. The only active organization is the Environmental Defense Committee. The students are involved in local pollution issues.

SURVIVAL:

If you dig the outdoors and natural-type settings this place is ideal. A very hang-loose, casual atmosphere surrounds the school.

Good doctor and infirmary on campus. Draft counseling on campus. No Help switchboard, "but if you need help, just yell." *The Mandala* is a small good effort for a campus newspaper. Lids go for $10, mescaline and acid for $2.50.

ENVIRONMENT:

Mental—People are reading *The Population Bomb* by Paul Ehrlich and *Lord of the Rings* by Tolkien.

Everyone talks about ecology.

Physical—The campus is rural and dry. Soft hills covered with sagebrush, sparse grass and red dirt. You can see a white mountain rising in the distance. Little air pollution.

Buildings are one-story tan brick with dark wood supports, red and yellow doors. They are not very big but there are a lot of them. The major eyesore is the flagpole.

Students are always taking off to go somewhere—kayaking, hiking, or skiing at Snow Bowl. Some ski expeditions to Aspen. The school does things like sponsor trips through the Grand Canyon.

ARKANSAS

Arkansas State University

State University, Arkansas

Straight rural southerners.

SERGEANT PEPPER SECTION:

6,302 students, of which 372 are graduate students. 23% out-of-state. It's very easy to get into ASU, in-state requires a high-school diploma (and not even that all the time). Transfer students have to have a 2.00 GPA.

ACADEMIC BULLSHIT:

ASU is one of only about 15 schools offering a degree in Printing. Printing department offers two degree plans—B.S.E. and B.S. Short description of several good courses:

Cold Type Composition—The operation of the VariTyper, Headliner, IBM Computer Cold Type machines and other cold type systems are studied in this course.

Lithography and Offset Printing—Camera work, platemaking, masking, sheet and web-fed presses are studied in this course. Students actually go through whole job procedure by themselves.

Scheduling and Estimating—A study of plant scheduling systems, estimating various printing jobs, and cost systems.

The Radio-TV department at ASU is rated fourth in the country by many agencies. The B.S. degree plan is offered. Short description of several good courses:

Television Directing—Theory, techniques, and practices in directing for television. (ASU has an elaborate, privately-owned television station called KASU, Channel 12.)

Advanced Television Practices—Special practices in television station operation. (Except for the chief engineers, students actually manage and operate the TV station.)

Broadcasting Seminar—A study of the latest developments in radio and television and their social influences and significance.

The most popular graduate course is Business. Lots of Education graduates and Science graduates. No Pass/Fail.

Darrell Cunningham of the Radio-TV department and Steve Tricarico of the Geography department are popular professors.

The only student-initiated course to date is "Black History." No Free U. Not much student-professor interaction. Independent study for those with a 3.0. No study abroad.

BREAD:

Tuition is $150 per semester in-state; out-of-state is $285.

Average price for a dorm is $500 per semester with room and board. Average price for apartments is $140. Greek housing is $500 per semester.

Loans and scholarships are available. Many campus jobs are available at $1.30 an hour. About half the student body has cars—a date costs $10. Most students are well dressed.

BROTHERS AND SISTERS:

Ratio cats : chicks—2.5 : 1.

"The kick here is getting drunk and shacking up." Most are straight although a few of the Arts and Liberal Arts majors are looking a little hip. Girls aren't liberated and must be in at 1 A.M. Lots of students leave for the weekend to go home, the others stay and date. Since ASU is located in a dry (that's no liquor—remember the prohibition days?) county, students go to Memphis, Tennessee, for action. Hangs are people's apartments. 5% of the campus are marijuana users—a lid goes for $25. No hard stuff. No revolutionaries (although one person thought they had one). There has been no political action except on the part of the Political Affairs Club until this year. The 150 blacks staged a couple of sit-ins against the playing of "Dixie" at school athletic events. University police consists of five or six Barney Fifes. Outside pigs have never been called in. 22% of the student body commutes from surrounding areas. Most girls on campus have to live in dorms.

SURVIVAL:

Difficult. No BC pills dispensed from student health (in fact no pills of any sort except aspirin) but they are sometimes available in town. No draft counseling, Free Clinic, abortion referral center or suicide prevention center . . . but lots of football heroes. The campus paper is the *Herald of ASU*—straight establishment-type reporting.

ENVIRONMENT:

Mental—Straights are talking about sports and hips are reading Tom Wolfe's *The Electric Kool-Aid Acid Test*.

Physical—It's a middle-class rural and urban populace—all white except for 150 blacks. The climate is hot in summer, cold in winter with rainy spots. Lots of hunting, fishing, swimming and boating in the area. Campus architecture is nothing to shout about.

CALIFORNIA

California College of Arts and Crafts
Oakland, California

This place is an artist's dream. Everyone is creative and productive. Students are congenial and everyone knows everyone else at least by sight.

SERGEANT PEPPER SECTION:

1,365 art students go here, 85 of whom are graduate students. Most of the students are from California. It's easy to get in, you need a 2.0 GPA, no SATs. Sometimes the grade requirement is waived.

ACADEMIC BULLSHIT:

This place offers a wealth of creative courses which include drawing, film making, art and environmental design, print making, sculpture, photography, television, graphic design, industrial design, interior design, art history, ceramics, metals, textiles and a few standard courses. There is a very close relationship between faculty and students. Blacks are being recruited; in 1970 there were 27 blacks, 3 Chicanos and 6 Indians. There is a significant amount of independent study. CCAC has its own campus in Mexico. Most classes are very informal and are workshops or studios.

BREAD:

Heavy bread. It's $720 per semester. 370 students received aid in 1970 in the form of scholarship, loan or employment. There were 29 work-study jobs and 140 student jobs on campus. Competition for jobs is stiff. There is a used-book store.

Nearby apartment costs approximately $70 per bedroom—they are dingy. There is a dorm which is restricted to freshmen women.

BROTHERS AND SISTERS:

Almost equal number of cats and chicks. The mellow arty hip style predominates here. Everyone is an individual. Most students dress in old work clothing as their clothes get messed up in the workshops. Bohemian values are firmly entrenched, no formal dating but lots of sexual activity. Lots of friendly pets roam the campus.

CCAC students have easy access to Berkeley and San Francisco as far as meeting people. There's a hang across the street from campus called the "Rockridge Tea Shop" which serves health foods.

SURVIVAL:

CCAC has no survival services of its own but it's easy to survive in the Bay area. In fact, it's a delightful place to survive. The CCAC students melt into the Berkeley hip scene on weekends. Everyone on campus smokes dope and it goes for $15 a lid; not much heavy stuff.

ENVIRONMENT:

Mental—Everyone does their own thing in a very happy relaxed atmosphere.

Physical—CCAC is built on a hillside in a residential area of Oakland. There is a fenced-in garden with a pond and a number of small lawns and a plaza where students sit sketching and drawing. But the buildings have a cluttering effect. One new building is outstanding—it has a large mural with the signs of the zodiac and other mystic symbols on it. One building is a complex of studios.

California Institute of the Arts
Valencia, California

A fantastic new school of the arts which opened in October of 1970. The Institute consists of six schools: Art, Music, Design, Theater and Dance, Film, Critical Studies. The 1970 student body included 600 students. The maximum by 1973 will be 1,500. There is no fixed curriculum and there are no grades. It's a combination of the Chouinard Art School and The School of Music in Los Angeles.

The Institute's criteria for selection of students differ in each school. Art students must present exhibits of their work and students in the performing arts are required to take auditions. "Talent counts most in every field."

California Institute of Technology
Pasadena, California

One of the two best science institutions in the country—kids have an average I.Q. of 135. Dr. Strangelove types. "Science has no soul. Don't come here unless you absolutely have to" . . . from a C.I.T. student.

SERGEANT PEPPER SECTION:

1,537 students of which 780 are grads. All male except for 39 women grads. 846 out-of-state and 260 foreign students. Ten blacks.

Some say Cal Tech is better than M.I.T.—a nationally-known school. Applicants need about a 3.6 GPA and a Math ACT score of over 750. Very hard to get in. Students are the top kids.

ACADEMIC BULLSHIT:

The whole school is on an honor system and kids take it seriously.

Best courses in each department are: Physics—"Physics" with Professor Leighton (overview of most essential topics—individual research emphasized and term projects required. One student did "Ill-fated love story of an electronpositron pair."); Chemistry—Professor Waser's courses; Math ("Introduction to Abstract Algebra"); Humanities ("Induction" with Professor Thompson. He is a professor of philosophy, math, engineering—"When you see Thompson you see a mind that truly impresses yours.").

Professor Feynmann is the campus idol—he's a Nobel laureate "and he's usually up in the clouds but he comes down and mingles with us."

Physics is the best department on campus. The department has two Nobel laureates, Gell-Mann (theoretical physics) and Feynmann. Everyone has to take two years of physics. Facilities include a two-million volt linear accelerator and a synchrotron. The emphasis is on research and all the students go into physics hoping they will think of something new.

Particle physics is the most important field in the department. Its aim is to find "a systematic way of categorizing all elementary particles"—that's what goes on all day and every day at Cal Tech, folks.

Biology is also a very important department. The major research projects include further research into the genetic code and split brain experiments (operations on brains of epileptics involving the disconnection of one half of the brain from the half that is controlling it).

Studying constantly. Emphasis on learning rather than grades. Very easy to initiate a course. A few informal study groups substitute for a Free U. One course in black literature.

Professors are willing to spend any amount of time with students. In Biology, independent study is standard. Instead of regular classes, a student maps out his entire own curriculum.

Students and professors work together in every area.

BREAD:

$2,385 a year. Lots of loans and scholarship money. The school "digs up bread if you're qualified." Of course, to get a big scholarship you have to be outstanding in relation to the others at Cal Tech. It boggles the brain.

Campus jobs include that of a tour guide for VIPs who come to check out the place—$2.00 an hour. National Science Foundation grants. Half have cars.

BROTHERS:

The men (the term "cats" just doesn't fit geniuses) live in houses which have names and stereotypes and cost $1,130 a year, but are not frats. Every student gets into one. There are 50–90 in each house. The food is the same and is prepared by a central kitchen. Dinners are waited. Old houses all separate but connected and surrounding a beautiful flowered and treed courtyard where kids play croquet. Houses have arched hallways and a quaint European aura. Each house has an R.A.—the big daddy. The houses have "images"—Fleming House gets the jocks, Dabney gets the longhairs, Lloyd is the most diverse house, Blacker takes in eggheads, Rickets gets the beer drinkers and Page is full of "toads." Oh, well, geniuses aren't perfect.

Houses have parties every weekend—some stag, some exchanges (usually miserable flops). All sorts of interhouse sports are also popular. But the C.I.T. man's favorite activity is "everybody descending on somebody who's fast asleep and spending the night in a bull session."

Guys admit that "we don't really know how to date and are sexually frustrated."

They look like scientists, short hair and quite a few hornrimmed hermit types. Slacks and T-shirts and casual. All friendly and superarticulate and very shy with chicks. Some guys never go out.

Students are liberal and rational but not active. The pervasive philosophy is positivism. The administration and the students talk about any issues that come up. The most political thing that ever happened was the day the food was so bad that everyone took their macaroni and cheese to the president's door. Classes were briefly canceled during the days of the Cambodia holocaust. About 60% are sympathetic to anti-war programs.

For excitement, C.I.T. students take advantage of the Los Angeles scene. The school has a couple of programs for Los Angeles high-school students.

SURVIVAL:

Brilliance begets survival. Mensa types of the Dr. Strangelove variety. There's an art student in an old greenhouse darkroom. Few creative art opportunities. A draft counselor is paid by the Institute. People eat at the "Coffee House," a small coffee house in an old house—it's open from 9–2 and serves 35¢ hamburgers. *The Cal Tech* is mediocre.

About 30% are regular smokers. Open market—lids for $10.

ENVIRONMENT:

Mental—People study, think and discover. Free reading tastes run to Tolkien and Brautigan. The Cal Tech Ecology Action Committee is very small—the action in ecology is more centered in the curriculum.

Physical—Los Angeles climate—warm most of the year, lots of smog. Cal Tech is just off the road from downtown Pasadena. It's a light green tree-lined residential area.

The campus has a Spanish flavor. The buildings are of old yellowed concrete with inlaid designs and wales of arches, authentic cracks and mostly old-world flavor. The campus is very quiet. The energy accumulated within its walls seems to flow in harmonic circles that ripple in the languid quad pool. The library is a black monolith that is the only whisper of the cybernetic age.

Not much traveling except when the geology department takes kids on field trips to Rainbow Basin or Baja.

Cal State at L.A.

Los Angeles, California

A big gloomy dismal commuters' school in the middle of Los Angeles.

SERGEANT PEPPER SECTION:

20,993 students of which 6,200 are grads. Almost 100% in-state. The largest number of minority students of any university in California. 2,000 blacks, 2,500 Chicanos, 2,000 Asian students.

Easy to get in. C averages and 1,000 combined on SATs.

ACADEMIC BULLSHIT:

General academic level is mediocre.

Best departments are Psychology, Art and American Studies. The Psychology department has all sorts of groovy machines—like an EEG and many others. Students get to fondle them. The Art department is best in ceramics—they have 30 pottery wheels. The Student Art Council is autonomous and is responsible for all sorts of excellent lectures and shows.

Take Gomez for psychology—there's lots of sensitivity training and encounter-group stuff—in his "Social Psyche," there's an emphasis on the parapsychological and the existential.

Bellman for "Negroes in the New World" (sounds like an eighth-grade course in explorers) is recommended.

The graduate departments are mainly for those who are older and have jobs to acquire new tidbits of knowledge—Home Economics, Industrial Studies, Public Health. Some Pass/Fail—many exams.

Classes are big and usually boring. A few student-initiated courses such as "Film."

There's a new Experimental College. The popularity varies with courses and instructor. Some of the current courses are "Yoga," "Guerrilla Theater," "Birth Control," "Non Verbal Group Therapy," and "Eating Wild Plants." The only close relationships between professors and students are in the Fine Arts department. They have their own building and work, eat and play together.

Study abroad and independent study.

BREAD:

In-state tuition is $47 a quarter, out-of-state is approximately $300 a quarter. Scholarships are practically nonexistent, a few loans. Since this is a commuter's school, many students have jobs off campus. Most people live in their homes in a 15-mile radius from campus. Most are also married. There is one privately owned residence called Marianna Residence—$1,100 for room and board per person for a one-bedroom apartment that must be shared by three. Very unpopular. Housing in the area is hard to get. Most places are the plastic apartments that run $150 for a one-bedroom furnished apartment. The community is not receptive to students and it is difficult to scrounge. Everyone has wheels. The school resembles a traffic jam; parking is 25¢ a day.

Students are usually lower-middle-class and don't have fancy threads.

BROTHERS AND SISTERS:

Ratio cats : chicks—3 : 2.

It's a very dull group. A large % are from another generation— plodding on to get a job. Average joes. Chicks wear stockings, makeup and set hair. Cats wear slacks, shirts and sneakers. There's a recent appreciable amount of guy freaks with medium-long hair and beards and round sunglasses. But mostly sport shirt types. The average age is 25. Over 50% have establishment jobs and are married. Many younger kids are active in fraternities and sororities —they have turtle races and do their goodwill bit (book drive for "our boys in Nam").

There's lots of dating among frats and sororities. But not very liberated—the dating scene is beautiful downtown Los Angeles. Chicks are uptight.

Hardly any political activities. Students are interested in school "as a means to an end, rather than a separate world."

A little action started with the student strike of 1970. A Community Action Group was started to go into the community and do anti-war work—250 signed up.

Students hang in L.A. "Garfano's Pizza Place" and the "Cabin Inn" are popular. Mostly straights. People go on real live dates in Los Angeles—blind dates and "double-dates" too. Dress up for the movies where it's too dark to be seen.

Not much drug use—about $10 a lid.

SURVIVAL:

If you can survive in L.A., you can survive here. It's very hard to meet a companion in this commuter school. Two creative outlets —excellent photography equipment and art studios. Draft counseling in the Experimental College. Los Angeles Free Clinic is ten miles away.

No health-food stores or other survival services.

The Ecology Action Group is starting to do good work.

ENVIRONMENT:

Mental—People talk about their kids and their jobs.

Physical—The campus is a dull untogether place. This poor section of Los Angeles looks like someone made a green Jell-O mold a hundred years ago, it rotted, turned gray and now hangs over the campus. The campus resembles a huge high school—concrete buildings, lots of parking lots. Smoggy and construction noise. Generally dismal.

One additional point. In the center of campus is a huge map entitled "War Board. Play along and try to guess the next moves on land, air, and sea." It is a map of Southeast Asia and has an up-to-date death count.

Chico State
Chico, California

Booze, fraternity parties and "Pioneer Week" are the watchwords here.

SERGEANT PEPPER SECTION:

8,000 students, mostly in-state. 150–200 blacks. "Eligibility Index" used to determine admission—grades, test scores and the like. Easy to get in.

ACADEMIC BULLSHIT:

Most of the radical and popular teachers are fired shortly after getting here. Some Philosophy professors were fired when they cancelled classes for more than one day for the October 15 Moratorium.

A good teacher is Dan Chandler, a very hip type (Marxist theory) in the Sociology department, who teaches courses in "Social Problems." This year it's "Ecology from the Social Scientist's Viewpoint." Dan was busted during the sit-in on First Street.

Mr. Cunningham in the Philosophy department teaches courses in "Introductory Philosophy," "Logic" and "Contemporary Morals," the last of which is a very popular course.

The school has a lot of Education and P.E. majors.

Most of the students I talked to thought of the place as a party school, where very little work was done and few departments were of high quality. They can take a week off for "Pioneer Week" in the spring and "Hi" week in the fall, just for socializing, so academics can't be that important.

Some Pass/Fail classes. About 100 students are passive, not much interaction between students and professors.

Chico has a Community Action Volunteers in Education—CAVE. Students get credit for tutorial and other programs such as setting up bum-trip clinics. Credit in the Psychology or Sociology department. Many of the projects involve work in Chapman Town, Chico's slum, where its blacks and third-worlders live.

About ten courses in black studies.

The Batwinger Indian Tribe runs a Free U with about 15 courses such as "Winemaking," "Basket Weaving," "Motorcycle Repairs" and "Astrology." Not much independent study. One study abroad program—five weeks of fun in Italy.

BREAD:

Tuition is $73 per semester in-state, $360 out-of-state. Loans are tight. More or less a rich-kid's school—almost no one receives financial aid. Many students have cars and go away on the weekends. Regular campus jobs.

Dorms cost $1,100 for room and board. No dope and booze. Curfew for girls in some dorms. The dorms are carpeted barracks. A new coed dorm, Whitney Hall, is nine stories high, the tallest building in Chico. It reminds me of a New York State mental hospital.

People with half a brain move off campus. Average price for apartments in older houses—$40–$50 per student, three–five in a house. Apartments rented on a nine-month basis. There is a giant new plastic student ghetto called "College Park." All the apartments look alike, two-story garden apartments. They cost $200 for a two-bedroom.

One commune I heard about was the Batwingers, though they are out of one house now and won't move into another until next fall. "Agora House" is a co-op, big house, lived in by students, formerly school-sponsored.

Dorm head residents and resident counselors take the rules seriously. Girls have to be checked in. No crashers on your floor.

Most typical arrangement is three–five students living in a house within walking distance of campus.

It's difficult to scrounge. If you qualify you can get staples at the "Food Commodities Store" in Chico. Expensive wardrobes aren't necessary—students have that college-shop casual look.

Average date costs $2—dance and drinking.

BROTHERS AND SISTERS:

Ratio cats : chicks—1 : 1.

Most guys have short hair. I was there on a weekend after a week when the frats do nothing but partying and the hips clear out to go camping. Still, estimates are that less than 10% of the students are hip. Some straight guys grew two-week beards for "Pioneer Week." Most of these students looked like Middle-Americans. Many girls have short hair that has been processed so that it curls around the ears—that astronaut's-wife look. Many others have the phony natural hair style, but few were free of the cosmetics-glamour bullshit.

Blacks seem complacent about politics.

The Joe College look was everywhere. For guys, college-shop

shirts and slacks, loafers or sneakers. For girls, blouses and jeans.
Very few longhairs. The hips dress pretty straight. No girls without bras.

"Reagan would want his daughter to go here."

Very few virgins.

Lots of fraternity interaction.

"Pioneer Week" is a big frat event. Organizations build exhibits
like log cabins and oil wells for which they get trophies.

The hippest people describe it as a friendly, quiet campus.
Apparently the state politicos like this school because it is expanding rapidly.

There are a handful of rock-throwers around. The blacks are
tame. The silent majority of straight-looking non-radicals prevail.
There are a lot of aggies and jocks who are outright conservatives
and call longhairs filthy names when they get drunk.

Reagan came to a $50-a-plate dinner in March. A couple of
guns were in a crowd that booed him at the airport and then
later downtown. One student was arrested. This was a must for
any campus radical—300 showed up.

The Batwinger Indian Tribe is a Yippie-like organization that
does everything radical on this campus. They run the Switchboard, sponsor the Free U, sponsored Ecology Week, raise bail
for the people who were busted at the first street sit-in, have a
Ken Kesey-like schoolbus they bring to campus every day. Their
leader, Pete Kinsey, was runner-up in a contest for student-body
pres.

Kinsey was on trial at a student tribunal for stealing a glass of
orange juice from the student cafeteria. A number of freaks in
orange suits broke into the tribunal throwing around oranges,
making a farce of the whole thing. Kinsey was acquitted.

First Street used to be the natural boundary of the campus on
one side. Now, the school has built extensively on the east side
of it and students have been trying to get it closed to traffic for
some time. It was closed off for Ecology Week, mid-April. At the
end of that week students and faculty sat-in to keep it closed.
Jocks and Aggies were out there beating heads; the local police
made 16 arrests on the felony charge of conspiracy to obstruct
traffic.

The latest protest movement is against the construction of tract
homes on land adjacent to Chico's gigantic Bidwell Park. A lot of
"Save Bidwell Park" stickers on cars.

Typical of campus politics, when James Rector was killed last
year, the school's flag was lowered to half-mast. Some conservatives made a stink. They wanted the flag flying full-staff.

Football weekends are very big. Meet at the "Keggers." Fraternity sponsored parties.

"The Oasis," a bar and pool hall, is popular among fraternity
guys. "The Coffee Mill," a store-front coffee house with about
30 seats, has live entertainment six nights a week—folk and rock.
There are occasional dances in the gym. There are two flicks in
town, occasional flicks on campus.

Lids go for $10. Straights don't smoke.

SURVIVAL:

Hard, unless you split on weekends. Planned Parenthood all the way in Oakland for BC pills. Some draft counseling. A drop-in health center for bad trips. There's a Switchboard. The campus paper, *Wildcat*, is conservative and dull. "Chico Health Food Store" is good.

ENVIRONMENT:

Mental—People are reading Huxley and Hesse. Credence Clearwater reigns supreme. Little ecology action.

Physical—The campus is near the center of a small city (20,000) in the central valley 100 miles north of Sacramento. Outside of town is a large agricultural area. Chico was known as the almond capital of the world not too long ago. There are even almond orchards on campus. The campus itself has a creek running through it but the buildings are institutionally ugly and the landscaping is like urban campuses. It is very hot in the summer—air conditioning is a must from April or May onwards. It rains frequently from December to March. Not one kind word for campus architecture. The Business and Social Science box is very ugly, but the nine-story dormitory monstrosity, Whitney Hall, is probably uglier. The old Spanish style administration building looks like a 1920s high school in a wealthy suburb. Newer buildings look like suburban factories. The campus is mostly new (and crowded). Chico is no longer the almond capital of the world because college expansion led to conversion of orchards into buildings.

Lots of camping grounds available. Feather Falls, an hour drive away, is a 500-foot waterfall, accessible after a four-mile walk. Skiing is very big. The Ski Club has facilities at the Donner Ski Ranch in Tahoe.

On warm days, and there are a lot of them, swimming and boating on lakes in the area. (Dorms have outdoor swimming pools.) One favorite spot for picnics is the "Sandbar," on the banks of the Sacramento River.

Humboldt State College
Arcata, California

This is the nicest of the California state colleges. People are into nature and themselves. The surrounding area is pleasant and it's only five hours to the Bay area.

SERGEANT PEPPER SECTION:

5,250 students, 69 are out-of-state.

To get in—must be approximately in upper third of high-school graduating class—they are presently overcrowded so it is hard to get in. There are only a few blacks, although last year's student-body president was black.

ACADEMIC BULLSHIT:

Dennis Winter, a Speech professor, teaches a course called "Communications and the Generation Gap," an encounter session between the teacher and the students who are almost all over 35 and not fully enrolled students (I guess this is Adult Ed.). He teaches a very popular undergrad course as well—"Communications Analysis of the Welfare System in Humboldt County." He sicced his 35 students on the welfare department to find out how they processed clients and how well they informed the community. I talked to some students who loved it. "Dennis is a hippie."

Tom Jones is another extremely popular teacher, and like Winter," he often holds court with some of his favorite students in "The Keg," a beer and billiards and burger joint where the more radical element tends to hang out. Jones teaches the senior seminar in History, and is a radical and a medievalist.

Dr. Fred Cranston is a fatherly physicist who teaches a general ed required course right now. His class cleaned up the highway between Eureka and Arcata recently. He was once called to help bail out a hippie busted for dope. He invited the guy home and the kid married his daughter.

The school has good departments called Division of Natural Resources (fisheries, oceanography, forestry and game management). Chamber music is big and there is a well-stocked chamber-music library. Large Education department.

Some Pass/Fail, especially General Education. Class size averages 30. As of next fall, there will be a cluster college, an experiment on the idea in Santa Cruz in students living together, with faculty having offices in the student housing. The cluster college will be alternative to the general ed requirements that fill up the first two years of most students' programs.

Next year, the school has "Project 100" for the purpose of recruiting 100 minority students who meet the regular qualifications.

There is a lot of student-teacher interaction. In 1970, there was a three-day retreat for students, administration and faculty. This resulted in the cluster college plan. Not much independent study, no programs of study abroad.

A very good Free U offering a wide variety of courses: "Child Nutrition," "Crocheting," "Ecology," "Winter Camping and Survival" and "Alternative Journalism" among others.

BREAD:

$1,000 out-of-state per year, $152 in-state. Loans and scholarships are tight, campus jobs are hard to find. A few students work in a local sawmill on the night shift. Cafeteria work pays $1.25 an hour. Work-study is available in the departments. Food stamps are available if you qualify. Students living in buses and vans.

Room and board in dorms $1,000 and up. People can break contracts and often do, so the dorms aren't filled up. Peer group discipline in dorms is being tried out. Dope and booze are illegal, but used a lot in the dorms. There are narcs in the dorms, so students have to keep cool. Dorms are coed, either floor-by-floor, or wing-by-wing. No co-ops. Lots of apartments (800 live in dorms, everybody else lives in apartments). Many students live in a school-run trailer park, six to a trailer. "Humboldt Village"—dreadful place.

Three frats, two sororities, rather isolated for general run of campus life.

Apartments are hard to get. $150 for three people is typical near campus. There are some fantastic bargains, like houses for $50, but these are handed down carefully from friend to friend.

I heard a story of one student who lived in the campus parking lot for three months in the back seat of a station wagon. He paid his $9 parking permit fee and was never caught.

Some students live in vans or VW buses. I was in one commune and heard of others. There are communes all around Arcata, in the forest. Trinidad, 15 miles north of Arcata, is a commune-heavy area.

An expensive wardrobe is unnecessary and dates are cheap.

BROTHERS AND SISTERS:

Ratio cats : chicks—2 : 1.

Lots of mescaline and grass. Easy to score. 90% smoke dope. There is a lot of long hair and beards here, but the straights are majority. Dress styles determined by the weather—it's 40° to 70° all year 'round, so people have good healthy-looking leather jackets and flannels. Most of the guys, hip or straight, have the slacks-sports shirt-loafer or sneaker look. Groovy things happen to shoes, though—a lot of sandals and boots. There are girls with short hair, store-shoes, coats and dresses. But most wear jeans. Bare feet occasionally. Among the hips, long hair here is often shoulder length. The beards are really full.

Clothes scene is straight, even for the hips. Most of the faces look 1950ish.

About 10% of the chicks let it all hang out. Fraternities are no big thing.

You can meet someone at a dance on campus, but few resort to this. "The Keg" is a pretty good bar where all types hang out, but it is more hip than the school as a whole. There are three theaters and two drive-ins. One of the theaters has an excellent series of flicks. Every month or two, a play or concert arrives on a tour of college circuit. There is a head shop in Eureka. A couple of coffee houses ("House of Jansch," "Olde Towne Coffee").

Local police chief is a law-school grad, and recently aced out FBI school in Washington. Local police are model department and not too tough on dope. County police are rough dudes. They do most of the dope-busting. Campus cops never do anything except give parking tickets.

When Reagan spoke at College of the Redwoods last month, HSC students trooped over and disrupted the meeting.

Max Rafferty came to HSC during the winter quarter, and was greeted by demonstrators in KKK outfits.

SDS is dead and the Student Mobe is very weak. 800 people marched on October 15. Bettina Aptheker drew 100 people at a speech of hers. There was talk of a strike about Cambodia. No heavy political scene.

SURVIVAL:

Easy. Humboldt is cool. Plenty of creative outlets—painting, photography and the like. There are 15 draft counselors in the office. They were broadcasting draft counseling info on the campus radio. BC pills available in town. Switchboard opened in fall of 1970.

Dull campus newspaper, *Lumberjack*. Many students grow their own gardens in their own backyards. Health-food stores in area. The underground paper is the *North Coast Rip Saw*—good. Small chapter of Women's Liberation.

ENVIRONMENT:

Mental—People are reading *Do It!* by Jerry Rubin, Tolkien and books on Indians. Sierra Club has a very large membership. A new group called "Hope" sponsored Ecology Week and is now giving away non-detergent soap.

Physical—Climate is damp, between 40° and 70° all year 'round. Cloudy. It rains like hell. Below campus, going downhill, is the small town of Arcata. Above campus is beautiful redwood forest that extends inland hundreds of miles. A walk away from class takes you into large expanses of gorgeous forest. This is the heart of Redwood Country.

When there is no wind, the pulp mills in Eureka make the air smell bad. The water in Humboldt Bay is badly polluted—there are no fish. Not much noise.

Lots of really far-out forest and mountains to explore in the area. Hiking expeditions posted on campus. Many go up the coast for camping. A lot of hitchhiking on Highway 101 in front of the school. Lots of beaches to spend weekends on, though you must dress warmly.

Founders Hall is the oldest building on campus, Spanish style. The most hated building is Engineering—described as a cement block, a fleshy pink concrete cube. Art and Music buildings are twins, new, large glass walls on one side. Most of the buildings are institutionally ugly from various periods. I liked the new dorms which are called the Jolly Giant Complex. They look like four-story ski lodges.

The town is a conservative area. Longhairs are discriminated against in housing, as are the few blacks. Also, local greasers have been beating up longhairs. One freak I met was chased once, and had been carrying a knife since, although this is atypical. When a woman drama teacher held a final examination in her house that consisted of dressed-up freaky-looking students roaming around playing with closed circuit TV, the neighbors called the police. Eight pigs showed up and the lady and her husband were evicted shortly afterwards.

San Diego State College

San Diego, California

One of the only state schools with a sense of community.

SERGEANT PEPPER SECTION:

16,000 students. Mostly in-state. Circa 400 blacks, 350 Chicanos. Need about a 2.5 and 1,000 SATs.

ACADEMIC BULLSHIT:

Best departments are Psychology, Sociology, and Engineering. Take "World Literature" with Jerry Farber (he is the author of *The Student as Nigger*) and sociology with Professor Mortidies. Art is more unstructured than most departments. Teachers allow students to express themselves—macramé, tie-dying and batik. The Drama department has a huge theater, puts on lots of productions and runs an Experimental Theater.

Only one course ("Math 3") given Pass/Fail. Large lectures, not much class participation. Student-initiated ethnic courses and women's studies. A limited Free U. Interdepartmental majors in Black Studies, Asian Studies, Latin-American Studies and Mexican-American studies, European Studies, American Studies and Russian Studies. There's a Black Studies Center. Upper division students can take three units of independent study and can also make up their own major if it is approved. Study abroad. Good programming in Telecommunication, Speech Pathology and Clinical Training.

BREAD:

$145 in-state, $890 out-of-state. Not much financial aid. Jobs are easy to get. Dorms are $500 a semester for room and board—three women's, two men's and one coed. Red brick "obsolete type." Many students live off campus in the College Village, which is approved housing, or in the 55th Street area—rents at about $125 for a one-bedroom. Many live at Ocean Beach—lots of old small houses for about $100. Rents are cheaper there than anywhere else. Freaks live in Mission Beach. Scrounging is easy at the beach.

Moderate clothes and lots of cars.

BROTHERS AND SISTERS:

Ratio cats : chicks—1+ : 1.

Students look robust and healthy—less uptight than some of the other California state schools. Quite a few cats with long hair. Casual dress—lots of different types but few outlandish freaks. Most are rather dull. Plenty of dating and virtuous chicks. 12 frats and 12 sororities; still important and host such events as barbeques, "Car Washes" and "Derby Day." Pledge pranks are popular.

Hangs are bars like "Rounder," "Ledbetter's," "Tijuana," the "Campus Chuckwagon" (smorgasbord) and the "Sports Arena," where concerts are held. Hips hang at Balboa Park and around the beaches.

Most smoke grass—lids about $10. Not much other dope. Score at the beach.

The school is generally quiet politically. The Young Republicans are the only group that is actually organized and does things. They had demonstrations against the strike and hold school-wide referendums.

The biggest issue was in April, 1970. Four teachers had been hired on a trial basis and were not given tenure after the two-year period. Two were terminated and two were not promoted. Students protested and took over the administration building for a week.

The response to the strike was primarily rallies and marches with about 500 students participating. The faculty did not, for the most part, support the strike. "This school is too big to be politically active." (?) Sentiment ranges from apathy to conservatism. 38 narcs were enrolled as students in 1970.

SURVIVAL:

Plenty of art and film facilities.

No BC pills or abortion referrals from student health. Thursday nights a volunteer draft counselor comes to the Aztec Center. Free Clinic in San Diego. The *Aztec Daily* is pretty good and is liberal at times. The local undergrounds are the *Street Journal* and the *Free Poor,* both radical and good.

Health-food stores in Ocean Beach. Women's Liberation has instituted a Women's Studies program that includes 12 courses.

ENVIRONMENT:

Mental—People are talking about the beaches and surfing and their courses. There are some good ecology programs and students are aware. Some campus trees were going to be torn down and ecology groups saved them. Earth Day decorated the entire campus.

Physical—The school is in a semi-urban area, just ten minutes from downtown. Hot all year 'round. Lots of smog and noise pollution from the freeway. The campus is white, lined with white walks, made of tall modern white buildings with outer archways and black glass. The back of the campus faces out into a sloping grassland, a panoramic smog-shrouded small valley.

Escapes are Mt. Helix (three miles away), where students take a break to watch the sunset, and the beaches.

Many commuters but fewer than most other California state schools.

San Fernando Valley State College
Northridge, California

"It's a commuter college, most people come here and go home."

SERGEANT PEPPER SECTION:

20,673 students of which 4,332 are grads. Almost 99% in-state. 500 Chicanos and 800 blacks.

For entrance you need a 2.5 GPA and 1,000 combined boards. Easy to get in. Constant transfers in and out.

ACADEMIC BULLSHIT:

Nothing too exciting. For limited interest there's "Marriage and Family Relations" (Dr. Campbell), "Jazz" (Professor Wilson—a professional musician) and "Afro-American Literature" (Professor Rhodes). The Art department is good.

Best graduate departments are Engineering and Psychology. Engineering is known to be creative (for engineering)—kids have creative projects and contests. They run a computer dating program.

Pass/Fail, tests, not much class participation, very difficult for students to originate courses. Students have no representation on the college board.

Experimental College is Free U—"Yoga," "Encounter," "Buddhism," "Parliamentary Procedure," and "Laboratory in Fantasy" (for aspiring artists) are offered.

Black Studies department offers many courses in Afric American culture. Pretty extensive. There is also a M American Studies program. There is heavy recruitment of blacks and Chicanos and minority scholarships are readily available. Limited independent study on the undergraduate level—more available to grads. Study abroad in many countries. Summer programs include a "Study Tour of Pre-Columbian Art in Mexico."

BREAD:

In-state costs $71 a semester, out-of-state $30 per unit (maximum is $445). Minority students get the loans and scholarships. Most students work off rather than on campus. There are only two dorms—they cost approximately $1,200 a year for room and board. Apartments cost $145 for a plastic furnished one-bedroom. Sorority or frat houses cost $100 a month for room and board. Most students commute from home or apartments away from campus.

Difficult to scrounge in the area.

Most students have cars.

BROTHERS AND SISTERS:

Ratio cats : chicks—6 : 5.

The campus is straight, conservative and ordinary-looking. Students have many interests outside of school, i.e., jobs and families. Chicks wear shirtwaists and look inexpensive and local. Cats wear slacks, loose shirts and that smiley athletic look. No real freaks but many plastic hips. No sense of community—quiet campus. Dating off campus. Most events on campus are fraternity sponsored.

There have been a few peaceful demonstrations in the past—one resulted in the creation of a Black and Mexican-American Studies program.

Temporary strike after Kent State massacre. VIVA is the right-wing group on campus—they work with administration and police. SRAF (Student Revolutionary Anarchist Family) is a group of communal radicals.

Social life is the Los Angeles scene. "Buffalo Chips" is a groovy place, all types and 75¢ hamburgers.

Grass is widespread. Lids go for $10.

SURVIVAL:

Same as in Los Angeles. Survival services in the city, however, and you'll need them. Student health gives BC pills. Draft counseling course in Experimental College. Los Angeles Free Clinic and Hotline (24-hour telephone line—they connect you with the help you need). The cafeteria has slop food.

The campus paper, *Daily Sundial*, is a liberal bore.

ENVIRONMENT:

Mental—People are talking about the sad state of America. The environmental awareness group is pretty active. They sponsored an Ecology Week which was a success. There's a big program to get the oil out of Santa Barbara. Students are aware of and interested in ecology.

Physical—It's hot in the San Fernando Valley—90° in spring. Soft sloping valley look. The campus is flat and square with lots of lawns. Only 12 years old. Modern white concrete, two four-story buildings. Everything is clean, white and hot.

Zuma and Malibu beaches are the popular escapes. 90% have cars. They go all over California. 75% commuters.

San Francisco State College
San Francisco, California

San Francisco State is a college of contradictions. The strike in 1969 plummeted the campus into the headlines, characterizing the students as hard-core revolutionaries. But a stroll leaves the impression that a striving middle-class career-oriented study body characterizes the campus. Both elements exist in this large diverse campus. Then there's that sometimes semanticist and patriot, S. I. Hayakawa, thrown in to produce an air of the theater of the absurd.

SERGEANT PEPPER SECTION:

17,857 students go here, 70% of them undergraduates. It is relatively easy to get in if the application is made early in January since admission is decided on a first come, first served basis. A GPA above 3.2 automatically makes a student eligible for admission but a GPA of 3.20 with an ACT of 11 and a SAT of 512 is also eligible! There are many transfers from junior colleges. There are only 4% out-of-state students.

ACADEMIC BULLSHIT:

Most of the classes are of typical state school mediocre quality with a few exceptions. Before the 1968–69 strike, many undergraduate departments were ranked comparable to Berkeley. But since the strike many departments have gone down in their quality. The English department is still very good (one English class goes to a Santa Cruz mansion on weekends and does plays). Another very good department is Film, even though it is short of funds. This department specializes in creative films rather than commercial ones.

The graduate departments give only M.A.s, M.S.s, and M.B.A.s. State has large English and Education grad departments. The Education department tends to be innovative—students can take "Education-Administration," "Educational Technology," "Elementary Education," "Higher Education," "Secondary Education" or "Special Education" (very good). The Business graduate program is well integrated into the community business structure and finds its grads establishment-type jobs.

The Film graduate department is well suited to independent film makers. Animation courses taught by Hilberman are exceptionally good. However, the department is very selective and underfunded. To get a Masters in Film, a student must scrounge up his money to make his own film.

A popular course is Tom Ryther's "Ecology of the Bay Area" (Sociology). All of the AFT profs who struck were fired and rehired, are usually radical and popular.

Pass/Fail courses were instituted with the strike. Most student-initiated courses are under the Experimental College or the Ethnic department. Titles include "Antidotes for Opium Eaters" and "Asian-American Communities and Urban Crisis." Several courses in ecology.

Teachers who participated in the strike are close to students and those who didn't tend to be distant.

The big strike last year was in part over an attempt to get a Third World College. It was instituted after the strike was over. They offer a large selection of courses in Asian Studies ("Cantonese," "Philippino," "Chinese and Japanese cultures in America"), Black Studies (history, psychology, literature, journalism, philosophy, etc.), Mexican-American Studies and Native American Studies. Around 800 students are enrolled, but attendance is low. A student can major in Ethnic Studies. The department has been very heavily politicized. The administration is now trying to disband the department and put the courses in individual departments, claiming that the present courses don't meet academic standards. There is a special admissions program for minority students, which admitted about 3,000 students this year.

Independent study is possible; both tests and papers are used. Study abroad with the California state college program—Colombia,

France, Germany, Ghana, Greece, Israel, Italy, Japan, Lebanon, Netherlands, Peru, Portugal, Spain, Sweden and the United Kingdom.

Classrooms are informal, no dress codes or regulations.

BREAD:

State costs $62 a semester for residents and $30 a unit for out-of-state. Most students live off campus and commute. Expensive clothes and cars aren't necessary (public transportation provides service to the campus area).

Some work-study is available if you apply early in the year. Few scholarships and loans, and limited campus jobs. Short supply of used books in campus book store.

There are two coed dorms on campus which cost approximately $580 for a semester. No regulations to speak of. Only 3% of the students live on campus. There are 83 on-campus apartment units for married students. Most students live off campus in apartments, $50 to share a bedroom in the student areas. Dates are off campus and the cost is subject to preference.

BROTHERS AND SISTERS:

A few more chicks than cats.

Playboy said this was one of the most liberated campuses. But the mistake that the dirty old glossy men of *Playboy* make is assuming that a liberated campus would embrace their Bill Blass he-men. A Bunny would never fit in here.

State students look casual. Hair on guys ranges from frat-short to long, although very long (shoulder-length or longer) is very uncommon. Dress styles have been described as "suburban Marxist," not hip. Some girls have their hair fixed up, but most girls have quite natural hair. A substantial number of girls don't wear bras. Some nylons, but jeans are more prevalent. Not much lipstick. A male quote: "One of the nice things about this campus are the short skirts of the girls." A guy or girl could wear just about anything here and wouldn't stick out unless they were unusually high fashion.

Social life is centered off campus. Very liberated—many couples live together. Few fraternities. The only place to meet there is the eating place (commons) and at demonstrations.

State's long embattled strike overshadows all current political feelings. The students struck because Hayakawa wasn't going to give in to their demands for a Third World School. There was so much unrest, they closed the school early for Christmas vacation. After vacation the radical students called a strike. Most students didn't go to class. After a few weeks, the AFT teachers and a few others went on strike. Teachers going on strike is amazingly rare and usually ineffective. The students wanted to force the school to shut down, so there were continual clashes with outside cops (the Tac Squad), beatings, rock throwing and helicopters. Daily confrontations for weeks. A black student who was trying to set a bomb was seriously hurt. People were messing up the books in the library. Hundreds were arrested, sometimes in sweeps. In February, when the new semester started, things had quieted down and people were back in class. Students were tried downtown; one was expelled from the University, some suspended. A lot went to jail. Some still are there complaining that they've been forgotten. This year there is a switch to activism in ecology, Women's Liberation, a little support for Fatah.

The students have a revolutionary consciousness but the wind was knocked out of them last year with the strike. "People are exhausted, disgusted, tired, trying to avoid activism and confrontation."

Though they say they're against "capitalistic competition," there do not seem to be any plans to go out and join the working class; they are all basically planning for the professions. One guy said that he went to Israel with radicals who here advocated to each his share, socialism, etc., but once on the kibbutz, where they all shared equally, they were discontent. "There are a lot of people realizing that they're not Che Gueveras, they're just middle-class kids who are screwed up."

Women's Liberation is active and has been demonstrating for child-care centers. The BSU is active also.

Everyone smokes grass. Lids are $10–$15.

Two college presidents have bit the dust since the start of State student demonstrations. Last year fascist S. I. Hayakawa was selected for that Oscar. He has given a very bad performance so far and it is fervently hoped that he, too, will go to Ethiopia, although he seems to enjoy any type of publicity he can get and they don't have much TV in Ethiopia. If you see Hayakawa on campus (he'll be wearing a Tam O'Shanter) avoid him; he's not above picking fights with students.

SURVIVAL:

Survival is easy in the Bay area. Much entertainment (old flicks at the "Surf," rock concerts, plays, speakers), abundant health-food stores ("Glee's" in Stonestown is closest to campus) and stimulating rapping. No BC pills on campus but Planned Parenthood in the area. Students seem very satisfied with their health center. No draft counseling on campus but plenty in the Bay area.

ENVIRONMENT:

Mental—Students discussing ecology activism this year. Everyone is reading *Siddhartha* by Hesse and *The Population Bomb* by Paul Ehrlich.

Physical—S.F. State is in a residential area of San Francisco—it's an urban campus and Bambi would get claustrophobia. There is air pollution and all the other big-city evils. The buildings are all post-office modern and a drag. They are long and flat, multistoried vintage 1953 modern.

A delightful out-of-sight escape is Golden Gate Park. On sunny days the wooded area is packed with sunshine lovers. It is a commuter's school—people do their own thing and blend in with the Bay area.

San Jose State College

San Jose, California

San Jose State is one of those party schools full of blond sun-baked Californians. Some departments are good, but nothing is too hard—people are pretty busy drinking beer and watching television. The average age of the student is 24 and many are married—it's cheap and job preparatory.

SERGEANT PEPPER SECTION:

23,478 students attend this state school; 17,000 of these are undergraduate and 6,000 graduate. In-state requirement is upper-third standing in high school; out-of-state must have something called an "eligibility" index which would place him in upper one-sixth of a California high-school class. There are ways of getting around the administration which is much like the Pentagon in that it works in strange and mysterious ways. About 12% are out-of-state students.

ACADEMIC BULLSHIT:

This place isn't exactly a brain trust and kids laugh about how easy it is. None of the graduate departments are recommended. The best undergraduate department is Art. It is geared toward individual work and students have a lot of freedom. Courses in ceramics, jewelry and pottery. English and Business are also reputed to be good departments.

One of the most popular courses is Dr. Sperling's "Contemporary Issues." This class originated the burying of a new 1970 Ford Maverick to protest pollution. Another popular professor was Dr. Rutherford who has been fired for his recent part in the school strike. Most courses on the grading system—a few are allowed to be taken Pass/Fail.

A good student-initiated set of courses called the New College is only one year old. You can take just about anything—one girl took communes for credit. The experimental college is like a Free U with the usual courses (try "Experiment in Euphoric Living"—sounds like a real stunner!). Not much of a relationship between students and teachers ("the teachers have lost sight of the reason for their existence"). Tests are still the archaic method of selection, "when the occasion arises for an assignment." There is independent study and study abroad in several countries. Class rules are nonexistent—no dress codes and smoking is allowed.

BREAD:

In-state tuition is $74 per semester and out-of-state is $515. Scholarships and loans are available but tight. Work-study is available but the jobs are lousy. Some campus jobs, clerks and dishwashers for $1.65–$2.00 an hour.

Anything goes dresswise—casual is the rule. Dates are about 50¢, the price of three joints. No used-book store to rave about.

BROTHERS AND SISTERS:

Ratio cats : chicks—1⅓ : 1.

SJSC has mostly former fraternity boys who have gone hip this year. Many wear jeans and work shirts. Some have the rich hip look of bell-bottoms, boots and leather hat. Coleman moustache look. Chicks don't use much makeup but still have that Hollywood starlet suburban housewife appearance—that careless look that takes two hours to prepare.

People are still dating here and think of screwing as having "affairs," but it is getting hipper. Dating is casual and the chicks are liberated. Fraternities exist but are dying out. Three years ago they ran the school. They advertised for rush this year saying, "Join a Minority Group." "Jonah's Wail" is an actors'-workshop-type place where hips go. All types dig the "Red Ram" (rock concerts) and the SU. Straights go to the "Loft" and the "Garlic Factory" (beer joint). Dates consist of rapping and getting stoned in groups.

Most students are apathetic toward revolutionary thought—they might not have even supported the first American Revolution. They are among those "working through the basic channels for change." What radicals there were (Harry Edwards, who organized the black athletes' boycott of the Olympics), left. No one could tell us the jail conditions—they've never been there. The biggest thing this year was the burial of that Ford Maverick.

SURVIVAL:

BC pills can be obtained through Planned Parenthood in the area. A lid goes for $10 and you can score most anywhere. Hard dope is out but mescaline is increasing in favor.

The student health service is very good. Abortion counseling and suicide prevention are in the community. Draft counseling is provided by Tom May who is supposed to be good.

Some pets frequent the campus. Two natural-food stores—"Heidi's" and the "Nutrition Center."

ENVIRONMENT:

Mental—Not too stimulating. People are reading Huxley and Brautigan, though, so there's hope.

Physical—Sunny and clear tomorrow through forever. Despite the good weather the campus is miserably landscaped; the average cemetery is more attractive. The campus has few trees and the lawns are almost all minute rectangles. Noise pollution from nearby San Jose accompanies jets. The architecture is 1955 industrial-park businesslike modern. Narrow hallways inside with little black plastic plaques on doors circa the military establishment. An aesthetic wasteland. Morris Daley Auditorium, a gray stucco building with red brick trim, is refreshingly funky in the middle of campus. The decor in the new snack bar is "functional comfy." The Union also has a new listening room—it's the only building on campus with warmth.

Escapes are Santa Cruz, Yosemite, Berkeley and San Francisco.

Sonoma State College
Rohnert Park, California

Sonoma State is becoming increasingly popular with Californians. It's the most hang loose of the California State Colleges and lets students initiate many of their own campuses. It's a very hip rural place with people digging nature, drugs and their own things. Its country location permits it to exist without many pressures of conformity.

SERGEANT PEPPER SECTION:

Out-of-staters have to be in upper one-sixth of class. If you're over 21, some requirements can be waived.

The school is hard to get into only because it is so popular. SATs and grades vary and students are admitted on a first come, first served basis. There are 3,502 students and the school eventually hopes to contain 15,000. Get it while it's small. Only 2% out-of-state as not that many people know about it—it's new. The nearest city is Cotati—small and hick.

ACADEMIC BULLSHIT:

It's a free and unstructured school—plan your course and find someone to teach it. Popular courses are "Yoga," "Nature Survival," and "Organic Farming." "Spontaneity is what matters—dealing with the here and now." Many classes meet outdoors or in students' apartments.

The school excels in its Humanistic Psychology program, both on a graduate and undergraduate level—they took 24 applicants out of 1,500. Next year they are offering 60 courses in this department.

Four graduate programs include Psych, English, Political Science and History.

Any five professors can get together and form a college. Papers and grade-yourself are what's happening. Student-initiated courses like "Pornography" and "Karate" are given for credit. Many professors are popular, especially philosophy prof Stan McDaniels who teaches "Eastern Religions Philosophy." Some faculty-student relations are about as close as you can get. Independent study is fine—study abroad, including a new program with India.

BREAD:

It costs $66 for in-state and $500 for out-of-state students per semester. Living is expensive as housing supply is short. There are no school-owned dorms and privately-owned coed dorms run about $1,150 per year. Apartments run from $60–$100 per person in Rohnert Park. In town, about 20 miles away, students can get old houses and fix them up. Some kids live in converted chicken coops and tents in the hills. Work-study is available but limited—jobs are very scarce. Not everyone has a car. Many hitchers. The school has a formal hitchhiking stand. Heavy competition for loans and scholarships. Only a raving nonconformist needs fancy wardrobe—two changes are cool.

BROTHERS AND SISTERS:

Ratio cats : chicks—1 : 1.

Everyone is hip. Jeans, work shirts, boots and long hair abound. There is no formal dating scene. People go in groups, many living together. No Greeks. Everyone is liberated.

The hip place is the "Inn of the Beginning." It has a stage where anybody can perform on weekends. A new head shop arcade has just opened called "Cotati Company #2." There's a straight place —pizza parlor that plays 1950 music and features "Timmy and the Teen Tots."

Entertainment is usually in the Bay area although some Bay bands play Cotati occasionally. Nearby Mendocino for artistic recluses! Lids go for $10 and everybody smokes and balls in a healthy environment. Political apathy—more a return-to-nature-and-learn-self-subsistence type school. A few Third World clubs. There is a good minority-student program called Hidden Talent which recruits Third Worlders and offers courses in black music and history.

SURVIVAL:

Dr. Harry Horowitz, a professor in the Psych department, draft counsels. Abortion referrals and suicide prevention center are both well organized. Complete birth control information in community, V.D. clinic, too. This school is prepared for you.

Pets roam the campus—there are even horses around. The campus newspaper, *Steppen,* is a good political paper. The underground papers from Berkeley are available. Health-food store called "Trade Winds" in Cotati. Escapes are back-to-nature types—beach, mountains and of course Berkeley for a different kind of trip.

ENVIRONMENT:

Mental—Read Paul Ehrlich's *The Population Bomb* and the *Environmental Handbook* and be concerned about ecology.

Physical—Sonoma State is rural—rolling elephant hills, eucalyptus trees, farming land. This area was once the poultry capital of the world. Mostly drab concrete buildings, "San Quentin of the north." New, plastic, built in 1960, anti-riot types with dark glass windows. They had the Tac Squad in for a security check and it passed with flying colors.

The University of California
Power to the People

Nine campuses: Berkeley, Davis, Irvine, Los Angeles, Riverside, San Diego, Santa Barbara, Santa Cruz and a medical center in San Francisco.

Admission is very selective—must be in top 12% high-school class. Out-of-staters need B+ average, B in-state.

BERKELEY
Berkeley, California

Berkeley is a campus community located ten miles from San Francisco. It is the heaviest politically of the University of California campuses. Revolution is happening everywhere. Sex and drugs are a way of life, cats and chicks are natural-looking and wrapped in old clothes. The most relevant education can be imbibed from just living in Berkeley. There is an honest and somewhat successful attempt to offer classes that are responsive to society's needs, both through the bureaucracy and through the students' own initiative. Berkeley is a mind opener and a very freaky place.

SERGEANT PEPPER SECTION:

This campus is the answer for 29,000 students, 90% from California. Admission is highly selective for both in- and out-of-state students. Average SAT score is 600 for incoming freshmen. About 25% of the students receive financial aid. There are no rules governing living accommodations. A high percentage of foreign students attend, but not many Third World people. 25% of students live in dormitories. Greeks are going coed and dying out.

ACADEMIC BULLSHIT:

Berkeley has good undergraduate and excellent graduate departments for those who are on a formal learning trip. Its over-all rating in graduate-school standing is #1 by the American Council of Education Surveys. A student guide to courses is offered. Strongest undergraduate departments are Physics, Mathematics, History, English and Anthropology. Especially good grad departments are Law (no grades given), Public Health, Criminology, Journalism and all the Sciences. Independent study is allowed for those with a two-year 3.0 grade average.

Recommended: "Social History of China and Japan" (Schurmann, "Criminology—Etiology of Crime" Diamond—a shrink), "Political Science—American Role in the Far East" (defensively taught by former Johnson advisor Scalapino), "Psychology—Small Group Structures" (sections are T encounter groups—Sampson), "Rhetoric" (Bendich—he was Lenny Bruce's lawyer), "Journalism —Reporting of Public Affairs" (Bayley—a former NET vice president). The faculty has over ten Nobel Prize winners teaching science.

The most interesting courses offered are those given by the Center For Participant Education and the Free University. The CPE courses are worth credit although this must be arranged through the department and a condition of relative paranoia exists.

CPE offers "Seeding and Cultivation," "Country Music Workshop," and "Getting in Touch" (nonverbal communication). The Free University is super-freaky—no credit, just elucidation. Courses like "Body Massage," "Basic Auto Mechanics," "Glassworking," "Yoga" and "Wilderness Living and Survival" are a few of the choices. Everything the impudent snob needs to know.

Class attendance is necessary only in the small classes. Fybates are available—3/$5. Second-hand books are plentiful at "Moe's" or "Shakespeare's" on Telegraph. Xerox is 2¢ a sheet. Students are allowed one Pass/Fail course a semester outside of their major.

A new Ethnic Studies program was begun in fall, 1969, in Black, Chicano, Indian and Asian-American areas. It's a hodgepodge and the word is that the University is shafting it.

BREAD:

Tuition $325 per year in-state, $1,525 out-of-state. If tuition doesn't go up, Berkeley will continue to be the ideal hang for those short of bread. Digs are only expensive close to campus and the Berkeley Tenants' Union is striking to hopefully change that. Cheap housing is available within five miles of campus. Transportation is by hitching or motorcycle. Some cars exist. Dorms are despised and called the "Twelve Tombs." They are for Rich people who, like sterile atmospheres. No dorm regulations and some of them are coed. Many people are forming communes.

Work-study is available for low-income students—15 hours a week while school is in session and full time on the holidays and vacations. Loan money is freely available but scholarships are tight. Jobs are plentiful in the area.

Dating is no financial strain, a cup of capuccino and a walk along Telegraph Avenue and rapping costs 40¢.

BROTHERS AND SISTERS:

Ratio cats : chicks—1.5 : 1.

The sexual activity is heavy. Meeting people is easy—at supermarkets, in classes, in political organizations and laundromats on Telegraph. Chicks are the natural types, no makeup, bras or coiffed hair. Everyone wears old clothes, faded jeans, tie-dyed torn shirts, bright-colored home-knit shawls, mufflers, hiking boots. People generally prefer to look as unprosperous as possible and spend their bread on stereo equipment and books.

A typical date consists of going to hear a speaker or attending an art flick and then hitting Telegraph for that necessary cup of cappucino (for sustenance). Drugs are here, grass is part of life. A lid of grass is $10 and a cap of acid is $3 in the area. Students can usher and see plays free in San Francisco. Rock concerts are plentiful in San Francisco. Greeks (the few there are) can meet at beer joints and the library.

Preparations for the revolution and ecology action to save what earth is left are the two biggest causes. The organizations run from YAF to SDS. Women's Liberation is quite active, recently picketing to be allowed to join a men's karate class on campus (down with male chauvinism). The current cause is the Berkeley Tenants' Union strike against landlords who blitz the area with high rent increases yearly. Political information tables like G.I. resistance and the Young Socialist League are set up in Sproul Hall area at noon.

Political History:

1964. Berkeley started the current wave of student power with the FSM led by Mario Savio and Jack Weinberger. A filthy speech movement (in defense of word mongers) followed in 1965.

1967. A demonstration at the Oakland Induction Center made news, and subsequently the trial of the Oakland 7.

1968. The Third World Liberation Front staged a mostly unsuccessful strike demanding a Black Studies and Chicano Studies program which they got (the program is turning out to be a shuck). Eldridge Cleaver created another crisis among the Regents by teaching "controversial" "139X."

1969. It was students against administration in the People's Park Battle which occurred when students turned a muddy parking lot into a lovely park. The University didn't dig it because it was University property—riot and one death resulted. The park was cemented over and exists as an empty parking lot now.

In 1969 the issues were the emergence of Women's Liberation, Ecology Action and the Berkeley Tenants' Union Strike. ROTC still offers two- and four-year programs but there have been bombings of the facilities in recent years.

The jail conditions are vicious and the guards at the local clink, Santa Rita, are brutal. The campus cops aren't bad but the Alameda County Sheriff's Department is known for clubbing, gassing and kicking—"The Blue Meanies."

Berkeley organized an efficient strike against Nixon's Cambodian action. The campus is very political.

SURVIVAL:

The Gay Liberation Front is active. BC pills and diaphragms are given out at Planned Parenthood near campus. They also give free pregnancy tests and abortion referrals for careless lovers. A free hippie clinic exists for those sick without bread; they sponsor RAP sessions with a psychiatrist for those that feel they want it. University student health is good with about a half-hour wait and free prescriptions.

The student government has hired a full-time draft counselor and there are many other counseling services available. There is an off-campus Suicide Prevention Center.

Health foods are plentiful and restaurants also serve macrobiotic and health foods. A very successful Food Conspiracy exists in which students group to buy produce and meat from farms and ranches rather than stores.

ENVIRONMENT:

Mental—Read *Zap Comics*, the *Whole Earth* catalog, *Been Down So Long It Looks Like Up To Me* by Richard Fariña, *The Electric Kool-Aid Acid Test* by Tom Wolfe, *Quotations from Mao* and something about Marxism before you arrive. Read anything.

The *Berkeley Tribe* exists as a good means of underground communication. Radical thoughts circulate in the air. Pets are everywhere.

Physical—The climate is temperate with rain. You can eat a bag lunch outside ten months a year. The architecture is mixed, some pre-World War II monstrosities and some modern eyesores and some in-between alrights. There are trees and streams on campus. Tilden Park, a luscious adventure in nature, is close by. The setting is cluttered with buildings but there is still some open air left. Escapes are plentiful. Mendocino is an art colony with communes to the north, Big Sur is to the south, skiing is four hours away at Squaw Valley. Charters traverse the earth—Mexico City, Japan, Europe during the summer. Most students prefer a picnic in the country to city sightseeing.

DAVIS
Davis, California

Davis started out as an agricultural school in 1906 and it hasn't changed much. The students think you mean student government when you ask them about politics. The atmosphere is stagnantly efficient and many girls still wear bobby socks and pleated skirts.

Agriculture, Veterinary Medicine and Engineering are the biggest fields, and fraternities are still alive. 15% of the men join frats and 20% of the students live in dormitories. The nearest city is Sacramento, just a short distance away. Most students are from nearby suburbs and many go home for the weekend.

SERGEANT PEPPER SECTION:

12,000 students, same requirements as for all of University of California.

ACADEMIC BULLSHIT:

The emphasis on the Sciences produces strong departments in those fields. The Veterinary and Agricultural departments are excellent. The Law school and Medical school are gaining a good reputation. There is a very good intern program in Sacramento for those interested in California government and the Republican style political science.

Independent study is allowed and encouraged.

A few unusual institution courses are offered, including "Viticulture" (the science of wine-making—difficult but interesting) with "Amerine History" courses with Prof. W. T. Jackson and "Rhetoric" courses with John Vohs. Titles such as "Environmental

Horticulture" and "Animal Resources Problems" exist in the catalog. A student guide to courses called "Student Viewpoint" is offered. Pass/Fail.

Students or people in the community can initiate courses. An Experimental College exists that is allowed to give credit if you get a prof's O.K. Last quarter they offered "Flying Saucers," "You Are What You Eat," and many ecology courses. The Ethnic Studies program is new but a shuck at this time although the administration is being very cooperative.

BREAD:

The cost of living in Davis is about half that of Berkeley. You can get a tuna-fish sandwich for 35¢ (75¢ in Berkeley). The tuition is the same at all University of California schools ($312 in-state for three quarters, $1,526 out-of-state). The sterile dorms are $110 a quarter for room and board. Apartments usually go for about $200 close to campus and can be split four ways. Housing is a lot cheaper if you are willing to drive 15 minutes to campus. In the outlying areas of Woodland and Dixon a house rents for $120. There is married-student housing available.

A few students have cars but everyone has a bicycle. The campus looks like a mammoth bicycle race. Davis' most original contribution is its bus transport system—old red London double-decker buses that run on campus. Quarter tickets can be purchased at a low price and riding on the red giants is a delight.

Work-study is available but limited. Jobs are available on campus. About 20% of the students receive financial aid. Loans, especially emergency loans, are easy to get but scholarships are, as usual, tight. Cost of an average date is $5 for a movie and coffee. Clothes and dating are casual.

BROTHERS AND SISTERS:

Ratio cats : chicks—1 : 1.

This school is still in the early 60s. Guys wear short hair, sideburns are unusual. Chicks wear skirts and sweaters and an occasional "hair-do." They look like an ad for Montgomery Ward. Cats and chicks meet at the dorms and in their classes. Fraternity beer busts are a big thing.

The Davis students talk about school spirit a lot (remember that?). Their drug awareness is in a state of expansion and those that buy get a lid for $12. No one seemed to know the price of acid. Student government and clubs are "status groups" and intra-mural sports are supported. A few people shack together but they really can't admit it yet.

The few cool people here hang at the "Coffee House," a beat barnlike structure on campus. They play "Old Style Berkeley Music" there. The only visible minority students were Orientals.

Like we said, politics means student government to Davis residents. An SDS exists as does a Women's Liberation Front—but they aren't well organized or active. Davis students are lukewarm liberal—and by the way, the underground paper is far right.

SURVIVAL:

Contraceptive devices aren't given out on campus but there doesn't seem to be a need for them as yet. There is a Planned Parenthood in nearby Woodland. There is a Suicide Prevention Center.

Draft help in Davis. Student health has a hospital and the facilities are so-so, free prescriptions. Some students grow their own health foods but this is rare.

One unusual club is "The Latecomers" for older students. The main function is socializing.

ENVIRONMENT:

Mental—The mental environment isn't very stimulating although some students are reading Herman Hesse and *Zap Comics*.

Physical—The school has many lovely trees and flowers but the architecture is functional. The dorms are all alike—wooden boxes. On the outskirts of campus a lake and arboretum exist.

Most go home or skiing to the close-by Sierras for the weekend. They then go back to Davis for a rest.

IRVINE

Irvine, California

Irvine has all the personality of an empty locker. Supposedly it is the easiest of the University of California's campuses to get into, its main attraction being its proximity to Disneyland (lots of new rides this year). Irvine is smack dab in the center of John Birchland—Orange County—and the campus and school are uptight. Most of the 5,000 students go there to learn a skill.

There is a great building program going on, evidence of the fact that the Regents like Irvine. It's one of two UC campuses that haven't given the Regents too many headaches (the other being Davis). The school has few minority students or out-of-state students—just lots of rightists. Many students live in dorms although there is a severe shortage of student housing as of now.

SERGEANT PEPPER SECTION:

Irvine has only 5,000 students. Same academic requirements as other University of California campuses, but not that selective.

ACADEMIC BULLSHIT:

Irvine is just starting out. The classes are usually dull lectures, note-taking and tests. Better than average departments so far are those in Art, Dance and Social Sciences. A new course called "Comparative Cultures" has attracted followers. "Biology 40" is the house Mickey. There are no experimental courses or colleges. Pass/Not Pass courses are allowed in any course except those required (thanks a lot); a C gives you a pass, anything lower gives you no credit. There is a new Ethnic Studies program, not much as yet. The school is a diploma mill. Some independent study.

BREAD:

Irvine is basically expensive, because Orange County is expensive. A car is a necessity and many students commute. Even though the campus is 1,500 acres, Los Angeles is the place to go, usually, for entertainment. The dorms are usually full. An apartment runs $140 for two-bedrooms away from campus. Students like to live in Laguna Beach nearby.

Work-study, loans and scholarships, and campus jobs are all limited. An expensive wardrobe isn't necessary. You get the impression that everyone is saving their money to invest it.

BROTHERS AND SISTERS:

Ratio cats : chicks—1 : 1.

Sisters are straight—mid-50s type. Cats are a mixed breed. Most look like they live in conservative Orange County. Chicks wear not only bras but girdles. Dating is structured and cliquish. Sex may be happening but there really isn't a campus feeling, so if it is, it's quiet. There aren't any Greeks but there is some parent involvement (just as bad). Not much interest in sports or school spirit, just getting that degree.

Laguna Beach living is fun in an unhip manner. Bars, "Thumper" and "Whales Tails," are considered par for an evening. No birth control information dispensed on campus but Planned Parenthood in the area. Draft counseling on campus, no organized abortion referrals. Health service is excellent.

There are very few radicals but if you want to meet a straight go to "Finnigan's Rainbow," "The Attic," or "Pier 11" in Newport Beach. "Spritz's Garden" is also recommended for squares. Grass is the only dope and it's available. No foreign flicks in area except on campus. One good book store, "Bird in Search of a Cage." A new good twice-quarterly literary magazine called *Incantations* on campus.

The Revolution is a dirty word to the students and the community. SDS is the only political group (30 members) that is active (unless you count Young Republicans). SDSers are considered hairy freaks by most of the unthinking mass. This campus is apathetic and antiseptic.

The only stirring events that have happened were this year. SDS asked permission to hold their convention on campus; request denied—this caused a small ripple. Early in the year two officers held a black at gunpoint for speeding. The small BSU (30) protested this as did the few campus rads. Pigs stay off campus (looking for community "pinkos"). There are 60 blacks and 70 other minority students.

SURVIVAL:

Nearly impossible, but a small underground is just beginning to develop.

ENVIRONMENT:

Mental—The students don't know of any good books offhand.

Physical—The climate is fair and there is a lot of L.A. smog drifting over. The campus looks like a modern golf course that is expanding. Modern drab buildings abound. Students go on UC charters for escape or to the mountains to ski.

UCLA
Los Angeles, California

UCLA is the school of clean hippies. Everyone wants to be cool and they try but their clothes are the newest hip and their mind is the plastic hip. When they visit Berkeley they are afraid of picking up germs.

A sense of community is sadly lacking as most students are commuters. However, L.A. offers many cultural diversions—theater, museums and "stars." Students who don't commute usually live in boxlike dorms or expensive apartments near campus.

SERGEANT PEPPER SECTION:

UCLA is very overcrowded and will take only those with high grades and high SAT scores (600). 30,000 students attend UCLA. 3.4% of the students are black, 2.8% are Mexican-American and .3% are Indian.

ACADEMIC BULLSHIT:

Most interesting courses (undergraduate) are "Human Relations" with Faber ("UCLA can drive anyone into an identity crisis. This course helps you out"), "Journalism" with Robert Kirsch, any of Robert Hirsch's English classes (come to his classes stoned), "The Aesthetics of Rock" by Fagin, "Jazz" with Tanner, "Political Science" with Wolfenstein (he plays the guitar in class) and any courses in the Film department. Its graduate and undergraduate departments are excellent in many fields, especially Law, Medicine, Philosophy, Chemistry and Theater Arts.

The Experimental College gives no credit but offers "Esoteric Arts and Crafts" (magic), "Funky Guitar Stuff" and "Parapsychology." C.S.E.S. is student-originated and is a series of lectures and workshops on a study of society and education.

Pass/Fail is allowed as is independent study. Class attendance isn't vital as most classes are huge (some have closed-circuit television). The Ethnic Studies program is two years old and trying hard.

BREAD:

In-state is $112 and out-of-state $526 per quarter. UCLA doesn't take much bread if you are a commuter. Dorms are high—$1,100 a year for board, a group bathroom and a pad slightly bigger than a breadbox (which you have to share). The dorms are coed, separated by the floors. Visiting hours and open weekends, if you decide to split.

The best place to live is in Venice or Santa Monica. Venice was the scene of Muscle Beach in the 50s and is the most integrated community in Los Angeles. It's 20 minutes away and next to the ocean. Lots of high living in Venice. Groovy digs can be had (including old houses) for little bread. Santa Monica has boring modern structures but the rent is lower than in Westwood Village. The Village (an upper-middle-class commercial nucleus with dress stores, shoe stores, and grocery stores) is no relation to New York's Village. Apartments in the Village run $150–$225 for a one-closet within walking distance of campus. Another popular area to live is Beverly Glen. It's about 20 minutes from campus and it's like living out in the country. It's hard to get a place there, they are in demand.

A car is necessary and parking is available only if you are related to God. Public transportation? The only convenient way to attend UCLA is by parachute. Dates are financially open-ended: some chicks are demanding. Students are ultra clothes and class conscious.

Work-study is limited and campus jobs are nearly nonexistent. Loans and scholarships are tight.

BROTHERS AND SISTERS:

Ratio cats : chicks—1 : 1.

Chicks and cats are carefully garbed though increasingly hip. Hair is long for both sexes.

UCLA has definitely progressed since 1966 when it got uptight because USC swiped the coveted Rose Bowl bid. Although the campus is changing it will probably never be a focus of violent confrontation because it is too spread out and the majority of students commute. Greeks still exist but are dying.

Dudes range from the business-executive majors who wear wingtips (loafers without socks in the summer) to the blatant Hollywood hippie with wide collar shirts from expensive boutiques on Sunset Strip and classy fringed leather jackets. The in-between wear starched work shirts. Chicks come in all kinds—Theater Arts majors wearing tight bell-bottoms and expensive boots, sorority girls with pantihose and scarves, collegiate plain janes with training bras, and hippie barefoot types. Hips meet at the "Gypsy Wagon" on campus and squares hang at "Mom's" beer joint. The school is marriage-oriented—pinning is out but engagements are in.

UCLA used to be into Making It above ground, but now protest is becoming visible. During Berkeley's People's Park, 1,000 students took over the administration building for the night. In January of 1970, students protested the recruiters from G.E.

SDS now has the most momentum of any group on campus. The unhooked Women's Liberation Front is nudging for child-care centers. The two radical Mexican-American groups are MECHA and Nuestra Familia. The BSU isn't very militant although there are some Panthers on campus. In 1969, two Black Panthers were killed on campus.

The major political confrontation was the firing of Angela Davis, an admitted Communist professor, in the fall of 1969. She was reinstated after the students and the Regents supported her right to teach. She was not rehired to teach in fall of 1970.

In the fall of 1969, a black worker was fired from the food service after a dispute. 30 students crowded into the dean's office and detained him for ten hours. These students are presently on trial for this. The school keeps a file on activists and turns them over to the pigs.

There was confrontation during the strike. Students broke windows and liberated the administration building. 200 pigs came on campus on motorcycles and hassled students, breaking arms and heads.

"There are still more here that aren't with it than that are, but things are looking up."

SURVIVAL:

Dope is available and $10 buys a lid. The Overpopulation Information Center gives out information on birth control every Monday on campus. Planned Parenthood and cooperative doctors are available in the area. Draft counseling and The Resistance is on campus. There is a free hippie clinic in Los Angeles. The *Free Press* is a good underground newspaper published in L.A.

ENVIRONMENT:

Mental—UCLA is getting with it so read Hesse, *Woodstock Nation* by Abbie Hoffman and any books on Marx (Karl) you can find.

Physical—UCLA is a structured campus, Spanish and modern architecture among plotted grass. There is no rural feeling—it's urban. The visual thing on campus is called the "Inverted Fountain" located between Franz Hall and the Music building. Instead of shooting the water into the air, the water flows downward and drops.

It has smog, traffic and too many people, just like L.A.

RIVERSIDE
Riverside, California

Riverside is an hour from the mountains, an hour from the sea, an hour from L.A., an hour from Palm Springs and in the middle of nowhere. The campus is mostly straight, trying to get in on a little of the political action when they can. Everything is so cozy with the administration that they can't seem to produce any confrontations. During Berkeley's People's Park rages, Riverside students sympathized by occupying the administration building. The Chancellor sent them coffee and doughnuts. Most students want to grow up and live in the suburbs.

SERGEANT PEPPER SECTION:

People at Riverside are gung-ho students, not much interested in the world around them. The school houses 5,000 students, about half living in dormitories. They consider Los Angeles to be their nearest cultural center; this gives you an idea of their level of culture.

The school is medium-hard to get into—you need a 3.0 from high school and a 525 average on your SATs.

ACADEMIC BULLSHIT:

Riverside has two excellent departments: Agriculture and Entomology (bugs). Dr. Cortez teaches a popular Mexican-American Studies program, one of the only experimental classes. Study is oriented toward life sciences and physical sciences and students are studiers.

There is a new Chicano and Black Studies program, undistinguished so far. A Free University exists and offers such courses as "Cinematography" and "Yoga." No fybates and no cheap Xerox service. Class attendance is only vital in language classes. Independent study is offered in every department, Pass/Fail classes allowed. Black and Chicano Studies departments have been started this year with courses in history, psychology and political science.

BREAD:

Tuition in-state is $312, out-of-state, $1,500 per year.

BROTHERS AND SISTERS:

Ratio cats : chicks—1 : 1.

The campus has straights with wing-tips to heavy bushy hips. The majority of the chicks are collegiate Bobbie Brooks, studying and husband hunting. Some people cohabit but it's not prevalent. From the mouth of a hip chick—"I like it here—I'm not forced to be a radical. . . . You can study and ball and go down to the County Pound and look."

Most students live off campus in surrounding areas. They stay there on weekends and take in campus entertainment and L.A. sights. The University sponsored a grass bust in June, 1969. It was originally scheduled during the People's Park strike in May but the dean of students notified the suspects ahead of time. The bust was, however, completed in June, at pressure from the Riverside city fathers.

Greeks are nearly nonexistent but they still have sports heroes and bouncing cheerleaders.

The local hip hang is "Betty's Record Shop." For squares, hit "Frank's Bar" for juice freaks.

Brace yourself—the Young Republicans are the most active club. The Black Student Union is like a country club.

Last year during People's Park, the students occupied the administration building. It took them three hours of standing outside to decide to do it. The campus is apathetic except in the area of ecology where a group called "People's Lobby" is fighting smog. The 300 minority students aren't radical.

SURVIVAL:

Dope is available at $10 a lid and $3 for acid. You can get BC pills at the health center but it's a hassle. No abortion referrals or IUDs anywhere. Student health service is bad—"Yesterday I had to scream and kick to get an appointment." Good draft counseling on campus.

ENVIRONMENT:

Mental—Read Alan Watts and Herman Hesse.

Physical—The nicest natural feature are the mountains close by—for climbing and seeing. But it's nearly ruined when Los Angeles smog rolls in between 3–5 P.M. The campus is open, grassy and functional-looking (ugly).

The chief eyesore is the belltower. The chancellor wanted one because Berkeley had one. It is a large cement building with 48 bells with a range of four octaves. It emits clear-toned dull thuds. The yellow-orange brick buildings around it look like they have a bad case of jaundice.

SAN DIEGO

San Diego, California

(La Jolla, California)

San Diego is a campus of friendly Californians. The school was originally founded as a marine station and the underground is, for the most part, underwater. The school is located in La Jolla, a conservative beach resort outside of San Diego. Students quietly attend classes and are hung up on academics.

SERGEANT PEPPER SECTION:

UCSD is selective (4,000 students) but only medium-hard for state residents to get into.

ACADEMIC BULLSHIT:

The Science departments are excellent and students can take courses at Scripps Institute of Oceanography. The Medical school and the Philosophy department are also good.

Interesting undergraduate courses are "Art 1A" (Brach), "African Arts and Communication" (Wilton). There are student-initiated courses on such things as "Film" and "The Future of Faith." The school is modeled on the Oxford College system and students feel that faculty are very responsive to them. The new Third World College is student-initiated.

Beware of the Language department—it's hard and cantankerous. Class attendance is important only in seminars. Tests are 50% take-home and others are open-book. A liberal approach to grades and tests. Independent study is very popular and encouraged. A Third World College was started in the fall of 1970. Pass/Fail.

BREAD:

Tuition is $312 in-state and $1,500 out-of-state. It's not that expensive to attend UCSD but most of the students come from homes where their parents rip off over $25,000 a year.

Dorms are $1,100 a year and going up. Half the students live off campus in apartments and half live in the dorms. The most popular places to live are Del Mar and Cardiff, outlying areas. You can get an apartment in these areas for $70 a month. Cars and dune buggies are popular, and an expensive wardrobe definitely isn't necessary.

Work-study is fairly available as are campus jobs. You can scrounge by eating cheaply at the bars in Pacific Beach—19¢ and 31¢ meals.

BROTHERS AND SISTERS:

Ratio cats : chicks—2 : 1.

The brothers and sisters are friendly, outdoorsy and low key. They aren't politically active.

Traditionally there have not been many females on campus but this is changing. The school is in an expansion program—new colleges will be built each year until there are 12 (there are now three). UCDS is isolated and in the country—an ivory tower. Students don't date that much as they claim they are too studious.

Mostly straights, some hippies and a handful of radicals. They dress very casually. There are no Greeks. Hip places to meet are the "Heritage" and the "White Whale." Students can go into San Diego for diversions, which, except for the zoo, are expensive.

This school has a dearth of political history, left or right. The radical groups have small membership on campus. Third World College demands made by the minority students last year are awaiting the Regents' final approval. The big issue was when rightist organizations and Governor Reagan were giving Marcuse trouble— students supported his right to teach.

SURVIVAL:

Grass is freely available for $10 a lid, but other drugs are on vacation. The most popular health-food store is in Escondido (the students are trying to organize one on campus). Planned Parenthood is in the area. Student health is parochial and prudish. They refer you to a town doctor for birth control information. Abortion referrals are handled in a center in downtown San Diego. Draft counseling is in the area and on campus. A free hippie clinic operates out of San Diego.

The two underground papers are the *Street Journal* (Marxist rhetoric) and the *Free Door*. The campus AM station is dynamite —like an FM rock station—KSDT.

ENVIRONMENT:

Mental—Students do their "homework" and don't read outside books.

Physical—The campus is rather new and antiseptic looking. The prettiest sight is the water tower with a far out mural painted on it. The Basic Science building is a bummer—take a map or your lunch if you enter in basement.

Students escape to the beach or to Torray Pines Park. They can also camp out on the 20 acres of University-owned eucalyptus woods. The weather is beautiful.

SANTA BARBARA
Santa Barbara, California

Santa Barbara has changed in the last year from a sun-'n-fun-goodies place to a politically-active environment. A bank has burned, a student was killed and the community of Isla Vista, home of 8,000 students, has begun to organize.

SERGEANT PEPPER SECTION:

13,147 students, 2,005 graduates, 535 students out-of-state. 300 blacks, 200 Chicanos (1.5%). Not difficult to get in, C–B average in high school, average board scores—lots of junior-college transfers.

ACADEMIC BULLSHIT:

"Most significant was the difficulty everybody had in thinking of any departments that weren't terrible in some way or another." Anthropology was the best in 1969–70, but all the good professors have left due to administrative pressures. The Biological Science department is considered excellent with an emphasis on marine biology. Psychology department is the worst. The Drama department has courses in all facets of production including guerrilla theater.

Favorite professors include Professor Stuurman, who teaches English ("The Bible as Literature"). He opens every class by saying "If there are any Christians in this class, I'll probably offend them." Professor Garrett Hardin, the famous population biologist, teaches "Human Ecology."

Santa Barbara is becoming more and more progressive educationally. Pass/Fail is now used and papers are as prevalent as tests. Classes are large and impersonal. No student-originated classes for credit. No Free U. The Black Student Union created a Black Studies department with courses like "African Philosophy" and "Black Education." The BSU is active in the community and has established a liberation school to tutor underprivileged black children in the community.

Anyone with over 125 units can apply for independent study. There is a program called "Creative Studies." If you have a B average and show creative promise you can join the program—you plan your own program. There is also a Creative College for exceptionally "creative" students. It is a very small project and open to all kinds of experimental teaching.

Study abroad all over (Beirut, Bordeaux, Ghana, Hong Kong, Israel, Nairobi, Lund, Norway, Mexico, Padua, Paris, Madrid, U.K. and Tokyo).

BREAD:

UCSB costs $167 in-state and $567 out-of-state per quarter. Over 50% of the students have scholarships and loans. Jobs are hard to get and pay poorly. Some work-study if you are eligible.

In the summers, students and street people can crash. Meals can be gotten from the dining commons for free with a little know-how. Health-food stores offer a dinner of rice and vegetables for 37¢.

9,000 people live in the Isla Vista community. Apartments are ticky-tacky prefabs—$80 a month per person.

Dorms run $672 per year for a double and $771 for a single. The University-approved private dorms are lax in rules and nicer. "People smoke joints in the lounge watching TV."

Few studio apartments or houses.

People have cars but there's nowhere to use them. Lots of bikes and feet. Expensive wardrobes aren't necessary.

Dates are cheap—beach, parties and body painting.

BROTHERS AND SISTERS:

Ratio cats : chicks—1 : 1.

The kids are tanned and good-looking, smiling and holding hands and generally furthering the impression of Isla Vista as a youth utopia. Political speeches are given on a sloping lawn outside the cafeteria and the kids are pretty well divided as to those "on the lawn" and those "off the lawn." On the lawn, the guys have medium-long hair, shorts or jeans, sandals or no shoes and beards, and the girls have jeans or hip dresses, suede vests, long hair and beads, sneakers or sandals. Nobody outlandish or really freaky. The freaks are the Isla Vista street people who have dropped out or come from somewhere else.

The others have short hair, wear slacks, girls wear skirts, but nobody is disgustingly straight. Quite a few well-coordinated and outfitted sorority-type chicks.

Plenty of apathetic beach types, but generally growing political awareness etc. has resulted in more open minds and looser dress and life style. Very radical living. Community is very together, and is into all sorts of hip things like food co-ops and building parks and health foods, etc. "Avant-garde in life style," "becoming radicalized."

Not much dating—mostly living together. "Everybody's making love freely and openly." Fraternities still exist but are dying out.

Bill Allen, Anthropology professor, had done a lot to organize and radicalize the campus. He was fired in 1970 and the students staged a sit-in in the administration building, forcing the school to close down and demanding a hearing. Panic resulted when the dean hit a student in the face with his bull-horn when the student called him a pig. The pigs thought the dean was being attacked and charged the crowd.

Since that incident police harassment in Isla Vista has been common.

The Bank of America incident was a community incident rather than a campus one. At Kunstler's address the police were there, fully equipped beforehand with riot equipment and sirens, etc. News cameras, etc., "seemed to indicate that a riot was expected." "Police harassment was the major issue. The pigs stopped people late at night and hassled and searched them." "Entered apartments illegally, etc., all the time." The fire was started by only a few, and while not many participated, everybody "watched" and their sentiments were "right on!" While the Bank of America was burning, the fire department wouldn't come! So, it burned down.

SDS is no longer, but the Radical Union has gathered popularity. They got behind Bill Allen and the moratoriums and have made a move to incorporate Isla Vista.

This past quarter, everybody's been together on opposition to Nixon. When Reagan closed down UCSB in 1970, SB students had a protest at General Motors and on the freeway. The day preceding things were not as quiet. The food service equipment was smashed, many windows broken, the ROTC building was the victim of a "pee-in."

Rock throwers are a very small minority.

Local hangs include "Borsodi's Coffee House," the "Taco Bell" (where to score) and the "Sun and Earth" (where the freaks hang).

SURVIVAL:

Not enough creative facilities except in Music department. BC pills not available from student health (which is the worst). Abortion referrals are possible in the community. Draft counseling is done through the dean's office. Switchboard operates suicide prevention center and hippie clinic. There are plenty of pets on campus. The newspaper, *El Gaucho,* is radical and good.

A lid is $10 and easily available. A lot of smack freaks among the street people. Acid is $2. No big busts.

A great health-food store, the "Sun and Earth," is stocked with grains, nuts, fruit, yogurt, freaky atmosphere, rice drinks and a garden in back. The "Juice Factory" makes organic juices.

ENVIRONMENT:

Mental—Students are talking about the Isla Vista community and ecology. They are reading Hoffman and Rubin.

Physical—Isla Vista is a student community, set apart; the campus is in the center. To the west is the ocean and to the north are the mountains. The town is student-run except for the realtors. It has a "soft, organic open air atmosphere." It's like a beach resort, no tall buildings, open and airy. The water is 40 feet away.

Buildings are the Acme brick motif. One beautiful circular lecture hall with a white undulating roof is called "The Moon Crater." There's not much air pollution—just the smell of salt water. Escapes include the beach, Red Rock (an area in the hills with waterfalls and hiking trails) and Los Angeles.

The Isla Vista Community is trying to organize itself. Merchants have donated land to the people. Perfect Park was built, and corn and oats were planted. There are Ecology Survival Centers on every block.

SANTA CRUZ

Santa Cruz, California

Santa Cruz is a highly experimental unstructured campus just ten years old. No grades are given. The school is located on the coast of California on 2,000 wooded acres. Flowers, woods and meadows abound. "Power to the imagination" describes the campus which is modeled after the Oxford system of "cluster colleges."

SERGEANT PEPPER SECTION:

Admission is highly selective for the 3,000 students; the average boards scores of incoming freshmen are 630. Less than 5% are Third World and foreign students. 65% of the students live in dormitories.

ACADEMIC BULLSHIT:

The "cluster college" system makes for an intense course of study. There are six colleges, each with a specialty such as Social Science or Performing Arts. The graduate school is miniscule although a Ph.D. in the "History of Consciousness" is offered.

Several undergraduate courses are favorites including "Wine Appreciation" and courses in ethnic studies. There is a high percentage of visiting faculty members. Students can teach and initiate courses within the system. Field projects are offered in such places as the U.S.S.R. and Israel and are worth up to five hours credit. There is a Free University in Santa Cruz for those who are artsy-craftsy inclined. No grades are given and the academic environment is highly responsive to student desires.

Class attendance is important in the smaller classes. There are almost no tests and big lectures are composed of about 40 people. The opportunities for independent study are infinite and emphasized on the lower as well as the upper level.

BREAD:

Since most students live in the plush, colorful dorms, it is an expensive place to learn. Dorms run $1,200 a year, have few regulations. Off-campus housing is cheaper and students are beginning to group together and rent farms. 7–15 students can go in together on this—it's a very groovy idea. Cars aren't necessary as an orange tram called the "elephant train" transports students around campus. Hitching is popular. Date costs are miniscule—coffee or nature dates in the woods are the usual. Old, sloppy clothes are worn. The work-study program is severely limited. Loans and scholarships are scarce. No community jobs.

BROTHERS AND SISTERS:

Ratio cats : chicks—1 : 1.

Most are backwoods hip, into the natural environment, hiking, health foods and the outdoors. A full set of hair (head and face) is necessary for a cat. Hand-me-downs and ponchos for chicks. Kilo cleaning parties are preferred to powderpuff football.

Dating and going together aren't the most popular alternatives. Most people prefer doing things in small groups of around six. Entertainment is self-generated and students put on interpretive dance shows, mixed-media happenings and gospel concerts. The sexual revolution has arrived. Greeks are nonexistent. It's a suitcase school—a lot of weekend traveling.

The biggest issue at Santa Cruz last year was the Case of the Geodesic Domes. The students built two beautiful domes which they wanted to place on campus as their Home. The administration got uptight and a hassle ensued resulting in removal of the domes from central campus.

There is a highly vocal radical movement. Key leftist organization is "The Bakery and Delicatessen." Ecology action and Women's Liberation exist in a disoriented way.

No one has ever been arrested (it's true) and local pigs have not yet been noted on campus. It's radical but apathetic because of location. Santa Cruz struck against Nixon's Cambodia policy.

SURVIVAL:

A lid goes for $12, a cap of acid or a dose of mescaline is $2.50. No birth control devices are available as there is no Planned Parenthood in the area. No mental-health counseling—progress is hurting in these areas. Abortion referrals are through the grapevine only. Draft counseling through The Resistance. Student health is nothing to rave about, no hospital, limited infirmary. Pets are all about.

There's an organic horticulture project on campus which grows flowers and macrobiotic food and distributes them free. Health foods are served in the dining halls.

Local hangs are the "Bookstore" and the "Catalyst" in the city of Santa Cruz.

The school has an underground paper, *Stevenson Libre*, in addition to a community underground paper, *Free Spaghetti Dinner*. Foreign flicks and art flicks are at the "Nickelodian."

ENVIRONMENT:

Mental—The environment is heavy with nature-loving types. They are into growing things and wood sculpture. Read seed catalogs, *Autobiography of Malcolm X* and Buckminster Fuller before you come.

Physical—The campus is the most beautiful one in California. Trees, environmental sculpture, wood and Stonehenge type buildings everywhere. The rainy season is heavy with a little fog but just serves as a refreshing element. Forests and brown picket fences surround the hill which the campus is built on. Peace and no noise pollution.

Chapman College
Orange, California

The most impressive thing about Chapman is that they run the "World Campus Afloat"—a year of travel and study.

SERGEANT PEPPER SECTION:

1,700 students on the regular campus. Not hard to get in—you need 950 SAT scores, about a 2.0 and average ACTs. About 45 blacks and a few Chicanos.

ACADEMIC BULLSHIT:

Since Chapman is affiliated with the Disciples of Christ, two courses in religion are required of all students.

Take "Western Civilization" with either Bergel or Gooseville ("they bring in slides and records and emphasize cultural history") and Philosophy with John Miller ("he's the most controversial teacher here").

Traditional academia—exams and papers, no Pass/Fail, and no student-originated classes. A Free U just started and offers courses in handicrafts, politics and the occult. There are a few isolated courses in black studies but no major. The faculty is apathetic and not really into getting to know the students.

But wait! Can you dig the World Campus Afloat? Its aim is "to make the study of life and culture relevant by participating in all aspects of it." In other words, a great trip complete with tours, sex and fun—for credit!

450 students from 230 colleges are accepted each semester. Chapman students have priority. Requirements are a 2.0 GPA and the bread (some scholarships are given out). Fees are $3,500 for three and a half months (tuition and room and board on the ship).

Fall semester the ship leaves from New York and goes to major cities (for three–four days each) in England, Holland, Portugal, Turkey, Italy, Tunisia, Greece, Spain, Guinea, Brazil, Argentina, Chile, Peru, Mexico and then back to Los Angeles. The European trip group is usually composed of drinkers and straights who are going there to make the scene.

Spring semester the ship leaves from Los Angeles and goes to Honolulu, Japan, Hong Kong, Bangkok, Singapore, Malaysia, Ceylon, Bombay, Kenya, Tanzania, Capetown, Senegal, Casablanca, Spain, Portugal and returns to New York. This group is usually hipper and more intellectual—a lot are into Eastern religions.

Students and professors are as close as you can get—eating, studying, living and traveling together. The ship creates some psychological problems for the students as they are enclosed in an enforced environment. It can be depressing when all you see forever is a cold, vast ocean. There are an M.D. and a shrink on board who are extremely competent.

Curriculum is very flexible—usually at least one course is offered in each major field. There's a library on board and the students learn about each country (language, history and culture) before they get to it. There is assigned reading and visiting professors come from different ports to speak. The best professor on the ship is John Plott who is an expert on Eastern religions and takes students overland through India.

In port, a day is like this:

Morning . . . . City orientation tour and sightseeing.
Afternoon . . . . Functional tours (universities, museums, factories).
Evening . . . . Theater or participation in the country's culture (folk dancing).

Students have to attend a certain number of tours and can do their own thing the rest of the time. They can go anywhere any time in port—even go overland and meet the ship in the next port.

Ship life is close at sea. There is communal living and a few rules but they can be ignored. However, each semester about five kids are sent home for dope. Flicks, dances, swimming and sports on the ship. It's a luxury liner converted into a campus.

Students complain that most professors aren't that good but say that "while experience doesn't necessarily increase academic awareness it adds another dimension to one's life." The ship is a first step toward a radical curriculum change in terms of interdepartmental study and international study.

BREAD:

$800 a semester. Loans and scholarships "if they like you." Jobs at about $1.50 an hour. Dorms cost $750 for room and board a year. Four dorms, one is coed. They are mostly doubles and singles. The dorms look like dull motels and open into grass lawns. Chicks have enforced hours. Anyone can live off campus but the community of Orange is expensive and uptight. Many kids work off campus, especially at Disneyland. About half have cars and they are essential if you want to go anywhere in Los Angeles.

BROTHERS AND SISTERS:

Ratio cats : chicks—about 1 : 1.

Chapman is a "safe" institution—a place where parents like to send their kids (after all, it's affiliated with the Church—God, mom and apple pie). Less than one-third of the kids smoke.

Students dress conventionally—the freaks are in an unhappy minority. The campus is notorious for ugly fat chicks, "sweathogs." Plenty of traditional dating—chicks are virgins and uptight for the most part. The fraternities still wield a big influence in dorm life.

Entertainment consists of flicks, "Spring Sing," going to "Lucky's Pizza" or Disneyland.

BSU was organized in 1969—there is heavy recruiting for blacks (the school is infested with middle-class blacks and athletes).

The campus is in the middle of Orange County—this makes for conservative thought. The YAF is really in there and invites speakers to campus (most on campus admire them). A little liberal sentiment is creeping in—about 40% struck during the strike—a hard core of 25 occupied a building and fasted for two days—accomplished nothing.

SURVIVAL:

Hard in Orange County.

Some students are into the creative bag—there are darkrooms. The medical facilities are poor and they don't give BC pills. There are no survival services. The paper, *The Panther*, is a conservative rag.

ENVIRONMENT:

Mental—People don't read.

Physical—The climate is hot and smoggy (dangerous ozone counts of late).

The campus is in the middle of right-wing Reagan-land. It looks like a rundown high school. There's a quad of chipped salmon-colored structures and a "shady quad" in back.

"What's the ugliest building? You mean aside from all of them?"

Students leave Orange County as fast as possible and escape to Mexico and Big Bear. 60% are commuters who live in a secure and protected atmosphere with their parents.

The Five Claremont Colleges

Claremont, California

Claremont Men's College
Harvey Mudd College
Pitzer
Pomona
Scripps

INTERCOLLEGIATE ACTIVITIES:

POLITICS—In the spring of 1969 the BSU tried to get the administration and faculty to begin a Black Studies Center. Rallies, day and night, petitions and talks. Largest turnout ever. Blacks also demanded a 10% black quota for all campuses as well as a 10% Chicano quota.

A Black Studies Center was put into operation in 1970. It has a headquarters, staff, major and many courses: "Black Business," "Economics," "Education," "Literature," "Languages" (Portuguese, Swahili), "History," "Arts," "Theatre," "Political Science," "Psychology," "Race," "Black Church." At least two (and often more) courses are offered in each of the above fields.

A Mexican-American Studies Center also started this year. It has five–ten courses (major) including "History of the Southwest," "Sociology of Mexican-Americans," "Chicano Revolution," "Economics of Mexican-Americans."

Claremont Men's and Harvey Mudd haven't filled the quota. Claremont Men's has been under much and heated protest because of this. Rallies went on in the spring of 1970, as well as some threats by BSU members.

On the October 15th Moratorium, students organized for canvassing and marched on General Dynamics Corporation.

The only other event has been the sit-ins at ROTC at CMC. This has happened a few times—earlier in the year and during the Cambodia thing. The students, seven of whom sat-in, were tried by their judicial courts just recently. Earlier in 1970, Pomona suspended a few students for obstruction. A few rock throwers—some windows broken.

Generally, the campus is not active. No one knew of any political organizations on campus. Pitzer and Pomona are the most active.

The schools are over-all conservative—especially grad schools. The administration also likes to keep things down. During the sit-in they turned off the air conditioning, hoping to sweat the kids out!

ECOLOGY—Not much awareness or action. Individuals have been very active. Pitzer more concerned than most of the other schools. GASP, Group for Abolition of Smog and Pollution, mostly professors who are lobbying for bills to be passed.

Students for Environmental Action—about 200 people involved at one time or another. They conduct paper drives and do planting on campus.

INTERCOLLEGE GROUPS, PROGRAMS, COURSES—Very few clubs or groups on campus that involve the whole school. Only a few: Moratorium Committee, Ecology groups, ski club. New School.

NEW SCHOOL—Started at Pomona. Like a Free U. Interest has dwindled terribly this year. Only a few courses left. Subjects have been "Breadbaking," "Poetry," "Meditation," "Radicalism," "Photography," "Folk Dancing." Next year, the New School will be temporarily discontinued. Instead there will be a Center for Social Change. The Center will emphasize community work, like working with Ralph Nader. It will have a news team, and hopefully a bus in order to operate a traveling classroom and resource center, and be a base for guerrilla theater and art studio. It won't be for credit at first but hopefully will later become part of the curriculum. Pomona and Pitzer may not give it their sanction (or whatever) because they are afraid that if it becomes used as a political vehicle they will lose their tax exemptions.

URBAN STUDIES CENTER—Offers major in Urban Studies. Includes: (1) "Application and Social Uses of Social Science Methodologies" and (2) "Comparative Urbanization."

GRADUATE SCHOOL—Offers about ten courses open to all: "Communist World," "Polit. of Urbanization," "Japanese," "Oriental Philosophy," "Public School Teaching."

HEALTH SERVICE—Baxter Infirmary. Kids are satisfied. They dispense BC pills.

The Counseling Center has five psychologists. Lots of talking, very little actual therapy. Lots of kids go there, and many go to outside psychiatrists.

FREE CLINIC—Planned Parenthood has a chapter in Montclair. Students are trying to get a chapter on campus.

McAlister Religious Center offers counsel and aid to anyone who needs it.

DRAFT COUNSELING—Also in McAlister Religious Center. There is a specific office, funded by the student bodies. The chaplain is in charge. The office is associated with a Los Angeles lawyer.

VOLUNTEER TUTORING—An all-campus program—kids go out into local schools and tutor some amount of time every week. About 300 kids are involved.

NEWSPAPER—*The Collegian*—"it gets out the news," fair— pretty liberal and pretty uninteresting.

The Spectator—a more radical occasional newspaper of literary works, political opinion, cartoons. Excellent.

ATHLETICS—Not much emphasis. The campuses share the athletic fields and equipment.

ENTERTAINMENT—CMC—Friday night flicks. Free to all but Pomona. Thursday night dances. Occasional picnics and folk music festivals. Friday night—Keg in the woods nearby (called "The Wash"). Other movies. About two a week. Theater and dance and music programs. Not many outside rock groups or entertainment. Speakers weekly.

LOCAL HANGS—"People stay around campus. There's nowhere to go in Claremont."

"The Hub"—snack bar in CMC student center is the most popular eating place.

"The Coop"—snack bar—center of Pomona is usually very popular.

The colleges are situated in one large rectangular area, bordered in back by a highway and dumplike rock quarry, on one side by a woodsy area known as "The Wash" (used for parties and other nocturnal outings) and in front by the small downtown part of Claremont (one street of shops). Each campus has a distinct personality, atmosphere and appearance. The architecture and layout is completely different at each. Pomona is the largest, Scripps next, the others are quite small. Students stay on their own campuses pretty much except to go to classes. Meeting others from other schools is difficult as there is no central place to mingle. If you have a friend at another college, that is the only "in." The students are different at each. But the kids at each college are definitely into different things. It is not together, for a place so small.

CLAREMONT GRAD SCHOOL—$1,900 tuition, about 1,000 grad students, 50% men, 50% women. Only about half of those are around—others are elsewhere, writing theses, etc. Best grad departments are: Economics (conservative, theoretically oriented); Government ("huge lump of conservatism," mostly professors, advocates of classical political theory); Philosophy (one of the best in the country. Students and faculty are exceptional. Students free to do exactly what they want); John D. Lincoln School of Public Finance.

Problem with grad school is that the full-time faculty is limited. Many professors also teach undergraduate courses and there is bitterness as a result.

Grad school funds have stopped so there are very few fellowships or aid from the school. Facilities are also bad for the same reason.

The school is known for the World Center for Study of Ugaritic —a Near-Eastern language important for biblical study, history and archaeology. Many old texts were written in this language. There are only two other places in the world to study it. Also, other Middle-Eastern languages are taught.

Graduate school has a building, and residences, which are horrible and overpriced. Most try to live off-campus. Residences referred to as "Dickens' London."

OFF-CAMPUS HOUSING—Undergrads can only live off-campus if dorm quotas are filled. Then, it is difficult to find a place. Old houses are mostly available, some in the barrio (the local slum). Rents are inexpensive—about $120 for two-bedroom apartment. Some school-owned houses rent for $60 a month but the only way to get one is to know someone leaving.

Claremont is a "submerged island in the middle of suburbia." Weather especially beautiful in the winter. Lots of smog, except in winter. Very quiet scholastic atmosphere.

Program of Special Directed Studies to start next year—for underachievers from terrible economic backgrounds who are thought to be bright and to have potential. They will go to whichever school best meets their needs and interests. Program is well financed.

CLAREMONT MEN'S COLLEGE
Claremont, California

CMC prepares men to go out and conquer Dow-Jones.

SERGEANT PEPPER SECTION:

794 men. 50% out-of-state. A few blacks, a few Chinese.

SAT combined scores of 1,200. 56% of the 1970 freshmen were in the top 10% of their high-school graduating class. The school looks for students who did well in political science, economics and business courses.

ACADEMIC BULLSHIT:

Claremont specializes in business and government classes. Most popular are Dr. Diamond's "Political Philosophy" (how politicians think, what they base their priorities on) and Dr. Snortum's "Theories of Personality" (the most popular professor). Best departments are Economics and Political Science. The Economics department patterns itself after Milton Friedman's monetary school. Most students go on to Law or Business graduate school. You can take a Washington, D.C., semester and live there for a semester. A 3.0 is required. Pass/Fail used, papers and tests. Some student-originated courses (one was called "Educational Theory and Innovation") and studying of different modes of teaching—they came up with some innovative ideas and are putting together a book. Fairly close relationships between students and professors. Lots of independent study and a junior year abroad at the London School of Economics program.

BREAD:

Tuition is $2,200 a year. Aid is fairly easy to get but campus jobs are hard to find. Dorms cost $1,200 a year for room and board. They are long, low two-story buildings that look like old motels—pink and beige plaster.

BROTHERS:

Many of the students are into business and government and reflect that in their conservative manner and dress. Friendly and fairly straight, less freaky than Pomona, more freaky than Harvey Mudd. Plenty of dating and loving with chicks from the Circle. Lids are $10 and some smoke.

The student body is politically apathetic and the administration is extremely conservative. Most demonstrations in the Circle are over CMC—they don't recruit enough blacks and they have ROTC. In May, 1970, there was a trash-in at ROTC—75 participated. The school is open to all recruiters from war-related industries.

ENVIRONMENT:

Physical—Bauer Center has the largest classrooms—it's a rectangular building connected to a huge circular saucer-type building. The campus is routine and businesslike, like the school itself.

Harvey Mudd College
Claremont, California

Science eggheads for the most part.

SERGEANT PEPPER SECTION:

420 students, 50% in-state, seven black students. Science whizzes only. Average math SATs are 730, math ACTs are 740. 88% of the applicants are in the top 10% of their class.

ACADEMIC BULLSHIT:

Excellent in the sciences, especially physics, engineering, and math. The best courses are "Systems Engineering" (engineering of whole systems of activity, such as planning the transportation of a whole city from scratch), "Modern Physics" with Professor Stoddard (mind boggling—dealing with what had been before unexplained in science), "Complex Analysis" with Dr. Busenburg, "Organic Chemistry" with Dr. Myrhe and "Humanities" with Professor Davenport (interaction of arts and technology).

Like the other Claremont schools, Harvey Mudd has a few excellent programs.

New Freshman Program—A special faculty will just teach freshmen, emphasis on interrelated fields. Courses will mesh together, attempt to relate physics to math to chemistry to engineering and all to humanities.

Summer Engineering Clinic—Companies send in engineering problems, students work on and solve them, get paid. Any interested engineering student can participate.
Example: try and design better prosthetic (false) arms and legs.

Sloane Foundation—Received an initial $600,000 to experiment with. Some has been used to create new freshman program, special physics program. A group of students formed to decide what to do with it. Also used to finance special projects proposed by students.

Physics Colloquium—Seminar series (weekly) of profs, visiting profs and students, reporting on what they are doing and what they are finding. Can be attended by anyone.

Conference Physics Major—Originated by a professor, who, with a group of students, arranged to get it in the curriculum. Instead of taking regular physics courses, the group of nine students does independent study at their own speed. They meet once or twice a week for a total of six hours, study what texts they want, discuss and choose problems.

No required work, no exams or grades. More difficult than

regular program. Starts in junior year—two year program. Exam at end. Counts. All day lab once a week.

Senior Seminar Project to be completed at end of junior year.

Research—Profs Bell and Tubbs (Optics and Astrophysics) are studying F *Value*—by studying the probability of electrons to go from one state to another in neon lamps, it is possible to predict the % of materials in stars—students extremely interested in this project, work in it over summer.

Academic pressure is intense. All freshmen courses are Pass/Fail. Exams and heavy class participation. Many student-originated courses and independent study projects.

Student-professor interaction is very big in the Chemistry department. But all the professors are approachable and available.

BREAD:

Heavy. $2,350 a year. 75% of the students are on some form of aid. But Harvey Mudd College is in financial difficulty so they suggest that students apply for state scholarships first. Jobs are very difficult to find if you're not on work-study.

Dorms cost $1,070 a year for cats, $1,400 for chicks. In the new dorm, there are suites of three bedrooms, a living room and bath. The North Dorm is conservative while the South Dorm is more hip. The few girls live at Scripps.

BROTHERS AND SISTERS:

Ratio cats : chicks—20 : 1.

Science egghead types—that asocial genius look, ugly faces garbed in dull clothes. Then others look plain conservative—short hair, slacks and shirts. A few longhairs. About one-third of the guys go out. Most drink rather than smoke.

Inactive and politically conservative. The least political campus in the Circle. The school paper always finds it hard to find a reporter from Harvey Mudd College. It was the only school in the area to hold classes during the strike. One student said, "I pay $3 an hour to go to classes here. I can't afford to strike." The campus is rectangular with beige tile buildings that line a long grassy central area. Looks like a computer.

PITZER COLLEGE

Claremont, California

One of the five colleges in the Claremont Circle, Pitzer is known as a rich bitch's school—many nouveau riche Beverly Hills types. The school has many extremely creative courses in the Social Sciences. Pitzer was formerly a girls' school and went coed for the first time in 1970.

SERGEANT PEPPER SECTION:

700 students. 60% of the students are from California. 34 blacks, 16 Chicanos and 1 Indian.

Grade average must be about a 3.2 and combined SATs of 1,200. Pitzer is the easiest of the Circle colleges to get into gradewise. Selection is heavily based on creativity. One of the questions on the application is "If you could design a course, what would you do?"

ACADEMIC BULLSHIT:

Pitzer is oriented toward the Social Sciences. The best departments are Anthropology, Psychology and Sociology. The most popular English teacher is Mrs. Ringler—she delves into the nature of the alienated artist in America. Mr. Ellenhorn's "Group Dynamics" course is like a good sensitivity-group experience. Professor Ingabell's "Poverty and Minority Youth" course studies the causes of poverty and the resulting conditions faced by minority youth. Students are assigned to minority schools in the area to tutor. Guy Carawan teaches "American Folk Music and Folk Life Studies." He brings in performers and shows films like one on the folk singing at Texas prisons. Mr. Carawan, who is the folklorist in residence, takes about a dozen students to Appalachia for a semester. They live with local families, survey the region and travel. Each student works on a project in the area and keeps a journal. Sounds terrific. What a mind-blower! Professor Parks of the Art department takes students to Tuscararo, Nevada, a small rural community, and they work creatively with any tools that are there (like scrap metal, clay and stone).

A social science research course is available to students who want to take a semester to do a project like "The Anatomy of a Political Campaign" or a dig. Students can use the school's TV station to make a film.

The school is very unstructured and creative educationally. Projects are favored rather than tests and papers. Classes are small and participation is important. Every year a three-day conference is held during which time students discuss what's wrong with Pitzer, how they want to change it, and what new courses they'd like. Suggestions are implemented. (The Free U and Black Studies department are listed under *Pomona*.) Pitzer recruits heavily for minority students. The average age for professors is 35 and professors and students have dinner together. Profs talk to students and are always available. Study abroad.

BREAD:

Tuition and fees are $2,450 a year. If you qualify, loans and scholarships are easy to get. Pitzer takes its quota of rich kids and has enough money for the poor kids. Jobs are hard to find and pay about $1.60 an hour.

Room and board is $1,400 a year. The dorms are three-story connected apartment-looking types. Icky modern inside. No hours or rules. Only seniors can live off campus. The food is said to be excellent. About one-fourth of the students have cars. Students dress casually but have expensive rags in their closets.

BROTHERS AND SISTERS:

Ratio cats : chicks—1 : 14 (1970 is the first year Pitzer has taken cats).

Pitzer is the most experimental of the five colleges. The chicks are the most radical in the school and have long hair, wear jeans, shawls and boots. Have the *active hip* look. And like to ball. The best-looking chicks in the Circle. Lots of dating and the chicks are liberated.

Lids cost $10 and most smoke.

Pitzer is constructive on political issues. They were active in the Student Strike and have a town council which votes upon issues.

ENVIRONMENT:

Mental—People are reading books on sociology and Rubin's *Do It!* Pitzer and Cal Tech are doing a study on pollution. There is an Ecology major which includes courses in politics and population, man and machines and human ecology.

Physical—The classrooms are in one complex of four connected two-story "mausoleum" green brick buildings with outdoor as well as indoor halls. The campus is small—primarily little round putting greens surrounded by stone.

Students escape all the time, "Anywhere."

POMONA COLLEGE
Claremont, California

The most active of the Circle.

SERGEANT PEPPER SECTION:

1,267 students of which 829 are in-state. 10% black. A B+ average and combined SATs of about 1,300 are needed. Motivation is an important consideration.

ACADEMIC BULLSHIT:

Pomona emphasizes the Social Sciences, the Natural Sciences and the Humanities. Most popular courses are "The Impact of Freud and Marx on Contemporary Thought," an interdisciplinary literature course which stresses application of theories in other fields, "Biochemistry" with Dr. Cornell, "Shakespeare" with Mr. Young (lots of interpretation), all the Chemistry courses (heavily endowed as are other departments like Zoology and Biology) and all the Psychology courses (experimental research—rat experiments are common). The Religion department is excellent and has courses such as "Oriental Heritage," "Life and Death of God," and "Transformations and Utopia."

Pass/Fail is allowed for two courses a semester outside of the major. Lots of class participation with small classes. Some student-originated courses like the "Experimental Living Project" where 25 students live with a faculty member in the dorms and have seminars on a topic of their choice. As much independent study as you want. Study abroad.

BREAD:

Tuition is $2,000 a year. School is only liberal with money for minority students. Campus jobs at $1.50 an hour are tight.

Dorms cost $650 a semester for room and board. Coed. Old looking adobe buildings. 24-hour open house in the dorms. Check Frarie Hall—it looks like a medieval refectory.

BROTHERS AND SISTERS:

Ratio cats : chicks—7 : 5.

Pomona is the most freaky and hip of all the schools. Chicks wear jeans, shirts and long hair. Cats have really long hair. The cats outshine the chicks intellectually—Pomona is called "the Stanford of Southern California." Lots of dating and living together.

Students at Pomona are liberal. They demonstrate occasionally —like in ROTC demonstrations. The Claremont Liberation Army is the unofficial group that puts things together when there is an issue.

Plenty of people smoke but there aren't any real dope freaks.

ENVIRONMENT:

Physical—the classroom buildings are old, early part of the century, ivy strewn. Gardens are full of palm trees, pine trees and luxuriant foliage.

SCRIPPS COLLEGE
Claremont, California

The arty element of Claremont College.

SERGEANT PEPPER SECTION:

526 chicks. Half from out-of-state. 10% blacks.

Scripps is interested in some kind of exciting person with a lot of outside activities. Average combined SATs are 1,200. 62% of the freshmen in 1970 were in the top 10% of their class.

ACADEMIC BULLSHIT:

Scripps has a good Humanities curriculum. Favorite courses are weaving and ceramics (teachers are professionals and facilities are excellent), graphics (lithographs and woodblocks). The Fine

Arts department is the most extensive of all colleges which includes majors in Dance, Theater, Sculpture and Environment Art. Each student has to take four seminars a year for three years. They are small groups to discuss special topics.

Everything is on a Pass/Fail distinction basis. Small classes and much participation. You can create your own classes and over one-fourth create their own majors. Scripps has a study-abroad language program in Tours, France.

BREAD:

Tuition is $2,310 a year. Loans and scholarships are available on need. Some campus jobs at $1.65 an hour. Dorms are $1,400 a year. They are old with a Mediterranean garden atmosphere, porches, arched doors, green shutters on the windows. Finishing-school lounges with pianos and fireplaces. Antique wood benches line the entering halls, candles in little pockets on the walls. No hours but cats can only be in chicks' rooms from 1 P.M. to 11 P.M.

The hippest dorm is Grace Scripps—"we are promiscuous dope smokers." The Kimberly dorm chicks "got off the time bus in the 50s when the dorm was built."

About one-fifth of the chicks have cars and most have expensive threads.

SISTERS:

Chicks are noted for individuality. Many more wear skirts and dresses than at other schools. Hip mod types with tailored bells and silk blouses and shawls—arty. Some chicks have that rich eastern conservative look.

Social life is slow. People don't go out that much except when Cal Tech or HMC cats come down. Most dates are in the form of small private parties.

Chicks are apolitical. Extremely cautious, weigh everything and do nothing. Lids go for $10. A minority of chicks smoke but they smoke an awful lot.

ENVIRONMENT:

Physical—The campus is exquisite. The buildings are low, of beige brushed plaster with porches, courtyards and gardens. Long rectangular grassy areas fill the center. They are lined with fruit trees and luxuriant bushes.

Mills College
Oakland, California

Parents send their daughters to Mills to be protected, refined and properly prepared to lead a cultured lawn-partied life. Afternoon teas in this ivory-towered atmosphere breed something akin to a Radcliffe girl of 1900. However, in all fairness, this image is changing slightly. 1969's valedictorian, Stephanie Mills, scored a media coup when she announced in her commencement speech that "the most humane thing to do would be to have no children" in light of world conditions. And Mills girls have been making a concerted effort to catch on intellectually to what's going on in the world. Many of the girls are approaching awareness although the school still has its share of Junior League types.

SERGEANT PEPPER SECTION:

The average SATs: 575 verbal; 550 math. 50% of entering freshmen carry a B average with them from high school; 67% attended public schools. Recent admission of more blacks, Chicanos and American Chinese and Japanese has lessened the importance of high-school grades as a criterion. Admissions pays more attention, in their own words, to a girl's future plans in the arts. In reality, it's how close a girl's self-description comes to fitting the latest edition of the "Mills Girl."

Mills is a girls' school with 950 girls, 50 male graduate students. 800 undergraduate women live on the campus. No undergraduate may live off campus unless married or living with parents. There are 80 students living on campus in apartments. Half out-of-state students.

ACADEMIC BULLSHIT:

Best undergraduate departments are Art, Music and English. Art: "Drawing and Design" from Wayne Buckley, a long-haired bearded character. Works in mixed media, round pieces, light and sound. A warm, alive person.

"Ceramics" from Eunice Prieto, widow of the late ceramics heavy, Antonio. She's a quiet, conservative potter who can dig other people's work and help them along.

Good Music department.

Graduate departments again are Art, Music and English. Mills graduates can have a good scene *if* they already know what they want to do and can generate enough energy to keep going without any outside help. Mills has the facilities and sometimes the sense to let you alone. Therein lies the real merit of the college.

Popular professors include Dr. Scherril, who teaches undergraduate courses in "Ancient History," "Early Roman History," and "Medieval History." She is into the life of historical peoples and "tells the gossip that makes that shit real." Wayne Buckley's "Painting and Design" course was described as the "vitamin pill" on campus. So much latitude that unless you've a clear vision you may wobble.

The Pass/Fail option is open and used extensively. You need a 2.0 average, consent of the instructor. It may not be used in your major. Because of the Pass/Fail, there is no folklore about "gut" courses. If you want an easy load, you use your Pass/Fail option.

The only student-initiated course was called "Psychology of Chicanos," run by some of the Chicano students with nominal faculty participation.

Student initiative in courses is primarily through suggesting courses to the faculty. The Ethnic Studies program as a whole is in large part due to student pressures.

There are no non-credit courses on campus or nearby. A wide variety of arts and crafts courses are offered for fractional credit (four credits is a full load). There are a shit-load of such courses all around the Bay area, but none closer than eight miles (Berkeley).

The student-faculty ratio is roughly 12 : 1. Many of the classes are small, with ten students. 125 students is the biggest class anyone has ever seen. Some of the faculty live on campus in "Faculty Village." There is even a children's school on campus, presumably for faculty children. Students often invite faculty members to eat dinner in the dormitories. Classes are sometimes held in profs' homes. Many of the faculty are really cool, but the cooler faculty tend not to want to make a career out of teaching at Mills.

The Ethnic Studies program has about five black and five Chicano-Asian-Indian courses. Next year the program will be expanding to about 15 courses. The Black Student Union complains that the school only grants one-third of the money requested, and that it hires professors who are miles away from the interests of the black students (for example, one South African). Some black professors are popular among the black students, but other courses are ignored by them, and cater to whites.

Most of the classes are small. All the finals are take-homes except for art courses where slides are shown as part of the test.

Mills is phasing into Stanford's study-abroad program—at present, study abroad available only in Germany.

BREAD:

Mills is one of those expensive private schools. It costs $3,700 per year, including room, board and health services.

26% of the student body are on Mills scholarships. Campus jobs are really tight—waitresses get average wage and a few lab assistants are needed—that's it. Some loans. Mills girls aren't poor and behind their levis in their closet lurk expensive dresses.

SISTERS:

The 50 male graduate students seem to be completely satisfied with their 1 : 18 ratio.

Mills girls are as a whole pretty straight in their mode of dressing. Very few freaks on the campus and few braless chicks. Many wear jeans, flowery shirts and ski sweaters. A lot of long hair and about half of these tie it into a pony-tail. More than half the girls go on to graduate school and are career bound, they are not just in a marriage prep state of mind.

Dates are hard to come by unless you have friends in the Bay area. The Mills girls are referred to as "the meat rack" by surrounding schools. The administration buses the lovelies to various schools for "mixers" but many times the girls complain that their chosen partners are too straight. "If I have to go to one more fraternity party . . ." Not all the girls date. One party with Berkeley and Stanford students on campus included (bleahh) a panty raid. Virginity is rampant.

Most students are still under their parents' financial and social perceptions and there isn't much political activity except in the area of ecology.

The only militant event occurred in 1969 with a 9 A.M. rally of the BSU which Kathleen Cleaver addressed—200 people marched on the dean's office and demanded action on BSU demands for a black wing in the dormitories, an Ethnic Studies program, and more money for black student needs. Ethnic Studies is now in its first year. A black wing was denied—something about federal housing laws.

There is no campus police force and local jail conditions are, at present, irrelevant to activity at Mills.

A few dopers who score at campus apartments or at Berkeley. Some students do attend class stoned which is pretty surprising for Mills.

Cultural activity is excellent. There are dozens of good speakers —a chamber orchestra.

SURVIVAL:

Lids go for $15. The health service is very efficient and plush. No suicide prevention or BC pills. Girls use the Planned Parenthood in the area. The *Mills Stream* is the campus paper—published weekly and naively. Typical articles include "Students Work with City Government," "Groundwork for April 22 Earth Day," an editorial urging students to "wear gas masks of gauze to dramatize their consciousness of air pollution . . ." and that "studies be made of local industries—which are the big polluters?"

The library is terrible. Books are inadequate and outdated.

ENVIRONMENT:

Mental—Students discuss the academic pursuits and read Heinlein's *Stranger in a Strange Land*, and Hesse's *Steppenwolf*.

Physical—The 175-acre campus is a hilly, heavily wooded area with a very low density of buildings and students. Most of the buildings have large lawns around them. There are many tall eucalyptus trees all over the place as well as a high density of other handsome California trees. A stream runs across campus, fed from a small lake. Besides that, there is a pond and a fountain. (Actually, the lake is a disappointment, because it is rather mucky, has Interstate 580 a hundred feet up a slope on one side, and trailer offices and parked cars on another two sides.) There is so much room that one hardly ever sees any kind of crowd.

The buildings are expensively built, though there are some temporary structures and shacks that are exceptions. The wood and concrete chapel, which was built recently, is stunning.

Occidental College
Los Angeles, California

Occidental is a small, cohesive, liberal private school in the suburbs of Los Angeles. Students are open, nice and generally passive but aware.

SERGEANT PEPPER SECTION:

Private school. 1,800 students, 100 grads. 684 out-of-state, 56 blacks, 15 Chicanos.

Difficult to get in—1,300 combined boards, activities, and "lots of potential"; interview important. Easier to get in from out-of-state.

ACADEMIC BULLSHIT:

Popular courses include "Cinema" by Maria Kinder ("Freaky flicks, every student does a nonverbal project"); "Social Psyche," Dr. Cole, one of the campus father figures; Professor Bammel's "Modern Culture and Religious Quest" ("ephemeral and interesting current events"), and Professor Grigsby's "Urban Law Enforcement," study of pigs—get to go down to the station and meet the policemen. There's a P.E. class in "Scuba Diving." A General Studies program is to go into effect next year, promises to offer relevant type education. Good departments include Pre-med program, Biology ("Marine Plankton Ecology") and Religious Studies. The graduate departments ("You have to be perverted to go here for graduate school") aren't the best—except for English which is quite good. Some Pass/Fail, many papers, no student-initiated courses. A Free U—"Rock Music," "Possibility of Change," extensive black studies courses which include "Black Man in America," and "Popular Arts in Black America." A few Indian and Chicano courses.

Occidental is recruiting minority students—they want to have 15% minority. Students are trying to organize fund raising for minority scholarships.

A very close relationship between students and teachers. Dean Cully, "the father of the school," knows all the boys by name.

Lots of independent study. Any student can make up a course and take it with the approval of the professors. Study abroad in France, Germany and Japan. There are also international fellowships—you can go anywhere in the world to pursue your major field.

BREAD:

Expensive—tuition is $2,200 per year. 50% on scholarships but school is in bad shape financially so these are getting tighter. No work-study but many campus jobs at $1.50 an hour.

Dorms are $1,200 a year for room and board. Lots of people are moving off campus into funky old places—old apartments go for

$140. Area slowly becoming a slum. Hard to scrounge. Most kids have cars and well-made, hip clothes. Dates cost $10 for folk-singing places if your entertainment isn't self-generated.

BROTHERS AND SISTERS:

Ratio cats : chicks—3 : 2.

"You sort of bump into people here and stay with them like molecules. You run out of new people."

Cats have hair to the bottom of the neck, jeans, clean shirts, sandals and that well-brought-up look—clean but hip. Chicks wear jeans and polo shirts and print dresses. Mostly hip but no real hips. Generally really nice straightforward kids. Some fraternities but going down. Some dating and sexual activity but not as much as in the larger California schools.

People hang at "Tommy's," an incredible hamburger place, "Amilio's," a pizza place and "Zap's," a health-food store and restaurant. "Zap's" is the hip place.

Political activity has increased a lot in the last year. In 1969, Occidental students held a hunger strike as a protest against Navy recruiters. 46 students sat in at the office. In October of 1969, there were Moratorium Day activities. There was constructive peaceful type activity to protest Nixon's decision on Cambodia. Blacks have tried to organize now and then, nothing very impressive. "The campus is safe, quiet and nice. Lots of talking, not much doing."

SURVIVAL:

Occidental is a slow pace, do-your-own-thing place. There are plenty of creative outlets—dark-rooms and studios. Lots of grass, easy to get, lids $10, keys $150. Lots of mescaline and acid. "Always a threat of a big bust, but it never comes."

No BC pills given out at student health, "All they ever do is put a thermometer in your mouth." The chaplain is the draft counselor. Campus is overrun with dogs. The *Occidental,* the campus paper, is a drag but the Los Angeles *Free Press* is superb. No Women's Liberation.

ENVIRONMENT:

Mental—People are talking about the relevance of student political action and are reading *The Student as Nigger.* There are lots of speakers and good cultural activity in art, music and drama.

Physical—Hollywood rents the campus to make flicks. Occidental is in a suburban area in the conservative community of Glendale. The community regards the school as "hippie haven of communist ideals." It is surrounded by hills and the weather is nice, but if you value your lungs stay out of Los Angeles. The campus is a small close-knit place built around a rectangular quad with stone benches and flowers. The cafeteria is like a refectory with high-backed chairs and wooden tables and long benches. Herrick Chapel is an architectural masterpiece. It's a high-ceilinged building with a circular podium and a circular indented ceiling above with a stained-glass window in the center. Quiet and inspiring. There's an outdoor Greek Theater and an Art Barn. There's a black flag on the Art Barn. "What is it?" "I don't know, maybe a concept piece."

The administration building is ugly, nonfunctional and sinking (into the ground).

University of the Pacific

Stockton, California

Evolving into an interesting place.

SERGEANT PEPPER SECTION:

The University of the Pacific is composed of the College of the Pacific and the "Cluster Colleges"—Raymond College, Callison College and Elbert Covell College as well as six graduate schools and a Conservatory of Music. 2,705 students, of which 500 are grads. 100 black and 200 Chicanos. Admission is more selective at Raymond College than at the others. In general, you need about 1,000 SATs and a 2.0 GPA and lots of bread. Connected to the Methodist Church.

ACADEMIC BULLSHIT:

Best departments in the College of the Pacific are History, Foreign Languages and Biology. Best courses are "Religion and Modern Culture" taught by a team of three professors (it correlates the chapel program and has a lot of speakers) and "Group Dynamics" with Don Duns ("It's semi-encounter oriented"). It also has a Teacher Corps—one of the first education departments to institute it. Students teach and learn at the same time and there is lots of ghetto teaching.

The best graduate schools are the Dental school, the College of Physicians and Surgeons (in San Francisco) and the McGeorge School of Law (in Sacramento).

Raymond is a three-year liberal arts program that doesn't allow majors. It has 250 students and is seminar oriented. The faculty eats with the students. There is a curriculum of 23 required courses and four courses of independent study—all Pass/Fail. Innovative testing is encouraged. The students are more hip than in other colleges.

Callison College emphasizes the non-Western world. It especially prepares students interested in international law, business, the ministry and the diplomatic service. Students are required to spend their sophomore year in India. It's all Pass/Fail and students must do a community project in their first year.

In Elbert Covell College, everything is taught in Spanish.

The Conservatory of Music offers the Pacific Music Camp for four weeks each summer—much personal instruction.

The whole school is on a 4-1-4 system—in January the students do a month-long independent study project—like a marine-biology exploration study. Study abroad in Germany, Spain, France and Austria.

BREAD:

Tuition is $2,400 a year for Raymond, $2,040 a year for the other schools. Loans and scholarships are easy to get but most students don't need them. Jobs go at $1.50 an hour. Undergraduates are hired as T.A.s in freshmen courses for credits and pay.

Dorm room and board is approximately $1,200. There are primarily doubles and coed dorms. Callison and Raymond have their own dorm quads in order to maintain their small community atmosphere.

Campus apartments are across the street. One-bedrooms cost $110, doubles cost $200. You can find a few old Victorian homes in downtown Stockton for $50 a month per person.

Most people have cars, and chicks dress up in costly threads.

BROTHERS AND SISTERS:

Ratio cats : chicks—1 : 1.

Students are conservative college types—they look casual. Cats have short hair and moustaches. The freaks go to Callison and Raymond. There's plenty of dating—some living together off campus but for the most part people are uptight about sex and don't talk about it.

About 60% smoke and there is lots of dexadrene. Lids go for $15.

There are about 800 people in fraternities and sororities—they are into the whole Greek bit. They come out on Thursday night to sing gross songs. Sororities set dress codes and make their chicks wear skirts to class.

Everyone hangs at coffee houses in Lodi—one is in the Congregational Church. Straights go to "Pepe's Pizza," "Straw Hat Pizza" and "Mickey Grove" (zoo and park). Some go to the "Islander" which is for rich kids who can pay $2 a drink. Freaks go into San Francisco, Berkeley and to the levee of the Calavaras River behind the school.

Students love the openness of the administration—"You can just walk into the President's office and talk to him." Many upper-middle-class moderates.

The BSU is moderate—they asked for a Black Studies department and got it. Many people are in the Community Involvement Program—they go into ghettos and tutor and run educational and recreational programs. Students requested that the administration allow 200 economically disadvantaged students admission and help finance them—permission was granted.

There haven't been any sit-ins and students laughed at the thought. Amnesty was granted for those students who wanted to drop out and strike but few took advantage of the opportunity. There were discussions in class. Students mobilized for the first time in May, 1970, into a group called "People's Alliance for Peace Rally"; about 1,000 joined.

SURVIVAL:

There's a small but good Art department.

Student health is excellent—there's a brand new infirmary across the river—doctors are starting to give out BC pills. The YMCA offers CO counseling and legal aid. Free medical care at the Stockton Free Clinic. The Chapel is one of the few popular ones on a college campus. It's very liberal and religion is dynamic. Services are packed. Music and words are innovative.

The *Pacifican* is uncensored and cool.

The kids at Callison had a special health-food diet for awhile.

ENVIRONMENT:

Mental—People are talking about their studies.

Physical—The school is right near downtown Stockton—there's an urban environment on one side and boondock farm lands on the other. The weather is generally agreeable but very hot in the summer. There is no smog but peat dust blows in from the asparagus crop.

Buildings are made of old red bricks covered with traditional ivy.

People escape to the skiing resorts and to San Francisco. There are many lakes in the area—1,000 miles of water.

University of Southern California
Los Angeles, California

USC is a private school with wealthy students and a concerned, responsive faculty. Greek Week and Song Fests among fraternities and football games are still big (T.G.I.F.). But there's hope—things are changing. Professionally oriented school.

SERGEANT PEPPER SECTION:

24,107 students, 4,091 grads, 7,745 part-timers. About 12% minorities.

You need a B average and good board scores. Athletes get in with significantly less.

ACADEMIC BULLSHIT:

Popular professors include Professor Buscaglia ("Exceptional Education"—he has students go blindfolded for a day to experience blindness), and Professor Boskin ("History of the American Negro." Students do projects like mixed-media presentations.).

The Urban Semester is an unusual project. There are no scheduled teachers or classes. "Classroom is the community." Students do community work, such as the Free Clinic or a prison farm. It's worth 16 units. An unusual and freaky course is Professor Elwood's "Philosophical and Religious Movements in Southern California." Elwood has compiled a huge list of freak churches in southern

California—witches, mystics, flying saucer believers and erotic love cults. Students observe and try to dig.

USC has two excellent undergraduate departments, Cinema (includes trips, speakers, superb facilities, editing, animation, photo journalism, etc.) and Urban Studies like the Urban Semester. USC also has one of the best Dental schools in the country and a good Law school.

The school is leaning more and more toward progressive, relevant education. They have the bread to hire good professors—all they need is more perception.

One Pass/Fail course outside your major is allowed.

Creative projects and tests rather than papers. Classes are large with the exception of senior collegians. Some student-initiated courses. A Free U—"Rock and Roll Appreciation," "Narcotics," and "Love" (taught by Professor Buscaglia—"people I never thought would smile at me do now").

There is an extensive Ethnic Studies program—a concentration in Afro-American and Asian-American Studies courses such as "Race Relations," "Afro Literature," "Mexican-American Thought" and "Ethnic Studies in American Culture."

USC students were the first student body to vote a voluntary fee of $4 on themselves to raise money for minority scholarships.

Some dating between young professors and students. The older professors are detached and conservative.

Some independent study. Study abroad in Vienna, Japan, France and Tunisia.

The USC faculty and administration try to be very helpful to students and there is a lot of communication. The school's former rich WASP image is changing a lot.

BREAD:

It's expensive—$1,000 a semester for this private school. 60% of the student body are on financial aid. 350 minority students on scholarships. "Sure, you can get one, if you can kick, punt and pass." Majority of well-heeled students. Many students have part-time jobs on or off campus. Many students commute. Some students live in dorms which are $550 for room and board per semester. 600 chicks live in sororities, 1,300 cats live in fraternities. The cost is about $130 a month for room and board. A small number of students live in modern, expensive apartments, $250 up. Some funky places are available in the Hoover Redevelopment Project. "Ellis Island" is a famed commune with lots of crashers. Scrounging is hard in L.A. except with friendly freaks. The YMCA provides free food often and Ellis Island provides shelter.

Most students have status type cars. Expensive wardrobes are nauseatingly omnipresent—coordinated fashion-show chicks. Dates are expensive if you go to Westwood for dinner and a flick. Best book store in town is the "Free Press Book Store" on Fairfax.

BROTHERS AND SISTERS:

Ratio cats : chicks—3 : 1.

It's that L.A. plastic look—semi-starlet. Matching threads for the chicks who are pretty straight. The hips even wear expensive tailored jeans and have all had their teeth and eyes fixed. Neck scarves, bows, side curls. Natural blonds. Thin healthy-looking types. Cats have super-short hair, wear slacks with shirts tucked in, socks and shoes. More hip cats than chicks but not that many. Everyone is clean. Kids are socially oriented, and only recently have begun to have a political awareness. Longhairs and fraternity types don't mix.

Plenty of dating and sex—people are still discussing virginity—pros and cons.

Fraternities are the #1 influence on campus, the last stronghold of fraternities in Los Angeles. The football team keeps going to the Rose Bowl.

There wasn't much political activity before the Cambodian involvement. In 1968 at Alumni Park there was a demonstration by draft resisters. Fraternities tore down their displays. The 1969 Moratorium grossed about 1,000. In March, 1969, students struck and professors allowed students to drop out to work on anti-war projects. Many students wore armbands, 25% dropped out in the "Peaceful Campus Campaign." The YAF actively opposed the strike. Students at USC think of themselves as representing the "average American." (God help us.)

Hangs include Westwood, "McKeever's," a beer and pool place for fratters. Freaks go to "Alice's Restaurant." A guy about 40, Kesey type, called Serena, takes care of the kids. "Alice's" has a work bench and equipment in one corner for making things, random paintings on the wall.

The graduates are the most conservative and view everything as a "big investment."

SURVIVAL:

Pressures of conformity to date-and-mate life style are great. The education is fairly good but the atmosphere is not as yet very political.

Cinema people dig that department. Art department is sufficient for a creative outlet.

Draft center is sponsored by the Student Association and the Law school helps. Student health doesn't dispense BC pills and has lousy service. There's a suicide prevention number and a Free Clinic in downtown Los Angeles.

Lids go for $10—most smoke grass occasionally. Scoring in the dorms. 60% of football team smokes. No health-food stores. Women's Liberation is just starting up.

The campus paper is *The Trojan*—good and liberal.

ENVIRONMENT:

Mental—People don't read that much. The ecology group, P.R.O.B.E., circulates petitions.

Physical—USC is an urban campus in an ugly part of Los Angeles (an ugly part of California). It's right off the freeway in the middle of a slum, veiled in smog.

However, the campus itself is beautiful—lots of lawns, athletic fields, arched and old columned buildings. Some nice red brick buildings. Feeling of spaciousness and tranquility. Helicopters patrol the area and donate smog, fog, pollution and sickness. Eyesores are the Physics labs—already condemned. Escapes are beaches and shopping. 50% commuters.

Stanford University
Stanford, California

Stanford is a campus of concerned intellectuals. It has seen a rapid change in the last two years from a fraternity-party environment to one of increased radicalization. Called "the Harvard of the West," the school has stringent eligibility requirements which make the student body a haven for the Mensa type intelligentsia. Stanford also is very expensive and is composed of students with extremely wealthy parents. It has some of the top research departments in the world, especially in the Sciences. Stanford is losing its ivory-tower incubator environment daily and is approaching a kind of Berkeley environment, only richer.

SERGEANT PEPPER SECTION:

Stanford requires over 1,200 combined SAT scores and grades in the top fifth of your high-school graduating class. Extracurricular activities (remember student government) are also valued.

12,000 students, half grads and half undergrads—Stanford is big on turning out scientists and professors. Half are out-of-state students. Private school.

ACADEMIC BULLSHIT:

Law, Medicine, Aeronautical Engineering are some of the best graduate schools in the country. But you have to really dig studying. In the Law school they originated the Environmental Law program which is concerned with land use, government agencies and the state water plan. All courses are optional and Pass/Fail is also optional. The Medical school has a radical program which is oriented toward community service. Engineering is fine.

Undergraduate courses in History (radical professors) and Psychology are worth your time. Paul Ehrlich, the famous population-control expert, teaches "Man and Social Responsibility." Ehrlich is the author of *The Population Bomb* (don't hatch one, get sterilized). Pass/Fail is very acceptable outside your major. Almost anyone can initiate a course provided he gets faculty support. Students can even hire a professor to be paid from Associated Students funds. Some recents—"Human Sexuality," "The Stock Market" and "Yoga."

There's a Free U in Menlo Park—the Mid-Peninsula Free University—"Revolutionary Politics" and "Gardening" and many more.

There is a Black Studies program with a major offered in the field. 232 blacks attended Stanford last year and recruitment of blacks is pursued heavily. There are 68 Chicanos who are trying to get some courses in Mexican-American studies.

Tests and papers are both utilized. Independent study is very popular and creativity is encouraged.

Study abroad is fantastic. Stanford leases five campuses—Germany, Great Britain, France, Italy and Vienna. 80 students, usually sophomores, attend for six months at a time. Two professors from Stanford go to each campus. The program is financed completely by Stanford and includes a three-week vacation and field trip. 90% of the students attend at some time. Students can also work on a ship at the Scripps Institute of Oceanography.

BREAD:

It's impossible to scrounge here. You need heavy bread at $715 a quarter. Nothing is cheap, not even Xerox. There are no used-book stores. "Used things aren't reliable. They figure if you're rich enough to come here, you're rich enough to buy new stuff."

Dormitory room and board will cost $380 plus. Apartments run $65–$95 to share. The campus bought trailers recently and they cost $325 per quarter per body but aren't popular.

Big corporations give prospective employees scholarships—also rip off University donations. Campus jobs are hard to get but can be obtained if the student is persistent enough—most common is hashing in the dorms for $2 an hour. Lots of cars and bikes.

The average cost of a date is cheap—from zero to a couple of dollars for a movie. Women are expensively dressed hippies—although the need for expensive clothes is decreasing.

BROTHERS AND SISTERS:

Ratio cats : chicks—3 : 1.

Stanford has a lot of hip intellectuals. About half the boys look hip, wear jeans and sandals with medium-length hair, few with shoulder-length hair. There is also an established very straight community—madras and Sta-prest. Girls wear flower-print hip dresses, long hair—very few in hip capes and Indian prints. Hip but not radical looking. Dating in frats but rumor is that Stanford men don't date, they study. Girls are liberated (does this mean wasted talent?). Some coed fraternities—most of these are going communal. Delta Tau Delta is the football jocks' house and still strong. No sororities.

The hip hangout is "Rozottis"—a far-out bar where you can lie out in the back and rap. Straights hang at the "Oasis Bar"—lots of grads. Students hang around the fountain, called "the claw," in the center of campus. The coffee house is the center for quiet hips.

Students are sort of rational revolutionaries. They react to issues —getting ROTC off campus. Students are very strong about the land uses of their school but few "rock throwers." One major demonstration resulted in a large portion of the research of six professors be:ng burned up. Last year there was a big sit-in against the counterinsurgence research being conducted by the University. Students want vacant land used for low-cost housing instead of industrial project—organization is called "Grass Roots." The most active club is "The New Moratorium," an anti-ROTC group that registered last year and is "the movement." The "Free Campus Movement" is a bunch of right wingers. SDS is defunct.

In April of 1970, radicals set a Science building on fire to protest ROTC on campus. The entire life's work of six scientists was lost. In May, 1970, students struck. They held peaceful meetings and voted against the decision of Nixon to enter Cambodia and in support of getting ROTC off campus. Students formed a brigade which went to Washington to try to talk to Nixon. There is much cultural activity—many speakers.

Lids go for $10 and you can smoke on campus. Acid prevalent among younger kids—some uppers. Most smoke.

SURVIVAL:

BC pills available from student health. Health service is excellent, big hospital and excellent psychiatric service. Excellent draft counseling run by Allen Strand, a field worker for the C.C.C.O., who primarily does C.O. counseling. Three others are hired for draft counseling also. Advice on how to drop out of ROTC. Office is always busy. Everyone wants out.

Stanford Daily is an extremely good liberal paper.

ENVIRONMENT:

Mental—Study a lot and read Kurt Vonnegut and R. D. Laing.

Physical—Lots of trees, airy, spacious informal campus. "Palm Drive is the last tradition. It's the stately road leading up to campus, all lit up at night, lined with palm trees and a church in the middle." There's a lake for student use. Dorms vary from army barracks type—Wilbur-Stern—to cozy old Lagunita. Beige stone buildings with red tile roofs, lots of arcades and arches. Lots of land.

Students are very concerned about ecology and hold teach-ins and fairs. The eyesore is the Hoover Tower, referred to as "Hoover's Last Erection."

Escapes are the beach or mountains, Big Sur or Monterey. Esalen Institute (awareness and sensitivity training) has an office on campus. It conducts many workshops in gestalt psychology, encounter groups and bioenergenics.

California Western University*

San Diego, California

Cal Western is one campus of the privately-owned U.S. International University. Other campuses include Elliott Campus, and

* A campus of U.S. International University.

the School of the Performing Arts in San Diego, Colorado Alpine campus in Steamboat Springs, Colorado, and campuses in England and Kenya. The school is on a one-year accreditation—someone checks it every year before accrediting it.

SERGEANT PEPPER SECTION:

2,200 students, of which 330 are grads. 1,200 are out-of-staters. Eight blacks, three Chicanos.

Easy to get in if you can afford it (students have gotten in with a 1.5 average) but the kids seem more intelligent and aware than in many of the California state colleges with more stringent requirements.

ACADEMIC BULLSHIT:

Best departments are Education and Business. Teachers come from all over to take the fifth-year program—it emphasizes the freedom of the classroom and establishes intern programs with school districts in the area. The Business school stresses general knowledge rather than specifics. Science has an excellent Chemistry department. Take Dr. Wadia's "Introduction to Anthropology" (he uses his own case studies with the American Indians and native Indians rather than texts), Dr. Kim for "Oriental History" and Dr. Schmige for "Philosophies of Life" ("he knows everything about everything"). The Law school is ranked (academically) the third best in the state, behind Boalt and Stanford.

Good informal relationship between students and professors. Students can spend a year at one of the other USIU campuses. Dr. Kim takes 30 kids to Asia for a "Quarter in Asia" program.

BREAD:

Tuition is $2,100 a year. Not many who go here need loans and scholarships but a few are available. A few campus jobs at $1.40 an hour. Work-study mostly in food service.

Dorms are $350 for room and board a quarter. Guys have three dorms, long three-story buildings with chalet type roofs jutting out in the center. Girls have suitelike rooms which open into little courtyards. Only seniors or those over 21 can live off campus. Dorm rules—no overnight guests of opposite sex. Off-campus houses are mostly at the beach—Ocean Beach—two-bedroom houses go for $150–$200 a month.

Most have cars and there's a hassle with parking.

Scrounging is discouraged on campus.

BROTHERS AND SISTERS:

Ratio cats : chicks—1 : 1.

Cats are good-looking with stylish long hair (an inch), sideburns and moustaches—mostly semi-hip blonds. Chicks are straight to casual looking. A college campus unaware of the changes in the world outside yet not super-straight or traditional.

Dating pattern. Chicks not especially liberated.

Kids hang at the beach and at "Denny's" (coffee shop) and "Red's Pizza House" in Ocean Beach. Ocean Beach is the center for the hip subculture. Straights go to "The Long Bar" in Tijuana, Mexico. "The Unicorn" in La Jolla shows art flicks.

Lids are $15 and a large percentage smoke occasionally. The term "freak" is regarded as negative, almost in its old sense.

The politics of apathy. The administration is conservative and staid—they won't tolerate protests and students are afraid. President Rust got uptight this year as he viewed the radicalization of college campuses and watched such liberal measures as increase of women's visitation in men's halls happen at his university. He issued a document known as "the document." It stated a bunch of regulations (i.e., hair could not be unreasonably long). A student couldn't register for classes until he signed "the document" promising to adhere to the rules. About 1,000 students protested this. The faculty was incensed. No strike activity. Each year there is a convocation—two days of discussion and seminars on contemporary issues.

Students are conservative for the most part.

Athletes are welcome. Many teams.

SURVIVAL:

Nice art studios in a strange but beautiful Art building.

No BC pills or abortion referrals in student health. No draft counseling. Free Clinic and Crisis number in San Diego.

School paper is the *Western Tide*—"tactful and good"—devoted to the arts.

The cafeteria serves health foods at meals.

ENVIRONMENT:

Mental—Students discuss their courses. The Ecology Awareness Physical Emergency Committee runs a newspaper and can drives.

Physical—Beautiful climate all year 'round. Campus is lovely. Tree-lined, and ocean breezes—large acreage of woods and sand. Overlooks the ocean on one side. Buildings are modern.

Escapes are the beach and Mexico.

San Diego School of the Performing Arts*
San Diego, California

Students love this creative campus—they do scenes in the hallways, practice all the time and perform all the time. They put in an incredible amount of work and if they don't have enough to do, they'll ask for more.

SERGEANT PEPPER SECTION:

152 students, of which 13 are graduates. 36 are from out-of-state.

* A campus of U.S. International University.

It's difficult to get in—you must appear to have professional promise—students audition in their own fields. Each year students must audition to be readmitted.

ACADEMIC BULLSHIT:

The departments are separated into each creative field.

ACTING—During the four years students take a year of acting, speech, makeup, application of makeup, dance for actors, music, voice, stage speech, scene study, pantomime, acting workshop production, fencing and stage fighting, directing, acting internship, and the general education courses of English, "Philosophy of Life," "History of the Theater," "Greek Drama," "European Drama," "Elizabethan Drama" and "Shakespeare." 43 students are Acting majors—it's the largest major in the school.

Phil Phillips is one of the most popular professors. He has worked with the Royal Shakespeare Company.

In the fourth year the school helps students secure local acting jobs.

DIRECTING—Much the same as Acting, with more emphasis on costuming, design, lighting and commercial theater orientation.

TECHNICAL MAJOR—Many courses similar to the Acting major —and lighting, stagecraft and costuming.

MUSICAL THEATER—Courses similar to Acting—later emphasis on music, dance and musical theater production.

MUSIC MAJOR—Music is one of the more conservative departments—theory, piano, history, opera and composition are required. The best teachers are Dr. Lloyd and Mrs. McKenzie. Zoltan Roszynai, the conductor of the San Diego Symphony, teaches orchestra and conducting courses.

DANCE—Students take acting, voice, music, makeup, pantomime, design and more. Professor Tygett (a well-known choreographer) and Elaine Thomas (with the Royal Ballet Company) teach.

One of the best classes is the speech class with Dennis Turner. You learn how to speak onstage and how to sight read by looking at words.

Students put on Musical Theater Workshops, dance and ballet programs, instrument and voice recitals and plays.

The Summer Theater puts on three musical productions at the San Diego Zoo, using professional companies—auditions are held first at Performing Arts. Students get credit, room and board and small pay.

Grades are based on what you have done, how much you have progressed. There is an extremely close relationship between students and professors—they have parties together and share problems.

BREAD:

$630 a quarter. Scholarships and loans are hard to get. You need a 3.2 average to get a scholarship. You're not allowed to have a job while at school.

Students live in the dorms at the Elliot campus 25 miles away until they are 21 and can live off campus. They commute every day by car or special bus. Dorms are $350 for room and board per quarter. Dorms are like apartments—two doubles and a living room and bath. Dorms are in the middle of nowhere and on stilts.

Most kids have cars and you need them. Students dress in costly threads—in artsy ways.

BROTHERS AND SISTERS:

Ratio cats : chicks—about 1 : 1.

Students are artistic looking, carefully dressed and dramatically arrayed—antique clothes and older arty type things. Kids look avant-garde but not freaky. Cats have short hair and wear jeans and jackets—faces on both sexes are striking. Students work and live together—casual sleeping together but no overinvolved relationships. But kids do not as a rule date each other—theater is their life—there are endless stories of couples separating to take jobs in separate cities. Everyone is sexually liberated (except music students). They are warm, friendly and open.

Local hangs include the "Holiday Inn," down the street. The entire school assembles there for breakfast—that's it. The whole social life of the school is confined to the Performing Arts building—there is no time to go anywhere else. It's a very closely knit group and seems to be snobbish and elitist to outsiders. Everyone smokes but they don't have time to smoke a lot. Lots of speed, especially around exam and production times.

SURVIVAL:

Easy if you're creative. Elliot Health Clinic is O.K. but no BC pills. Survival services in San Diego.

ENVIRONMENT:

Mental—Everyone is discussing their performances.

Physical—The campus is one huge building in downtown San Diego. Urban area—hot and smoggy. There are two theaters in the building (one with stage and one with floor), a students' acting studio, two dance rooms and lots of practice rooms.

Kids rarely want to escape; they are caught up in their work.

Whittier College
Whittier, California

Nixon went here; assume the worst. Freshmen still look back on Orientation Week with nostalgia—especially the "barn dance, the snake dance, the rock fight, etc."

SERGEANT PEPPER SECTION:

2,089 students of which 161 are grads. 282 out-of-state. 3% blacks. B average and 1,000 total on SATs—fairly easy to get into.

ACADEMIC BULLSHIT:

The best departments are Political Science, Sociology and Biology. There is a new Science Center. The Biology and Sociology grad departments are O.K.

Most popular courses are "American Government" by Dr. Burnett ("he makes material relevant to contemporary society"), "Juvenile Delinquency" by Dr. Browning ("he is a humanitarian and develops the thesis that juvenile delinquency is created in the minds of Americans, and results in a stigma against the child that forces him further into crime"), and "Racial and Minority Groups" by Professor O'Brien. The Sociology department has opportunities for field work in girls' or boys' "correction homes," geriatric wards and mental hospitals.

Class participation is fairly important. There are lots of exams and quizzes and limited Pass/Fail. Very limited student-originated classes (one was added last year—"Black Man in America"). No full-time black professor, though. ("Our school is conservative. It gives you the impression that it wants to show how good it is by helping so many blacks. They want to mold them before they can become politicized.")

Close relationships between professors and students in the Sociology and Political Science departments. Everyone really digs the chaplain. Study abroad in Copenhagen—exchange program with Fisk and Howard.

BREAD:

Tuition is $1,550 per semester. Some Whittier scholarships. Jobs are easy to get at $1.45 an hour. Waitress jobs are most popular (lunch and dinner are sit-down and waited).

Men's dorms cost $450 for room and board a semester. They vary from one "prison camp" that houses 88 and looks like a reformatory to a smaller old type house that beds 20.

Girls' dorms at $490 for room and board a semester. The women's dorms are nice and have more facilities. Chicks have to live on campus till 21. They have hours. Cats can be in chicks' rooms every other Sunday from 4 P.M. to 10 P.M.

Carousel Court is a bunch of school-owned apartments. Four-person apartments cost $490 a semester with a meal ticket. Off-campus housing consists of plastic units at about $150 a month. They don't rent to longhairs. No scrounging—the community and students hate freaks.

One-third have cars. Chicks are well dressed and have "party dresses."

BROTHERS AND SISTERS:

Ratio cats : chicks—1 : 1.

From our correspondent: "The feeling I had most intensely at Whittier was an increasing desire to get as far away as possible."

It's like a small exclusive boarding school, shut within itself. The students are friendly but "guarded." Removed detachment. Old-line-family types who haven't had good years lately and have produced not-so-bright kiddies. No hips—mostly conservatives. Chicks have short hair and wear shorts, Whittier T-shirts and Villager dresses. Lots of Pat Nixon faces plastered on their well-groomed bodies and neatly-shaved legs. Cats looked ordinary, jeans, shirts, short hair—some moddish suit types. The WASPy look is "in."

Chicks complain that the boys sit in their dorms all night. "When we first got here we thought it was a girls' school." Society (like fraternity clubs) parties and flicks are most popular forms of entertainment. Chicks are incarcerated. There are five cats' "societies" and five chicks' "societies." About 175 men and 175 women are in them. Coat-and-tie dinner dates are still popular. The "MonaKai Party" is rated by *Playboy* magazine as the fifth best party of the year. It's put on by the Lancers' Society and is decorated Hawaiian, held in a parking lot and is dress-up. (Boola-Boola.)

Blacks have done the most protesting; most of the campus is conservative and apathetic. Recruiters come on campus and no one protests. About 100 struck with the Cambodia decision. During the strike 20 kids had a Hunger Vigil where they gave up lunch and stood outside with peace signs. The right-wingers threw things at them. Campus Crusade for Christ—called College Life—is an extremely right-wing group which has 60 members. They picketed the strike with signs saying they were "against the yellow men who are the manifestations of Satan."

Cats do smoke grass—$10 a lid. Pills for exams—drugs aren't big.

Local hangs include "The Spot," a fountain type place in the Student Union, "Bob's" (hamburgers) and the "Experiment" (coffee house idea where people can perform). "Wardman Theater" has 49¢ flicks. It's down the street. There's not much to do in Whittier.

SURVIVAL:

Nigh on impossible. No BC pills in student health and the doctor is afraid to examine chicks. The Unitarian Church in Whittier provides draft counseling. Chicks can go to the Whittier Free Clinic for pills. The *Quaker Campus* is a fairly liberal paper for the school. Kids aren't into organic foods.

ENVIRONMENT:

Mental—People read text books. Little ecology awareness. Students spend four hours a day studying.

Physical—The community is older and very conservative. Hills in the background. The school slopes downward. Campus is small and dull. Smog. Lawn mowing goes on all day and provides an incessant whirrrr.

Buildings are semi-Spanish types. The gym is ugly.

BRITISH COLUMBIA

Simon Fraser University

Burnaby, British Columbia

"When Jerry Rubin spoke in 1969, the students jeered at him."

SERGEANT PEPPER SECTION:

5,494 students, mostly from B.C. You need a C+ from B.C. schools and U.S. students need 3.2–3.5 GPA.

ACADEMIC BULLSHIT:

The best departments are Physics, Biology and Philosophy. The Political Science and Anthropology departments have extremely popular courses. The introductory English course with Ralph Mand is also very popular. "001," "002" and "003" are Science courses for non-scientists—they draw 500 people—and are contemporary problems related to science (i.e., ecology, and scientific developments).

No Pass/Fail, not much class participation and no student-originated courses. No ethnic studies. A Free U exists in Vancouver but has nothing to do with Simon Fraser. Independent study is restricted to fourth-year students. 40% of the faculty are American.

BREAD:

$225 a semester tuition. Financial aid is on the decline and job situations are awful—the going rate is $1.44. The average student spends $40–$80 a month on rent. 600 live in the dorm. Two-thirds of the students live at home. One group of 25 students lives close by on a farm with chickens and a garden but few farms are available. Some scrounge and live in vans but this is rare. More than half the students own cars. The social unit here is the car pool. Nobody could get up the mountain on which the school is located by foot or bike. Many middle-class students do the college-shop-threads thing.

BROTHERS AND SISTERS:

Ratio cats : chicks—2 : 1.

Lots of commuters—burdened with books, spending the hours between classes in densely-packed lounges trying to read assignments, living at home and dressing quite properly. There are, however, of late, a large number of moderately long-haired students.

But they look like the Beachboys after they grew long hair—they are still clean-cut-looking surfers.

There is almost no eccentric dress, few chicks go braless. They all have short hair. Solid middle-class dating tradition with some cohabitation. People hang at "The Pub" which is open on campus every Friday night. The drinking age is 19. One member of the party has to be a member. Try the "White Spot" and "McDonald's" for plastic burgers. There is practically nothing going on, or near, the campus—it's a dead residential area and a barren, desolate mountain.

Lots of dope all over Vancouver—4th Avenue is the hippie scene.

Simon Fraser was started in 1965 with an experimental but vague outlook.

In the late fall of 1968, students sat in at the administration building for a variety of demands including the University's refusal to admit draft dodgers. The pigs peacefully arrested 114.

The big event was the Political Science and Anthropology department strike in 1969. The PSA was the most radical department and also rather sloppy administratively. The administration decided to impose a tenure committee from outside the department on PSA. The PSA department struck and the radical students supported them. This controversy alienated the students from the administration on campus.

At the 1970 graduation, students did freaky things like kissing the chancellor's foot while receiving their degrees or reading the names of the Kent State and Jackson dead.

SURVIVAL:

Not many artsy-craftsy types.

BC pills given out at student health. Lots of shrinks available. All survival services are listed on the "Help Yourself" page of the *Georgia Straight*. The campus paper, *The Peak*, is left-wing and fairly good.

ENVIRONMENT:

Mental—People are reading McLuhan and *The Peter Principle* and always talking about how hard it is to get work. Off campus in Vancouver SPEC (The Society for Pollution and Environmental Control) is very active.

Physical—The campus sits desolately on a 1,200 foot mountain in Burnaby, a suburb of Vancouver. There's a spectacular view of ice-capped mountains all year round. The oil refineries of Vancouver pollute the air.

The campus looks like a glass case. The buildings are so impersonal that they don't even have nicknames. On top of that mountain, the great gray dungeon of concrete buildings are named "Rotunda," "Lower Library," "East Concourse" (right off the drawing board).

Escapes are Stanley Park in the city and skiing.

University of British Columbia
Vancouver, B.C.

Better than Vietnam.

SERGEANT PEPPER SECTION:

20,767 students, mostly from B.C. (6% from other provinces and 2% from the U.S.). 13% grads.

In Canada, students need a C+ average and good Department of Education exam scores. No first-year students are accepted from out of B.C.

ACADEMIC BULLSHIT:

The School of Architecture is rather unusual because it is more concerned with philosophy than with the draftsmanship involved. It is a subject of controversy within the Canadian architectural profession. The Community and Regional Planning school is into environmental sculpture and guerrilla theater. Chemistry and Medicine have excellent facilities.

Most popular courses are Bill Willmott's "Centro 260" which he fills with his insights into Southeast Asia, Samuelson's "Sociology" course which gives students a chance to work on contemporary social problems, and Suzuki's course on "General Genetics."

Mostly traditional academia. No Pass/Fail, large courses (even tutorials are usually too large for discussion), no student-originated courses, except some non-credit courses in sex education. There's a Free U in Vancouver with some interesting offerings. For awhile a man named Karl Buran was a one-man counter-university. He gave lectures in the SUB. Not much independent study or study abroad.

BREAD:

Tuition is $457 a year. Financial aid is only available to Canadians or landed immigrants and U.S. students must always finance their first year here themselves. Canadians with a 70% average automatically get one-third of their fees remitted. Jobs are very difficult to find.

Dorms are bland and cost $800 for room and board. 2,858 live in them. Basement suites are very popular although illegal (says the University). You pay $110 a month for room and board and eat with the family you live with (attics, too).

Some people rent houses for $250 (five split it). If you have to scrounge, go to "Famous Foods" for bulk food bargains.

Most kids have cars—lots of Mustangs, Camaros and Triumph Spitfires. Many middle-class students are into costly threads.

BROTHERS AND SISTERS:

Ratio cats : chicks—3 : 2.

Lots of commuters. The majority of kids are clean-cut and

middle-class. There are lots of freaks but they are confined mainly to the Art department. A minority of chicks are liberated. The 12 fraternities and 9 sororities have had trouble getting pledges lately. There are a lot of noon shows on campus rather than evening entertainment. A fair amount of student theater, and lots of rock concerts. Wolfman Jack can be heard late at night on XERB from Tijuana.

Lots of dope on campus, mostly grass. Alaskan dope is great and sells for $20 a lid. Narcs are known to sit around the cafeteria but there haven't been any campus busts.

Fourth Avenue is the main hippie street. Many students live in that area called Kitsilano. One place there is Harri Krishnal's "Last Chance Saloon"—a coffee house.

Intelligentsia go to the "Cecil Hotel" downtown to booze. Aggies and engineers go to the "Frazer Arms" near school to get drunk.

In 1968, Jerry Rubin visited UBC. After a speech he asked the crowd what building to take over. Somebody yelled out one, and students took over a building, held a party there and smoked dope. The campus still hasn't recovered from this shock. The Vancouver student movement is made up of freaky Maoists. Pigs haven't been on campus.

SURVIVAL:

Better chance than in Vietnam or Cambodia.

The Art department is very good and there are lots of darkrooms around. Lots of medical facilities since there is a Medical school on campus. They sell condoms in the johns of the SUB buildings. Getting an abortion can be a real hassle in British Columbia. All types of suicide services are available in Vancouver.

The campus paper, the *Ubyssey*, is literate and good (cynical as hell). There are two good restaurants for the vegetarian health trip—"Naam" and "Golden Lotus." The Women's Caucus is city-wide—they put out birth-control books. A part-time day-care center was established on campus.

ENVIRONMENT:

Mental—People are talking about their disenchantment with U.S. radical issues being laid on Canada. Many students feel it is just another form of U.S. imperialism. Canadians can't seem to make up their minds about draft dodgers.

The ecology movement is off campus but is very active.

Physical—The University is located on Point Grey which juts into the water from the city of Vancouver—it's separated from the urban scene by a large area of university-endowed lands. Rainy and cold. When you walk across the street from the campus, you can walk down a deep wooded slope to the beach.

The campus is the basic large multiversity block and cube architecture. The nicest thing about the campus is the view of snowcapped mountains to the north.

Students ski a lot at Mt. Grouse and Mt. Seymour. Stanley Park is a beautiful large park in the city, with a zoo.

COLORADO

Colorado College
Colorado Springs, Colorado

One of the few private schools in Colorado. Paul Webb, our researcher for the south-central area said, "If I could go to any of these schools, I'd go here." The campus paper carries a ski report every day. A party school.

SERGEANT PEPPER SECTION:

1,600 students. Few minority students. Difficult to get in—fairly high grades and 1,200 SATs are average. Some preference given to children of alumni.

ACADEMIC BULLSHIT:

Colorado College is a small liberal-arts school with an emphasis on the individual. Students say the best departments are Chemistry, English and History. There are no graduate schools.

Popular courses include "Philosophy" with Harvey Rabbin ("he's easy to talk to"), and "Religion" with Douglas Fox ("he's stimulating and communicates in an understandable way.").

Some Pass/Fail, lots of class participation and no student-originated courses. Students can take a single course for a period of concentrated study. An interdepartmental major in Asian Studies is offered—it's directed at Asian history, philosophy, art and religion.

Some dating between teachers and students. Study abroad in conjunction with other colleges' programs.

BREAD:

$845 a semester tuition. Loans and scholarships are fairly easy to get and jobs at $1.45 an hour are easy to find.

Dorms cost $950 a year for room and board. Students are supposed to live in the dorms or with their parents until age 21 and most do live in the dorms. There are no dorm hours but limited visitation (you can't have a chick in your room overnight). Apartments are $60 for a decent one-bedroom. Three dorms are coed. Many students have cars and bikes and some hitch.

Used books at "Clauson."

BROTHERS AND SISTERS:

Ratio cats : chicks—3 : 2.

This school is nearly as hip as Boulder. Students are easy-going

110

skiers. Lots of long hair, moustaches, jeans, tie-dyed shirts and boots. Chicks are for the most part braless and wearing jeans. There is little formal dating—just usually rapping and getting high or taking a walk in the country. Hip chicks are liberated, and balling prevails. The fraternities and sororities are strong—but they are losing membership.

Hangs include "Giuseppe's" (a 3.2 beer joint—18-year-olds can drink 3.2) and "Melba's" (a 3.2 place for straights).

Pretty heavy dope scene—score from freaks. Lids go for $15, acid and mescaline for $4. Few busts but the pigs are watching.

The campus is hip culturally and beginning to be hip politically. A Committee for the Moratorium ran the Moratoriums and about 1,000 students showed up.

400 supporters demonstrated after Kent State and six arrrests were made when students sat in at the local draft board. The only violence so far was when a bomb was thrown at the ROTC building after Kent. Pigs are only called on campus when an Army dude from the nearby base rapes a chick.

SURVIVAL:

The school has many facilities for creative arts. Health service is poor—a couple of shrinks and no BC pills. The church organizations do draft counseling. Survival services in town. The school paper, *The Catalyst*, has gone underground because the administration didn't like what they were printing and cut off their funds. Health-food stores in town.

ENVIRONMENT:

Mental—People are reading Tom Wolfe and Kurt Vonnegut and talking politics. The Ecology Action Committee had very good Earth Day activities. They are trying to get local grocery stores to sell bio-degradable products.

Physical—The climate is warm and nice in the summer, snowy in the winter. The campus is urban—a city street divides the campus in half. Big and flat lawns and trees. The older buildings are done in stone and are Gothic church style. The newer ones are of mixed designs.

Escapes are mainly ski resorts—Vail, Loveland, Aspen and Taos. Everybody skis. Denver is only an hour away if you desire a big city.

Colorado School of Mines

Golden, Colorado

Technically a good school but ROTC is required.

SERGEANT PEPPER SECTION:

1,750 students—few minority students, 1,100 out-of-state. Admission is very selective—it is based on (1) pattern of course work in

high school, (2) grades, (3) rank in class, (4) SATs, (5) other
test scores, (6) personality factors, (7) physical and social maturity and (8) desire to become an engineer.

ACADEMIC BULLSHIT:

This school is primarily for engineers who are interested in fields
related to mineral resources. Many fine courses in engineering
aspects of chemistry, ecology, geophysics, math, metallurgy, mining,
petroleum studies, and physics. Students say Geology is the best
department. Best professors include Jim Brown in Physics ("you
can talk to him") and Dr. Williams in Chemistry ("he really
makes you learn").

Lots of academic pressure—an emphasis on the technical nature
of things. No Pass/Fail, many tests, classes of 25, no Free U and
no Black Studies. A few student-originated courses like "Film
Making" and "Modern Art." Seniors do independent study in the
form of a research project. Most students take six weeks of field
study during the summer.

BREAD:

$230 in-state per semester, $605 out-of-state. Financial aid is
tight but jobs at $1.45 an hour are easy to get. Dorms cost $400
per semester for room and board. Many cats live in them. There's
no visitation for the 25 chicks. Fraternities are still booming and
they cost $450 a semester. Some students live in apartments at $50
for a one-bedroom. Most cats have cars and there's plenty of
parking.

BROTHERS AND SISTERS:

Ratio of a million to one (there are only 25 chicks).

A bunch of straight engineers who like Lawrence Welk, Nixon
and the defense industries.

They wear ugly shirts, and Sta-prest pants and 1950s shoes.
About one-third are still into drinking and fraternity blackballing.
The frats are very strong and control the student government (and
people are still concerned about student government). Colorado
School of Mines men hate professors who talk out against the war
—as it is "unpatriotic.'"

They date the 25 chicks who attend the school and also townies
and girls from Temple Buell.

ROTC is required. No demonstrations as yet (naturally). The
Young Republicans are fairly active and put out their own paper.
The few hips hang at "Washington Park" and "Exodus." Straights
hang at "Mr. Lucky's" and the "Galaxy."

The drug scene is very light—a few smoke and lids go for $15
in Denver.

SURVIVAL:

Hard.
Student health is fairly competent and shrinks are available.

Survival services in Denver. Most students eat in the school cafeteria and the food is baked barf. "The Mule" is the mascot and surrounding chicks' schools refer to it as "The Ass." The campus paper, *The Ore-digger*, is a drag.

ENVIRONMENT:

Mental—People are reading *Fanny Hill* and *Catch 22* and talking about job recruiters.

Physical—Golden, Colorado, is a town of 8,600, 15 miles out of Denver. The campus is spread out over 207 acres. The weather is cold and dry in winter and warm in the summer. The buildings resemble old high schools—cream-colored square-cement blockers. The eyesores are the ROTC barracks.

The escape is mainly skiing—ski resorts all over the area.

University of Northern Colorado

Greeley, Colorado

Most people are interested in getting their teaching certificate at this school. It is rated the third best teachers' college in the nation. The campus is nauseatingly collegiate. Those freaks that exist are always hassled by real live cowboys. As of late, someone was cramming oranges into the urinals in the Student Center every Sunday. To combat this fiendish crime the administration is going to close the johns.

SERGEANT PEPPER SECTION:

Colorado State has 8,624 students, 1,211 of which are graduate students. It's relatively easy to get into—entering freshmen must be in the upper half of their graduating class and score 19 or above on their ACT. Transfer students need a 2.0 GPA. 25% are from out-of-state.

ACADEMIC BULLSHIT:

This school's best department is Education, especially Special Education. Popular courses in this section include "Introduction to Educating Exceptional Children" and "Speech Correction." Dr. Napier teaches "Education of the Blind." She herself is blind. Graduate courses in Special Education and Music are good.

Tommy Thompson is a meditation freak who teaches English. He always turns his courses into an experience in mysticism. Leika and Pingstone teach freaky art classes.

Grades are used at Colorado State—no Pass/Fail.

No student-initiated courses and no Free U. Relationships with the teachers are whatever you make out of them. There is a Minorities Studies program—it deals only in areas of Black and Spanish Studies. Tests and papers both. No independent study and not much study abroad. Lax dress codes except for P.E. and business classes—girls must wear dresses.

BREAD:

In-state pays $123 tuition a quarter and out-of-state $273 a quarter. Living is cheap in Greeley—if you can consistently make $100 a month you can get by easily. Greeks cost $80 a quarter for board and room. Apartments range $42 up monthly and dorms range $283–$333 quarterly for room and board. Scholarships and loans are limited. Approximately 700 students are employed on campus and make about $1.45 an hour. The "Corner Book Store" has used books.

Dates are cheap because guys are in the minority and can usually get the chick to go dutch. Most students walk, not that many cars.

BROTHERS AND SISTERS:

More chicks here; ratio cats : chicks—4 : 5.

On the whole, everyone looks straight with one or two lukewarm hips here and there among the guys. Greek guys usually wear jeans, bell-bottom jeans; when they wear slacks, they wear "straight" slacks. Button-down shirts and T-shirts are worn by the guys. Girls usually wear dresses and bras and some are into those ugly brown loafers (but that's just a few) and they just look comfortable. Their clothes seem to be "straight" utilitarian with some eye for fashion. Guys don't have long hair—just sideburns and moustaches here and there. Lots of levis worn around here. A freak or two can be spotted by his work shirt and somewhat longer hair.

The Greeks live. They are the closest thing to being a dominant force on this campus of all the Colorado campuses. Only organized group on campus. Practically all student-body presidents have been Greeks with just a couple of exceptions. A lot of pick-ups here (too many girls for the usual dating game to be played). "I don't know any male here who couldn't get laid within 24 hours if he weren't particular." "There's more balling than people like to think." A lot of chicks live with a guy for two or three weeks and then go back to their regular place.

Freaks meet at the "Belly of the Whale" (a campus coffee house run by The Ecumenical Presence). Freaks and cowboys go to the "Library" (a 3.2 beer bar). If someone hassles you there because of your hair, the bartenders throw them out. But freaks sometimes get jumped by cowboys as they leave. Freaks hang in the "Bruin Lair" (also 3.2 bar). Theater majors go to the "Columbine Coffee Shop."

Lids go for $15. About every frat house turns on. Patches of grass are growing along the South Platte River. You can score on campus or at the 3.2 bars.

Movies and rock concerts are the main entertainment, sometimes in Greeley, sometimes in Denver.

The students are apolitical and apathetic. Most want their teaching certificates and their freedom (or imprisonment, however you consider a teaching job). "They couldn't give a rat's ass about anything." About 1% active leftists.

There were a couple of minor demonstrations—one involving

the Afro-American Student Union and one involving the grape strike before 1970. In January of 1970 there was a demonstration. Most town cops are decent. If you get hassled about your hair, call Meyers'—it's sort of a clan which live about three miles west of town. They'll protect you.

The only radical professors are in the Art department.

First-quarter freshmen women must keep hours—Sunday–Thursday, 11 P.M. and Friday and Saturday 1 A.M.

One campus newspaper happening deserves mention.

In October, 1969, Ed Quillen, the editor started the famed hippie hoax. He made up a story and printed it in the paper saying that hippies were planning to move into Wyoming and take it over by outvoting the small population there. One of the students at U.N.C. was from Casper, Wyoming, and sent the article home to his soon-worried parents. The hoax mushroomed and was carried by the A.P. wires. Editorials appeared in the *Wall Street Journal, The New York Times* and Denver *Post* about this horrendous hippie conspiracy. It was never revealed as a hoax UNTIL NOW and people still believe that hippies want to take over Wyoming—Wyoming residents are still on the lookout for them.

SURVIVAL:

Dope is available and BC pills from Planned Parenthood in Denver. No Free Clinic here, but again, in Denver. There is a suicide prevention center in Greeley called "Somebody Loves You, Baby" (SLYB). Draft counseling at The Ecumenical Presence (group of campus churches). Student health is bad, free medicine but you'd better not have anything serious.

Campus paper is the *Mirror,* run by a former SDSer but not radical.

"Greeley Health Foods" for the natural foodist.

ENVIRONMENT:

Mental—The sports page is the most widely read in the school newspaper. The P.E. department is the most opulent in the school. "Nobody will fool around with the P.E. Department, even the President of the College is afraid of them."

Physical—The old or central campus has a lot of grass and trees. The new campus has rolling grass fields—ah, nature! But then come the buildings. They look like a hospital and have no windows and are on an artificial atmosphere control system. "If it breaks down you gotta clear everyone out or they'll suffocate. You feel like you're on a missile base."

50% of the campus splits from Greeley on weekends. They go westward. Skiing is really big.

Colorado State University
Ft. Collins, Colorado

This school is a rural sterile place with the only hope being a few freaky nature lovers. The Colorado Board of Agriculture governs the school. Say no more.

SERGEANT PEPPER SECTION:

14,500 students attend Colorado State, of which 2,500 are graduate students. It's easy to get in, no definite requirements except that freshmen should be in the upper half of their graduating class and have acceptable recommendations from high school counselor. Transfer students need a 2.0 GPA. SATs required, usually with a combined score of about 1,000. 35% out-of-state students, 200 blacks, 250 Chicanos, 20 Indians.

ACADEMIC BULLSHIT:

Veterinary Medicine is their best department; along with Cornell's it is one of the two top departments in the nation. Biology and Microbiology are also important because they are major centers for ecology research. Engineering is also nationally known.

The most popular professor is Meyer Nathan of the History department. "He's an important liberal on campus and everyone likes him because he cares."

Pass/Fail just started in fall of 1970. There are no student-initiated courses. The Free U exists but is looking for a home. Not much interaction between students and teachers. Most teachers would rather be doing research in the laboratory than be in the classroom. No Third World College. 1950s type tests, few papers. No specific study abroad but CSU does handle applications for students who want to study on the World Campus Afloat.

Some dress codes—especially in Home Economics and Business classes—chicks have to wear dresses.

BREAD:

Tuition is $142 in-state per quarter and $435 out-of-state. Dorms run $966–$1,050 for the year, apartments $100 a month for a furnished two-bedroom, and a few three-bedroom bungalows go for $185 up. Work-study is tight; however, over 3,500 students receive some form of financial aid—partial scholarships and loans. Some campus jobs but no central department on campus to do the hiring.

Most students walk, some bikes and cars. Dates cost an average of $5. No used-book or record stores.

BROTHERS AND SISTERS:

Ratio cats : chicks—2 : 1.

The campus is about evenly divided between freaks, Greeks and —cowboys! These cats have short hair, wear cowboy hats which warp upward, levis and western shirts. They look at freaks with vicious contempt and threaten to castrate them. This category of human being so far has proved socially unredeeming. The chicks wear bras, hair spray and perfume—very few foxy ones. Sororities have been actively preserved against the tide of change.

People are into Friday and Saturday dating and going to 3.2 bars for a big evening. Popular bars are "Giuseppe's," the "Green Onion," and the "Black Mine." Freaks hang out in the "Ramskellar" to the left of the entrance door.

The Athletic department is trying to build the school into a Big Ten type. CSU spent three million on a new football stadium which is used only four or five times a year.

About 40% smoke grass, 5% into harder stuff. Hard stuff (acid, speed) easier to get than the soft stuff.

The campus is apathetic and apolitical. "The only thing that stirs them up is what band is playing at the local 3.2 place and how much time they can get off from school." Sort of a rural agricultural mentality—the main topic is "can you get as drunk on 3.2 beer as on regular?" SDS died from apathy.

The Black Student Alliance has presented a couple of lists of demands to the administrators with no success. In November of 1969, the students demonstrated for the case of having beer served on campus. They took over the ballroom in the student center, threw popcorn around, had a light show and drank beer. They got their demand.

In February of 1970, the Black Student Alliance demonstrated against the racial policies of the Mormon Church during a basketball game with Brigham Young. "Hang the niggers" and "Kill the niggers" was yelled from the stands. The pigs were called in and six black students were suspended. Cameron Bishop is a well-known radical in the area. He supposedly blew up power towers in the Denver area which supplied power to the Coors Brewing Plant (Coors doesn't hire minority people and makes porcelain warheads for bombs used in Vietnam). Bishop is on the honorable list of FBI's Ten Most Wanted Dissenters.

Campus police are into parking tickets and drug busts. They are also citizen-watching at Ft. Collins. It seems that many townspeople have guns and have threatened to use them on students if any more trouble appears. The area is saturated with narcs.

Another glum note: The first weekend in May is known as "College Days." The cowboys come into town, get drunk and are all over the place. The only group with political potential is the BSA.

SURVIVAL:

Good luck. Quotes from the catalog:

1. The University does not allow a person to attend class unless he is registered for the class either for audit or credit.

2. Students are expected to attend all classes for which they are regularly registered.

3. All work missed by students shall be made up if required by the instructor.

4. If a student finds it necessary to be absent from class or late in attendance, he is expected to offer a satisfactory explanation to the instructor.

In determining the number of absences a student may be allowed, the instructor is expected to give first consideration to the effect on the work. Some students may be allowed several absences, others cannot afford to take any. Whenever absences are a cause of delinquency, the matter is reported to the Office of the Associate Dean of Students.

"Western Health Foods" has natural foods but their prices are phenomenally high. BC pills are given out without question at the student health service but besides that, student health is useless. No Free Clinic in Ft. Collins but one in Denver. Draft counseling is done by the Rev. Bob White of the United Campus Ministry.

No underground paper but the moderate campus paper, *The Collegian,* is somewhat good.

ENVIRONMENT:

Mental—Greeks are into beer discussions, freaks reading *Tales of Hoffman.*

Physical—The campus is rather unattractive. There's a big veterinary clinic on it and whereas most schools have a beautiful tower or bell as a prominent landmark, CSU has a 200-ft. chimney. South Hall is described as "A pink, ugly, army barricade—the ugliest building ever conceived." One other eyesore is the Burlingame Railroad—it runs through the campus—freight trains only. Corporate sterile architecture. They have about 50 newly-planted trees running in a straight line parallel to the Student Union—unimaginative and dull. Students do like the Moby Gym—it looks a little like a two-layer cake that is beginning to fall.

The campus is very cement in distinct contrast to the beautiful Colorado scenery surrounding it. Hardly any air or noise pollution.

People escape by going skiing, mountain climbing and motorcycling. For meditation, people go to Poudre Canyon, Poudre River and Horsetooth Reservoir.

University of Colorado
Boulder, Colorado

The Berkeley of Colorado. This is an ideal place for students who dig nature, the relaxed life, dope, sex and other students.

SERGEANT PEPPER SECTION:

20,387 students go here, of which 3,500 are graduate students. In-state applicants have to be in the upper half of their graduating class and need a 1,000 combined SAT and a 23 ACT. Out-of-state students need to be in the upper half of their graduating class and score 1,050 SAT and 24 ACT. Transfers need a 2.5 GPA. 1,200 minority students.

ACADEMIC BULLSHIT:

The best grad and undergrad departments are in the Sciences. Physics is fantastic ("They have great defense contracts, that's why they have such great facilities"), Chemistry ("They also have a lot of government contracts") and Psychology. Students really like the Philosophy department but the University never provides enough space for them. Prof. John Visvader is very popular in this department.

Pass/Fail, grades, tests and papers. Student-initiated courses are independent study classes and are for credit. There's a Free U with "Astrology," "Organic Gardening" and 48 other courses. They put out an underground newspaper—*Boulder Express*. No Third World College. Most classes are big and impersonal. Some grad departments have good student-professor interaction. Study abroad in France, Spain, Germany, Italy, Portugal, England and Russia.

BREAD:

Total yearly cost for in-state students is $429; $1,400 for out-of-state.

Dorms go for $890–$1,020 a year for room and board for a double room. Sororities cost from $400–$550 a semester and frats cost approximately $100 a month for room and board. No such thing as a commune at the moment—a couple co-ops. As for off-campus housing, since September–October of 1969 the BTU (Boulder Tenants' Union) has been in existence. At the time, there was a hassle over housing and over 400 students had no place to stay. If you aren't rich, then rents are exorbitant. A lot of the old houses and apartments are being torn down and replaced with relatively expensive townhouses and apartments—it costs $75 per person to live in a relatively dinky (small) townhouse with four other people. At one time, you had to give a $500 damage deposit before you moved in; now it's down to approximately $200.

Insufficient adequate low-cost housing around—costs $60–$70 a month for a single room and you don't always get cooking privileges. Or $80 a month for a room about 10 by 15.

Work-study, scholarships and loans are tight. Some campus jobs at $1.50–$2.00 an hour—hashing, library, the usual. You need about $150 a month to get by in Boulder.

Most students have cars and parking is a tremendous problem on campus. A date costs approximately $5. Both used books and records can be purchased at "Duck Soup."

BROTHERS AND SISTERS:

Ratio cats : chicks—7 : 5.

There are Greeks here but for the most part it looks like Berkeley—heavy hip types, mostly freaks. Lots and lots of hair and beards and fringed leather jackets and old jeans, chicks without bras wearing all kinds of good stuff.

Dating is still popular with the Greeks, but the majority of kids (freaks) are with it. Chicks are very liberated.

Freaks can meet everywhere on campus, including the fountain area and the hallway just outside of the book center. Off campus it's the "Brillig Works" (book store), the "Raven Book Store," "Duck Soup" and "The Hill," a place where spare-changers hang.

50% of the campus turns on and a lid goes for $15. You can buy drugs on the "Hill," but be careful, there are four full-time narcotics investigators on campus all the time.

Entertainment is balling, "Your place or mine."

"There are just too many rich kids here for a lot of political activity." The school had the reputation of a party school a few years back and it's still that way a little. SDS was kicked off campus last year. Women's Liberation is just forming and is starting to be quite active.

Political activity in 1970 included two significant events. In March, the Black Students Association and the United Mexican-American Students presented a list of demands to the administration, such as minority control of minority funds, partial minority control over the hiring of minority faculty and more minority students. The administration offered a compromise and both groups accepted it immediately. In April there was a sit-in at the administration building led by the Student Mobilization Committee. It lasted 13 hours and it was aimed at abolishing ROTC and ending all defense-related research. Then the SMC tried to organize a student strike to get their demands, but it failed.

Then there are the "Mad Bombers of Boulder." It all started this past March and is still happening. There are two bombers. One is a guy who wants the Colorado legislature to pass some anti-dynamite legislation. He goes around the mountains near Boulder exploding bombs, usually going off at around 8:00 in the evening and people hear a big explosion and say, "Oh, that's the Mad Boulder Bomber."

There has also been another set of bombings, by an unknown group which is more political in nature—there have been a couple of explosions in campus buildings—in the Air Force ROTC building, and in the basement of the Behavioral Sciences building. A police car was also bombed—this bombing received some of the highest approval of them all—and so was the Security Bank of Boulder. Also, a lot of bomb scares and buildings on campus had to be evacuated. Still not over as of yet.

SURVIVAL:

Boulder is cool—survival is easy. Plenty of drugs, cohabitation and smiles. BC pills at the student health center with a hassle. Planned Parenthood in the area. "Rapline" is a suicide prevention center. Communications Center in Boulder for runaways and counseling. Draft counseling is given on campus, and there is a Resistance office in Denver. Student health is lousy. Lots of health-food stores—"The Health Foods Store," "Green Mountain Grainery," "Bicopia," and "Natural Foods Store."

ENVIRONMENT:

Mental—Good stimulating atmosphere. People are reading Douglas' *Points of Rebellion*. Dig the "Alfred E. Packer Grill." It's located in the UMC and is named after the only man ever convicted of cannibalism in the U.S. Every year they have an "Alfred E. Packer Day" and sell special Packer Burgers for lower prices.

Physical—"In winter you ski and smoke dope, in summer you lay in the sun and blow dope." 76 degrees and no clouds. Mountains overlook the school and make it scenic. The only bummer is the cars parked all over the place. It looks like a retirement village for students—it's utterly beautiful. It is Italian-Spanish with everything made of red brick.

There is, however, pollution brought to you by the Dow Chemical Company in the area (they make warheads).

Escapes are the mountains.

In the winter the class schedule is a hassle as people try not to have any Monday, Wednesday and Friday courses so that they can have a four-day weekend.

Temple Buell Women's College
Denver, Colorado

A finishing type school.

SERGEANT PEPPER SECTION:

1,030 chicks. 14 blacks, 14 Chicanos. Easy to get in. You need average grades and about 1,000 SATs. 750 from out-of-state.

ACADEMIC BULLSHIT:

This used to be Colorado Women's College and was a junior college until 1960. It's a finishing school of sorts with an emphasis on a proper, not too bright, young lady. It's all liberal arts and the best departments are the Arts (theater and studio art, art history) and Sociology. There is no graduate school. An innovative program is New College which opened in 1970—everyone goes at his own speed and there is no "failing." It is voluntary.

Favorite classes include Sociology with David Torbett ("he's a very interesting person) and "Religion and Ethics" with Charles Spring ("he has lots of personal contact with his students"). Some Pass/Fail, small classes (average size is 12), class participation is important. Some student-originated courses ("Chinese and Oriental Art") and no Third World studies. A new Free U in Denver offers "Leather Work," "Encounter" groups and a few more. Independent study is easy to get. Study abroad in Geneva, Madrid and Vienna.

BREAD:

$3,189 a year—this includes tuition, fees and lunch on campus. Loans and scholarships and jobs are all easy to get—jobs pay $1.45 an hour.

Dorms cost $700 a semester for room and board and most live in them. First-semester freshmen have curfews—12 P.M. on weekdays and 2 A.M. on weekends. Men are allowed in rooms once a week. Freshmen can't have cars, most others do.

SISTERS:

Most chicks are just getting lukewarm hip. Many rich chicks who couldn't get into a sister school. CWC, before its name change, was considered comparable to Stephens. Temple Buell, as CWC is now called, is trying to shake that finishing-school image to no avail. Chicks still wear bras and dresses to school—some are beginning to wear jeans and sandals around campus.

There is lots of dating and quite a bit of balling. Chicks date cats from the other schools in Denver, especially the Air Force Academy. (Ick!)

Hip chicks hang at "Washington Park" and go to "Mr. Lucky's" (a nightclub) and "The Pub" (a 3.2 beer joint) on dates. Straights go to the "Galaxy." Lots of chicks smoke dope but have to be very careful as the school will kick you out if you get caught. The administration kicked out a teacher who advocated sexual freedom. These chicks aren't exactly intellectuals and aren't too politically aware. There was limited support for the Moratorium in 69. And the school shut down for a short time after Kent State. But there has never been a real demonstration (too uncouth!).

SURVIVAL:

If you're lightheaded it's easy.

The school has excellent facilities for the creative arts. Student health is pretty competent but no BC pills. Survival services in Denver. No one "brown-bags it"—all eat in the dining hall. *The Western Graphic* is a drag.

Chicks don't want to know about Women's Liberation.

ENVIRONMENT:

Mental—People are reading a little Brautigan and Tom Wolfe. About 50% of the students took part in Earth Day activities.

Physical—Denver is cold and snowy in the winter and hot in the summer. The campus is in a residential area of town and is stretched over four square blocks. Noise pollution is bad since the school is near the airport.

Most buildings are stone Gothic style. The eyesore is a huge mural in the Fine Arts building done by Temple Buell's sister—it's a horrible 70 feet long.

People escape to the Air Force Academy for weekends (yes—"to"). They also go skiing at Vail and Loveland.

U.S. Air Force Academy
Colorado Springs, Colorado

As the brochure states: "Mission: To provide instruction, experience and motivation to each cadet so that he will graduate with the knowledge, character and qualities of leadership essential to his progressive development as a career officer in the U.S. Air Force."

30% drop out. Why not more? Because if you drop out after two years, you are immediately inducted into the armed forces.

Learn to kill. Come to the Air Force Academy and let Uncle Sam foot the bill.

SERGEANT PEPPER SECTION:

Sergeant is right. 4,000 future disabled vets attend the Academy. They try to include a few minority students (Why kill only WASPs?) and they have succeeded in getting about 100 blacks and 100 Mexican-Americans.

ACADEMIC BULLSHIT:

Cheating was popular in 1968 but the administration purged the school of unpatriotic cheaters (they hope). "Groovey" teachers are Lt. Hayes (he talks about sex and psychology) and Major Kiley in English (could you dig addressing your teachers as "Major"?).

Engineering and War Machines are their best departments. Students originated two courses in 1970—"Soviet Studies" (get those commies) and "Far East Asian Studies" (get those gooks). There are lots of drills and target practice sessions. Study abroad in Cambodia and Vietnam.

BREAD:

It's free—all they want is your life in return. No jobs or need— cadets go to school all year 'round with one month's leave. They all live on campus and must be at ease in their barracks by 7:15 P.M. weeknights, 10:45 P.M. Fridays and 1:30 A.M. Saturday night-Sunday morning. No chicks or booze in the rooms and can't leave the base on weekdays. Only seniors can have cars. Schoolbooks are free, too.

CADETS:

Cadets will be cadets. They must have scalped short hair and wear armed forces ugly uniforms. No one will talk about dope but one cadet estimated (behind closed doors) that about 10% of them have turned on. They are afraid to talk because in 1970 SDS came in, talked to cadets, and misquoted them.

Cadets have a terrible time getting dates—they use the facilities of the whorehouses in Colorado Springs a lot. Some get a girl at Temple Buell nearby or at a pickup 3.2 bar. Most cadets are dying for a date (no pun intended).

Cadets can't participate in any demonstrations. The Air Force Academy punishes them if they do (spankings, expulsions and eight months of 160 hours a month marching around with rifles). If you admit to smoking grass, they kick you out.

SURVIVAL:

Not for long. Student health has shrinks who are able to examine your head and find out why you signed up. No draft counseling, needless to say. You eat in the mess hall. Their mascot is the "Falcon" and their magazine is the *Talon* (open aggression). Their satire paper is called the *DoDo*.

ENVIRONMENT:

Mental—Cadets read crotch novels (dirty books). They talk about war.

Physical—Colorado is cold in winter (with snow) and warm in summer. The academy covers 15 square miles. The school buildings are clustered together out in the country. They are made of steel, glass and cement. Aerodynamic architecture with parade grounds in-between.

CONNECTICUT

University of Bridgeport
Bridgeport, Connecticut

Apathy.

SERGEANT PEPPER SECTION:

8,200 students (some are part-time). Not hard to get in. You need fairly good grades, SAT scores of about 1,000, and a recommendation. Transfers need a C average. Most students are from the New England area.

ACADEMIC BULLSHIT:

Students say the best departments are Theater Arts, Philosophy, the College of Business and College of Nursing. Dr. Degrood in the Philosophy department is a leading Marxist in the country. Favorite professors include Dick Allen, who teaches "Creative Writing," and Warren Bass, the head of the Theater Arts department.

Some Pass/Fail, no student-originated classes. A new Free U teaches "The Revolution" and "How to Live Off the Street." The student-faculty relationship is poor and there is no separate Black Studies department (few blacks on campus). Some independent study. Study abroad.

BREAD:

Tuition at this private university for the semester is $825. Some financial aid is available in a packet—scholarship, loan and job. There are a fair number of jobs available. Dorms cost $550 a semester for room and board. Apartments go for about $125 a month. Most students live in the dorms.

Lots of people have cars but parking is difficult.

BROTHERS AND SISTERS:

Ratio cats : chicks—about 1 : 1.

There are three types of students here: the dopers, the pseudo-freaks and the whisky trippers (or straight-straights). Some of the straight-straights still wear Ivy coats and ties, jocks wear cut-off sweatshirts to show off their muscles, straight chicks wear mini skirts and freaks wear jeans and tie-dyes. The pseudo-freaks wear long hair and beards. People aren't very friendly on the whole and are slightly paranoid. "Why are you talking to me, what do you want from me?"

125

Social life is in-between formal dating and hanging out. It's a suitcase school. Every weekend people split to pick up chicks. There's no place to go after 11 P.M. in Bridgeport. Most people gather at each others' digs or go into New York or Boston for dates. Everybody balls. Fraternities "are here and they're here to stay, unfortunately—they are not dying out at all." "Signifynothing" is an anti-frat organization on campus. Everyone is into drugs. About 75% smoke grass (about once a week). You can score from bikers and freaks near campus. Some hard drugs.

Local hangs include "Columbia Court" (where freaks live), "Milford Beach" and the Student Center (bridge, poker, pinball machines and juke boxes)—freaky freaks hang here, really weird people (whoever heard of a freak who was into bridge and pool).

Most students are armchair liberals; the strike almost got them going. The activists come from New York and New Jersey (they're rebelling, but they still don't want to lose daddy's money). The only really active political group was the University of Bridgeport Students for Peace and Freedom (the Strike Committee). Women's Liberation is active and is into day-care centers and more dissemination of birth control information. The school is basically apathetic. They had a demonstration to get a coed dorm in 1969—it succeeded. Some participation in the Moratoriums; in October, 1969, about 1,000 marched on the federal building.

The first real activism came with the Cambodia-Kent days. President Henry F. Littlefield refused to send a telegram denouncing the war to Nixon, so the students took over Cortright Hall, the library, the Computer Center and Fones Hall. The strike went on, canvassing, leafletting, and rallies. The action lasted four weeks. There was no violence. All the letters and petitions to congressmen that the Strike Committee had gathered were mysteriously burned by someone.

SURVIVAL:

Student health doesn't distribute BC pills. An organization called "Fish" has survival services. Rabbi Wallich gives excellent draft counseling. Even the dogs on campus are apathetic. *The Scribe* is so-so—borders on liberal.

ENVIRONMENT:

Mental—People are smoking dope rather than talking or reading.

Physical—It starts snowing two weeks before Christmas and rains a lot in the spring—lots of mud. Bridgeport is one of the 15 cities with the highest rate of air pollution in the United States. United Illuminating, Avco and G.E. are polluters. Long Island Sound and the Housatonic River are both polluted.

Both modern and old traditional buildings adorn the campus. Georgetown Hall looks like an octopus. The campus as a whole looks like a bunch of city blocks.

Escapes include Easton and "The Devil's Den" (waterfall and woods). Lots of bike clubs hang around campus. The clubs get along with the freaks.

Connecticut College
New London, Connecticut

A small fine New England liberal arts college.

SERGEANT PEPPER SECTION:

1,500 students, of which 143 are graduate and special students. Two-thirds are from out-of-state.

It's relatively difficult to get in. You need a grade point of at least 3.2 and SATs totaling 1,200. 3% blacks.

ACADEMIC BULLSHIT:

Connecticut College provides an excellent academic environment. There can be a very close relationship between students and professors if the student shows any degree of initiative at all. Professors eagerly reciprocate and students feel there is excellent communication.

There are some exciting things happening in the History department. The Asian History section boasts some very fine scholars in the fields of Indian, Japanese and Chinese history—can be a major. The European and American sections of the department are also very good (especially courses like "History of the Afro-American in North America," "Modern Japan," and "Borderlands of Civilization." Philosophy offers excellent traditional courses. The Psychology department is good and oriented toward experimental psychology. The Psychology department offers an excellent but small graduate program in Experimental and Perceptual Psychology. They do research in underwater perception in conjunction with the Navy.

Most popular professors are Lester Reiss (Philosophy) and Ronald Glassman (Sociology—teaches "Crime and Delinquency").

Some Pass/Fail, no student-initiated courses or Free U. Many black studies courses. An occasional midterm. Generally a final but most often papers. "Last semester I had ten of them to write and this is not at all unusual."

Independent study for juniors and seniors. Study abroad at Cambridge University in England. Seniors are required to take comprehensives in their majors after four years.

BREAD:

$2,600 a year tuition. About 20% of the students receive some aid but scholarship funds are deplorably scarce. Campus job preference is given to financial-aid students—average salary for the year is $200.

Dorms cost $1,250 a year for room and board, and cooperative housing runs $750. Cars and expensive wardrobes aren't necessary.

BROTHERS AND SISTERS:

Ratio cats : chicks—1 : 25.

Connecticut College went coed for the first time in 1969. The

127

chicks are New England lukewarm hip, dressed in blue jeans and T-shirts. Hair is long, sometimes electric. The cats are straighter and have shortish hair, wear jeans and boots.

Connecticut College chicks split on the weekends to Brown, Wesleyan or Trinity because social life on their own campus is dismal. Fixups, mixers and searches are the order of the day. "Dating" is nonexistent. Weekending is the thing. The chicks are liberated and individualistic. Entertainment is small parties. Lids are $15 and enter the campus from all over (the college is located midway between Boston and New York). Grass is popular, some mescaline.

Women's Liberation is in the educational stage. The political history was nonexistent until the Kent State Massacre and the Cambodian decision. Strike action was peaceful and productive. There's never been a "disorderly demonstration." The only radical club that exists is called "Rally" and was started in May, 1970.

SURVIVAL:

Connecticut College is on the honor system. Students have to sign a pledge before each exam promising not to cheat. They are responsible for disciplining themselves and each other. A worthy idea. Most students like it and it works fine.

The only hangup to survival is the dearth of males, but if chicks don't mind traveling on the weekend, it's cool.

Student health is adequate. BC pills to chicks over 21. Certain faculty members pioneered the draft counseling movement in New England. The campus paper, the *Satyagraha,* is moderately left of center. No organic garden scene. Closest city is New London, Connecticut (32,000).

ENVIRONMENT:

Mental—"No two people read the same books on this campus if they can help it."

Physical—Climate is typical New England—very cold winters, pleasant spring and autumn, rather hot summers. The campus and local area is semi-rural, a lot of "free" land. Lots of trees. Polluted Thames River and Long Island Sound.

Architecture is neo-Gothic.

"Everyone here must find his own escape. Some people go to one of the many nearby schools. Others go to Boston or New York." 97% live-ins.

University of Connecticut at Storrs

Storrs, Connecticut

Getting there.

SERGEANT PEPPER SECTION:

13,692 students of which 2,983 are grads. Entering freshmen

should be in the upper fourth of their high-school class, have SATs of 1,100 and have taken a college prep program in high school. Transfers should have a GPA of C. 22% are from out-of-state. 243 blacks.

ACADEMIC BULLSHIT:

There's a new honors program called "Inner College" for a small number of undergraduates that is very good. The Agriculture school is excellent and the English, Philosophy and Economics departments are good.

"This school is too big and diverse for any one professor to be really popular." Tabb, an Economics professor, was mentioned as being very well liked.

Pass/Fail is allowed (and you have nine weeks into the semester to decide if you want to take the course Pass/Fail).

Student-initiated courses in Inner College only (a course is offered on macrobiotics). The Free U is called The Experimental College and offers about 25 courses (T-groups, astrology and the usual). The student-professor relationship is very remote ("If you're lucky enough to see him other than in class, you should consider it an extreme honor"). There are various classes on black studies and some independent study is allowed. Study abroad in Spain and France.

BREAD:

Tuition in-state is $153 per semester, out-of-state is $503. Some financial aid is possible, mostly in the form of loans and jobs.

Dorms cost about $500 a semester for room and board. Apartments go for about $140 a month for a three- or four-room apartment.

Hitching is the most popular form of transportation as parking is tight unless you park your car in the fraternity lots. Expensive threads are a must.

BROTHERS AND SISTERS:

Ratio cats : chicks—4 : 3.

90% of both sexes are straight. The first thing they do when they arrive is go immediately to the Book Store and buy a blue windbreaker with an official "U Conn." insignia on the left—a blue windbreaker without the insignia just doesn't make it. Chicks wear expensive pants suits and skirts and nylons. They wear maxi coats that have zippered detachable bottoms. Straights wear loafers. About 10% of the campus is hip and the freaks are casual. They wear old sweatshirts, old pants and beads. The Engineer and Business people wear coats and ties. In the winter, people wear huge Arctic type fur coats. In the summer, chicks sunbathe and the cats walk by and check them out.

The fraternities do the dating thing (parties and beer) but they are dying. People go to "A's" (the airport restaurant) and the "Rock Garden." The "Rock Garden" is a vicious pick-up place—

all the cats sit around waiting for the music to start and when it does they make a mad dash for the prettiest chick. Straights hang at the "Snack Bar" in the Student Union. Freaks hang at the "Campus Restaurant."

There are three types of chicks here—the first group are free and liberated, the second are virgins and the third are in the great middle ground that can be moved. The majority are in the third category. They want to know you—you have to explain yourself and whip out a whole list of credentials to make sex meaningful to them. This process is a long, hard road. They will ball only if there's a chance of marriage. There's an excellent chance to pick up, get laid and get the clap. It's beginning to become worker oriented.

Hips are into grass (60% use it regularly). There are virtually no hard drugs here. You can score at fraternities or on campus. In the fall of 1969 there was a major drug bust here and everyone was flushing it down their toilets at the same time.

The majority of the students are uninformed liberals and are apathetic. "You have to jam information down their throats, rattle their heads around and sometimes they start to catch on." There also seems to be "a written or unwritten University policy to rip off any leaders" (expulsion, suspension or court actions). There are the usual political groups on campus. SDS is extremely ineffectual —"some of the best-meaning klutzes around." There have been Dow and ROTC demonstrations.

In March of 1970 there was a trustee meeting at the school to decide strategy against student demonstrators. Students were massed outside the building—there was an assistant professor with them who gave pigs taking pictures the finger. One of the trustees saw him flip the pig the bird—the trustee was "mortified" (his own words). They suspended the professor. Signs went up all over campus with a finger painted on them; there was even one big papier-mâché finger. The campus erupted over the Kent and Cambodia issues. 4,000 rallied and struck. ROTC was taken over and painted and there was some trashing.

SURVIVAL:

Chances are getting very good.

The infirmary is good only for diseases that are treatable with cough syrup. "Very often kids buy $3.98 first-aid kits and other kids go to them in the dorm rather than to the Infirmary." "The only kids who get fast service are the athletes." Planned Parenthood nearby. The Campus Christian Foundation gives draft counseling. "The only people who look up to jocks are sorority chicks and that's from a prone position."

The Connecticut Daily Campus is middle-of-the-road. *The Nutmeg Crier* is the local fascist rag.

The closest city to campus is Hartford.

ENVIRONMENT:

Mental—People are either studying or talking politics.

Physical—Winter has some really nice snow here and then it becomes slush for months. Spring is rainy and becomes sunny and beautiful as soon as it's time to go home. The worst thing about the campus is the wind—it's freezing.

There isn't any air pollution but you can't swim in Coventry Lake any more because of the pollution. Swan Lake on campus was cleaned up on Earth Day and they found a bicycle in it.

The Student Union, School of Education and School of Business Administration look like blocks of marble thrown on top of each other. The ROTC building is made of cinderblocks painted red—"neo-fascist" architecture. Mirror Lake is the only good-looking part of the campus. The swan (Horatio Godfrey) is at Mirror Lake. There are only ducks at Swan Lake.

Escapes are "Diana's Pool" (get stoned there) and "Hall's Pond"—skinny-dipping.

Trinity College
Hartford, Connecticut

Trinity is becoming a pretty groovy place considering that Connecticut still has blue laws and many of the trustees are into war-related things.

SERGEANT PEPPER SECTION:

1,460 full-time students and about 400 grads who attend on a part-time basis. Entering freshmen need 1,100 on the SATs and should be in the upper fourth of their public-school graduating class or the upper half of a private-school class. Transfers need a B average but they don't accept many transfer students due to the lack of turnover (90% of all the people who start here go on to finish). 80% from out-of-state.

ACADEMIC BULLSHIT:

The best departments are Engineering, Math, Science and Music. Students don't like the Art department as they feel it should be expanded and should include more specialization. The most popular courses are Dr. Higgins' "Psycho-Pathology" course (he is also the most popular professor on campus), Dr. McDowell's "Religion" course (one of the people) and Dr. Ogden's "Creative Writing" course (he brings a lot of poets in).

Traditional academia. One course a semester is Pass/Fail and juniors and seniors can originate courses. (Some have been "Swahili," "Mandarin Chinese" and "Revolution.") No Free U here as people here don't like to sit around in a class and not get credit. The student-professor relationship among the popular teachers is very good. No separate Black Studies department but they have two or three black courses like "Pan African History" and "Black Politics." Independent study is mostly for seniors. Study abroad. The "Open Semester" program lets you go away for one semester and do your own project for credit.

BREAD:

Tuition and fees for the year are $2,468. Financial aid is very squeezed at the moment. The school is helping about 20% of their student body. Most of the jobs are awarded to those on financial aid. Other jobs are hard to find. They pay $1.60 an hour. Dorms cost $1,160 a year for room and board. Apartments cost $150 a month on the average.

Most students drive either cars or bikes. It's impossible to scrounge—private schools cost too much.

BROTHERS AND SISTERS:

Ratio cats : chicks—3 : 1.

The school suffered a shock in 1969—it went coed. The cats are much happier since this addition although many of the professors haven't adjusted to the change.

Students are divided between pseudo-hips and straights—there's a small minority who are into the preppie coat-and-tie look. The most common threads are old levis, loafers and sport coats. There still aren't enough chicks for all the cats so Road Trips are still happening. Dating is usually a group thing on weekends; for a lot of people the academic tension is so great that they don't feel free until Friday.

Lots of success-oriented people who only have time to study and ball nurses from the hospital or chicks from the airline school.

The fraternities are dying fast and are becoming more like eating clubs. The hard-core preppies are also being rooted out.

Over half the campus has tried grass and about 35% are constant users. About 10% use acid (even many of the faculty). There's never been a bust. There are also a lot of boozers. The big weekends like Fall Weekend, Winter Weekend and Spring Weekend are excuses for the jocks to pass out drunk.

Local hangs include "The Green Onion" and "The Loft" (coffee houses) and "Zip's Bar" for fraternities.

The school image has changed from that of a rich boys' play-school to an intellectual community. The students are intellectual activists. They don't move until a specific issue comes up. There are a large number of artists here who are apolitical except in their artistic expression. There are about 100 silent conservatives and 20 hard-core radicals on campus. The radical caucus is called "Cabaret Votaire"—they are very interesting and intelligent people. The Trinity Coalition of Blacks includes those who are militant and talk rhetoric and those who are just liberal.

The first time students came together to protest was in 1968 when they took over the administration building and kept trustees inside against their will to demand a fund for black scholarships and more black admissions. This marked the turning point of the old conservative Trinity into a new, aware campus. The Moratoriums witnessed leafletting, canvassing and teach-ins. In April, 1970, there was a firebombing of the administration building for no apparent reason—they never found the culprit who perpetrated the dastardly deed—$40,000 damage.

The campus struck after Kent State. Local merchants sent food to help the kids and a lot of that food found its way into the surrounding poor districts. True community spirit arose. The strike was effective and lasted for two weeks.

The campus pigs just try to protect students from local rip-off artists; they just sit around watching the tube and playing with their walkie-talkies. The Hartford pigs usually don't come on campus because they aren't invited. But on Bottle Night, 1970 (a Trinity tradition in which the people throw their bottles in the quad on the last day of class), a lady said there was a riot and Hartford pigs came running in with bullet-proof vests.

SURVIVAL:

Student health service is awful; unless you are half-dead the doctor won't look at you. "They haven't gotten into birth control problems yet as chicks have only been on campus two years" (it only takes a second). Planned Parenthood is in Hartford. McCook Hospital is a Free Clinic for the unemployed. Draft counseling is done in the chapel and at the Trinity College Action Committee. Sports are very big but jocks aren't heroes. *The Tripod* is a middle-of-the-road college paper. *The Other Voice* is the underground rag.

ENVIRONMENT:

Mental—People are starting to talk politics.
Physical—The climate fluctuates between scorching hot and freezing cold—very humid. Practically all the elm trees are diseased.

Hartford is in the top 30 cities as to air pollution. Living here is like smoking a pack and a half of cigarettes a day. The Connecticut River is undrinkable and unswimmable.

The architecture is traditional and comfortable. The Life Sciences building looks like a big stone castle.

If you want to escape, you have to go way out of Hartford.

Wesleyan University
Middletown, Connecticut

Students are fragmented into political trips, drug trips and academic trips.

SERGEANT PEPPER SECTION:

1,456 students of which 276 are grads. Very difficult to get in. You need recommendations, an interview and three ACT tests. Most Wesleyan students are in the upper 10% of their high-school class and about 1,350 SATs. The competition is tough. Transfers need a B-average. 82% from out-of-state.

ACADEMIC BULLSHIT:

Education is very innovative lately at Wesleyan. They have eliminated course requirements and are going to build a new art-theater-music complex and a science center. The tutorials are becoming very popular and letter grades have been eliminated in two of the College Plans. The student-professor relationship is very good. "The main problem is that if you haven't done a paper you gotta hide all over campus so you don't bump into your professor. They are all over the place."

The Anthropology department has all the freaks in it. Ethno-Musicology, Art, Math and Science are the best departments. It is rumored that "the Chemistry department makes the best acid on the East Coast." Many students are here for a Master of Art in Teaching program.

The most popular professor is Dr. David McAllester in the Music department. He's the father of "Ethno-Musicology" on campus. He teaches a class called "North American Indian Vocal Techniques" which you can take over and over again for credit because it "took the Indians years and years to learn their things." He's about the only university-wide popular professor. The librarian for the Psychology department, Michael Millen, is also very popular. He and several students have organized an experimental off-campus education commune.

They have student-initiated classes which are taught for credit—one was on "Anarchism." The Strike Committee started an "Open Summer" program. It included a Free U for students and townspeople at the University. It also started the Gnu Knoll Day Camp which provided recreation facilities and education for 225 Middletown children, a breakfast program which fed 500 children for the summer and a high-school program.

The Third World College is known as the "Afro-American Institute." They offer 20 black studies classes including a major. Wesleyan is hooked up with the Institute for the Future—kind of a Buckminster Fuller computer type thing that computes solutions to social and environmental issues.

BREAD:

Tuition and fees at this private university are $2,910 a year. The University says that it will cost a student a minimum of $4,700 yearly to go here and so far the University has enough money so that if a student is accepted by the admissions committee and he happens to have need he is sent to the Financial Aids Office which provides for his need. They have $1.4 million available in scholarship money. Around 80 jobs are available under the work-study programs and 700 regular jobs.

Dorms run $1,250 a year. Most students live in the dormitories but a few live off campus in apartments that cost $65 a month. Cars are the most popular form of transportation and there's plenty of parking available. Scholarship students aren't allowed to have cars. 80% live on campus.

BROTHERS AND SISTERS:

Ratio cats : chicks—26 : 1.

Wesleyan just went coed and Wesleyan males are reveling in the change.

Students are very freaky. Practically everyone has long hair. They wear anything. Lots of air force jump suits and brown penny loafers. No one does the coat-and-tie scene but some of the jocks do wear "Wesleyan University" T-shirts. "The clothing here is just casual, comfortable and colorful."

The social life is very informal and activities take place in a small circle of friends that do things within themselves. Most guys visit Connecticut College to find a chick as there are so few at Wesleyan. There's a sizable number of people living together. The chicks don't go to school—they try to get jobs at Middletown. Much of the campus isn't getting any action at all—over the 1970 year there was a 200% increase of pubic lice from two known cases. Most action happens on the weekends. Guys bring the girls in in droves for the weekend, ball them, send them home for the rest of the week and forget them till the next week. Kind of like a male chauvinist cattle drive. The usual date is a party and a joint. On rainy days couples go belly-sliding down Foss Hill. Fraternities are on their way out. The only hang is "O'Rourke's Diner," where you can go any time from midnight to 6 A.M. and find a Wesleyan student.

Drugs are well imbedded here and there is a serious debate in the Religion department whether or not acid is a religious experience. Dope is in all the fraternities and has been smoked in every building on campus. Over 95% of the students use dope regularly. Hard dope passes through Middletown. Police have only been on campus for one bust.

There are a lot of apolitical freaks here who aren't committed to any political action. It's hard to get any concerted action going here because the administration and trustees are very cool and very liberal and they give in to many student demands (and if you're an SDSer who thrives on confrontation, forget it). The campus is fragmented between the academic trip, the drug trip and the political trip. The kids are fairly content, the war is far away and so is repression.

Students work constructively. 150 of them from the Strike Committee stayed over during the summer of 1970 to work with residents of Middletown in a project called "Open Summer." Others are into Eastern thought and want to go to India and Nepal, but they are a minority. On the whole, students here are into community action and are getting more positive results than most other colleges.

The only together political club on campus is the blacks' organization—the Ujama Society. Wesleyan has an enlightened admissions policy and is almost 10% black.

SDS is defunct and has splintered into the Student Action Movement (close to the black house) and Union for Progressive Action (UPA—Marxist). But neither group is really into anything.

Only one bad racial incident took place. It was in November, 1969. Two blacks and a white cat got into a fight in the dorms and repercussions took place over the next two weeks. It ended in suspensions, expulsions and a firebombing.

The usual action took place during Moratorium days. On April 20, 1970, two weeks before the strike, people were playing songs at full blast on their record players. Someone called the radio station and said that the Lawn Avenue Dorms (where all this was taking place) were liberated and so people came down there out of curiosity. A bonfire was started. Then someone placed a false fire alarm and when the firemen arrived they decided to put out the bonfire. This foolishness died off around 2:30 in the morning. The incident was known as the "Lawn Avenue Revolution."

NEW HAVEN—CAMBODIA—KENT—THE STRIKE—MAY, 1970— The strike had to do with a lot of things (such as the long-time apathy of most Wesleyan students and the restlessness that that breeds). Some people went to New Haven and were set in motion by that, others by Cambodia—and Kent was the icing on the cake.

April 29. Three buildings were firebombed on campus.

April 30. A volunteer fire watch by students all night long.

May 1. Panther rally in New Haven.

May 3. A free concert on campus by the Grateful Dead who arrived late. While waiting for them to arrive there was a free mike and people went up to it and planned the strike. There were meetings that night about the strike.

May 4. Town Meetings. 800 students there with an open mike again. There were pro- and anti-strike talks. A vote on the strike passed before news of Kent had arrived.

May 6 or 7. The faculty voted to support the strike, but not to stop classes.

Hardly anyone attended classes after that. They had meetings every day which were packed and they had an open mike. Meetings were really well-attended for two weeks and then things died down. A strike newspaper came out every day. They worked in the high schools and did the usual things that happened everywhere else. They also had a draft tie-up—calling up the draft board and tying-up their lines. This was and still is a period of the best race relations in the school's history—people are very close. Most whites were unsure whether the blacks would join the strike, but they did (as long as they felt that the whites were sincere and in support of the Panthers). Had the three National Demands and a lot of workshops, especially to learn about the history of the Panthers. From the strike there was the spin-off of 150 kids staying here for the summer to do things for the community (Open Summer).

SURVIVAL:

The infirmary has very bad service as far as drugs and sex are concerned. Don't go there for VD or bum trips. Sometimes they give out BC pills.

Helpline in Hartford for survival services. Planned Parenthood also in Hartford. The Selective Service Information and Counseling Center in downtown Middletown does draft counseling. *The Argus* is informative and moderate. "Wayne's Natural Food Store" is on Conn. 66. "Sights and Sounds" is the local head shop.

ENVIRONMENT:

Mental—People are talking about the political situation.

Physical—Fall is fantastic until mid-November and then it gets cold. January, February and March are hell. Spring is nice even though it gets quite muddy (but people like playing in the mud). The Wesleyan smokestack pollutes the air—the sewer plant also pollutes. The area surrounding the campus is filled with lovely grass and trees. The new Science building is an enormous square corporate architecture building that can be seen from near and far.

People escape to Miller's Pond to skinny-dip. Students also go to Wadsworth Falls and to Pine Cemetery to escape (externally).

Yale University
New Haven, Connecticut

It finally went coed, but it didn't help. However, Yale does have its points. According to *Time* magazine in August, 1970, the alumni "forked over $4,643,322, the biggest sum ever raised by Yale's annual alumni fund campaign—or that of any other American university."

SERGEANT PEPPER SECTION:

9,600 students of which 5,000 are graduate students. 8% of the freshman class is black. 40% prep school. Very difficult to get in. You need good grades, SATs of about 1,400 and recommendations.

ACADEMIC BULLSHIT:

Yale is one of the best schools in the country for book learning—graduate schools of Medicine, Law, Dentistry and Forestry are excellent. The Law school is located on Wall Street. Eugene Rostow teaches economic law. A good six-unit course on military law is offered (learn to defend the Movement). Professor Wiseman teaches an experimental course in "Legal Filmmaking" (lawyers attempt to communicate their thing to the community). The graduate school of Music has a library of electronic music composition and an electronic music studio which can be hooked up to a computer—far out! The graduate Art department has a course in graduate art for McLuhan freaks and the Madison Avenue crew. There's also a course in bookprinting taught by Professor Eisenman where students plan, illustrate and execute limited editions of books.

Groovy undergraduate courses include "Chinese Politics" with Professor Bernstein, "Biology" with J. P. Trinkaus (he grosses kids out), "Ancient Drama" with Professor Segal (the guy who had the best seller about boy meets girl at Harvard), "Cartography" (map reading for those who are always getting lost) and the interdisciplinary major, "Study of the City" with an internship program for non-suburbia-bound students.

Yale's Black Studies program was the first in the country; it's really good. It is a large department with courses in "The Economics of Slavery," "Urban Anthropology" and "The Psychology of Prejudice."

Yale has a system of Pass/High-Pass, etc. which is just another form of grades. There are some student-originated seminars.

The University is divided into 12 residential colleges and people go to school with those in their college (like the Oxford-Cambridge system). There's a Free U in each college with courses like "Gourmet Cooking" and "Metal Sculpture," but these are not very popular. Faculty are available for conferences and talks but there is no real contact with the "Stars." Seminars are better than lectures, though. There is independent study in the junior and senior years and some "Scholars of the House" are given free reign for their senior year. Some write books. They don't have to take any courses. Study abroad and you can work anywhere abroad in a special five-year B.A. program and get a draft deferment. "Yale students are snowed under with tests and papers, but free time would only confuse them."

BREAD:

Tuition for undergraduates is $2,350, $3,600 for grads, which includes room and board. About three-fifths of the students receive some financial aid. If you need money, and can stay in, Yale will take care of you. They have a big endowment fund (over $12 million in scholarships, loans and work wages were given to students in 1969–70). Jobs pay $1.60 an hour. Room and board costs $1,250 in the dorms. Most students are satisfied with the accommodations that the paternalistic administration provides, although a few freshmen cats complain of being stacked two or three in a room. Freshman chicks are segregated in cushy Vanderbilt on the old campus but other chicks are distributed evenly. Chicks don't have overnight visitation privileges so many cats stay over anyway and escape from first-floor windows (games!). The upperclass dorms are luxurious (for college) suites. Off-campus housing in New Haven is a real hassle—$125 for a plastic one-bedroom. All freshmen live in a segregated area and then live in the residential colleges their sophomore year. There are a couple of communes (Roachdale is a commune corporation).

Freshmen aren't allowed to have wheels but many "garage them." New Haven is clogged with autos and parking is an exercise in patience.

Buy used books at "Yale Station."

BROTHERS AND SISTERS:

Ratio cats : chicks—4 : 1.

Yale abounds with an unhealthy number of wit pickers—sarcastic and indifferent types. Dinner is a daily chore—a mental fencing match. Memorize *Games People Play* or survival. Dress is Ivy—cats still wear cuffed chinos, button-dowr shirts (preferably without chest pockets from Brooks or Oxford from J. Press), and weejens. Cats have fashionably long hair and moustaches. Few bells and T-shirts. They always send their clothes to the laundry (Yale students are not earthy). Chicks wear Ladybug clothes, coordinated skirts and sweaters, and bras and nylons. Spring print bermudas and tank tops are popular. Conservative and expensive threads.

Dating is not informal—there's a lot of dating tension. Chicks expect to be "courted" and don't bring more than $1 with them on dates in case of "emergencies." The cats say there is too much "ogling" and not enough "touching."

Some chicks shack up with cats but don't actually move in. Lots of bridge dates, TV and Yale Repertory Theater-goers. Hangs include "George and Harry's," "The Exit" (coffee house), "Hungry Charlie's" for beer and burgers and Dwight Hall on Sunday nights. Chicks are super-straight and aren't into dope. Supposedly 90% of the cats have tried grass, but it doesn't look like it did much good. Eggheads (hard-boiled, not freaks). A few pushers but dope isn't a way of life. They still drink here.

Demonstrations at Yale occur by accident. The University has a habit of co-opting all the issues. In spring, 1969, there was an anti-ROTC demonstration, the University dropped credit from it and eventually ROTC packed up. The 1969 "grape strike" in sympathy with Chavez folded. Yale still has the traditional spring freshman riot where they pour water on other students, set fire to trash cans for "fun" and search for the biggest bra. The famous Yale strike in 1970 was like a college weekend. It centered around the New Haven Panthers and the question of Yale's expansion into the community. President Brewster agreed that the Panthers couldn't get a fair trial in New Haven, Agnew got pissed at him and from then on Brewster was in solid with the students. About 25,000 students from all over came to the New Haven rally. Yale students stayed in their rooms because they were afraid something would happen. The Panthers, however, kept it cool.

SURVIVAL:

Each college has its own creative-arts facilities. The gym has a sauna, steambath and an ice-skating rink. The mental health service "will put you together." Chicks can get BC pills. Draft counseling is done at the Law School. Religious type draft counseling by the famous William Sloan Coffin. The *Yale Daily News* is out to lunch. Women's Liberation has been getting some action from faculty wives who feel there is economic discrimination against women on campus and are interested in getting day-care centers.

ENVIRONMENT:

Mental—People are skimming *Seize the Time* by Seale and are reading *Love Story* by Erich Segal (the Yale classics professor). ZPG started here and the Forestry school started an ecology center. Vanderbilt dorm has a little-people's garden and a together group called "Sunshine" throws *ad hoc* environmental protests.

Physical—During the winter, it's cold, bleak and rotten. The place defrosts in the spring. It's an urban campus with quads. United Illuminating is your friendly polluter. Architecture is medieval Gothic.

People escape to girls' schools, to Cape Cod or to New York, Rome Camp at Sperry Falls or Sleeping Giant State Park. Others trip at the cemetery on Grove Street by digging the bodies.

DISTRICT OF COLUMBIA

American University
Washington, D.C.

What's in a name?

SERGEANT PEPPER SECTION:

15,347 students, half from out-of-state. Admission is selective. Most applicants need a C+ average and around 1,100 on the SATs. The English and math achievement tests are required. For admission to the School of International Services students must have a B average, rank in the top fourth of their class and score at least 1,150 on the SATs. Only 100 are admitted.

ACADEMIC BULLSHIT:

American University supports the flag. It trains people best to be future politicians, diplomats or hard-hats. The best department is the International Service department—a big help to a future in politics. Students have all of Washington to use as a resource. The Business school, the Law school and the School of Government and Public Administration are all good.

The most popular professor is Dr. Brady Tyson in the International Service department. He teaches "Latin-American Studies." Dr. Lester and Dr. Church of the Philosophy department teach "Introduction to Eastern Philosophy," a very popular course also.

Traditional academic structure. Some Pass/Fail, tests and papers, class participation is encouraged and classes are large. Some student-originated courses like "The University in Revolution" in 1970 and some black studies courses. There's a Free U in downtown Washington. There are a few black studies courses but not much interest in them. Not much recruitment of black students because bread is tight. The school has an immense foreign student population and they are considered the minority students. Most professors encourage friendship with the students and relationships are usually very close. Lots of independent study.

American University is the host to Washington Semester, a semester in which other college students come to Washington to study.

BREAD:

Tuition is $900 per semester and going up. Loans are easy to get but scholarships are tight—only students with a B average who

141

rank in the top of their class are eligible. Jobs are easy to find on and off campus—the average wage is $1.65 an hour. Dorms cost $500 for room and board a semester. No one is required to live in the dorms but most of the freshman and sophomore girls live in them. No rules and one coed dorm. Most other students live in apartments or large houses. Lots of cars and expensive threads (plastic hip) for the chicks.

BROTHERS AND SISTERS:

Ratio cats : chicks—1 : 1.

This campus is hip but in the structure hip. Over half the campus are longhairs and most students wear jeans and T-shirts. Yet many are aspiring to government jobs and won't be so anxious to join the revolution (and waste all those contacts?). The chicks are liberated and most people ball. The six fraternities and six sororities do their thing and don't affect the mainstream of campus life. The campus is into drugs and it's estimated that 80% smoke grass —there's lots of acid and speed, too. In 1969, narcs busted students in the dorms at 5 A.M. and future busts are always possible.

Local hangs include the "Mary Graydon Center" for everyone, the "Zebra Room" on Wisconsin Avenue for straights, the "Waffle Shop," the "Grog" and the "Old Stein" on Connecticut Avenue.

American's students are liberals. They did all the right things— participated in the Moratoriums, the rallies and the like. The first demonstration was the take-over of the Ward Circle building over curriculum changes. A group called "The New American University" held it for two weeks and conducted what they hoped were relevant classes. It petered out and there was no confrontation. SDS tried to take over the president's office when there was University opposition to American housing out-of-towners for the Moratorium, but frat rats dragged the SDSers away.

The biggest opposition so far has been over a program called "ADJUST"—it's a training program for policemen on the campus. When Jerry Rubin spoke here in 1970, the campus reacted to ADJUST and other political issues. There was trashing and arson and $3,000 worth of damage. After the Cambodia announcement students did leafletting on Ward Circle during rush hour. Riot police with tear gas came in and started a week-long battle with the students. There were arrests and beatings. American University is getting more and more political.

SURVIVAL:

The creative students are into playing with plexiglas. The Music building has a listening room with a huge record library. The infirmary is "run by witch-doctors with rattles and masks." The nurses run the show and give out lots of aspirin. No BC pills. Draft counseling in the Case Spiritual Life Center. A free hippie clinic is in operation in Georgetown. There's a 24-hour emergency phone service set up by the Psychology department. *The Eagle* is trying to be a radical paper but just isn't making it.

American University students are really into health foods. Many are honey and wheat-germ freaks and there's a groovy health-food store ten minutes away in Bethesda, Maryland.

ENVIRONMENT:

Mental—People are reading *Do It* and *The Godfather*. Ecology activity is minimal.

Physical—Washington, D.C., ugly. Polluted by FBI, government officials and politicians.

The area surrounding the University is a rich suburban neighborhood where many top government brass reside. The campus is pleasant and grassy and most buildings are whitish stone.

It's a suitcase college and many students go home to New York or New Jersey on weekends.

Catholic University of America
Washington, D.C.

The administration is very uptight about admitting freaks and has requested that all applicants submit a picture of themselves (cut hair if you want to get in).

SERGEANT PEPPER SECTION:

5,855 students, many of them graduate students. Applicants should rank in the upper third of their class and have SATs of about 1,150. And you need—get this—a statement of good moral character from a minister, rabbi, pastor or other responsible reference (your local pusher).

ACADEMIC BULLSHIT:

Catholic University is basically a graduate institution but has some good undergraduate courses as well. Best overall departments are Speech and Drama (one of the best in the United States), Psychology and Engineering (gets a lot of war-machine contracts). The Law school and the Theology department are also considered among the best in the nation.

The most popular courses are the "Psychology of Revolution" and the "Impact of the City on Man," both taught by Professor Statman ("he's very original, spontaneous and his course is enlightening"). Other popular courses are "Magic and Witchcraft" taught by Anthropology professor Dr. Kenny and Gregory Des Jordin's "Political Philosophy" class. Pass/Fail is allowed, lots of tests and papers. Class participation is important in the graduate schools and the average class size is 40. The school is not very responsive to student-originated classes although a couple of classes were suggested by students, one in 1970 called "Black English." No Free U and no Black Studies department. Catholic University does have cross-enrollment with four other schools, one of which, Howard University, has the most complete Black Studies department in the country.

Students and faculty enjoy a fairly close relationship and can often be seen rapping together at the "Shanti" coffee shop. Independent study is available but very restricted—you need a 3.3 GPA and must be a senior.

BREAD:

Tuition is $2,000 a year. Loans and scholarships are pretty available (the Catholic Church has a lot of bread). They are based more on need than merit. Some campus jobs at $1.65 an hour but there are many more available off campus. Many students are on work-study.

Dorms cost about $1,170 for chicks for room and board (single room) and $850 for cats. Most people do live in the dorms. In the past, all students were required to reside on campus and the rules were super-strict. There were no parietals at all. In 1970, students demonstrated for less regulations and won them. Now students can live off campus and the men's dorms have parietals. People are quickly moving off campus. But dope and sex in the dorms still goes on. Apartments run about $65 per month per person.

Scrounging is unheard of—most of the students have bread or jobs. Most have cars and bikes. Three years ago expensive wardrobes were a must—even cats wore swank sports clothes. But the campus is in the throes of a big change and now informal threads are becoming very acceptable.

BROTHERS AND SISTERS:

Ratio cats : chicks—about 2 : 1.

The byword here is transition. The upperclassmen still are collegiate and straight while freaks are in abundance among the freshman class. In the past two years chicks began wearing pants and shirts for the first time—even a few pairs of jeans. Cats are starting to wear levis instead of cotton pants and button-down shirts. The campus administration is trying to screen out freaks by making applicants enclose a picture. The majority of the students are still straight but hips are encroaching.

Most chicks are still unliberated and the virginity index is still quite high. Living together would mean expulsion. Sexual activity is at a low (and remember, if you do, only the rhythm method). The drug scene is a real variable. Some students have never even seen the stuff and others smoke regularly. Lids go for $20 and hash is getting very popular with the heads.

The five sororities and fraternities are still a big force. The frats get a whole dorm floor to themselves. Students consider Greek Week a gas.

Dates cost about $10, dinner and a flick or a fraternity party are the most common. The freaks stroll around the Washington Monument and rap. Local hangs include "The Rathskellar" in the Student Union building, "Shrine Cafeteria," "Fred's" and the "Shanti"—a student-run coffee and sandwich shop.

The first big issue on the campus took place in 1969. One of the priests was refused tenure because he advocated birth control. Pressure from local churches got him fired. Students struck, the campus was shut down and the administration was forced to give him tenure. There were also protest activities in connection with Biafra—on Good Friday in 1969, students burned a cross on the steps of the National Shrine on campus. 1970 was the most active so far. There were massive demonstrations for less dorm restrictions and academic reform. Students here are only aroused if an issue affects them directly. There was limited support for the student strike. The campus is polarized between upperclass conservatives and the younger radicals.

SURVIVAL:

There are two health centers on campus, one for guys and one for girls—naturally, no BC pills. Draft counseling is excellent at the Law school. *The Tower* is a typical college newspaper. The *Ogre* is the underground rag—it's filled with mostly anti-Catholic University comments. No one is into health-food stores or Women's Liberation.

ENVIRONMENT:

Mental—People are reading *Sun Signs* by Linda Goodman and *Portnoy's Complaint*. Few are interested in ecology.

Physical—Icky Washington weather. Highest crime rate in the nation. Air and noise pollution.

The most dominant building on campus is the National Shrine —the huge church in front of the campus. The other buildings are square brownish stone structures with red tile roofs.

Catholic University students stay around school on weekends.

George Washington University
Washington, D.C.

Come to Washington—see a politician.

SERGEANT PEPPER SECTION:

14,556 students. Hard to get in—the two most important things are good high-school grades and personal recommendations Most freshmen have SATs of about 1,150.

ACADEMIC BULLSHIT:

George Washington affords students a chance to get a good academic background. The best departments are Political Science and the Department of Public and International Affairs. The White House is only four blocks away and many professors are active in politics. The Institute for Sino-Soviet Studies offers specialized graduate study in that area. Other unusual majors offered are Latin American Civilization and Speech Pathology. The Medical and Law schools are good.

The two most popular courses are "Philosophy of Literature" with Dr. Levine ("it's a new course and the readings are relevant—Kafka, Camus, Sartre and Mann") and "Constitutional Law" with Professor Morgan ("he makes it interesting"). These two are always packed.

There was a Pass/Fail system which was changed to an "Honors, High Pass, Pass, Fail" system. If a student does D work he receives a D because D is passing. Lots of papers and tests, some class participation and many large lecture classes. Some student-originated courses like Afro-American courses. There's a Free U in conjunction with all the Washington, D.C., colleges. It's about six blocks from campus and attendance from George Washington is sparse. A few black studies courses are offered in "History" and "Folklore." A march on the administration building over black admissions led to the setting up of the EOP minority recruitment. Relationships between students and professors aren't good as professors live away from campus. The Chemistry department is the exception —the faculty there are more open and responsive to the students' needs. There is independent study for those that qualify. George Washington has a special sophomore year in Paris and hooks its students up with other study-abroad programs. "Internship on the Hill" is for kids who are interested in working in Congress.

BREAD:

Tuition is $950 a semester. Loans and scholarships are tight and go mostly to blacks. Campus jobs are limited in part because the cafeteria has union workers. The book store and the libraries are the major student employers but most of the students have campus jobs on the "Hill." Average wage is $1.65 an hour.

Dorms cost $1,250 a year for room and board. Freshmen are required to live in the dorms. Commuters can't live near the school as the rents are too high, but they do rent places in DuPont Circle. People pay about $50 apiece. Only those with a lot of bread can afford the $100-plus rent per person in the immediate campus area. Usually about six people go in on a house. Scrounging isn't popular as most kids have bread, but some can do it by pushing and panhandling. Cars and motorcycles are big. Expensive threads hang in the closets.

BROTHERS AND SISTERS:

Ratio cats : chicks—2 : 1.

This campus is hip. People wear dungarees, sandals and T-shirts. Lots of freaky chicks go braless and cats have beards and moustaches. Chicks are liberated and there is lots of cohabitation by twos and in communes. Fraternities have recently lost all their strength.

Dating is super-casual. People rap and smoke and ball. The big hang is the University Center which opened in January. It has bowling, billiards and a rathskellar. Straights go to the "Tom

Foolery" bar or to "Quigley's" (sandwich shop). The drug scene is very heavy—nearly everyone smokes and lids run $20 an ounce. Many also drop acid at $3.00 a tab. Mescaline is on the upsurge. In 1969 there were big busts in the dorms.

The campus is fairly active politically. Student government was abolished in 1969 because it was such a farce. The Strike Committee in 1970 and the Black Student Union have been the most influential political forces so far. In 1969 there was a takeover of the administration building demanding more black admissions (they got it) and a take-over by SDS of the Institute of Sino-Soviet Affairs charging complicity (the students also charged that the Institute was taking a hard anti-Communist line). Some of the SDSers were suspended.

In November of 1969, there were demonstrations on Election Day, protesting the Chicago Conspiracy (TDA—The Day After) which included a march to Watergate apartments (where John Mitchell lives). There was tear gas, brick throwing, clubbings and arrests—it was even violent by Berkeley standards. About 50 George Washington students took part. There was also sporadic violence and 20 arrests during the student strike.

SURVIVAL:

Many students are into the creative arts, especially photography (get the pic of Tricky Dick). The biggest complaint about student health is that it is understaffed and slow—but the facilities over-all are competent. No BC pills but shrinks are available. The law students are great for draft counseling. If they can't handle it they'll send you to the Washington Peace Center. There's a Free Clinic in Georgetown. Students eat their lunches in the University Center cafeteria or in the sandwich shops—"Quigley's," "Leo's," or the "Gallery." *The Hatchet* is a liberal campus paper. *The Quick-Silver Times* is a groovy underground rag.

ENVIRONMENT:

Mental—People are talking about national politics and reading *The Godfather* and *Do It!* The ecologists at George Washington have a suit in conjunction with the Law school against the D.C. transit for its pollution.

Physical—Washington, D.C., is polluted by drunk politicians who may breathe on you. The weather is terrible—cold, snowy winters and hot summers. The crime rate is the highest in the nation—pigs travel in threes (which means you should travel in sixes). Air and noise pollution are bad. There is no campus to speak of—the school is in the middle of a semi-commercial area. The old red-and-tan brick buildings are cramped together. Thurston Hall, the girls' dorm, is referred to as "the Zoo."

There is a lot of weekend traveling to Boston, Ocean Beach, Maryland and Fun City. About half are commuters.

Georgetown University
Washington, D.C.

Getting political at last.

SERGEANT PEPPER SECTION:

7,925 students of which over 7,000 are from out-of-state. Hard to get in. You need high grades and SATs of about 1,200.

ACADEMIC BULLSHIT:

This school has an excellent undergraduate Foreign Service school, an excellent History department and very good Medical and Law schools. The Language departments are also praised by the students.

Favorite courses include "The Development of Civilization" by Professor Quigly, "International Relations" by Professor Ello (an expert on the Soviet Union), "Fifteen Film Directors" by Professor Segal.

Some Pass/Fail, lots of tests and papers, and class participation varies from course to course. There are a few student-originated courses—like "Wine and Cheese Tasting"—but they aren't for credit. A Free U was started in 1966; students say it is the largest in the United States. Many students participate in it. There isn't a Black Studies department but there are a few courses—like "Black Theology," "Black Literature" and "Black History." There's cross-enrollment and students can take black studies courses at Howard University which has an excellent Black Studies department. Independent study and study abroad. There are special programs called "International Projects for Foreign Study"—in Asia, Africa, Latin America and Western Europe.

Since Georgetown is a Jesuit institution, 12 hours of theology are required of all Catholic students.

BREAD:

$2,100 a year for both in- and out-of-state. Loans and scholarships are tight but there are lots of jobs both on and off campus at $1.50 an hour. Dorms cost chicks $1,100 a year for room and board—cats, $1,250. About half the students live in the dorms. There are parietals. The other half of the students live off campus in houses or apartments which run $60 a person.

Georgetown students aren't into scrounging. Their parents have a lot of bread. Most have cars or cycles and expensive threads. The cats are still into spending $10–15 on a date—like dinner and a flick or a discotheque.

Used bookstores in the Georgetown area.

BROTHERS AND SISTERS:

Ratio cats : chicks—3 : 1.
The campus is still, unfortunately, straight. Chicks wear dresses

or pantsuits. Cats wear new jeans and slacks. Only about a fourth of the campus is hip—they wear rags. But then, things are progressing as three years ago some cats still wore sport coats and ties to classes. The community around the campus is very hip. The chicks on campus aren't liberated but the freshman chicks are just getting into it.

Local hangs include "1789" (jock bar), "Walsh Lobby," "Cellar Door" on M Street (coffee house) and the "Charlie Weismuller" delicatessen.

Grass is on the upswing but booze is still happening. Freshmen smoke, seniors drink. Little hard-drug culture. Grass runs $20 an ounce. Most students score in the area.

Georgetown has been known in the past as a very conservative campus but it's getting more vocal. The fact that Washington, D.C., is a focal point for political action is finally getting to Georgetown students. Radicals from off campus come on campus to recruit. Most active political groups include the Radical Union, the Black Student Alliance and the Georgetown University Community Action program. There have been three incidents so far.

The first was in 1969 when Mayor Joseph Alioto of San Francisco came to campus to speak. SDSers (most from off campus) broke down the doors and kept him from speaking—he was rushed out the back door for protection. The disruption was held because of his handling of the San Francisco State strike. Students also tried to block freeway construction that would have torn down a black residential area and struck over Cambodia.

SURVIVAL:

The infirmary is adequate—no BC pills, of course, but shrinks are available. Draft counseling by AFS in the city. The Georgetown Legal Aid Society run by the Law school does free legal work. There's a Free Clinic in the basement of a church at Wisconsin and Q Streets in Georgetown. *The Hoya* is a conservative student newspaper. Students read *The Quick-Silver Times*—a good underground rag. Women's Liberation has about 20 members. They tried to integrate (sexwise) an all-male rooting section called "The Animal Section." They also made a study on the admission of women to Georgetown University and are pressing for further admissions.

ENVIRONMENT:

Mental—People are reading Hesse, Cleaver and *Portnoy's Complaint*. Not much ecology support.

Physical—Politiciany. The area around the University is residential and it's a very hip community with many street people. The campus is small and buildings are gray stone. It's an urban campus.

Students escape to Virginia Beach, Williamsburg and New York.

Howard University

Washington, D.C.

Fast becoming militant and activist.

SERGEANT PEPPER SECTION:

8,862 students of which 4,311 are out-of-state. Most applicants should graduate in the upper half of their high-school class and have average SAT scores of 850.

ACADEMIC BULLSHIT:

This is the only national institution mainly for blacks in the United States. It is supported partially by the federal government. Good graduate schools of Pharmacy, Engineering, Architecture, and excellent Dental, Medical and Law schools. Students dig the Afro-American department and the Sociology department. The most popular course is "Social Recreation" taught by Professor McKnight. It's a course in Physical Education which prepares you to go out into the community and help those children who need help in their programs of physical education. Another popular course is the "Introduction to Afro-Americanism Study" by Mr. Rigsby.

Some Pass/Fail, lots of tests, quite a bit of class participation and a Free U in the D.C. area. Most of the black courses were student-originated—one really popular one was "Black Politicians." The Black Studies department is excellent and every student at Howard seems to have taken at least two or more courses in black history. In the past there wasn't much interaction between students and professors but as of late they are working very closely together for the black cause.

Study abroad in Spain, Germany, France and Africa.

BREAD:

Tuition in-state and out-of-state is $310 a semester. Loans and scholarships are tight—lots of campus jobs at $1.65 an hour.

About one-fourth of the students live in the dorms which cost $1,000 a year for room and board. 24-hour visitation in the dorms. Most students live off campus in the surrounding area—apartments go for $150 for a one-bedroom.

Kids have cars and take buses. Chicks wear expensive threads.

BROTHERS AND SISTERS:

Ratio cats : chicks—circa 1.5 : 1.

Most students dress neatly in conservatively hip threads. The majority of the chicks are clothes conscious, the cats aren't. It's about evenly divided hairwise between naturals and unnaturals. Dating and living together is happening. Dates are casual, getting stoned and going to a flick is the usual. Fraternities used to be a big thing but their prestige is fading.

Local hangs include the "Campus Corner" and "Al's."

The drug scene is also fading. Students say they are too involved in politics and the cause.

Political action is diffused through Washington, D.C., rather than concentrated in Howard. There were building takeovers in 68 and 69 over the curriculum, and demands for more community action. Howard students worked on the Mississippi Project to set up medical clinics there and took part in their own separate Moratorium days.

In April, 1970, there was a demonstration protesting the overthrow of the government in Trinidad. In May, 1970, when the students at Jackson State were killed, Howard closed down for the rest of the semester.

SURVIVAL:

Good chance if you are an activist black.

Students are interested in Afro-dancing. The health service is adequate. Law students do draft counseling in Johnson Hall. Survival services in Washington.

The Hilltop is a good militant campus paper.

ENVIRONMENT:

Mental—Students are reading *Soul on Ice* and *Soledad Brother.* Everyone is talking about black issues.

Physical—The school is located in an urban ghetto. The buildings are old and dingy. There isn't much weekend traveling.

FLORIDA

University of Florida
Gainesville, Florida

Fun in the sun.

SERGEANT PEPPER SECTION:

21,000 students. 3,000 out-of-state. 86 blacks and 400 Cuban-Americans. One-half of the students who get degrees from the University of Florida didn't start there, three-fourths of those who start, don't finish. SATs combined score of 1,000 required of in-staters, 1,200 out-of-staters. 2.5 high school GPA. 5% are admitted on special criteria by the State Board of Regents, mostly blacks and jocks.

ACADEMIC BULLSHIT:

Interesting courses are "Cybernetics" (how man lives with his computer society), "Southern History," and "Contemporary Moral Issues" (class size limited to 15). Best departments are Engineering, Agriculture, Journalism and Education.

Popular professors include the Reverend Father Michael Gannon (teaches Florida history—the most active instructor on campus) and Manning Daner (Political Science department).

You can opt for one Pass/Fail course per quarter. University College flunks out one-half of the freshman class—tons of papers, tests, etc. If you make it through the first two years, you're home free. Classes range from 5–300 people. No student-originated classes. No Free U (any more).

Some black studies courses. Minority recruitment has started in the last two years.

The college structure at University of Florida (15 different colleges specializing in different fields) allows each unit virtual independence. In the Journalism college, the innovative instructors don't last long. In Arts and Sciences, the old ones don't last long. Interaction between students and professors depends on the student. Independent study varies from college to college. Some study abroad in western Europe.

BREAD:

In-state tuition is $150 per quarter, out-of-state is $450. The money market is tight, few loans and scholarships. Campus jobs at

$1.45 an hour. Students can scrounge. Some live in the hip ghetto and sponge off friendly brothers. Common practice is for a chick to offer herself free of charge to a cat in exchange for room and board (slavery!). Dorms cost $130 a quarter. Hips pay about $50 for "ghetto" digs and straights in Sin City pay $150 for an apartment.

Straights have the wheels, hips have bikes or walk. Straights dress up to impress. Hips wear unbleached muslin and tie-dyed shirts. Straights and dorm rats play pool or go to flicks for dates. Hips get stoned or hit Union flicks.

BROTHERS AND SISTERS:

Ratio cats : chicks—3 : 2.

University of Florida is stratified. 8,000 straights live in Sin City and shell out from $50 to $80 a month. University housing shelters 5,000 single and 2,000 married students. The north side of campus is called the "ghetto." 6,000 hips live in dwellings that start at $40 a month. Never the twain(s) shall meet.

Dorm rats look like whoever they are emulating this month. Sin City straights have sporty shirts, sunglasses and good tans. Chicks have straight hair and big sunglasses. Sandals everyone.

Hips wear tie-dyed muslin, frizzy hair, beards, old T-shirts and dungarees.

About one-fifth of the kids belong to fraternities or sororities but they are declining.

One-fourth of the campus is married and another one-fourth lives together. Sex is free and plenty of chicks are liberated.

Straights meet at "Sin City Lounge," "Thirsty Gator," "Dubs," or around the pools in the apartment complexes. Hips meet at "Anthony's" or at Union dances. They hold "come togethers" on the plaza every weekend.

The campus has been politically apathetic so far. Dow demonstrations in 1967. Only activity was in reaction to the Indochina war and Kent State murders. There was a candlelight march of 7,000 kids, one building was taken. The strike lasted one day. Hardcore radical group of SDSers and YSAers who always announce they are going to strike and don't. The BSU is afraid of having their charter lifted.

SURVIVAL:

O.K. for the South. There's plenty of cottage industry among the hips. The health service (for a change) is good. Free BC pills. Suicide and Crisis Intervention Center. No draft counseling on campus.

Gainesville is a drug haven. Lids go from $5 down depending on the quality. Score in the "ghetto." Use is all over town.

"Mother Earth's" for health foods.

The *Florida Alligator* is a competent student newspaper, straight slant.

ENVIRONMENT:

Mental—People are discussing the Indochina War and the beach.

Physical—Gainesville is a community of 60,000, 20,000 of which are students. Warm all year 'round. Clean air. Small-town environment. Buildings are red brick Gothic.

Escapes are Atlanta, Miami or the ocean. Some go to the Itchetucknee River for tubing (floating in groups in inner tubes down the river).

University of Miami
Coral Gables, Florida

Sun-tan city.

SERGEANT PEPPER SECTION:

18,000 students, about half out-of-state. 242 blacks. Easy to get in. The main requirements are a 2.0 average and SATS in the 1,000 range, but the University of Miami will take you with a lower average if it has room.

ACADEMIC BULLSHIT:

The main party school in the country has for a long time been trying to raise its level of academics and a few departments are good. Their School of Marine Biology is the tops in the nation. The Law, Engineering and Medical schools are all good. University of Miami has an unusual Hispanic-American Studies program.

Most popular courses are "Philosophy 319" (aesthetics) with Dr. Jack Painter ("everybody really digs this guy") and "Psychology 103" with Dr. Shemp Faber.

Some Pass/Fail. No student-initiated courses or Free U. Black Studies department is in the planning stage. Classes are so big that many of them are done by closed-circuit TV. The faculty is evenly divided between the young thinkers and the older conservative ones. Independent study is allowed and there is study abroad.

BREAD:

Tuition costs $1,000 a semester at this private school. There's aid for those with a 3.0+ GPA but it's tight for others. Jobs are easy to find. Dorms go for $500 for room and board per semester. Two-bedroom apartments go for $200. A growing hip population and camaraderie among the students help those without bread to scrounge. But most of University of Miami kids are dirty stinking rich. They drive Corvettes and have the latest threads.

Most dates require expensive entertainment; it's go to dinner and a nightclub at the beach hotels.

BROTHERS AND SISTERS:

Ratio cats : chicks—2 : 1.

"Everyone here has money to burn, they are always dressed fashionable rich hip. Even those with the hippest threads sometimes go shaggy and dirty just to assimilate." Most chicks go braless or swing often. Hair is long to the shoulder. People are very concerned with suntans and beach parties.

Hangs include the "Varsity Inn" and the "Steak and Brew."

As to sex, "every guy is expected to get his chick every other night. It is important to most students to date constantly. In fact, with the cost of living, most guys and gals find it a necessity as well as a pleasure to shack up together."

Frats are on the way out.

The "Coconut Grove" hip group is really into dope and the best grass in the nation comes through Miami. Lids go for $25 and tabs of acid go for $2.

Miami was politically dead for years. But since the anti-war sentiment has grown, so has campus activity. In 1969, for the first time, University of Miami had mass demonstrations during the Moratorium, Kent State and a black strike. The administration is still recovering from those activities.

Pigs were called in for the first time during the Kent State days.

SURVIVAL:

The hip group in Coconut Grove is into creative counter-culture. University of Miami does not give out BC pills in student health. Full-scale draft counseling in the Grove Peace Center. The HELP line refers you for survival services.

The Miami Hurricane has a professional style but low-key approach to problems. There are lots of health-food addicts at the school.

ENVIRONMENT:

Mental—People are reading *Woodstock Nation* and *Playboy*.

Physical—The climate is—Florida beach weather. The campus is in Coral Gables and the city is always moving, lots of traffic and out-of-towners. The air is slowly getting dirty. Most buildings are modern.

"Escapes include a hop to the islands or a weekend at a Miami Beach hotel."

New College
Sarasota, Florida

New College is a new experimental unstructured private school composed mainly of inner-directed individuals. Classes are tutorial and personal. Students initiate many of their own courses and there is a great sense of community. It's located in an isolated section of Florida and generates its own interests.

SERGEANT PEPPER SECTION:

This private school is on the quarter system. They have study-abroad programs everywhere with special programs in India and

Colombia. Eligibility requirements revolve around the individual. "Who knows what the requirements are, although in general, I think you should have your high school think you are God. If you've done some far-out creative thing in high school, you're in. They also weigh heavily on good letters of recommendation. SATs scores average about 650."

400 students in all, 15% in-state and 85% out-of-state. 4% minority (black). Undergraduate program only. Nearest city is Sarasota and the town is small.

ACADEMIC BULLSHIT:

Creative, hang-loose tutorial type classes. Very close relationship between students and professors. You can create your own course and get credit for it. Some students started a health-food store and got credit. "You have to realize that course titles around here mean nothing; one religion course is called 'Monday Night' because it meets Monday night." The Math department and the Religion courses ("Heroes, Fools and Saints," a mythical approach to religion) are recommended. Last semester a group of freaks sort of took over a dorm and tried to start a Free College with such courses as "Freaking." They got a professor to sanction it and got credit for just living communally in the dorm. Film-making is student controlled and student paid for.

One professor comes highly praised: Marshall Barry, an Economics professor. His main course is called "Project Real"—a hit-the-community-and-do-something plan—on-the-spot economic training in the ghetto.

Close relationship between students and professors. "I can think of several instances where they had downright sexual relations."

BREAD:

It costs heavy bread to go to New College—$2,600 for tuition alone. But there are many loans and scholarships and if they want you they'll subsidize you. Dorms run about $160 per quarter for very fine rooms, each with private outside entrance, patio and private bath. That's living. 75 students must live off campus and living accommodations in Sarasota are expensive and scarce.

Most kids walk, a few have bikes and cars. Old clothes are the habit—boots, jeans and shirts. Lots of campus jobs, softest are library clerk at $1.30 an hour and campus security officer at $1.75 an hour.

Dates consist of rapping, drinking and screwing in the dorm rooms. Big dates are a movie at $2 a shot.

BROTHERS AND SISTERS:

Ratio cats : chicks—1.5 : 1.

New College is big on thinking rather than acting. There are radicals in thought and everyone is very hip aware but they are not activists. There are one-and-a-half cats to every chick and the chicks call the shots. All are liberated. Everyone dresses experimental hip—beards on again, off again, tie-dyed faded jeans and old shirts, scuffed boots and sandals. Clothes are unimportant and unnecessary since Florida is so warm year 'round. A few cats have pony tails and all the chicks have long, straight hair. Organized mating and couples the rule. No Greeks (naturally). One person didn't even know what Greeks were. He thought it was a euphemism for gay. Right on! Chicks suffer from underwear famine.

Grass is big at $10–$20 a lid but it is shared more than sold; it's a friendly thing contained in the campus, no connections in town, which is probably why there haven't been any busts. Hard drugs are scarce. No scenes to meet people at—just the dorms.

No big political activity. "Seems like somebody was demonstrating against something (I honestly can't remember what) and got hit over the head with a guitar. That's about all the political activity around here."

SURVIVAL:

You can score on campus. No dress codes, very relaxed and informal. Many classes held outside. BC pills available in town. Student health is adequate and nursie dispenses Darvon like M and Ms. Draft counseling is done by students and by hired counselors— fine scene. Pets abound.

ENVIRONMENT:

Mental—Read Tom Wolfe's *The Electric Kool-Aid Acid Test* before arriving and books on ecology. The campus newspaper, *Captain Jack*, is a small, good effort.

Physical—Out of sight. Tropical, palm trees, breeze, sandy beach. "At night you smell orange blossoms and sometimes the smell of the orange juice factory which is something else if you've never smelled an orange juice factory."

The dorms are futuristic motel type cool—all concrete with lots of overhangs and angles. Landscaped courtyard with row of trees, airy and restful looks. Escapes are the beaches and state parks— but you really don't need one. New College is a trip in itself.

Rollins College
Winter Park, Florida

Rollins is a small independent Florida college. Academic tradition and Republican sentiment. Getting a little hip, though, at last.

SERGEANT PEPPER SECTION:

1,100 students go to this small independent college. It's fairly easy to get into presently because of economic difficulties. Average SATs 1,100 combined. Only 40 graduate students and 1% minority students. 25% out-of-state.

ACADEMIC BULLSHIT:

Rollins has good departments in Theater, Biology and Behavioral Sciences. The students put on many theater productions. Biology department takes trips to the Florida Keys. The only graduate program offered is in Business. Arnold Wettstein teaches "Religion" which includes mysticism. He takes students on sensitivity retreats. Dr. Paul Douglas, director of the Center for Practical Politics, is also popular.

No student-initiated courses and a limited Pass/Fail option. No Free U. Very close relationship between students and teachers because the college is so small. No Black Studies program as such but new courses concerning blacks were initiated in 1970. There is independent study for a five-week winter term available to juniors and seniors. Study abroad in Colombia, England, Spain, Costa Rica, Switzerland and Germany. No dress regulations in class.

BREAD:

Tuition is $2,115 per year; $1,085 for room and board on campus. Loans and scholarships are decreasing. In 1970 about 18% were receiving financial aid. Limited work-study and campus jobs. One used-book store in the area.

BROTHERS AND SISTERS:

Ratio cats : chicks—1 : 1.

Students are mostly straight with a few lukewarm hips. Each year's freshman class is more hip. They come from mainly middle-class–upper-class southern and northeastern families. Chicks not liberated, sexual activity curtailed because of stringent dorm regulations. Greeks are still very important. Casual clothes are worn; most students have cars. All the action (what there is) is on campus. The few radicals hang in their digs. Straight people meet at something called a beer bust. Beach parties are also popular. Little hard stuff, fair amount of grass available on campus for $15 a lid. No revolutionary action—campus is primarily Republican. Few demonstrations with at the most 250 people. Even so, Rollins is the most progressive place in central Florida.

Outside pigs never called in. There has never been a bust. The most important political happening was when two students were arrested for flying the American flag upside down in 1970.

SURVIVAL:

Possible intellectually but difficult socially and impossible politically. No BC pills from student health, no hippie clinic (or apparent need for one), no draft counseling service. Health service very poor. Pets aren't allowed on campus. "The *Rollins Sandspur* is the campus paper—slightly left of center." No health-food stores. The closest big city is Orlando, Florida.

ENVIRONMENT:

Mental—Studying and talking about **Greek rush.**

Physical—Rollins is a traditional Florida campus—palm trees, slight breeze, sunny weather. The campus is located on 65 acres of ground near suburbia. Spanish and Mediterranean type architecture abound. Most students live at the school and escape to the beach.

GEORGIA

Emory University
Atlanta, Georgia

A fine southern school in Maddox country.

SERGEANT PEPPER SECTION:

5,500 (2,800 of which are grads). Difficult to get in for a southern school—B average and about 1,200 SATs are required. About 75% are from out-of-state.

ACADEMIC BULLSHIT:

Emory is one of the best southern schools. The Medical and Dental schools are some of the finest in the nation. Law school has a good regional reputation. It has a program which admits black students with low SATs which has been extremely successful, almost to the point of indicating that entrance requirements have no meaning.

History, Religion and Chemistry are the most popular undergraduate departments among the students. Take G. P. Cuttino for "English Law," Bell Wiley for "The South during the Civil War," Dr. Bianchi for "Religion" (he is a former priest married to a former nun, who wrote a column defending the Panthers for a national magazine), Dr. Fenton for "Hinduism and Buddhism" and Dr. Mandel for "Chemistry." Emory was the home of Thomas ("God is dead") Altizer until 1970.

Some Pass/Fail, no student-originated courses, no Free U and a major offered in Black Studies. Some independent study and study abroad.

BREAD:

$700 per quarter. Georgia residents can get $1,000 a year in aid. Some financial aid to others is available. Lots of campus jobs at $1.40–$1.60 an hour. Dorms cost $135 per quarter for room. Apartments usually are $100 a month for a one-bedroom (two can share). Frats are about $100 per quarter for room. Half the students have cars (except for freshmen who aren't allowed to). College-shop clothes and dates run about $8.

BROTHERS AND SISTERS:

Ratio cats : chicks—3 : 1.
The campus is split between the hip and the straight. Southern

frat types are still around but are fading fast. There's been a big change since 1968 when the alumni magazine ran pictures of supposed "longhairs." There's a lot of semi-hips and about 200 freaks. People still date and sex is "heavy." Fraternities still import some verrrrry rich type chicks and Atlanta provides opportunities to meet others. The freshman chicks are the most liberated. The school was totally fraternity-oriented as recently as 1969, but now it's beginning to change. In 1970 some "even pledged blacks although most blacks avoid rush."

Straights hang at "Manuel's" (beer joint) and "Lum's." Freaks gather at "Dooley's Den" (the snack bar beneath the cafeteria) and "The Twelfth Gate."

60% of one boys' dorm had tried grass and 35% had tried harder stuff according to a survey done in 1970. Score in the Tenth Street area—lids go for $20.

Freaks attend rock concerts at the Sports Arena or go to flicks in Atlanta. Straights dig frat parties.

Most students want to grow up to be doctors and lawyers and don't "give a hang about politics." The YSA has about ten members and Young Republicans have about 50. Women's Liberation has been boycotting the Miss Emory Contest.

This is Maddox country. In 1964 some nurds organized Affirmation Vietnam which drew 40,000 to Atlanta. A few scattered Dow, Maddox and CIA protests.

The first real demonstration on campus was in 1969 when the Black Student Alliance disrupted University worship and read a list of demands—no consequences. Whites started supporting them (they wanted more black admissions, a black house, a black advisor, and black studies). The University agreed.

The Moratoriums in 1969 drew about 1,000 students. Anti-ROTC rallies and some strike action after Kent State.

SURVIVAL:

Student health is the "take two aspirins and rest" type. No survival services. The United Campus Ministry does good draft counseling as does the Atlanta Workshop in Non-Violence (A-WIN).

The *Emory Wheel* is liberal. The *Right Angle* is ultraconservative and the *Spare Change* is the underground paper. People aren't into health foods.

ENVIRONMENT:

Mental—People are talking about frat parties and reading *Soul on Ice*.

Physical—Emory is far enough out of Atlanta to still have plenty of trees. The University owns a lake across the street from the campus where the president lives. Georgian marble buildings with red tile roofs.

People escape to downtown Atlanta, Stone Mountain or Kennesaw Mountain.

Georgia Institute of Technology
Atlanta, Georgia

Georgia Tech is known for its football team and jocks. Give me a S - H - I - T.

SERGEANT PEPPER SECTION:

Difficult to get in. B average plus about 1,200 SATs. ACTs required. 7,800 students, 2,000 graduates. National student body but most from the South.

ACADEMIC BULLSHIT:

This is supposed to be the best institute of technology in the South. Best departments include Electrical Engineering (computer and microwave research done), Aero-Space Engineering (the program is closely tied to research at Lockheed in Georgia) and Technical Engineering. No Pass/Fail yet. Some student-initiated courses in the Science department. Free U offers "Photography," "Wine Tasting," "Bartending" and "Black Students and Society." No Third World College—just some black studies in the Social Sciences department. Mostly independent study and special projects in the Science departments. These students get to know their faculty members rather well. Students aren't allowed to smoke in class but can dress the way they want. Some study abroad.

BREAD:

In-state costs $165 per quarter, out-of-state is $400 per quarter. Most people live in dorms or fraternities. Dorms are around $100 a quarter, fraternities around $90 a quarter and apartments about $100 a month. You need expensive possessions to make it socially here (functional obsolescence)—expensive threads and cars. A date costs $10 for the guy. Some loans and scholarships and work-study.

Campus jobs like mail service and janitorial jobs in dorms pay about $1.75. Some used books at the "College Inn Book Store."

BROTHERS AND SISTERS:

Ratio cats : chicks—40 : 1.

The brothers and sisters are described as "apathetic reactionaries." Most are straight, fraternities are popular—jocks are the style. "Heavy sex in the fraternity houses" (I can almost see it). The only hip area is around 14th Street. All the teenie boppers and rednecks hang at the "Varsity." There's a small underground in Atlanta. Most popular entertainment is "drinking and women." Stone Mountain is the local necking place.

The Young Republicans are the major political club and they mostly drink beer. The Tech Action Committee (what is it?) is active also. No demonstrations or activity on campus at all.

SURVIVAL:

Better in Atlanta than in other areas of the South. Still not much cerebral action or political concern—isolationism. A couple of health-food stores, "Health Mart" and "Natural Foods Shop." Lids are $20 and available in the 14th Street area. Heavy dope is unusual. No BC pills on campus and a poor student health service. Pills and abortions are available in Atlanta. No draft counseling service. The campus paper, *Technique,* is described as "pathetic."

ENVIRONMENT:

Mental—People talk about their football team and are reading a lot of science fiction, especially Heinlein's *Stranger in a Strange Land.*

Physical—Tech is an urban campus in the middle of downtown Atlanta. 60% of the students are commuters. The campus architecture covers a wide range from turn-of-the-century to modern. The escapes are all in the country—Stone Mountain (20 miles away), Calloway Gardens (50 miles away), Lake Lanier (50 miles). Air pollution is starting to become noticeable.

Mercer University
Macon, Georgia

Southern Baptist again.

SERGEANT PEPPER SECTION:

Mercer is fairly easy for cats to get into, a little more difficult for chicks. Average grades and SAT minimum of 800. 1,900 students, of which 427 are graduate students. 10% blacks.

ACADEMIC BULLSHIT:

Mercer has graduate schools of Law and Pharmacy. The Walter F. George School of Law is one of the best law schools in the southeastern United States (one of the only law schools in the southeastern United States).

The History and English courses are adequate.

As to popular professors, "Dr. James Lamar Cox is one of the most brilliant men in the South and teaches Christianity" and "Dr. John Bunyan Sheppard has a very fresh, lively point of view in our Christianity department." A Black Studies plan has been adopted but not initiated yet. Some Pass/Fail, mostly grades. Independent study is offered to seniors. The Free U died last year from apathy.

BREAD:

Tuition is $505 per quarter for everyone and going up. Students have to live on campus until they are 21. Room rent and health fees run about $375 per year. Apartments are fairly reasonable.

Most upperclass cats have wheels—freshmen not allowed to have them. Average date is $5 for a cat. Loans and scholarships are fairly easy to get. Work-study and campus jobs are available at about $1.45 an hour.

BROTHERS AND SISTERS:

Overall ratio cats : chicks—1.5 : 1.

"About 90% straight and narrow right down the line, but there are all types here as on most campuses. . . . Students like to be relaxed and informal, but there is *very* little really hip dress on campus. . . . Few really short-haired eggheads, but just as few really long-haired types. The school is moderate, with some on both sides of every fence, most leaning fairly conservative."

"There is much dating and a very good amount of sexual activity, though some are still hung up with the Victorian ideals of their parents. The girls very recently liberated themselves from University control, but they are still, and will always be, controlled by their men.'"

Greeks still exist.

Protests are peaceful. Campus took part in mourning for Kent State students.

There are very few real radicals or even hips on campus.

SURVIVAL:

No drugs—no one knew where to score. Everyone boozes—beer and parties. Draft counseling rumored to be available somewhere. No health-food stores. No BC pills or abortion referrals anywhere! Health service terrible. The *Mercer Cluster* is a good straight (liberal, though) student newspaper. People meet at the "Coop."

ENVIRONMENT:

Mental—People are reading Skinner's *Walden Two*.

Physical—The campus is spacious and nice—lots of trees and grass. Pollution exists from the nearby paper mill. All the buildings are red brick. The major eyesore is the ROTC building.

HAWAII

The Church College of Hawaii

Laie, Hawaii

Brigham Young comes to Hawaii. Another Mormon college—
"smoking and alcoholic beverages not permitted on or off campus,
courtesy, modesty and chastity required of all students." The student as Mormon.

SERGEANT PEPPER SECTION:

1,194 students, all undergraduate. 643 students out-of-state, including 397 foreign students.

ACADEMIC BULLSHIT:

This college is a liberal arts and teacher education school. Best
courses include "Western Civilization" and "Biological Science-
Ecology." One class a semester can be taken Pass/Fail. Sixteen
hours of religion are required, and Jerry Roundy, head of the
Religion department, is very popular with the students. If any 10
students get together (close together?) they can originate a course
during the interim term (the school is on a 4-1-4 program).

Very close relationship between students and teachers—it's
almost a total campus community.

The Polynesian Studies courses are very good. Next to the college is the Polynesian Cultural Center, a tourist attraction which
helps support the school. There is also a "Center for Pacific Island
Studies."

Some independent study and study abroad. "No smoking in class.
Girls must be 'modest,' interpreted as dresses no shorter than 2"
above the knee, no low necklines."

BREAD:

Mormons from the Pacific pay $200 a semester. Mormons from
the mainland pay $250. Non-Mormons pay $375 a semester. Work-
study is available at the Polynesian Cultural Center. Lots of loans
and scholarships for Mormons.

Few students have cars and dates are cheap (and chaste).

BROTHERS AND SISTERS:

Ratio cats : chicks—1 : 1.

"Everyone is straight, but that is Hawaiian straight, casual not stuffed shirts." As to sexual activity—"There's an average amount for a religious school."

Hangs include the beach and dances in the gym.

As to drugs—"A small group of about 20 are suspected by the administration of being involved, 6 of them were recently expelled." Main events include drug dismissals.

Students are Mormons—no political activity.

SURVIVAL:

Student health is bad—there's one part-time doctor. BC pills distributed only to those married. Hawaii has legalized abortion.

"I doubt if more than 4 or 5 students here would resist the draft. Official policy is that all should do their military service."

The Ke Alaka is a moderate campus paper.

Kaneohe is the nearest city to campus—27 miles.

ENVIRONMENT:

Mental—People are reading the Bible.

Physical—It's summer all year 'round in hula land. The only air pollution is when the Hawaiian volcanoes blow.

People escape to the beach (400 yards) or the sugar-cane fields (50 yards).

IDAHO

University of Idaho
Moscow, Idaho

Peas and potatoes area.

SERGEANT PEPPER SECTION:

6,354 students of which 984 are out-of-state. Grads from Idaho high schools are admitted, out-of-staters must be in top third of their class. Non-resident transfers need a 2.3 GPA average.

ACADEMIC BULLSHIT:

The best departments are Agriculture, Mining, Forestry and Engineering.

The most popular professors are Dr. Skrbek who teaches a course, "Revolutions," to about 50 people in the Political Science department and Dr. Davis, an assistant professor of English who teaches black studies to about 70 people. An interdisciplinary course called "Man in the Space Age" is popular.

12 credits of Pass/Fail are allowed, an average of 250 people attend big lectures, 20 attend discussion groups. No Free U, no student-originated courses—the Black Studies department has three courses. Study abroad in London, Avignon, Paris and Stockholm.

BREAD:

· Tuition is $150 per semester in-state, $400 out-of-state. A few loans and scholarships and campus jobs.

Dorms cost about $850 for room and board a year. Freshman guys and all girls under 21 must live in the dorms. There are rules against booze and dope but people break them discreetly. Governor Don Samuelson was wondering out loud at a western governors' conference if liberalized rules and coed dorms would lead to orgies. People can live off campus at some places for $30 a month.

It's pretty easy to live cheaply here. Most people walk and expensive clothes aren't necessary.

BROTHERS AND SISTERS:

Ratio cats : chicks—2 : 1.

The majority of students are straight as a Hereford cow. There is a definite double standard. The girls are almost all farm or small-town provincial types. Middle-America clothing on everybody. A

167

few freaks, though, with colored T-shirts, faded dungarees and boots. Fraternity guys have shaggy hair and moustaches. A few freaks carry knives—a holdover from the days when jocks would ambush any longhair they could find.

Dating and no balling without "meaningful relationships." Beer and dope are big parts of fraternity life.

There are 19 fraternities and 14 sororities. Dates consist of bars and ice cream, Keggers at Robinson Lake and dances in the Student Union.

Politically apathetic. There are about 80 activists who have undergone semi-annual name changes for the last three years. There was a sit-in in spring of 1968 over student desires not to have fees raised to cover a new football stadium—the fees were raised anyway during the summer. This group of 80 has done all the Moratoriums. The day after Kent State, the wooden ROTC buildings were burned down—25 trucks in an armory in Lewiston, Idaho (close by), were also set on fire.

Idaho is a place where 3.2 beer can be consumed by 20-year-olds. Students come from Pullman and all around to drink beer in Moscow. The "Rathaus" is popular with WSU (Wazoo) Greeks. "The Spruce," with beer, television, billiards and burgers, attracts freaks. People also go to the bars in Pullman. "Rico's" has plain decor, and good sandwiches. "Charlie Brown's" is the plastic-hip place.

SURVIVAL:

Hard here in the wilds.

The Art department sucks. Student health is poor but one doctor does give BC pills. Campus Christian Center does draft counseling. No survival services in Moscow. Lots of dogs on campus. The *Argonaut* appears semi-weekly—one Spiro fan has a column called "Middle America." The diet here is overloaded with home products—peas and potatoes.

ENVIRONMENT:

Mental—People are reading Hesse and Wolfe but mostly are talking about frat parties. The first symposium on ecology was held in 1970.

Physical—Moscow is a town of 14,000 in the wheat country of northern Idaho, 80 miles from Spokane, Washington. The summers are hot, the winters snowy. There is farm land all around. No serious pollution locally. The campus eyesore is the new high-rise 12-story Theophilus Hall—it looks like a cubical approximation of an erection. The area around the old administration building is a gentle slope with lots of shade trees and green lawns. People go home to escape or to Wallace for whores ($10 a trick).

ILLINOIS

University of Chicago
Chicago, Illinois

The graduate school here is the old apprentice type of learning. "The difference between the University of Chicago and other universities is like the difference between English Justice and French Justice—at other universities the professors consider you innocent of stupidity until you prove otherwise while here you are presumed guilty of stupidity until you prove yourself innocent."

SERGEANT PEPPER SECTION:

10,137 students of which 5,578 are grads. Very difficult to get in. If you aren't in the top 25% of your class, don't bother applying. Over 75% of the 1970 freshman class were in the upper 10% of their high-school class. 668 was the Verbal SAT mean and 673 was the Math mean. Transfers need at least a B.

ACADEMIC BULLSHIT:

University of Chicago is one of the best graduate schools in the country. The intellectual level of both undergraduate and graduate classes is very high. Undergraduate courses are murder.

Economics under Milton Friedman is one of the best conservative Economics departments in the country. Majors are offered in such unusual subjects as "Scandinavian," "New Testament," "Russian Literature" and "Indian Civilization." University of Chicago has one of the best Theoretical Population Biology programs in the country. Physics, Business, Law and Medicine are all excellent. Grad students have little contact with the undergrads and rarely have any idea of what is happening with them. Grads never teach undergrad classes.

Pass/Fail is offered on a limited basis. It's not a good thing for some reason to be a popular professor here because for some reason or another you won't get rehired if you are. Saul Bellow has conducted undergrad courses and Bruno Bettelheim has done things in the Social Sciences. No student-initiated courses for credit. A limited Free U. The faculty is pretty far removed from the students except in the Humanities. A few black studies courses. Some independent study and study abroad.

BREAD:

Tuition is $775 a quarter at this private school. Some financial aid but it is tight. There are sufficient jobs on campus and in the Hyde Park area. Work-study was started in the summer of 1970.

About half the students live in dormitories, which cost $1,310 for room and board a year.

Realtors are real fuckers on the South Side. Rents are high, the places are run down, poorly heated and have poor security. A one-bedroom may go for $100 or $160 a month and you might even find a three-bedroom for $160 a month. You have to know some-one to get a good price. Most people get around by feet, but some have cars. Parking lots open at 8 A.M. and by 8:15 they are full.

The Student Co-op has used books on campus.

BROTHERS AND SISTERS:

Ratio cats : chicks—3 : 2.

The majority of the students are intellectual freaks. Amazing metamorphoses occur here. A new straight chick comes to campus and within a month she is a freak. Cats have long hair and chicks either have no bra or the no-bra bra. No one is gung-ho about clothing, they just wear whatever is comfortable.

People hang in cliques. Cats feel there are a lot of unnecessarily ugly chicks here. People go to flicks, to "Jimmy's" (a bar for grad students listed in your friendly yellow pages as "Woodlawn Tavern") and to "The Blue Gargoyle." Chicks are definitely sex-ually liberated ("The only virgin in Hyde Park is in the 7th grade and ugly"). There are two types of chicks, the big city foxy lady and the uptight chick who came to grad school here from a small midwestern college (20% of the chicks).

Dating transcends color and has for a long, long time.

Grass and mescaline are big here, especially with the grad stu-dents. Lids go for $20. There's a little opium from the East Coast. But people are a little paranoid because of the Chicago pigs.

There's a small subset of graduates that are activists and really into politics. 80% of the grads are leftists. The reason more aren't terribly active is that there isn't much of a sense of community here. People go home from school and do their own thing. The administration works hard at expelling the radical leaders. Also, many graduate students have vested interests (the amount of time they've spent on their education) and they are afraid of expulsion. There are two types of grad here, (1) the one who has done very well at an important school like Columbia and Berkeley—he tends to be very radical, and (2) the good student who comes from a rinky-dink school to the big city—he is a little straighter. About 5% of the students are into SDS-PL and most are on the intel-lectual left. Women's Liberation is very big. The strike and admin-istration-building take-over in 1969 were because of the firing of a woman professor. The group has picketed the Playboy Club and taught a course on Women's Liberation at the Business school. The Afro-American League and the Movement for a New Congress are both big. The Students for Violent Non Action (SVNA) is an outgrowth of the now defunct Chickenshit Brigade. The SVNA has ten members and is a put-on—they were originally too chicken-shit to sit-in in a building so they went around disrupting classes instead. Their idea of "hitting" the G.E. recruiter was to overwhelm him with enthusiasm and take away all his literature so he wouldn't be able to talk to anyone. They organized the first nude swim at Ida Noyes Hall. They also held a counterdance to the Washington Prom (a very straight dance where Miss University of Chicago was crowned). The counterdance was called the Lascivious Costume Ball and they crowned the person who had the most obscene costume (the winner had a Green Beret costume).

This school has been politically active for a long time. In 1960, there was a group on campus known as the "Vice Squad." They were a bunch of "crazies" who were very violent—they threw a gargoyle at Queen Elizabeth when she spoke here and set off dynamite caps in the crowd in opposition to the football spirit. In 1962 there was a sit-in over housing discrimination in Hyde Park. This was one of the first sit-ins at a U.S. campus.

In 1966 they had scattered demonstrations against the draft and University complicity with I.D.A. (Institute for Defense Analysis).

In 1969 there was a huge hassle over curriculum. It started as a protest when Professor Marlene Dixon was denied tenure in the Sociology department and ended in a demand for a more relevant curriculum. SDS got involved and the administration building was seized. The administration said that anyone who went into that building would be expelled. Students still went in as did professors who held some free classes there. Classes were held there like a marathon for 16 days and nights. This was after the Democratic Convention. The faculty was afraid the pigs would come and kick the shit out of the students so they prevailed upon the administration not to call them in. The strike finally collapsed from within and the administration swooped down and kicked out 45 leaders. Marlene Dixon was rehired for a year as a cop-out.

In May, 1970, the school was shut down because of Kent State. The strike lasted a few days. The Stevenson Institute for the Study of Foreign Affairs was accused of complicity with the War Machine. Students moved their stuff out of the office and trashed some of the furniture (this might not have been so bad except that it was made by Frank Lloyd Wright).

"The campus cops keep students from being beat up or raped by the people in the surrounding ghetto." It has the highest ratio of pigs per area of any area in the city. The average time for waiting for the cops to arrive if you're white is five minutes and an hour if you're black.

It is unsafe to walk in Hyde Park if your hair is long—even groups of up to seven won't insure safety. Chicks get hassled at 53rd Street. Racial tensions are bad in Hyde Park and if things ever explode they might decide to rip the school off. There's no saving University of Chicago because it is surrounded by ghetto on three sides and Lake Michigan on the fourth. The administration keeps buying up contiguous buildings, tearing them down and leaving them like No-Man's-Land to insulate the school. Some people are trying to get a race issue started accusing the University of racism but it has never caught on mainly because this is a white middle-class university and blacks aren't into the "map" of things.

SURVIVAL:

Student health, or Billings Hospital, is slow and poor. They misdiagnose a lot but do dispense BC pills. Free Clinics are being set up in the area and the Abortion Counseling Service is in Hyde Park. *Chicago Seed,* the underground rag, has all the survival services. Draft counseling is available all over campus. Sports are a farce. They're building a new library on the site of the old football stadium. *The Chicago Maroon,* the campus paper, walks a delicate line between students and faculty.

ENVIRONMENT:

Mental—People are talking politics.
Physical—The weather is awful. Chicago weather. Hyde Park is #1 in sulphur dioxide pollution in the country. The heating is turned off at 10 P.M. in the Southside "3 Flight Apartments" and it is cold. The campus is in the middle of the ghetto—Gothic type architecture with gargoyles. On the south side of the school is an area called "Midway Plaisance." It is really beautiful—a long area of grass, with trees on the perimeter, that looks like they should have jousting matches there. Prince Valiant country—but that's the only relief from the prevailing urban decay.

University of Illinois

Urbana, Illinois

Illinois is becoming more and more radical but still a Big Ten fraternity stronghold.

SERGEANT PEPPER SECTION:

31,267 students of which 8,500 are graduates. 15% out-of-state.
Freshmen must have completed at least six semesters of high school, submit either SAT or ACT scores, and be in upper one-fourth of their class. As long as there is space open in his chosen curriculum, there is room for him.

ACADEMIC BULLSHIT:

The best departments are Engineering, Agriculture and Computer (the best computer school in the nation). In these departments the professors give the students a lot of individual help. No one seems to know of any exciting or particularly great courses or professors. Some Pass/Fail and all you need is a professor's sponsorship to get credit for a class you want to originate. If you can't get credit, it can be a Free U course. Third World studies started in various departments in 1970. The University requires that every student take a final examination in all classes. Some study abroad.

BREAD:

Cost in-state is $380 a year, out-of-state $1,088. Lots of loans and scholarships if you need it. The Student Economic Opportunities Program takes in kids who can't afford the cost and gets them jobs or loans or scholarships. Jobs can be gotten through some departments at $1.50 an hour.

Dorms cost around $1,100 a year for room and board. You must be 21 to get an apartment. They cost a whole lot of bread—two-bedrooms for $285 a month. You must live in the dorms or in the approved housing for four years. Dates cost about $8 and lots of people have cars. Books cost a lot.

BROTHERS AND SISTERS:

Ratio cats : chicks—2 : 1.

They have their freaks here, but most of the kids are straight—the big thing for guys is jeans or slacks, button-down shirts or T-shirts and brown loafers without socks (in the spring). No one would be caught dead wearing white socks (very gauche). The straights' hair isn't especially long, but there is a beau brummel in every crowd who dares let a stray hair or two grow. The straight chicks wear their dresses and skirts and every now and then get into some pants. Lots of people wear those ugly University of Illinois T-shirts (which in the past were mainly gray but with the whole psychedelic craze are turning up in other colors). As to the freaks (who are very few), long hair, no bra, tie dyes, jeans, hair bands, shoeless and on strike. On the whole, there isn't that much dating (there are more than 10,000 more men than women on this campus). The Greeks are deeply into the dating game—maybe 25% of the campus dates—while most everyone else is spontaneous. A date consists of going to a movie, and then to a bar or an eatery afterwards.

As for the girls being liberated—"Any girl *wants* to do it, but is *waiting* for the *right guy*." The hip chicks will do it. Not that much shacking-up here. The chicks are either just off the farm or from Chicago (so they are either naive as hell or know it all).

Intervisitation in the dorms just started about a year ago on campus—more pregnancies have been registered with the health center than in previous years. It is easier to find a chick who will have sex now than it was two years ago when things were extremely difficult—all the sorority houses lock their doors at night.

Greeks exist here and they prevail! There are 58 fraternities (an average house has a membership of 35–40 though some houses have over a hundred while others have much less) and around 30 sororities. It is a Greek campus. For a while they were beginning to wane slightly (especially with the black movement) but they are now slowly beginning to get their power back. Some of the

Greeks are trying to change their image and appear more liberal. They are collecting money for the bail funds for people who were busted during the current disturbances and some houses had strike banners flying.

Hangs are mostly the fraternity houses, "but they hate outsiders." The freaks are on a big paranoia trip and don't take well to newcomers. Radicals run the coffee house called the "Red Herring." Frats patronize "Kam's & Sam's" (bar).

A lid costs $20 and is easy to get—even frats turn on. But weird though it seems, acid is more popular than grass. At least one-third are regular acid-heads. Scoring through contacts.

A lot of students are politically apathetic because they are unaware. The frats are conservative. Young Republicans, Young Democrats, Black Student Association (straight, nonmilitant), Radical Student Union (most active group), SDS and Women's Liberation all exist.

The school has the reputation of being the most conservative school around but things are changing. In 1968, the blacks gave 32 demands to the University. Some were granted. Also in 1968 there was a major demonstration by radicals who tried to close down a building where Dow was recruiting.

Some recent political events:

March, 1970. G.E. recruiters on campus. G.E. has a war contract so the radicals were demonstrating against them. On the first day the radicals surrounded the building where the recruiters were. The pigs then surrounded them and got rid of the demonstrators—some rocks were thrown, some heads were bashed by the pigs and there were some arrests.

That night:

A rally was held by the students and they got some bail money.

The State Police were called in.

The 2nd day:

Students went into the town and rampaged against the businesses that exploited them.

That night the National Guard was called in (no bullets, but they had bayonets).

The 3rd day:

A 10:30 curfew was imposed—there were confrontations during the day—there was a sit-in in the Union—rallies were held at night.

The 4th day:

A curfew again. General demonstrations during the day. Things were cooling off.

May 5, 1970. On May 3 (a Sunday) Edgar Hoult (a black man) was "accidentally" killed by a pig—the next day was the Kent State massacre.

Tuesday the 5th—big rallies were held announcing a strike for Wednesday, Thursday and Friday. That night the National Guard was called up and placed on alert.

Wednesday—there was an 8:00 P.M. curfew. 50 State police were called in. There was an incident at the Student Union over a garbage truck—the truck's path was blocked by some students. The police beat up a professor and arrested him. The students went into the nearby business area. The National Guard arrived.

Thursday—more demonstrations—another rally—curfew revoked—the National Guard was around every building (though there was freedom of movement). The students wanted to lower the flag to half mast, but the National Guard wouldn't let them do it, and then the administration ordered it to be half-masted. That night the American flag was burned—students booed. Students also booed students who advocated violence.

Friday—National Guard still around—lots of milling around at school. No curfew. "Impeach the Asshole," "Strike" and clenched fists written and painted all over the campus. Boycott of the cafeteria. Free food given out—there was a confrontation between students and Guardsmen, state police and local police in the park next to the Physical Plant Service building. The students chased a pig car. They were monitoring police radio. Teamsters refused to cross student picket lines. The National Guard finally cleared the park while people in the nearby dorms turned up their record players and played "Street Fighting Man."

SURVIVAL:

Getting easier. Plenty of dope, sex and politics are opening up. BC pills through student health and Planned Parenthood in area. No suicide prevention center. Draft counseling by student government, and the Draft Resistors Corps in the area. It's a Big Ten school so football is still important. The campus paper is the *Daily Illinois*—a bore. Two underground papers—*Walrus* and *Greek*. No health-food stores. The closest "big city" is Chicago.

The merchants in the area are big exploiters, especially around Wright, Green and 6th Streets. Two of the dorms have "had trouble with the black community" and so lock their doors at night.

ENVIRONMENT:

Mental—The largest computer in the world is being built here—called "Illiac IV." It will have a mammoth data bank on everyone in the country, is funded by the Defense Department and will be used for "defense-related things." Stop it before it multiplies.

Physical—"Spring is when the monsoons come." Hot in summer, cold in winter, lots of rain. The campus is very spread-out—the University is located both in Champaign and Urbana. Boneyard Creek is an open sewer which might be considered an eyesore—it's polluted. The Assembly Hall is pretty—looks like a mushroom. Air pollution only from wheels.

People escape to Allerton Park, 20 miles away and Scott Park. Hardly any commuters.

Lake Forest College
Lake Forest, Illinois

Lake Forest was one of the first colleges to actively recruit blacks. They visited black high schools recruiting over ten years ago.

SERGEANT PEPPER SECTION:

1,300 undergraduates. There are no cut-off points for admission but most students score around 1,150 on the SATs and are in the top 25% of their class. Transfers need a C+ GPA. 76% out-of-state. 8% black.

ACADEMIC BULLSHIT:

The Sciences are the strongest departments on this campus. The best department is Physics. Dr. Jeong has his own laser-beam lab. The Chemistry department has great equipment and good teachers. Psychology is also good. Favorite professors include George Mills in Sociology (he is so wise that he freaks you out with what he said six months later), Michael Croydon in Art and Charles Behling in Psychology.

Some Pass/Fail, independent study and an occasional Free U. The student-professor relationship is far-out, really fine. Kids often just drop in at their faculty members' homes.

Black studies, but no major in it. Study abroad.

The only dress rule is that you can't go barefoot in the dining hall.

They have a thing here called "Gentleman's Pass" in which a student can go to a class just four or five times a term, rap with the professor for a few hours, hand in a paper and get a "Pass" for the course.

BREAD:

Tuition for this private college is $2,539 a year. There is financial aid but money is tight. People on financial aid get first crack at campus jobs. They also get quite a few calls from estates in Lake Forest who need caretakers. Campus jobs pay $1.50 an hour.

Dorms cost $800 a year for room and board. Apartments are expensive and run about $150 a month for a one-bedroom. People use wheels or feet. Freshmen and sophomores aren't allowed wheels. Expensive threads are big with the chicks.

BROTHERS AND SISTERS:

Ratio cats : chicks—5 : 4.

The school is freaky-looking on the whole, although there is a large minority of chicks who are "well dressed" in the old *Seventeen* look. Frat rats wear slacks, sport coats and loafers. Freaks wear typical threads, chicks go braless.

Social life is almost nonexistent. Kids have to play for fun in groups. People are interested in talking sense (a good interpersonal relationship) or balling ("We're all here to amuse each other." "People who don't live with someone are the exception."). Everyone knows everyone and there is tremendous pressure to mold your life around a clique for security. Frats are nearly dead.

Hangs include the Commons and "The Lantern" ("a together bar in town").

"Grass is so imbedded here we even stuff our mattresses with it." "At least 99-44/100 have tried grass here—they're so pure they float." 30% are every-nighters. Mescaline and hash are big. It's easy to score and lids cost $20.

The school has mostly apathetic liberals. The few blacks are the activists. Whites are turned off by politics and into the cultural revolution instead. They are usually co-opted before anything happens because when they want something the administration gives it to them. The only together group on campus is Black Students for Black Action. They request rather than demand and are on good terms with the administration.

The school was moderately active during the 1970 Student Strike. "The student body wanted a strike and asked the faculty. They granted it. The faculty called up the Army base and asked if the kids could have permission to block the entrance. It was granted. 100 students remained at Ft. Sheridan for 10 hours, trying to get busted." The faculty then passed the students' non-negotiable demands.

SURVIVAL:

Student health is terrible, nothing is free and the staff hates longhairs.

No Free Clinic but the Drug Information and Rescue Center on campus is open 24 hours. Draft counseling from George Mills in the Sociology department. *The Stentor* is like a high-school paper. There's a health-food store across from Fort Sheridan.

ENVIRONMENT:

Mental—People are starting to talk about politics.

Physical—Weather is horrible all year 'round except for the fall. The air is cleaner here than in Chicago but still polluted. Lake Michigan is polluted.

The campus is done in a "Gothic Revival" style. The older buildings are really fine, the Castle, especially (a small building with four towers in its corners). The freshman girls' dorm, Deerpath, looks like a county jail and is slowly slipping into a ravine.

Northwestern University
Evanston, Illinois

In the process of metamorphosis.

SERGEANT PEPPER SECTION:

6,500 students. Difficult to get in. The school is very selective and wants mainly "students who will succeed." They get 7,500 applications and only take about 1,700 freshmen. You need high grades and SATs in the 1,300 range. Transfers need a B average. 70% out-of-state students.

ACADEMIC BULLSHIT:

There is no intellectual community as such and the departments are dependent on the professors as to whether or not they are good. Philosophy is good and into existentialism and phenomenology. The German, Theater and Journalism departments are popular with students. The grads are all generally good and are in Chicago.

Favorite professors include Peter Todas in Philosophy (he organized the Peace Commencement, a separate graduation commencement here), Jack Burnham in Art (he teaches stuff like "Metal Sculpture" and you have to literally beg to get into his class), Edward Hall in Anthropology and Arthur Simon in Math.

Some Pass/Fail, a few student-originated courses and a Free U called "The Experimental College" which teaches classes on "Photography," "Wine Tasting" and "Guerrilla Warfare." Professors aren't really approachable. You need a B average and upperclass status for independent study. Study abroad through the French, German and Spanish departments. Northwestern has a program of African Studies which they say is one of the most comprehensive programs in the country.

BREAD:

Tuition for this private university is $800 a quarter. This university is one of the most heavily endowed schools in the country. They have enough money to meet the needs of the kids on aid. On-campus jobs are tight and pay $1.50 an hour.

Dorms cost $1,200 for room and board. Apartments are $60 a month.

People either have wheels or hitch.

Straight chicks are into expensive rags.

The "Great Expectations" bookstore in Evanston has a lot of used books and many hard-to-get philosophy texts.

BROTHERS AND SISTERS:

Ratio cats : chicks—3 : 2.

Freaks here are definitely in the minority. The upper-middle-class slightly-hip WASP from the Midwest prevails. Cats wear $15 bells and flashy shirts. Frat rats and Sallies wear their own T-shirts and their lavaliers. The few freaks there are wear jeans and work shirts and don't care about their threads

Frats and sororities are still big, but not as big as before. There's a lot of loose dating. Most chicks are sexually but not intellectually liberated—they are out to grab a quick husband. Straights hang in the fraternity houses. Freaks hang in "The Grill" in Scott Hall and around stores like "The Spectacle" and "The Male Bag." About three-fourths of the campus has tried grass and half are regular users. It is definitely into the frats—they are big dealers. The jocks are heavily into grass and get wrecked the night before a "big game." There are federal narcs on campus. Most every campus bust has been thrown out as a violation of civil liberties.

The campus has become much less conservative in the past five years. They used to have "Rites of Spring" every year where the jocks would throw water on three or four freaks in Deering Meadow. But 4,000 out of 6,500 students voted to strike in 1970. The student body, essentially, is liberal. Many worked for the peace candidates in 1970. The activists publicize the fact that Northwestern has stock in Dow Chemical.

There are a few YRs and SDS people. "For Members Only" is the black organization—they aren't too militant.

Political history started with "Bitch-Ins" in 1966 where students would come together and air their gripes about the school. In 1968 they had their first real mass action, with an anti-Dow demonstration. 500 attended this peaceful protest. In spring of 1968, blacks occupied a building and presented demands. The U capitulated to most of their demands and they left. In 1969 they had hassles with the pigs over Dow demonstrators. This was followed by a bad racial incident. A black cat was accused of fooling around with a white chick. Some white frat rats started messing with a black chick. The blacks trashed the frat house, some frat brats were knifed and some blacks were beaten.

There was support of the Moratoriums and the student strike lasted a week. Some students occupied the ROTC building and the pigs came to bust the students. 200 other students surrounded the pigs and succeeded in getting the administration to call off the pigs and give the students a school trial.

SURVIVAL:

Student health in Searle Hall ("Sterile Hall") is pretty good except they over-mother you. Some doctors give speed out for diets. BC pills are dispensed. The shrinks are terrible. No Free Clinic but survival services in nearby Chicago. Draft counseling in Scott Hall. *The Northwestern Daily* is more liberal than radical.

ENVIRONMENT:

Mental—People are either talking about their social life or politics.

Physical—The climate is shitting—"It's cold and freezing and it affects your head, it's like 'death point,' all you want to do is stay inside." The campus has 160 beautiful green acres with trees and grass, bordering on Lake Michigan. The architecture is split between the old and the new. The administration building is groovy if you dig modern architecture. It's concrete and U-shaped with a clock tower on it. The Alice Miller Chapel has a reverse stained glass window. You can see it from the outside but not from the inside (the ultimate in plastic churches).

Escapes include the Shakespeare Gardens on campus and the rooms in the library.

One-half commuters.

Roosevelt University

Chicago, Illinois

"It's really incredible trying to hold a class when the 'L' goes by."

SERGEANT PEPPER SECTION:

6,800, of which 1,500 are grads. 3,000 of these are part-time and attend in the evening.

Freshmen need average grades and average board scores. Transfers need a C. Most students are Chicago commuters. 12% black.

ACADEMIC BULLSHIT:

All the evening students are business types so the Business department is good. The Philosophy department and English department are good. "Experimental Psychology really sucks."

The College of Continuing Education is very good. It gives a degree in General Studies for a student over 25 who can get his Bachelor of General Study faster than within his normal four years. He can also get credit for "actual life experience."

Pass/Fail is allowed in subjects outside your major.

Popular professors include Norm Leer in English and S. D. Klemke in Philosophy.

Students can initiate classes in a program called "Innovative Studies" (one course was called "Revolution Evolution"). No Free U.

Roosevelt has been offering a program of Afro-American Studies for the past 25 years and you can major in it. There is also a Jewish Studies program in which you can major. Independent study is available for those past the freshman level.

BREAD:

Tuition at this private university is $50 per semester unit (15 units = $750). Financial aid is available for those who really need it. People usually work off campus. The dorm costs $1,200 a year for room and board—it only houses 350. Most students are commuters and live off campus. Apartments run $80–$120 a month.

Transportation is the "L" and the subway.

BROTHERS AND SISTERS:

Ratio cats : chicks—about 1 : 1.

Most students are just interested in getting a degree. At night it's mostly Rush Street types (Rush Street is a street with bars that cater to swingers). They wear expensive pseudo-hip clothes. The rest of the campus is somewhere between Rush Street and freaky. There is no social life on campus (except picnicking in Grant Park across the street from campus). Chicks are liberated sexually.

People hang with the same friends they've known for years, at the cafeteria, in the "Yacht Club" (near the school) and on Northside (freak types).

About half the students turn on often. Grass goes for $20 a lid and $240 a key. People smoke joints inside the school building at times. Psychedelics are big and there is a small number of smack freaks.

The evening students are adults and not into community action. The full-time students are liberals, lots of talking and no action. The administration is conservative and is preoccupied with getting trustees and keeping them. The only active group is the Black Students Association.

As to political history, "Most students don't care what happens to the University at all . . . you never see them . . . they walk in the front door, go up the elevator, walk into their classes, go down the elevator, out the front door and then go home."

Blacks demonstrated in 1969 for more black studies and more facilities. They took over the eighth floor of a building, and a dean rushed out the back door scared shitless. A couple of Weathermen poured red paint over the head of a General Motors recruiter in the Placement Center. There was a disciplinary hearing over this and five Weathermen showed up with squirt guns and popcorn. A fistfight broke out between the professors and the Weathermen and one administrator got hit in the face with a pie.

The Moratoriums were well supported. In February, 1970, when Fred Hampton was killed by the Chicago Police Department, students disrupted classes and pulled fire alarms and marched to downtown Chicago. The largest number of involved students here, 400, supported the 1970 strike, but it wasn't very effective.

Chicago pigs are the worst, as shown at the Democratic Convention. As soon as they get you in the paddy wagon they spit on you and kick you in the ribs and scare the chicks by telling them they are going to put them in a cell with a six-foot lesbian. The matrons are supposedly a bunch of dykes.

The "Red Squad" is part of the Chicago Police Department. They took pictures of everyone on Earth Day, including eight-year-old kids. They wear work shirts and have hair that encroaches on their ears—beware, they are provocateurs.

The 11th and State jail is known as the "Lock-Up." You get a slice of greasy bologna between two slices of stale bread for all meals.

Cook County Jail is totally fucked. Roaches, fifth, shitty food and overcrowded.

SURVIVAL:

The Health Service is good, but most students go to their own doctors. Lots of Free Clinics are springing up in Chicago—you can find them in *The Chicago Seed*. AFS does draft counseling. *The Roosevelt Torch* is slightly Marxist oriented—good. *The Chicago Seed* is a really good underground paper.

ENVIRONMENT:

Mental—Most students are rapping about their social life.

Physical—Cold in the winter, hot in the summer, ridiculously strong wind. Humidity is bad. Air pollution is terrible—main polluters include Commonwealth Edison and the steel mills. The Chicago River and the Des Plaines River are almost gone because of pollution.

Roosevelt University is in downtown Chicago in a ten-story building that used to be a hotel. The johns are hideous. The eighth-floor women's john has a shower and smells.

Escapes are Lincoln Park and the forest reserves outside Chicago.

Southern Illinois University
Carbondale, Illinois

Southern Illinois University is still a sportsy conservative school but inroads on television mentality are definitely starting to protrude.

SERGEANT PEPPER SECTION:

21,553 students of which 2,996 are graduates. 7% out-of-state. In-state have to be in upper half of graduating class; out-of-state in upper two-fifths. ACTs required. Transfers need a C average.

ACADEMIC BULLSHIT:

Best undergraduate departments are Education (one of the biggest in the nation) and Design (Buckminster Fuller teaches here). Design is fantastic.

Doug Allen is a popular professor on campus (with the radicals). He teaches Philosophy. Both grades and Pass/Fail. No student-initiated classes but you can set up your own major. The Free U is called "The Free School"—small but interesting. There's a Black Studies program that is expanding. Independent study is called "Reading Classes"—you just read and read and read. The traditional academic environment except for design.

BREAD:

In-state is $116 per quarter, out-of-state is $255. Limited loans and scholarships. 8,000 students employed on the campus. Wages range from $1.45–$3.00 an hour. Only juniors and seniors are allowed to have cars. Dates cost about $5.

BROTHERS AND SISTERS:

Ratio cats : chicks—2 : 1.

Lots of straights but some freaks. But the freaks are the identity-crisis types—beards, beads and bermuda shorts and loafers. Hipper freaks are wearing headbands. Foxy chicks wear levis, T-shirts and no bras. Straights wear "the ugliest thing I ever saw in my entire born days"—gray T-shirts that have SIU in big blue letters across the chest. The penny loafer is considered to be a mark of excellent taste in all the right circles.

Freaks meet at "Magnolia Lounge" and the "Cafeteria" or on the lawn of the "Dairy Queen." Straights watch *The Dating Game* on TV in the Student Union. The student government is leftist (blacks and whites) but it is powerless. Most others are conservative.

There were some demonstrations in 1965 having to do with coed study hours, the right to have cats on campus and the right for freshmen and sophomores to live off campus.

Although this part of the country is very conservative, Chicago is also the headquarters of the Weathermen. There is little middle ground. The fraternities are concerned with partying only. Only about 2,500 on campus know what's happening in the outside world.

The Duck Front is an umbrella group for all the radicals on campus. They got their name from the saying, "That when the shit starts flying, you had better duck." There are approximately 16 radical groups in it. Women's Liberation is into the male chauvinist bag and gives abortion referrals. The Veteran Students are the reactionaries—they carry American flags and beer cans to demonstrations. The Board of Trustees is composed of conservative lawyers, doctors and bankers.

In the fall of 1969, a black chick was elected homecoming queen. The Veterans Club insisted she didn't win and elected their own white chick. There was nearly a riot at the school.

In January, 1970, Abbie Hoffman gave a speech. A riot ensued.

In February, 1970, Woody Hall (the administration building) was occupied by thousands of students who then went into town to trash. The students were protesting the Vietnamese Studies Center on campus which is funded by AID and may be a CIA front. In May, 1970, there was a protest against the Indochina War. There were four firebombings. Wheeler Hall (the ROTC building) was ransacked. There were rallies and marches. There were about ten heavy police charges. Possible big demonstrations in the future. Professor Doug Allen spearheaded the opposition to the Vietnamese Studies Center.

SURVIVAL:

Drugs are easy to get at $15–$25 a lid. About 25% turn on. ACLU gives draft counseling. Abortion referrals are available from Women's Liberation and 2 PG. The Matrix is a religious group which helps with drug problems. The student health service is a "standing joke on campus." BC pills available. Basketball heroes are the big cheese on campus. The *Daily Egyptian* is the campus paper—they carry San Francisco's Art Hoppe. There's a health-food store in a shopping center near campus. The closest city is St. Louis.

ENVIRONMENT:

Mental—People are talking about TV, basketball and student activity.

Physical—The climate is hell in the summer and snow in the winter. The area is nice for naturalists—couple of lakes nearby. Trees and a veritable forest on campus (near the University Center). Great for guerrilla war tactics.

The University has a ton of land, not that much is cluttered with buildings—lots of wide open spaces. A couple of older buildings have steeples, while some of the newer ones are corporate sterile.

Not that much air pollution except what comes from the campus physical plant.

Escapes include many lakes in the area and Giant City—a state park. Mostly live-ins.

Wheaton College
Wheaton, Illinois

Billy Graham went here. It's a Christian school—no dancing, card playing or booze. The following message sent to Wheaton students by a fellow-traveler student traveling in Europe was posted in a showcase bulletin board:

> Greetings from Suisse. We are now on our way to Zurich. It's beautiful. The tour is progressing well. God is using this group in a fantastic way. I trust Dave is keeping you posted. With the Iron Curtain countries approaching fast we covet your prayers.
>
> George

SERGEANT PEPPER SECTION:

1,772 students of which 111 are grads. Freshmen need about 1,100 SATs and fair grades. The most important requirement is that you be a Christian Fundamentalist. It's an independent Christian school that is supported by a number of evangelical denominations. (Make that very clear on your application.) 75% out-of-state. 38 blacks, 5 Indians, 8 Mexican-Americans.

ACADEMIC BULLSHIT:

Lots of Christianity courses. The school's motto is "For Christ and His Kingdom." 14 hours of Bible are required as is daily chapel. If this bums you out, don't apply.

Best departments are Bible, Chemistry and Philosophy. The grad students are mostly in Theology but there is no seminary here. Favorite professors are Dr. Weber in Bible, Dr. Voget in Sociology and Dr. Leedy, a groovy grandfather type in the Botany department.

Pass/Fail is available. No student-originated courses and no Free U. Most professors really try to get close to the students and there is a fair amount of interaction. No Black Studies department but a few black courses in the Sociology department.

Some independent study and study abroad.

BREAD:

Tuition for a quarter at this private school is $573. Packaged financial aid is available and at least 800 of the 1,800 students work on campus for about $1.60 an hour.

Dorms cost $1,000 a year for room and board and most students live in them. A furnished one-bedroom apartment goes for $170 a month. Most students have wheels except for freshmen who aren't allowed to.

BROTHERS AND SISTERS:

Ratio cats : chicks—1 : 1.

This is a small enough place that the kids would recognize a stranger if he came into the dining hall. People are Christianity freaks, straight looking. No one is clothes-conscious. People wear Wheaton College T-shirts and letterman jackets. They just revoked the girls' dress code in 1970.

The trouble with the social life is that you can't even get any privacy to neck, not just to ball. The social life is formal and the dorm rules are stringent. If a girl is ever allowed into a guy's dorm room, the door must be open. Dates are campus sporting events or classical concerts. People still dig "The Lettermen." "A philosophy professor once said there was so little sex on this campus that he thought it was unhealthy." The double standard is big; cats try to make a townie chick, but they want to marry a nice virginal Wheaton College chick.

There's hardly any drug use here and the kids who use it are super-secretive about it. About 5% of the school turns on. They buy it from their local high-schooler or score in nearby Chicago.

The administration is conservative and so are the students. On the application for admission they ask about five questions concerning your religious beliefs ("Why do you believe in God?"). They will only take Jews who believe in Christ. Faculty members must sign an oath of faith as they don't want any atheists.

The Young Republicans are pretty strong. SOUL (Soul Organization for Urban Leadership) is a black and Puerto Rican group—their hero is Tom Skinner, the black evangelist. The Rifles are an offshoot of ROTC—really gung-ho cadets. The liberal group on campus is the Johnathan Blanchard Association. He founded the school in the 1860s and was an abolitionist and a pacifist.

The administration tries to stop any protests. The town of Wheaton is an "All-American City."

In the fall of 1967, a few students protested the Veterans Day chapel service. The ROTC cadets came into the chapel and sat in the front rows. Students stood outside with protest signs, and jocks covered the signs with umbrellas so the cadets could pass unscathed. Students demonstrated against mandatory ROTC again in 1969. It was cut down to one mandatory year from two (wowee).

In 1970, the student government dissolved itself because it felt it couldn't do anything the way student government was structured. The freshmen were very upset because they felt the student government wasn't providing any spiritual leadership.

In May, 1970, a memorial service was held for the Kent State four. Many students wrote letters to Billy Graham and Nixon.

Campus pigs shine lights on kids necking on Front Campus. They are very hung up about finding kids making out.

SURVIVAL:

God and country.

Student health is O.K., no BC pills. No survival services except North Park Psychological clinic 20 miles away for suicide prevention. No formal draft counseling. Jocks are BMOC. *The Wheaton Record* is censored by the administration.

ENVIRONMENT:

Mental—People are seriously discussing Billy Graham—they worship him.

Physical—The climate is like Chicago. Cold in the winter, humid in the summer. Occasional air pollution.

The architecture is a hodgepodge. Blanchard Hall is the historic sight—the original building in the school.

People escape to The Arboretum or to Chicago. (Going to Chicago is fulfilling a death wish.)

INDIANA

Indiana State University

Terre Haute, Indiana

Blacks and whites are still fighting each other rather than the power structure. Wake up, ISU!

SERGEANT PEPPER SECTION:

13,300 students, 10% out-of-state.

In-state need to be in the upper 70% of their high-school class and have comparable SATs. Out-of-state should be in the upper half of their graduating class and have comparable SATs. Transfers should have a 2.0.

675 blacks.

ACADEMIC BULLSHIT:

Best undergraduate departments are Education and Physical Education. Popular professors include John Cooper (Art professor)—he is the originator of the School of Hopper Art (and was also just fired—he may be back), Eugene Dyche (Philosophy) and David Crispin (Educational Psychology).

Traditional academia—they have no Pass/Fail but have been working on it for four years. No student-initiated courses. Not much interaction between most professors and students. No Third World College, but a few departments. Mainly tests. Independent study exists "mainly for people with an I.Q. of 200, who you can always find in the library stacks."

BREAD:

In-state tuition is $256 per semester, out-of-state is $512.

Poor campus—some financial aid. Most students come from working-class families (as opposed to middle-class). Campus jobs are available.

Most students live in dorms. They cost $462 a semester for room and board (no intervisitation allowed). A one-bedroom apartment goes for $80 a month.

Most people walk, dress casually and lay out $5 for a date.

BROTHERS AND SISTERS:

Ratio cats : chicks—about 1 : 1.

The campus is straighter than hell. A comparison has been made.

187

The well-dressed ISU male buys his clothes at Schultz—Gant shirts. If he wants to blow minds, he buys flares, stripes and checks. Chokers and track shoes are big. Lots of Plain Janes and bras. Then there's the Hopper People. They started when John Cooper (Art professor) bought some hoppers (those square things after used autos are squeezed) and started painting on them (Hopper Art). Every time Cooper held a Hopper Art Show it was a peace and love happening. His mystical followers are called Hopper People.

About two-thirds of the campus is into the dating game. A lot of frosh chicks get married here. Greeks are still big—most social functions at school are Greek activities.

About 20 real freaks. They hang at the off-campus "Wesley House." Frats hang at the "Grill" in the Student Union during the day. About 10% of the people turn on. $20 a lid—demand outweighs supply even though grass grows wild along the banks of the Wabash River.

A majority of whites come from rural or small-town backgrounds or from the Calumet area (the Indiana part of the Chicago megalopolis). Blacks are from the inner urban area (Calumet and Indianapolis). The most organized club on campus is the YRs. No strong militant left. The administration is always telling people to work through proper channels.

This campus is still having racial problems. Witness:

April 23, 1970. Two black girls in the dorms placed a poster that had "More power to the people, less power to the pigs" on a bulletin board on the 22nd. The white chicks in the dorms thought that "pigs" meant them—they asked the black chicks to remove the poster and they refused—that night someone wrote "nigger" on their door. The next morning the black chicks went to the dorm director and asked for an all-hall meeting to find out who wrote it—the director refused so the black chicks planned a sit-in in the dorm cafeteria that night until someone confessed.

The white students felt that their white women were being threatened so they came to save them with baseball bats and guns—small fights broke out and then the rains came and cooled things off. At 7:30 that night LeRoi Jones' *The Slave* (a play about a racially-torn campus) was being held at the theater and most of the blacks went there. After the play the blacks destroyed the lounge in the dorm. Then they traveled across the campus to a dorm classified as the "easiest defensible position" on campus to make a stand. White frats gathered across from them with bats, rocks, guns and tire tools. City pigs were called in—state pigs were placed on alert. The whites moved toward the blacks and were turned back by the pigs. The whites regrouped, refused to disperse, were gassed by the pigs and then left. The next day the campus was very tight—the Greeks were making defense plans for their houses—the campus was turned into an arsenal.

May, 1970. A strike was called in protest of Cambodia and Kent State. 500 students participated in a memorial service held at noon in the quad around the flagpole (the flag was lowered at half mast). Half-way through the service the pigs came in and raised the flag. After the service 75 circled the pole and lowered it again. Terre Haute pigs came and arrested. No blood.

At night frats will beat up freaks if it's dark and deserted.

SURVIVAL:

Chances not too good. Not yet enlightened.

BC pills for married only—no survival services. The school shrink is an administration fink. Wesley Foundation does draft counseling. The school paper, *The Indiana Statesman,* is run by YRs, a piece of shit. "Good to wrap your garbage in."

ENVIRONMENT:

Mental—People are discussing sports and marriage.

Physical—Terre Haute has all four seasons in one day. The humidity is for shit—"like breathing water." The city has 26 times the amount of air pollution that is safe for a city of its population —air polluters are the pharmaceutical companies, Central Nitrogen, coke-producing companies and the campus physical plant.

Concrete everywhere—except where there's red brick. "The administration gets some kind of insane sexual kick by building tall shiny new buildings." The dorms are named after three politicians who were caught for embezzling.

A small, blah-looking campus.

Escapes are a bunch of "itty bitty" parks in the area or going home for the weekend. Shades State Park is a really great park.

University of Indiana
Bloomington, Indiana

Some of the best-looking chicks around. Definitely the hippest place in Indiana.

SERGEANT PEPPER SECTION:

29,000 students. 73% from Indiana.

In-state should be in upper half of graduating class and have comparable SAT scores. Out-of-state should be in upper quarter of high school class. Transfer in-states need a 2.0 GPA; out-of-states need a 3.0.

ACADEMIC BULLSHIT:

Traditional academic atmosphere. The Music department is second only to Juilliard. Good Business and Political Science departments. Many graduate schools—Law, Medical, Business, Optometry and Dental.

Most popular professors include Gary Scrimgour (Literature), Phillip Appleman (English) and Bernard Morris (Political Science). But the administration has tried to fire many of the radical professors and many are leaving the school.

Pass/Fail allowed. In the Foster Quadrangle (a university within the University) students can initiate courses like "The Analysis of Rock Music." The Free U is alive and well and into the unconventional. They hold classes every night in things like "Student Unrest" and "Political Cartooning."

Classes are usually small (30–50) or medium-sized (75–400) students. Some interaction between professors and students but not much. A new Black Studies department. In the big classes (over 600) there are those archaic T-F multiple-guess exams. Independent study is pretty loose. Study abroad all over.

BREAD:

In-state tuition is $325 per semester, out-of-state is $745. Loans and scholarships aren't too prevalent since last year when the Indiana legislature cut over a million dollars in University funds because they were upset with the students.

Plenty of campus jobs but usually few openings. About $1.50 an hour.

Most people walk and dates are about $5.

Dorms go for $1,050 a year for room and board (most students live in dorms). Fraternities are about the same. Ratty apartments go for $150 a month for a furnished one-bedroom. There's a lot of farm land around and some people are beginning to rent farmhouses for around $100 a month.

BROTHERS AND SISTERS:

Ratio cats : chicks—1 : 1.

About one-third freaks here and the chicks are really good-looking. No bras, chokers and jeans. Cats have beads. Even the straights wear blue jeans but they wear collared shirts. Frat rats wear T-shirts and V-neck sweaters. Straight chicks wear all sorts of hair ribbons.

Dating is both structured and casual. Flicks, rock concerts and parties. About 50% of the chicks are liberated and will dispense their favors.

The Greeks are still strong—32 fraternities and 18 sororities but they are changing. There's no antagonism between the freaks and the Greeks. Many of the Greeks are into the Movement.

Most hangs attract both Greeks and freaks. Freaks sit on the curb on Kirkwood Avenue a lot. Everyone digs "The Gables," a traditional eatery next to campus. "Dunn Meadow," in front of the Union, has Jordan Creek running through it. "On nice days it's packed with Frisbees, dogs and little kids wading in the polluted water."

Over 50% of the campus smokes grass; about 20% dope at least once a week. People drop acid a lot. Drugs are falling off with the radicals and revolutionaries but new dopers are replacing them. Scoring through friends. There's an FBI bureau in town.

Protests and demonstrations have been fairly conservative so far, but IU is the intellectual oasis in the state and leftist sentiment is growing. The conservatives are apathetic and the radicals are energetic. But the vast majority of students are nonviolent.

The most active political group is the New University Conference which was started by a group of T.A.s who are pushing for radical change within and outside of the University. The BSU is beginning to work with the white radicals. Women's Liberation is very vocal—they want a day-care center and legalized abortions.

There have been demonstrations against Dow and discriminatory Greek racial practices since 1967.

In spring of 1969, the tuition was doubled. There were mass demonstrations and a 10,000-person-strong campus rally. Riotous conspiracy charges were placed against many students.

During the October, 1969, Moratorium, a large group went to Washington. Clark Kerr visited the campus and a Yippie in a red devil's costume ran into the class and pushed a pie in his face (what that had to do with the war only the Yippies know for sure). In the fall of 1969, the campus beauty contests were outlawed because they were judged inherently racist.

In February, 1970, some students supported the G.E. strikers at a G.E. plant in town. A couple of bombings at the plant and subsequent arrests.

There was window breaking and a strike in opposition to Nixon's Indochina war. The short strike had the support of 75% of the campus. The campus is quite left for Indiana.

SURVIVAL:

Easiest place in Indiana to survive. Many good vibes.

Lids go for $15, tabs of acid for $3.

BC pills given out at student health—service is pretty good. Student government is establishing a legal-aid thing. The student government has a draft counseling service. (The student government's much to the left of campus—a bunch of Marxists.)

Pets are everywhere. Sports are big (it's a Big Ten school). *The Indiana Daily Student* is fairly good.

ENVIRONMENT:

Mental—People are talking about national issues—they're hip.

Physical—The monsoon season strikes in the spring—it once rained for a 26-day stretch—lots of snow and slush in the winter, humid in the summer, nice in the fall with thousands of trees turning all sorts of colors.

All the buildings are gigantic. The school is a haven for limestone and trees. Most of the buildings are made out of limestone. The Center building in McNutt Quad has spiraling staircases. They have a statue of Adam and Eve on campus—someone cut off Adam's nuts. Everyone is always painting on Ballantine Hall. Maxwell Hall has gargoyles.

There's a real forest to the east of Bryan Hall—out of sight.

Escapes are lovely. Brown County State Park (autumn leaves) and Nashville, Indiana—an artist's colony. Stone quarries are all over.

University of Notre Dame
Notre Dame, Indiana

One of the last bastions of male supremacy around.

SERGEANT PEPPER SECTION:

7,500 students, all male. 1,300 of these are grads. Entering freshmen need a teacher's evaluation, good grades and SATs in the 1,100 area. Transfers need a B. 81 blacks, 7 Chicanos. 92% out-of-state.

ACADEMIC BULLSHIT:

Academically, this is a bad place for freaks. There is practically no opportunity for self-expression. Work is upheld as the standard.

Notre Dame is supposedly ranked ninth in the country for undergraduate education. Best departments are Theology, English and the General Program (200 kids are enrolled in it and it is a sequence of different type classes). 12 hours of Theology are required for all Catholic students.

Favorite professors are Father Dunne in the Theology department (he teaches "God in Time and Memory") and Rudy Gerber who teaches "Philosophy of Revolution."

There's a new "Non-Violence Program" that is "student-initiated." The Free U teaches "Pottery," "Guitar," "The History of Locomotives," "Baseball Trivia" and "How to Live Like a Gentleman on $7,000 a Year."

Some Pass/Fail, independent study and study abroad.

The student-professor relationship is very good; much of the faculty is very student oriented.

The Black Studies program offers a double major possibility (one in Black Studies, one in something else).

BREAD:

Tuition at this private school is $1,000 a semester. The school is in somewhat of a bind as to financial aids. Most of the students have to work in the summer to earn enough for school. There are 1,200 jobs on campus.

Dorms cost $1,050 for room, board and laundry for the year. About half the students live in dorms. The others pay about $60 each for an apartment. Cars are the most popular form of transportation among the upperclassmen. Freshmen and sophomores aren't allowed cars and walk.

BROTHERS:

This school is all men and they aren't very happy about it. Students keep pushing for Notre Dame to go coed. There are a few chicks in classes on an exchange program from nearby St. Mary's but that's it.

Cats wear contemporary clothing—fads. Some are into anachronistic Ivy League threads. They have medium-length well-trimmed hair. There are about 400 freaky looking people on campus.

The few chicks that are there play the field and try to go out with as many cats as possible. When they do get involved, it's in terms of marriage. The cats are preoccupied with the chicks' appearance.

Notre Dame is a haven for male supremacists and male chauvinists. The campus is sexually repressed and there are a lot of gay people. Only the freaks are into interpersonal relationships and balling.

Entertainment consists of flicks, athletic events and drinking. People hang at "Frankie's" (straights) and "Corby's" (a jock bar). There is some usage of grass here, though they have a very strong ingrained tradition of drinking Budweiser. In 1970 there were only about 15 freaks into grass and then all of a sudden people got interested in ecology and turned on to grass. It is $5 a lid or free (it grows wild in South Bend since hemp was planted in the area during World War II).

Over the past five years the school has changed from a rah-rah superconservative school to a more open place. The old Catholic conservative tradition is being replaced by a new Catholic liberal contemplative thing. This is being done mainly through the Non-Violence Program (classes on nonviolence based on the New Testament) which has started a sanctuary for draft resisters on campus. Kids are willing to work through the system to get the changes they want. There is an idea stressed on campus that politics should not destroy humanism (a person should not let his political hate dehumanize himself).

All political people are deeply into nonviolence. Political clubs are elitist with a strong leader. There is the YAF, the Committee for Political Action (liberal), the Committee for a New Congress (worked for peace candidates in the November election) and the Afro-American Society (separatists for the most part).

Notre Dame has always had a good football team and pushes athletics. These jocks are typically bean-head right-wingers. Sports reigned supreme until 1967 when demonstrations against ROTC started. In 1969, students demonstrated against a CIA recruiter. He was scared and split. There was some support for the Moratorium.

On November 17, 1969, Father Hesburgh made his famous "15-minute policy" speech that earned him praise from Tricky Dick. There was a demonstration against the CIA and Father Hesburgh made a speech giving the students 15 minutes to either split or get expelled. For this he was congratulated by Nixon who apparently didn't read the second half of the statement in which Hesburgh said he was only doing this because he felt that otherwise troops might be called in and he didn't want that.

Students supported the strike in 1970. There was canvassing, leafletting and demands of ROTC off campus. They got 23,000 people in South Bend to sign an anti-war petition.

SURVIVAL:

The infirmary is poor—they dispense downers. There's no Free Clinic or survival services. Draft counseling through the Non-Violence Program.

Intercollegiate sports are still very big here. Jocks are gods and football is the end-all.

The Observer is a fairly boring campus paper.

ENVIRONMENT:

Mental—Some talk about sports, others about politics.

Physical—The climate is terrible with really harsh winters. Spring is nice. Drewry's Brewery is a big polluter. The St. Joseph River is almost totally polluted—they dump sewage directly into the river.

For the size of its student body, Notre Dame has a massive campus. The administration building is Gothic and has a beautiful gold dome with Jesus Christ on top. When the sun hits it, it's outta sight.

The campus has a lot of natural beauty, trees, grass and lakes.

Escapes include The Dunes (a state park) and Leeper Park in town.

Purdue University
Lafayette, Indiana

Purdue is all rules and regulations, law and order. You have to have permission to set up an info table and you can only sit at your table—the campus pigs are always harassing the few freaks. Everyone belongs to a Greek house (pledge or die). A bastion of Midwest farm conservative leanings (and the girls are considered hogs).

SERGEANT PEPPER SECTION:

25,037 students of which 5,231 are grads.

Fairly selective. In-state must be in upper half of high-school class and have good SATs. Out-of-states must be in upper fourth of class and have good SATs. Transfers should have a B average.

ACADEMIC BULLSHIT:

Purdue is known for its Engineering department. It is one of the best in the country. "All our engineers are sought after but I don't know if they'll ever be executives, they might just be able to function as machines."

The Creative Arts department is also good—no grades and no core requirements (also no money). The Speech Therapy graduate school may be the best in the nation. Physics and Agriculture are also good graduate departments. Students seem to like their teachers—especially in the Art, English and Math departments.

No Third World College—just a black history course. They have a special counselor who counsels blacks—he's white. But they are getting a genuine black "black" counselor to replace the white "black" counselor.

Independent study in the Humanities.

High academic quality in most courses.

BREAD:

In-state is $700 a year, out-of-state $1,600 a year. Good chance for a loan or scholarship and plenty of campus jobs.

Room and board in the dorms is $1,100 a year. Apartments are expensive—$80 a month for a single. Houses are about the cheapest if you get a tribe to share them with. Dates cost about $8 and most people walk rather than drive. "Von's" has cheap books.

BROTHERS AND SISTERS:

Ratio cats : chicks—2 : 1.

One of the last all-Greek campuses around. There are 42 fraternities and 15 sororities and everyone belongs to a house.

When the kids here aren't being totally square in their appearance, they move on to complete plasticity—for the well-dressed Purdue male this year, it is checkered pants and saddle shoes. They sometimes wear *ironed* blue jeans (done at the laundries). Some are growing their hair and are wearing choker bead necklaces. Chicks are beginning to dig blue jeans and bell-bottoms and wear either penny loafers or low-cut (sailing) tennis shoes, old army jackets and work shirts with embroidered collars. A lot of people are wearing wire-rim glasses (especially the ROTC jocks). One way to tell a freak from a straight chick is that if she doesn't wear a bra, she is a freak. They have a couple freaks, but nothing to write home about.

Very little balling happening here. They still pin people. They have gigantic parties at which someone gets pinned. A couple years ago there was a big uproar on campus when the paper said it wasn't going to devote any more space to announce pinnings—the paper had to relent. There is a really structured dating thing here for most of the people. They usually go to a movie and then get a couple of beers (if they're over 21). After football games they have a thing called "Victory Varieties" and in the spring they have a thing called "Pop Stars Concerts"—both go over very big. At 1970's homecoming they had Montovani who was an overwhelming success here.

To make sure everyone remains a virgin while at Purdue, police cars patrol the golf course and other balling areas (the car is still a popular place for lovemaking).

Football heroes are everybody's dream. White jocks are conservative; black jocks are starting to get into grass. Anyone who has an athletic scholarship must stay out of politics or they'll lose it.

All the Greeks meet at the "Sweet Shop." It's segregated by choice—Greeks sit on one end, unaffiliated in the middle, and freaks on the other end. It has been bugged with 22 microphones. The few freaks hang at "Will's" near campus.

About 500 people smoke at Purdue. Some of the frat guys are substituting grass for beer. Indiana grass (poor quality) goes for $10 a lid—good grass goes for $20 a lid.

The kids are apathetic—all middle America. About 75 on the Far Left (more than on the Far Right). Escapism is big here—getting smashed. All the organizations are represented—even the Yippies. The BSU isn't militant. Women's Liberation chicks get together and take their bras off in the basement of a church. The Lib girls are working on getting rid of the Miss Purdue Pageant and the Auction Dance (in which chicks are auctioned off and have to spend the entire night with the guy).

The few radicals have led a few protests against Dow and the CIA. In the fall of 1968, during the national anthem, the black cheerleader gave the black salute while on the playing field. After that the cheerleaders weren't allowed out onto the floor—she eventually resigned.

After the invasion of Cambodia, students (1,000 strong) broke windows in the armory. A rally was held and they went to the administration and presented three demands: (1) end ROTC; (2) end classified military research on campus; and (3) the administration should make a statement on the University's position on the war. The administration refused all three demands and told the students they'd be suspended if they didn't leave the building. At that time there was an Army-ROTC awards ceremony so the students left the administration building and went to that. They stayed there awhile, left, came back when they saw someone getting busted and sat-in on the floor. The pigs came in and moved out the students (no one was arrested—the pigs just got to beat the shit out of the students)—there were approximately 100 students. That night there was a rally, a street dance and students marched down to the courthouse in downtown Lafayette.

The administration refused to close down for a strike after the Kent State Four. But the majority of kids don't give a shit. Greeks had banners saying "Grand Prix Week" and "Delta Welcomes Mom" on their houses—no peace posters. The country was in turmoil and Purdue was playing Greek Week.

SURVIVAL:

Hard. It's a very conservative school. Be prepared to have to join a Greek house (this may be the last big Greek campus).

Drugs are easy to get but there are a lot of busts. Student health is terrible. One frat house burned down and two badly-burned Greeks had to wait an hour to see a doctor. Selected doctors give out BC pills (but Purdue girls won't need them). The Psychology department has a hot line. Women's Liberation will give out abortion referrals.

The University ministry does good draft counseling.

The campus newspaper, *The Exponent*, is lousy. Flicks are the most important form of entertainment here and in Indianapolis.

ENVIRONMENT:

Mental—-People are talking about pledging and pinning. Freaks are reading Rubin and Hoffman.

Physical—Cold in the winter, hot in the summer and always wet. They put wires up around the grass so as to "rotate it." The Agriculture department burns animals (usually dead) which pollutes the air. The Purdue physical plant also pollutes. Some companies dump raw sewage directly into the polluted Wabash River.

It's an old, pretty campus. All the buildings are red brick. "They have a contract for 150 years to use nothing but red brick."

"The campus has been scientifically designed so that no matter what direction you're walking, the wind will be blowing in your face."

"They built a new dorm which holds 800 people and it's all filled up, but they still use the old ones which have 1200 vacancies."

One nice eyeful—the fountain outside of the executive building. There's a mural on a wall in the west foyer in the Union building and in the far-right corner there are cleaning instructions printed on it.

IOWA

Coe College

Cedar Rapids, Iowa

Coe is a small midwestern liberal arts school. Strong emphasis on academics. Atmosphere is liberal for Iowa.

SERGEANT PEPPER SECTION:

Coe is affiliated with the United Presbyterian Church but is not much for religious atmosphere. Average grades plus SAT score of about 1,100 combined. 1,126 students, all undergraduates. 60% out-of-state. A few minority students.

ACADEMIC BULLSHIT:

Very liberal academically.

The faculty has just abolished all graduation requirements. Students need take only the two-course sequence called "Introduction to Liberal Arts" during their first year, and then complete 36 courses before graduation. Majors have been abandoned and replaced by the "Concentration." Students are encouraged to design interdepartmental majors.

If a student wishes to spend time off campus doing work in his field or any other related area, he may get four to five course credits for the time spent off campus. Many other off-campus programs are available, including a semester in Washington, D.C., New York, Costa Rica, Newberry Library in Chicago, etc. Coe belongs to the Associated Colleges of the Midwest (in the ACM are also Carleton, St. Olaf, Beloit, Knox, Macalester, etc.) and the ACM offers a barrage of off-campus programs.

Good departments include Physics (only nuclear accelerator in a small midwestern college), Business and Music. Pass/Fail (called Satisfactory/Unsatisfactory) is used.

Dr. John Chapman in Economics and Dr. Pat Alson in History are popular.

Student-initiated courses as of this year. Some were: "A Scientific Approach to Student Activism" and "Racial Traditions of America." No Free U.

Coe's teachers and students are very close. Professors frequently have their classes in their homes.

The blacks have an organization called Afro-American-Self-

Education Organization. They have a house on campus and conduct seminars and talks on campus.

Lots of independent study and study abroad.

BREAD:

Total annual tuition for all students is $2,000. Annual cost for room and board is $1,000. Most students live in the dorms. The college has a policy of meeting the financial needs of any student who qualifies for entrance but cannot meet the cost. Loans, scholarships, work-study and campus jobs. An expensive wardrobe isn't at all necessary. Some students have cars. Average cost of date for a cat is $7.

BROTHERS AND SISTERS:

Ratio cats : chicks— 1 : 1.

The campus borders on lukewarm hip. The heavy hips have not made it in Iowa yet. Active dating and sexual activity. Greeks are dwindling. People meet at the Union snack area called the "Pub." The Student Senate sponsors a coffee house in the basement of a pad near campus that is popular.

The drug scene is fair to middling. Several busts on campus in 1970. Lids go for $15.

The most frequent entertainment is the movies in town. The students are not revolutionary but are aware. Two hundred marched on the draft board to protest Nixon's stand in Cambodia. No active political organizations.

Since the college is dependent upon the community for alumni funds, a mere threat of violence without the actuality is usually effective. Students occasionally march on the administration building.

SURVIVAL:

Coe is a midwestern student sanctuary. Student health is very good since the largest private hospital in the state is located across the street. BC pills and abortion referrals not available through school but in city. The campus is establishing a counseling center for students for things like suicide prevention. The college chaplain and citizen groups in town sponsor draft counseling services.

The *Coe Cosmos* is the student newspaper and is fairly well-respected.

The "McCready Health Food Store" is close by.

ENVIRONMENT:

Mental—Students read.

Physical—The college is located in a city of 110,000 people (Cedar Rapids). The climate varies greatly and the city has the most air pollution of any city in Iowa. A strong smell can be detected several days of the week. The major contributors to the pollution are Quaker Oats, Pennick and Ford and Iowa Electric.

Most of the buildings are new and modern. The Student Union, five years old, has won a couple of architecture awards. The college is planning to build a new Fine Arts center.

Escapes include Chicago (250 miles away) or ski resorts in Illinois. There's not a lot of travel. Most students live on campus.

Drake University

Des Moines, Iowa

Drake is in the center of Des Moines. Des Moines is in Iowa.

SERGEANT PEPPER SECTION:

Drake is a small midwestern independent college that has traditional ties with the Disciples of Christ Church but is now independent. 2.5 GPA for entrance and ACTs required. Transfers also need a 2.5. 5,000 students, 250 of which are grads. 35% are out-of-state students.

ACADEMIC BULLSHIT:

Drake has a good Law school and an excellent Pharmacy.

Moot Court Day and Supreme Court Day rank high as unusual activities imparting knowledge and practical experience. Speeches have been given by Harold Hughes of Iowa, Governor Robert Ray and, this year, Hubert Humphrey. The remainder of the event is the handling of famous cases with students serving as lawyers, judges and jury. Also have a Campus Legal Aides Service designed to aid students in court problems, landlord problems, suits, etc. Very active—handled over 200 cases last year and the student opinion and reaction was high and very favorable. Also assists in charges brought against students for violation of university rules.

The best courses in Pharmacy are the higher level chemistry courses. They also offer practical experience in local pharmacies, and have undertaken a drug program run by the students whereby students receive professional counseling if they call a certain telephone number when having a "bad trip."

The Business school is straight and adequate. Business courses that are good include all accounting courses plus excellent courses in "Insurance," "Personnel Management," and "Marketing." "Consumer Behavior" and "Marketing Research" are the best in the Marketing department. "Personnel Management" is excellent because of the professor—it's taught with a social slant with business having the role of helping to alleviate the poverty problem, military-industrial complex and pollution. "Life Insurance" and "Health Insurance" are the two courses in the Insurance curriculum—final consists of passing the first CPA exam, and thus is useful to students.

The Education program is also good. Popular professors include Frank Wilhoit in "Political Science" and Peter Gunther in "Business."

Pass/Fail is used but grades are the main procedure. There is a

Free U which consists of student courses for one hour credit; topics depend on the result of a student poll. There are no grades, just credit. One course taught was "Drug Use" moderated by Dr. Phillip LeVine, Pharmacy professor and head of the Des Moines Drug Abuse Council. There is a very close relationship between students and teachers—much interaction. Independent study is allowed those who have a 3.5 average and a recommendation. There are about 65 black students—no Third World College. Study abroad in Italy, England and France.

BREAD:

Drake costs $800 a semester for everyone. Dorms run $500 a semester for room and board. Apartments are about $110 a month for a one-bedroom. Fraternities and sororities average $450 per semester. There are MANY loans and scholarships available. Work-study and campus jobs are average—$1.50 an hour. Assistants to professors get paid more. Expensive threads aren't necessary.

BROTHERS AND SISTERS:

Ratio cats : chicks—1 : 1.

"Most guys are straight, although the heavy hips are growing in number. Clothing and haircut seem to be dictated by *Playboy* and *Esquire* fashion supplements. As the heavy hips grow in number, however, straights begin to let themselves go—they are starting to conform. Most subconsciously identify with movie images and hero types. After *Easy Rider,* people got hip for awhile."

"There is a lot of dating. This is a very social-conscious school. From what I gather, there is also an availability of sexual activity and quite a bit of sleeping over. Girls are not liberated—dorm hours enforced. They have to live in dorm until they are 21."

Greeks still exist and play a major role in campus political and social life. There are large numbers of heavy Greeks.

Places to hang include:

"The Kennel"—basement atmosphere typical. Juke box, card games, good place to go between classes. Everyone hangs here.

"Vic's"—grungy atmosphere. Nice furniture but dirty floors, etc. Greasy food and muddy coffee. Good place to sober up, just by looking at the waitresses and your order. Radicals only.

"Hubbell"—very nice atmosphere. Carpet, nice furniture, good food. Straights.

Students are liberals. All the regular clubs exist. A few SDSers who changed their name to "The Movement." They had the normal Moratorium Day activities in 1969. There was an "Anti-Military Ball and Concert" in 1969. Some students struck after the Kent State tragedy. No outside cops have been called in as yet. The drug scene is pretty active for the Midwest. You can score on campus.

Most popular entertainment is weekend rock concerts in Greenwood Park.

SURVIVAL:

Drake is way above places like Utah in survivability but isn't
really with it yet. No BC pills, abortion referrals, or health-food
stores. Draft counseling is run by local advisors and the Wesley
House Foundation. It's quite successful. The *Times-Delphic* is a
good campus newspaper. The underground paper, *Breakthru*, is
also good. The biggest hindrance to surviving is the location of the
campus—smack dab in the center of the residential area of Des
Moines, Iowa.

ENVIRONMENT:

Mental—People read. Douglas' *Points of Rebellion* and the *Tales
of Hoffman* are popular.

Physical—Drake has a typical midwestern climate with plenty of
trees and fresh air in the campus area. However, the campus is
surrounded by a suburban area. The campus is a cross between
attractive modern architecture and ivy-tower type buildings. The
major eyesore is Iowa Hall (Art building)—it's an outdated
wooden building with poor heating and little ventilation.

Greenwood Park is about three miles from campus with a lake
in the center—serene and passive place. Except for nature lovers'
visits to surrounding parks, most entertainment consists of flicks in
suburbia and parties.

Parsons College

Fairfield, Iowa

Known as "The Second Chance School."

SERGEANT PEPPER SECTION:

1,200 undergraduates. Entering freshmen must be high-school
graduates and take either the ACT or SAT. Most freshmen come
from the top 70% of their class (Big Top). Some have board
scores of 500 combined. Parsons does not actively seek the lower
third of class rank even though it is advertised as "The Second
Chance School." They look at the individual and will accept him
because they feel the student has potential and that his mind was
messed up for some reason and he got bad grades. Parsons will
consider students as transfers who have been academically dismissed. 75% out-of-state. 75 blacks. A few Indians.

ACADEMIC BULLSHIT:

In June, 1967, Parsons lost its accreditation and didn't get it back
until April, 1970. Although it was charged that this was due to
academic reasons, Parsons people say this was untrue. They hold

that it was politics. President Roberts was stealing some of the finest professors from other schools since Parsons was making a financial profit and he could afford to offer outrageous salaries. Other universities resented this so Parsons lost its accreditation officially because (1) the library didn't have enough volumes, (2) the admissions policies were too lax and (3) housing wasn't good enough.

The student-professor interaction here is very good, much better than at most schools. Professors consider the students a challenge. Best programs include the Social Science program (the second in the state), Business Administration, Education and Foreign Service. Popular professors include Dr. Rutgers in Chemistry and Dr. Barton in History. Colonel Hackett, in Math, is a former West Pointer —freaks beware.

No Pass/Fail, student-initiated courses or Free U.

Parsons has tutorial assistance which is given by all professors. Professors, while not teaching, must be in their offices from 8–5. The students come first.

No black studies courses. Independent study in the upper divisions. Study abroad. Smoking is allowed except in the theater, and you must wear shoes and a shirt in the cafeteria.

BREAD:

Tuition at this private college is $845 a semester. About a third of each incoming class gets financial aid in package form (scholarship, loan, job). Campus jobs pay about $1.65 an hour. Dorms cost $550 for room and board a semester. Apartments are in old two-story houses which have been converted into a bunch of bedrooms. They run about $80 a month per person. Some people rent farmhouses in the countryside where they swim for the summer. Most students have cars. Dates vary in price.

The best bookstore is the "Fairfield News Center" where you can pick up the Los Angeles *Free Press*.

BROTHERS AND SISTERS:

Ratio cats : chicks—3 : 1.

People are kind of weird here. They try to put forth an image, a veneer, so that they can deal with others better. They don't seem like real people. Most students are from the northeast and fads hit big about two months after being on the East Coast. Straights wear bells, jeans and loafers without socks. Freaks wear normal freak dress although chicks usually wear bras.

There's really nowhere to go in Fairfield so the students live for the free flicks over the weekend. The school is still a party school, but it used to be even more so. They have campus drinking organizations dedicated to getting drunk every weekend. The fraternities are all but dead and those that remain are composed of freaks.

Local hangs include "The Den" (a bar for both jocks and trippers) and "The Snack Bar" in the student center. Some go to the "Aardvark," where new singers try to get their acts together before going into the big time.

Sexual action is kind of weird. In 1970, there were a large number of gay cats (estimated at 150). The fact that there are three cats to every chick for the rest makes action limited. The chicks have affected heads from the ratio in their favor.

Most students have tried grass and about half of the school trips regularly. Score in Iowa City at $15 a lid. Speed is big. The administration is cool about dope but the townspeople are uptight. Army vets sometimes come on campus and act as informers.

Parsons lacks real political commitment because of all the dropouts who are afraid of getting bad grades. There's a smattering of views. Nobody really does anything, they just want their diploma. In the city of Fairfield there is a really active chapter of the Minutemen.

In January, 1969, a bug was placed in a student's room and a cop disguised himself as a janitor and was in a student's closet for two days listening. They finally busted the student for dope, but charges were dropped.

During the Kent days of 1970, there was a lot of rapping between students and professors. Some kids went to D.C. A good percentage of the student body wrote home to their representatives on official school stationery which Parsons provided. There was a march through town. Maxwell Taylor was their commencement speaker and the professor who was forced to give him his honorary degree read his speech in a monotone.

Security cops are "campus rejects." Their things are parking tickets and some busts. If they want you, they'll look up your schedule, walk into your class and call off your name. The town tries to get "undesirable students" in the position where they'll either go to jail or leave town on the noon train.

SURVIVAL:

The student health service hates freaks. No BC pills without parental permission.

The Freak Out Control Center is on campus in the religious center—for drug rescue and suicide prevention. The campus paper is the *Portfolio;* funds for it were cut in half in 1970.

ENVIRONMENT:

Mental—People are just starting to talk.

Physical—Summer is hot and there are tornadoes in the spring and summer (although there hasn't been one for five years). There's a low level of air pollution. The Des Moines River is polluted but it's 25 miles from here.

The old campus is ivy-covered collegiate. The new buildings are functional and windowless. The basement of the Howard dorm reeks from stink and is called "The Pit." The student center is cool and looks like a pagoda.

Escapes include Iowa City and the State Parks. 80% live on campus.

KANSAS

Kansas State University

Manhattan, Kansas

General Westmoreland got a standing ovation at commencement last year. Racial violence for two years running. The blacks are the main campus radicals. White students out of American Kansas Gothic.

SERGEANT PEPPER SECTION:

13,149 students, of which 1,855 are grads. 18% out-of-state. In-state just must have graduated from an accredited Kansas high school. Out-of-states must be in upper half of graduating high-school class. Transfers need a 2.0.

ACADEMIC BULLSHIT:

Their best departments are Agriculture, Home Economics and Psychology. The Agriculture school is one of the best in the nation —"Grain and Milling Technology" is the only course like it in the U.S. The Psychology department, in conjunction with Engineering, has an environmental lab set up to test human reactions.

Popular professors include Steve Grolin, History (he is just another member of the class), Shel Edleman, Sociology (works a lot with sensitivity sessions), and Gil Browning (teaches psychotherapy and personal awareness).

Kansas State University has Pass/Fail. Many independent study courses—one was for 15 units and the students went to Berkeley to live and observe. Other students are trying to set up a College of Ecology. There is a Free U called "University for Man." 70 courses from "Auto Mechanics" to "Psychic Mind Power." 2,000 people attend the UFM World College. Just a black history class. Tests prevail and some study abroad.

BREAD:

In-state tuition per semester $231, out-of-state $526. Fair amount of loans; one out of three applicants obtain scholarships. Not enough student jobs. Work-study depends on D.C. spending.

Dates cost $5–$10. Most have cars. Dorms are $900 a year for room and board. Greeks run from $110–$130 a month. One commune so far—Laramie House, which rents for $200 a month and

205

is split ten ways. Apartments run $125 a month for a one-bedroom.
Some old houses for $200 a month.

"The Door" has used records.

BROTHERS AND SISTERS:

Ratio cats : chicks—1.5 : 1.

The students are generally straights—jeans, pullover sweaters
and button-down shirts. Plain Janes of the American Gothic paintings. Couple of freaks. Dating is big and straight arrow—dancing
and shows. Greeks still are big but dwindling. They hang at
"Kite's" and "Mr. Kay's" (bars). The few freaks hang at
"Mother's," and "The Door" (record shops) and the "Chocolate
George"—an aesthetic trinket shop.

KSU just built a new football stadium and a new athletic building (sports are big business). They are trying to get artificial turf
for their football field.

The students aren't even liberal. In the spring of 1964 the music
students wanted a new place to play their music because the Music
building was old, so they burned it down (lost a couple of
Stradivariuses). In 1968 there was a confrontation between minorities and the administration. Nichols gym burned down.

There have been some real confrontations between blacks and
administrators. In 1970, a black ran for AS President. During the
run-offs, some of the Ag teachers let their classes out early if they
promised to vote against him—he lost.

In the fall of 1969, the University started to try to change. They
began to create a new distribution of power within the University.
Clubs are the Black Students Union, Young Republicans, Young
Democrats. Women's Liberation is new.

"Bob's Motel" is local balling place.

SURVIVAL:

Around 600 kids smoke grass. They usually live in the coed
dorms (Moore Hall and Van Zide Hall). Lids go for $20, acid for
$3. Scoring is hard because Ft. Riley, a military base, is just down
the road. G.I.'s are the sources and there are a lot of busts. Opium
comes into Ft. Riley from Vietnam. More wild marijuana grows
in Kansas than in any other state in the dis-Union. Sometimes it
grows between buildings on campus.

Student health is atrocious and is called Student Death Service—
rumors of a student who died of a brain concussion they diagnosed
as a small bruise. They don't give out BC pills, but do give sun-
burn advice through the school newspaper. Manhattan City, a
county clinic, gives out birth control information. The Mental
Health Service handles abortion referrals and suicide prevention.
Also Crisis Center. The UFM gives draft counseling advice as does
Bruce Woods of the Baptist Center.

The campus paper is the *Kansas State Collegian*—alright. No
health-food stores. Kansas City is the nearest big city.

ENVIRONMENT:

Mental—People are reading *Quest for Identity* and *The Electric Kool-Aid Acid Test*.

Physical—Trees, trees, trees—greenery and more beautiful green trees, green grass, green trees. Not much pollution of any kind in Kansas. A stream goes through the campus but it is getting polluted with trash and beer cans.

Anderson Hall, the administration building, looks like a midwestern stone prairie church—pointing tall. The president of Kansas State University lives on campus in a Hansel and Gretel house.

Escapes are Tuttle Creek Lake, a man-made lake, and Pillsbury Crossing, a shallow stream with a waterfall.

Hardly any commuters.

University of Kansas
Lawrence, Kansas

Kansas University has many contradictory elements: grass that grows wild, Minutemen shopkeepers and freaks who snipe and set fires.

SERGEANT PEPPER SECTION:

17,576 students of which 3,395 are grad students. 32% out-of-state. In-state just needs to have graduated from an accredited Kansas high school. Out-of-state must be in upper half of graduating high-school class. Both must take ACTs. SATs average 1,000 combined.

ACADEMIC BULLSHIT:

Engineering, Business, Pharmacy, Law and Medicine all adequate. No one seemed too excited about any of them. The Medical school is in Kansas City proper.

Popular professors are John Chotlos, Psychology guru, Harry Schafer, Economics, and Verdu, Oriental Philosophy. Pass/Fail used. No student-initiated courses for credit. A Free U that has classes on "Sunsets" and one on "Guitars." Hardly any interaction between students and professors. Tests and papers. A certain local freak will write papers and take tests for you for a fee—seen at "Rock Chalk Cafe." Lots of independent study, just get a faculty sponsor. Study abroad mainly for language proficiency.

BREAD:

In-state $550 per year, out-of-state $1050 per year. The students voted a fee increase on themselves for a new building in 1970.

Some work-study, tight loans and scholarships. All campus jobs pay about $1.65 an hour. Dorms go for $900 room and board a year, fraternities $120 a month. Freaks all live in apartments ($100 a month) or houses. Possibility of a rent strike in the future because of exploitation.

Dates are about $5—not that many cars.

BROTHERS AND SISTERS:

Ratio cats : chicks—1.5 : 1.

There is a large freak (long hair, artsy-craftsy) element at the school. Boots, ponchos, no bras. The rest of the school is neat sideburn fraternity type. 80% of the campus is mid-50s—dating, dancing and necking. The "Yuk" and "Red Dog Inn" are the popular beer joints.

The sexual revolution has made a hit. Everyone is balling (especially sorority chicks) but not many cohabiting couples. Freaks survive selling dope to frats. Freaks hang at the "Rock Chalk Cafe" —egg salad, french fries and Coors. They also live in the Oread area near campus. Straights hang at the "Jaywalk Cafe" and "Wagon Wheel."

The underground paper, *Vortex,* supplies the prices of dope. Lids go for about $15—much of the stuff is homegrown (grass grows wild in Kansas). There was even an article in *The New York Times* about the tremendous amount of dope smoking at Kansas University. Even the faculty smokes constantly.

The main entertainment is flicks, rapping and smoking dope.

The students are rather apathetic, as a whole, but freaks recently made the transition from dope to politics (not presuming a relationship). They are on the verge of really getting things together.

In the spring of 1969, there was a pig convention at Kansas University. Freaks liberated the microphone, took pictures of pigs and upset them. A $160,000 suit was filed against 25 students for violating the pigs' civil rights.

In February, 1970, things started to happen. There was a sympathy strike for the Chicago Seven. In March, the BSU presented a list of demands to the chancellor which asked for more representation in most areas of the University—the chancellor rejected their demands. In early April a student strike was called to protest the denial of promotions to two radical teachers. The night before the strike began, Anchorage Savings was bombed.

On April 20, 1970, the Student Union was set on fire. There had been trouble in the black community and a curfew was imposed on the city. The freaks challenged the curfew, set up barricades in the street, and set them on fire. National Guard was called in and there was gunfire. Students shot out all the lights in the area. Freaks were evicted from a place called "The White House" and it was set on fire. Pigs busted lots of people for curfew. Police used double-O buckshot. Things finally died down. KU will probably continue to be political considering the atmosphere of Kansas. A lot of people have front license plates that say "Kill a Commie for Christ."

SURVIVAL:

Except for the dearth of outside stimulation, KU is getting there. Plenty of dope, Planned Parenthood in Lawrence and abortion referrals in Kansas City. The Peace Center on 7th Street gives draft counseling. Sports heroes are still big (rah). The University

Daily Kansan has mostly wire stuff in it—underground *Vortex* is good. Health foods are available from the "Downtown Health and Foreign Foods Store."

ENVIRONMENT:

Mental—People smoke dope rather than read.

Physical—Hot in summer, snow for six months in winter. Lots and lots of trees and hills. Little air pollution.

As to campus buildings, "They have a general policy here, anything that looks aesthetically pleasing is torn down for more practical things." Summerfield Hall looks like a computer from the outside. There's a new $2 million library which is atomic blast-proof in case of war. Strong Hall and Murphy Hall were built backwards. A factory whistle goes off close to school twice daily.

KENTUCKY

Murray State University
Murray, Kentucky

"Intercourse is illegal before marriage in Kentucky. Murray is a dry city. Nearest bar (beer only) is 12 miles away. It is owned by a black man and the few blacks, radical types, and solid people go there. School motto: 'Keep America bigotted: Elect Wallace.' Most are southern conservatives. Straights play tennis 24 hours a day, 7 days a week." Ugh.

SERGEANT PEPPER SECTION:

Murray State is easy to get into. The catalog says that all Kentucky high-school graduates will be admitted. Out-of-state students have to meet minimal requirements. There are 6,538 students of which 762 are graduate students. Only 25% out-of-state. 2% blacks.

ACADEMIC BULLSHIT:

Murray State has adequate Journalism, Physical Education and English departments. P.E. is really strong with all sorts of courses in "Basketball Officiating" and "Football." Murray State seems to be in a bad way. I quote: "Our most popular teacher is Dr. Ray Mofield. He teaches 'History of Journalism' and uses no notes. He uses humor going on topic and off again while still referring to journalism." Can I watch?

No Pass/Fail—grades everywhere. One black studies course was taught last year but the teacher escaped. Students have suggested courses in black studies but the administration has turned them down for what they referred to as "a lack of competent teachers." Of course there aren't any competent teachers, they won't hire any.

Three tests per semester per course (Omigod). No study abroad. No Free U. Not much interaction between students and teachers and no smoking in class and no . . .

BREAD:

$130 in-state and $380 out-of-state per semester. Apartments range from $65–$95 a month. Dorms are overpriced at $120 a semester. Fraternity houses charge $200 a month.

Limited work-study and campus jobs at $1.45 an hour. Loans and scholarships are available.

$5 buys a big date—booze and a flick. Most students have cars but an expensive wardrobe isn't that necessary. Bells and body shirts on out-of-staters—Kentuckians wear "farmer type" clothes.

BROTHERS AND SISTERS:

Ratio cats : chicks—1.5 : 1.

The campus is generally conservative with Spiro Agnew and Martha Mitchell campus heroes to 90% of students. They are mostly from farms and narrow-minded. Most out-of-state students from New York, New Jersey and Illinois are up to it. They smoke grass, drink and party while Kentuckians are either studying or going home to work on the farms.

Fair on dating, but nowhere to go. Good sexual activity as northerners are cool. Southerners think sex is solid as long as they hit church on Sunday.

Greeks on campus but not that important.

Drugs are not big on campus. The nearest outlet for grass is Carbondale, Illinois, two and one-half hours away. Lids go for $20.

Basketball players are still making it with the jock image.

Most are ultra-conservatives. STEAM is the radical organization, known as radical because many northerners belong.

The biggest political event happened in May, 1970. A pregnant, unwed chick was thrown out for breaking a Kentucky statute outlawing fornication. She went to court over it. Students have tried to pressure the student government to support the girl but they won't because of administration pressure.

SURVIVAL:

Very difficult. Parties are the big entertainment, drinking and screwing by the lake. There are no draft counseling services. The draft board in town is only open one day a week and the women in it still think World War II is going on. No chance of BC pills being dispensed in the Bible Belt. One doctor for whole school constitutes student health. No suicide prevention center and no abortion referrals although there is an illegal abortion specialist in town who's good, reasonable and silent. No pets on campus. Fairly good campus paper considering the atmosphere, *Murray News. Dawn* is a new underground paper.

ENVIRONMENT:

Mental—Most people are reading that best seller, *The New English Translation of the Bible.*

Physical—The climate is hot and humid April–October. Mild winters with little if any snow. Murray is surrounded by Kentucky lakes. There are two types of buildings. The older, circa 1925, ones have an enchantment about them. The new ones are corporate sterile—five-story white boxes with few windows and they are starting to yellow. Major escapes are the lakes—15 miles away— and bars which serve beer only.

LOUISIANA

Tulane University and Sophie Newcomb College
New Orleans, Louisiana

These two colleges have separate curricula and faculty but are part of the same university. Tulane is one of the most progressive schools in the South. And one of its greatest assets is that it is in New Orleans.

SERGEANT PEPPER SECTION:

6,000 students, of which 1,500 are graduates.

Admission is harder for Sophie Newcomb College and chicks need about 1,200 SATs and high grades. Cats need about 1,000 SATs and high grades. 60% of the Newcomb College freshmen and 40% of the Tulane freshmen are in the top 10% of their high-school graduating class. 30% from Louisiana.

ACADEMIC BULLSHIT:

Sophie Newcomb is one of the best women's colleges in the country. Tulane is also academically excellent.

Many good departments—Architecture, Engineering, Law and Medicine. Students said there were no "favorite courses" but that everything was good. The most popular professors are Andy Antippas in the English department and Gordon Gallup in the Psychology department.

Student-initiated colloquiums that you can take for one quarter. Some Pass/Fail. Tulane is small enough so that there is still good interaction between students and teacher. Traditional academic crap—tests, papers and busy-work. Independent study allowed and study abroad in Europe and the Middle East.

BREAD:

$1,050 a semester tuition. Very slim offering of loans, scholarships and work-study. Campus jobs are available at $1.50 an hour. Most students live in dorms and fraternities. Dorms are average price—room and board costs about $1,000 a year. Apartments are $100 a month. Most students have cars.

BROTHERS AND SISTERS:

Ratio cats : chicks—2 : 1.

"Students here range from super-fascist drill-team members to constantly tripping 'hippies.'" Most are evenly divided between lukewarm hip and straight. 18 fraternities and 9 sororities exist and are still very important socially. Lots of dating and more chicks are becoming liberated.

Local hangs include the whole French Quarter and it's like a world apart—very freaky in its own way. Hips hit "The Raven" for beer and "Eddie Price's" for hamburgers near campus. Straights hang at the "Hob Nob Inn" (beer) and the "Maple Hill Restaurant" (big meals).

Lots of dope on campus. $15 for a lid, score in the University sector or the French Quarter.

Most popular entertainments are "drinking and wenching."

Not many revolutionaries and the ones that there were were "purged" last year after the ROTC demonstrations. The Tulane Liberation Front has the politicos. In spring of 1969 at the anti-ROTC demonstration, six students were expelled. In spring of 1970, there was an anti-administration demonstration in which a building was seized and held for a day.

SURVIVAL:

New Orleans is one of the easiest cities to survive in in the South —less repression than many other cities. No "official" prescribing of BC pills at student health. A Free Clinic and a Family Planning Agency are run by Tulane. The *Tulane Hullabaloo* is a liberal college paper.

ENVIRONMENT:

Mental—People are doing things in New Orleans and reading Rubin.

Physical—Warm climate and plenty of trees and water. New Orleans is in the middle of swamplike ground at the mouth of the Mississippi River.

Escapes are the French Quarter (15 minutes) or to the Gulf Coast (one hour).

MAINE

Colby College

Waterville, Maine

Colby is a small New England college that is big on educational innovation. But there still isn't much of an intellectual environment. It's the ivy-tower thing—with drinking, skiing and rapping at campus eateries. The administration is trying to improve the quality of the student body.

SERGEANT PEPPER SECTION:

Colby is fairly difficult to get into—average 1,300 combined SATs and in top one-third of high-school graduating class. In 1970, 54% were in the top tenth of their class. 1,506 undergraduates attend, many from out-of-state (82%).

ACADEMIC BULLSHIT:

The English department is very good. The best course is "Shakespeare" taught by the chairman of the department. It is extremely thorough and inclusive and students must have a consuming interest in Shakespeare. "Twentieth Century Literature" and "Twentieth Century Poetry" are also recommended. Good minds in the Sociology department. Material and approach toward education are more important than presentation. The Philosophy department has a very good staff—two professors who get the highest student evaluations of any teachers in the school. Highest of the high are "Contemporary Philosophy," "Advanced Symbolic Logic," "19th Century Philosophy" and "Seminars on Nonviolence" (Gandhi).

Most popular professor is Stephen Marks of the Sociology department, who teaches "Social Change: A Theoretical and Empirical Approach with Current Reference to the Third World, Blacks, and any Type of Action that Can be Considered Social Change." Requires student presentations followed up with in-depth study of topic. In this Seminar, students read books like *The Electric Kool-Aid Acid Test, Education and Ecstasy.* He has encouraged students to find their own topics and submit special reports.

Professor Reuman is very popular in the Philosophy department. As of September, 1970, one out of every five courses taken is Pass/Fail. There are occasional student-originated courses, especially in the Sociology department. No Free U but the school has workshops for "Printing," "Silk Screening," "Leather," "Pottery," "Photography" and "Film."

214

There is an extremely close relationship between popular professors and students due to small classes. A few Third World courses. Both tests and papers. Independent study can be done on a special topic for three credits. Study abroad in many countries.

Professors and students are responsive to one another and communicate well.

BREAD:

Tuition is $2,100 per year for both in-state and out-of-state since this is a private school. It's rough for people without bread—loans, scholarships and work-study are very tight. Scholarship people can have a job at $1.45 an hour. Dorms are about $500 per semester for room and board. Apartments run $125 a month for a one-bedroom. Three-fourths of the students have cars. An expensive wardrobe isn't necessary.

BROTHERS AND SISTERS:

Ratio cats : chicks—1 : 1.

The chicks: 2% heavy hip, 15% hip, 63% lukewarm hip, 20% straight and conservative. Homemade clothes and weaving. More concerned with comfort than pure appeal. Jeans, some skirts, groovy jewelry, whatever is functional and not atrocious. Lukewarm hip category obviously concerned with how they look (carefully construed unconstrued look). They work at it. Some jeans, mostly bell-bottom slacks that are too short, loafers or glamour-girl shoes, skirts, blouses that are see-through with colored bras. Put up their hair. Straights: blouses, skirts, nylons, loafers—constantly worried about how they look. Fidgety and good posture.

The cats: heavy hip 10%, hip 40%, lukewarm hip 40%, straight conservative 10%. Differences between the clothes can be deceiving. You can distinguish the first two (if you're lucky) by boots which are worn out and functional. Hair and face growth is prominent. Lukewarms usually have some sort of polished boots on, not usually as high; all three categories wear jeans of one sort or another. Hair usually long. Lukewarms usually have some sort of groovy glasses, optical or sun. Straights wear Brooks Brothers or something like that, pants or slacks with cuffs, and short hair.

Lots of dating and sexual activity, especially among the hips. Fraternities are dying out and turning into communes. The big hang is the "SPA," in the lower part of the library. A bar in town called "Big John's" is another hang. Heavy drug action—not much H—mostly grass and acid. $10 buys a lid. Best entertainment is that which is self-generated or flicks in town. Waterville isn't an entertainment mecca.

The campus is politically aware but not revolutionary. SDS and the student government are the most active groups.

Every time there's a demonstration, the administration refuses the demands and attempts to take credit for student suggestions. There was fair support for the strike in May, 1970, and in February, 1970, the blacks occupied a chapel, made demands which were refused. No student has ever been arrested. Campus cops are harmless watchmen.

SURVIVAL:

Fairly easy—good chances in academic world. Boston is only three hours away if you dig the urban scene.

Birth control advice is available from a list of doctors that have been collated by students. There's a 24-hour drug clinic and a school shrink who is always on call. Some draft counseling. The *Echo* is the campus paper. It's anti-establishment and good.

ENVIRONMENT:

Mental—People are discussing student political potential and reading *The Electric Kool-Aid Acid Test*.

Physical—New England chilly, snowy weather—with a fair amount of spring and fall rain—green and lush. Lakes nearby.

All the buildings on campus are pseudo-Georgian with the exception of the three connected dorms which were designed by Design Research people.

Air pollution is bad. Scott Paper is located in Waterville and covers the town with a smoky shroud.

Escapes are Boston, Sugarloaf (for skiing) and the hills and woods all around the college.

MARYLAND

Johns Hopkins University
Baltimore, Maryland

"Most cats are lunch meat."

SERGEANT PEPPER SECTION:

8,862 students of which 4,311 are out-of-state. Very hard to get in. You need excellent grades, approximately 1,350 SATs, great recommendations and a successful personal interview.

ACADEMIC BULLSHIT:

Johns Hopkins is primarily a graduate institution famed for its excellence in Science, Engineering and Medicine. Three-fifths of the undergraduates are in either Engineering, Business Administration or Pre-med. There's a lot of studying and students' lives revolve around their school work. The faculty is among the highest paid in the country, but students complain that teachers are always writing books or taking sabbaticals.

The most popular course on the undergraduate level is "The History of Art" taught by Dr. Stanton. Another popular course is "Negro History" taught by a white, Hugh Davis Graham. Popular professors include Dr. Dfeffer (Political Science) and Professor Pepper (Art).

The school is trying to expand its Humanities and Arts departments and will probably have more to offer in those fields in the future. At present the most outstanding course offerings are in the Sciences.

Some Pass/Fail, not much class participation on the undergraduate level and no Free U. Student-originated courses are prevalent but the subject matter is that which is usually offered in the regular curriculum in other schools. ("Victorian and Modern Literature"). No Black Studies department but a few token courses. Dr. Wickiore is the school chaplain and teaches "Black and Urban Studies," a groovy course.

There is good student-faculty interaction between the young radical professors and the students. They usually go out to coffee and socialize. About 40% of the students do independent study. Anybody that wants to, can do it. Many undergraduates take graduate courses and do projects.

Study abroad in London, France, Rome and Bologna.

BREAD:

Tuition in-state and out-of-state is $2,250 a year. Loans and scholarships are fairly easy to get and campus jobs are prevalent at $1.50 an hour. Many kids substitute teach in the area—you don't even need a B.A. to do this.

Half of the students live in the dorms (freshmen must). They cost $1,025 for room and board a year. The other half of the students live off campus in apartments that are dirt cheap—about $50–$60 per person. A few still live in fraternity houses. Most students walk or take buses.

Expensive threads aren't a must although some cats still have them.

Scrounging is easy as far as rents and food go, but tuition is very high.

BROTHERS AND SISTERS:

Predominantly cats with 50 chicks.

The average student has short hair, a neatly trimmed beard, wears Sta-prest pants and trudges around in loafers. There are a few freaks who wear jeans, T-shirts and sandals, but they are in the minority.

Sex is just about dead here. The eggheads are more interested in studies than chicks. Half the students are goal-oriented graduate students. Dating doesn't even go on much. If a guy should by chance want a date, he usually makes the scene at nearby Goucher where the students are straight but female. Fraternities are folding.

Few hang out anywhere except the library but some have coffee at Levering Hall, the Student Union or at "Pecora's Pizza." For relaxation the cats go to "Peabody's Bar" and "Bud's Beer Garden." Most students are into school work too heavily to try drugs. Some undergraduates, especially freshmen, smoke grass and drop acid occasionally. There are lots of student informers and four students were busted in their dorms at 2 A.M. in 1970. Lids go for $15, tabs of mescaline for $3.

Students are apathetic and conservative. One cat referred to them as "lunch meat" (constant studiers). They do some constructive work (it was a big McCarthy campaign center). The only real incident happened in 1970 over military recruiters. There was a sit-in the day the recruiters came, then students camped out in front of the administration building for three weeks. Finally there was a referendum and recruiters were voted off campus—it was the first time any group was barred from campus. Students, however, voted also to keep ROTC.

SURVIVAL:

Hard unless you are really into studying.

Student health is just O.K. The Friends Committee in Baltimore does draft counseling. Survival services are available from the "Switchboard" in Baltimore. *The Newsletter* is the campus paper—it won't turn you on.

ENVIRONMENT:

Mental—No one reads anything but text books. An environmental-engineering group did some garbage and waste studies—that's it for ecology.

Physical—Baltimore is a very urban, very commercial city. It is located 45 minutes north of Washington, D.C. Air pollution is bad —there's always a gray haze hanging over the city. The campus, however, is set off from the city and is really beautiful. It's so natural-looking in parts that it seems like a park. There's an abundance of well-kept grass and trees. The buildings are simple red brick structures.

People study on weekends.

University of Maryland
College Park, Maryland

It took awhile but the University of Maryland finally became politicized with the Cambodia-Kent issues.

SERGEANT PEPPER SECTION:

32,444 students of which 85% are residents of Maryland. About 500 blacks. Not hard to get in. Applicants should have at least a 2.0 GPA and be in the upper half of their high-school graduating class. Average SAT scores are 1,050. Transfers from Maryland must have a C average, nonresident transfers need a 2.5.

ACADEMIC BULLSHIT:

Students feel the best department is the College of Business and Public Administration. Other good departments are the Education school and the graduate school of Dentistry, Law and Medicine on the Baltimore campus.

Best courses include "Europe in the World Setting in the 20th Century" with Dr. Harris, "Creative Writing" with Dr. Fleming and Professor Davis' Chemistry courses.

Traditional academic methods. Some Pass/Fail, lots of papers and tests and not much class participation. (The school is too gigantic for this.)

The school puts up bureaucratic barriers to students originating classes although there are a few. A Free U exists which has little support. There is no separate Ethnic Studies department but a Black Studies major is offered on an interdepartmental level. Most courses are taught by whites. Minority recruitment is not heavy. Some educational opportunity grants have been set up for the purpose of bringing in more blacks to Maryland. Professors and students aren't close as T.A.s teach many of the classes. Lots of study abroad.

BREAD:

Tuition is $506 a year in-state, $1,006 out-of-state. Financial aid is very available for in-state students. Campus jobs are easy to come by and pay $1.80 an hour.

Dorms cost $900 a year for room and board in-state, $1,000 for out-of-staters. Most students commute and live off campus. Fraternities and sororities are still happening and some frats are going coed. Most juniors and seniors live in apartments that run about $65 a month per person. There are some communes in the Silver Springs area. All the commuters have cars and parking is disgusting. University of Maryland students are pretty good at scrounging. For a long time a bunch of guys lived in the College Park Fire House. Other students crashed for a whole year with friends in the dorms.

BROTHERS AND SISTERS:

Ratio cats : chicks—1+ : 1.

The campus is somewhere between hip and straight. Most students dress cheaply and comfortably—a middle-class commuter's college. Conservatives dig the Greek scene, the chicks still wear Bobbie Brooks coordinates. Freaks ball and commuters date. Freaks live together in communes and straights live at home or with roommates. Greeks still control student government. Dates are cheap and include drinks at the "Varsity Grill," dancing in Georgetown, or just rapping. Local hangs in the College Park area include "Hungry Herman's" (dig the submarine sandwiches), "The Mall," "Howie's," and "The Rendezvous" and the "Doughnut Shop" on Route 1. Drugs are around but the school isn't submerged in them. About half have tried grass—it's in the dorms, frats and apartments and runs $15 a lid. Heavier drugs circulate among the hips and mescaline is getting popular.

This campus has the usual array of political clubs from SDS to YAF. There has been a small group of hard-core activists for about two years but the majority of the campus had been passive until the recent Cambodia-ROTC riot. Before that there were a few scattered demonstrations, one to protest dining-hall food (students came to hear the rock band), another was a BSU walkout over the usual demands.

For the November, 1969, Moratorium, students got permission to house out-of-town peace people in the campus chapel. After they arrived, riot pigs came and made the students leave. Four students were arrested for trespassing.

In March, tenure became an issue when two young popular left-wing philosophy teachers were fired. There was publicity and rallies over this, which led to a sit-in at the Skinner building. It was legal because the doors were left open and there was no trashing or looting. At first the police didn't come, but took a "wait and see" attitude. Finally at 3 A.M. the police came and 87 people were arrested. After that, things were peaceful until the Cambodia announcement.

The next day a rally was called in front of the library to get

ROTC off campus. It ended up with the trashing and vandalizing of the ROTC building with damage estimated at $15,000. Then the students congregated on Route 1 (a major thoroughfare), milling and blocking traffic. At about 4 P.M. the riot police came and began clearing the area and arresting students for throwing rocks. As soon as the kids were arrested it changed from a Cambodia-ROTC issue to a "pigs off campus" issue. About 2,000 kids then marched down to the police station, protesting the arrests. Clubbings, beatings and more arrests followed. Violence kept up, and that night tear gas was used to disperse students. After that it became cat and mouse with tear gas and arrests for a few days until the National Guard was called out. The rioting went off and on for several weeks. The Guard stayed until early June. There was a (Cambodia) strike at this time that was 50% effective. During the rioting there were many complaints of police brutality and 470 people were arrested.

SURVIVAL:

Student health is mediocre—no BC pills given out there but referrals are made. A gynecologist was recently installed due to student pressure. (One gynecologist?) Shrinks are available for consultation. Draft counseling in the Student Union. A Legal Defense Fund was set up after the Skinner building sit-in a year ago. There's a HELP switchboard in the area—dial 362-HELP. *The Diamondback* is an adequate campus paper with a leftist slant. A minority are into health foods and there is a health-food store in the College Park area. The Women's Liberation group isn't into the basics—they're protesting the auctions of sorority girls. Some chicks broke away from Women's Liberation and formed the Radical Women Caucus.

ENVIRONMENT:

Mental—People are reading *Portnoy's Complaint, Sister Carrie* and poetry by Allen Ginsburg. ZPG organized Earth Day but students really aren't into ecology yet.

Physical—Washington, D.C., area. See Catholic University for description.

College Park is suburbia. The area is a little quieter and more open than D.C. The campus is big and peaceful. The architecture is simple—buildings are square red brick three-story structures. Lots of grass gives the place a roomy look.

Students travel on the weekends to Ocean City or D.C.

MASSACHUSETTS

Amherst College
Amherst, Massachusetts

Some of the most sought-after cats in the East. Marlboro man appearance, clubby personality. And who do you know?

SERGEANT PEPPER SECTION:

1,245 students, 1,218 cats and 27 chicks. 1,055 out-of-state, 85 blacks, 10 Puerto Ricans, and a freshman from New Mexico who wears a serape and is considered an ethnic. Very difficult to enter. Only 18% of all applicants selected. The admissions committee loves sons of alumni. Average SATs are 667 verbal and 668 math. Very big on the well-rounded individual—lots of preppies.

ACADEMIC BULLSHIT:

Education is excellent, classes are small and the faculty is very distinguished. A complete curriculum of liberal arts is offered. Almost 100% go on to graduate school. Popular courses include all English courses by Marx ("he gets standing ovations"; "he'll talk to anyone, anytime about anything"), Political Science courses with Earl Latham ("his mind is a steel trap") and Economics with James Nelson. The English department's Leo Marx is often the liaison between the faculty and the students. Benjamin DeMott of the English department is a super cynic but the students are masochists and eat up his condescending manner. American Studies in the undergraduate department has an excellent multi-disciplinary approach.

Amherst cats aren't that excited over their courses as a rule and opt rather for dating and sports. The school is big on grades. Small classes and constant discussions. Black Studies is a department but for now is taught by all whites. Blacks think it sucks. The school is shooting for 10% blacks but so far is a WASP upper-middle-class school.

Professors and students are "close in proximity but not in social action." The professors are generally intellectual snobs. Independent study for juniors and seniors. You can take a year off with no credit for field study if it is approved.

BREAD:

Heavy. $3,800 a year including tuition, room and board. Fraternity costs run about $150 a year more. Two-thirds of the students live in dorms, one-third in frats. David Eisenhower lived in a well-guarded Northampton house. Only 20 people a year can live off campus.

Money is tight, but if you get in, they'll take care of you—loans and scholarships. More jobs than takers at $1.50 an hour. 15% of the people work. 35% of the students have cars. Inexpensive clothes worn but Brooks Brothers suits are stashed in the back of the closet.

Dates cost zero. The average date is going out with a Smith or Holyoke girl and drinking beer at a frat. "Why take a chick to a movie when you can go by yourself and enjoy it more."

BROTHERS AND SISTERS:

Ratio cats : chicks—45 : 1.

Cats are generally lukewarm hip and have that "Amherst cowboy" look complete with jeans, lumber jackets, work boots and moustaches. Modified Marlboro man, young cool he-men. Clubbish. Little educational discussion, more about who screwed who. Almost zero freaks except a few Darien, Connecticut, refugees.

Dating is the mode. Crappy pattern of game playing, name dropping, and screwing. It's hard for the Amherst male to overcome his country-club background and talk real talk to chicks. But Amherst men have the ideal social set up—surrounded by schools made up of all chicks (Smith and Holyoke).

Frats still exist and have parties and long weekends. Students are divorced from the political world. Apathy laced with lethargic action describes the political history of the last three years. In February, 1970, 250 blacks (some not from Amherst) took over four buildings for 12 hours at night. They demanded greater funding of the J College Coordination of Blacks (at Amherst, Smith, Mt. Holyoke, University of Massachusetts and Hampshire), more money for summer programs for black kids in Springfield, Massachusetts, a 5-College Black Studies Institute, and a summer program for blacks as college preparatory. Nothing much happened except that they got some expensive furniture for their lounge—not much support for the 1970 student strike.

Cats hang at "Log's Bar" in Amherst (half-assed freak types) and "The Pub" (post-graduate blazer types). Mixers at Smith and Holyoke. Average date is beer at the fraternity house, hopefully followed by instant Kharma and bed.

Not too many are into drugs but you can score on campus. $20 for a lid, $4 for mescaline.

SURVIVAL:

If you like the semi-intellectual prep-school chicks in the area—you're in. They all want Amherst males.

Student health is a bummer—the doctor thinks everyone is a hypochondriac. Draft counseling at the Valley Peace Center. No herds of pets. The paper, the *Amherst Student,* is liberal and used to dump on David Eisenhower a lot. No health-food stores.

ENVIRONMENT:

Mental—Cats are reading Hesse but "people don't talk about books, they talk about sex."

Physical—Amherst is a small rural New England brick town. Setting is rural, meadows and woods. Red brick, ivy-covered halls abound on the campus along with large wooded unfenced lawns, settled and relaxed looking. Frats have large gracious-looking mansions. "No one goes anywhere on the weekends, we stay here and hustle female counterparts." Smith and Holyoke girls can take classes at Amherst and vice versa.

Boston College
Boston, Massachusetts

A Catholic enclave in Boston.

SERGEANT PEPPER SECTION:

10,124 students of which 3,009 are grads. 30% out-of-state. 187 blacks, 8 Indians, 44 Chicanos.

You need fair to good grades, 1,000 SATs and good recommendations from high school.

ACADEMIC BULLSHIT:

The best undergraduate departments are English, Biology (especially molecular) and Math. The best graduate departments are also English and Biology.

Most popular courses include Richard Hughes' English courses, "General Endocrinology" by Solomon ("she is a dynamic person who knows her material well") and the "Art Workshop" by Macomber.

Some Pass/Fail, a little class participation, no student-originated courses, no Free U, and no ethnic studies (just a few black courses). Independent study after the sophomore year. Study abroad at the usual European hot spots.

BREAD:

$2,240 a year. Loans and scholarships are available but it's not Give-away Day. Some office jobs at about $1.60 an hour. Dorms cost $1,200 a year for room and board—about 25% of the people live in them. Girls' dormitories are old decrepit houses 20 minutes' walk from campus. Men's are on campus. Another fourth of the students live in superexpensive apartments. The rest commute. Lots of car pools and a few bikes.

BROTHERS AND SISTERS:

Ratio cats : chicks—2.5 : 1.

"Nice kids." Not an intellectual group or one that is suave— just nice kids. Chicks wear casual dresses and little make-up. Some dress in levis. They are pleasant but not too bright. Cats wear clean casual clothes and have that relaxed comfortable look. Very few freaks.

The school is 75% Catholic. There is dating but "the sex life here is pathetic. The good old Catholic hang-ups make *Portnoy's Complaint* look small-time." Chicks are gun-shy the first two years and "they put out grudgingly with enough hang-ups to wilt one's enthusiasm." Male undergrads are constantly "trick-or-treating—pranksters in the old frat style."

People hang at bars like "Fathers 1 & 2," Commonwealth Avenue, Cambridge, and go to flicks, concerts and plays. Not that much drug culture—lids go for $20 and are easy to get in Boston.

Students are aware but not active. The 1970 strike was looked upon by most as a holiday. Pigs have never been called in and there haven't been any busts.

SURVIVAL:

Chestnut Hill is only six miles from Boston and it is nearly as easy to survive in Boston as it is in Berkeley. Boston has Project Place which provides all the survival services.

Boston College has good facilities for film work.

Student health is O.K. but no BC pills or abortion referrals—"God wouldn't like it." *The Heights* is their weekly paper that is moderately leftist. It lost its funding in 1970 for being "too radical."

ENVIRONMENT:

Mental—People are reading *The Peter Principle* and *The Godfather*. The Boston College Ecology Committee is just getting started.

Physical—Suburb of Boston. Upper-middle-class area. Big houses and lawns in neighborhood. The older buildings on campus are large yellowish-gray stone Gothic structures. The main eyesore is Fulton, the Management building. It is described as "a neo-modern Sing-Sing."

Escapes include Florida, Bermuda, the Cape ("which is a god-awful mob-scene composed of frantic Massachusetts people and savage New York and New Jersey people slugging it out to relax").

Boston University

Boston, Massachusetts

A big social school.

SERGEANT PEPPER SECTION:

22,000 students of which 5,000 are grads. 80% are out-of-state. The admissions man had "no idea" about the percentage of minority students.

Fairly easy to get in. You need middle 500 SATs and fair-to-middlin' grades. Lots of transfers.

ACADEMIC BULLSHIT:

The training in classical instruments in the School of Fine Arts is outstanding. The undergraduate department of Political Science is good. The graduate schools of Social Welfare, Medicine and Law are very good.

Best courses include "American Foreign Policy" with Bottome, and Philosophy courses. Also Howard Zinn's courses in Political Science.

Interesting programs are the College of Basic Studies, a two-year program with team teaching for students who are slow starters, and the Division of General Education featuring team teaching for whiz kids.

Some Pass/Fail, little class participation. Some student-originated courses ("Women's Liberation" and "Revolution").

The Free U is called the "Communiversity"—courses like "Justice in America" and "The History of Revolutionary Poetry." There's an Afro-American Center but no major is offered as yet. Independent study is mostly for juniors and seniors. Study abroad.

BREAD:

$2,000 tuition a year. Loans and scholarships are tight. Campus jobs pay up to $2 an hour.

40% of the undergrads live in dorms. Chicks have to live in the first year. 45% live in apartments and cheap apartments are hard to find in Boston. It's impossible to scrounge in Boston—things are too expensive.

Lots of cars even though parking is limited and costs 50¢ a day. Cheap threads and entertainment are fine.

BROTHERS AND SISTERS:

Ratio cats : chicks—5 : 4.

There's a cross-section of everything. Hair is generally long and there are few freaks or Brooks Brothers suits types. Feeling of multiversity throngs. Mostly hip "SOCS" (they were in their heyday in the eary 60s when fraternities were king, but they were born too late and now must pretend to care about "relevant issues").

Lots of dating and sexual activity is on the rise. More and more chicks are getting liberated.

Fraternities exist off campus and are dying fast.

Local hangs include the Charles River, the Union, the "Dug-Out" (straight bar) and Harvard Square. There are lots of women in Boston—all over. BU males complain, however, that most chicks desire a Harvard or MIT male. But, fortunately for BU males, there aren't enough of those gems to go around.

Drugs are fairly light here, people are getting away from chemicals. You can score anywhere in Boston—grass is $20 a lid, acid and mescaline are $3 up.

Political action has been heavy in the last couple of years. In the fall of 1968, an AWOL G.I. was given sanctuary for a week until the FBI carted him off.

In 1969, there were SDS-sponsored demonstrations against General Electric—riots and arrests. The administration building was taken over for two days nonviolently.

Many students participated in the student strike in 1970. Their demands were to establish a black college, increase minority enrollment to 15% and end court injunctions against demonstrations. 75% of the students were out of classes for two days but not all were active.

SURVIVAL:

All survival services at Project Place in Boston. The School of Fine Arts has good facilities. Student health is adequate. The Draft Counseling Center is on Bay State Road. *The Boston University News* has turned out some good newsmen.

ENVIRONMENT:

Mental—People are reading *The Politics of Experience* and *Woodstock Nation*. Ecology Action files reports against polluters.

Physical—A big drab urban campus in downtown Boston—all the big-city ills. Buildings are Gothic cement. Newer buildings are large tasteless slabs.

Escapes include skiing, New York and home.

Brandeis University

Waltham, Massachusetts

Superintellectual heads, liberal politics, bagel bodies and Jewish ethnic personalities.

SERGEANT PEPPER SECTION:

2,800 students, of which 600 are grads. Two-thirds out-of-state. 10% blacks. Brandeis requires that applicants have 500ish SATs, and B average, but most have 675 SATs and are in the top 10% of their high-school graduating class. The admissions committee favors the "inner-directed self-starter."

ACADEMIC BULLSHIT:

Brandeis is a very intellectually-oriented high-pressure place. Best courses include "Theater Arts" by Halpern ("he excels at dealing with plays from a production standpoint"), "Social Psychology" from Gordon Fellman ("he's brilliant and has sex appeal"), "Shakespeare" by Leviton ("every lecture is a gem") and anything in the Near Eastern and Judaic Studies department (the best department of its kind in the U.S.). The Biology department has much impressive gadgetry and is a very fine department. The Sociology department is the most hip because it includes Gordon ("you can call him 'Gordy' ") Fellman who teaches civil disobedience in the classroom, and Neil Friedman who helped start the

1970 National Student Strike and suggested Brandeis as strike headquarters.

Some Pass/Fail (mostly pass) as grading is very permissive. *Very* generous in grading and lots of interacting with professors. Small classes. Student-originated classes which include "Ceramics," "Homosexuality in America," and "Witchcraft." Full credit. A very good Afro-American Studies program. Blacks have their own office, lounges and generally receive reverse-prejudice treatment.

Independent study for seniors and honor people. Junior year in Israel at the Hebrew University.

BREAD:

Heavy gelt. $2,650 a year tuition. A third of the students get financial aid. Loans are usually the deal. There are a few work-study jobs at $1.70 an hour. No way to work your way through Brandeis.

Dorms are $1,300 a year and most students live in them. Bad food and modern two-person cubicles. No coed dorms yet. Dorm rule #22 says, "Be discreet," and most are. Some live in apartments at $60 a head. 20% have cars and lots use public transportation. Dates are middle-priced at $2 for an on-campus play to $8 for a movie in Cambridge.

Dress is casual.

BROTHERS AND SISTERS:

Ratio cats : chicks—1 : 1.

The majority of Brandeis students are lukewarm hip and wear blue jeans, work shirts and boots. The nice Jewish boy becomes a nice Jewish hippie at Brandeis. Chicks are tidy-looking and natural. No suits and ties and no electric hair freaks. Moderation is the word.

The dating scene is prevalent, not as ritualistic as in the early 60s, though. "People are more head oriented than sex oriented." Chicks are Jewish-liberated. "The Jewish mother lurks behind the pretty coed!" Lots of propriety.

School politics are actively liberal. Dow demonstrations in 1967. In 1969 blacks took over Ford Hall for 11 days with 10 non-negotiable demands such as an Afro-American department, more blacks on campus and an Afro-American lounge.

In March, 1969, there was a sit-in to support the black demands, many of which were granted. President Abrams granted amnesty to black demonstrators. In 1969 an AWOL soldier took sanctuary and was protected by students until Christmas vacation when everyone left and he was arrested. In 1970, Brandeis became the National Strike Information headquarters. The Sociology department looks on strikes as field work.

Straights meet at Hillel (brack!!!) and hips through demonstrations. Local flicks in Gerstenzang Quad are popular. "Cholmondley's Coffee House" in the Castle on Friday and Saturday nights is cheap. Lots of musicians on and off campus.

Most have smoked and lids go for $20. Little mescaline and acid.

SURVIVAL:

The chosen people have always managed to survive and for those chosen who are intellectually oriented, it's a snap at Brandeis. Lots of head stimulation.

Student health is a bummer—aspirin for pneumonia. BC pills off campus. Some campus chaplains give abortion referrals.

Psych counseling is good. Rabbi Axelrad in the Bethlehem Student Chapel is great for draft counseling. Project Place, 37 Rutland, in Boston, provides all Help Switchboard services. The school newspaper is the *Justice*—a series of superintellectual editorials.

ENVIRONMENT:

Mental—People read Cleaver and Hesse and talk politics. There's a small non-militant group of ecologists who are in their formation stage.

Physical—Brandeis is in a suburb of Boston—typical eastern weather. Neighborhood is mildly rolling and woodsy. Campus is described as "a medieval castle, an American Jewish historical tomb." Pleasant light classrooms, though. The campus is only 23 years old. The Castle, a gingerbready medieval romance place, is a combination dorm and snack bar—storybook funky. Picturesque campus.

Escapes are New York City and Boston—these are urban people.

Emerson College
Boston, Massachusetts

Most students here are professionally oriented and see the school as vocational training rather than Kulture Kamp like the Ivy Leaguers.

SERGEANT PEPPER SECTION:

1,600 students of which 1,100 are out-of-state and 200 are grads. 7% minority. It takes a C+ average and 1,000 SATs to get in— not particularly selective. Transfers need a 2.5.

ACADEMIC BULLSHIT:

The best undergraduate departments are Speech Therapy and Mass Communications. Speech Therapy is rated second in the country—it has a good faculty, good training facilities and excellent programs. They operate their own Speech and Hearing Clinic. Mass Communication is so good that sophomores in the program work at WRKO (Boston rock AM station) and WNAC (TV station). Good place for future Walter Cronkites, script writers, reporters and all those mass-media types.

Education is also very interesting—students learn to do children's plays on the primary- and secondary-school levels and to use drama as therapy for disturbed children.

The Graduate School of Dramatic Arts is also good for would-be actors, directors or drama teachers.

Popular courses include "The Family" with Dr. Mosca ("it's a good basic course to refer to for the rest of your life"), "Western Civilization," with Coffee ("Great—he makes it come alive"), "Abnormal Psychology" with Corea ("Everybody at Emerson's a weirdo—this course helps you to understand them better").

Favorite professors include Bill Corbett in English ("He's a doer, not just a talker"), Walter Littlefield of the Speech department ("he's active in Massachusetts politics and is really liked") and Ken Crannell in Speech ("he's very talented and inspiring").

Not many Pass/Fail courses, student-originated courses, and no Free U or ethnic studies. Emerson people don't want relevance—they want jobs. Classes number about 30 and participation is very important. Students and professors have a lot of interaction—there are dinners together and even dating. Some independent study and study abroad.

BREAD:

Tuition is $1,000 a semester—$70 per credit for grads. Hardly any money available for loans and scholarships but there are lots of campus jobs and jobs in Boston. Most students live in apartments and the usual cost is about $100 per month per student. Most apartment buildings are old, gloomy crapholes well-stocked with New England's most gregarious cockroaches. Anything that's decent is sky-high. Freshman chicks have to live in dorms and the cost is $1,150 per year for room and board.

Transportation includes your feet and the MBTA (Massachusetts Bay Transit Association). Only a masochist would own and operate a car in Boston—driving is only slightly better than suicide.

Dates cost about $6 for a flick and coffee. Used books at the "Book Clearing House" on Boylston Street in Boston.

BROTHERS AND SISTERS:

Ratio cats : chicks—1 : 1.5.

Emerson people are into preparing for professional jobs so that they can take their place in society. There are two types—the collegiate straight (these cats dress in Sta-prest and drink beer) and the new hippy (who wears jeans, smokes dope and is aware). But all are basically middle-class in their ideals and aspirations. People hang around in groups. Sexual activity is good and generally friendly rather than overintellectual or serious. Girls aren't really liberated but aren't hung-up either.

Hangs are the Wall (the low stone wall next to the sidewalk on campus), "The Smoker" (campus snack bar) and "Ken's" (a Boylston Street delicatessen).

The drug scene is light—about one-third smoke. Not many

heavy drugs. Lids go for $20, acid and mescaline for between $2.50–$5.

The students are committeeish in their approach to politics. In the spring of 1968 the students boycotted classes in support of the dean of women who had been fired—they made ten demands—they got nine of them except for the reinstatement of the dean.

In 1969 there was another student walkout, this time in support of EBONI—the black students' group—nothing was decided. Emerson students are very businesslike. Sit-ins last from 9 to 5.

There was limited strike activity in 1970—lots of committees.

SURVIVAL:

Good chance just because it's Boston.

Students are into the creative arts—films, painting and photography (but at home). Student health is O.K. All the survival services are in Boston—especially at Project Place. No Women's Liberation as Emerson chicks are basically tuned in to American folkways.

ENVIRONMENT:

Mental—People are reading *The Godfather* and *Everything You Ever Wanted to Know about Sex.*

Physical—Boston weather is gloomy. The campus is in super-urban downtown. Tons of air pollution. Water pollution also The buildings are old brownstone townhouses—the campus is a facility rather than an environment.

Most people stay in Boston on the weekend because a lot is happening. Vacation favorites are Florida and Puerto Rico.

Hampshire College
Amherst, Massachusetts

This newest addition to the Amherst circle opened in 1970 and is alive and well. It has 251 freshmen and 17 seniors, and a 1 : 1 ratio between cats and chicks. 20 blacks. It's hard to get in and you need high grades and high SATs.

There are no grades. There are exams at the end of each year and Pass/Fail is the rule. Students originate and teach some classes and the faculty is very flexible.

The first two years consist of a group of seminars. The third year you develop an area of concentrated interest, and the fourth year you study one area. Bread for everything during the year is $3,800. No dorm rules. Lots of creative-arts facilities.

The campus is totally rural in setting—the administration building is an old farm house.

Hampshire people can take classes at the University of Massachusetts, Smith, Amherst and Mt. Holyoke.

Harvard University and Radcliffe College
Cambridge, Massachusetts

Go—so you can say you went there. Many superintellects who play mental cut-throat games.

SERGEANT PEPPER SECTION:

15,364 students of which 9,350 are graduates. 80% out-of-state. About 400 undergraduate blacks. As to getting in—just be the best and you may have a chance. These schools don't only want top grades and 700ish board scores—they want interesting extracurricular activities too—the cream of the crop. At Radcliffe, it helps if your mother went. Almost zero transfers.

ACADEMIC BULLSHIT:

Harvard has the best graduate departments in the nation in many fields—Law, Medicine, Geology, Comparative Literature and Economics. Business and City Planning are outrageously good. Harvard can afford to buy the best faculty around. And professors insist that the school's quality is due to the students rather than the faculty—which is cool. All the above-mentioned graduate departments also have cool undergraduate departments as do Math and Science. All the leading institutions of capitalism recruit first at Harvard.

The Social Relations department is very wide-ranging—it includes Anthropology, Psychology, Economics and Criminology in its curriculum. The Economics department has a food solid faculty and is quantitatively oriented—45% of its grads go to business school, 45% to law school.

Favorite courses include "Principles of Economics" with Eckstein ("he's generally interesting" which, coming from these students, is a rave review), "The Modern Industrial Society" with John Kenneth Galbraith (we all know Galbraith. right? If you've read *The New Industrial State* you've done the course. But come to the lectures and you'll learn a lot about government and the corporate mind from an insider. "He is the most fascinating, clear-minded person here!" His lectures draw about 400 people), "The Human Life Cycle" with Erikson (studies famous individuals [Martin Luther King] and you write a life history including their psychological twists and turn-ons and -offs. This course is so popular that only seniors usually get in).

Popular professors include Galbraith, Edwin Reischauer (Far-Eastern Studies—ex-ambassador to Japan), Hilary Putnam ("an intellectual radical") and Elliott Forbes (conductor of the Glee Club and Choral Society).

Some professors are radically oriented but as a whole, teaching fellows are the radicals of the community.

Lectures are big but tutorials and discussion sections are small. "The problem here is that everyone is so capable, you are afraid to speak out." Inferiority complexes are rampant. The Afro-

American Studies department so far is a whitey shuck. Few student-originated courses but lots of independent study. There's a Free U that's held in different dorms and run by teaching fellows and students—it offers "Revolution," "Astrology"—kind of an in-crowd affair. Harvard has the money to buy minority students and it does heavy recruiting. Not much of a study-abroad program—once you get in here, they expect you to stay. Professors and students are generally close on the graduate level. Many professors date Cliffies.

BREAD:

Tuition is $2,600. Loans and scholarships are very available. The school is so loaded that a month's interest on their endowment would be a small fortune. Lots of jobs at $2 an hour. Dorms cost $1,300 a year and almost all undergraduates live in them. Frosh cats are in large dorms—frosh Cliffies in "hell holes." Dorms have open rules. 40% of the dormies live in new coed dorms.

Harvard sophomores usually move into houses that are socially oriented and closely knit. Juniors and seniors get single rooms in the houses—there are ten houses that rent for $360 per house.

Apartments are more grad-student territory and incredibly difficult to find and pay for. Rents are $260 and up for a two-bedroom unfurnished place. Only a fool has a car here. You walk, ride a bike or take the MTA.

Dates aren't expensive and the Harvard Bookstore has used books.

BROTHERS AND SISTERS:

Ratio cats : chicks—5 : 1.

Bright, interested, aware, slightly snobbish people. Cats are mixed—preppies, athletes and hip overachievers. The Cliffies are usually natural-looking and attractive—to refute the old theory that they are ungainly and ugly. Cliffies date Harvard students and professors and many times marry them. "Radcliffe girls are so busy seeing how they are growing that they are neurotic—they introspect too much for their own good." Undergrads don't work that hard as the administration protects them. Graduate school is often a rude shock.

Cliffies wear blue jeans, no makeup and few bras. Cats are slightly more uptight—wear neat shirts and slacks and have fashionably long hair. Harvard graduates are known to be slightly cloddish—all that brilliance doesn't necessarily beget grace.

Chicks are liberated and there is lots of sexual activity. Dating is very informal—includes coffee and a flick. Harvard cats date lots of Cliffies and some Wellesley people and lesser locals. The biggest hang is Harvard Square. How to get a date? "Be cool and pretend you don't give a shit." Entertainment abounds in Boston.

Boston is the clearing-house for drugs in the area. You can get anything you want. Grass and acid are popular. Lids go for $20, acid and mescaline $2.50–$5. Score through friends.

No fraternities, a few clubs, but they are dying.

Harvard and Radcliffe are both what Tricky Dick refers to as "radical hotbeds" but many claim Cliffies are actually much more intellectually radical than Harvard men. SDS is fairly big and has 100 Cliffies in it. They will actually throw things and riot. They took over University Hall in 1969 demanding a raise in workers' wages, an Afro-American department and an end to Harvard's role as slum lord. PLP has fewer people than the old SDS umbrella but it is more violent. In the fall, 1969, they disrupted a Center for International Affairs meeting and threw people down stairs.

The Moratoriums drew peaceful marchers. There was a lot of activity during the 1970 strike—rapping, picketing, leafletting and canvassing. Classes were suspended and Pass/Fail was available. Many activities extended through the summer.

The thing to remember about getting busted at Harvard is—it's less dangerous than at Berkeley. After all, a pig might be breaking open the head of a famous windbag's son and this could bring down a lot of shit. Pigs are still rough, but not as rough as at a people's college. They aren't called in that much.

SURVIVAL:

Easy in Boston.

Creative arts are very popular, especially drama and the choral society. "Stillman Infirmary is a real horror story." No BC pills. Many anti-draft groups in Boston do excellent draft counseling. Project Place has survival services.

The Harvard Crimson is a liberal, witty paper.

Political grandstand observers.

Health-food stores in Central Square.

Women's Liberation hasn't had much impact. "There's a conflict between being the hated stereotype female and fighting it and therefore possibly losing a chance to find a man."

ENVIRONMENT:

Mental—Stimulating. People are reading all kinds of esoteric things and *The Electric Kool-Aid Acid Test*. Ecology groups in Boston are really happening.

Physical—Boston weather. Plenty of air and noise pollution.

Nice old buildings on campus. Old red brick neo-classical dorms at Radcliffe, nice red brick super-mansion dorms at Harvard except for the grad dorms which are yellow cubicle-sized aborts. Harvard houses are neo-Georgian efforts. The eyesore is William James Hall, a gray-white skyscraper slab. The administration building, Holyoke Center, is a huge maze where you can get shuffled around all day if you make the mistake of asking a question.

Escapes include sleep, dope and sex.

Vacations include skiing, the Cape and home.

Winter is super-gloomy—hibernation is in.

Massachusetts Institute of Technology
Cambridge, Massachusetts

Tech men wear gray pants and red socks and act like Giles' Goat Boy.

SERGEANT PEPPER SECTION:

3,891 students. Most from out of state. 90 blacks. One important qualification—you must have 790+ in Math SAT scores. That's right, 790+ in Math and 680+ Verbal. Decisions are made quantitatively (of course). Grades, personality and tests are put on a grid and if the grid shows an 85% chance of your getting a 3.5 average your freshman year, you get in.

ACADEMIC BULLSHIT:

At MIT they have a humanities requirement. The foremost scientific institution in the United States. Dr. Strangelove types may apply.

The most popular course is "Introduction to Automatic Computation" which teaches basic computer programming, a must around MIT. An experimental offshoot of the course describes itself as a "direct communication between students and a large-scale digital computer." Then there's "Electrical Engineering," "Physics," "Math," "Nuclear Engineering," "Metallurgy" (welding) and "Psychology"—all of which are excellent.

The general comment about classes is that "the people who teach here know what they're talking about, but aren't good teachers"—apparently they are victims of quantitative, nonverbal professional lives. Naturally people identify their major by numbers —"My major is 9."

Popular professors include Noam Chomsky in linguistics, Louis Kampf, Chomsky's disciple, and Jerry Lettvin of the Biology department. Chomsky and Kampf sympathize with the radical left.

The "Management Program" is similar to business administration but designed for institutional and governmental work as well as private business. They emphasize the quantitative approach to management.

The Nuclear Engineering department is the finest—NASA recruits like mad.

Academically excellent but very difficult. All frosh take all courses Pass/Fail. Less than 10% of the classes have finals. Not much interaction between undergraduates and professors, more among grads and professors. If a group can interest a professor in teaching something, it's taught as a "special topic" with full credit. No Free U as no one has time to learn outside of MIT. No active recruiting for minorities as MIT doesn't give a damn about color. If a small green being fit the admission grid, he'd get in and have his hands full studying.

Lots of independent study.

BREAD:

. $2,500 tuition. If you need money, you get it—although it depends on your grades after your freshman year—quantitative again. Campus jobs at $1.75 an hour. One enterprising trio put pinball machines on campus (including a Computer Quiz Machine) and are cleaning up.

Dorms cost $1,080 a year (no weekend meals) and about one-third of the students live in them. Frats are better living than the dorms and cost $1,270 a year. Apartments are super-expensive in the nearby area and cost $80 apiece. There's one coed dorm but only 30 people are in it. In the women's dorms, if the girl you know gives you a special button you can get past the desk and go upstairs, rather than doing it in the road. "Old Sid lived there a month and a half"—he had a button.

25% have cars. Inexpensive clothes put on in an absent-minded fashion. Nonverbal dates popular—especially flicks. $5–$10 dates usually consist of flicks, snack, and "maybe breakfast." MIT eggheads date BU and Simmons girls.

BROTHERS AND SISTERS:

Ratio cats chicks—15 1.

Scientific types—absent-minded, red socks and gray pants, wrinkled cotton shirts, some sideburns. No spiffy dressers or freaks. "Most hardly ever fuck and seldom date." Chicks are very very ugly.

Frats exist and are composed of 29 houses with about 1,200 undergrads. They have stayed strong because of the tight housing situation. No real hangs—fixups are big. "Most freshmen have never had a date in their life." Grass is getting very popular and it's very easy to get at $20 a lid.

The main political club is the Rosa Luxembourg SDS which screams a lot and makes demands. Mildly hip demonstrations. In November of 1969, "The November Action' people from the Boston area came to MIT to protest war research. In May, the student strike came to MIT—they canvassed. The faculty canceled a week's classes and after May 4 anyone could take Pass/Fail or grades.

SURVIVAL:

Good chance if you're a computer.

Photography is big and most dorms have great darkrooms. Chicks can get BC pills at student health which is pretty all-round competent. The Undergraduate Selective Service advisor is in the main building. AFS committee in Boston Project Place in Boston takes care of all survival services Three free trips to the campus shrink, then referrals—lots of people go. Last year (1969–70) there were reputed to be 18 suicides at MIT. Tense. The school newspaper, *The Tech,* lambasts war research.

ENVIRONMENT:

Mental—People are using slide rules and reading *The Peter Principle,* and *Everything You Wanted to Know About Sex* Topic: The War.

Physical—MIT is in a run-down urban section of Cambridge next to the polluted Charles River. Weather stinks and buildings are gloomy and depressing. Lawns are flat and classrooms are monumentally ugly. The student center looks like a German fortress. Little travel except home on vacations.

University of Massachusetts
Amherst Massachusetts

Politically it's a hotbed of apathy.

SERGEANT PEPPER SECTION:

18,865 students of which 3,779 are grads. 5% are from out-of-state, 535 blacks. In-staters need a B-ish average and SATs of 1,000. Out-of-state people need better grades and scores and lots of luck. Many in-state transfers.

ACADEMIC BULLSHIT:

If you've been rejected from Ivy League schools and want that kind of an education, the U of Massachusetts is a good choice. Chemistry is the best undergraduate department—Math, Psychology and English are also excellent. Music is good, too—not many majors but a very good staff that gives intensive instruction. You can also major in Education here.

Best courses include "Criminology" with Stanfield ("you learn about the rotten court system"), "The History of Film" ("it's the most interesting"), and "Abnormal Psychology" with Harmatz ("he brings in his personal experiences as well as really interesting material"). Howard Gradlin of the Psychology department and John Nelson in the English department are very popular with students for their political views.

The best graduate department is Chemical Engineering (within the Engineering department). The Astronomy and Physics departments offer good training in radio astronomy.

Some Pass/Fail, lots of tests, big classes and some student-originated courses. A few black studies courses and no Free U. Seniors with a B average and approval by their advisor can take independent study.

BREAD:

Tuition in-state is $100 a semester, $200 out-of-state. Financial aid is super-tight; the legislature doesn't want to spend too much money on troublesome students. Jobs at $1.40 an hour are hard to get.

One-half of the students live in dorms that cost about $1,000 a year for room and board. One complex, the Southwest Residential College, has 7,000 people in a high-rise (22 floors) and low-rise (six floors) dorms. Many of these are triples. Several dorms are coed, not many rules. Apartments run $60 per person per month and you have to be 20 or have parents' permission and the University's O.K. to live in them. There are 18 fraternities and 13 sororities and 1,000 people live in them. They cost about $1,300 a year.

A minority have cars, and the majority thumb.

BROTHERS AND SISTERS:

Ratio cats : chicks—1.5 : 1.

These students are rather dull middle-class conservatives and Boston's suburbia hips. People are socially and politically fairly conservative compared to other schools in the area—drag-ass types. Few freaks and few dress-ups. Compared to Berkeley most people put you to sleep. Dating is the thing—little living together and not too many chicks are liberated or concerned about it. Beer and parties or flicks are the average dates. The fraternities are dying.

People hang at "The Drake," "Log's" (freaks—a grungy downer place) and "Mike's" (frat types)—all in Amherst. A light drug scene here—mainly grass—score on campus for $20 a lid and $2.50 for mescaline.

Politically the school is a "hotbed of apathy." No demonstrations or support for anything is the rule. The only exceptions so far were in 1969 when blacks marched on the administration building with the usual demands (no results), and in 1970 when they took over the Mills House dorm. It is now a black dorm and cultural center.

The strike "went strong for maybe 3 days and as soon as people found out they could take Pass/Fail, they split."

SURVIVAL:

The best offering in the Creative Arts department is the ceramics studio. Student health is good, some doctors give BC pills. Shrinks are poor. Draft counseling is good at the Valley Peace Center in Northampton. There's a HELP Switchboard in the South College building 24 hours a day. *The Collegian* is a daily—good editorials. The underground paper is the *Carbunkle Review*—the usual rhetoric.

ENVIRONMENT:

Mental—People read best sellers. The Ecology Group doesn't do much.

Physical.—Amherst is a small town in a rather rural setting. As you drive into town from a woodsy area, you see Amherst first, a small red brick colonial place, and then, wham-o, there it is—a modern planned city with modern concrete slabs and huge flat sterile areas in-between them—that's the U .f Massachusetts.

There are a few 1870–1900 dull buildings still around, but they seem ashamed to be still hanging around. Most people go home for vacations

Mt. Holyoke College
South Hadley, Massachusetts

Amherst says "Smith to bed, Holyoke to wed."

SERGEANT PEPPER SECTION:

1,800 females of which 50 are grads. 16 exchange men. 83% out-of-state. 87 blacks. Black students got 38% of the 1970 freshman budget. Hard to get in, must show "serious academic interest." 90% of the applicants are interviewed. Most are within the top 10% of their high-school class. Average combined SATs are 1,300. They will allow qualified transfers.

ACADEMIC BULLSHIT:

All the liberal arts departments are excellent. But the chicks complain that "there are very few enjoyable courses and it takes a lot to get innovations through."

Students do like Leonard Delonga's Art classes. "He is an artist and is beautiful to listen to. He teaches you to feel your subject, to try to get its essence." People come from Smith and Amherst to take his classes. Jean Grossholtz's Political Science courses are popular ("She's a very dynamic person—she organized teach-ins for the strike") and Larry Flood's Political Science courses are also popular.

The Theater Arts and Speech classes are personal and good—especially those taught by Cavanaugh. Not much Pass/Fail, and not much class participation (it's supposed to be there but doesn't happen much). 20 is the average size for a class.

No student-originated classes, no Free U, and no student push for either. There's an interdepartmental major in Ethnic Studies but it's a shuck—honky racist imperialist jive-ass mother-fucker.

Sophomores can take independent study. Study abroad.

BREAD:

Tuition is $2,200, room and board is $1,350. Tight financial scene, and available mostly for minority students. Jobs at $1.50 an hour are easy to get if you're needy. Everyone lives in the large brick mansionlike dorms. Cars and hitching serve for transportation. Bicycles are big for local spooning.

SISTERS:

Holyoke chicks are the children of suburban eastern parents. Dress is casual, blue jeanish, work shirts, bras. Chicks aren't as good-looking as those at Smith and Wellesley. Lukewarm hip with a fringe of straights "We are middle-class girls. We'd like to be freaky but we won't try it. We'd like to leave college, but we won't do it." Typical neurotic college girls with typical good manners and typical concern for the underprivileged that stops where the action begins. The followers of tomorrow who will be good wives and mothers and send their daughters to Holyoke.

They date guys from the Connecticut River Valley cluster of colleges—Hampshire College, Amherst and the University of Massachusetts. Dates are casual, flicks and a burger. Girls go away on weekends and do it up with Fred Yale or Irving Dartmouth. A telling saying at Amherst, "Smith to bed, Holyoke to wed." Holyoke chicks are serious about who is qualified breeding-and intentionwise to sleep with them. "By the time you get a piece, it hardly seems worth it." Light drug use, grass at $15 a lid.

"The Monarch" is a roadside bar in S. Hadley that's a hang. But people meet mostly on fixups and blind dates.

No political action as "it's more important to find a man." Some strike activity, leafletting and teach-ins during the student strike. "There were also Peace Vigils in 1968 in South Hadley but these unfortunately did not bring peace in our time."

SURVIVAL:

Students aren't into creative arts—it's not an artsy-craftsy sort of place. Theater is good. Student health is bad and one doctor always describes your problems as "you're pregnant." No BC pills. Survival services in Boston. No Women's Liberation on campus. Girls are locked into wife-and-mother game preceded by serious-girl-friend-and-fiancée game. Graack!

ENVIRONMENT:

Mental—People are reading *The Making of a Counter-Culture* and D. H. Lawrence's *Women in Love*. Topic of conversation is the hope of totally eliminating dorm hours. Ecology people made a sign on Earth Day.

Physical—Hilly meadow and forest rural area. Boston weather. Campus buildings are out of *Pride and Prejudice*. 19th century American Gothic, huge red stone blocks with gray trim. Large, expansive lush lawns—the college has 800 acres of land, most of it unfucked by buildings.

Escapes are mostly other schools on the weekend. All live-ins.

Northeastern University

Boston, Massachusetts

Concrete environment.

SERGEANT PEPPER SECTION:

13,730 students full time. 20,785 part-time people. Not hard to get in. You need B grades and about 1,000 SATs There are a lot of transfers from junior colleges.

ACADEMIC BULLSHIT:

No departments are particularly outstanding. Math, Sciences and Engineering are O.K.

Students disagreed violently as to which courses were best, no consensus.

Not much opportunity for Pass/Fail. Class participation isn't happening Some student-originated courses—"Racism." Afro-American studies offers a major. Lots of recruitment of blacks. Not much independent study, "everything is too structured " Study abroad.

BREAD:

Freshmen pay $500 a quarter (they go three quarters). Sophomores and up pay $800 a quarter (they can only go two quarters a year). Financial aid is available. Sophomore year up, you study a quarter, work a quarter. The school helps you find jobs.

About 50% are commuters, the rest live in dorms, apartments and fraternities. Dorms are $432 a quarter for room and board and hard to get into. Guys' dorms are old and run-down, girls' dorms are modern. Apartments are about $70 a month.

The campus is in the heart of Boston—most people use public transportation. Most students are middle-class and lower-middle-class and don't have costly threads.

BROTHERS AND SISTERS:

Ratio cats : chicks—2.5 : 1.

Every type of city dweller. Full range of hair from ex-Marines to freaks. Clothes are casual and functional.

Dating is straight arrow—night people are heavily married. Chicks aren't really liberated and are husband hunting. About 16 fraternities still exist, but they aren't important.

People hang in the campus snack bar—not a hang-out campus. All types of city entertainment in Boston. All drugs are available, lids for $20.

It's a diploma mill. People don't care about politics. There was a little bit of action for the strike.

SURVIVAL:

Students aren't into creative arts

Survival services available from Project Place in Boston.

The Northeastern News is for shit.

ENVIRONMENT:

Mental—People are reading *The Godfather* and talking about the War.

Physical—Urban downtown Boston. Plenty of air and noise pollution. All campus buildings are grayish-white high-rise types, efficient sterile containers with no lawns to alleviate what looks like a hospital complex.

Zero travel on the weekend.

Smith College
Northampton, Massachusetts

Planned feminine opulence. Debutante country-club atmosphere. Girls are refined, athletic and Pollyannaish. Their major interest is apprehending a man.

SERGEANT PEPPER SECTION:

2,650 students·of which 137 are grads. All chicks. 86% out-of-state, 76 blacks and 3 Puerto Ricans.

Very difficult to get into this sister school. The total record is important and 1,400 boards and very high grades are the average. Socially-oriented girls (deb society types) are the usual.

ACADEMIC BULLSHIT:

The academic environment is excellent. The chicks like the Art, Political Science and Economics departments best. Favorite courses include "Introduction to the History of Art," with Helen Searing, "Introduction to Political Science" with Weinstein. Sockrey's Economics courses and "Horticulture" by Campbell (a ladies' gardening course for those who plan to recreate Versailles in Darien, Connecticut). Other popular professors include Phillip Green and Donald Robinson who are politicos and Kathy Portugues who is leading the Women's Liberation at Smith. The best graduate department is the Education of the Deaf program.

Smith chicks have a good opportunity to learn but they care more about their social life, or lack of it, than their courses. Classes are small and the chicks do yak a lot, but it's mostly b.s. A few black studies classes. Very close relationship between students and teachers, but there is a dating taboo. Some independent study. Study abroad in France, Germany, Italy, Spain and Geneva. All are junior-year programs.

BREAD:

Smith runs about $3,455 a year and that's heavy bread. But if you get in, help is available in scholarship aid and small loans. Plenty of jobs at about $1.60 an hour. All chicks must live on campus at $1,375 a year for the dorms which look like red brick mansions. Men can stay in the dorms for three days if they are civil and the house mother likes them. About 15% have cars, lots of locked bikes. Chicks dress casual on campus but have expensive wardrobes in their closets.

SISTERS:

The girls at Smith don't like being called chicks. Most are private-school deb-trained types. They are polite, soft-spoken and athletic. Not intellectually oriented like their Radcliffe sisters, the most important thing is getting a man. They dress lukewarm hip, blue jeans and inexpensive casual dresses. About 20% go in for

242

the Lord-and-Taylor-Voguish look. Hair is long and neat, few blonds and redheads. "Everyone knits and plays the piano." Small talk and smiles. They seek Amherst and Yale men on the weekends. No living together in the down-home Berkeley way. Hot long weekends and cold weeks. Most girls are up for sex if they can meet someone they like. Mixers are the rule ("and like oil and water—ghastly").

The college is apolitical. A little action for the student strike in May, 1970, but that's it. Committee-oriented.

Smithies don't hang-out anywhere. "That's vulgar."

About 50% use grass regularly. It's scored through friends at Amherst. Busts are rare. Lids go for $25, acid for $5. The girls feel mildly "naughty" about smoking dope.

SURVIVAL:

Most girls who apply to Smith and get in like it. The atmosphere is isolated and calm. The sheltered girls' school bit.

No BC pills at student health but available in town. Physical and mental help at student health is very good. Great listening room in Josten Library. No pets. *The Sophian* is the campus paper —genteel and liberal. Women's Liberation has about 50 members, but most Smithies don't want to be liberated—their rendezvous with destiny is at the country club.

ENVIRONMENT:

Mental—The girls are reading radical stuff—*Seize the Time* mostly. Some ecology action through D.I.E. (Drift into Eco-Action). They return bottles.

Physical—Northampton is a red brick, rural New England small town. Environs are rolling meadows, woodsy areas, and romantic 19th century landscape. Thoreau would have liked it. Some air pollution. Buildings are a series of mansions connected by large open lands. Paradise Pond is fit for 1840s picknickers. Rowboats and stables. Very plush. Students fly home for vacation.

Tufts University and Jackson College
Medford, Massachusetts

A coed college in the Boston area. The schools are separate only administratively.

SERGEANT PEPPER SECTION:

6,000 students. 76% out-of-state, 7% minorities (mostly black). Fairly difficult to get in but the admissions department makes decisions based on individuals rather than on class rank. Average SATs are 1,300. Most students are from suburban high schools and in the top 10% of their class. Qualified transfers are welcome.

ACADEMIC BULLSHIT:

Best undergraduate and graduate departments are English, Biology, European History. The Fletcher School of Law and Diplomacy—a school for international law and foreign-service type preparation—is of outstanding quality. It has ties with Harvard.

Dr. Richie of the Drama department is flamboyant and really popular with the students. His courses pack them in since Tufts students are quiet and vicariously dig his enthusiasm. Take Mulholland for "Revolution Since 1815"—he's young and cool. Mark Seiden of the English department enjoys students so much that they occasionally live in his house. Students also dig Lee Elioseff of the English department.

Some Pass/Fail, not much class participation. Typical class has about 30 people. A Free U called Experimental College with far-out courses like "Hatha Yoga for the West," "Chemistry for the Curious," for credit. Some independent study and study abroad.

BREAD:

$2,300 tuition per year. They buy talent and give scholarships to especially bright students or minority students. Campus jobs at $1.60–$1.90 an hour.

About two-thirds of the students live in the dorms at $1,110 a year for room and board. Large unstructured dorms. Apartments tend to be $60 a month per person—upperclassmen mainly. A few fraternities—no communes. About one-third have cars. Inexpensive wardrobes and cheap dates.

BROTHERS AND SISTERS:

Ratio cats : chicks—5 : 1.

Tufts people are friendly and open. Very few fancy clothes or freaks. Blue jeans, casual shirts, long straight brown hair on most chicks. Cats have moderately long hair and are neat. Suburban types, don't blow their noses on their sleeves. Courteous liberals. A relaxed dating pattern. A few live together; the freshmen are the hippest and were weaned on the pill.

Fraternities are dying.

Everyone hangs on campus—"like high school—it's close-knit." Entertainment is flicks and parties.

Some grass, nothing heavy and no blown minds.

The politics of apathy. SDS is small and nonviolent. Tufts did the "typical moderate stunt" in response to the historic student strike of 1970. Classes curtailed but not stopped. Discussions, canvassing.

SURVIVAL:

Easy as long as you're not too political. Hang loose. No artsy-craftsy types, unfortunately. The infirmary is solicitous but lacking. Some BC pills given.

Boston is next door for survival services—Project Place.

The campus mascot is an elephant named Jumbo " 'Why not Dumbo?' I asked, and got a cold stare.")

The campus newspaper is *The Observer* (an appropriate description of a Tufts undergrad). Not much interest in health foods. No Women's Liberation.

ENVIRONMENT:

Mental—People are talking about courses, student power and are reading R. D. Laing's *Politics of Experience* and *Portnoy's Complaint*.

Physical—Urban setting. The school is open and hilly. Much air pollution—all the fixtures of gracious urban living. Traditional New England campus, colonial red brick ivy-covered buildings. Grounds immaculately maintained by pixies—people eat their trash. The University Library is an architectural triumph—medieval modern horizontal concrete structure.

Little weekend travel. 5% commuters.

Wellesley College
Wellesley, Massachusetts

Refined minds in a luxurious setting.

SERGEANT PEPPER SECTION:

1,750 students. New England students comprise 24% of the campus. 120 blacks, 3 Mexican-Americans and a couple of Indians.

Very difficult to get in—SATs of 1,300 and high grades. For minority students, the potential and ability to grow academically are considered. One of the only schools that recruits Southwest Indians and gets them to come.

ACADEMIC BULLSHIT:

Wellesley offers us fine liberal arts education. Best departments are Anatomy (history rather than studio), English and Economics. Favorite courses include "Introduction to the Literature of Music" (with Mr. Herrman)—it's a good course on history and theory of music, "Painting and Sculpture of the 19th Century" (with Mrs. Janis who forgets the class is there when she sees a slide— she really digs her subject), "Astronomy" with Birney and Hill (good telescopes and night labs), "Modern Poetry" (Miss Craig), "Modern Drama" (take Garis if you like Ibsen) and "Political Science" with Mr. Sederberg (he was active during the strike).

Very few graduate students. There is cross-registration with MIT. Wellesley girls can take classes there and vice versa, but not many do.

Some Pass/Fail, casual class participation, small classes and no student-originated courses or Free U. Afro-American Studies exists as an interdepartmental major and is not very structured.

Close relationships between professors and students when you get to your major. Some dating. Independent study is reserved for upperclassmen—you can take two or three courses a semester. Lots of study abroad.

BREAD:

Heavy bread. $3,400 for tuition and room and board (there are payment plans but most can afford to pay all at once).

If you have financial need, you can get aid, there is almost always a higher percentage scholarship than loan. Jobs are easy to get if you're on scholarship. In 1969, over one-third of total student earning came from babysitting at 75¢ an hour. Otherwise library, department work, lab clean-up and waitressing pay a fat $1.50 an hour.

1,650 students lived in dorms and 100 juniors and seniors lived off campus in 1970. The dorm supervisors "overlook everything—men, grass, booze." All the freaks live in Tower Court and Stone and Davis have the best food. Apartments are expensive in the neighborhood.

30% have wheels, the rest have bikes or hitchhike.

SISTERS:

The sisters can take classes at MIT to meet guys but they usually consider themselves far superior to MIT cats—they prefer Harvard and Yale men.

Wellesley girls are "well-bred"—many are Junior League types. "It takes the first half of your freshman year before you can bring yourself to pick up chicken with your hands."

They are just getting to be lukewarm hip and wear work clothes, no makeup and have long straight hair. Wellesley chicks are more intellectual and politically aware than Wheaton, Holyoke or Smith girls but not quite up to their sisters at Radcliffe. Many Wellesley coeds had Wellesley mothers making for a lot of stuffiness.

Lots of dating with Ivy League men—some chicks are so brave that they pay fees at Wellesley and live with their boy friends in Cambridge (not many). The girls on the whole aren't liberated and they blame it on school restrictions ("the situation works against the development of independence"). Dates include flicks and parties in Cambridge, dinner near Wellesley, or just rapping. There are two extremes here—the "never been kissed" and the continual baller, but in either case they really don't talk about it—it's "private."

People hang at "The Well" in Alumnae Hall (a snack bar), the library, the "coffee mixers" (on either Saturday or Sunday night—come meet the man of your dreams) and Cambridge.

The chicks are liberal but apathetic, and too scared to participate in politics. Sad but true—YAF is relatively active and holds picnics. The Young Republicans hold meetings with Harvard Law people to help Massachusetts candidates. But most chicks are liberal. They did a little canvassing during the Moratoriums and a few got worked up enough to go to Washington during the strike. Genteel politics, all in all.

Some smoke—others drop acid but grass is the most popular. Grass users add up to about one-third of the Wellesley chicks.

SURVIVAL:

There are a lot of creative people here—girls are into music and writing. For photography enthusiasts, MIT has one of the most outstanding Photography departments in the nation. There's a good listening room in Jewett Art Center and they have an excellent classical record collection. Student health is described as "just O.K." —no BC pills and shrinks are lousy. All other survival services can be obtained from Project Place in Boston. The *Wellesley Weekly* is sort of "bleh." Women's Liberation was born and died here in 1970.

ENVIRONMENT:

Mental—People are reading Vonnegut and Hesse. The ecology group is under the auspices of the Outing Club which held Earth Day activities.

Physical—Boston weather. The campus is in a woodsy suburban area, gorgeous tranquil forests and plush homes nearby. 19th century medieval architecture, red brick with gray stone trim—looks romantic. Lawns are lush. There's an idyllic little lake (Lake Wahan) that's still swimable and most buildings look like castles. Wellesley, all in all, is a super country estate—one of the most beautiful campuses anywhere.

Escapes include home, the Bahamas and men's schools on the weekends.

Wheaton College
Norton, Massachusetts

Wheaties like their academic environment but deplore the absence of men. 43% of the 1970 class were preppies.

SERGEANT PEPPER SECTION:

1,191 women with a trace of exchange men. 887 out-of-state, 19 blacks, all undergraduates.

Difficult to get in. High grades and combined SATs of 1,200. They also look for extracurricular activities. The interview with prospective applicants is very important.

ACADEMIC BULLSHIT:

A small personalized stimul.ting academic environment. The best departments are Art, History and English.

Take "Hispanic Literature in Translation" with Mr. Ruiz ("he has a terrific grasp of art, philosophy and literature as background stuff and he discusses dreams and magic as they relate to the reading—a total experience"). "Introduction to Art History" (some field study in Boston), "The American Political System" with Goodman, and "Politics and American Literature" with Pearce. Richard Pearce is a very popular professor. He ran workshops during the strike. Other popular and active professors are Ed Greer ("Urban Studies" and he's young and single) and Peter Stangle ("Economics").

Wheaton has very good facilities for science studies and for experimental psychology.

Classes average about 30 and there is a lot of interaction between students and professors. Some Pass/Fail and some student-originated classes (as to topic). A few courses on ethnic studies. Independent study for seniors.

Study abroad for the junior year though "it's not encouraged because people never come back. They prefer to be alive and well in Switzerland rather than Norton, Massachusetts."

BREAD:

$3,650 for tuition, fees and room and board per year. Students have to live in dorms. But they are loose—no house mothers (occasional sin in the dorms). The dorm food is excellent—100% superb. Tight money—not much financial aid although some is possible. Some campus jobs at $1.40 an hour—outrageous wages. No scrounging—after all you have to kick in $3,650—the rest is peanuts. Lots of cars and nice party clothes hidden away in the closet.

SISTERS:

These are girls, not chicks. The majority are lukewarm hip—work clothes, cut-offs, no makeup—"well-groomed suburban-background types that don't stir their coffee with their fingers in public."

The main problem is lack of men. Lots of knitting goes on. The Wheaties have to export themselves to Boston or New Haven for weekends. Weekend dates include flicks, plays or concerts. Sex —Wheaties have heard of it and estimate that half of them indulge. No living together like down-home Berkeley. Sex is confined to Friday and Saturday nights. People meet at mixers and fixups.

Politically, there's "very little demanding" at Wheaton. During the strike, classes were suspended for three days and canvassing went on.

Very light drug scene. $20 a lid and few takers. No acid or mescaline.

SURVIVAL:

Alright except for the sex scene. Girls play bridge and study a lot. Creative arts are big—especially dance and drama. Student health sucks—no BC pills or advice. The school psychiatrist "really messes up your messed-up mind." All other survival services are in Boston. Many cats in dorm rooms.

The Wheaton News takes stands on issues of little consequence.

ENVIRONMENT:

Mental—People are reading *The U.S. in Vietnam* by Kahn and the works of Richard Brautigan.

Physical—Beautiful campus. Rural, forests, meadows and clean air. Norton is a small town. Climate is snowy in winter, nice in spring and fall.

Campus buildings are red brick New England 19th century prim and proper. Enough ivy on buildings to be respectable. The eyesore is plastic Clark Gym that looks like a refugee from San Jose State.

Escapes include men's schools (train to Boston costs $3.60 and runs four times a day), skiing and home.

Williams College

Williamstown, Massachusetts

All men—how archaic!

SERGEANT PEPPER SECTION:

1,250 students of which 88% are out-of-state. 7% black. Very hard to get in. SATs are around 650 verbal and 700 math. Applicants are generally in the top 10% of their class. 38% preppies. It's easier to get in if you're not from the East (old melting-pot theory).

ACADEMIC BULLSHIT:

A small excellent school. Best undergraduate departments are English, Chemistry and Physics. An excellent graduate program in Development Economics.

Best courses include all English literature offerings by Hunt ("he's alive and very intense and exciting," "he uses his knowledge to help people"), and "The Sociology of Religion" with Little ("he's a great guy and enjoys the students").

Pass/Fail is rare. Some class participation and no student-originated courses. Afro-American Studies is a program of courses but not a separate department. Lots of interaction between faculty and students—both in and out of class. Independent study in your senior year and study abroad.

BREAD:

$2,250 tuition a year. Financial aid is available as are jobs at $1.30 an hour. 95% of the students are in University-owned dwellings including ex-fraternity houses. Room and board are $1,250 a year. The dorms are nice old buildings with large comfy rooms.

Most students have cars or cycles. You don't need costly threads.

BROTHERS:

Alas, all males with just 50 semi-precious exchange girls from Vassar.

Students wear levis, long hair and look backwoods-casual with tweed stuff in the closet. There are a few 1962 smoking-jacket type swingers but they're almost museum pieces by now.

Cats have to go to Bennington, Smith or Skidmore to find chicks. Very small number live with chicks. The sexual situation isn't as bad as Dartmouth. Fraternities are outlawed. Mixers and fixups and "keep your eyes open and brush between meals." The drug scene is moderate, lids go for $20, acid is $3 a shot.

"Williams men are apolitical and sort of out of it." People go other places to demonstrate.

In 1968, Lady Bird Johnson spoke here and there was a peaceful demonstration. In 1969, blacks took over the administration building and "raised a lot of hell." They demanded black housing and got it.

Many students made it down to Washington for the strike and the Moratoriums. Campus and local cops' action demonstrates that someone does hire the handicapped.

SURVIVAL:

There's a good darkroom on campus. Student health service is good, especially the shrinks. Draft counseling at Seeley House. *The Williams Record* is middle-of-the-road.

ENVIRONMENT:

Mental—People are reading *The Politics of Experience* and *The Electric Kool-Aid Acid Test*.

Physical—Boston weather. It's very woodsy near campus but there's a grungy industrial town that is also close (N. Adams).

The campus itself is semi-rural with nice woods and meadows. Buildings are brick structures with pleasant lawn areas surrounding them.

People escape to Florida, Boston and girls' schools.

MICHIGAN

Michigan State University
East Lansing, Michigan

"The most perfect expression for this school is 'bullshit.'" A party school, still in the 1950s.

SERGEANT PEPPER SECTION:

37,894 students, of which 7,904 are grads. Average grades and SATs to get in—the school admissions office likes to make it seem like it is much more difficult to get in than it really is. Out-of-staters need high grades and 1,300 SATs or 98 percentile or higher on the NMSQT. Transfers need a 3.0. 17% out-of-state. 1,000 blacks.

ACADEMIC BULLSHIT:

This school is the most pretentious that we've come across. They talk about their high standards and lofty programs when in fact they have neither—their academic program is poor. There is presently an excessive emphasis on publishing for the faculty because the school is trying to lift itself up by its bootstraps from its beginnings as an "Aggie type" college to something of more prominence —but can you get that by giving out machine-graded multiple-choice tests? (Even in some grad departments.)

The only two departments that the students seem satisfied with are Psychology and Math. "Political Science and Philosophy are wretched." "There is an increasing emphasis on starving the undergrad departments and beefing up the graduate departments."

Popular courses are "Beginning Psychology" by Fitzgerald, and "Child Psychology" by Harris. "Social Science 231" is like a sensitivity training session. Popular professors are Charles Larrowe in Economics (he's the faculty sponsor of SDS) and Walter Adams (the former acting president of MSU—teaches in the Economics department). Some Pass/Fail, few student-initiated courses and hardly any student-professor interaction.

The Free U offers "Hitchhiking" (people told about their hitching experiences and then had a race to see who could get to a certain place fastest by hitching), "Leather Working," "Anarchistic

Movements" and "Self Defense." The Center for Urban Affairs is
the Black Studies department.

Everything is tests—and especially archaic multiple-choice ones.
Some independent study.

BREAD:

In-state is $184 a quarter, out-of-state is $420. Some financial
aid and lots of jobs are available. Buses are the most important
form of transportation (the place is so huge that some classes are
20 walking minutes apart and the buses are a necessity). Dates
cost about $7 and the "Man and Nature" store sells both used
records and used books.

BROTHERS AND SISTERS:

Ratio cats : chicks—7 : 5.

This campus is completely apathetic—it's amazing, considering
the fact that University of Michigan, a radical center, is so close.
The freaks here are about two months behind other campus freaks
and at that they're not too freaky-looking. Everyone wears MSU
shirts or football jerseys with the number 69 on them (how
daring!). A conservative campus with a few hip inroads. The
majority of the kids live in dorms (17,000) and play the dating
game. Lots of Greeks but they're in deep financial trouble and are
dying.

A bunch of freaks set up 100 tents on campus in 1970 and
named it People's Park. The freaks hang there and at "Brody
Grill." Freaks live in certain dorms—Snyder Hall, Phillips Hall
and Mason Abbot Hall.

Many of the kids are into dope—it's quite prevalent with the
Greeks—lids go for $20, tabs of acid for $2.50. People are selective
about their doping, though, as busts are prevalent.

The campus is somewhat between apathetic and indifferent politically. "As long as you make your girl, get your bottle of Ripple
and do something 'groovy' on the weekend, it's cool."

There are about 100 activists and the only group with any
coherence on campus is the Black Liberation Front. But no one
really cares about anything here. Brief political history (none of
the actions had much support):

1965. Five students disrupted the Career Carnival at the school
(Marine recruiters were there).

November, 1966. The Orange Horse Affair. Three nontenured
instructors (two of whom didn't have their Ph.D.s and were
saying that they weren't even going to bother getting them)
were not rehired by the administration. (In other words, they
were fired) and without being given any reason. There were student protests and a sit-in at Bessey Hall. One or two of them had
written poems for a local avant-garde magazine that were considered pornographic (called the "Orange Horse Affair"). It was
considered terribly shocking and the Mothers for Decency protested. They were never rehired here.

Spring, 1969. Demonstrations against Oakland Police recruiting on campus. 300 people sat in the Placement Center in the Student Services building and that killed the second day of their two-day recruiting program. Their main accomplishment is that when Oakland pigs come to recruit now they are a little more secretive and they don't give too much publicity that they are there.

October, 1969. The Moratorium—6,000–8,000 kids marched on the state capitol from MSU. Half the school's administration was marching with the students. Acting-president Adams made classes optional (for the first time in MSU history).

February 17, 1970. There's a little group of maybe 40 who see themselves as revolutionaries. They met in the Union building after the Chicago Conspiracy verdict had come in and then they went off campus to city hall and broke some windows (this was the first incident of trashing in MSU history). They had five-ten minutes of rock throwing at city hall.

May, 1970. The culmination of the ROTC issue, Cambodia and Kent—also People's Park. April, 1970 (two weeks before the strike), students pitched tents across from the administration building and got together a thing called People's Park. Rock bands came and they had pot, wine and orgasms. The police kept ripping off their tables and in turn they had to rip off some other tables which the pigs in turn ripped off, etc., etc.

May 1. A night rally was held and some trashing was done to the administration building. This was a reaction mainly to the Cambodian invasion. During the rest of May there were two other incidents of trashing on campus and during one of these nights there was a fire in the ROTC building, but unfortunately the building did not go up in flames.

May 4. That night students organized themselves into a Strike Committee and called for a strike the next day (in response to Kent). A strike began and was about 33% effective for the first week. There was a supposed strike going on, but there wasn't that much visible support for it.

SURVIVAL:

Chances are alright if you don't think.
Student health is bad "unless you're in the athletic department." BC pills are given out by one freak doctor. The Listening Ear and the Free Clinic are in Lansing.
Don't get draft counseled in the Student Services Building—a former Major handles cases. Go to the Draft Information Center or the Resistance.
Sports are very big—especially football (it's a Big Ten school). The campus paper, *State News,* is a real drag.

ENVIRONMENT:

Mental—People aren't talking.

Physical·—May–October see nice weather. The rest of the year is bad news. MSU pollutes its own air. Red Cedar River, which flows through campus, is polluted with sewage (ugh! "You can see human feces and if you fall in the river you need a tetanus shot").

The campus is gigantic and looks like a "luxury reformatory"— nice natural beauty but ugly buildings.

Escapes are Lake 66 and The Arboretum (it has long-horned cattle).

University of Michigan

Ann Arbor, Michigan

One of the best state schools in every respect.

SERGEANT PEPPER SECTION:

38,328 students, of which 10,835 are grads.

20% out-of-state. It's hard to get in. "The admission of all students is selective and is based upon ability, preparation and probability of success in the applicant's chosen field of study." Generally in-states need a B average, SAT scores that place him in the top quarter of students nationally and a "commendable personal record. . . . All new transfer students are expected to compare favorably with the students already enrolled in the university." 3% black.

ACADEMIC BULLSHIT:

Most students really dig their classes at Michigan—it has a very high quality of academic excellence. Graduate schools of Near-Eastern Studies, Psychology and Economics and Law and Medical schools are all excellent; Michigan bases its reputation on its graduate schools.

The Residential College is a separate college within the College of Literature and has very good courses. Many courses in the Science and Arts college are student-taught and student-initiated. Lots of Pass/Fail and independent study. The Near-Eastern History department is supposed to be one of the best in the nation. Nursing and Engineering are also praiseworthy. The only department students don't seem to like is Education—"It's very bad and very disorganized."

Popular classes are "Psychology 454" (a T-group), "Psychology 506" (a class on racism) and "History 573" (the "History of the American City" taught by Sam Bass Warner, Jr.).

Popular professors are Warner, Fritsof Bergmann in Philosophy and Dick Mann in Psychology.

If you're in good standing you can take one course a semester (junior year up) Pass/Fail if it's not in your major.

In the College of Literature, Science and the Arts they have a thing called "Course Mart" in which students or faculty can initiate a class and have it given for credit. A couple of them are "Little Wars" about guerrilla wars and "Anthropology of Women."

The Free U offers courses in "Communal Barbering," "Phenomenology of Sexuality," "Macramé," "The End of the World" and "Astrology."

The higher up you go the better the relationship with your professors. The relationships with T.A.s are generally good. They have an Afro-American Studies program which you can major in. It's an "interdepartmental concentration program." Lots of independent study.

BREAD:

Tuition is $480 a year in-state, $1,540 a year out-of-state. Financial aid is available. Most students can find work in the dining halls or residence halls at $1.50 an hour.

Room and board in the dorms is about $1,225. Fraternities cost $1,100 a year. There's a co-op (10–12 houses) where you work a little to pay part of your way. $620 there for room and board. Ann Arbor has the highest standard of living in the country and apartments are very expensive. A single can go for $120 a month. Houses that would rent for $165 a month in Detroit cost $350 here. "Conditions are shitty and the landlords are incredible vampires." There is a Tenants' Union which had a pretty effective rent strike in 1968–69. The Union is mainly controlled by International Socialist people.

Dates can cost as much as $7 since some theaters raise their prices for the weekend. Walking or bicycling is the most popular form of transportation here. The "Students International Record Shop" sells used records.

BROTHERS AND SISTERS:

Ratio cats : chicks—3 : 2.

A freaky campus. 90% of the cats wear their hair Beatles 1964 length. Lots of people wear purple rags and work shirts, jeans and sandals. A moderate amount of chicks are braless. There are some straights—they wear pressed shirts and pressed cuff pants. Structured dating still exists but like frats it s on the decline. Dates are taking in the flicks at Cinema Guild and Cinema II. The double standard is dead—sex is an accepted thing even by those who don't indulge.

No one hangs at the Union—it's practically deserted. "The Canterbury House" is a quasi-church turned hip—they have cheap food and radical flicks (Newsreel) and concerts. Any organization that's denied office space at the University (like the Gay Liberation Front) is given space here. Freaks also hang at "Pizza Loy's" (dig the submarine sandwich), "Mark's" on South University Avenue and at "The Ugly" (undergraduate library) in the basement—the second and third floors are for straights.

65% smoke dope regularly—"it's incredibly prevalent here." The campus is relatively free of busts—"We'd go insane if there was one big dorm dope bust, there's such a lack of paranoia here." Score on South University Avenue or if you're new in town ask some freak if you can crash and most likely you'll be smoking dope before the night is over. Lids go for $15.

The University of Michigan has traditionally been radical and made big news when they discovered a campus connection with the CIA a few years back. "Most of the kids are tired peace creeps here—when you need them, they're there but they're not paranoic enough to be able to feel the subtler forms of repression. Their strong point is their emotions—they can relate best to blatant repression." Tom Hayden went here and was editor of the *Michigan Daily*.

People are more into the environmental-political thing as opposed to the social-conscious political trip.

Two of the active political groups are ENACT (Environmental Action for Survival—they push the line of being nonpolitical) and RE-ENACT (a radical offshoot of ENACT—they espouse more radical solutions to the environmental problems than ENACT).

There's the usual New-Mobe, YSA, I.S. (control Tenants' Union), Women's Liberation (pushing for repeal of abortion laws and want day-care centers), the American Revolutionary Media, and the most powerful groups, the Black Action Movement (90% of blacks on campus) and SDS (one of the first chapters in the U.S.).

The *Michigan Daily* –the school paper—is a political group in a sense—if any action wants to be guaranteed to at least get off the ground, they need the paper's support.

SDS, Yippies and Crazies all have their own collectives.

Political History:

Spring, 1969. A lock-in on a Navy recruiter (150 people sat in the corridor of the Engineering building, thus preventing passing into the recruiter's room). It was the first time that people were prevented from seeing any recruiter.

Spring, 1969 "Bookstore" issue. Ann Arbor is notorious for high prices That is one reason why a Tenant's Union was formed—so there was a Tenant's Union and the people started thinking about setting up their own bookstore because they were always getting soaked by all the bookstores in the area. Just before summer vacation the students had a referendum and they voted to set up their own bookstore, but the Regents overruled them. So school was out and in September the kids took up the issue again and asked the Regents to reconsider. They did, but had a 4–4 tie which meant defeat because it was on a motion to reconsider their (the Regents') previous vote. Rallies were held and the students took over the Literature building— one thousand were outside supporting the sit-in. Cops were called in and were on campus for the first time in the history of the University. 107 people were busted amidst police brutality. A call for a strike followed and a one-day strike (that's all that was called for) gathered 5,000–7,000 who honored it. The next time the Regents met, they passed the bookstore issue and the bookstore was set up in 1970.

October 15, 1969. They had the Moratorium and it was 80–90% effective. Rennie Davis gave a speech. The Moratorium created a whole lot of motion on campus and things started to build.

January, 1970. There was a conference on repression held here. Jerry Rubin was here for it. Trashing hit the campus for the first time after that conference. They trashed the ROTC building sometime after the conference.

February–March, 1970. Recruiter actions were held against the Navy, Allied Chemical (sprayed DDT in his room and he was given a dead fish), DuPont (he was locked in his room) and G.E. recruiters.

February 17. The G.E. recruiter's office was stink-bombed and that effectively closed down his recruiting for the day.

February 18. A recruiter was locked in by 120 people. The police were called in and they arrested a chick. Spontaneously, SDSers and a bunch of other people fought the pigs to save her from being arrested.

Also that day, the verdict on the Chicago Conspirators came out and a march was scheduled for that night. People were mad, first the busts earlier that day and then the Chicago Conspiracy verdict. Even though it was raining, 3,000 people showed up at the march. There was some trashing (some store windows and bank windows) and undercover men who were marching were arresting people as they trashed places. When the march reached city hall the pigs jumped all over the march and everyone split.

February 24—Dow recruiters were supposed to be recruiting that day and because they didn't want to have trouble they held a conference with students to explain themselves and ended up exposing themselves for what they were.

March, 1970. During the entire first week of March there was an environmental teach-in at University of Michigan. Since it was the first one ever held in the United States (and in the world) there were reporters and photographers from all over the country and the world at the school. The day before the teach-in was supposed to begin (with all these photographers and reporters there), 500 students sat-in the Literature school building protesting the suspension of an SDS student. Their sit-in was successful because the suspension was removed. For the rest of the week a bunch of ecology actions were taken at the school.

End of March, 1970. A BAM strike was called. This was the culmination of two months of movement by the blacks over a set of eight demands (some of which were: 10% black enrollment by 1973–74; more recruiters in black high schools; more Chicanos; tuition waivers; control over black studies; that the black community center should be in the black community; control of the community center; and amnesty).

Previously BAM had twice gone to the undergrad library and pulled down all the books from the shelves as part of their protests.

The Regents had rejected them once before and the March Regents' meeting was considered do-or-die for them. Just before the strike a white group came out in support of them. On Thursday, March 19, there was a big demonstration in front of the administration building while the Regents were meeting on campus. The pigs were brought in to break things up. Rocks were thrown. *The very first rock was thrown by a plainclothesman* (he provoked all the brutality that followed by throwing that rock—he instigated all the violence by throwing that rock), says our researcher, Jim Zane. As far as my informants know the University has not filed charges against him yet. That day the strike was called.

March 20. 60% of the classes were closed and a march was held that went around campus and disrupted classes.

March 27. The strike was successful by this time (the school was pretty well shut down that week) and by Wednesday, April 1, the Regents and the University met all but three of the Blacks' demands (no black community center, no tuition waiver, and didn't get recruiters). The strike movement was radical at the beginning and then got watered down as it went along and became somewhat liberal. The workers at the school respected BAM picket lines and didn't cross them. This fall or winter the contract between the workers and the school is up and the workers sort of expect reciprocity from the students— if it happens, there could be an excellent worker-student alliance at this school.

May 1, 1970. 100 people from Ann Arbor went to New Haven (the largest contingent from any place other than the East Coast) for Bobby Seale.

May 4, 1970. Mass meetings were called because of Kent and a strike was called for May 6 (the first day of the summer semester). The strike wasn't going well (mainly because the people who go to summer school are hard-core students and can't get involved in politics even if they were so inclined). 30% of the school honored the strike the first day (which was considered a victory because they didn't think that many people of these hard-core students would strike).

May 7, 1970. A memorial service for the Kent people. After it was over some of the kids took over the ROTC building and made it into a community center. Gay Lib Front was given an office, they started a day-care center there and other stuff. They held a community dinner there that night and over 2,000 people came to it, both students and community people. "People's Art" went up on the walls with VC flags. There was a fire in the building that night but they put it out because the ROTC building had become the "People's" building. The strike was called off that night. After numerous bomb and pig scares, people split from the building on the night of May 8. The radicals decided that they should work with the high-school kids instead of trying to get something going at the University during the summer.

Campus Police—certain of their people are always taking pictures. A lot of them are provocateurs.

FBI and *CIA* people are known to be on campus.

Washtenaw County Sheriffs—they are the big pigs here They have two types— the regular ones wear khakis while the tactical unit wears all black like SS officers. The sheriffs are quick with the stick and are using dogs lately. They're the personification of all that's bad in pigs.

Ann Arbor Police—they're a little better than the sheriffs. They at least have 10% humanity.

SURVIVAL:

"Is there a student health?" "Oh, God, yes." The service is terrible although BC pills are dispensed there and at Planned Parenthood. You can get an abortion at the University Hospital if you qualify. Ann Arbor has a Suicide Prevention Center and a Legal Self-Defense Center. Draft counseling is available through Ann Arbor Draft Counseling and the Canterbury House.

There are masses of dogs all over the campus. It's a Big Ten school. Football and baseball are still popular. The *Daily Michigan* is a terrific paper—one of the best campus papers in the United States. Even their sports column is political. Underground papers are the *Ann Arbor Argus* and the *Big Fat Magazine*. There's an organic-food store across from "Mark's."

ENVIRONMENT:

Mental—People are talking about politics.

Physical—The climate has a lot to do with the Movement at the school. School starts in early August and ends in late April (both warm times) so the best times climatically for a political activism are bad times school-yearwise. (People don't get worked up over things at the beginning and the end of the school year.)

Pollution is beginning to happen.

The campus is old and comfortable-looking. The main eyesore is the new administration building. From the outside it looks like a torture chamber—it has little slits that are supposed to be windows. The yard at the back of the administration building is trippy—it has different types of architecture including different pillars and mobiles.

Students escape to "The Arb" (Arboretum)—it's a gorgeous huge park.

Wayne State University
Detroit, Michigan

A cross-section of America. The great commuter school in the sky.

SERGEANT PEPPER SECTION:

31,756 students, of which about 8,300 are grads. Applicants should have a B average and good SATs. Transfers need a C average in their college work. 90% are in-state.

ACADEMIC BULLSHIT:

The best departments are Theater (fantastic) and English. Monteith College is an experimental college that was originally set up by the Ford Foundation. It's very progressive—no tests, no class attendance, no major is necessary. You are graded on what you say in class. There are 900 students in the College and a very close relationship between them and the professors. Some interesting courses offered in this college are "Film Making," "Happenings" and "Basketweaving."

The Physics and Engineering departments are being built up through war contracts. The History department is reactionary.

Most popular professors are Paul Sporn of the English department and Louis Tsen, who teaches "Cinema." Some Pass/Fail, no student-initiated courses.

The Indochina Institute was started during the Kent-Cambodia days. It's student-faculty initiated and is a series of seminars and lectures on Asia. The Free U has classes on things like how to play the blues harmonica, how to make toys, and guerrilla theater. Many classes on black studies but no separate department. Seniors and grads take independent study. Study abroad is a junior year in

Munich or Freiburg, Germany. Students can dress any way they want except in the department of Pharmacy where men must wear shirts and ties.

BREAD:

Tuition in-state is $176, out-of-state $490 per quarter. Some financial aid—lots of jobs. Many students work part-time as substitute teachers (requirements are that you must have completed 135 quarter hours).

There's only one dorm—it's for chicks. Most kids live at home and commute—you need a car and "if you don't get here by 10 A.M. all the parking structures are filled and you have to wait at least an hour." It costs 50¢ a day. Most students are poor and don't have expensive rags. The "Blood Bank," run by "Open City," buys and sells used records. "Marwells" sells used books. Lots of cheap ethnic places to eat, especially the Chinese place, "Hoe-Hoe."

BROTHERS AND SISTERS:

Ratio cats : chicks—about 3 : 2.

There are two types of people at Wayne State University. The commuters and Greeks and the freaks. 90% of the campus are conservative commuters who are into the dating-studying bag. They go to movies and restaurants (usually drive-ins), have hot-shot cars. The big thing to do is to drive your suped-up car to a drive-in and show off your date to all your friends who are in their hot-shot cars showing off their girl friend at the drive-in.

There are about 3,000 freaks who are students and lots of community people who hang out around the campus. They wear army jackets and cowboy boots or tennis shoes. The commutes dress straight and some have embryonic moustaches. Sally commuter digs Revlon. The freaks go to the "Bronx Bar," the "Traffic Jam" bar and to the flicks presented by the Wayne State Cinema Guild. "Boone's Farm Apple Wine" is the drink for freaks. Dopers are even into wine. Freaky chicks are liberated.

On Sunday morning freaks hit "Alvin's Delicatessen" and have a hot pastrami sandwich on a Kaiser roll. They also dig "Johnny's Home of Good Food" and hang out around Prentis Street.

The straights have bake sales in State Hall.

Lots of dope. You can get a great placebo high by walking into the Eastown Theater. Lots of mescaline and cocaine. Score anywhere but be careful—narcs permeate the scene.

90% of the students are politically apathetic and interested in grades only. They usually work and go to school—it takes them five and a half years to graduate so they don't have the time to get involved in politics. Extrémes on both ends exist from arch-conservatives to Trotskyite movement people. Lots of Young Republicans: RNAs—blacks' Republic of New Africa—they want five states in the south to be given to them. White Panthers "they're into the rock 'n' roll, smoking dope and fucking in the streets."

Michigan

There are many other groups—all of the groups are fairly small and unorganized.

Wayne State University had always had the reputation of being a hotbed of radicalism. They've always had a small radical element here. (Detroit is a labor city and has had radical workers.) Many, many demonstrations over the years.

Spring, 1968. (These important events happened over the past couple of years. Most were discovered and exposed by the school paper.) Discovered that WSU had hidden cameras in the bathroom to check up on homosexual activity. This pissed a lot of people off.

Discovered that WSU was keeping security files on certain students and faculty. WSU denied that they were keeping such files and said that they (the files) did not exist. Finally a person from the newspaper took a school VP (who had denied that the files ever existed) to the room where the files were kept, opened the drawer and the VP was face to face with the files. So the University agreed to destroy the files. Most people feel that WSU still has and is keeping the files except now they are better hidden.

Fall, 1968–Spring, 1969. A black nationalist militant took over the editorship of the school paper and a lot of black militants were working on the paper. While the year before the paper was a cultural-political paper, it now became a mainly black political paper. The paper was sent off campus and it was used to attempt to get the black workers at the Dodge plant together.

Big heavy year politically at WSU—people were coming together politically.

1969. They've had four big Moratorium things here at which WSU usually will close down classes and have big conferences. Kent caused the whole school to be closed down and only conferences were held.

Fall, 1969. Sit-ins at Mac Hall (nickname for Mackenzie Hall) over Air Force and Dow recruiters. These sit-ins were handled by the Student Mobilization Committee (the YSA front) and instead of addressing themselves to the real problem (recruiting by these people on campus) they wanted to use these actions to try to build the Movement—so they failed (and are always failing because they are never addressing the real problem).

A little while later there was a Navy recruiter on campus who was given an office in the University Center building. While there a couple of Weathermen came in carrying VC flags. Another Weatherman then entered with a cherry pie and put it in the Navy recruiter's face because "violence is as American as cherry pie "

May, 1970. Kent mobilized the people here. There was a call for a strike. Things began to build up here and the president of WSU closed classes until the end of the week and seminars were held.

A lot of kids were shocked about Kent. A lot came to the realization that the next time it could be them who might get killed.

Different and various strike committees arose spontaneously (everyone felt that something had to be done so all these different strike committees got organized). Because there were so many different strike committees going at the same time and not working together (and therefore rather ineffective), SMC-YSA decided to step in and organize all these committees into one. They also decided to indoctrinate these people with their Trot line. People got so fed up with them that most everyone left the Strike Committee and it fell apart.

May 10–12. Rally held on the Mall. 500 people attended and they then marched over to the Engineering building and broke a few windows and trashed the place.

May 15. A big rally on the Mall (8,000 people there). A lot of people not from WSU were there (a lot of radicals, street people, community people, and hangers-on live nearby WSU and WSU seems to be a focal point for these people to gather at). There was a big march downtown to protest the war, Kent killings and Jackson killings. There was a large rally in downtown Detroit with people trying to confront the police but the monitors prevented anything from happening. They then returned to WSU with kids carrying VC flags and on the way back to school they trashed a police car (which visibly upset two cops who were still in the car as it was being turned over and having its windows broken). There was scattered violence until school closed for summer.

Police. Cops are really uptight in Detroit. Five or six of them have been killed recently, so you can't mess around with cops like you could in the past. They're really uptight— handle with care.

Tactical Mobil Unit. The tough pigs. Have riot equipment, drive blue-and-white cars while regular Detroit pigs drive black cars.

Campus Police. Called "plastic cops." Get special training like "What to do if you find a couple screwing in the bushes." Have a lot of special equipment they never use. They take off their badges for demonstrations (supposedly so they're not stolen, but mainly so they can brutalize without having their number taken). There's a big conflict between WSU and the community (WSU is encroaching upon the community— grabbing their land) and even though the community is right next to the University, WSU won't allow community people to use WSU facilities (like the swimming pool or the athletic fields). So the campus police usually try to hassle community people or keep them off WSU.

SURVIVAL:

Student health is hurting. "If anything serious, they tell you to see your own doctor." No BC pills. Survival services in Detroit. Open City Switchboard refers you to lawyers (Legal Self-Defense), Planned Parenthood, suicide prevention, people who will help you split to Canada because of the draft, and a Free Clinic. There's a draft counseling page in the school paper, other draft help at the Detroit Draft Counseling Center, Newman Center, North Central Detroit Draft Counseling Service and the Interfaith Draft Counseling Center.

Lots of stray cats and fat pigeons in the area. "The only good sports team is the fencing team." *The South End* is an excellent, super-good, fantastic school paper—into both the political and cultural bag. *The Fifth Estate* is a good underground paper. Call Open City (again) for health-food stores.

ENVIRONMENT:

Mental—The gap—straights talk about grades, freaks discuss politics.

Physical—Snow in the winter. Every other winter the school is closed down because of it. Hot and humid in the summer. Spring is the nicest time of year.

The school is in Detroit and there are few trees in Detroit and even fewer trees on campus. Very polluted. "If you drive a cycle, your face gets full of grime."

Zug Island is the place to go if you want pollution. It's owned by Great Lakes Steel—makes 5–10% of all the steel in the United States at that plant. Reddish clouds always hang over the plant. Lake Erie, Detroit River and River Rouge (someone dropped a match in it in 1969 and it caught fire) are polluted. Everything is polluted in Detroit.

The campus is concrete sterile. Trees inside cement and gravel instead of grass. The place is utilitarian. The University Center building looks like an IBM card.

Everyone commutes.

MINNESOTA

Macalester College
St. Paul, Minnesota

In 1970 a groovy experiment was tried. 30 kids lived in a house with a professor and his family and they could do anything they wanted for credit—all student-initiated. It's called "Inner College" and is going to be continued.

SERGEANT PEPPER SECTION:

1,980 undergraduates. Macalester actively recruits National Merit Scholars. It's very difficult to get in. You need good grades and SATs of about 1,300. Transfers need a C or better. 65% of the students are from out-of-state. 260 blacks.

ACADEMIC BULLSHIT:

Their Speech department is first in the nation for small colleges. Students are happy with many of their departments—Psychology, Philosophy, English and Political Science especially. Favorite professors include Mike Obsatz in Education and Mike Greenburg in English. They have Pass/Fail, student-initiated courses. Interaction between young faculty members and students is very good. No Black Studies department but a few courses. Lots of independent study and study abroad. General requirements were abolished here last year—you just have your major and distributive requirements in three areas—Physical Sciences, Social Science and Fine Arts.

Hubert Humphrey lectures here every once in awhile.

BREAD:

Macalester is on the 4-1-4 plan and tuition for the year is $2,050. The school will meet anyone's financial need if they are accepted here. All the National Merit Scholars are given full scholarships. (DeWitt Wallace of *Reader's Digest* fame gives a lot of National Merit Scholarships through his *Reader's Digest* Foundation—his father was once president of the college.) Lots of campus jobs at $1.40–$2.40 an hour.

Most students live in dorms that cost about $1,000 a year for room and board. Apartments go for $70–$80 a month for a one-bedroom. Few people have cars.

BROTHERS AND SISTERS:

Ratio cats : chicks—1 : 1.

Students here are bright and hip. They wear a lot of tie-dyed shirts, splotched pants and boots. Some wear expensive leather stuff, semi-hip clothing. Chicks go without bras. As to social life, "I didn't know we had it." The coed dorm has helped things along a little. There are no fraternities or sororities. Chicks are all liberated—"if a chick hasn't lost her virginity before she gets here, she won't be after her first month."

Dates are flicks, riverbanking and balling.

Local hangs include "The Grill" in the Student Union, "The Green Room" in the Drama building, and the Chapel, a hangout for the God Squad (a bunch of freaks really into religion at the school).

The Twin Cities are the headquarters for drug use for the entire state and Mac College is the center for the cities. 50% of the kids are regular users and 75% are experimental users. Psychedelics are mainly mescaline. Contacts on campus.

Students are liberal. "You'll never get a radical movement at Macalester because they give them everything they want." Political clubs aren't big. The Black Liberation Affairs Committee went from moderate to militant.

In the spring of 1969, students demonstrated against housing discrimination in St. Paul. In the fall of 1969, people set up a table next to the Army recruiters, and the Army people got so upset that they haven't been back yet. The Moratoriums drew a lot of people.

In April, 1970, Jerry Rubin spoke on campus and everyone was turned off. In May, 1970, the school was closed down because of Cambodia and Kent. Students marched on the state capitol in St. Paul and some went to D.C.

There's a yearly snowball fight at Christmas.

SURVIVAL:

Winton Health Service is O.K. but sometimes they diagnose things wrong. The cough syrup is great, codeine and vodka really get you off.

There's suicide prevention on campus in the Psychological Clinic. Planned Parenthood in the area. Draft counseling at the Macalester Draft Information Center, the Twin Cities Draft Information Center and from various professors on campus. The biggest sport is Frisbee.

A squirrel comes into the Xerox room in Old Main at 3 P.M. and they save peanuts for him.

The Mac Weekly is a drag.

ENVIRONMENT:

Mental—People are talking about politics. Faculty meetings and some trustee meetings are open to students.

Physical—The only bearable climatic times are from September through November. Some air pollution. Northern States Power is the biggest polluter.

Ordinary brick buildings. The Mall is a nice-sized grassy area. The Chapel is a brownish glass building, hexagonal in shape.

University of Minnesota
Minneapolis, Minnesota

One of the largest schools in the United States.

SERGEANT PEPPER SECTION:

42,996 students. Entering Minnesota freshmen need a college aptitude rating of 50. Applicants with a rating of 70 or over are practically assured of admission in the College of Liberal Arts. Nonresident freshmen must take the ACT and "must show above average promise and superior high-school records." Most students are in-state.

ACADEMIC BULLSHIT:

Most popular departments are Anthropology, the School of Social Work (it does a lot of innovative things) and the Social Science program. On the graduate level, the Journalism, Engineering and Medical schools are good. The graduate schools are better than the undergraduate departments here. Some Pass/Fail and student-originated courses through independent study.

Most popular professors are Mulford Q. Sibley ("he's a political scientist who's a utopian socialist"), Mischa Penn (Humanities) and John Berryman (Humanities). The Free U offers "Guitar Workshop," "Music Theory" and "Poems of Protest."

Interaction between students and professors is hard because some undergraduate courses have 600 students. The Afro-American Studies department offers eight courses and the American Indian Studies department has courses. You can also take "Mortuary Science" if you are so inclined.

Independent study and study abroad are available.

BREAD:

In-state tuition is $174 a quarter, out-of-state is $421. Money is tight but available for "critical need." "Non-critical need" students have to hustle for bread. Aid is always packaged. There are tremendously large opportunities for student employment on campus—$14 million worth of it a year. Pay is about $2.00 an hour. Dorms cost about $1,000 a year for room and board. 10% of the students live in them. Apartments are high—a furnished one-bedroom goes for $150 a month. More and more communes in the West Bank area are opening up. Most students are commuters and drive cars.

Used records on Washington Avenue South. Groovy cheap books at the "McCosh Bookstore."

BROTHERS AND SISTERS:

Ratio cats : chicks—1+ : 1.

On the whole, the campus looks straight but it is getting freakier every month. All chicks wear slacks and there are scattered fraternity and U of M T-shirts. Tie-dyes are picking up and you see a fair amount of work shirts, jeans and boots. All of the chicks who are halfway freaky don't wear bras. Dormies and frats are more into dating than others. Lots of flicks and parties.

The Greek system is on the way out. They have been losing money for years and their influence is dwindling fast.

Local freak hangs include the lounge of the West Bank Student Union and the whole West Bank. Straights hang at the "Whole," a coffee house in the Student Union. There's a lot of grass use on campus. The climate is good enough to grow Panama Red. A significant number of students are regular users. Mescaline and acid are big. Score through friends.

The majority of students are liberal and anti-Vietnam, but inactive. There are few violent types here.

Active clubs include the YAF, the Students for the Preservation of the American Republic (another right-wing group), SDS, YSA, Students Against the Selective Service (a good anti-draft group that does draft counseling), the Afro-American Action Committee (reasonably militant) and Fight Repression with Erotic Expression (FREE—a gay group).

From 1967–69, there were protests over Dow recruiters, black demands and the War. In the spring of 1968, 2,000 people participated in a one-day strike over the War. In 1969, blacks occupied a building for 36 hours. They got Black Studies, some black faculty and partial control of the King Memorial Scholarship Fund for the black community. 5,000 students marched on the courthouse to support three blacks who were arrested for the above incident. About 10,000 turned out for the Moratoriums.

In the spring of 1970, there was a huge hassle over the "Red Barn Incident." The Red Barn is like "McDonald's"; it tore down some little stores to build a restaurant. People protested and demanded that the land be given to the community. Pigs came and busted students.

Students struck over Cambodia and Kent. The strike was about 15% effective (7,500 students). They were allowed grade options.

The worst pigs in the area are the Minneapolis Tactical Squad. The local jail was built in 1889 and is archaic.

SURVIVAL:

Student health is rated as competent. BC pills are dispensed. The YES (Youth Emergency Service) is open 24 hours and refers to all survival services. Draft counseling is done by AFS, the Twin Cities Draft Information Center and Students Against the Selective Service.

Sports still have a following.

The Minnesota Daily is somewhat to the left and interesting.

There are health-food stores in downtown Minneapolis—"Pavo's" and "The People's Pantry."

ENVIRONMENT:

Mental—People are talking about the war and are listening to a fantastic AM rock station—KQRS (1440 AM).

Physical—Winters are so cold that "you've got to be a little slow of mind to stay here." The summer is humid and hot. There's some air pollution but it's small-time compared to smog city, Los Angeles.

The architecture is all mixed up. The ROTC building looks like a medieval fort with its round towers and front door that resembles a drawbridge. The Mississippi River runs through the campus, but your view of the river is three piles of coal and oil refineries.

Escapes include "The Riverbanks" and the state parks.

MISSOURI

University of Missouri
Columbia, Missouri

The big football game and subsequent panty raids are the biggest thing going. The Minutemen originated in Missouri.

SERGEANT PEPPER SECTION:

21,082 students of which 4,146 are grads. In-state need to be in upper two-thirds of high-school class, out-of-state need to be in upper half. Transfers need a 2.0. 24% out-of-state.

ACADEMIC BULLSHIT:

University of Missouri at Columbia is known for its School of Journalism—a practical newspaper approach. Students enjoy the undergraduate History department. Most professors are right-wingers but a few are good. Chesney Hill teaches a good class in international law, Goff teaches a course in forestry called "The Environmental Crisis" and Dr. Warren Fleming is good in zoology. A few Pass/Fail courses allowed.

160 students are involved in Free U courses like "Metaphysics," "Nutrition" and a "Harmonica" group.

Not much interaction between students and professors—no Third World College. Tests rather than papers. Some independent study in an Arts and Sciences major. Study abroad—the Archeology department has summer field trips to Central America. Traditional academia.

BREAD:

In-state is $220 a semester, out-of-state is $620. Limited loans and scholarships. 2,000 students on the campus job payroll. Most students have cars. It's hard to scrounge at MU.

BROTHERS AND SISTERS:

Ratio cats : chicks—1.5 : 1.

"Nobody's trying to be hip up here—it's still 'hep' on this campus." Only 1% are freaky. Most are conservative. Chicks wear dresses and shorts. 2,000 Aggies wear jeans. Lots of ugly brown penny loafers. Dating is casual—going "out" rather than balling is the thing. Fraternities still do their thing, but they are dying.

Straights meet at the "Heidelburg" (a bar) and the few heads gather at "Osmosis" (a coffee house) and "McAlester Park" on campus. About 3,000 maximum that have tried grass. It's tight as of late—goes for $15 a lid. Big busts in May and September—mostly dealers.

Most of the students are apathetic—Midwest farm conservatives.

In spring of 1968 there was a panty raid. 3,000 students were involved. One student got shot by a pig. Fortunately, the pig was aiming to kill and not firing a warning shot so the student was only injured. The pig was suspended from the force for a week, but the local Optimist Club reimbursed him for his lost salary.

There have been a couple of SDS incidents. In spring, 1969, the *Free Press* (underground paper) got busted—a big demonstration ensued. The Moratoriums fizzled.

The main problems have been about intervisitation in the women's dorms. It isn't allowed. The Greeks staged a mass intervisitation in 1970 and were suspended.

Radical professors get canned and the University administration hates organizing. The radical group on campus is the CCS (Committee for Concerned Students). The Aggies always beat up a couple of demonstrators.

SURVIVAL:

Hard.

Grass is tight and sex is sparse. Conservative minds prevail. Football players are the End (and the Center and the . . .). Student health is terrible, and only open from 8–5 (don't get hurt after hours). Women's Liberation gives abortion referrals. FISH takes phone calls 24 hours a day—can be a suicide prevention center. Draft counseling is done by the Peace Information Center in town. Health foods at "Columbia Specialty Foods."

People go to flicks for entertainment.

ENVIRONMENT:

Mental—People aren't discussing much of anything.

Physical—The summer is hot and humid and the winter is "colder than a witch's tail." Lots of trees and rivers in the area. Air pollution is terrible—the borderline sulphur air content is dangerous. A nearby nuclear reactor also drops crud into the river.

The nicest buildings are the Union building and the Francis Quadrangle area. The Union building is made from beige stone and has a tall clock tower—Oxfordish. Lots of cowpaths. The town makes its living by exploiting students. The Minutemen originated in Missouri—if you're a freak don't travel on the back roads.

The "Osmosis" coffee shop is a world unto itself. Not only do they have music, they are a drug rehabilitation center and a cultural exchange area.

St. Louis University

St. Louis, Missouri

A Jesuit university in the midwest. During the October Moratorium, the president of the school said a mass for peace.

SERGEANT PEPPER SECTION:

10,774 students, of which 4,198 are graduate students. Fairly difficult to get in. B average and 1,100 SATs combined. Most students were in the upper two-fifths of their high-school graduating class. 40% from the St. Louis area.

ACADEMIC BULLSHIT:

One of the leading Jesuit institutions in the country. Best departments are Psychology, English, History and Philosophy. Good graduate schools of Medicine, Law and Divinity. Psychology is clinical and operates a Psychological Clinic which offers services to the community and the students. The Philosophy department emphasizes the historical approach as opposed to the analytical.

Traditional academic emphasis. Mostly grades, stifled Pass/Fail option. Popular professors include Dr. John Napoli and Father Dan O'Connell in the Department of Psychology and Dr. Vincent Ponzo of the Philosophy department.

Student-initiated courses if you can get together three students and a professor. Some black courses—"Black Metropolis," "Black Religion" and "Black History" but no Third World College. Not much in experimental curriculum except for the Free U which offers things like "Bhakti Yoga" and "Violence in America and Other Crazy Stuff." Study abroad.

BREAD:

Tuition is $875 per semester. Hardly any loans or scholarships or work-study is available. Impending financial depression. Jobs are available at $1.65 an hour. Kids have cars and dates can run up to $10.

Dorms are $550 a semester for room and board. Apartments average $150 a month.

BROTHERS AND SISTERS:

Ratio cats : chicks—2 : 1.

Most people are straight. Blue jeans are gaining a little favor though "most of our kids look as conservative as they think." Lots of casual dating but not much sexual activity. A few fraternities and sororities but nothing big. All the radicals in the area go to Washington University.

Very little drug action and lids go for $20.

Most kids are white middle-class apathetics. The only activities so far were in connection with the Kent State murders and black demands. In May of 1970, 400 kids struck to protest Kent State and Cambodia. There were teach-ins all week. 300 students marched downtown but it was nonviolent. Later that month the blacks, dissatisfied with the administration's action on demands they had presented, declared their own strike. A few small fires were set and the blacks blocked the doors to the administration building. No decisions were made.

The SLU Community for Peace is a new active group.

SURVIVAL:

SLU is in the middle of St. Louis so you must be an urban rat. BC pills can be bought from student health. The acid rescue squad is helping with bad trips. The draft counseling service is student-run on a volunteer basis. The *U. News* is a liberal campus paper. *Hardwolf* is an underground paper that appears occasionally.

ENVIRONMENT:

Mental—People are discussing their classes and reading *The Autobiography of Malcolm X*.

Physical—St. Louis University is in the middle of St. Louis' ghetto. No trees, water or natural anything. Air pollution courtesy of Union Electric. Buildings are a combination of modern three-story jobs and restored brick 1920 types.

People can escape to Forest Park, two miles away.

About half commute.

$tephens College
Columbia, Missouri

$tephens is a rich-bitch school. Girls' schools are a thing of the past. No man is allowed in unless "escorted" by a chick.

SERGEANT PEPPER SECTION:

2,000 undergraduate students, 1,987 chicks and 13 cats. Mostly out-of-state. It's a private women's school—only a few men are admitted in Fine Arts. Overall grades and test scores individually considered. Transfers need a 2.0.

ACADEMIC BULLSHIT:

$tephens is very strong in the Arts—especially theater, fashion design and dance. There are very few required classes and you don't have to major in anything. They have a resident theater company in the Theater department and a resident dance company in the Dance department. Photography is also very interesting and loosely structured.

Popular professors are Dr. Whitehill in Religion, James Burkhart, "Contemporary Social Issues," and Tom McKeown, English. All three are very interested in the students.

No Pass/Fail system and few student-originated courses. Interesting regular curriculum courses are "Sensitivity Training," "Sexuality" and "Freedom and Equality." No Free U as such.

There is a very close relationship between students and professors—one professor to every 14 students.

One course in black culture. Either tests or papers—anything goes. Field studies similar to independent study. You do related work in the community. Study abroad under the Institute for European Study.

BREAD:

Tuition and board and room come to $3,250 a year. $tephens is a residential campus. If you are enrolled, you must live on campus. Financial aid is somewhat limited but students can make around $700 a year at a job. You need heavy bread to go to $tephens. Most chicks hitch because you aren't allowed to have a car until your senior year.

SISTERS:

Ratio cats : chicks—1 : 153 (some odds).

It's a four-year college with the image of a two-year finishing school.

It looks like a giant sorority with casual standards—everything goes. Skirts, blouses, knee socks, liberated breasts—no real freaks.

Blind dates. Remember blind dates? Well, that is the main social situation for the poor chicks at $tephens. Entertainment is drinking and partying. Balling is frequent. Most chicks date MU Greeks. There are six sororities on campus—it's one of those cliquish girls' schools. A lot of chicks hang out on their North Campus near the post office on Walnut waiting to be picked up. 75% smoke dope and 50% are regular users. There's a possible death penalty for pushing in Missouri. Lids are $15—big busts every May. (When a young pig's fancy turns to busts.)

No activists—evenly divided between liberals and conservatives. Women's Liberation is pushing for legalized abortion—a small chapter.

In spring of 65 there was a panty raid with MU. $tephens was the home team.

In February of 1970, Women's Liberation gave an abortion referral to a pregnant $tephens chick (her parents approved the abortion). The administration expelled the chick "until her problem disappeared."

The number of males is never to exceed 20. There are 25 blacks.

SURVIVAL:

It's a girls' school.

Everything costs heavy bread. Even prescriptions at the Health Center. No survival facilities of any kind—Planned Parenthood in town. *$tephens Life,* the weekly newspaper, is a high-school sheet. The closest big city is Kansas City.

ENVIRONMENT:

Mental—Chicks like cats and the arts.

Physical—The weather is constantly changing. The campus is trying to protect its grass and has those insipid signs all over—"Don't Tread on Me," "Protect the Downtrodden."

The school looks like a new high-rise housing development surrounding a park. $tephens owns town land and a lake. The top floor of the library has wall-to-wall carpeting, a fireplace in the middle and cushions.

Girls escape whenever they can.

There are rules:

1. Aren't allowed to smoke on campus.
2. Can't go barefoot on campus.
3. Have to wear a dress for dinner.
4. Can't wear pants before 1:00 on Sundays.
5. No living off campus.
6. Must be a junior and have the permission of the dean to get married.
7. Junior and senior possibly can have key privileges if they have a good GPA. Otherwise, girls must be in by 11:30 during the week and 1:00 on weekends.
8. Must have their parents' approval before the school will allow them to travel beyond a 50-mile radius from the school. Also need their parents' approval if they are planning to spend the night at a girl friend's home in town and you also need a note from the girl friend's mother to give to the school—you need to tell the school where you'll be, how long you're staying there, and the telephone number. The college checks up on you by calling up—so you had better be there. When you go out on a date, you have to check out and leave the name of the person you are going out with.

Washington University

St. Louis, Missouri

Washington University has been the scene of heavy political activity lately. The campus is aware and active.

SERGEANT PEPPER SECTION:

11,257 students of which 2,340 are graduates. 80% out-of-state. No specific GPA is needed by an entering student. Everything is considered. Transfers need a C+ average.

ACADEMIC BULLSHIT:

Washington University's Medical school is nationally known. Good departments are Engineering, Architecture (the Buckminster Fuller Design Institute) and Fine Arts. The school is heavy on technical science so the Chemistry and Biology departments are good.

Popular professors include David Hadas, English (guru type and "magical"), Garland Allen, biologist, and Barry Commoner, the famous ecology man.

Limited Pass/Fail option, student-initiated courses known as General Studies (one on counter-cultures). A small Free U. There's a small group of good teachers at Washington University. A Black Studies program of sorts. More tests than papers, independent study. Study abroad in France, Germany, Spain and Japan.

BREAD:

It's a private school—$2,250 a year. Approximately 35% of the freshmen receive aid.

Scholarships go to students in the top 10% of their graduating class. Work-study is available—some jobs from the placement center. Informal dates cost $2. Casual wardrobe.

BROTHERS AND SISTERS:

Ratio cats : chicks—2 : 1.

People have a lot of hair, work shirts, sandals; freaky but not quite like Berkeley or Boulder. The students are hip, into thinking and doing. The chicks are liberated. 80% of the school is from Missouri. Dating is informal, Greeks are on their way out.

Freaks hang at "Holmes Lounge" (check out the ceiling) and in the head shops in St. Louis (Euclid-McPherson area).

Drugs were pretty big two years ago but are fading due to political activism. "You can't face a National Guardsman stoned." The laws are really tough and dope is tight—lids go for $25. About 50% turn on. Scoring only through close friends.

This school has everything politically but is mostly semi-activated. There are 2% extreme rightists, 8% legal rightists, 10% engineering students, 20% fair-weather friends (go to rallies if weather is nice), 40% semi-activated people (leftists with reserve—he'll give his bread to pay for the bomb but won't light it), 20% revolutionary left (complete collapse by violence believers). All the %s keep fluctuating depending on the current situation.

Many political activist groups but also a community spirit. As of late, students have had town house meetings where everyone is allowed to speak—like Athenian democracy. Pretty spontaneous.

In the past there have been demonstrations against Dow and harassing of blacks. In March, 1969, the first outside pigs were called in to quell a disturbance at a trustees' meeting. Three students were charged with disruption. A sample heavily political year:

> *Spring, 69.* An attempted firebombing of the AFROTC building—the cat couldn't light the fuse and he kept on going back and forth trying to get it started.

Feb. 25, 70. In the wee hours of Sunday morning the Army ROTC building went up in flames—totally demolished. Students gathered outside and cheered the fire on. "Good colors." They cheered the flames and booed the firemen.

The next week the feds were on campus investigating because it was a federally-funded building and federal property. The FBI was called in.

Students had a rally and anyone who spoke was buttonholed by the pigs and interrogated. The campus quieted down for awhile.

April, 70. A planned ROTC demonstration meeting of students who were upset that nothing was being done about ROTC. They had no plan except for occupying the administration or ROTC buildings. They went out and found the doors to the administration building locked, and that there were riot pigs all over the place (over 200 cops with 30–50 cars parked all over. The pigs were concentrated in the quad and the ROTC areas.

Pigs swept the campus—students threw rocks and did minor damage and occupied South Brooking for awhile.

There was a whole week of disruptions—they had meetings in Holmes Lounge every night to map out strategy for the next day. The students just milled about that week trying to cause disruptions—they went to ROTC classes and disrupted them every day. There were a lot of photos being taken. Pigs were constantly on campus.

On Wednesday, pigs chased some students around campus and the chancellor asked the pigs to leave because they hadn't been invited on campus by him.

Students tried to board up the ROTC building but failed and were chased by the police.

Then the administration got a restraining order on the second or third day of this first week of disturbances.

On Friday of that week classes were canceled.

Nothing happened on Saturday and Sunday.

The Second Week. A bunch of students were suspended. Legal actions were started—ROTC faculty and students charged students with violation of University judicial procedures. At the same time, federal D.A. Barrett decided to make a test case against Washington University of the 68 Civil Rights Law (thus the whole University is under federal investigation)—the Justice Department is using Washington University as a test case, i.e. the federal government vs radicals. There is a grand jury investigation and the county grand jury has been sending out indictments. FBI agents are here for this thing also.

Meetings were held during the week.

The chancellor suspended 15 students on Wednesday of that week. There was talk of strike, but spring break arrived and things cooled off. Students returned from break, but there was no strike.

An *ad hoc* committee recommended that everyone get reinstated except for three students.

Nothing more happened until the Kent State murders and
that night the remaining ROTC building went up in flames and
the kids went on strike.

Every night of the disturbances the student crowd ranged
anywhere from 200–1,000 students.

SURVIVAL:

Tight dope but heavy political and sexual action.

Student health is mediocre—referrals for BC pills. No suicide
prevention clinic. Free Clinic in St. Louis area. KDNA (free
radio station FM with Help Switchboard). Draft counseling everywhere. Tons of tiny dogs on campus. Not much on varsity sports.
Student Life, campus newspaper, is so-so. *The Outlaw* is a
politically left paper.

"Tong's" is a good health-food store. St. Louis is suburbia—
town shuts down at 8 P.M. on weeknights.

ENVIRONMENT:

Mental—People are political, reading Hoffman and Rubin.

Physical—The fall and spring weather is very erratic—hot in
summer, cold in winter otherwise. Many trees—a green city. But
the air pollution is terrible—filthy—awful—cars, Monsanto Chemical Plant and chicken plucking.

The administration building looks like a medieval castle. The
quad behind it looks like a palace courtyard—stone buildings.
A really attractive campus.

Lots of camping areas around—rivers and farmland in the area.

MONTANA

University of Montana
Missoula, Montana

Where are we? The nearest big city is Spokane with 200,000 people—it's 200 miles away. Where are we?

SERGEANT PEPPER SECTION:

8,200 students. 1,910 out-of-state. 50 blacks, 62 Indians. All high-school graduates in state accepted. Out-of-state freshmen should have standing in the upper half of their high-school class. Out-of-state transfers need a 2.0.

ACADEMIC BULLSHIT:

The best department is Creative Writing which is part of the English department. The turnover is great as all the good people find it hard to take Missoula for too long. The graduate and professional schools in Forestry, Journalism and Geology are good. The Music department is interesting for this neck of the woods. They put on an opera every year and have frequent recitals.

Take Bob Curry's Geology course in "Population and Environment," Sister Madelene de Frees' and Cesar Vallejo's courses in the Creative Writing department, and Professor E. W. Feiffer's courses in Zoology (he has been studying the effects of defoliation in Vietnam)

Pass/Fail in Physical Education only. Large classes, papers. Black Studies was student-originated. A Free U called "Fun-do" with courses in "Gourmet Cooking," photography and art. An Indian Studies program started in 1970. The Kyi-Yo Indian Club is active and sponsors a conference every year—there is an Indian advisor on campus.

The Black Studies program (three courses) has been recruiting blacks from outside the area, especially Chicago. Independent study in most departments. Study abroad.

BREAD:

Tuition is $134 in-state and $375 out-of-state, per quarter. Only scholarships that are easy to get are athletic ones. Elks and the Chamber of Commerce give them to flag-wavers. Very tight town for jobs, especially for longhairs. During the summer you can get a job fighting fires. Jocks get first grabs at park jobs.

The 2,400 dorm spaces cost $280 per quarter for room and board. Freshman students under 21 must live in dorms unless they have parental permission to leave. Mediocre visiting hours. 394 units for married students. Apartments run about $40 per person. In the warm months, a few freaks live in buses.

Clothes are informal and most of the bright clothing that the straights wear looks like it was given to them by their parents. In winter, people dress for the weather, not for the fashion.

Minimum dating expenses—flicks cost $1.50.

BROTHERS AND SISTERS:

Ratio cats : chicks—2 : 1.

Most students are still into the straight scene. The town of Missoula is very repressive, locals beat up freaks and applaud jocks. The only safe place for a freak is on campus or in the State of Montana's one head shop, "The Joint Effort," which is in Missoula.

Freaks and jocks both own shitkickers (cowboy boots). The freaks carry knives to protect themselves from local rednecks who aspire to be amateur barbers. Hip chicks look like straights except they have long hair and carry ethnic purses. In warm weather, everyone wears cut-offs, T-shirts and sandals. Hips don't make much of a point of dressing differently. 10% have long hair (half-way to shoulders). Most everyone comes from a small-town Montana background. There's a double standard between hips and straights for sex—lots of cats go to the whorehouses in Wallace, Idaho. There are ten fraternities and seven sororities that have their own social scene.

The "Oxford Hotel" has a lunch counter and bar populated with old timers and students. Calves brains and eggs cost 85¢. "Eddie's Cafe" attracts professors and hip students. "The Heidelhaus" and "Monk's Cave" are two straight bars. "The Copper Commons" in the University Center is the big on-campus hangout.

Late at night one of the AM stations plays a good selection of heavy music—it's great when you are cruising around on one of the town's many dirt roads stoned out of your mind.

They do get good concerts and speakers at the University.

Lots of dope among all elements of the community of students. Lids go for $15.

The political scene in the town of Missoula can best be described as conservative. Demonstrators from campus have to be careful. Back in 1965, 260 peace marchers were pelted with eggs. In 1968, when Martin Luther King was shot, a local realtor put a sign in his window saying King had associated with Communists. There was a sit-in at the realty office; 20 were maced.

After Kent State, about one-fourth of the students went on strike. They occupied the ROTC building and the school closed it down for three days.

SURVIVAL:

Hard in Missoula itself, so-so chances at the University. Hips are into creative writing. Student health is described as puritan. Two of the doctors are willing to give unmarried women pills, but they do it only for girls who are having "meaningful relationships." The Trip Line is staffed by amateurs The *Montana Kaimin* is good.

ENVIRONMENT:

Mental—Freaks talk dope and politics

Physical—Missoula is a town of 50,000 in a valley surrounded by mountains. The campus is in a residential area of the city across the river from downtown. The weather is terrible—cold in the winter and hot in the summer. Wilderness outside of the town. Pollution is terrible. The Hoerner-Waldorf paper mill does the trick.

Escapes are skiing and home. Very few commuters. Montana's population has not been increasing as much as the national rate. Many University of Montana grads leave the state.

NEBRASKA

University of Nebraska
Lincoln, Nebraska

A large mass-oriented nondescript midwestern university.

SERGEANT PEPPER SECTION:

19,100 students on the Lincoln campus. Fairly easy for a Nebraska resident to get in—average SATs and grades. Not too hard for out-of-staters either. 4,500 graduate students. 15,000 of the students are state residents. 400 blacks, 200 Chicanos.

ACADEMIC BULLSHIT:

The best department on campus is English with a preponderance of young teachers. Economics is a small good department—relevant economics. Psychology is also good. Dentistry, Law and the School of Social Work are the best graduate departments. Graduate schools are into job placements.

"So damn many requirements in the different majors that no one has time to take anything else." Hardly any Pass/Fail used.

Ivan Volgyes, a Political Science professor, is the most popular professor on campus—he's a "liberal."

As to student-initiated courses, "a student has to stick pretty much to channels here, which are the various student-faculty groups, or he hasn't got a prayer " A very small Free U which teaches mainly "Sky Diving."

No close faculty-student relationships and no Third World College. Not much independent study or study abroad. Lots of tests. Old traditional learning

BREAD:

U of Nebraska costs $216 per semester in-state, $475 out-of-state. Dorms run about $100 monthly for room and board. Many students live in the traditional Nebraska dwelling, the white two-story house. Cost is $60 per person, average. Modern apartments run $120 for a one-bedroom. Fraternities cost about $150 a month.

Scholarships are limited but available for state students—not for out-of-state. Loans are available. Not many campus jobs and they pay $1.25–$1.60 an hour. Average cost of a date for a guy is $6—flick, bar, party. Feet or cars usually. Some work-study.

BROTHERS AND SISTERS:

Ratio cats : chicks—1.5 : 1.

Most people are straight. Guys wear levis and sweat-shirts, and dark suit and tie for dress up. A few hip chicks. Hips are described as "scruffy-looking people by most of the campus." "Some girls think they are liberated, many girls say they are liberated, but few girls understand what it means to be liberated." "Since we have so many kids from small towns in Nebraska, there's not that much dating." Greeks still live. "Straight people with money go to the classy bars around town." Not much grass—lids go for $16. Best bars are the "Grill," "Casey's" "Duffy's" and "The Rail." People dig frat parties.

Students are academic and dull. They don't know what the term "revolutionary" means.

Political activity included a listing of a giant "panty raid in 1949 which resulted in several suspensions. In April of 1969 the first demonstration occurred—200 black students demonstrated. The strike against Nixon's stand in Cambodia was about 40% effective. The city pigs have never been called in. The city has a brand spanking new jail—the County City Jail. It's clean, bright, and well managed." Do they take lodgers?

SURVIVAL:

Easy if you are straight, midwestern and retarded. Little dope and sex. No Free Clinic, hard to get BC pills, some abortion referrals through campus ministers. Suicide prevention handled by floor assistants in dormitories. Draft counseling is "pretty straight. It's manned by kids who depend on books and pamphlets for information. They are darn anxious to give out their pamphlets." Pets aren't allowed on campus. The *Daily Nebraskan* is the campus paper—it's so-so. Not much of an underground anything. No health-food stores. The big city is Omaha, 50 miles away.

ENVIRONMENT:

Mental—People talk about midterms, finals and grades.

Physical—Urban. The campus is three blocks from the downtown area. Bordered on three sides by railroad tracks. The climate is hot and humid in summer, cold and dry in winter. Trees are being cut down to make room for parking lots—a concrete and asphalt university Some air pollution. Architecture is very diverse —there is a gigantic concrete football stadium and an ancient coliseum that looks like a big barn—some 80 years old, some new, some brick with little grass, others marble with lots of grass.

People go home to Omaha and Kansas City to escape. Half the students live off campus, one-fourth with their parents.

NEVADA

University of Nevada
Reno, Nevada

A political vacuum—"1901" times. Military Science is required. Even the music here is 20 years old.

SERGEANT PEPPER SECTION:

5,988 students (and 1,412 correspondence-course students). 888 grads. About one-fifth are from out-of-state. 80 blacks, 100 Indians and 10 Chicanos. Easy to get in—you need about a 2.3 average and ACT tests.

ACADEMIC BULLSHIT:

Lots of boring requirements. The best departments are the School of Mines, Agriculture and Mechanical Engineering.

Favorite courses are "Mystical Romance" taught by Dr. Jim Lewis (an emphasis on the Tolkien trilogy—he's the hippest professor on campus) and "The Bible as Literature" taught by Dr. Hettich (the professor is an actor—he reads and performs) and English courses by Dr. Hawdavay ("under the guise of teaching English he develops an elaborate design for living and presents varied perspectives on life").

The Art department is excellent although many of the best professors left. Three Pass/Fail courses during four years are allowed, grade emphasis and not much emphasis on class participation. The African studies seminar in the Political Science department was student-originated. A few courses offered at the Free U in music, art and guerrilla warfare.

The BSU has about 80 members and started the African studies course. There is recruitment of Indians with E.O.P. funds.

Relationships between students and teachers are fair. A number of younger liberal professors are on a first-name basis. Students can spend a semester at the state capitol. Not much independent study but study abroad. There are two-year programs in Agricultural Air Services, Fashion Trades and Parks and Turf Management.

BREAD:

Tuition is $218 per semester in-state and $618 out-of-state. Scholarships are difficult to get unless you are an athlete or an Indian. Some jobs at $1.65 an hour.

Room and board in the dorms is $521.50 a semester. Officially, students must live in the dorm till they are 21, but this can be circumvented. There are five dorms—two women's, two men's and one coed. Frosh chicks have 12 and 2:30 A.M. hours. The Manzanita dorm for women is a huge red brick structure with tons of character. Nye dorm is coed and the epitome of luxury.

The College Inn (off campus) has approved apartments from $1200 a year. Unfurnished houses on the other side of town go for $125. Rents are expensive.

Many students are hired by gambling casinos. Over half have cars. The "Book Stall" has cheap used books.

BROTHERS AND SISTERS:

Ratio cats : chicks—3 : 2.

The school is divided between fully-costumed cowboys (Ag and Mining students with broad shoulders, broad grins and narrow minds) and average straights with everybody faces and nondescript clothes. There are a few guys with inch-long hair, moustaches and groovy smiles. A few freaky chicks with jeans and stringy hair. Freaks stopped being ostracized in 1970.

Dating consists of getting drunk and going to a flick. Plenty of fraternities but they aren't terribly important—but they are still super-selective and go through your background.

Hangs include "The Mouse House" (a bar for hips and straights who dig the rock scene and martinis), "Shakey's Pizza" (for Anthropology students), "Harrah's" (gamblers go there to play 10¢ craps but gambling is not heavy among students), and the Aggies go to western type places that play country blues.

The cowboys from east Nevada are conservatives and up tight. The Californians are more liberal but the school is trying to limit the number of kids coming in from California. Are the kids aware? "One kid I questioned didn't know what a Chicano was."

Sit-ins are unheard of. However, in the spring of 1970, students sat outside the dining commons to protest bad food and that shook up the administration. On Governor's Day, an annual ROTC celebration, a peace march of 150 disrupted the proceedings. After this the Nevada Board of Regents passed a *Code of Conduct* setting up stringent punishments for students and professors who demonstrate.

All this was caused by the minor disturbance at the Governor's Conference—"the community is sure that foreigners, radicals and Jews are here." During the strike a group called the United Student Alliance presented a list of demands and got nowhere.

About one-third smoke dope. There are lots of pills, but other dope is not really heavy. "Nevada is tight."

SURVIVAL:

Hard.

But the Art department is good. No BC pills or shrinks and student health is lousy. A small draft counseling committee.

Survival services in the Public Health Center and a Free Clinic. The campus paper is the middle-of-the-road *Sagebrush*.

ENVIRONMENT:

Mental—People are talking about their horses.

Physical—The front lawn is decorated with an exhibit of World War I cannons.

The school is located in a residential area four blocks from the center of the Reno action. It's one peaceful acre away from the narrow trafficked roads and cheapy neon flashing attractions. There are mostly old two-storied red brick buildings interspersed with the modern institutional variety. There's a freaky beautiful zigzag-roofed all-glass library with marble columns.

Freaks escape to Pyramid Lake (beautiful and desolate desert with limestone formations) and everyone goes skiing at Tahoe.

Sierra Nevada College

Incline Village, Nevada

This is a new school built on a new concept. It was started by Friedrich von Brincken, a successful corporation lawyer, and William Cox, a Hollywood writer. The idea is to write it off as a tax deduction. The president describes the college as a "Capitalist communal effort." It's a four-year college; this is the first year. It will be accredited in three years when it graduates its first class.

SERGEANT PEPPER SECTION:

There are no definite requirements for eligibility. They are looking for talented, versatile, motivated students. Its first year of operation, 1970, saw 50 students enrolled, undergraduates only. Most of the students are from the Nevada-California border Tahoe area.

ACADEMIC BULLSHIT:

The school's two strongest departments are Communicative Arts and Business. Communicative Arts prepares a student for a professional career in theater, music or art. Piano or guitar lessons are given to any interested students. The students are all taking part in building and maintaining the college itself. John Corbett, the photography instructor, is big on nature study and tree preservation, etc. and is hoping to get grants to make studies. He takes his students on field trips to Truckee and Virginia City in search of artifacts. There was participation in Earth Day—a poster at "Eagle Thrifty" (the supermarket everybody goes to and meets at) said, "This is a Tree—Our most precious exhibit." It is hoped that with a grant the students will be able to start their own ecological projects. Some projects have included studying growth rings on trees to predict wet and dry years and collecting arrowheads.

Drama students built and wired their own stage. Writing is taught by former Hollywood screenwriter, Gilbert Ralson. The total production is emphasized. The drama coach also teaches a course in heraldic design for those who wish to have the mark of their lineage.

Mr. von Brincken, the president (a corporation lawyer), teaches about 15 business courses. Many of his students are local business-men who desire further education in certain areas.

There are also courses in Humanities and Science. In history, the professor has the students find the books they want to read and has them bring in passages that interest them. He plays music of the era, shows films and "inspires creativity." Other courses are tailored to fit the student. One girl wanted to major in Math so she and the professor are building a computer. "If a student is interested in something, we'll try and do it." All the faculty are professionals in their field and thus feel especially qualified to instruct. They all express their disdain for college graduates who immediately start teaching. Students are free to initiate any course they want to. Grades are used, but aren't considered im-portant. The faculty and students are all on a first-name basis. They drop over to each others' houses for parties all the time. Most of the morning is spent in the library where people wander in and out, joke and drink coffee.

Projects are the rule rather than tests. Students can smoke in class and dress as they please. Professors get expenses only, no salary. "It's a labor of love."

BREAD:

Tuition is $500 a quarter. The school hopes to build a dorm in the future. Most students live in cabins in this mountain area or in trailers. Two–three can share a trailer at $180 a month. Cabins are about $100. There are a few private scholarships offered and the regular loans. Most students have a job on campus and a few also have jobs in the area in the ski lodges or casinos. There is no used-book store, or new-book store for that matter. Texts are borrowed at the moment.

BROTHERS AND SISTERS:

Most of the 50 students are women.

Everybody wears boots, jeans and shirts and long sweaters. Everyone looks casual and athletic and artsy-craftsy rather than hip. They are all skiers and party-goers. Skiing is the big activity as Squaw Valley is only 15 minutes away. "Baron's," a pizza and beer joint, is the local hang—it's about a mile away. Popular sports besides skiing include water sports, jogging and mountain climbing.

SURVIVAL:

If you like skiing, this is the place for you. Nothing is struc-tured, it's very free. The nearest hospital is 40 miles away, but there is a nearer emergency service. There is a health-food store in Tahoe City. Everybody smokes but it's a quiet drug scene. Lids go for $15 and sources are freaks who come up for a weekend of skiing. Reno is the closest city to campus—it's 40 miles away.

ENVIRONMENT:

Physical—Elevation 6,800 feet. Snow and about 20° all winter, beautiful and sunny—up to 70°–75° in the summer. There are pine trees all over the area which surrounds Lake Tahoe. The campus is composed of three slant-roofed cabins that were meant to be a community center and were quickly transformed. It's on about a quarter of an acre, surrounded by forest, a mountain in the background. Icicles drip from the roof, the air is clean and smells refreshing. The water is cold and clear—waterfalls and hills nearby. "When it rains, the sun shines." "Sometimes snow on 4th of July."

The three cabins are connected by a wooden staircase. The theater has a stage on one side, easels on the other and a fireplace warming both in the center. Downstairs is a basement loaded with theatrical and photographic and art supplies. A small classroom and a darkroom are in the third building. Everything is still in the works.

NEW HAMPSHIRE

Dartmouth College

Hanover, New Hampshire

The animals of the Ivy League.

SERGEANT PEPPER SECTION:

3,263 students of which 134 are grads.

Very difficult to get in. You need excellent grades, SATs of about 1,300 and good recommendations. The catalog states: "Entering classes consist of approximately 800 students. Since several thousand candidates apply for admission each year, many hundreds of whom possess academic qualifications sufficient to promise successful completion of college courses, the selection of students is made on a competitive basis."

95% are from out-of-state.

ACADEMIC BULLSHIT:

Dartmouth offers fine educational facilities, if that's what you dig. The Medical school and the graduate departments of Business and Engineering are very good. Most undergraduate departments are good, especially Math, English, Business, Theology, Psychology and Art. The most popular courses are "Psychology 10" (abnormal psychology) and "Science 10" (a course on colors with slides and movies). Peter Bien in the English department and Minsky in the East Asian department are both well liked.

Some Pass/Fail, few student-initiated courses and no Black Studies department. A Free U called the "Experimental Courses" which offers "Film Making," "Ballet," "Meditation," "The Experimental Theatre" and "The College as Employer."

The professors are very available—the fraternities invite them to cocktail parties. Some independent study and lots of study abroad.

BREAD:

Tuition for the year is $2,250. The school is pretty well-endowed and the money situation is not too tight. About 40% of the student body receives aid. Jobs on campus are very available and pay $1.65 an hour.

Dorms range from $365 to $635 a year for room, and board costs $750 a year. Houses go for $400 a month and farmhouses go for $200 a month. Housing is not sufficient in town—there is a big shortage. A one-bedroom goes for $185 a month.

Students drive cycles and foreign sports cars but don't wear expensive rags.

BROTHERS AND SISTERS:

Ratio cats : chicks—46 : 1. (Some chicks take classes on an exchange program.)

Dartmouth cats are fairly individualistic in their appearance in a pseudo-hip way. Frat rats spend their time going on "Road Trips" (which means getting a car and driving to one of the girls' schools such as Colby, Smith, Radcliffe or Skidmore) or they have things called "mixers." Then there's Green Key Weekend when 3,000 chicks come up and get it on with the guys. The frats have orgies in the "Pit" or the "Den." Freshmen can't go to these weekends so their year is a bit of a bore! Frats control everything socially. Non-frats are sort of on the outs with the college chicks—they are forced to find a "townie." Dartmouth used to be heavily alcohol-oriented but recently they turned on. Gambling was also really popular in the dorms in 1969—sometimes stakes go up to $300.

The drug scene is really open. When the administration finds out that a student is dealing they give him two warnings and if he persists, he gets suspended for a year. About 85% have tried grass and 60% are regular users. There are about 500 trippers. Freaks meet at the snack bar in Hopkins.

Most of the students are liberals but "there is no action taken here, it's an Ivory Tower." The president initiated the strike himself—he personally shut the place down. There's really no conflict at Dartmouth because students get what they want.

The political history is said to have started in 1967 when an ROTC cadet wore his uniform to a Wednesday flagpole vigil against the war.

In 1968, there started to be a lot of support for the California grape strike, and the students began to boycott the markets that carried the grapes. In 1969, 100 students took over the administration building in reaction against ROTC. ROTC was finally thrown off campus in 1970.

In the fall of 1969, blacks presented a list of demands—a Black Studies program, a black dorm, more black students and more black professors. The administration gave in to most of the demands.

There was quite a bit of support for the strike in 1970—70% of the students worked on some form of it. Many people went to Washington, D.C., and others went to New Haven for Bobby Seale. Some organized into CPW (Continuing Presence in Washington) for the purpose of using computers to go over the voting records of the people in Congress against the War.

SURVIVAL:

The main impediment to survival is the lack of girls. The

chicks in the schools that visit Dartmouth refer to them as "animals."

"Dick's House" is the name of the student infirmary. It gives very good service and free medication. No survival services in Hanover. Theology students give draft counseling. Sports (both intercollegiate and intramural) are big here but the spirit is showing a decline.

The Dartmouth is the oldest college paper and good.

ENVIRONMENT:

Mental—People are talking about student politics.

Physical—"You get tired of winter, you get tired of summer, fall is just short enough and spring is just fine." The only air pollution is from the college smokestack and the hospital—but there is heavy water pollution. The Connecticut River is one of the worst polluted rivers in the state. You could get a ton of scrap metal from it if you bothered.

Dartmouth used to have the largest gym and the smallest library in the Ivy League. Things have changed though. The nicest part of the campus is the whole surrounding area (there's a lot of skiing, horseback riding and canoeing in the area).

People escape to Union Village Dam to swim in the nude. Freaks go to the communes in the area—there are three in South Stratford.

University of New Hampshire

Durham, New Hampshire

Set in rural New England.

SERGEANT PEPPER SECTION:

7,376 students of which 2,185 are out-of-state. 1% black. Instate must be in top 40% of high-school class, out-of-state must be in top 20%. SATs are 500ish. About 550 transfers a year.

ACADEMIC BULLSHIT:

So-so in academia. Students maintain best departments are Philosophy, Zoology and Political Science. The Psychology department is obsessed with rat games.

Best courses include "Biology 409, Human Reproduction," with Wright ("People ask gross questions, and he gets down to the meat. He answers 'where do babies come from, momma?' graphically"), "The History of China and Japan" with Linden, "General Botany" with Schreiber (he gets standing ovations from reserved New Englanders) and "Criminology" with Palmer.

You can only take four courses in four years Pass/Fail. Class participation is just fair in quality—lots of polite listeners. Students both originate and teach classes such as "Racism on Campus."

No Free U and no Black Studies department (hardly any blacks).
Sophomores up can do independent study and study abroad is
available.

BREAD:

In-state tuition is $680, out-of-state $1,680 per year. Loans
and scholarships are tight but some packaged aid is available.
Work-study jobs are typical. Wages are $1.60 an hour.

Dorms cost about $900 a year for room and board. 60% of
the cats and 75% of the chicks live in dorms. Rules are O.K.
(chicks have no hours after their first semester freshman year).
Little scrounging. Many have cars (there are 2,000+ commuters.)

Threads are cheap and so are dates (for $5 you can eat, see
a flick and ball).

BROTHERS AND SISTERS:

Ratio cats : chicks—1.5 : 1.

Among the unusual personalities here we have Tonto's nephew
who plays hockey for the school, and the former Gerber baby.

As to a description of the other students, "they breathe a lot,"
(socially conservative and apathetic). Hair is moderately long for
cats and chicks look straight (a fair percentage still wear
makeup). There is no New Hampshire look. Most students look
like straight Berkeley types, relatively hip for New England.

Lots of dating and chicks eat shit because they're up for marriage. You can call a chick Friday night for Friday night and
she'll be grateful. Very heavy social pressure for chicks to get
married. Some living together but it's rare. There are 13 fraternities and 5 sororities, with less than 20% of the students as
members—they are on their way out.

Local hangs include the "Keg Room" on Main Street, the
Memorial Union building and the Library ("you never go to
study"). Entertainment consists of flicks, booze and some grass.
The drug scene is light, lids go for $15, acid for $4. Lots of
student narcs.

Politics for the most part are nonexistent. In May, 1970, the
strike and Chicago Three (Dellinger, Rubin and Hoffman)
brought the big-time to New Hampshire. When the strike started,
only one day of classes was left. Students felt gypped—many split
right away. The others stayed and participated in moderate
action—canvassing and teach-ins.

The only other semi-political event occurred in 1969, when
the "Unilateral Government"—enabling students to have a say
as to curriculum—was created.

SURVIVAL:

Facilities for pottery, jewelry making and photography. Student
health is terrible—one cat was told he had cancer when he had
a stomach virus. Doctors are well trained in malpractice techniques. No BC pills. Draft counseling at the Memorial Union.

"Kool-Aid" at St. George's Church in Durham has a 24-hour hot line. *The New Hampshire* is the most political thing about the school. Women's Liberation "is fairly loudmouthed but has made no inroads as yet."

ENVIRONMENT:

Mental—People are reading *The Population Bomb* and discussing the War and "boredom."

The Ecology group, UNHITE, ran Earth Day and is fairly active.

Physical—Typical New England weather, long cold dark winters, gloom and rain in the spring. Good setting for hatchet murders.

Durham is a small town in a rural area. The campus dorms look like red brick colonial hospitals. East and West Halls are 1918ish white frame barracks.

Kids don't have the bread to travel on the weekends. Some go home.

NEW JERSEY

Princeton University
Princeton, New Jersey

Times are changing for this former bastion of the conservative upper-class aristocracy.

SERGEANT PEPPER SECTION:

4,837 students, 333 of them are chicks and three-fourths of them are from out-of-state. Admission is very, very difficult—applicants need the SATs and three ACT tests. Princeton looks for the bright, WASP upper-class, slightly athletic applicant in most cases.

ACADEMIC BULLSHIT:

Princeton offers an excellent education and is rated in the top three Ivy League schools along with Harvard and Yale. The best departments are Math, Philosophy, Physics and English. The Woodrow Wilson School for International Affairs is fantastic. The graduate schools in Physics and Math are world famous.

Popular courses include Malcolm Diamond's "Problems in Religion," Steve Klineberg's "Personality and Culture," Arno Mayer's "European History" and Walter Kaufmann's "Hegel, Nietzche and Existentialism." Bill Wheatley of the Sociology department is a leading radical professor. He's been doing research on how Princeton operates as part of the military-industrial complex.

Some Pass/Fail, lots of busy-work (papers, tests, etc.), average class size is 20. Class participation is extremely important. Big classes are broken down into discussion groups of eight students.

Groups of students can petition The Committee on the Course of Study to originate a course. They must develop a reading list and a formal course structure. Some of the ones given for credit have been "Appraisal of the University Ideal" and "Economics of the Ghetto."

There's an Afro-American Studies program and a program in African Studies. They are two-year programs.

Upperclassmen can have a very close relationship with their teachers. Each student has to do two independent study-type projects before he graduates. In your junior year you have to do two 50-page theses and in your senior year a 100-page thesis. Study abroad is allowed.

BREAD:

$2,500 per year. If they accept you and you need financial aid, they will usually help you. 45% of the undergraduates are on financial aid which consists of scholarship funds, loans and campus employment. Campus jobs are very easy to find both with the University and in student agencies (there's a student hot-dog agency, a watch agency and a movie agency).

The dorms are the major housing (90% of the students live there) and cost $530 per year for room. Board costs between $690 and $900 per year depending on where you eat. No dorm rules and students are required to get permission to live off campus. Most students stay on campus because off-campus housing is expensive and scarce. The majority of the students are loaded with bread.

The parking lot overflows with Porsches, XKEs and Corvettes. Most have Brooks Brothers suits lurking in their closets. You can buy cheap records at "The Last Chance" in town (but Princeton students don't do anything cheap).

BROTHERS:

Princeton is one of the last eastern snob holdouts. The Princeton man starts out by being conceited because he got in. And the fact that most girls at schools in the East are dying to go out with a Princeton man doesn't help much. Some men belong to eating clubs which are the same as fraternities for all practical purposes. They select and reject, traumatizing the freshmen class. They control the social life and still have some that are designated as football eating clubs (Let's have a RAH). About half the campus smokes and some drop acid, nothing heavier.

Forced celibacy is the rule during the week unless you can grab a chick from one of the local high schools. Chicks from Wellesley, Smith, Vassar and Randolph Macon flock onto the campus in search of a man on the weekends. Dates consist of hitting New York, going to dinner and a party at an eating club, or flying kites on the grassy fields near the campus. People can sit and talk at the "Axe," a student coffee shop. About one-fourth the men dress up for school (cotton pants, dress shoes and a button-down shirt). Another one-sixth dresses freaky—beards, bells and old shirts, but not even the freaks are very freaky. The majority of the students wear levis and a T-shirt and has socially acceptable medium-length hair. But "the times they are a-changin'" and the number of freaks gets larger every year. Hangs include the "Axe," "Black Bart's" and "The King's" (bars), and "The Princetonian Diner" (the only place open late at night for food).

Most students are moderate but there is a small active radical faction who are always supported by high-school students in the area. Groups are UNDO (The United National Draft Opposition), SDS, the Bobby Seale Brigade, The ABC (Association of Black Collegiates) and the USA (Undergrads for a Stable America)—the right-wingers.

In 1969, the ABC had a sit-in to protest the University's investment in South Africa and to obtain a Black Studies department. This resulted in two Black Studies programs being initiated.

Walter Hickel came to speak in 1970 and was heckled. Several alumni had come to hear him and they were scandalized. The administration was furious and suspended three students.

The biggest issue to hit the campus has been the IDA (Institute for Defense Analysis) issue. The IDA makes weapons for riot control and does other military research. Students blocked work at IDA after the Cambodia decision. The strike over Cambodia was also successful—UNDO was formed to work for peace candidates.

SURVIVAL:

So terribly Vanderbilt and Mellon.

Little creative arts as academic work is too demanding.

The infirmary hurts rather than helps. UNDO does draft counseling. The FOR (Fellowship of Reconciliation) is a Quaker group in town which also gives draft counseling. The *Daily Princetonian* is literary and good.

ENVIRONMENT:

Mental—People are talking about national politics.

Physical—Princeton, New Jersey, is a small city located 45 minutes from Philadelphia. The countryside is rural and beautiful. Cold winters and muggy summers. All the Gothic buildings look tranquil, somehow.

Weekend traveling to girls' schools and to the Jersey shore.

Rutgers University

New Brunswick, New Jersey

"New Jersey is New Jersey."

SERGEANT PEPPER SECTION:

6,400 males, 2,800 females at Douglass College (sister school). Fairly difficult to enter. In-state must be in top 20% of high-school graduating class and have an average of around 1,100 on the SATs. One of only three universities in New Jersey. 15% out-of-state. 5% black.

ACADEMIC BULLSHIT:

The best Agriculture school in the world. The English department is also very good. John Ciardi has taught there. It has many good courses on modern Anglo-American poetry. Engineering, Math, Physics and Thermodynamics are passable.

The Microbiology Institute is one of the best in the United States. It frequently has Nobel prize winners on its staff. The

Medical school and the Graduate School of Social Work are well liked by the students. Popular professors include Renee Weber (Philosophy) and Warren Susman (History).

Mostly traditional academia. Tests, no student-originated courses and an emphasis on grades. Seniors have a Pass/Fail option for one course and first-semester freshmen are graded Pass/Fail. No Third World College, but a Transitional Year program for disadvantaged youth. A selected few can get independent study for their senior thesis, but no more than two or three per department are usually eligible.

BREAD:

$200 per semester in-state, $400 out-of-state. Dorms cost $1,130 a year for room and board. Fraternities are a little more expensive. Apartments run $150 a month for a two-bedroom unfurnished.

New Jersey state scholarships are readily available if needed. Work-study and campus jobs are available for those who need them. Expensive wardrobes aren't necessary but many students have cars. Dates cost about $5.

BROTHERS AND SISTERS:

6,400 cats. (Douglass College, the sister school, has 2,800 chicks.)

Most cats are lukewarm hip. They look casual, have sloppy hair and wear jeans. There are many straights and a few freaks. Cats date chicks from Douglass who aren't that liberated. Greeks are on the decline.

Hangs include the student center, which is usually filled with high-school freaks, "One Mine St." (a coffee house) and "The Ledge" (briefcase commuter types).

Lots of people smoke in the dorms and lids go for $15. Score at the student center but there are narcs all over.

Entertainment is flicks and dances.

Most students are liberal by Phil Ochs' definition, "10% to the left of center in good times, 10% to the right of center if it affects them personally."

The farthest-left group is the Radical Student Movement.

In spring, 1969, blacks presented a list of demands to the administration. The result was the Transitional Year program and the Urban University department. In the fall of 1969, a total of 15 SDSers sat in at a board of governors meeting. Outside cops called in for the first time. Most students were against SDS.

In the spring of 1970, Rutgers turned on and struck after Kent State. The RSM occupied the administration building, and the president of the university, Mason Gross, said they were his "guests." "His guests leave peacefully with demands for ROTC to go off campus. Faculty votes ROTC off campus, board of governors overturns faculty decision, faculty takes academic credit from ROTC. High noon comes to Rutgers. Issue not yet resolved. Much 100% Americanism activity goes on in New Brunswick, stirred up by the local American Legion post. After the initial catharsis, Rutgers men return to form and go home early."

SURVIVAL:

Student health is generally good. "Rap line" service functions as switchboard. One hip religious counselor does draft counseling. The newspaper is liberal and good.

ENVIRONMENT:

Mental—People are talking about "The War" and reading *Soul on Ice.*

Physical—Rutgers is an urban campus. City streets go right through campus which is bordered by residential and commercial areas. Small, old buildings, and large modern blahs. Architecture is Basic Brick Impressive.

No escape.

NEW MEXICO

Eastern New Mexico State University
Portales, New Mexico

A dry county.

SERGEANT PEPPER SECTION:

4,000 students of which 590 are out-of-state. 55 blacks.
Easy to get in—you need a C average and recommendations.

ACADEMIC BULLSHIT:

The best undergraduate departments are Music, Business and Anthropology. The best graduate departments are History and Education. Take George Agogino for Anthropology. Garland Tipps for Sociology and Henry Hahn for Psychology.

No Pass/Fail, lots of tests, few student-originated courses (one in 1970 was a Chicano culture course). No Free U, no ethnic studies and independent study only on the graduate level. Some study abroad.

BREAD:

Tuition is $170 in-state per semester and $440 out-of-state. Loans and scholarships are available. Jobs are hard to find but available if you hassle—$1.45 an hour average.

Dorms are $369 per semester. Freshmen have to live on campus—freshman chicks have hours and there is no visitation. Most students do live in the dorms. Apartments run about $60 for a one-bedroom—landlords don't rent to minority students or long-hairs. Most people have cars and motorcycles.

BROTHERS AND SISTERS:

Ratio cats : chicks—about 1 : 1.

Straight arrow for the most part—right out of Archie and Veronica comic strips. They wear nondescript cotton rags and look neat and clean. A few in 1970 began to look a little hip. There are more cowboy reactionaries than hips, though. Dating is still the thing, living together is impossible because the local community is the redneck fascist type and frowns on it.

There aren't any hangs as it's a dry and dull county. The few hips smoke grass and it sells for $15 a lid.

There are seven fraternities and three sororities that are fairly strong.

The only political action in the school's history was a demonstration against Cambodia in May, 1970. 400 showed up. The Portales City Jail is hurting.

SURVIVAL:

Hard.

Student health is lousy. No BC pills, abortion referrals or shrinks. No draft counseling or bail fund and no survival services in town.

The Chase is O.K. for a student newspaper, considering the school.

ENVIRONMENT:

Mental—Some are reading *Catch 22* and *Soul on Ice.*

Physical—Portales is a town of 4,000. The nearest big city is Albuquerque, 200 miles away. The campus is barren—a few lawns, no trees and lots of parking lots. Dust is everywhere and train whistles are always blowing. Brick and cement sterile buildings.

Those that escape go to Taos, Albuquerque and home.

New Mexico State University

Las Cruces, New Mexico

This campus owns more land than any other campus in America. But can you stomach the indigenous people—called cowboys?

SERGEANT PEPPER SECTION:

7,050 students, of which 1,269 are out-of-state.

20% minority students, mostly Mexican-Americans.

Easy to get in. Must have a C average from high school or an ACT score of 17. 38% of the students are married.

ACADEMIC BULLSHIT:

General academic level is mediocre.

Best undergraduate departments are Physics, Geology and Agriculture. Best graduate departments are Art and Education (emphasis on teaching mentally retarded children).

Popular professors include Dr. McCormick in Sociology, Dr. David Martin in Psychology and Dr. John Dupree in Journalism.

Ted Smith in Sociology is the most radical professor.

Big traditional type classes—tests, papers, some Pass/Fail, no student-originated courses and no Ethnic department. A Free U that offers "Relevant Reading Here and Now," "Essentials of

Alchemy" and a "Seminar in Inter-Personal Communication." Some independent study. Study abroad in Mexico and Europe.

BREAD:

$207 in-state and $522 out-of-state per semester. Loans and scholarships tight—scholarships given on scholastic achievement basis only. Many campus jobs at $1.30 an hour.

Dorms are $400 a semester for room and board. Apartments are much more popular and run about $70 a month. No coed dorms.

Some scrounging possible if you share. Food stamps are possible if you make less than $110 a month. Most kids have cars but no fancy threads. Straights date at $5 per evening—flicks and hamburger. Heads buy a chick a cup of coffee and go to hear a band.

BROTHERS AND SISTERS:

Ratio cats : chicks—2 : 1.

Most students are straight and training for that dream job (insurance salesman, teacher, social worker). Very, very few hips— maybe 3%. Some frats and many of that unusual breed of animal—the cowboy. He looks like a Marlboro Man, wears horsy smelling clothes and a wide-brimmed hat and threatens to castrate hippies. Lots of dating and kissing. Women have hymenphobia. The few hips hang at the "Cork and Bottle," a beer joint with a band. Cowboys hang at "Bonnie and Clyde's Truck Stop" which has a jukebox that plays western songs.

Several political and cultural groups. Students for Peace in Vietnam sponsored the Moratoriums—little turnout. Los Chuanos are trying to get themselves scholarships. The Black Student Organization put on a Black Festival in 1970. YRs, YDs, and YAFs have speakers. No big political activity.

SURVIVAL:

Hard. Little sex and drugs. Lids go for $10, $3 mescaline. $4 for acid but little demand. Student health gives psychological counseling, no BC pills. The Newman Center has off-campus draft counseling. Suicide prevention in town. No Free Clinic. No pets on campus. School newspaper is the *Roundup* and it is mostly filled with sports news.

ENVIRONMENT:

Mental—Cowboys and straights talk about rodeos and other sports. Hips read *The Population Bomb*. SCOPE is the ecology group.

Physical—The campus is in the suburbs of Las Cruces, which is in the middle of the desert. The campus owns mountains and part of a freeway—it's the biggest campus in the world. Clean, pure dry air.

Most old buildings are tan two-story stucco ones. Newer ones are three-story cream brick uglies. Unpaved parking lots.

People escape rarely. Some go to Sierra Blanca for winter skiing. Guadalajara, Mexico, for sunning. Mostly a commuter campus.

University of New Mexico
Albuquerque, New Mexico

"Lots of hip people and pretty women."

SERGEANT PEPPER SECTION:

15,692 students of which 2,617 are from out-of-state. Few minority students except for Chicanos (11.7%).

Easy to get into—you need a C average from high school.

ACADEMIC BULLSHIT:

Best undergraduate departments are Psychology, English and Sociology. Best graduate departments are History and Psychology.

Many graduate students in Psychology are working on a marijuana project with chimpanzees. Professor Ferraro conducts these experiments on the long-term effects of grass. Take Joe Fashing and Gil Marx for Sociology. One professor assigned a chick an erotic poem to read to the class—he was fired (after all the Regents read the poem too).

Some Pass/Fail, and some student-originated courses ("Violence and Non Violence"). No ethnic studies as yet but they are working on a Chicano Studies department.

A really good Free U called "Amistad" which offers "The World Game" (from Buckminster Fuller's idea), "Equal Justice in New Mexico," "Poetry Against Repression," "Elementary Draft Counseling," "Defense Contract," "Survival and Guerrilla Warfare" and "How to Laugh Your Way Through a Revolution" ("4 dead at Kent State [ha, ha], Cambodian War [ha, ha]. Maybe something's happening that we can look at as amusing. Be a happy revolutionary").

No independent study but study abroad in Ecuador.

BREAD:

$210 tuition in-state per semester, $525 out-of-state. Loans and scholarships are tight for all but Chicanos. Jobs are difficult to get and run about $1.45 an hour.

Hardly any students live off campus but there are dorms that cost $400 a semester for room and board. Apartments cost $80 for a one-bedroom. Fraternities run $500–$600 per semester. Most students have cars or bikes.

BROTHERS AND SISTERS:

Ratio cats : chicks—3 : 2.

This place is one of the hippest spots in the West. About half the campus is hip, into drugs and politics. Chicks wear jeans and no bras and cats wear tie-dyed shirts and jeans. Even the frat cats are hip—only about 25% of the campus is straight. Fraternities are losing membership—there are 15 of them and 9 sororities.

Cohabitation is common and all but the straight-arrow chicks ball.

The major freak hang is Yale Park, right beside the campus. The average date consists of smoking grass and taking in a band. Lots of chicks go dutch.

SDS is on campus and organized a child-care center in 1970. 1,000 students took part in the Kent State demonstration. The National Guard was called in and there were 11 bayonettings (they even accidentally bayonetted their own man, they were so scared). The War Resisters League organized Moratoriums in 1969 but attendance was slight.

There was limited support for the Kent State strike.

The administration has all the radical professors up against the wall.

Chicanos do a lot of in-community work.

Heads score all over—lids go for $10, acid for $2.

SURVIVAL:

Student health is terrible, no BC pills or abortion referrals and it closed down during the Kent State demonstrations. The Law school gives good draft counseling. A student organization called "MASH" gives first aid and helps people who have bad trips.

The Lobo is a good campus newspaper. There's a health-food co-op but it isn't too good.

ENVIRONMENT:

Mental—People are reading *La Raza* and *Do It* and are talking about Cambodia. The ecology group had a successful Earth Day and are gathering petitions to stop the Alaskan pipeline.

Physical—The school is right in Albuquerque—cold winters and hot summers. The campus is pleasant with an average amount of open space. The buildings are Spanish-style stucco cream colored structures.

Not too much traveling on the weekends except during ski season.

St. John's College

Santa Fe, New Mexico

Students are lost in Sophocles and Aristotle, knee-deep in the classics and out of touch with the world.

SERGEANT PEPPER SECTION:

262 students of which 48 are in-state. All undergraduates. Six minority students. Hard to get in. Most freshmen were in the

top two-thirds of their high-school class and had about **1,100** on their SATs. Recommendations are also important.

ACADEMIC BULLSHIT:

St. John's offers a very intensive education—discourse is emphasized and each student is expected to be very interested in his studies and do a lot of work. They try to develop intelligence by having students become thoroughly familiar with the classics. Students must take four years of a language, two of Greek and two of French, four years of math (starting with Euclid and leading up to the present), one year of music theory, four years of lab science and four years of Great Books (Homer, Freud, Mark Twain, etc.) plus many other courses.

Favorite professors include Mr. Robert Niedorf ("he's a philosopher"), Mr. Sacks for language ("dynamic") and Mr. Brown for math ("venerable").

Courses are only taken Pass/Fail, class participation is intense, classes are small. Students can originate non-credit courses like Hebrew, fencing and karate.

BREAD:

$2,300 a year for tuition and dorm. Loans and scholarships are tight. Jobs are easy to get at $1.50 an hour.

90% of the students live on campus. There are no dorm hours and visitation is from 10 A.M. to 1 P.M. on weekdays and 10 A.M. to 2 P.M. on weekends. No overnight visitation. A few students live in town in apartments at $60. Not many students have cars. Most walk.

"Ancient City" sells used books.

BROTHERS AND SISTERS:

Ratio cats : chicks—about 1 : 1.

This school is very small and people know each other very well —it's like a big family. Everything is informal and intimate. Most students are hip—long hair, jeans and tie-dyed shirts. Dress is casual. Lots of chicks are braless and dress in work clothes. Most are liberated, lots of balling. Dates are informal and consist of a walk in the woods. Most are liberal but there have been no big demonstrations yet. (The school was only started in 1964.) Pretty heavy drug scene and the administration doesn't kick you out if you are busted. Lids go for $15, acid and mescaline for $5. Hangs include "Claude's Bar" for heads and the local truck stops for straights.

SURVIVAL:

Student health is free and competent. Free shrinks and BC pills. Professor Steadman gives draft counseling. The campus paper, *Seven,* is straight.

Natural foods at "Ella Hanford's" in town.

ENVIRONMENT:

Mental—People are reading *The Environmental Handbook* and the classics. Everyone is really into ecology.

Physical—The campus is spread over 260 acres within the city limits of Santa Fe a short distance from Santa Fe Plaza.

The climate is warm and dry in the summer, cold with a little snow in the winter. The buildings are Spanish, stucco, one–two stories each.

People go skiing and camping.

Western New Mexico University
Silver City, New Mexico

A quote from the school newspaper, *The Mustang*, May, 1970:

One Small Voice

The ice cream social was quite a success. It was well attended (about 150 people) and the presentation of the questionnaire results was very informative. Maybe some people in this place will begin to realize that students are responsible young adults who will accept responsibility and utilize their powers and resources in a constructive manner . . . Meeting the new student body officers in the fashion that we did last Thursday was extremely interesting. While none of them really expounded on anything relevant to student problems, I believe the people who met them were impressed with the fact that they all want to help the students and work for the students' cause. I certainly hope the students let them.

But, was the ice cream social *really* a success?

SERGEANT PEPPER SECTION:

1,400 students of which 150 are out-of-state.

Easy to get in—C average from high school. 30% Mexican-American minority students.

ACADEMIC BULLSHIT:

The dean has a flattop.

Another "going to school to train for a job" school.

The best undergraduate departments are the Social Sciences, and Political Science. The best graduate department is Business Administration. Popular courses include "Social Problems" (Gwen Mulder) and "Economic Geography" (Gus Getner). Traditional schoolbook things—tests, lectures, no Pass/Fail. No student-originated classes or Free U. No Ethnic Studies department *per se*—a few courses. Study "abroad" in Mexico.

BREAD:

Tuition is $150 in-state, $420 out-of-state per semester. Loans and scholarships are tight. Campus jobs are easy to find. About one-third of the students live on campus. Dorms are $500 for room and board per semester. Most popular dwellings are apartments that go for $50 for a decent one-room place. Easy to scrounge. If your income is less than $110 a month you are eligible for food stamps.

Dates average $6 for a flick and food. Used clothes at the "Army and Navy Store."

BROTHERS AND SISTERS:

Ratio cats : chicks—1.5 : 1.

Most students are straight middle-class job seekers. The Chicanos aren't militant but are very study oriented. The cowboys here wear levis that are too long over scuffed cowboy boots, wide belts and fancy buckles and hats. Cow chicks wear dresses, nylons, tennis shoes and white cardigans. Also lipstick, eye shadow, pancake batter makeup and bleached, stiff blond hair.

The one hip place was busted and closed. So the few heads that exist gather at the "A&W Rootbeer" drive-in. Cowboys and girls gather at the "Casa Loma Bar" where they have cowboy bands.

Politically, they're confused. One week they had a Kent State and Anti-War teach-in, the next week a Pro-Vietnam and Cambodia teach-in. At least they're open-minded. Circle K (whatever that is) controls the student senate.

No demonstrations so far.

SURVIVAL:

If you're into creative things, the school does have good ceramics and print-making facilities. No BC pills or abortion referrals in student health. No draft counseling on campus or in town (ACLU take note!). Grant County Ministerial Association offers mental health counseling. Lids go for $13 (outrageous, considering how close to the border they are), acid $4, mescaline $2. Not much drug use.

ENVIRONMENT:

Mental—The few heads are reading Kesey's *One Flew Over the Cuckoo's Nest*. The Biological Society does ecology things.

Physical—Western New Mexico University is in Silver City which has a population of 6,000 (S.W. New Mexico). Hot and dry in summer, cold and dry in winter. Barren. No trees. Cacti. Some air pollution from a copper mine five miles away.

The small campus is built on the side of a hill. Many cream colored brick and stucco buildings.

People escape to El Paso (really?), Tucson and Elephant Butte Lake.

NEW YORK

Bard College

Annandale-on-Hudson, New York

Ginsberg hangs out here (Leary used to, too)—it's only 20 miles from Woodstock. Heavy scene.

SERGEANT PEPPER SECTION:

Bard bases its admission decision primarily on a personal interview. Grades have to be fairly good with about 1,100 combined SAT score. 700 undergraduate students, 55% out-of-state (mostly from middle-Atlantic states). 15 black students.

ACADEMIC BULLSHIT:

Bard emphasizes intellectual attainment and gives the students lots of freedom in which to develop. It's an undergraduate school. The best departments are Art, English and Drama. The Drama department stages a total play production which goes on the road —last year's play went to London. Good professors are Robert Kelly ("leads you on a poetic mystery tour") and Peter Skiff, who teaches "Energy and Entropy" ("a scientific madman who makes all that weird stuff seem relevant and delightful").

There are student-initiated courses—last year had "America in the 60s," "Student Revolution in the U.S." and a film workshop— all for credit. Half grades and half Pass/Fail.

Good interaction between students-professors since school is small. Independent study is well established. Black studies is on its first legs—about three courses. Study abroad.

BREAD:

Total average costs are $2,400 for tuition, fees and room and board. Some live off campus, but not many. Almost everyone lives in the dorms. Few loans and scholarships and hardly any work-study. Some campus jobs—building and grounds and dining commons at $1.45 an hour. Department assistants are the best jobs— $2.50 an hour.

Most people have cars—it's only 90 miles from N.Y.C.

BROTHERS AND SISTERS:

Ratio cats : chicks—1 : 1.

Students are constantly freaking out on one drug or another! An intellectual atmosphere with individuality the byword.

It's a heavy hip school—everyone's liberated, balling, smoking dope, learning. "This is a space school—no regular type dating." Jeans, boots and sweaters—old threads mostly. Dope all over— $20 a lid for grass. Everyone's a freak—hang at "Adolph's Bar," general mind zap. Revolutionaries abound—of the new-left-radical sort. The YSA is very big as are mobe committees. Women's Liberation is active and writes a weekly newspaper column. Demonstrations and drug busts—local jail is bad news. In 1969, big bust—50 arrests. Students are close-knit and have a real sense of community.

SURVIVAL:

Very easy—in fact, a pleasure—dope and freedom abound. BC pills available from student health, all referrals are available. A full-time draft counselor. Pets all over. Good campus paper, *The Bard Observer,* written by a "dope-crazed anarchist radical plastic American neo-journalist."

ENVIRONMENT:

Mental—Read books on political movements, on blacks, on anything.

Physical—"Old Hudson Valley crazy. Former rich. Lots of trees, mansions, woods, rivers. Near the Catskills. Rip Van Winkle. Thunder. Cold as a mother in winter." Far-out 500 acres rural type campus. New York City—hour and a half away.

Architecture on campus is Old Hudson Valley mansion type. 1890 Gothic-Victorian. The school is located on 500 acres of the Hudson River Valley and has 16 dorms scattered over the area. Some upperclassmen live off campus in nearby Red Hook or Rhinebeck. Rural type life.

Barnard College
New York, New York

If you can live through four years in New York and want to try it, go to Barnard.

SERGEANT PEPPER SECTION:

1,950 women. About 300 transfers a year (they come to New York to get married or get lost). Hard to get in—applicants should be in top one-fifth of their high-school graduating class and should have a combined score of 1,330 on their SATs. Less snobbish in requirements than the other sister schools.

ACADEMIC BULLSHIT:

Chicks can take courses at Columbia and they usually plot their schedules to do it so that they can meet guys.

Good departments include English, Ecology and Art. Popular Art courses include "Literature of Art" with Professor Novack ("free wheeling discussion of artists' writings"), "Baroque Painting and Architecture." Kathleen Stimson is recommended for English.

Other popular courses are "History of Buddhism" with Professor Olson, "Old Testament" with Professor Gaster, and "Metaphysics" with Professor Larson (a hip Women's Liberation type whom the students adore).

The new Ecology major combines conservation, urban planning and field work in New York City.

Studies are intense and difficult at Barnard but chicks seem to enjoy many of their classes. Pass/Fail is limited to four courses and students are "grade crazy" for fear they might not get into a good graduate school. Many people go through Barnard and never talk in class. The chicks are indignant that they have to take three years of gym. There's an Experimental College set up on the fourth floor of the "Paris Hotel"—a real craphole. 25 chicks and 25 cats from Columbia live there for a semester and rap about educational reform—workshops and seminars. "It's a non-directed commune for a couple of hours' credit."

There are many good urban studies and ethnic groups—"Stability in Africa" and "Psychology of Racism" to name a couple. Most professors are "amenable to contact but you have to make the effort."

Seniors can do a project for their whole senior year—such as a book. Some independent majors. Study abroad in France, Spain, Italy.

BREAD:

Tuition is $2,100 a year. Scholarships and loans go mostly to minority students. Campus jobs are available at $2.00 an hour. There's a job placement center for jobs in the city.

Dorms cost $1,150 for room and board a year, including laundry. There are two renovated apartment houses. The upperclassmen "fight to get them." No curfews and males can stay overnight in the dorms. Freshmen are stuck in a prison brick dorm called the Hewitt-Reid Complex—they are dungeons.

Apartments are $60–$100 a person in the area of 100–125th Street (from windy Riverside Drive overlooking the Hudson to Central Park West). You have to "snoop around for quite awhile to find one." Some people commute from up to 50 miles away. There's a big housing shortage.

No cars—it's an urban campus. People ride the subway for 30¢. No one is able to scrounge. However, "Rapoport's" gives day old bread away free.

SISTERS:

There's a whole barrage of types of chicks. First there's the Fifth Avenue type: stylish, long Pucci scarf, Gucci shoes, tailored double-knit sweater from Lord and Taylor, thick gold hoop earrings and an expensive watch. The Jewish liberal: navy-blue mini with expensive knit sweaters or a matching leather vest, long hair and thick-heeled shoes. Post-debs wear pantsuits. The freaks wear jeans, T-shirts, crocheted belts and sandals.

The chicks on the whole are sedate and passive. They complain that they can't meet anyone, but there's plenty of part-time cohabitation. Dates start when a cat calls and tells a chick to "come on over." They smoke and screw and the next morning the chick is lucky if she gets breakfast. "Around the junior year, everyone starts looking for a husband."

Most Columbia cats are cheap; the chicks have to pay for themselves. Dates are flicks at "Thalia." A date of a Broadway show is described as a "windfall." Spontaneous relationshipping.

Chicks go to Columbia rallies to meet the guys. Barnard is a political parasite of Columbia—"A strong left-hand wedding band movement afoot."

Lindy LeClair is the heroine of Barnard. She had a huge hassle with the administration about living with her boy friend. Barnard nominally supported the student strike and talked its way through finals.

New York has made most chicks numb. "What do you think about here?" "Being robbed, mugged and raped."

Places to meet are the "West End Bar" (people live there), the South Field (lay out on the grass and smoke dope) and the "Lion's Den" (the cafeteria at Columbia).

SURVIVAL:

It's extremely difficult to get through four years in New York and emerge unscathed and alive. But if you're the independent type you may enjoy it. New York has all the survival services (and they need them). Student health "won't do a pelvic." People in trouble can get help any time at the "Dawn," a coffee house. The only animals in the dorms are rats (and cockroaches). The campus paper, the *Barnard Bulletin*, is "polite and busy."

Lids go for $25 (Columbia guys are the suppliers). The quality of psychedelics is bad. Wine and beer are still very popular.

Women's Liberation is active. When *Mademoiselle* magazine asked Barnard girls to model, Women's Liberation stopped the girls from signing up. They are fighting for gynecological services at student health. They borrowed babies and brought them into the student center to give tangible evidence that pregnancy leads to children.

ENVIRONMENT:

Mental—People talk all the time about anything. The chicks are reading R. D. Laing and the *I Ching*.

Physical—Grim forecast, surrounded by Columbia cats, the smelly Hudson and the Harlem jungle. Everybody stays inside during the winter. The air is so polluted that as soon as you step outside your face gets dirty. Architecture is Institutional Old, a combination of Imitation Italian, Monumental Ick, and Modern

Functional. Urban sidewalk campus surrounded by black iron rail fence.

Escapes are "sleep." There are a lot of night people. Vacations at home or skiing at Stowe.

Columbia University
New York, New York

Urban, alienated, Ivy League assembly-line education. "The approach to learning is more scholarly than enthusiastic." The campus is so sterile that they had to form a Warmth Committee.

SERGEANT PEPPER SECTION:

17,040 students (total graduate and undergraduate) in the University. 2,700 cats in Columbia College. Admission is very selective. You need high grades and good SATs. 80% of the students are in the top two-fifths of their high-school class. The average SATs are 1,400. 65% of the students are from public schools; 35% are from private schools.

ACADEMIC BULLSHIT:

Columbia offers an excellent education—it has first-rate undergraduate and graduate schools—it's a super-intellectual place.

Best departments include Contemporary Communications with Fred Friendly, the former CBS news chief (take "Journalism for Poets, Protesters and Physicists"—many courses have established media people as guest lecturers); EthnoMusicology (take Professor England for folk music); Art History ("It has a lot of far-out aesthetic people and is a small responsive department which takes advantage of its proximity to New York City); take Gree kArt with Mr. Santomasso—"he makes dead stuff come alive"; English (take Lionel Trilling); and the Law school and Medical school (College of Physicians and Surgeons) are excellent.

Academic competition is tough as students are studiers. Pass/Fail is allowed for one course a semester. Few student-originated courses. A Free U at the "Paris Hotel" (see Barnard).

There is a Black Studies program but blacks are unhappy with the way the courses are taught. They feel they are too technically oriented.

Student-professor relationships are formal and distant—professors are usually accessible during their office hours—that's it. Independent study is allowed but the first two years you are usually too busy filling requirements. Study abroad is possible but by the junior year students are too beaten down to take advantage of it.

BREAD:

Tuition is $2,300 a year, known as the "high cost of Ivy." Scholarships and loans go mostly to the minority students except in the graduate departments where almost everybody is on a fellowship or research grant. Some students take jobs as taxi drivers at $4.00 an hour to see them through.

Room and board is $1,200 a year for the dorms—they aren't coed and don't have mandatory eating plans. Many students eat locally at "'Mama Joy's," "New Moon," or the "V&T." The dorms are shitty. Apartments between 100th and 125th Streets in the "knife point fear district" run from $60 to $100 per person. Dorms are so paranoid that students have to show their I.D.s with photos as they enter.

There is little scrounging in New York City—students are too intimidated by the "far out cost of living; in New York the only thing free is the air." (Cough!) The biggest bargain is the Staten Island Ferry which costs 5¢. Transportation is subway and buses—a car isn't practical because of congestion, vandalism and the "Midnight Auto Sales Company."

Costly threads aren't necessary as the plebeian look is in. Buy used books at "Salters." You can borrow records from the record library at Butler.

BROTHERS:

No chicks here.

Columbia College has fun-city intellectuals, messy and slightly odorous on summer days, dressed in jeans and ugly shirts with a full head of hair—here comes the cat from Columbia. Most students also wear ugly outgrown sport coats. Boots, wing tips and Weejuns exist foot by foot. During the winter there is a big surplus scene—army jackets, pea coats, and knit caps—they have topcoats to wear with those seldom-worn suits. Columbia does have a lot of freaks because "New York City gets to you."

Columbia cats "get it on" for Barnard chicks and other sister-school counterparts. They call a chick and tell her to "come over" but the chicks are paranoid of the dark so they have to fetch them. Bread is scarce, so many dates are dutch. 15% of the undergrads join fraternities in houses on 112th and 113th Streets but they are important only as a place to crash for a couple of years.

Dates consist of rapping, smoking and going either to "Thalia" to see an old Bogart flick or for a ride on the Staten Island Ferry. They also go to other flicks and plays and to Central Park for free concerts in the summer. "The West End" is the mecca for non-students and literary intellectuals; the "Gold Rail" is good for wine and beer; the "Lion's Den" is a hang for panhandlers; and the "Postscript" is a church basement coffee house at St. Paul's Chapel that attracts students. And then there's the rest of Fun City.

Politics broke open in the spring of 1968, with the now-famed Columbia Strike. SDS directed it (the students produced it) and it was aimed against United States and Columbia's racism in the neighborhood and war research. Mark Rudd led the student take-over of the buildings which lasted eight days. Pigs finally moved in and evicted the student squatters with clubs, beatings and arrests. The University was shut down. Since then a lot of politicos in New York have gone underground.

Since the big strike there have been guerrilla skirmishes with Dow recruiters, military recruiters and ROTC. About $40,000 worth of broken windows has amassed in the last two years. But outside of that the campus has really settled down—the Cambodian strike was merely a spring exercise which moderates took over. People collected signatures on petitions and got beat up by Hard-Hats.

All the New York City pigs are bad but the crack unit called "The Tactical Police Force" are real mothers. They are "physical giants with clubs, riot helmets and leather coats—they ride horses through crowds."

SURVIVAL:

Physically impossible, intellectually feasible. Students are into the creative arts as Columbia has a good school of the Arts. There's a club called "Filmmakers" that lends motion picture cameras and equipment. Student health is terrible—you may have to wait up to three hours to see a doctor and then he will try to farm you out to a private doctor—it doesn't give BC pills either. Students try to stay healthy. There are many survival services in New York City (and they need as much help as they can get!). Draft counseling is in Dodge Hall. "Dawn" handles bum trips and has shrink referrals. Students eat take-out a lot and snack from the Good Humor truck in front of the main gate. *The Columbia Spectator* is political and excellent. Dope is prevalent.

ENVIRONMENT:

Mental—People are reading *Do It!* by Jerry Rubin and *Eros and Civilization* by Marcuse.

Physical—Hibernate in the winter—it's too cold to go outside. Stay inside with the air conditioner in the summer—it's too hot to go outside.

Terrible air and noise pollution (and visual pollution—the Hard-Hats).

The buildings are bland institutional Gothic but it is one of the most spacious of New York City's campuses—it actually has a few patches of land where they attempt to grow green grass.

Escapes are anywhere. People frequent the "Cloisters" in New York City (30¢ for subway), Boston and the ski resorts.

Cooper Union
New York, New York

Cooper Union houses Architecture, Art and Engineering students who are totally involved in their creativity. It's an unusual place.

SERGEANT PEPPER SECTION:

1,250 students of which 50 are graduates. 50% from New York City. A few minority students.

Hard to get in. Must be in top one-tenth of high-school class, have 1,100 minimum SATs. For Art and Architecture students, a special entrance examination is given in New York (six hours long). These students must also submit a portfolio.

ACADEMIC BULLSHIT:

Only artists, architects and engineers go here—they are usually very high-quality students. Cooper Union exists "for the advancement of science and art."

Best courses include Professor Haacke's sculpture course, Professor Marsicano's printing class and all the professors who teach painting and drawing. Art professors are artists who teach a couple days a week for bread. All professors allow the students great freedom in their individual projects. "They treat students as artists here."

Physics is the best department in the Engineering section. There's a new doctorate offered called the "Philosophy of Engineering" and also a new program on air-pollution control.

Tests and papers are obsolete. "Artists and Architecture students do projects and engineers rarely get time to come up for air." Classes are small, participation intense. The Art school has a storefront children's workshop to teach ghetto kids how to paint and draw.

Independent study in your major. Students are totally involved in their work.

BREAD:

Stringent academic requirements but free tuition. There is a $100 student fee and, naturally, art supplies are infinitely expensive. The school is privately funded. Some campus jobs—secretarial and machine-shop cleaning.

There are no dorms and bread is usually a big worry for students here. Apartments can be $45 a month per person on the Lower East Side. Lofts are 10¢ a square foot—two or three people get together and cough up $200.

A lot of engineering students commute from home.

Expensive wardrobes and cars are a rarity.

BROTHERS AND SISTERS:

Ratio cats : chicks—3 : 1.

The art types wear work clothes covered with paint and plaster —the "slept-in" variety. Dirty T-shirts, jeans, denim jackets. Plenty of freaks and all are Bohemian in dress and values. The engineers, per usual, have that straight undernourished look. A lot of chicks make their own clothes—many interesting "smocks." Engineers date. Artists live with their old ladies (at her place).

There are no organized political clubs or groups. Most issues revolve around internal problems in the school. Current issues are the artists' need for more studio room, their dislike of the midnight close-down rule. A few small demonstrations against Hughes Aircraft. Not a political place.

SURVIVAL:

For artists, architects and engineers, this is the place. Do your own thing. Creativity is the word. Students take pride in what they do.

There are studios all over the place. On the fourth floor of the ancient "foundation building" there's the Cooper-Hewitt Museum, which is run by the Smithsonian. It has a far-out collection of textiles, wallpaper, photography and art. There is a gorgeous aluminum geodesic dorm also.

Survival services all over New York. On campus, Professor Bowman in Humanities does draft counseling. No BC pills or anything else from student health. People bring their own lunches. The campus paper is the *Cooper Pioneer* run by engineers—straight as a slide rule. Women's Liberation is just starting on campus. The students celebrated Earth Day with a "Free Organic Dinner."

ENVIRONMENT:

Mental—People create, form and produce. Readings include Gary Snyder and Hesse. Engineers don't read—they multiply and divide.

Physical—New York is an urban blight. Cooper Union is in the East Village, down the block from Andy Warhol's "Electric Circus," around the corner from the Fillmore and a stone's throw from McSorley's famous "Ale House." Of course, the Village is headquarters for New York's hip scene. During the spring panhandlers bloom.

Need I describe New York's air pollution?

It's a sidewalk campus—three buildings in the middle of the city. The "Foundation" is a mammoth old brownstone labyrinth of angular rooms and skylights. The elevator shaft is painted with psychedelic colors—it's a trip (up or down).

Hewitt is a rectangular solid block building—it houses all the workshops.

The Engineering building is in the modern New York style. It houses New York City's air-pollution-control center.

Cornell University
Ithaca, New York

Probably has the most beautiful campus in the United States.

SERGEANT PEPPER SECTION:

13,569 students, of which 3,931 are grads. Each college has a good deal of autonomy in selecting students. Generally high grades and SATs. "The College selects primarily for what Aristotle called the intellectual virtues, it considers academic ability, intelligence, creativity, independence, maturity and a promise of mental growth." Hard to get in.

ACADEMIC BULLSHIT:

The best departments are Fine Arts, Arts and Sciences, and Engineering. Rhodin in the Physics department, Dowd in Economics and Mattack in English are good. Engineering—"It stinks spiritually but is technically excellent—an autocratic authoritarian machine." Very good faculty at Cornell, especially those connected with Southeast Asian studies.

Charlie Ackerman of the Sociology department is by far the most popular professor. He teaches a course called "Deviants" which is otherwise known as "Nuts and Sluts."

Some Pass/Fail, few student-initiated courses. A new Free U at the "Ithaca Seed Company" (a local health-foods store). The freaks in Ithaca operate the Neighborhood College which is aimed at the local workers in downtown Ithaca.

Poor relationships between most professors and students.

A Black Studies program for blacks only.

Upperclassmen take independent study. Study abroad.

BREAD:

Cornell is really a weird place. The University is private, public and land grant—some of its colleges are public, others are private. Thus there are different tuitions at each school.

Tuition and Fees—

College or School	Semester
Architecture, Art, Planning	$1,175.00
Arts and Sciences	1,175.00
Engineering	1,175.00
Aerospace Engineering	1,175.00
Business and Public Administration	1,175.00
Hotel Administration	1,175.00
Law	962.00
Agriculture:	
In-state	375.00
Out-of-state	575.00
Human Ecology:	
In-state	412.50
Out-of-state	612.50
Industrial and Labor Relations:	
In-state	350.00
Out-of-state	550.00
Veterinary:	
In-state	412.50
Out-of-state	612.50

Tight money—not much financial aid. A relatively limited number of jobs at $1.85 an hour. Cars are the most popular form of transportation (freshmen aren't allowed to have them). Dates cost about $5.

Dorms cost either $500 or $800 for room. They sell ticket books for $500 for the academic year. Apartments are cheap—$40–$80 a month in the summer and higher in the winter. $160 a month for a two-bedroom place is considered very high.

BROTHERS AND SISTERS:

Ratio cats : chicks—3 : 1.

Most students are very bright. The campus is divided into three equal groups appearancewise—freaks, straights and a combination. A majority of the chicks are braless and wear jeans. Lots of army jackets and penny loafers and tie-dyed shirts.

Freshmen males never get a date—they can't even buy one. They don't have cars and chicks like only upperclassmen. They have to go to surrounding colleges or look around for local talent. There are too few chicks at Cornell to go around. The situation gets better as you get older.

Freaks are into group dating—collegiates into twosies. Flicks, concerts, parties. Living together cuts across cultural lines—most chicks are liberated. They get superiority complexes because so many guys want to date them.

48 fraternities, but they are becoming less popular. The biggest hang is "The Straight,"—Willard Straight Hall—one of three student unions on campus. Freaks hang in at "Noye's Lodge" and "The Commons." The "Chapter House" bar collects four guys to every girl.

Not much grass around to buy—mainly hash, which costs $40 for a quarter ounce. Most smoke. Dopers hang at "Dunkin Donuts" on Meadow Street.

Students are left of moderate—a crisis has to get them moving—basically apathetic liberals. A small group of hard-core radicals. The Black Liberation Front is militant but not without University provocation. The Ithaca Labor Committee is a group of students who want to get to the working-class people and take radical politics off campus.

Cornell had its share of demonstrations and sit-ins in 1968–69.

Spring of 1969, someone burned a cross in front of the Black Women's Co-op. There were black demands all spring, especially for an Afro-American Studies center. Finally blacks took over Straight (and held it for 36 hours). They had guns. Reason for guns was that in the early morning the frats tried to break into Straight and the police didn't stop them. A couple of frats got in and some fights broke out—one white and one black got minor injuries. Blacks said that throughout that day they were receiving threatening phone calls. Then they received a call from a member of the administration who told them that the white frat boys had armed themselves and might be coming after them. So the blacks felt they had to arm themselves for their own protection—that's the only reason they brought in guns.

The dean of the Arts and Sciences faculty said that if the A&S faculty wouldn't grant amnesty he would resign (he also said that he'd resign if the faculty wouldn't accept their other demands). The guns may have slightly influenced this decision. So the blacks left Straight. A majority of the students were sympathetic to the blacks, though a significant number were against what the blacks were doing and the University "buckling in."

The Arts and Sciences faculty then met and rejected all the blacks' demands. That morning President Perkins said that people would be expelled from Cornell if they seized a building. So about 8,000 students seized Barton Hall (a big gym—the ROTC building) and had a meeting. Tom Jones (then the leader of the Afro-American Society) said that Cornell had one day to live and that the blacks were going to take certain actions which he didn't specify. He wanted to know if the whites were going to support them (they'd go ahead with their actions even if the whites didn't support them). The SDS people there wanted to have their own separate meeting to decide on actions to be taken but a majority of the students there shouted down the SDS speakers and told them to stay at the meeting for an all-Cornell policy. The Arts and Sciences faculty was scheduled to meet the next day and the big thing that had to be decided at this meeting was whether the students should go out and take some actions in attempting to influence that meeting or whether they should wait and let the faculty have a chance to change their minds (the majority there supported this). 2,500–3,000 people slept over at Barton Hall that night. The next morning a lot of the students went out after their professors to talk with them and find out where their heads were and try to get them to accept the blacks' demands. At their meeting the faculty voted to grant amnesty.

A spin-off from this crisis was that a Constituent Assembly was created (a body elected by students, faculty, the administration and University employees) which was supposed to look at the University and see how it would and should be restructured. Their grand result was a report that established a Student Senate which has just been elected. The Student Senate's power is sort of nebulous and it can be dissolved by the trustees at any time they wish.

Another spin-off is that there has been some restructuring of different colleges and some easing up of required courses. Several professors left because of this crisis. They said that academic freedom was threatened here and that Cornell wasn't conducive to their studies!

At the end of the semester President Perkins resigned.

October, November, 1969. There was a lot of support for the Moratorium.

February, 1970. Some kids stopped G.E. recruiting here.

March 19, 1970. The National Mobilization Committee called for an anti-draft action to be held nationwide with tactics to be left up to the local people. 500 people from Cornell went up to Syracuse where the action was to be held. Cornell and University of Syracuse people planned and successfully executed a blocking of an induction bus as it pulled into the Induction

Center in Syracuse. 117 people were arrested (45 from Cornell). They also stopped the police vans that were taking the arrestees back to the jail. The police were forced to negotiate with them. The result was that the demonstrators allowed the vans to move on if no more arrests were made. (And that's what happened.)

April, 1970. Another black crisis. Earlier in the year a kerosene highway flare was thrown at the Black Women's Co-op. Then during Easter vacation the Afro-American Studies Center burned down (arson). These two incidents upset the blacks immensely and after the arson of the Center the blacks came out with a list of demands—a new Afro-American Center to be built for next year, buses to take them to a temporary center which was set up in one of the dorms, Cornell to help rebuild the Southside Community Center (which was burned down earlier in the year), and black guards hired to protect black buildings. Several blacks went into the campus store and broke some showcases and stole some goods. Cornell said that they couldn't identify anyone so there were no prosecutions. The next night the blacks burned their loot and they trashed windows around campus (big picture windows in the Library and windows in the white chicks' dorms). Bomb threats during the week.

White radicals had their own supporting actions. There was an injunction against gathering on campus. They tested it and found it was unenforceable. There was a curfew; it was tested and it also was shown to be unenforceable. There was a takeover of the atomic reactor by the whites (not much community support for them).

In the end the black demands were pretty much met—Cornell said it would build a new Center and said it would be hiring black guards for the rest of the semester.

April–May, 1970. Kent and Cambodia.

April 30, 1970. Strike called that night and lasted for a week.

May 1, 1970. Radicals set up barricades on all roads leading to the Cornell campus.

The strike was not against Cornell but against the United States government. They had three demands: (1) Free the Panthers; (2) End the war in Indochina; (3) End ROTC.

During the strike ROTC was trashed and so was a car belonging to ROTC.

On *May 7* a lot of the kids went to Washington.

During the week there was a lot of organizing on campus, with petitions and canvassing of Ithaca. The faculty voted several grade options so students could do political work (or stay at school). You just had to work it out with your professor. There was a faculty meeting which decided to keep ROTC.

SURVIVAL:

O.K. if you aren't a freshman boy.

Student health is very bad. Limited number of doctors who give out BC pills. Mainline is a drug rescue service. There's a suicide prevention service and Planned Parenthood in Ithaca. Cornell United Religious Work gives draft counseling—one of their members is being chased by the FBI for burning draft files.

"Some guy left a lot of money to Cornell provided that dogs be allowed to run free on campus." Dogs are all over the school. There's "no glorification of jocks here." The *Cornell Daily Sun* is the only morning paper in Ithaca—left of center. *The First Issue* and *Year One* are both radically-oriented pamphlets that come out irregularly.

Health foods at the "Ithaca Seed Company."

ENVIRONMENT:

Mental—People are talking politics.

Physical—Rains all year 'round. Cold from October to April. Humidity in spring and summer. The campus and surrounding area is one of the most beautiful natural environments around—trees, a stream and the view of Lake Cayuga—exquisite. Old beautiful buildings in general. The Uris Library has a nice tall clock tower.

The new wing of the Baker Hall Annex is an uncontested eyesore. Architecture students unfurled a seven-story banner that said "Mediocre" when the building was dedicated. The new campus store is somewhat underground and is like a bomb shelter.

The entire area is beautiful. Head in any direction for an escape —especially Taughannock State Park. The People's Park in Ithaca is two sidewalk blocks off Eddy Street. After 11 P.M. every night you see freaks there. It has its own mayor who sometimes negotiates with the mayor of Ithaca.

C. W. Post College*

Greenvale, New York

Plastic-hip commuters.

SERGEANT PEPPER SECTION:

11,000 students, about 20% out-of-state. 100 blacks. Easy to get in. Most students don't have very high grades and score about 950 on the SATs.

ACADEMIC BULLSHIT:

The best departments in this academically mediocre college are Education, Business Administration and Psychology. The graduate departments of Education and Biology are adequate.

The most popular course on campus is the one which is considered the biggest "mic" by the students. It's "Theater Arts." Geography is also considered easy and therefore groovy by these quiz kids. "We have a lot of boneheads here who just take the easy

* Long Island University.

courses." Dr. Lathstein's philosophy course is one of the only ones that's popular because it is interesting rather than easy.

Some Pass/Fail, lots of tests. Class participation good only in the Psychology department. Some student-originated courses like "Institute for Student Problems" and black studies courses. The Free U is nothing to write home about. Some black studies courses like "Afro-American History" and "Swahili," but nothing special there either. Independent study is popular. Study abroad in France and Italy.

BREAD:

Heavy for this school. Tuition is $960 per semester. There is a $60 per credit charge for semester hours over 18 credits. Loans and scholarships are tight. Campus jobs are mostly maintenance work and pay $1.75 an hour. Most kids don't need to work. Dorms cost $625 for room and board per semester. This includes laundry and infirmary fees. Most kids live at home and commute. There is one coed dorm and 24-hour visitation. Apartment dwellers pay $160 on the average for a one-bedroom. Some summer cottages are available in summer on the north shore.

It's hard to scrounge and most of the kids don't need to. Everyone has a car and parking is for shit. Some cats and chicks are into the "rich-hip" look but many have just casual threads.

BROTHERS AND SISTERS:

Ratio cats : chicks—1.5 : 1.

Varied looks adorn the campus but the rich-hip look predominates—$50 boots, $40 leather vests, brand-new jeans. Some freaks exist but not many. Hair is fashionably long. Chicks are the plastic-hip types who say they love balling and have done it once. Dating is still happening and people go to the city and dance or see a flick.

The biggest hang is the "Commuter Cafeteria." Eat at "The Rathskellar" or "The Burger King." No one stays around campus for entertainment; on the weekends, people attack Fillmore East.

Frats still exist but have been weakened by dope.

Students are rich and apathetic. They go to class and go home, blithely on their merry little ways. The only active group is the new Black Generation which has been pressing for the usual demands. Students became moderately active over Kent State and Cambodia, but most agitators weren't students at C. W. Post. That was the only time the outside pigs have been used so far.

Grass is very big—most everyone smokes. Lids go for $15. Acid and mescaline are just starting to arrive. Busts were frequent in 1969 but have been quiet lately.

SURVIVAL:

Photography is a fad here—everyone has a light meter on his shoulder. The health center is lousy, no BC pills dispensed. No draft counseling. No survival services here, but all are available in

New York City. *The Post Pioneer* is a conservative, boring paper that emphasizes sports coverage. Some are into natural foods and go to a store in Huntington, 15 minutes away.

ENVIRONMENT:

Mental—People are reading *The Godfather* and Abbie Hoffman's books.

Physical—The campus is located in a suburban community an hour from New York City. Typical terrible New York weather. The campus used to be the Post estate and is beautifully landscaped —gardens, shrubs and roses. Most buildings are two-story, red brick and simple. Other structures are old, dark wood ivy-covered units. It's a beautiful campus.

Everyone escapes on the weekends to Long Beach, New York City or Boston.

Hobart and Wm. Smith Colleges
Geneva, New York

A fine small liberal arts college. Hobart men tend to think of themselves as prizes far above the caliber of their female counterparts.

SERGEANT PEPPER SECTION:

1,549 students—all undergraduate. 50% from New York State. Admission is reasonably selective; the emphasis is on extracurricular activities in high school and recommendations. Average combined SAT scores are 1,200. Average student is in top third of graduating class. 6% minority students.

ACADEMIC BULLSHIT:

Hobart was a small Episcopalian liberal arts college for men that recently merged with the nonsectarian girls' school, William Smith.

The best departments are English, Political Science and History. The emphasis is on traditional academic endeavors. Be sure to take the courses on Shakespeare. 6 out of 36 courses may be taken Pass/Fail. Popular professors include Jack Krause of the Political Science department and Gary Campbell of the English department (specializes in poetry of the Romantics).

A student may virtually do anything he wishes—as long as he can get a professor to sponsor it, it's O.K. A Free U exists in informal structure.

There are close relationships between faculty and students—they smoke dope, drink and play Frisbee together. Most professors require papers rather than tests.

BREAD:

Lots. Annual tuition is $2,400 and rising. Loans and scholarships are tight since the school is low on funds. Some work-study, many campus jobs at $1.45 an hour. Expensive wardrobes are necessary only for rich jocks. About one-fifth of the students have cars.

Dorms and fraternities run $450 per year for room and board. Average apartments run $110 a month. A few communes. Most students live in dorms.

BROTHERS AND SISTERS:

Ratio cats : chicks—25 : 1.

Hobart men pride themselves as "elusive."

Most students are hip. There are lots of straights, but "a hell of a lot of freaks to counteract them. Long hair on dudes and braless wonders among the chicks."

Balling is commonplace, dating only exists among the frats (which are, by the way, declining). Freaks meet at the Student Union. Everyone hangs at the "Oaks" (a bar and restaurant).

Hobart students are becoming increasingly political. The two biggest organizations on campus are the Hobart Student Movement and the Strike Committee (spring, 70)—both leftist types.

Orderly demonstrations began about five years ago when Hobart males in business suits asked the trustees to allow them to have chicks and booze in their rooms. When this was granted, the young men's fancy turned to ROTC. There have been many demonstrations including a firebombing in the ROTC offices. ROTC was removed. Hobart and William Smith supported the student strike.

Spring clearance for grass usually runs about $15 (lid). Everyone smokes.

Entertainment is self-generating—indoor tripping in winter, outdoor appreciation in the summer.

SURVIVAL:

Survival sounds good. Any BC pills or abortion referrals can be found in Geneva (central New York). The faculty does draft counseling very efficiently. People brown-bag it for lunch or eat in the cafeteria. Dope and sex run wild. The campus newspaper is good. Almost all live-ins.

ENVIRONMENT:

Mental—People are talking about the sad state of the world.

Physical—Hobart and William Smith are located in the Finger Lakes region of central New York. The climate is poor—wet and windy in winter, hot in summer. Beautiful grounds, trees and waterfalls. Not much pollution.

Most buildings are brick. The Library-Chapel complex is Gothic.

For escapes, people flock to the secluded waterfall areas like Slate Rock, Glenora and Watkins Glen. Some men escape to neighboring women's schools—Wells and Elmira.

John Jay College of Criminal Justice*
New York, New York

It's not pigs off campus here, but pigs on campus.

SERGEANT PEPPER SECTION:

4,500 students of which 500 are graduates. John Jay accepts "civilians" as well as "those people involved in Criminal Justice as an occupation" (pigs). The school accepts nonmatriculated students—it's easy to get in. Applicants must take the SATs. John Jay used to be a police academy but now has open enrollment.

ACADEMIC BULLSHIT:

Pre-pig courses include "Methods of Security," "Crime Scene Laboratory," "Current Problems in Traffic Control," "The Patrol Function," "Criminal Law of N.Y." and "The Law and Politics of Race Relations" to name a few.

The best three graduate divisions are Forensic Science, Criminal Justice and Psychology. Other grad degrees offered are in the fields of Public Administration and Social Relations.

Favorite courses include "Laws and Police Science" (a survey of criminalistics—emphasis is placed on the value and assistance of various scientific aids to the police officer), and "Criminology" taught by Professor McNamara.

There's an extremely close relationship between big and little pigs. Students and teachers are very friendly. No Pass/Fail system, some student-originated courses and no Free U. No Black Studies departments but several ethnic courses such as "Afro-American History," "Afro-American Culture" and "Puerto Rican History and Culture." Some study abroad in Europe.

BREAD:

Tuition per year for residents of New York City is free, $220 for residents of New York State—out-of-staters pay $35 per credit. Loans and scholarships are very available for students enrolled in study programs related to law enforcement. Most of the students are cops and go to school in their off-hours. There are no dorms at John Jay—all commuters.

An expensive wardrobe isn't necessary—uniforms are in. Carry a club and gun to be really in.

PIGS:

Ratio male pigs : female pigs—10 : 1.

About the students, one pig said, "Since our school is made up of a diverse group of students it is hard to categorize our student body into one set description." Upon walking into John Jay, the overwhelming impression is one of fright. Radicals are trying to

* Part of The City University of New York.

send in an undercover agent to infiltrate the pig ranks but so far have been unsuccessful. Students are always demonstrating on the streets for law and order. It is rumored that J. Edgar Hoover knows each by name and has them on a special list.

The main political demonstration came after the Cambodian announcement in 1970. The president of the school gave the students the option of closing down the school. 25 pigs protested this.

Some pigs go to other schools for demonstrations, but they are inevitably on the wrong side. Dick Tracy is the local hero. Under "sports heroes" a pig answered, "our karate instructor is nationally known." Some pigs are known to turn on.

SURVIVAL:

Forget it. It's hard enough to survive in New York City, let alone John Jay.

ENVIRONMENT:

Mental—Lots of pigs walk around mumbling "10-4" to themselves. They are all reading *The Driving Code* and *The Godfather*.
Physical—Dangerous to your health. Proceed with caution.

Manhattanville College
Purchase, New York

Supposedly the foremost Catholic women's college in the United States. Manhattanville, however, doesn't like that image and is trying to discard its reputation as a rich Catholic snob school.

SERGEANT PEPPER SECTION:

1,200 female students of which 30 are grad students.

Difficult to get in. Must have an average of 1,200 combined SATs and good grades. Most students were in the upper two-fifths of their graduating class. 3% blacks. 4% Mexican-American.

ACADEMIC BULLSHIT:

Manhattanville has recently been trying to erase its "Catholic school" image. It's still Catholic, but they have been hiring non-Catholic professors for the first time.

The best courses are in the Humanities department. The East Asian Center allows students to choose an interdepartmental major in Asian Studies. The English courses in creative writing are very good. Popular professors include Dr. McDermott (Philosophy) and Dr. Johnson ("Introduction to Religion"—Dr. Johnson uses a philosophical approach which students dig).

Pass/Fail is rare. There are provisions for independent study and for student-originated courses. Classes are small and the teachers are very interested in students as individuals. A Black Studies program offers courses in sociology, economics, history and psychology but no Black Studies major is offered. Study abroad in Majorca, Spain.

BREAD:

Tuition is $2,300 a year. There are a large number of Manhattan-ville grants. Lots of jobs are available at $1.70 an hour. Most students live in the dorms and they cost $1,200 a year for room and board. Many students have cars and expensive wardrobes.

SISTERS:

These chicks are pretty hip dresswise. They wear minis and jeans, see-through braless tops and sandals. Some are still into the Villager bag but this is fading.

But the sad note is the lack of cats. There's a heavy emphasis placed on dating and social life. The chicks have to go through the mixer and blind-date trip and are shipped to nearby men's schools on the weekends. "Local hangs are not for meeting people because you run the risk of fighting a Townie. This is unheard of for the most part." Gracious! About half have smoked grass but it's hard to get on campus.

The girls are liberal—not revolutionary. There were two sit-ins led by the blacks. School was closed down two weeks early because of these in 1969.

SURVIVAL:

Hard with only chicks (unless you're a cat).

Student health doesn't give out BC pills but you can get them in White Plains. No other survival services besides student health are provided.

ENVIRONMENT:

Mental—Chicks study and hunt for guys.

Physical—A small women's college in upstate New York, fifteen minutes away from White Plains. Architecture is modern and squarish. There are lush woods and fields on the school land.

Chicks split every weekend for guys' schools.

State University of New York (SUNY)

Five campuses: Albany, Binghamton, Buffalo, Potsdam, and Stony Brook.

NEW YORK STATE UNIVERSITY AT BUFFALO
Buffalo, New York

The largest and most diverse of the SUNY campuses.

SERGEANT PEPPER SECTION:

23,764 students of which 6,844 are grads. Entering freshmen must have graduated from high school and have good grades and good SATs. Transfers need a 2.0 GPA. Most are in-state. 600 blacks, 200 Puerto Ricans.

ACADEMIC BULLSHIT:

There are many great departments, especially Philosophy, English and Law. The English department has a fantastic faculty and lots of independent study. The American Studies department is one of the more radical departments in the school. It looks critically at America through all phases of American society. They also have different colleges which are interesting and different—the College of Ecology, the Political Movements College and the Community Organizing College.

Pass/Fail is called Satisfactory/Unsatisfactory. "There are too many popular professors here to name them." Numerous student-initiated courses for credit—called "Bulletin Board" courses. Extensive Free U. Good relationships between teachers and students in the good departments. Many black studies courses. EPIS is a special program to bring minority students here. Independent study and study abroad.

BREAD:

Tuition is $531 in-state and $731 out-of-state per year. Some financial aid and campus jobs are available. Dorms cost $1,100 for room and board. A furnished efficiency in Buffalo goes for circa $100 per month. You can get room and board in someone's home for $25 a week.

Many students have cars (mostly Ramblers and VWs). Dates are usually inexpensive.

BROTHERS AND SISTERS:

Ratio cats : chicks—5 : 3.

The campus is divided into three types—the commuters (from Buffalo) tend to be conservative, the New York City arty kids have that expensive plastic-hip look and the real freaks wear overall work pants and tie-dyed shirts. The commuters are for the most part Catholic and virtuous. The freaks dig balling and cohabiting. Fraternities are dropping off fast, only one Greek group still owns their house. They get to use the Millard Fillmore Room in Norton Hall to eat in all by themselves from 11–1 daily (wow!).

Freaks hang at "The Rat," commuters, medical people and Greeks hang at "The Cafeteria." Freaks live in the Allentown area —near Allen Street. Freaks smoke a lot. Lids go for $25 and are bought communally but they are paranoic since the authorities are really cracking down. Score in Allentown. People smoke in "The Rat."

Students are seasonal revolutionaries—"9 months of the year we are revolutionaries and during the summer we take our classes." Buffalo is a notoriously conservative city bordering on the fanatic. Thus the community and school are divided. The radicals would like to use the campus like a Latin-American campus (to make forays on the city and then come back and use the campus as a sanctuary). Most kids are sympathetic to or intimidated by the radicals. Most support the values ideologically but they won't condone the manifestations of the protests. The most radical group on campus is the "Youth Against War and Fascism" (Maoists). Puerto Ricans have organized into PODER, a group which hangs around BSU. BSU wants a slice of the American pie while the radicals want to smash that pie—they don't trust the white radicals and so far are militant only in rhetoric. Women's Liberation succeeded in setting up a day-care center in 1970.

The political history started in 1968 when white radicals gave a list of demands to the president, Martin Meyerson. Meyerson managed to diffuse the whole thing. In March of 1970, the place blew up (not literally). 20 BSU members stopped a basketball game to protest the fact that there weren't any black coaches. There was a confrontation the next day around the new president's (Regan) office (over many of the usual demands). The campus cops came wearing full riot gear. Regan also called in the TPU (Tactical Police Unit) and charges of police brutality ensued. A strike was called (half the faculty struck) and 24 students were dismissed from the University. The University got an injunction against sit-ins. 300 Buffalo police were on campus for two and a half weeks (still in full riot gear). The strike continued and there was moment-to-moment confrontation.

Chronology of events (1970):

February:
24 = Sit-in at basketball game.
25 = Pig invasion of the campus.
26 = Strike called.
27 = Injunction against sitting-in or closing down of buildings by students.
28 = 1st firebombings started on campus.

March:
1 = Students blocked buildings in defiance of the administration for an entire week starting on this day.
8 = Rally in Norton. Everyone decided to move out to ROTC (Clark Gym). The police were stationed in there. Rocks and a molotov cocktail were thrown. An American flag was burned. Students kept circling the building and harassing the pigs while another group went over to Project THEMIS (special military underwater research) and trashed the windows there. Then came the pigs and beat the kids. They chased them—from THEMIS to Clark Gym to Hayes and then through the parking lots. Pigs just used their clubs and no gas (no time to use gas when you are beating someone). That night at 11:30 there was another big confrontation with the pigs and some of them broke ranks and were screaming hysterically, "Kill! Kill! Take Norton!" Luckily, one cop seemed to calm the rest down.
15 = Sit-in by faculty at Hayes.

May (Kent-Cambodia):

5 = Students had a big march and tried to get together with all the students in the Buffalo area. The march was stopped and the students built a barricade in the street and then were forced back onto the campus where they were tear-gassed all afternoon. A couple people were smashed in the face with rifle butts.

That night kids trashed windows in three banks next to campus. Pigs were called in. A fire was set in the ROTC building ($5,000 damage). Radicals tried to burn down Project THEMIS but failed. There were some trashings on campus (no trashing on private property). All buildings were very selectively chosen.

6 = Police were chasing students and firing tear gas. That night, high-school kids came onto campus with sticks and beat up radicals. Happened again the next night.

7 = The police finally came on campus and fired tear gas on top of the dorms and when the students came running out the pigs fired bird shot at them.

8 = Everyone was given the option to go home for the rest of the year and this caused things to quiet down. The problems lasted about a week. Professors who were on strike had their pay docked.

SURVIVAL:

Student health has pretty good service but doesn't meet all birth control needs. The school has shrinks and a number of counselors. There's a 24-hour switchboard and a Planned Parenthood in Buffalo.

The Buffalo Draft Counseling office is really good. Lots of people in the Buffalo area are really knowledgeable about the option of splitting to Canada since they are so close. There are dogs all over campus ("Irving" is the notorious sire of many a campus puppy).

The Spectrum is considered the second best college paper within the U.S.—considered fairly radical by some.

ENVIRONMENT:

Mental—People are talking about student politics.

Physical—"After a very cold winter, we have a spring revolution." Lots of snow in the winter, humidity in the summer. Buffalo is the second windiest city in the nation. "The nicest time of year is when you're away." Nice days in Buffalo are "2 days in spring and 1½ days in the fall." South Buffalo has Bethlehem Steel Corporation and terrible air pollution. Republic Steel is also a polluter and the Buffalo River is a fire hazard.

The school was constructed over a long period of time so the architecture is diversified. Most buildings are four-stories high. Capen looks like a bunch of yellow bricks thrown together in a square pile. There aren't too many trees on campus. Lots of buildings and cement.

NEW YORK STATE UNIVERSITY AT STONY BROOK
Stony Brook, New York

A freaky campus where the dorms are like brothels.

SERGEANT PEPPER SECTION:

8,825 students of which 674 are out-of-state. 170 blacks, 41 Spanish-Americans. In-state students must take either the Regents' Scholarship Examination or the State University Entrance Exam to get in. Admission is highly selective—average SATs are 1,200.

ACADEMIC BULLSHIT:

This campus is the hippest and the most intellectual of the SUNY campuses. The best departments are Psychology, English and Social Science. Best graduate departments are Psychology and Engineering.

The most popular course is "Deviance and Delinquency" taught by Dr. Good of the Sociology department. Another good course is Dr. Carlson's "Introduction to Biology." Both Drs. Carlson and Good were active during the 1970 student strike and are very well liked by the students. Chicks flock to "Courtship and Marriage" by Dr. Goodman for obvious reasons.

Some Pass/Fail but most grades. Many tests and not much class participation. Students originated the black studies course. The Free U is poor and is mostly research projects. No Black Studies department. Teachers-student interaction is best in the Biology department. Independent study is allowed but isn't utilized much. Study abroad in France, Spain, Germany and England.

BREAD:

Tuition in-state is $600 per year, $800 per year out-of-state. New York State residents can get a Regents' scholarship—almost 65% of the kids are on them. Loans are available from the EOP—it depends more on need than on merit. Campus jobs are tight and pay $1.65 an hour.

Most students live in the dorms. The campus is outside of town and most students would rather not commute. The town is conservative and doesn't like longhairs. Most dorms are coed. Dorms cost $1,025 for room and board a year. These rooms have 24-hour visitations. Few apartments and no fraternity houses. Most students walk since they live on campus, but some have cars. An expensive set of threads isn't vital, but some chicks are still into the Villager look.

BROTHERS AND SISTERS:

Ratio cats : chicks—1.5 : 1.

Everybody is hip and freaky for the most part. Students dress in dungaress and T-shirts. It is one of the freakiest and most casual campuses in the East. Chicks are liberated but there's not much cohabitation due to the dorm situation. But the dorms are like brothels—there's always a chick spending the night.

Dates are super-casual. Smoking and seeing a flick is the usual. Others go to the "Libery Diner" or "Fat Humphrey's" and eat for $5. People hang in the Student Union, the quads and the "Coach House." A big date consists of going into New York to the Fillmore East.

The drug scene is very heavy—the campus is literally flooded with grass and mescaline. In 1968–69, there were undercover agents on campus who led big raids on the dorms. The biggest bust brought 200 pigs on to campus. Grass goes for $15 a lid, acid for $2.50 a tab.

The biggest political action was after a bust in spring of 1969. It triggered action and students set fire to trucks and stoned buildings. The administration was hysterical and closed down school early.

There are many activists here. The main issue the last two years has been defense contracts. After the Cambodian strike, the administration decided to phase it out. The strike was mildly successful in that it started community action. SDS leads all the demonstrations and controls the student council called "The Polity."

SURVIVAL:

The biggest creative bag is music. Many students play the guitar or the piano. In the Student Union there's a groovy craft shop where tie-dying, pottery and jewelry-making are taught. The student health center is very poor—there are only 12 sick-beds and the nurses are very rude. Students staged a demonstration requesting that a nurse be fired because she refused to treat a student injured in a demonstration. Shrinks are available. No draft counseling office on campus. A bail fund was just set up by the student government —it comes from student funds. No survival services in the conservative community around the school.

The Statesman, the campus paper, is leftist and proactivist.

No one is into health foods.

A loose Women's Liberation exists.

ENVIRONMENT:

Mental—People are reading Abbie Hoffman and Ken Kesey. They are rapping on drugs and music.

Physical—Stony Brook is one and a half hours from Fun City. It's an open rich conservative suburban community. The campus was just started in 1957 and is always expanding—it looks like one big construction site. Buildings are three-story red brick structures.

Students travel to nearby schools on the weekends.

NEW YORK STATE UNIVERSITY
COLLEGE AT POTSDAM
Potsdam, New York

An isolated state college campus.

SERGEANT PEPPER SECTION:

4,500 students of which 1,300 are graduate students. Only 45 out-of-state. 20 blacks, 5 Indians. Not too difficult to get in. You need above average grades and SATs in the 1,100 range.

ACADEMIC BULLSHIT:

Best departments include Music, which is noted for its Crane School of Music, and Education, which is better for secondary-school teachers. Favorite courses include "Major American Authors" with Israel Kaplan ("Kaplan makes it, he gives us pause now and then"), and "Introductory Psychology" with Wolf.

Pass/Fail is allowed, lots of traditional tests, no student-initiated courses, limited black studies. "Teachers and students don't have much interaction; they'll talk over courses in their offices but they don't generally come on as human beings." Independent study in your major and study abroad in Tours, France, or Madrid, Spain.

BREAD:

Tuition is $260 a semester in-state, $330 out-of-state. Loans are easy to get but scholarships are nearly impossible. All campus jobs are work-study. Some work in the community of Potsdam (population of 9,000).

Most people live in dorms which cost $1,150 for room and board a year. They have either doubles or suites for six (few singles). "It sucks because if you dorm it, you must feed at the cafeteria." Dorms have lax rules. A few people live in apartments which run $70–$120 a month for a one-bedroom. The campus is flooded with cars—hardly any bikes.

Dates usually cost about $4 for a flick.

BROTHERS AND SISTERS:

Ratio cats : chicks—1 : 3.

"This place is where all the farmers' sons and daughters go to school; it's a conservative rural population." Most students are straight and "dumb and unaware, study = a degree = money slop-up-the-suds types."

"Maybe a hundred are interesting hip people."

Hair is mostly Joe College, about 25 shoulder-length darers. Girls dress straight Penny's.

The dating scene is bad for the chicks as there are too many of them. Cats have no trouble getting a date, moderate trouble getting a balling partner. "Women here don't really want to be liberated, one dorm voted open house, and we have an iron-virgin dictator for our Dean of Women." About one-fifth of the campus are Greek, but they are dying out.

Major entertainment is beer busts.

Drugs are just getting popular. Acid goes for $5 a tab, and grass is sold in nickel and dime bags. Few busts.

Most students are Middle-America conservative. "In May, 1968, we had a few broken bottles and gas, nothing constructive or destructive, and in May, 1969, they had real pigs on alert. Everybody went downtown to see if there would be a 'riot.' " A few students demonstrated against food prices and for the Moratoriums. In November, 1969, 60 people went to Washington to lobby for peace. There was a little action in conjunction with the 1970 strike.

SURVIVAL:

Student health is lousy—all sex referrals to Planned Parenthood, mental health problems referred to the St. Lawrence Mental Health Clinic on campus which is good. Draft counseling is done at the Potsdam Information Center. Everyone eats in the cafeteria and the food is lousy. The campus paper, *The Racquette,* is of low quality.

ENVIRONMENT:

Mental—The few freaks are reading *Woodstock Nation.* People are talking about campus politics.

Physical—The climate includes 33 inches of rain a year and four feet of snow. The campus is in the foothills of the Adirondacks, on hilly farm land. Not much air or noise pollution. The old administration building is nice with red brick and white trim. Other buildings are red brick and black glass.

Kids go home to escape.

The school has a resort in the hills which some kids use.

New York University
New York, New York
(Washington Square—downtown)

You are on your own in Greenwich Village to survive and learn.

SERGEANT PEPPER SECTION:

44,000 in all (uptown and downtown). NYU is the largest private university in the country. Uptown is the University Heights campus for Liberal Arts and Engineering. The Washington Square campus (downtown in the Village) has Liberal Arts, Commerce, a School of Arts and a School of Education. Ten other "colleges" are spread among the two campuses.

Difficult to get in. Average 3.0 GPA and 1,300 SATs (combined). Over half the students are from New York. 2,000 minority students. Many professionals and adults attend the adult education center.

ACADEMIC BULLSHIT:

The School of the Arts is excellent in Films. It's "not plumbing" and is spiritually oriented. "Film and drama are incredible." Olympia Dekakis (an actress) "teaches a fine acting course."

Popular courses include "Utopia" by Carse (each person must

boggle their mind and create their own utopia), "Philosophy of Democracy" by Hook (a former Marxist who turned rightist, good dialog), Clive Barnes, *The New York Times* theater critic, teaches "Critical Writing," Paul Simon (of Simon and Garfunkel) teaches "Songwriting," Bertell Ollman teaches "Socialist Theory." The Graduate School of Medicine is tied up with Bellevue Hospital. The Archeology program has many overseas field programs.

NYU can be very stimulating intellectually if you take advantage of the opportunities offered—it can also be a drag depending on what courses you take.

Undergraduate courses are large (150) but graduate seminars are smaller. No student-initiated courses except in the School of Continuing Education. There is a Free U called "Alternate U" on 14th Street.

There are scattered black studies courses. The program is looked upon as a flop. The majority of these are attended by 70% white. Roscoe C. Brown, Jr., is head of the Institute of Afro-American Affairs. The Institute has recruited minority students, called "King Scholars." Courses include "Race and News Media," and "Black Man in American Literature."

Most professors discourage intimacy and make themselves "generally unavailable to students." Some independent study and some study abroad. Some students take their junior year in New York—it's an open program but only ten students came in 1970 (masochists).

BREAD:

Heavy bread—$2,275 a year. Scholarships are tight and some students complain that the school awards big money the first year and then cuts back the second year. (Beware.) Loans are more available. Work-study at $2.00 an hour, but few jobs.

Some dorms are coed. Most cost $1,300 for room and board per year. There are 24-hour visitation rights. Some of the dorms are converted hotels—"real plaster walls and very homey." The new dorms are "cinderblock jail cells." Some students suffer at home.

The majority of the students live in apartments between 20th Street and Houston Street. A one-bedroom goes for about $100 a head. In the East Village, you can get a dingy eighth floor walkup for $60–$80 a month. Housing is scarce. Come early.

It's not easy to scrounge in New York. Subways and buses are used for transportation. An expensive wardrobe is optional ("it's necessary only if you want to shop on Fifth Avenue"). Average price of a date is from 30¢ (price of joints) to $5.50—rock concerts. Campus bookstore sells used books.

BROTHERS AND SISTERS:

Ratio cats : chicks—7 : 5. (Washington Square campus)

NYU is a large impersonal factory—survival and learning only for the fittest.

Chicks garb themselves in a lot of vinyl and plastic—the hip synthetics—heavy eye makeup and lipstick. They're stylish—square-toed boots and maxi coats, funky old raccoon type coats in winter and short minis in summer. Other chicks wear old jeans and shirts. Then there are the Verushka types—dressy shopping wardrobes.

Cats wear bell-bottoms, carry briefcases and trim their moustaches. Not much of the work-clothes look. They have bushy hair in the back of their neck, but no shoulder-length locks. A few fancy dudes wear men's boutique slacks and high-vented sports jackets.

Everyone complains that it's hard to meet people here—some mixers and fixups. Rallies are the spot to meet and greet. Fraternities are dying out.

Most people want to get learning, get married and get a job. They find politics too confusing. The most active club for freaks is the "Transcendental Students," a cross between Kesey's Pranksters and the Hell's Angels with 250 members. Some ROTC incidents. Continual bomb scares.

During the student strike in 1970, NYUers kidnapped a computer (worth $6 million) and attempted to ransom it to the administration for $100,000 to be used for the Panther Bail Fund. The plot plopped and there was a peaceful ending.

People meet at the Loeb Student Center, "Le Maison Francaise" (shows French flicks), "The Free Store" (experimental theater) and the "Integral Yoga" (meditation freaks). "St. Adrian's" is an artist-type gathering place. Most action takes place in "his apartment."

SURVIVAL:

Fine if you're a big boy. No warm cozy supportive people at NYU. The big city can be great if you take advantage of it (and it doesn't take advantage of you). You may die from smog, muggings and robberies but you'll "get culture."

Draft counseling is available on campus by the University Christian Foundation. Abortion referrals from Clergy Consultation Service.

The Health Service provides shoddy service. Planned Parenthood for BC pills. Then there's:

Dial-A-Prayer
Dial-A-Demonstration
Dial-A-Freakout
or
Call home.

The Mobile Health Clinic operates on the Lower East Side. People feed at the Loeb Center or nearby delis. Pets don't like it—have to be leashed. Lots of parakeets. The *Washington Square Journal* is a "left of center joke." The *NYU Ticker* puts out a really good literary supplement called *"Incantations."* Undergrounds are the *Village Voice* and the *East Village Other*, both good.

Lids go for $25, tabs for $5, easy to score in the Village.

"Nature's Cupboard" has health foods (Avenue of the Americas).

Women's Liberation is embryonic, not confrontation oriented. But they did occupy the office of Grove Press to protest *Evergreen's* Image of Woman.

ENVIRONMENT:

Mental—People are reading Tom Wolfe, Gunter Grass and Jacqueline Susann. Ecology hasn't made it on campus, they're too weak from the air pollution to protest.

Physical—The campus is brutally urban. Washington Square is in the heart of Greenwich Village, surrounded by pavement. No natural land for miles. Weather is awful, always, except for spring. The Commerce building looks like a mausoleum. Most buildings are a hodgepodge of undistinguished office-building types.

Escapes—well, there's the Empire State Building, Coney Island, Jones Beach or Fire Island (a hip upper-middle-class summer Bohemian Long Island). Skiing in Vermont. Buses go to Miami Beach (ugh). 70% commuters.

Rensselaer Polytechnic Institute

Troy, New York

Rensselaer Polytechnic Institute is called "Tute" for "Institute" by the students. Breeds good engineers but not geniuses like MIT.

SERGEANT PEPPER SECTION:

5,000 students of which 1,200 are grads. Very difficult to get in. Second only to MIT and Cal Tech in Engineering schools. Median SATs for frosh are 600 verbal and 710 math. Median ACT scores are 590 verbal, 660 chemistry, 690 physics, 730 math level I, 750 math level II. (How like an Engineering school to have all the statistics.) 70% of the freshmen are in the upper 10% of their high-school class. 55% of the students are from out-of-state. 38 blacks.

ACADEMIC BULLSHIT:

The best departments are Engineering, the Sciences, and Management. The Management department has grown a lot because people who can't hack it in Engineering and who like RPI go there. Architecture is also very strong. The weakest departments are the Humanities.

Favorite professors include W. K. Brown in "Literature" ("he really makes things interesting"), Dan Walkowitz in "History" ("he's the most brilliant professor and is really into politics"), and Bernd Forester for "Art and Architecture" (it is completely visual. You have two term projects—either a photographic essay on any subject or an analysis of your home community).

Lots of technical knowledge. Very limited Pass/Fail and not many student-originated courses. The Free U is called a "Free School" and is mainly rap sessions.

Both faculty and students are rather repressed here and grow together working for what they want. The classes are large but the relationships between faculty and students are good. Two or three black studies courses. Independent study in the Humanities and the Social Sciences.

BREAD:

Tuition for the year is $2,300. Two-thirds of freshmen receive financial aid and 80% of these get their total need met. The aid is a combination of loans, scholarships and jobs. Jobs go for $2 an hour. Dorms cost $1,000 a year for room and board—frats about the same. Apartments in Troy are really cheap—about $50 a head. Freshmen aren't allowed to have cars but lots of the upperclassmen have them.

"Dauber's" has used books.

BROTHERS AND SISTERS:

Ratio cats : chicks—14 : 1 (only 340 chicks).

The campus is straight-looking with a smattering of freaks, especially among the freshmen. People are wrinkled casual ("Everyone has perma-press clothing here but it doesn't always work"). The engineers wear blue jeans, button-down shirts and ugly shoes. Some chicks have that liberated braless look and others are really into clothes. The freaks are in Architecture and the School of Humanities and Social Sciences.

RPI cats like booze and girls (although they have a hard time finding them). There aren't too many chicks at RPI so the cats have to find them at Russell Sage. When they get one, there's no time to get acquainted. Sex is their prime interest. The administration seems to feel that sex and alcohol will divert people from politics. 30% of 1970's freshmen joined fraternities but they are on the verge of collapse.

Drunken frats go to "Petar's," "Shaker's" and "The Question Mark"—all three are on River Street. The freaks live on Washington Square and hang at "The Inside Out Coffeehouse" on 10th Street. Some freaks are buying farms in the area ("The Farm" is a hang for freak architects).

The freshmen are really into dope and you can score on campus. "A hell of a lot are usually on uppers for finals week." About 50% of the school smokes, but dope is tight and you can't always get it.

Half the campus is indifferent toward politics—they just want their degree and feel the University shouldn't be involved in politics (usually engineers). Another fourth are conservative and support Nixon's ROTC. The final fourth are liberals (who don't really see the relevance of their education). The most active leftists are in the Humanities and Social Sciences and the Physics departments. Women's Liberation has about 20 coeds in it; they are lobbying for a day-care center and helped get the New York State abortion law passed.

Political history started in April, 1969, when the black students presented a list of demands to the administration. A black dorm was set up. About 700 people participated in the 1969 Moratoriums.

In March, 1970, students presented four demands called "Requisites for a Technological University"—they were: (1) a new library; (2) doubling the budget for Humanities and Social Sciences; (3) the resignation of the dean of Humanities and Social Sciences; and (4) equal student/faculty representation on all trustee committees and all University committees. These demands are being considered. So far only the new library was promised.

The Peace and Freedom people demonstrated in April, 1970, to abolish ROTC.

After Cambodia and Kent, some students went to New Haven to support Bobby Seale. On May 6, students took over the Student Affairs building on the basis of the ROTC issue—they also demanded (1) that University complicity be ended, (2) stop political repression at home and (3) end the war. About 300 people supported the strike.

SURVIVAL:

The doctors are in the infirmary only a couple of hours a day. No BC pills. No survival services except for a Planned Parenthood in Schenectady. "Refer" is a 24-hour switchboard in Albany. Draft counseling through the chaplain's office in the Student Union. *The Polytechnic* is a liberal element on campus. Natural foods at "Nutritional Foods, Inc." on Fulton Street.

ENVIRONMENT:

Mental—Engineers are discussing their slide rules, activists are discussing politics.

Physical—The climate is miserable in winter—there is always half a foot of snow on the ground. In the summer when it's not raining, it's overcast. Allegheny Ludlum (steel and aluminum manufacturers) is the major polluter. Troy has 57 raw sewage outlets into the Hudson River.

Most of the buildings have green roofs. The People's Avenue Complex was a former reform school for chicks ("it's an architectural nightmare"). Social Science professors have their offices in this building just above the room where the band and chorus practice. They're driven out because of the decibel level. West Hall is a former Troy high school and "one of the biggest monstrosities in upstate New York." The frosh dorms are in the neo-penitentiary style. "Superficially it looks like a penitentiary." Frosh yell, "I am a hairy integral" from its windows.

The nicest spots on campus are the open green spots.

People escape to neighboring schools, especially Russell Sage.

University of Rochester
Rochester, New York

Rich Long Island pseudo-hippies.

SERGEANT PEPPER SECTION:

9,100 students, of which 1,400 are grads. 41% out-of-state students. Each applicant is considered individually. You should be in the upper one-fifth of your class and have 1,300 SATs but there can be deviations from this. 180 blacks.

ACADEMIC BULLSHIT:

The Medical school competes with Howard, Johns Hopkins and Case Western Reserve for number-one honors in the country. The Eastman School of Music is one of the best in the country—it's as difficult to get admitted here as to any other top music conservatory. Excellent pre-med courses. The Geology department has great relationships between teachers and students—you can drink beer in the seminars and professors play Frisbee with the kids.

Popular professors are Murray Colin Turbayne in Philosophy, Beck in Philosophy and Peck in English.

Lots of Pass/Fail and many student-initiated courses (known as "Bulletin Board Courses" because the student sticks a piece of paper on the bulletin board describing his course, the other students sign up and then they get a professor). Some interesting courses are "Soaring Flight" (gliders), "Human Ecology" and "Methods and Morals of Advertising." 25% of all courses in any one term have less than ten students enrolled. Faculty members are always complaining that students don't come to see them. Students like professors in the Geology, Philosophy and Optics departments. Various classes in black studies. Students can design their own major—a couple of students are majoring in Urban Studies. Easy to get independent study—study abroad.

BREAD:

Private and costly. $2,600 a year tuition (University of Rochester says a student should expect to spend $4,400 a year on living expenses). 45% of the students receive financial assistance. Campus jobs are available.

Dorms cost $1,250 a year for room and board. $65–$75 per person for an apartment. Dates cost about $5 and most have cars. The "Clinton Book Store" across from "Hippie" Park gives you a free used book if you buy one.

BROTHERS AND SISTERS:

Ratio cats : chicks—3 : 2.

The generalized undergraduate student: he or she is from Long Island, is loaded with bread, can't piss-off his parents no matter what he does because they love him so much, does things that he thinks are fun because he was conditioned to think they were fun. The professional type student (in Physics, Optics or Chemistry) is the one who asks the professor the exact question he wants to be asked, wears ironed clothes, carries a brief case and wants to start off making $14,500 a year. Then there's the intellectual—not really an intellectual but thinks he is. Grows his hair long and sprouts a beard, spends lots of money on cheap clothes (25 pairs of levis), goes to all the SDS rallies and fights for the microphone. When he gets it he doesn't know what to say so he repeats what the previous person just said. Has money and cuts his hair before vacation.

A moderate amount of structured dating—flicks and out to eat. Popular bars are "The Bungalow," "Kelly's" and "The Nugget." No Christian ethic concerning balling. "If balling is fun, fine, if it's more than that, then that's fine too." Frats are dying. Half the campus turns on—mainly hash and grass. Some pills from the Medical school. "You can get high just walking through the corridors of the dorms." Grass grows wild in Bushnell's Basin. Lids go for $20.

People hang at "The Bungalow," the dorms and Highland Park.

Kids are apathetic left—even when they demonstrate it's more of a game and social event (the kids' families are too loaded and feel they've got too much to lose if revolution comes).

"It's traditional—every spring we take over the Old Building." Blacks and Center for Naval Analysis demonstrations so far. In May, 1970, after Kent and Cambodia, students broke in and took over the administration building but they didn't know what to do with it. The National Petition Committee was started on this campus then; they had a goal of getting 20 million signatures and ten million dollars for work against the war.

SURVIVAL:

Health service is terrible—"it costs $35 a year and your health." BC pills dispensed. At Strong Memorial Hospital on campus there is a 24-hour switchboard for suicide prevention. Draft counseling at the Rochester Free School and the Rochester Friends Society.

Plenty of dogs on campus, so many that the city pigs are threatening to come on campus and bust the dogs. The *Campus Times* is good.

ENVIRONMENT:

Mental—People talk about student politics.

Physical—"There are two seasons—winter and the Fourth of July." Fall is usually nice. The Genessee River flows in front of the campus and there are lots of trees. Air pollution gets bad in some areas. The sewage outtake from Rochester is dumped into Lake Ontario and the water intake for the city is retaken from the Lake. Kodak supposedly dumps its shit into the Genessee River. The Geology department is superconcerned about the environmental scene.

The buildings around the quad are really nice and funky-looking—old and fine with lots of ivy. My favorite building is Rhees Library—it's a big building and the top looks like a wedding cake. It's called "The Nipple of Knowledge" because it has a shining red light on top of it at night.

90% live on campus.

Sarah Lawrence College
Bronxville, New York

Sarah Lawrence chicks are upper-class dilettantes who go Bohemian in style. Although the school is now coed, the chicks still go on menhunts on weekends to nearby men's colleges.

SERGEANT PEPPER SECTION:

720 students of which 100 are graduates. Over 50% from the East. 7% black.

Very difficult to get in—an "elitist" school. Many private-school chicks. Need excellent grades and combined SATs of 1,300. There's a long application form to evaluate your "potentiality for maturity."

ACADEMIC BULLSHIT:

Excellent departments—many innovate courses; things are changing all the time. Sarah Lawrence chicks have the opportunity for a wonderful education.

There is no structure. No majors, grades or required courses. Mostly independent study. Teachers write out comments on each student. The president of the school, De Carlo, was the former head of IBM's education division.

All classes start late. Favorites include "Courtly Love" (Mr. Spitzer), "Biology of Pollution" (Professor Mandel) and "Children's Theater" (Shirley Kaplan). In "Children's Theater" the chicks set up workshops in elementary schools in the ghetto and sponsor the "Sneaker Players" which perform for the kids (noblesse oblige).

The Theater department has a top-notch faculty. "Techniques of New Theater" is taught by Professor W. Finley, who's a member of the Shechner Performance Group in the city.

Music Composition and Creative Writing are also excellent departments.

You can do graduate work in almost anything, all you need is a professor to help you set it up. There's a great new program this year called the "Special Program in Human Genetics" for chicks who don't want to be M.D.s but want to be associate physicians. They specialize in areas of birth defects and inherited diseases.

No tests or old teaching methods—just individual projects. The class limit is 15.

Physical education is out of sight here. You can take "Yoga" or "Circus Skills" (juggling and tightrope walking).

There are nine black studies courses attended mostly by blacks. Courses such as "Ecology and Health Problems in the Ghetto" or the "Black Experience." The black students all live together in coed Brandt.

The ratio of professors to students is 1 : 7. Everyone is on a first-name basis. Frequent dating, balling and smoking. Students

341

have one-hour conferences with their advisor every week. They even visit them during summers.

Independent study is the rule. "Just visit the professor every once in awhile and tell him you are alive." "There are hardly any regular class hours."

BREAD:

Heavy. Most of the students come from very wealthy homes. $2,900 a year; not much financial aid possible. "The school is incredibly broke."

As for campus jobs—"Sarah Lawrence is the community center for baby sitting at $1.00 an hour until the baby goes to sleep, then it's 75¢. It's wish-fulfillment for the chicks." Some typing and food-service jobs are available at $1.60 an hour. Dorms are $1,400 for room and board for your own filing cabinet. Some chicks live in Tudor-style homes which the school has bought up. Most live on campus.

Scrounging? Forget it. It's the type of joint where chicks give their clothes to the maid.

Lots of cars. The school has free bikes you can borrow. Dates are often dutch-informal type.

BROTHERS AND SISTERS:

Ratio cats : chicks—1 : 7.

Sarah Lawrence recently went coed. For years it has had the image of high educational attainment and highly insane girls. The Sarah Lawrence chick is the avant-garde individual—the highly sophisticated keeper of tons of hidden "creative talent."

They dress in the latest old thrift-shop styles. In the winter, chicks are wrapped in funky old raccoon coats (which it took them a month to find), wool scarves, high leather boots and bell-bottom jeans. Eye makeup. Many are New York sophisticates—maxi coats, panty hose and copies of *Women's Wear Daily*. There's a small number of boarding-school types. They all bring second wardrobes for "New York weekends."

The cats have a lot of hair and wear T-shirts, jeans and boots. The guys are hipper than the girls but not so freaky looking.

Chicks at Sarah Lawrence have lots of "romances" and live with cats without a solid commitment—kind of flitting around. Chicks also fret about the lack of sex. The ideal is to be "in love" and live with someone—but when they do, they maintain separate residences for the purpose of fooling their parents. Cats who go to school here feel it's a "stud farm." "I feel like Don Juan."

The upperclass Sarah Lawrence chicks are friendlier and freakier than the sister-schools chicks. But they can be very aggressive and slightly frightening. Artsy-craftsy.

The students are liberals. Most are more Bohemian thinkers than active radical. They have marched against the War. In 1969 they held a sit-in at the administration building for ten days to protest the tuition hike and the elitist nature of the institution. The administration fed them and the students left to take showers and returned later. In 1970, they took part in community canvassing against the War.

Pastimes include cultivating artist talk, rapping at "The Pub" (a noisy jive scene on campus) and eating at the "Reisinger Caf." The chicks have an oral fetish—eat, smoke, rap.

SURVIVAL:

Except for bad dating odds for the chicks, it's cool. Students are very arty and have an electronic music studio with a Moog synthesizer. Art studios and workshops everywhere. Everyone has his own Nikon camera.

Yogurt and shrinks are Sarah Lawrence chicks' status symbols. BC pills and abortion referrals are available in Bronxville. Draft counseling by Professors Danny Kaisen and Eva Kollish. There's a menagerie of dogs and cats in the girls' rooms. The *Emanon* ("no name" spelled backward—how quaint) is the school paper—so-so.

Men brought drugs and politics when they came to the school. Lids go for $20. Everyone smokes but only cats buy it. Lots of mescaline. In 1968, lectures were given on "How to Stall in a Dope Raid," (strip naked, etc.).

Not much of a Women's Liberation. "The men are oppressed sex objects here."

ENVIRONMENT:

Mental—Stimulating. People read Rubin and Brautigan. Brandt House has a new greenhouse. There's a course on "Light Media and Producing Environments." Many night owls—midnight to 3 A.M. are big hours.

Physical—A lovely suburban campus in icky upper-middle-class anti-Semitic WASP Bronxville. Green lawns and trees and flowers.

The campus is a chaotic mixture of old mansions, Gothic buildings, Tudor residential homes and dorms. Lots of slate-top roofs and fine trees. A bizarre Hitchcock type trellis of knotted branches that leads to the administration building. Two-thirds of the girls split on the weekends to Fun City or to the men's schools. Chicks will visit the men's schools on any pretext.

Syracuse University
Syracuse, New York

Tremendously vast, uninspiring, fraternity-controlled place.

SERGEANT PEPPER SECTION:

17,151 students, of which 7,000 are graduates. The school tries to consider each applicant individually—ACT average and 1,200 boards should get you in. 50% from out-of-state.

ACADEMIC BULLSHIT:

Best departments are Philosophy, Religion, Political Science, Forestry and Law (grad). The New York State College of Forestry at Syracuse is one of the best Forestry departments in the country. The Religion department has Professor Yahanian, whose students think he is a theologian on a par with Martin Buber. Bharatti of the Anthropology department is into mysticism and derived much of his material from his personal experience as a Tantric student in Tibet. The Maxwell School has a good reputation of government service and for a fine Political Science department. The Philosophy department demands rigorous thinking, especially in the course on existentialism which deals mainly with phenomenology rather than art or literature-oriented existentialism. The course on "Plato's Republic" is well spoken of. Professor Michael O. Sawyer teaches "Constitutional Law" and is especially popular.

"Projection '70," supported by the College of Education, offers three credits for tutoring grammar-school kids from nearby black neighborhoods.

Some Pass/Fail, no student-originated courses and a loose Free U. (They work on an Indian reservation in Syracuse.) There are black study courses in eight departments. The relationships between students and teachers are good. Some independent study and lots of study abroad.

BREAD:

Tuition is $3,000 per year. Dorms cost $1,100 for room and board a year, the same as fraternities. A one-bedroom apartment near campus costs $100 a month (unfurnished). Some cars (juniors and seniors only).

Dates cost as much as $15.

Cheap records at the "S.O.S. Record Shop."

BROTHERS AND SISTERS:

Ratio cats : chicks—5 : 3.

Syracuse students are made up of those who were rejected from the Ivy League Schools. They are upper-middle-class, suburban and drive Corvettes. About half are hip and half are straight. The hip chicks wear expensive mini skirts and dresses—costly threads are a status symbol. Some freaks wear T-shirts and jeans and tie-dyed stuff. The "Toads" are the intellectual, stay-at-home study types, nonpolitical. They have short hair, wear white socks, baggy pants and penny loafers. The Forestry people are called "Stumpies"—they are usually very nice and wear tight dungarees, lumberjack jackets and stumpy boots (hiking boots). Everyone has a Syracuse T-shirt.

Average dates are flicks and a collegiate bar. A lot of chicks are not liberated until after their first semester here. It's hard to find a chick unless you fit into the norm which is that of the hip.

The Greeks died in 1970. "People are embarrassed to admit that they are in a House"—lots of anti-Greek sentiment on campus.

Half of the 1970 basketball team was suspended. Syracuse has run into a rash of great athletes with police records (robbery, usually).

"The trouble with this university is that nobody hangs out enough." There is no student union although the "Jabberwocky" at the bottom of Kimmel Dining Hall is a pseudo-student union. Freaks hang off campus on Marshall Street at "Carrol's" (burgers). The "Beach" (a small strip of land near the corner of Marshall and Crouse) is another hang.

About 70% of the people have tried drugs—25% are regular users. The pig department prides itself on the fact that no one has been acquitted on a drug charge in the last year. Most use drugs because they think it's cool (because everyone else does it). Big dope busts every three months.

Most students are unable to grasp the essence of political ideas—they are very middle-class in their politics. (The thing that broke the student strike in 1970 was when they defined the strike.) As long as they talk they are radical, but when it comes to action they disappear. No civil disobedience. They are concerned in their heads but not in their guts about issues. "They'll drive to the Revolution in their Corvettes."

The only together political group is the Black Student Union—Separatists and a lot of them have money, not many ghetto blacks.

Water fights every spring. In April of 1968, the pigs were called in to stop the water fights.

Political history began in 1968—there was a cafeteria boycott because of the food—some ROTC demonstrations. In spring of 1969, there was a boycott of classes over dorm autonomy. Big march for the 1969 Moratorium. There was quite a lot of action over the student strike in 1970.

Briefly:

May 5. There was an unofficial strike with barricades.

May 6. Big meeting in the quad to discuss the strike. They passed proposals that (1) SU be shut down, (2) $100,000 should be raised for the Panther defense fund, (3) ROTC off campus, (4) all University contracts with the government should cease. That night the chancellor announced that classes would be canceled for the next day and Friday.

The students knew that police weren't going to be allowed to come on campus by the chancellor and that their barricades would remain.

They began to organize groups of peace marshals (to guard against trashings), first-aid marshals, and legal-aid marshals to go around campus and make sure everything was O.K.

They organized and eventually canvassed the neighborhoods and tried to get into the high schools (and were successful at times).

May 7. Another meeting was held—had a big argument over the words "strike" and "shutdown"—the real radicals wanted a shutdown but the voice vote was too close to call. The next day the chancellor said that if there were any disruptions of classes, he would close the place down completely (so the students would have to leave and wouldn't have any place to stay). That night there was a fire at the construction site of the new Geology building. It was a normal fire—NOT arson.

May 8. 100–150 students took over the administration building over the Panther issue. They stayed there till midnight of the 9–10 when SU got an injunction against them. Syracuse chief of police Sardino stayed in the building with them for two days, rapping with the kids and finding out what was happening . . . he was cool. The students told him he would either have to get some rest or leave the building after he had stayed up two days rapping with them. He may have been occupying that building longer than any of the students there (he is a grad student in Sociology there).

May 9. A lot of kids went to D.C. though a lot of the other kids wanted them to stay at SU to man strike headquarters.

May 11. Classes were held. Options on classes for the students were announced and on Tuesday the consensus was that it was up to the individual professors to decide what to do. There were three bomb threats that day. Nixon was burned in effigy in front of the administration building that night.

May 12–13. Some people met with their professors, deciding what was going to happen with their course work. As soon as this was over with, things died down because the students had "nothing to do."
Workshops were held.

May 14. A dance marathon was held on the quad to raise money.

May 16–17. Barricades were removed that weekend and no one complained.

May 18. The campus was back to normal.

The local jail is known as the PSB or Public Safety Building (or Pot Smokers Building amongst the street people). It is filthy and unkempt. Freaks get harassed in it. There are no windows there. They totally control your environment. They may even bug your cell. The judges are down on freaks.

SURVIVAL:

If you fit into one of the many stratifications, you can survive. Student health is the worst—no BC pills. No free hippie clinic, but Planned Parenthood is near campus. "1012" is a 24-hour switchboard—drug rescues and suicide prevention. "Rap Center" gives draft counseling. The campus paper is the *Daily Orange*—"when it's 8 pages long it's an 8-page editorial, and when it's 16 pages long, it's a 16-page editorial."
"Good Foods Store" and "The Healthful Diet Shoppe, Inc." sell health foods.

ENVIRONMENT:

Mental—People discuss their social life and their philosophy classes.

Physical—Cold winters and humid summers. "No matter what kind of day it is, the sun will manage to appear five minutes before sunset." Air pollution from Solvay Process (part of Allied Chemicals) which makes things out of limestone—they pollute Onondaga Lake.

Lots of new buildings on campus—boxlike orangish creations. Crouse College is nice—it looks like a Gothic castle.

Escapes are Burnet Park Zoo and the Green Lakes State Park.

Union College

Schenectady, New York

Of Union, Skidmore says, "The close but gross school."

SERGEANT PEPPER SECTION:

1,620 students of which about 15 are grads. Difficult to get in. Students need about 1,300 SAT scores and high grades. The school desires a cosmopolitan student body and gives preference to those students who are applying from geographic areas of the country not adequately represented at the school. You also have to take the ACT tests and go through a personal interview. 40% are out-of-state. 40 blacks.

ACADEMIC BULLSHIT:

One unique thing about Union College is that they combine a Liberal Arts and Engineering curriculum on a small campus (this is unusual because Engineering is so expensive to teach). The school is moving from an emphasis on Science to the Humanities. Independent study is encouraged. Best departments are Engineering, Physics, Political Science, Psychology and Biology.

Some of the projects in the Comprehensive Education programs include study in France, in Bogota (students live independently with a Colombian family—they take prep work in Spanish and Colombian studies at Union for a term and then go to Colombia), in Vienna and in the Developing Countries.

Other unusual courses are:

THE STATE LEGISLATURE IN ACTION. A systematic analysis of various aspects of the New York State Legislature. Student research will be based on participation and observation. All students will serve as volunteer interns in the offices of New York State Legislators.

NUTRITION, HEALTH AND DISEASE. A study of the medical care system and health services available in the United States. Designed to gather concise information at the local, state, national, and international levels on recent innovations in the provision of health care. Individual and group projects will permit students to analyze the problems—social, political, economic, and otherwise.

LAND USE AS AN ASPECT OF REGIONAL PLAN-NING. A brief survey of planning practice to be followed by a careful, in-depth analysis of the historical, current, and projected land use along the Schenectady-Troy Road. Attention will be given to conflicts between public and private interests.

REGIONAL DEVELOPMENT IN THE CAPITAL DIS-TRICT. An analysis of the Troy-Albany-Schenectady area as a single unit. Student research will be based on a systematic study of those aspects, economic, social, cultural, and/or political, which either integrate or fragment this region.

POLITICS OF EDUCATION. A study of the crisis in educational policy-making participation, with special emphasis on the participation of the community in local school system politics. Field research in the Schenectady area.

EXPERIMENTAL EDUCATION IN THE UNITED STATES. An introduction to the problems of traditional classroom learning and an exploration of the major approaches to experimental education with special emphasis on field research into the structures, modes of procedure in the classroom, and the overall effectiveness of existing experimental colleges in the United States.

POLITICS OF DISSENT IN AMERICAN HIGHER EDU-CATION. An analysis of some of the major theories about the traditional functions of a university, some of the major theories about how the university should be politicized, and of two specific attempts to politicize the university at Berkeley and Columbia. Special emphasis will be placed on field research by each student into at least one national movement whose declared or implied aim is to politicize the campus.

And more in Science, in Economics, English, Political Science, "Disputed Questions." In the "Social Psychology" course they have a simulated pot party and a simulated pot bust once a quarter.

They have a few Master's degrees—some in the Sciences and one in the Institute of Industrial Administration—and an Interdisciplinary Doctoral program in Life Science and Biology.

Popular professors include Professor Allen in English, Professor Huntley in Psychology (he's an experimental psychologist) and Professor Scharlet in Political Science ("he seems to know everything"). No Free U or student-originated courses. Professors are friendly and accessible. A few black studies courses. You can create your own major.

BREAD:

Tuition and fees for three quarters is $2,445. Aid is very tight.

They used to have a backlog of money but it has been eaten up. There are about 150 jobs starting at $1.45 an hour. Most aid is packaged, a combination of scholarships, loans and jobs.

Dorms cost about $1,200 a year for room and board. A resident professor lives in each of the dorm buildings. Apartments are shared by many students who pay $40 a month per bedroom.

Hitching or cars are the most popular forms of transportation. "Lescron" sells used books.

BROTHERS AND SISTERS:

Union went coed finally after a long struggle—in 1970. The campus looks straight generally. Levi Sta-prest, jeans and T-shirts. The jock casual. The freshmen look hipper than the rest of the campus. The Engineering students are super-straight.

The social life is primarily through the fraternities with other colleges (Albany State, Russell Sage and Skidmore). Even with the chicks this year you still have to find chicks at other schools— no one dates townie chicks. Horniness runs rampant here ("everybody feels so horny here that when they finally get a girl they just about rape her"). The Beta Turtling Team is associated with the Beta fraternity—they have a tendency to gross out people and their favorite trick is dry humping on the floor in one big pile.

Fraternities are in their dying gasp.

Hangs are the "Rathskellar" (a snack bar on campus), the "Library Plaza" and "Diamonte's" and the "Union Inn" (bars for straights). 60% of the campus smokes regularly—hash, grass and mescaline are popular, some speed. Dope is very accessible through friends. Paranoia is evident only when the R.A. (resident advisor) is uptight about it. Lids go for $20, $8 for a gram of hash and $2.50 for a tab of mescaline.

The school is just beginning to emerge politically. The DAR once classified the school as a safe place to send your son, where he wouldn't run into the evil influences of drugs, sex and politics. The students are liberal McCarthy types with a small vote for Wallace.

The administration has a theory of "Give it to the students before they want it." On things that aren't really important. About 300 students participated in the Moratorium.

Nixon's comment about "bums" was made after he heard that Union College and University of Maryland students burned him in effigy after his speech about the Cambodian invasion.

Students struck over Kent and Cambodia and marched downtown to sit in at G.E. They demanded that the school (1) take a position on the war, (2) take a position on the ending of political repression and (3) get rid of ROTC. People went to D.C. to lobby, canvassed and petitioned.

The Union for National Draft Opposition started here and at Princeton (independently)—the idea was to get 100,000 people to sign pledges to turn in their draft cards when the total of pledges reached 100,000.

Union College was the central control for the college radio sta-

tions during the strike. The amateur radio stations tried to jam
them and did sometimes—one local redneck whistled "America
the Beautiful," "God Bless America," and "The Star Spangled
Banner" for three hours.

SURVIVAL:

Student health is O.K. "Refer" is a 24-hour switchboard in
Albany that gets you in touch with the survival services. Draft
counseling is done by the Schenectady Area Clergy Concerned
about Vietnam, and Simon Burrows, a Vietnam veteran who gives
counseling on campus.

"Wilson" is the most popular dog on campus—one day he had
the nerve to bite the dean of housing. Wilson was locked up in the
pound for two weeks while they tried to decide whether he had
rabies—the frats put up a sign which said "Free Wilson."

Football, wrestling and lacrosse are the most popular sports.
The official paper at school is *Concordiences*—their articles suck.
"If you ever had a nonpolitical paper, that's it." Underground
papers are the *Union Press* (sprung up with the strike) and *Lotus
Nexus* (for the Schenectady community—basically a cultural
paper).

ENVIRONMENT:

Mental—People are really starting to talk politics as of 1970.

Physical—The climate goes from winter to mud and the humidity
is terrible. May is the nicest time of year. Air pollution is wretched
—the Tobin Packing Company in Albany is a big polluter.

The campus has old colonial-type architecture—they are trying
to give the campus a traditional look and ivy grows all over.
There's a stuffed whale's penis in the president's office.

North College is a wooden frame building built in 1813 and
renovated in 1940. It is used for a dorm now and has sinks and
mirrors in the halls. The Chi Psi house is really nice and looks
like a Swiss chalet.

Escape is Jackson's Garden (part of the campus, it has a creek,
formal gardens, woods and a statue of Chester Arthur).

Vassar College

Poughkeepsie, New York

This pillar of upper-class instability recently went coed and
culture shock set in. Plus point: Jane Fonda, the activist movie
star, went here for one year and left.

SERGEANT PEPPER SECTION:

1,692 students, of which 1,600 are chicks. 70% of the students
are from the East. It's hard to get into any of the sister schools,
but Vassar is the "easiest of them to enter." You need 1,300 SATs

and a ranking in the top fifth of your high-school graduating class. It helps to have a mother who went to school here and to be pure WASP.

ACADEMIC BULLSHIT:

Vassar offers a fine educational opportunity if you like the celibate academic life. Each student is allowed a lot of independent study including six weeks every year between the school terms to develop a project. Some of the most recent ones were "Altruism," "Victorian Studies" and "Psycho-Biology." There are no comprehensive exams and self-motivation is vital. Vassar's strong in the traditional subjects and weak in the creative sphere. There are no applied-arts majors and you can only get half credit for things like dance.

Best departments are Psychology and Art History. Popular courses include "Sex and Violence in the Mass Media," "Justice" (Professor Schalk of the History department studies current trials), "The Creative Spirit in Children" (Professor McConnell) and the "Philosophy of Urban Existence" (Professor Bierman).

The Anthropology department offers "The Ritual Basis of the Drama" and the Psychology department offers courses in parapsychology.

Faculty : student ratio is 1 : 9. Classes are small and participation is important—"the chicks here aren't afraid to talk up, the problem is shutting them up." Black studies is autonomous and mostly off campus in the urban center in downtown Poughkeepsie (Vassar charters a bus to get there). The school's 70 blacks live in Kendrick Hall. Girls prefer spending a semester a year at cats' campuses rather than studying abroad (Yale, Williams). Junior year abroad in Europe and at the American University in Cairo.

BREAD:

Tuition is $2,100 a year. Room and board costs $1,300. Some loans and scholarships are available. There are unusual campus jobs such as washing the piano keys of the 56 Steinway pianos for $1.45 an hour or baby sitting. Cats can get jobs as guards. They wear hats and armbands and protect the chicks from "muggers."

The "Quad Dorms" are enormous solid buildings with single rooms. Comfy rooms and high ceilings. Easy aristocratic living. Students buy a lot of their own furniture. One dorm has Persian rugs, long heavy wooden tables and high-backed chairs. The food, however, is crud. Only the desserts are faintly edible.

Vassar students tried a coed living experiment (platonic coed roommates) but the administration found out and killed the experiment.

Chicks have bikes (they need college license plates) and cars but no motorcycles or scooters are permitted on campus. Also have fine clothes if just to hang in their closets.

Naturally no one would admit to trying to scrounge.

BROTHERS AND SISTERS:

Ratio cats : chicks—1 : 15.

A sad place—not enough cats for the chicks. Vassar has those upper-class WASP types all over. Post debs. Everyone knows someone who went out with Edsel Ford. The campus is suffering from culture shock because of the first male class in 1970. But the chicks say it makes the campus more "livable."

The chicks have that freshly-scrubbed look and take two showers a day for entertainment. They collect a lot of clothes. In the winter they wear jeans, old 1920s furs (mink), knit shawls and manage to look society "camp" (not funky). When they go home they wear suits and "party dresses." Lots of rings and little gold earrings and scarves. The spring uniform is cut-off jeans, T-shirts and sandals (they walk barefoot only on the cement, not on the grass).

Cats are on the grubby side—long burns, shoulder-length hair and handlebar moustaches. Jeans, T-shirts, boots and ski parkas.

Male chauvinism free and loose. There are a lot of buddy relationships between cats and chicks. A small number live together. Lots of blind dates and loneliness for the chicks. They do, however, get the pleasure of having tea in the parlor after dinner accompanied by piano versions of "Moonlight Sonata."

Weekend meat trucks—the chicks are bussed to men's schools. West Pointers come to Vassar for mixers. They stand stiffly "at ease" when introduced. The chicks dump on them.

Hangs include "The Dutch" (an off-campus bar with a cavernous atmosphere—bands play short sets due to the lack of enthusiasm in the audience), "The Brickton Diner" (a gross all-night joint), and "The Retreat" (a plastic cafeteria on campus). For culture it's the Mid-Hudson Philharmonic and the Classic Film Series. Students also go kite flying and tray sliding in winter on Sunset Hill.

Grass isn't obvious but there's a "small dedicated group who smoke dope." They go to Vassar Farms to trip (there's a farm in the back of the campus).

Chicks go to Yale for politics, Yale goes to . . . The Movement consists of a handful of people and two mimeograph machines. The two main political issues are: (1) the administration doesn't reappoint young radical professors and (2) Vassar may become affiliated with IBM and start VIT—"Vassar Institute of Engineering for Graduate Students." Students go to IBM a lot and ask for "tours" to harass them. IBM is uptight about this. The Cambodia decision strike was directed at canvassing and was rather ineffective.

SURVIVAL:

The cats brought politics and dope with them and have worn themselves out crusading. Except for the dating situation, survival is O.K. There's a groovy observatory for star freaks and a private golf course and a solarium (the chicks can tan their costly nude bodies). Three studios for arting and the school supplies materials. Student health gives sex lectures, cold pills. Chicks have to go in to town for BC pills. Professor Schalk of the History department gives informal draft counseling. Grass is available, as is acid—but things have quieted down since Leary left nearby Millbrook.

"House of Nutrition" on College View Avenue sells health foods.

ENVIRONMENT:

Mental—People are reading science fiction by Isaac Asimov and *The Godfather*. Pete Seeger leads the Hudson River Sloop Restoration Committee and charts pollution areas. Vassar students join in.

Physical—New York weather. Spring is a "profound number, people defrost." The campus is elegant—it's like living in a park. Quiet, sedate, rural settings and easy to get to it. Many fortresslike structures with turrets that look like European cathedrals. Maple trees and ivy-covered buildings.

Escapes include New York City (That's an escape?) which is two and one-half hours away—Vassar charters buses. Fallout shelter signs are all over the campus which could mean something. Vassar students also go skiing.

Wells College

Aurora, New York

Wells is a small well-established exclusive type girls' school. The main topic of interest is how to meet a guy. Then how to meet two guys. Then . . .

SERGEANT PEPPER SECTION:

632 chicks. No cats. All undergraduates.

Wells College is ranked #6 on the list of top girls' schools in the United States. The SATs are about 1,200 and grades of the A–B variety but compared to Smith and Vassar, it's easy to get in. 33% are from New York. Ten black students.

ACADEMIC BULLSHIT:

Wells has excellent academic credentials. The classes are small, relevant and interesting. Student : faculty ratio is 9 : 1.

Popular departments include History and Philosophy of Religion, Mathematics and Biology. History and Philosophy of Religion offers "Quest of the Historical Jesus," "Linguistic Analysis and Theological Existentialism" (sounds heavy) and "Prophetic and Wisdom Literature."

Best-liked professors are Mr. Shiflett (Math), Mr. Gilroy (Economics) and Mr. Zorach (Biology—he's an ecologist).

Wells has student-faculty teas every Wednesday afternoon to foster close communication.

Some independent study. Tests and papers required, study abroad. Students must wear shoes to class.

BREAD:

Estimated yearly costs, $3,650. Girls must live in dorms—the cost is included in tuition. Loans and scholarships are readily available. Half the girls have a campus job at $1.60 an hour. If you are on financial aid, you can't have a car on campus. Casual clothes are fine.

SISTERS:

All chicks and they are cooped up and anxious for "relationships." They date cats from Cornell (the catches) and from Hobart and other upstate New York campuses. Chicks are either sophisticated New York with a touch of hipness or pseudo-heavy-hip. The freshmen are the hippest of all.

A recent "health center survey" showed that 14% were regular pot smokers, 6% had tried acid, 15% took the Pill, and 42% had been deflowered.

The chicks at Wells complain that it is hard for them to meet cats—they are literally dying for the chance to increase that 42%.

Most of them are from upper-middle-class type families. But they try not to mention it.

The only hangs are the "Aurora Inn" (where everyone goes on dates) and the "Fargo Bar." Chicks hang on the campus on the weekend keeping watch for any signs of males.

Wells girls aren't revolutionaries. They are mild-mannered nature lovers. The only political event that has ever happened on campus was the student strike of 1970. There's a core group of about 50 who care.

SURVIVAL:

Fine for celibates. Mentally it's O.K.—beautiful tranquil setting. The school administration is liberal, student health dispenses BC pills. Their service is very good.

The *Wells Courier* is a readable newspaper. Lids go for $15 on campus only. Aurora itself has little drug traffic. No pets on campus.

ENVIRONMENT:

Mental—The chicks talk about where to catch a cat. They are reading *The Strawberry Statement* and *The Godfather*.

Physical—Lovely. Typical northern New York setting—trees, a large lake and lots of lush greenery. Different types of architecture on campus. Nearest escapes are Cornell (40 minutes), Hobart (45 minutes) and Colgate (two–three hours). New York City is four hours away.

NORTH CAROLINA

Davidson College
Davidson, North Carolina

"The most academically eminent church related school in the south [Presbyterian]."

Davidson College is a small men's college that is graduate-school preparatory. They list as one of their biggest demonstrations that time a few years back when the Greeks held a torchlight parade to protest the abolition of fraternities by the administration. The honor system and two campus police are in charge of law enforcement.

SERGEANT PEPPER SECTION:

1,000 men go here and there are no graduate programs. It's a hard school to get into—you need a B+ average and 1,100 combined on your SATs. No effort is made by the admissions department to stretch the requirements for minority students, except, perhaps, for basketball players (if you're a Harlem Globetrotter, apply).

ACADEMIC BULLSHIT:

This school is heavy on traditional academics—studying is the order of the day. As Jerry Rubin says, "Studying and taking tests is like taking a shit. You eat it, digest it and regurgitate it." The course of study is more or less dictated by the graduate school the student wants to go to—especially medical schools. Pre-med is a strong department, majors write an independent paper in the spring of their junior year and an experimental thesis during the spring term of their senior year. The English department is also good. The school lists one of its more unusual and interesting courses as "Religious Literature 101"—a real stunner!

The school is very regional and the students come mainly from North Carolina, South Carolina, Florida, Virginia and Georgia. Pass/Fail is used in some courses. There is a close relationship between students and teachers because of the size of the school. Hardly any student-initiated courses. Popular professors include Mr. William Jackson, Assistant Professor of Political Science and Dr. Earl MacCormac, Associate Professor of Philosophy.

There is a Free U run by the school with some interesting courses—"Beyond Conception" (seminar on abortion and birth control) and another one on astronomy. The types of courses that conscientious schools offer in the regular curriculum.

Mostly WASPs with 26 blacks. Independent study is allowed inside the major. Study abroad in Germany and France.

BREAD:

Private schools mean bread. Pay through the nose at $1,550 a year. Almost everybody lives in the dorm at $300 a semester. Those few that live in apartments pay about $70 a month. If you need aid, the college guarantees it relative to your need through loans or scholarships or work-study. Campus jobs in Charlotte include working at a foam-rubber plant for $2.10 an hour. No "used thing" stores. Dates are expensive since it means commuting to a women's college and "showing her a nice evening." 60% of the students have cars.

BROTHERS:

This is a boys' school and you know what condition they must be in. Private girls' schools house delectable southern belles who definitely aren't liberated. Most cats are very straight. "The crew cuts just left but there are few with hair covering their ears. The admissions office goes in big for the all-American boy look and most of the students do, too. To look cool everyone reads the ads in *Playboy* and *Esquire,* tones them down a little, and buys his clothes accordingly." They do, however, wear jeans and sweat-shirts in class.

Davidson is a suitcase college—everyone splits to the girls' colleges on the weekend. 60% of the upperclassmen belong to fraternities, but it's gone down from the 85% of last year. They are nonresidential.

"Hattie's" beer joint is the local hangout. The few radicals frequent the College Union.

Most of the students smoke grass, but that's it. Lids vary greatly in price. Drinking, movies and music are the entertainment. There are only about three radicals on campus. The only active club is the Vietnam Moratorium Committee.

Students try their fellow students on all charges—even those "caught" taking LSD. Little outside law enforcement involvement.

SURVIVAL:

If you can afford to go here, you probably don't need much help surviving. The infirmary is dangerous beyond the cold or flu stage. Draft counseling services include "just several very concerned individuals who can give someone the information. There is a Friends Committee 30 miles south in Charlotte." Pets aren't the rule on campus.

The Davidsonian is the paper. It's liberal and usually anti-administration. However, it did get the All-American rating for five straight years. There are no health-food stores.

ENVIRONMENT:

Mental—Read *Autobiography of Malcolm X*. People discuss the relevance or irrelevance of fraternities and integration—pros and cons.

Physical—Davidson is out in the country with only a polluted creek to remind anyone of civilization. There are still more trees than people. The students are very concerned about ecology, especially about the polluting effects of the Duke power plants. The air pollution is still light.

The buildings are ante-bellum Classical revival. "The major eyesore is the design of the Fine Arts building. Whoever gave that man his instructions in perspective should be re-examined for professional competency." Escapes include the city of Charlotte, the mountains 120 miles away and the beach 100 miles away.

Duke University

Durham, North Carolina

Duke is one of the nicest schools in the South. It is located in the middle of a lush forest and the campus is very much a separate community. The school is composed of thinking liberals.

SERGEANT PEPPER SECTION:

Duke is very difficult to get into. You must have a combined SAT score of about 1,200 and be in the top tenth of your high-school class. It is one of the few southern universities that ranks as a major national university.

The school has about 7,000 students, of which 3,500 are graduate students. 85% of the students are from out-of-state. The school is Methodist but admits students of all religions. 1% black.

ACADEMIC BULLSHIT:

The school is very good in the traditional academic fields, especially Pre-med. The Divinity school is also very good. Popular professors include Dr. Warren Lerner, who teaches a course entitled "History of Socialism and Communism," and Dr. John Altrocchi, who teaches "Abnormal Psychology."

Student-initiated courses like "The University and Society" and "Film as Art" are given in the dormitories for half credit. Students can also band together and form their own seminars as long as they get a professor to sponsor them. There is no Free U.

Both Pass/Fail and grades are used. Both tests and papers.

There is a close relationship between the younger faculty members and the students. There is no Third World College but a skeletal Afro-American Studies program. A good deal of independent study and wide-open study abroad wherever you can arrange it.

BREAD:

Bread is heavy—tuition is $2,100 a year. Dorms are about $400 for a double per semester (add $25 if you want air conditioning). Off-campus apartments vary greatly—from $15 per month for a dive to $65 a month for fancy digs. Little work-study but many scholarships and loans. Campus jobs are available at about $1.80 an hour if you want one. "Anyone who is willing to take jobs and loans can get through here."

Dates and threads vary greatly—can either adjust to an expensive or a reasonable way of life. Flicks run $1.75 a ticket.

BROTHERS AND SISTERS:

Ratio cats : chicks—2 : 1.

This is a school of intelligent gentle concerned people—mostly straight in appearance but not oppressively so. No flaming radicals but a few hips. Most everyone has tried grass though are not constant users. The social life is rather stilted since the women's campus is about a mile away from the men's campus. Greeks still exist but are on the way out.

There aren't any hangs for the freaks which do not exist. Straights hang in the Union lounge and around the quad. They have a wide variety of beer/pizza places like "Bat's" and the "Ivy Room."

Grass is easy to get on campus or in the local ghetto but it's expensive—$20 a lid. The harder stuff is easier and cheaper to get than the grass.

All the entertainment takes place on campus. Durham itself is an anti-college town.

SDS, Young Democrats, Young Republicans, and Young Americans for Freedom all exist. Women's Liberation is quite active.

The main political event occurred in February of 1969. There was a takeover of the administration building by 65 black students over demands for black studies and more black students. Police were called in, the usual riot, tear gas and clubbings. Outside cops hate Duke students while campus cops are the old-style feeble types.

SURVIVAL:

It's easier to survive at Duke than most southern schools because the students are very bright and are not southern rednecks. Both BC pills and information are available from the very fine student health service. Free prescriptions for acute conditions on all medicines. There is a good abortion referral service on campus too. There is extensive draft counseling available five days a week by specialists.

The school newspaper, *The Duke Chronicle,* was just named the best "daily in the southeast." It is controlled by pragmatic radicals and is very good. The underground paper, the *Protean Radish,* is also good.

ENVIRONMENT:

Mental—Duke students are into the issues and discuss them. They are reading Hesse's *Steppenwolf*.

Physical—Duke has an outstanding campus. It is located in the middle of a forest. There are rivers which the campus has fought to keep unpolluted and a cultivated garden and many streams. The climate includes mild rainy winters and nice autumns and springs.

Most of the campus is neo-Gothic. Women's college is Georgian. Some of the newer buildings are neo-neo-Gothic which is rather unique and attractive. Eyesores are three nondescript Science buildings apart from the main campus which are pretty ugly—Engineering, Life Sciences, and Physics.

Escapes include the beach, which is three hours away. Or Duke Forest itself right on campus. Nearest decent urban areas are D.C. and Atlanta (four and seven hours, respectively).

East Carolina University

Greenville, North Carolina

There are separate bathroom facilities for students and faculty—indicative of a lack of fraternization.

SERGEANT PEPPER SECTION:

10,000 students of which 1,500 are graduate students. Most graduates of North Carolina high schools are admitted. The average freshman SATs are 1,000 and GPA is usually 2.0 16% out-of-state.

ACADEMIC BULLSHIT:

Best departments are Education, History and Art. The Graduate School of History is fairly competent but bugged with political overtones. The Art department is excellent in the Commercial Design department. Dr. East of the Political Science department is very popular. Most of the good professors went out with a political purge in 1970.

Traditional academic shit. No Pass/Fail, no student-originated courses and no Free U. Little independent study. No smoking in class. Many papers and tests and one black studies course taught by a white.

BREAD:

Annual tuition is $330 a semester in-state, $700 out-of-state. Loans and scholarships are tight and go primarily to in-state students. Work-study is available only to those in extreme financial need. Very few jobs. Dorms cost $1,000 for room and board. About 50% of the cats and 65% of the chicks live in the dorms. The rest live in apartments which rent for $140 a month or fraternities which are the same price as dorms.

Most have cars and costly threads are important only to the few frat rats.

BROTHERS AND SISTERS:

Ratio cats : chicks—about 1 : 1.

Most students are southern straight—there are a few freaks "who dress radically, i.e. no bras, see-through blouses, extremely short skirts with no panties, long, long hair for shock value" (from a southern correspondent). Chicks like to think of themselves as sexual objects and balling is starting to be commonplace. Frats are dying.

Freaks hang at the "Mushroom" (head shop) and "The Id" (booze hall). Straights hang at "Lum's." Dates include rapping and going to "The Id" or a flick. Grass is getting very popular— you can score anywhere in town—grass goes for $20 a lid. There have been a few half-hearted demonstrations.

SURVIVAL:

Could you survive in North Carolina?

The health service is poor and no BC pills are prescribed—no survival services. "No draft counseling services in the open." ACLU and others helped to set up underground facilities. However, these have been forced to operate off campus.

ENVIRONMENT:

Mental—People study and drink.

Physical—Greenville is a city of 26,000, about 100 miles from Raleigh, North Carolina. The campus is in a rural environment— there's a mall with grass and trees—little else. The major eyesore is the heating plant which belches black smoke into the air.

There is nowhere to go. Drugs are the main escape for the freaks. Straights go home.

University of North Carolina
Chapel Hill, North Carolina

A good southern university whose biggest problem is too few chicks.

SERGEANT PEPPER SECTION:

16,000 students of which 85% are from North Carolina. It's easy to enter in-state. Average boards are 1,150. Out-of-states need about the same boards and a B average. 3,000 grads. 3% black.

ACADEMIC BULLSHIT:

University of North Carolina and the University of Virginia are considered the South's two top state universities.

The Liberal Arts department and the Chemistry department are both very good. The Creative Writing program includes publishing instructors and writers in residence. The German department is rated #1 nationally. Most professors teach both graduate and undergraduate programs.

Popular professors include Father James Devereaux, a Jesuit priest who teaches Shakespeare and Dr. William Peck who teaches the "Psychology of Religion." Some independent study and Pass/ Fail used. Undergraduate courses range from an independent study seminar of four students to 300-student lectures. Black studies was instituted in 1970 but there are fewer than ten black faculty members in spite of apparently sincere efforts of the University to recruit. Both tests and papers. Study abroad in Germany, France and Spain.

BREAD:

$170 in-state and $400 out-of-state per semester. The University guarantees that no one will have to leave for lack of bread. Loans, scholarships and jobs that pay $1.65 an hour.

Dorms cost about $200 a semester—all students must live on campus their first two years. Apartments (scarce) run between $40–$75 for a one-bedroom.

There are the usual two subcultures—hips and straights. Straights spend bread on dates, have expensive wardrobes and cars.

BROTHERS AND SISTERS:

Ratio cats : chicks—3 : 1.

University of North Carolina's main complaint is its lack of chicks. Consequently, cats go in search of them on the weekends and in return chicks come to the campus for the cats. Women's rules have been liberalized recently to include self-limiting hours, visitation and off-campus apartments allowed for juniors and seniors.

Many hips dress casually sloppy, while straights have that freshly-ironed ordinary look. Very heavy dating scene in the embryonic liberated stage. 20% are Greeks but they are dying off. Sports figures are still very popular—especially basketball jocks.

People hang at the same places—"Harry's" (a delicatessen-restaurant), "The New Establishment" (a large dingy second-floor room that serves beer), "The Blue Angel" (food, beer and local performers) and the "Carolina Grill." People date to the sports events. About half smoke. Lids cost $20. Heavy drug scene in the high schools.

Few revolutionaries. Lots of liberals. There were about 4,000 students involved in the student strike over Cambodia and 1,000 students went to Washington to lobby.

The only major confrontation was a cafeteria workers' strike in

1970. Most students supported it and the state patrol was called in twice.

SURVIVAL:

The biggest drawback to survival is the school's location. Chapel Hill is nowhere, man. It's 350 miles from Atlanta. Chapel Hill and Durham (12 miles away) are both culturally impoverished. Drugs are available but expensive. No BC pills or other survival services except draft counseling offered by the school. BC pills and Switchboard (for bad trips) are in town.

The cafeteria food is terrible and no one eats there—they eat in town. The school paper, the *Daily Tar Heel,* is very political for the South. Student health service is good.

ENVIRONMENT:

Mental—People are just starting to talk politics and to read.

Physical—The campus and surrounding area are pleasantly wooded but quickly being polluted. The Chapel Hill sewer plant dumps waste into the creeks and new apartment developments are causing erosion in drainage bases.

The campus is mostly traditional—Georgian with some modern buildings with linear type designs. 60% live on campus.

Escapes are the beach (200 miles) and Greensboro, North Carolina (another University of North Carolina branch that is 90% female).

OHIO

Antioch College
Yellow Springs, Ohio

Antioch is a way of life. Five intense full active years of learning. One term of every year is spent working in the real world but you can be prepared for it by taking a course called "Futureshock." One of the best things about the college is that it teaches you how to survive in a completely unstructured and chaotic situation. A real sense of community in the college.

SERGEANT PEPPER SECTION:

2,000 students of which 130 are grads.

Incoming freshmen must take the SATs and any three achievement tests. Antioch considers "intellectual capacity and motivation, personality, character traits, health, emotional maturity, depth and breadth of interests and seriousness of purpose" in a prospective applicant. They continue, "We seek young men and women who are ready to assume responsibility for their own lives."

Transfers must have no more than two years of college and at least a B average.

91% out-of-state.

ACADEMIC BULLSHIT:

Antioch is very fine. It's one of the oldest Bohemian liberal schools in the United States. The students originate practically all of the courses. One term of every year is spent off campus—in the real world. The school helps you find a job. For Antioch students the world is their college. It takes five years to graduate.

Every department is good—especially Education, Biology, Literature, Psychology and Art.

The Antioch-Putney Graduate School of Education offers a one-year graduate program to develop "teachers for schools and workers in community education."

So many interesting courses—"Film Aesthetics," many ceramics courses, "Modern German Literature on the Left," "Europe in the 20th Century" (case studies on how history is written), "Poetry Workshop," "Independent Study in Rock Music," "Philosophical Studies: Law, Order and Justice: The Chicago Conspiracy Trial in Legal, Philosophical, and Social Context," "Futureshock" (for students moving out of Antioch to the World), "Readings in

363

Psychology: The Psychology of Colonialism," "Television-Anti-Television," and millions of others.

There are no grades—only a system of a professor granting "credit or no credit." Most courses are student-originated—staff members (secretaries, clerks, etc. can also originate them). No need for a Free U—that's what the college is.

Two of the most popular professors are Keith McGary (Philosophy) and Ben Thompson (Education). The classes are small and there's a lot of interaction between students and professors. The Afro-American Studies Institute is only for blacks. Its aim is "correcting the emotional or personality damage done to African-Americans in the ghetto, as well as increasing the specific knowledge and skills necessary to reconstruct and develop the Afro-American community in modern society."

Students do a project to get course credit. Students are encouraged to do independent study for a full quarter on a project of the student's own choice. When students work off campus for a quarter they write up a paper of their experiences.

Study abroad is called "Antioch Study Abroad." You can go anywhere in the world. Students take up independent study or classes or go to work and then evaluate themselves and send in a report to the school.

Tons of freedom in classes. No structure, no meaningless formalities.

BREAD:

Tuition is $2,871 a year (this includes health fee and community government fee). Room and board in the dorms is $680 a year—people are on campus only two of the four quarters. Apartments are hard to get and rents are considered high—about $85 a month for a single. A few communes around (but the dorms are like communes).

Last year 38% of Antioch's students received financial aid. But there are usually more applicants than aid. About 15% of the students get part-time jobs either on campus or in town during their study quarters. They do work away from campus for that one quarter.

You need no expensive clothes—bring rags. Dates are dutch. The "Epic Book Store" has used books and Indian cigarettes.

BROTHERS AND SISTERS:

Ratio cats : chicks—about 1 : 1.

Antioch students are the essence of hip in the mid-50s Bohemian way. Sort of as you might imagine Ferlinghetti and Ginsberg were in their twenties. Everyone looks plain and simple and comfortable—like workers. They are very natural. Beats. People look contented in an arty way. Everyone is an individual and most are quite mature for their age. There are a few new-fangled freak types and a few straights, but most are old-style beats.

No dating—just grouping. "Hey, I'm going down to the Little

Theater, does anyone want to come?" Flicks are popular and so is the 6:30 TV news in McGregor Hall—you participate in the news—people boo or hiss the news and everyone tries to quiet down the next person. There are free midnight movies on campus. Chicks and cats are liberated—professors are liberated, secretaries are liberated—everyone is liberated.

The whole campus is a hangout—especially the Union and the coffee shop. Everyone smokes but grass is tight. In the good old days (before Operation Intercept) lids went for $6–$8. It is generally felt that dope had a head-start here. Students lately have been trying to define what drugs are considered no good and how to stop people from pushing the hard stuff on campus.

Everyone is sort of political to a degree but the majority are more into a cultural thing. Artistic alternates to life styles—the majority are far to the left. Approximately 200 of the 1000 students on campus at any one time are solidly into radical politics. They want "to open other people's heads, not just get them to accept a new philosophy."

Four years ago the students helped organize the workers' union here and the union people have supported students ever since.

The president of the college, James Payson Dixon (Chairman of Dick Gregory's new political party), is a good man. When students demonstrated against the administration in 1967 (they discovered that Antioch had three contracts with Dow and the Defense Department), Dixon called for a Vietnam Assembly—he organized it.

Antioch has supported the Moratoriums by closing down the school and giving the staff a paid vacation.

After Nixon's Cambodia decision, the students had a mass meeting and made four demands on the administration: (1) drop the contract the school held with the Air Force; (2) pay all workers while on strike; (3) the college should take a stand on the War; and (4) the college should donate $50,000 to the Panthers' defense fund. No action was taken on the last three demands.

The problem with politics here is that any time there is an important issue that needs to be resolved, it gets diluted with extraneous issues, is diverted and is talked into the ground. Most Antioch students go to other places for their political confrontations. They go to other schools and get arrested there. The workers on campus are aligned with the students.

Women's Liberation is very strong and militant here.

SURVIVAL:

A pleasure here. Freedom of everything.

The Antioch infirmary is part of the Yellow Springs Clinic—prescriptions are free—BC pills prescribed. Cats can buy rubbers in the school book store. School shrink. Women's Liberation gives abortion referrals. Draft counseling by the Radical Studies Institute.

Dogs all over the campus—they go to the midnight movies and to all the important meetings. Mutley is a rather well known dog in some campus circles—he knows where all the meetings are and has been getting into a lot of fights lately.

ENVIRONMENT:

Mental—People read everything and rap constantly.

Physical—The climate is nice here in the fall but the winters are frigid. The Glen Helen part of campus is out of sight—greenery everywhere.

Most of the buildings are rectangular, short and red brick. Antioch Hall (the administration building) is very unusual—it looks like the home the Addams Family lived in—pointy "lookout" type things on its top. There's a jungle gym just south of Science Hall.

People escape to the Glen Helen area, or to Cincinnati. Very few commuters.

Case Western Reserve University
Cleveland, Ohio

A schizophrenic school—the Caseys are conservative bores and the Reserve kids are hip and cool.

SERGEANT PEPPER SECTION:

9,951 students of which 4,394 are grads. Admission is based on a variety of considerations. The most important factor is a "high degree of demonstrated academic competence." Their first admissions guideline states, "The general pattern of your performance throughout secondary school, particularly as it relates to the level of courses you have taken." Fairly high grades and board scores needed.

66% out-of-state, 3% black.

ACADEMIC BULLSHIT:

Excellent curriculum. The Art History department is one of the finest in the country and "going stoned to a lecture on Hieronymous Bosch is great."

Dennis Dooley of the English department teaches a course on American language in which you read *Rolling Stone* and *Zap Comics*. There's a Division of Metallurgy where they have glassblowing. The Medical school has excellent facilities and a lot of bread.

Dennis Livingstone in the Division of Special Interdisciplinary Studies, teaches two great courses—"Science Fiction and Public Policy" and "Futurology." You read Herman Kahn type things. Livingstone is into gestalt psychology.

Professors are accessible and if you want a close relationship you can find it. Limited Pass/Fail. The 4-1-4 program of CWRU means that you can take a month of independent study for the month of intersession and receive credit.

Free U that teaches "Blues" and "Parapsychology" stuff.

Scattered black courses. Junior year abroad in Belgium, France and England. In the summer they're gone to Spain and France for language and Guatemala for archaeology.

BREAD:

Tuition is $2,290 a year. Financial aid is available and is packaged to split between loans, scholarships and work. Average dorm price is $1,325 for room and board. An apartment near campus may go for $80 a month. Freaks live in Coventry Road and digs are pretty cheap.

You don't need a lot of bread for other expenses. On-campus flicks run $2 a night. Most have cars and parking is miserable. Rags are casual.

BROTHERS AND SISTERS:

Ratio cats : chicks—2 : 1.

There are two types of students at CWRU—the Case type and the Reserve type. The "Casey" is much more conservative than the Reserve. "The 'Casey' has short hair, wears white socks, plain pants and slide rule tie bars. They have those pen and pencil plastic things in their pocket." There are only 50 chicks at Case. The Reserve people are either hip Greek types or freaks. Freaks wear tie-dyed shirts and jeans.

If you're without a companion of the opposite sex you have a miserable social life. There's a little of every type of dating pattern—the flicks-and-a-burger dates, the getting-stoned dates. Very few liberated chicks (even freaks). "The Vast Virginity."

Greeks are solid on the Case side and fading on the Reserve side.

There are no real hangs in Cleveland and it's a tough city socially. "Severence Center" is a big shopping place and college people go there on Saturday. Freaks live in the area around Coventry Road in Cleveland Heights.

Most Reserve people come in as heads and turn on the Case people. If you're busted for drugs the Reserve administration makes no judgment on you, but if you're enrolled at Case they'll expel you. Score in the Coventry Road area at $15 a lid and $7 per gram of hash.

CWRU is a Jekyll and Hyde place politically. Caseys are pro-war (the anti-war effort is anti-corporate and screws them up) and the Reserve kids are liberal. About 50 hard-core revolutionaries. The YSA is big and are to the right of the Movement. They are very well organized and have well-oiled machinery. They get involved in things at the beginning and place people in positions of power. The American Student Movement are Maoists and the furthest left. The Afro-American blacks are militant and separatist. Women's Lib is in the education stage and is working with a coordinated Men's Liberation Front.

There has been a lot of student opposition to the University Circle Development Foundation—it controls most of the land around campus and is always trying to put it to commercial uses. In the University Circle area there have been 16 unexplained fires of businesses that UCDF wanted to buy. Big turnouts for the Moratorium. In February, 1970, the Student Mobilization Committee held its national convention here. The YSA took it over. In April, 1970, there was an AT&T stockholders meeting in the Public Auditorium in Cleveland. The radicals convened—some police action.

There was big action over the Cambodian decision. Students presented five demands: (1) end ROTC; (2) close the University; (3) end campus complicity in war effort; (4) the University should make an anti-war statement; and (5) the University should offer legal aid to the Panthers. The ROTC building was occupied. The next day a busy street in Cleveland (Euclid Avenue) was occupied and the police were called up. CWRU served as part of the Ohio Coalition which was the communications network for Ohio during the strike. There was quite a lot of strike activity.

SURVIVAL:

Good on the Reserve side. BC pills given out at student health but the health service is usually mediocre. Switchboard and Drug Clinic in Cleveland, Law students have a Draft Counseling Service. The campus paper is the *Observor*. It's liberal and good.

Many health-food stores in Cleveland.

ENVIRONMENT:

Mental—Caseys are studying and Reserve students are talking politics.

Physical—Bitter winter, hot, muggy summers, few nice days here. Terrible air pollution—many buildings are black from it and you can smell it. Republic Steel and Ford are two big polluters. The Cuyahoga River is so polluted it's a fire hazard—it was the first river in the United States to be declared a fire hazard and caught fire last summer. "The feeling about Lake Erie is that if you can't swim, you won't drown, you'll dissolve."

Campus buildings are ugly because of all the pollution dirt on them. "The Case dorm looks like a home for juvenile delinquents." The Olin building is another eyesore and looks like a concrete slab monolith. The nicest-looking building on campus is the coed dorm called Mather House—looks collegiate.

People escape to Cleveland (?) and to the Lagoon (next to the Art Museum).

Denison University

Granville, Ohio

"Most of the people on this campus are 1950s types preserved in butch wax." "Life at Denison University is a dried flower arrangement under bell-glass."

SERGEANT PEPPER SECTION:

2,097 undergraduates. They have a double standard for eligibility and discriminate against women. High grades and scores for both. Frosh must take the SATs and three ACT tests. 66% out-of-state. 43 blacks.

ACADEMIC BULLSHIT:

Best departments are Chemistry and Psychology. They have some of the best equipment in the country. The English and History departments are also good.

Most popular professors are Burkett, Camoin and Sonsolo of the English department. "Theories of Personality" is a psychology class taught by Professor Tritt—it's like an encounter group.

Pass/Fail is O.K. for juniors and seniors. There's a course on black culture that is the only student-initiated course.

The Free U is called the "Experimental College." It offers such courses as "The Aesthetics of Diving," "Computer Music" and "Black Psychology."

There's a close relationship between professors and students. Many professors who teach upperclass courses conduct them at their homes. No Third World College but about ten black-related courses.

Independent study is called "Directed Study" and anyone above a sophomore who has a certain minimum GPA can take it. The month of January (on the 4-1-4 system) is also devoted to independent study. Study abroad.

BREAD:

It's a private school so bread is heavy. Tuition and fees per year are $2,320. Some aid and only a limited number of available jobs.

All chicks must live in the dorms. They cost $300 a semester for room and board. Apartments run about $60 a month per person.

Most students drive white VWs. 65% of the school is Greek and this requires a middle-cost wardrobe. Used books at "Huzza Huzza," the local plastic-hippie store.

BROTHERS AND SISTERS:

Ratio cats : chicks—11 : 9.

Most students are straight. Villager outfits for chicks, Gant shirts for cats. $15–$20 bell-bottoms. One chick spent an entire night painting flowers on her thigh and calf. Chicks have that impeccable made-up look. "They spend 4 hours making themselves look natural." "About 50% of the cats come from prep schools and 60% of the chicks have made their debuts. They are all Ivy League rejects."

A few freaks, hair, beards, and fringed leather jackets.

As to sex, "No matter how horny you get Denison chicks aren't worth it." Get in your time machine, Martha, it's back to 1959. Frat rats only want virgins for wives. 65% of Denison people marry other Denison people. Chicks who graduate and become airline stewardesses are considered real class. "There's a lot of pinning and when you get pinned, your brothers put you on the hood of a car, drive you to a pond, drop you in, put you back on the hood and then drive you around the women's dorms three times honking their horns." Sounds like a gas.

Most entertainment is fraternity parties, flicks and booze. Everyone converges on the Student Union at ten in the morning and nine at night. Straight hangs are "Powell's Place," "The Stein" and "Tony's." Freaks go to "The Market." The fraternities are on to grass and it goes for $15 a lid.

The whole area is Wallace country.

Students are changing from middle-of-the-road Republicans to liberal Republicans. They love John Lindsay. Denison University prides itself on "being a place of rational discourse." There are about 75 hard-core leftists who are Yippie types and known as the "Festive Left."

A smattering of students participated in anti-war activities in the middle 60s. In 1968 HEW told Denison University to recruit more blacks or lose federal funding. In the spring of 1968 was their Peace and Education Day—450 turned out—the biggest turn-out yet. In 1969 a whole bunch of frosh freaks arrived and brought the cultural revolution with them. In 1969 blacks demanded rights and threatened to leave. In March, 1970, blacks led a strike but no demands were met. The Denison University trustees are thick-headed. Someone tried to burn down the ROTC building with lighter fluid in May, 1970, but failed.

SURVIVAL:

Hard, unless you're a liberal Republican. No health-food stores or interest in organic living. Student health service runs from poor to shitty. "Mono is diagnosed as a cancerous growth on the neck." "Asthma was diagnosed as arthritis of the rib cage." Everything costs. No survival services—some BC pills in town. Quakers run the Draft Counseling Service on campus. Pets on campus and they are more interesting than most of the people. *The Denisonian* is a drag.

ENVIRONMENT:

Mental—People are talking about pinnings.

Physical—Rains a lot and is humid—good thunderstorm action. Many, many, many trees. Plenty of air pollution.

The nicest building is the Swasey Chapel—it has a domed tower and is out of sight.

The Beta House made it into Ripley's "Believe it or Not." Most buildings are made of red brick and are square-like. Check the "lollipop clock" near the main quad. It's a very attractive campus.

Slayter Hall has an elevator out of 2001. It's all white except for a blue carpet, and when it starts moving it sounds as if someone had flushed the toilet and you're being washed down the tubes.

Escapes are Hocking Hills—caves and waterfalls in a big state park—and Black Hand Gorge—a great cliff.

Kenyon College

Gambier, Ohio

Kenyon is an oasis of turned-on freaks in the Middle-America Midwest.

SERGEANT PEPPER SECTION:

957 undergraduates. Entering freshmen should take a college prep major in high school, need recommendations from high-school officials, good SAT and ACT scores. 60% out-of-state, 15 blacks.

ACADEMIC BULLSHIT:

Kenyon is a small liberal arts college. The school doesn't require any particular classes. At the end of four years you take comprehensives in your major. Classes are small and students and professors are very close. Best departments are English, Political Science (most people are traditionalists and are into the philosophy side of political science) and Religion. The students like practically all the professors—especially Dr. Kullman in Religion ("he's the charismatic prophet here"), Dr. Baker in History ("everyone takes his course in Medieval History"), Dr. Haywood of the German department, and Drs. Crump and Roelofs of the English department. All these professors are really into their subjects, enjoy them and pass them on to their students.

Pass/Fail in your senior year. A Free U called the Experimental College exists with courses in photography, jazz and chess.

There are three or four black courses. "All classes are pretty heavy on writing papers." Independent study on the Honors program.

BREAD:

Tuition is $2,635 a year for men and $2,660 a year for women. There's a real squeeze financially so loans and scholarships are very tight. A number of campus jobs at average wages.

To make bread, the school insists that most of the kids live in the dorms at $305 a semester—average cost.

Many have cars and dates are cheap. Inexpensive clothes are the rule.

BROTHERS AND SISTERS:

Ratio cats : chicks—5 : 1.

This is the first year Kenyon has gone coed and the cats are very happy about it. There are a ton of freaks and even the Greeks don't look like Greeks. Everyone dresses casual—jeans, button-down shirts, boots, penny loafers, no one gives a shit about appearance. Some freaks have short hair and some Greeks have long. A turned-on group.

There's not much dating since there are so few chicks. Gambier is in the middle of nowhere. Sexual relationships are casual and free. Most chicks are from Ohio but aren't backward like most Ohio chicks when it comes to liberation. All relationships are free-wheeling and unstructured.

Fraternities exist but most are cool and hip. Most of the senior freaks have gone through dope and have stopped using it. The freshmen usually come on big on dope and then stop using it after a while here. All types of dope are readily accessible although you may have to wait two hours while your order is filled. Score on campus. The administration is cool and is just concerned that drugs may be harmful.

The main hang is the "Coffee Shop" in Pierce Hall. People go to Columbus for big-city fun.

Students are liberals. They have become radicalized during the past two years with the giving up of booze and the inroads of dope. The president of the college is a master at placating students. "It's the Magic Mountain, a fantasy insulated world here."

In May of 1970, there was a lot of anti-war activity which included teach-ins and canvassing. Constructive action.

The Community Action Peace Committee was formed by students at Kenyon, Antioch and Oberlin. They staged a march on the state capitol in Columbus to mobilize people for nonviolent action against the War. They are setting up a Medic-Aid to train people to treat injured rioters. They sent a group of 300 students into the neighboring town of Mt. Vernon (described by a national magazine as an "all-American city") to talk about the War. They opened up some minds and got the ministers in Mt. Vernon to hold a pray-in and give sermons against the War.

SURVIVAL:

Easy at Kenyon. People are individuals, into their own thing and there's no peer group pressure.

Contraceptives are available in town. All survival services are in Cincinnati and the school's student health suffices. Chaplain Brogan is a very good draft counselor.

The campus paper is the *Kenyon Collegian*—a handout type thing.

ENVIRONMENT:

Mental—People talk about student action and read all the usual freak books.

Physical—Fall and spring are wonderful here. Winter is a cold, muddy, dreary introspective drag. Lots of trees, greenery and squirrels on campus. Very slight air and water pollution.

Most of the buildings are Gothic stone. Pierce Hall has a lovely tower that stretches upward and has stained-glass windows. Eyesores include the dorms. "Hallways in the women's dorms must have been designed by a drunk. You run into the walls."

There's no need to escape from Kenyon since there is so much land. But you can always go to Mohican State Park, 20 miles away.

Miami University

Oxford, Ohio

Quiet academic life is the rule at Miami. Away from it all in Oxford about the only things to do are to get drunk at the frat house and study for tests.

SERGEANT PEPPER SECTION:

11,580 students of which 1,020 are grads.

In-state must graduate from an accredited Ohio high school and have an acceptable class rank. ACT scores, high-school recommendations and special abilities are taken into account. All these are taken into consideration for out-of-staters, and they should be in the upper 25% of their class and have at least 1,100 SATs. No more than 20% can be admitted from out-of-state in the freshman class. Transfers need a 2.5 GPA.

ACADEMIC BULLSHIT:

Popular departments are American Studies and Philosophy. American Studies is an offshoot of the English department and all the freaks take courses. Most Philosophy professors hold their courses in the living room of the dorms—take Benjamin and Momeyer.

The graduate programs are expanding—the Applied Science department is supposed to be good.

They have a student leadership class in the Education department.

A Free U occasionally—usually during a strike.

No student-originated classes, not much interaction between students and professors except in the Philosophy department. 12 classes on black studies scattered among the departments. Some independent study. Miami has its own European Study Center where students can study for a year.

No smoking in class and in the dining halls. Cats have to wear a coat and tie on Sundays.

BREAD:

In-state tuition is $240 a quarter, out-of-state is $560. Loans and scholarships are fairly available. 905 students received $430,900 in grants, University scholarships and alumni scholarships in 1969. If you want work, you can get it here for $1.45 an hour.

Room and board in the dorms costs $330 a quarter. All freshmen must live in the dorms. All women, until they are seniors or 21, must live in the dorms or in University-approved places. Apartments are $150–$190 a month for a two-bedroom unfurnished place.

Dates are cheap but most people have expensive clothes.

373

BROTHERS AND SISTERS:

Ratio cats : chicks—about 1 : 1.
From the catalog:

Motor Vehicles
    Oxford is a small town and all students live within walk-
ing distance of classrooms. There is no need for students to
have motor vehicles in the village. They have proved to be
a detriment to scholarship and a temptation to waste much
time. It is positively forbidden for any student while enrolled at Miami University to have or to drive a motor
vehicle without proper University permission. This does not
apply to the use of one in the student's home community,
if other than Oxford. Students who find it necessary to use
a motor vehicle must consult the University Security Office
regarding permits.
    Students who feel it desirable to bring a motor vehicle to
college, but who have no real need for one, should select
another institution.

Cuts down on the mobility.
Oxford is into the straight-tending-toward-plastic-hip look. Frat
rats want to be hip—they wear "Mod Squad" clothes—tailored
bell-bottoms, new tailored army jackets, and new hip Gant shirts—
an occasional tie-dyed shirt. The semi-hip chicks wear choker bead
necklaces, mesh knee socks and the sorority outfit (no saddle
shoes any more). Approximately 100 freaks on campus. Miami
chicks aren't into balling—"they ball the guy they're gonna marry."
Sexual fulfillment is better across the street at the Western College
for Women.
Greeks used to be big but are declining. Miami University is
known as the "Mother of Fraternities." People are still getting
pinned; it's staid and stuffy.
Straights hang at two bars—"The Boar's Head" and the
"Purity." Freaks hang at the United Campus Ministry House and
under the water tower in the middle of town.
Political history really stretches back. It includes the following:

1890. The students rolled snowballs in front of all three (at
the time) buildings. They then poured water on them (which
froze) and the buildings were locked up because of that . . .
it was a prank.

Fall, 1956. Miami played one of the Big Ten teams, Indiana,
for about the first time in their football history. Miami won the
game and the students went wild with ecstacy. They ran into
town, caused a ruckus, and beat the shit out of anyone who
could be identified as being from Indiana.

Panty raids have always been big here—they usually get around
2,000 to attend.

Fall, 1965. 50 people in a Dow demonstration. Tried to sit-in in the building but they couldn't get in, so they marched around the building and were jeered by the students. It lasted through the afternoon.

Spring, 1969. "The Famed Motherfucker Incident." An organization named "CASE" was formed that wanted more social rights and academic freedom and were protesting the trustees. 1,000 marched on the trustees meeting at the school with their signs asking for abolition of women's hours and different social reforms. One sign said "Up Against the Wall Motherfucker" and that caused a couple of trustees to faint. These students were prosecuted. An outgrowth of these prosecutions was that students barged into faculty meetings yelling obscenities—they were put on social probation. This was the beginning of real political activity here.

April, 1970. There was an Anti-War Teach-In. After it was over, students led an assault on the ROTC building and occupied it. About 500 people sat-in. The National Guard was alerted and stayed just outside of town on the Nike base. State police came in and were cool but the Butler County sheriffs freaked and got out of hand, firing tear gas and mace point blank at people. 176 people were arrested.

Some smoke grass. Occasional busts. Frats are into it. Scoring from friends or in Cincinnati.

SURVIVAL:

Not too easy. The school is very conservative. Hailed as the "Cradle of Coaches" (the cradle and the mother), Miami does the football thing.

Student health gives out BC pills only if you are getting married. They always keep you overnight no matter what you have. No Free Clinic, no suicide prevention, no drug counseling and no Planned Parenthood in Oxford. ZPG gives some birth control advice. Draft counseling is done by the United Campus Ministry and by Rick Karg, an Economics graduate student.

Thousands of squirrels on campus. *The Miami Student,* the campus newspaper—liberal rag. There is nothing to do in town but go to movies (which are usually rated G).

ENVIRONMENT:

Mental—People are talking about the effectiveness of student protest.

Physical—It's hot and muggy in the summer, cold in the winter, but moderately. Students love the trees on campus—"they are the most precious resource we have." Farm country—no pollution.

Architecture is Georgian—three-story red brick buildings with white columns and porticos. They are big on seals. They spent $18,000 to put a seal in the middle of campus—called the "Hub." The "Beta Bells" which chime every quarter of an hour are a major gripe. Students once had buttons saying "Ban the Beta Bells." Then there's the John D. Millet Assembly Hall, which was named after a former president of Miami University. Students didn't like him so they renamed it Jefferson Assembly Hall. Then they found out Tom had slaves—now they call it Assembly Hall.

Steeplelike things on top of the buildings house birds' nests.

It's impossible to escape this collegiate place without a car (and you can't have one). No commuters.

Oberlin College
Oberlin, Ohio

9% of the school is black—Oberlin has always tried to attract blacks. They were in the forefront of the Abolitionist cause and were the northernmost point in the Underground Railroad. The town is 40% black so black students are not surrounded by a white sea.

SERGEANT PEPPER SECTION:

2,496 students—all undergraduates. They treat each applicant on an "individual basis." Transfers need a B. 85% out-of-state. 9% blacks. No commuters.

ACADEMIC BULLSHIT:

Very good library and a computer for the students to play with. Many good courses and departments. The Conservatory of Music is excellent as is the Religion department. The History and Art departments are good but stuffy. Popular professors are Dendler (teaches "Sculpture" in the Art department), Papworth (Anthropology), Thompson (Psychology), Capitan (teaches "'Philosophy of Art" and "Philosophy of Values"—he's unique, fresh, easygoing and leaving the school) and Goulding (Communications).

There a Pass/Fail system—one course per semester. Student-originated classes for credit both in the Experimental College ("Survival," "Yoga," "The American Indian") and for the "Ad Hoc Classes" in which students ask a professor to teach a class.

The relationship between professors and students is described as "A pedagogical one—the condescending instructor." Professors are conservatives and uptight about their status (they usually are Oberlin people who have gotten their Ph.D.s). An Afro-American department began in 1970. Many more papers than tests. Usually no finals. The school operates on a 4-1-4 system so that the students can do independent study for the month of January. No credit or grades, very unstructured (one student learned how to play the sitar). Study abroad in Austria, France, Russia and Taiwan for a few.

BREAD:

$2,400 a year. If a student is admitted and needs aid he will get it. The school's budget has more aid per capita than any other school in Ohio. The majority are given scholarships and the average loan is $500. Campus jobs can bring in $300 a year.

Dorms cost $560 a year for room and board. Few apartments. No fraternity houses.

Expensive clothes aren't necessary and most students have bicycles rather than cars.

BROTHERS AND SISTERS:

Ratio cats : chicks—about 1 : 1.

Students dress casually. The straightest people on campus go into the Music Conservatory. Quite a sizable freak population. Lots of intense 1 : 1 relationships and most chicks are liberated. It's groupie type functions in the freshman year (people run in packs) and pairing off becomes prevalent in the sophomore year. Entertainment is parties, dope and sex. "No segregated hangouts for freaks and straights, everyone hangs together." If they congregate anywhere it's in "Wilders'" (the Student Union). Drugs are well ingrained in the school. 50% use grass weekly. 95% have tried it.

The school has always had a bunch of politicos leading rallies. But most students are nonactivists who give their support to the radicals. SDS was big five years ago but folded in 1970. The Oberlin College Alliance for Black Culture is the blacks' political organization. They are separatists. Women's Liberation is pretty active here. They held a conference in 1970 and chicks came from all the surrounding campuses to attend.

The political history dates back to 1833 when Oberlin was founded and it immediately became involved in Abolitionist issues. They allowed anyone into their college regardless of race, religion or sex. It was the first college in the nation to be coed. The latter half of the 1800s witnessed many women's crusades on campus.

In the fall of 1967 there were big demonstrations against Navy recruiters coming on campus. The town pigs did gassings. The students surrounded the Navy recruiter in his car (he had to go to the bathroom something fierce and the students offered him a blanket and a bottle but he refused). They finally let him go to the bathroom in a gas station and he escaped.

During the Cambodian and Kent State issues, Oberlin struck. The administration was very cool and let them organize and canvass. Thousands of committees were set up and people were very responsive. Oberlin students (750) went to Washington, D.C., to lobby. The college became an official refuge for Kent people who were allowed to live here.

ENVIRONMENT:

Mental—People are discussing the war and activism.

Physical—"The climate here is shitty—rainy and unpredictable *all* the time—spring comes late and is mushy and snowy." The land is flat with trees and creeks. The main creek is called "The Stinking Plum" in the summer and "The Raging Plum" in the spring.

Some air pollution from Cleveland. The Plum Creek is polluted and bubbles (industry dumps all its shit into it).

The campus is small and buildings are made out of yellowish stone with a tinge of orange in it. People are equally divided as to the merits of Peters Hall—some consider it freaky while others call it a Gothic horror.

Escapes are the Arb (a wooded area on the southern part of the campus) and the Quarry.

Ohio State University

Columbus, Ohio

Ohio State University became politically aware with the National Student Strike of 1970.

SERGEANT PEPPER SECTION:

45,262 students. Out-of-state must have "demonstrated high academic promise." In-state must graduate from an accredited high school. Average freshman ACT scores are 22. Most students are from Ohio.

ACADEMIC BULLSHIT:

Big university type school with fairly good graduate programs. One of the worst things about undergraduate courses is that they are taught by T.A.s who are usually more concerned about getting their degree than educating the students. Best departments include Fine Arts, the School of Social Work and the Law school. Bernie Mehl in the Education department is very popular. "What he does in class is attack the students mentally and you learn from being attacked" (Masochists unite!). Some Pass/Fail, no student-originated classes and a poor Free U. A few black studies courses and some independent study. Not much participation in class.

BREAD:

Tuition and fees in-state is $510 a year, $1,100 out-of-state. About 20% of the cats and 40% of the chicks live in dorms that cost $1,000 a year for room and board.

Rags are cheap if you're a freak. Lots have cars and dates range from $7–$20.

BROTHERS AND SISTERS:

Ratio cats : chicks—2 : 1.

Students vary—there are the straight Greeks, the hip Greeks, and the freak freaks. The well-dressed male straight Greek wears plaid pants, a monogrammed shirt, a V-neck sweater, wingtips, carries a briefcase and studies at night. The hip Greek wears bell-bottoms, body shirts, brown loafers, peace symbols and bush jackets. Sorority Sallys wear opaque knee socks, coordinated outfits, gold jewelry and $30 purses. The hip sorority chick wears a tucked-in body shirt, sandals, jeans and a bra. There's a goodly number of freaks who make the no-bra tie-dyed scene. Freaks are comfortably unkempt while Greeks are oppressively immaculate. "If a hip Greek buys a leather jacket, he spends every night brushing it."

Frats have their own society and do the dating scene—flicks and the "Draft House" for a beer. About 50% of the chicks have balled—most want to get married.

Dope is very available, especially hash. Score in the "Inner City." There's a new drug on campus called "Soper"—its chemical name is metha qualod—it's legal. Freak places to hang are "Pearl Alley" (a group of stores on 13th and High), "Mr. Christian's Dilemma" (freak bar) and "The Coffee Shop" in Hayes Hall. Straights hang at the "Draft House" and the "Travel Agency" (both bars).

For most kids "life is a big football game" but some political awareness is coming, but the Movement so far is very diluted. "Many kids want a revolution as long as they're not inconvenienced."

The group called "Majority Alliance" is a conservative group which is allied with local businessmen. They want all demonstrators expelled. The Afro-Americans are militant as is the Ad Hoc Committee for Student Rights. Women's Liberation has existed for three years; they are pushing for day-care centers and give abortion referrals.

In 1965 there was a free-speech controversy on campus but there were no riots. In 1968, blacks took over the administration building demanding black counselors and black studies. Some of the blacks were expelled and the demands weren't met.

The major political activity so far came with the student strike in 1970.

March 13, 1970. The blacks gave a list of demands to the administration which were somewhat repetitious of those of 68—more recruitment and financial aid for blacks, more black faculty and a center for black studies—two of the blacks were charged with violating the University's disruption rules and went on trial before the OSU Disciplinary Committee.

April 20–21, 1970. A student-government-sponsored careers exposition had the FBI and Columbus Police Force included— called Prospectus 70—SDS said they didn't want the recruiters on campus and they staged two days of protests—five students were arrested the second day—on April 24 a group of students marched to the administration protesting the arrests and presented 11 demands to the administration—amnesty for the arrested students and students in the March 13 thing; an end to ROTC; removal of all city and state police from campus; the immediate dismissal of three administrators; 50% student representation on all faculty committees on curriculum, recruitment and University finances; and six other demands. A strike was called for April 29.

Wednesday, April 29. The strike began. They decided to shut the school down symbolically by closing some iron gates at an entrance to the school—pigs came into the area to clear it and overreacted with tear gas and then retreated to the administration building. The students then went to the administration building and about 1,000 of them surrounded the place. There were two buses outside that had brought in highway patrolmen and several police cars. The students let some air out of the tires and someone opened up the engine compartment of the bus and started fooling around. The crowd cheered. Then 20–30 highway patrolmen came running out of the building lobbing tear gas, which the students threw back into the administration building. The crowd was moved off to High Street where they opened fireplugs, flooding the street. A curfew was ordered. Police tried to clear the streets that night and street fighting ensued. They lobbed tear gas into the fraternity houses. Pitched battles lasted close to midnight. Store windows were broken. Seven people were shot that night.

April 30. The National Guard was brought in. Tear gas was all over campus. Whenever people congregated they were dispersed with tear gas. Another seven people were shot. Philip A. Wright, Jr., a National Guard captain, was given a bullhorn to talk with the protestors. Instead he mounted a makeshift podium—a garbage can—took off his helmet, took off his pistol, took off his tear gas cannister, and dropped them all at his feet. He told the 5,000 kids to stay together and be peaceful and was cheered by the kids. His reward was to be publicly criticized by his commander before the press and his fellow guardsmen and to be reassigned.

OSU reopened to all its students on May 19, but was a closed campus. Tons and tons of pigs all over. Students had to have I.D.s. Visitors had to have official permission and I.D.s to get on campus. It was just like Berlin—you needed a visa to get in.

SURVIVAL:

Easy if you know the right people.

There's a Planned Parenthood in Columbus and a suicide prevention center near the University. Operation Switchboard helps in all crises. The Psychological Center is a Free Clinic in town run by the University. Abortion referrals from Women's Liberation. Quakers in town give draft counseling. Student health is lousy. Pets run wild on the Oval. A lot of people still dig sports here. The *Ohio State Lantern* is a moderate rightist paper—it has "Peanuts."

ENVIRONMENT:

Mental—People are talking about the world situation and football games.

Physical—Cold in the winter, hot in the summer. Mirror Lake on campus is stagnant and smells like sulphur (composed of 50% water, 50% crud). Water and air pollution.

The architecture of the buildings takes in everything. They have red brick, granite, stone and "whatever they make buildings out of, they have here." Functional and nondescript. Orton Hall is nice—it's made out of big stones and is castlelike. There's a museum inside and it has fossils—check the gigantic mastodon and the Glyptodon *(clavipes)*.

OKLAHOMA

Oklahoma State University
Stillwater, Oklahoma

Stillwater breeds still minds.

SERGEANT PEPPER SECTION:

17,492 students of which only 1,568 are from out-of-state. Eligibility requirements are that you are either in the upper-half ranking of the National ACT scores, the upper half of your high-school graduating class, or have a B— average. Few transfers.

ACADEMIC BULLSHIT:

The best undergraduate departments are Pre-veterinary, Home Economics, Agriculture and Education. The best graduate departments are Engineering, Home Economics and Agriculture. The Engineering department gets a lot of government contracts (at present they are studying the electrical content of thunderstorms).

Take Mrs. Mickle for English and Mr. Shaw for History. No Pass/Fail, not much class participation, no student-originated courses, Free U, ethnic studies, independent study or study abroad.

BREAD:

Tuition is $14 per credit in-state and $36 per credit out-of-state per semester. It's easy to get loans, but scholarships are tight. Jobs are available at $1.30 an hour. Dorms cost from $400–$500 a semester with food. 7,000 live on campus. Most students live off campus in apartments that cost $70–$120 for a one-bedroom.

Lots of cars and rags are cheap.

BROTHERS AND SISTERS:

Ratio cats : chicks—about 2 : 1.

Straight arrow with a few cowboys and about 2% hip thrown in. Cotton pants and shirts for the cats, dresses and bras for the chicks. The cats have that frat-type personality. There's a lot of dating and about one-fifth of the chicks are liberated.

Fraternities are still very strong and are gaining in membership. The fraternities control student government.

Straights hang at the "Coachman's," "Slope's" the "Family Dog" and "West Olive"—all bars. Juice and country music is the main entertainment.

Very few are hip and very few of those are into dope. Lids go for $15 and acid goes for $5. Small-town paranoia of dope and frequent busts.

The campus hasn't heard of politics yet. Their first demonstration was a gathering of 400 (out of 17,000) people in response to the Kent State Massacre. The YAF occasionally has speakers.

SURVIVAL:

Hard.

Student health is O.K. but doesn't give out BC pills or abortion referrals. Draft counseling is done by "the Army recruiting office, the Air Force recruiting office and the barber shop." No survival services in Stillwater. *The O'Collegian* is a drag.

ENVIRONMENT:

Mental—Sterile on the whole. Those that can read are reading Tom Wolfe and *Portnoy's Complaint*.

Physical—The climate is cold and wet in the winter, hot and humid in the summer. Stillwater is a small town 80 miles from Oklahoma City. The campus is suburban. Buildings on campus are square red brick, two–five stories. The major eyesores are the animal barns where they keep cows, horses, pigs, sheep and chickens for the Agricultural department. They smell.

Escapes are Oklahoma City and Tulsa.

University of Oklahoma
Norman, Oklahoma

The best chance of survival in Oklahoma.

SERGEANT PEPPER SECTION:

17,607 students of which 4,449 are from out-of-state. The dean wouldn't give us the minority statistics—he considered it "private information."

Oklahoma residents need to have either a B— GPA in high school and rank in the upper half of their high-school class, or a rank in the upper half of the National ACT scores. Out-of-state applicants must be in the upper half of their high-school class or rank in the upper half of the National ACT scores.

ACADEMIC BULLSHIT:

Best undergraduate departments are Engineering, Zoology and Social Sciences. Best graduate departments are the Medical and Dental schools. Take Ted Langford for English and Steve Blevins for anthropology. Pass/Fail is allowed for one subject per semester outside your major. Class participation isn't important and there are no student-originated classes, no Free U and no Ethnic Studies program. Some independent study and study abroad.

BREAD:

Tuition is $12 per credit-hour per quarter in-state and $30 per credit-hour per quarter out-of-state. Loans, scholarships and jobs are all hard to get (jobs pay $1.40 an hour).

Dorms cost $420 for room and board per semester. Students are required to live in dorms or married-student housing until they are 21. Apartments run for $75–$150 for a one-bedroom. Lots of cars, inexpensive rags. "Shirley's Book Stall" has fair prices.

BROTHERS AND SISTERS:

Ratio cats : chicks—about 2 : 1.

This is the hippest of the Oklahoma campuses but it's still not hip as we know it. About half the campus is super-straight arrow—the others have embryonic moustaches and wear levis. Chicks are just beginning to wear pants. There's lots of dating and a few liberated women. Fraternities are still strong but are losing power.

Hangs include the South Oval (grassy area on campus), the "Renaissance Fair" (has a leather shop, used books, food, beer and bands on the weekend) and the "Organ Grinder" (bar). Hips are definitely into dope and it goes for $15 a lid. Acid tabs go for $3.

The campus is just starting to dig politics. 3,000 demonstrated after the Cambodia-Kent State week. They were led by the black student-body president.

Pigs were called in in 1970 when students with an NLF flag marched during the ROTC parade. They beat up a few students.

SURVIVAL:

Some facilities for the creative arts. Poor student health facilities, no BC pills or abortion referrals. Some shrink help. Student government has draft counseling on campus and the Mennonites have a service in Oklahoma City. There's a Crisis Center in Oklahoma City. Oklahoma has the lowest suicide rate in the country.

The Oklahoma Daily is ignorant. *The Jones Family* is a radical underground paper.

ENVIRONMENT:

Mental—People are just starting to talk politics and are reading Jerry Rubin's *Do It!*

Physical—Norman is 20 miles from Oklahoma City. It's hot and humid in the summer and cold and wet in the winter. Norman is suburbia. The school is pleasant on the eyes, lots of trees and brick buildings.

University of Tulsa
Tulsa, Oklahoma

An Oklahoma commuters' school.

SERGEANT PEPPER SECTION:

6,540 students. 75 blacks. Easy to get in—you need average SATs and high-school graduation recommendations.

ACADEMIC BULLSHIT:

Traditional academic busy-work. Students like the English, Engineering and Anthropology departments best. Take Harold Hill for religion and Jim Matthews for English ("Matthews is very easy to talk to"). Pass/Fail is optional for one course. The average class of 25 does not include much participation and no ethnic studies or Free U. There is a month in January called the "short semester." Students can originate their own course of study—there are a few other student-originated courses. During January (the Mini-Mester) they have study abroad.

BREAD:

$900 per year. Loans and scholarships are fairly available if you hassle. Jobs are easy to get at $1.50 an hour.

Dorms cost $900 per year for room and board. First semester freshman girls have hours. There is visitation one day a week. About one-sixth of the students live on campus. Apartments are the most popular digs—they cost $60–$110 for a one-bedroom. Lots of students also live at home.

Cars and bikes, no costly threads.

BROTHERS AND SISTERS:

Ratio cats : chicks—2 : 1.

The students here are mostly straight with a few lukewarm hips and cowboy conservatives thrown in. Most wear cotton pants, shirts, loafers and have short hair. The chicks have "bubbles" and wear Villager type rags. It's rumored that there was one liberated woman. Dating is still happening—dates consist of a hamburger and a flick. Chicks can buy liquor at 18 but cats must be 21. People gather at the "Port Richards" beer parlor, and the "Library" (beer parlor with pool tables). A few hips are making inroads—they take part in a heavy dope scene. Lids go for $15 and mescaline for $5. There are lots of busts.

Most students are anything but political. There are minimal Young Republicans and Young Democrats. The biggest demonstration was in response to Kent State—about 500 kids led by the Student Committee for Active Concern had a peaceful rally.

SURVIVAL:

Student health is pretty competent and gives free medicine.

Shrinks are available. No BC pills or abortion referrals, though. AFS on campus gives free draft counseling. There are a couple of drug rehabilitation centers in town run by the Psychiatric Foundation. Good cheap food is available in the cafeteria.

The Collegiate, newspaper, is a drag.

ENVIRONMENT:

Mental—People are talking about their studies and reading Norman Mailer.

Physical—The campus is in Tulsa. It's split into the Law school which is downtown and the North Campus (Engineering and Physical Science) and the main campus (which is suburban). The buildings are constructed of flagstone and have long, narrow windows and slanting roofs.

People escape to Oklahoma City or Dallas.

OREGON

Lewis and Clark College
Portland, Oregon

A lovely wooded campus in Oregon. Lewis and Clark makes an attempt to be responsive to its students.

SERGEANT PEPPER SECTION:

1,750 students, 50% in-state, 29 blacks, 1 Chicano. Average 3.2 GPA and 1,100 combined SATs, but no definite requirements.

ACADEMIC BULLSHIT:

English, Political Science and History have excited young professors on their staffs. Music is known for its performance. It's possible to get a master's in Health and P.E. and they have a Law School.

Alan Kittell is the most popular professor. He's young, hip, and teaches U.S. foreign policy.

John Brown in History and Jerry Blum in English are also well liked. Courses are small and are taken more for the teacher than for the title. Pass/Fail, tests and papers, no student-originated courses.

Small intense discussions; faculty : student ratio is 1 : 15. Free U teaches "Leathercraft," "Witchcraft" and "Jewelry-Making." A few black studies courses. The school gets some of the top black students from the deep South. Very good relations between students and professors. Independent study allowed. One student is studying fraternities at the University of Washington.

Fantastic study-abroad program. 150 students abroad in 1970. Different countries all the time—students live in hostels and homes and must study the culture and the language of the country. Also have domestic programs (Washington, D.C., for politics, New Mexico for study of Indians).

BREAD:

Tuition is $1,900 a year. The school is rich and has many pious old benefactors. 40% receive financial aid. A few campus jobs at $1.50 an hour.

Dorms cost $1,000, room and board. Two-thirds of the students live on campus. Fraternities can get dorm floors. One rather hip house with 14 students living in it. Well-heeled students. The lower campus is a heavily wooded area where students have built lean-tos and an occasional shanty. About one-third of students have cars. Chicks wear bright middle-priced dresses to class. Mom and Dad buy lots of college wardrobe clothing for their kids. Dates cost around $5—hamburgers and flicks.

BROTHERS AND SISTERS:

Ratio cats : chicks—1 : 1.

Lewis and Clark has the type of people you see at a ski resort— straight with a few plastic-hip touches. Chicks wear conventional short dresses. Cats wear Middle-America hair, sport shirts and slacks. A handful of freaks—but less than 5% are hip-looking. Greeks play a small role. Not much cohabitation or sex except among the hips.

Not a heavy political scene at all. Quiet conservative upper-middle-class kids. Some students canvass for local elections. President Howard endorses Nixon on Indochina. Some keggers at the radical professors' homes to raise money for the Moratorium. The Student Strike Committee took the weekend off to go to the beach three days before the May 20, 1970, general strike.

Students eat at the "Trail Room" (student center). Burgers are 35¢. The dining room on the main floor of the student center is the only cafeteria. Hip types throw airplanes, jocks throw ice cubes.

A very good speakers program. In spring of 1970, they had Saul Alinsky, Gene McCarthy, Judith Crist, and Bruno Bettelheim. Students go into the city—Portland—for other entertainment.

SURVIVAL:

Grass is easy to get at $10 a lid—no other drugs. Not many smoke. Darkroom and a few inadequate art studios. It's hard to get BC pills, but possible. Bad health center. The chaplain is with it—he does draft counseling and recently wore a long paisley robe to marry a student couple, on a cliff on the Oregon coast.

Survival services in Portland.

The paper, the *Pioneer Log*, is liberal and amateurish.

ENVIRONMENT:

Mental—People are reading *Cat's Cradle* and the *I Ching*.

Physical—The campus is a beautiful former estate outside of Portland. It's wooded and surrounded by a lovely uncrowded suburb. The old manor house is now the administration building. Lots of tall Douglas fir trees; in lower campus a stream runs down a ravine to the Willamette River. Ivy grows on the buildings and trees. You can hear frogs at night. The old stable is the offices of the Math and Psych departments.

Beach and skiing are most popular escapes. The school has a ski lodge at Timberline. Only 5% commute.

Mount Angel College
Mount Angel, Oregon

This small Catholic college was recently taken over by experimentalists. People live in free houses, grow their own food, and freak. Very cool place.

SERGEANT PEPPER SECTION:

Undergraduate only.

300 students. 50% from Oregon, the other 50% from California and Hawaii. 12 Mexican-Americans, 2 blacks. Admission requirements are very vague. Lots of transfer students.

ACADEMIC BULLSHIT:

The Creative Arts department is excellent for a small school. All the art teachers are practicing artists. The Education department is reasonably good. The Art, English and Behavioral Science departments are experimental.

Popular courses include Jim Shull's "Art History" course, and Erickson's "Law and Social Change." The largest classes have 20 students. Lots of Pass/Fail. Some student-faculty jointly-taught classes like "Modern Poetry." No such thing as a teacher-student relationship. All relations are person-person. Teachers don't think of themselves as a separate community. The school president lives in a dorm room. Sexual relations, dope relations and rapping relations with the faculty. There's a lot of independent study. One student got credit for two months of screwing around Berkeley ("Experiences and Analysis of American Subcultures, 1970"). No study abroad as the school can't financially handle even out-of-country postage.

BREAD:

$435 per quarter. There are 25 scholarships each year for freshmen. Only work-study jobs at $2 an hour. Wages are low but so is the cost of living. Rooms cost about $25 per person per bedroom in houses and farms nearby. One art teacher lives in a treehouse. One chick lives in a teepee on campus.

Dorms are $936 for room and board—coed but rotten food. But only 87 of the 175 rooms are occupied. Students can offer a farmer a few dollars a month to live in his second house which is used by farm laborers during the summer. There's a food commodities store nearby. Homemade candles and clothes are sold. Very easy to scrounge.

BROTHERS AND SISTERS:

Ratio cats : chicks—1 : 1.

All the cats are hip—shoulder-length hair, faded jeans, boots. Most chicks are straight, Catholic and studying elementary education. They dress drably. A few jocks who call the hips "rugheads."

Students are a mixture of out-of-area hips, Catholic chicks and local farmboys. Small gossipy social scene—"Who's balling whom" raps. Some cohabitation, but most chicks are frigid.

Lots of heads, great deal of mescaline and grass. No busts since 1967. Lids go for $12. Informal dating.

In the summer of 1967 there was an Upward Bound program with 40 minority students on campus in the dorms. Many townspeople and trustees are bigoted and sent the pigs in on a bust. The kids were busted for dope. Financial support in the community went down sharply. To survive, the school revamped its curriculum. It de-emphasized its nature as a Catholic school and was taken over by experimentalists; the school is still broke but is beginning to attract hip California people. No political action.

SURVIVAL:

Easy. Students are into the creative arts. Large exhibits of student art work in the corridor of a building on campus. The health service consists of one nurse. Survival services from Portland. The campus paper is head-oriented and provocative. Some students are doing organic gardening on one acre of donated land.

ENVIRONMENT:

Mental—Students read R. Crumb's underground comics and Hesse. They gossip all the time—the word-of-mouth circuit is incredible.

Physical—Rainy Oregon climate. Rural farming area settled by German Catholics—they still have an annual Octoberfest. Mt. Angel has 1,900 residents. Air pollution from paper mills. The campus has brick buildings and large unmowed lawns. Fields surround the campus on three sides. Portland is 40 miles away.

Oregon State University

Corvallis, Oregon

Oregon's "technical school." Students are from small Oregon towns and still dig football weekends.

SERGEANT PEPPER SECTION:

15,244 students, 15% out-of-state. 50 Minority students. Residents need around a 2.00 PA and 900 combined SATs, out-of-staters need about a 2.7 and the same board scores.

ACADEMIC BULLSHIT:

The state legislature insists that the University of Oregon be the center for liberal arts and Oregon State University the center for technical studies. Best graduate departments are Oceanography, Forestry and Engineering, and "Dr. Hogg teaches an introductory anthropology course with 200 people and an advanced course, 'Afro-American Culture.'

"Dr. Crowe in Political Science teaches 'Revolutionary Theory,' 'Urban Violence,' and 'Politics and Values.' These are seminars limited to 30, but 200 try to get in. Seminar on 'Drug Abuse' (30 people) is also a favorite.

"Dr. Adolph's 'History of Southeast Asia' is well liked.

"There is an interdepartmental course in Ecology.

"A new interdepartmental major is American Field Studies. Courses are team-taught by people in relevant fields."

Some Pass/Fail, mostly multiple-choice tests, lectures have 150 students. No free U, but the Computer Center offers two videotape courses in computer programming. Black literature is taught by Dr. Richard Astro.

Students and professors are separated by caste. Some independent study and study abroad.

BREAD:

Tuition in-state is $408 per year, out-of-state $1,335. Loans and scholarships are easy for those with a 3.0 or higher. It's hard to get campus or off-campus work if you look hip. Some work-study—science lab pays best. No students are economically roughing it.

Dorms cost $921 for room and board. About half the students live off campus in plastic apartments. Apartments run $50 apiece. The 12 co-ops are the cheapest places to live on campus. Most students are uptight and wear "college casual" clothes. The school co-op buys used books.

BROTHERS AND SISTERS:

Ratio cats : chicks—3 : 2.

Straight cats have crewcuts, wear slacks and penny loafers. Heavy footwear needed sometimes because of rainy weather. Girls wear dresses, Middle-America hairdos. The only freaks are high-school kids who begin.

The few hips do smoke. Straights go to keggers or frat parties. Nonsurplus coats modeled after the pea coats are popular.

Flicks, rock concerts and plays.

No braless babes. Kissing and necking. 33 fraternities and 16 sororities. Everyone drinks beer. College Joes get drunk at the Beaverhut. PJ's is the hipper place. The Commons in the M.U. is a big hangout. There is one hippy corner—the straights avoid it. One parent sat down there and her son whispered, "Don't sit here, this is where the hippies sit."

Political activity is just dawning. In 1969, there was a 30-people sit-in over the denial of tenure of Frank Harper, a radical English teacher. The police were called in.

In March, 1969, black athletes protested that they were required to shave off their beards and moustaches. 47 blacks walked off campus. A boycott of classes by students was about 30% effective and then tapered off.

SDS is a rather loose organization. They get together once in awhile if there's a political issue.

In May of 1970, somebody protested Cambodia by throwing a fire bomb into the ROTC building. It did $200 damage (ROTC is very big here—all three branches and strong adherents).

SURVIVAL:

So-so. Oregon is nice, whatever the school. Crafts center in the basement of Memorial Union—facilities for ceramics and weaving. The art facilities are crummy. BC pills in the health center. Abortion referrals in Eugene or Portland. Sensitivity groups and a counseling center in student health. No draft counseling. No suicide prevention center. There's a leash law for the dogs. The newspaper is the *Barometer*—Administration, Inc. The *Scab Sheet* underground press comes out only in time of crisis.

Lots of dope in high schools. Heavy marijuana and mescaline scene. Couple of dorm narcs. One narc described as wearing black suit, black tie and white shirt, sideburns and short hair, has been snooping around the Commons.

There's a fine garden-supply store run by hips in Albany, the next town.

ENVIRONMENT:

Mental—People talk about fraternities and read Tolkien and Hesse. Eco-alliance is in the information stage.

Physical—Corvallis is a small city (30,000) in the middle of the rainy Willamette Valley. Zillions of Grosbeaks (finches) that sit in elm trees and rap in the spring. Rural area and pure college town. The Willamette River is polluted.

The campus is typical land-grant-college style. Lots of spaces between the buildings, which are huge red brick affairs. Spacious lawns. The administration building is World War II surplus that never got torn down.

For escapes, people go to the beaches in Seaside and Newport, less than an hour away. Some ski at Mt. Hood or go to Portland for culture. Football weekends are big.

Most students go home for a long weekend and go home when they graduate.

University of Oregon

Eugene, Oregon

The University of Oregon is a spacious, clean campus in a spacious, clean state. Students are hip, wholesome, open and friendly. It's a very nice place.

SERGEANT PEPPER SECTION:

14,829 students go to the University of Oregon. Admission is selective, average freshman SAT scores are 1,000 combined. Less than 1% minority students. 5,014 of the students are nonresidents and there are a large number of foreign students.

ACADEMIC BULLSHIT:

Good courses include many of the "Search" courses (student-initiated).

"Can Man Survive?" A Search course sponsored by Sociology, Biology and Anthropology is the most popular course with 2,000 students and meetings in the basketball court. MacGregor, a Sociology prof, teaches one 3-hour lecture section. The class breaks up into action groups to work on various ecology projects.

"Seminar on Human Sexuality" is also extremely popular. Enrollment would be large except that it is kept down to 100 students. Whatever Art Pearl teaches is extremely popular. He is an Education professor who was active in the McCarthy campaign. This term his course is "Life Styles of the Poor." Definitely the most popular prof on campus.

John Froines, Assistant Professor of Chemistry and one of the Chicago Seven, is popular also.

There are no degree requirements in Sociology and Political Science. Good graduate schools in Medicine and Dentistry. Pass/ Fail is used extensively. Some tests, some papers. Large classes. Lane Free School has many interesting Free U courses. A few courses in ethnic studies including "The Negro in American History," "Sociology of Race Relations." Not much faculty-student interaction.

BREAD:

Tuition in-state is $369 per year, $1,000 out-of-state. Loans, scholarships and campus jobs are very tight.

Dorms are $900 double, $1,080 single, for room and board. Married-student housing $42 to $91 a month. Co-ops are cheaper than dorms and attract a lot of small-town-straight students. There are communes outside of Eugene where students live with nonstudents. Two miles away from school is countryside.

Apartments cost $50 per person sharing if you're lucky. Most apartments cost $170 for a new two-bedroomer. Trailers also $50–$90.

Not too many city communes evidenced by the fact that old fraternities and sororities stand vacant instead of turning into communes. Very few people live in motor vehicles. One guy lived in an abandoned mail truck behind an abandoned frat. There are a few gypsies who live in cars, Berkeley style, many with California plates. They don't stay long, though.

Dope and booze are taboo in the dorm but some of the counselors are cool. There is a lot of dope in the dorms, and overnight guest rules are frequently violated.

Many students have cars and also bikes. Parking near campus is difficult. Threads are casual.

Flicks and concerts are popular—not much to spend money on—30¢ hamburgers are the most popular snack.

"Koobdooga Book Store" on 13th Street has used records and is the best book store in town. "Books Unlimited" on Franklin Boulevard has used books exclusively.

BROTHERS AND SISTERS:

Ratio cats : chicks—3 : 2.

A majority of the faces are straight, healthy, milk-drinking. A large minority are hip. Straight girls have shoulder-length hair, hip girls six inches longer. Few crewcuts (jocks only). Lot of full beards—tend to be neat on shorthairs. Straights wear desert boots and sneakers. Hips wear work shoes and boots. Many girls wear sandals or store shoes. Hip girls notable—for hair length, capes, ethnic pocketbooks, bright-colored dresses. Almost everybody in this town, hip or straight, male or female, wears blue jeans. Chinos are second, striped bell-bottoms third.

About one-third of the chicks are liberated and braless. 20 frats, 13 sororities—seven close-downs in last two years. Campus is not a big frat scene.

Local hangs include the "Odyssey Coffee House" on Willamette downtown, which has live entertainment Friday and Saturday, a rather hip clientele and sandwiches, soup, dessert. Open till midnight week nights. One big room with about 50 seats, piano. Owner, Bill Wooten, longhair, ran for state senate in Democratic primary.

"New World Coffee House"—good food, gourmet items, lot of teas. Chess and rock records. Popular lunch place. Lot of straights and hips go here.

"People's Cafe"—has natural type food as well as ham and steak. Very good meals for around $1.25. Abstract expressionists, tie-dyes, water-colors on the walls. Crowded weekends with longhairs.

The "Fishbowl" is the snack bar at the Student Union which is in Erb Memorial Union and called "ERB." Lot of nonstudents, dope-pushers, speed-freaks hang around here.

Good local and nationally-known folk, rock groups go to the "Attic." Light shows sometimes.

Abundant theater on campus—University Players and several other groups. Two or three small theaters in town.

There was a Renaissance Fair here last fall and there will be one this spring.

Football weekends are big.

School is definitely on the concert circuit—live entertainment on campus—Ike and Tina Turner, John Hammond, Mason Williams, many others this year.

No active political organizations but increasingly radical student body. Spring, 1969, sit-in in administration building over control of student-government budget and other issues. Ended in promises. Student body president elected for 1970 was a war-resister who had been busted for disrupting draft boards.

This year there have been numerous small acts of violence against ROTC—rock-throwing, demonstrations. Also, several big ones. Students have been active in off-campus strikes, opposing recruiters for military and polluters.

In January, 1970, Women's Liberation activists threw blood at ROTC registration table.

When Weyerhaueser Company sent recruiters on campus in February, the radical action theater put on an impromptu dramatization of immorality of pollution. The Weyerhaueser 18 were threatened with discipline concerning their actions that day. One has been tried so far and acquitted on appeal.

Fire bombs went off in the ROTC administration office in spring, 1970.

On April 15, 1970, the faculty voted by a narrow margin to keep ROTC. Some students got into the ROTC building and trashed it rather thoroughly. A torchlight parade went to the ROTC building. Some rock-throwing. Four arrests on serious charges—inciting to riot, with $25,000 bail later reduced to $3,000. The total of arrests connected with this is now up to ten. Tear gas on campus, first time.

The school was closed for two days after Nixon's Cambodia decision.

Lids go for $10–$12. Pushers all over the campus.

SURVIVAL:

A pleasure.

Students are creative—there are art studios and darkrooms for student use.

BC pills available to students over 21. Student health does abortion referrals. Draft counseling is in the basement of the student center, called the "University of Oregon Draft and Military Information Center," open 13 hours a day, 5 days a week.

Newly-opened White Bird Free Clinic on Lincoln has a wide range of services and much support from community doctors.

Notice on bulletin board: "All forestry areas are free to live in and love in as long as there are no permanent dwellings." Notice in co-op: "Do you have a billy goat to ball my nanny?" The Psychology department runs a Crisis Center. Lots of pets on campus. Very good campus newspaper—*The Emerald*—good articles on cultural events. A lot of students live on farms or communes in nearby area. They grow their own food.

Women's Liberation is in the movie-and-lecture-sponsoring stage.

ENVIRONMENT:

Mental—Read anything by Ken Kesey—this is Kesey's home town. Also popular are Rubin and Hoffman's books.

Good ecology group—"Can Man Survive?"

Physical—Eugene is a town of 90,000, 100 miles from Portland.

Lots of rain with moderate temperatures. Many of the buildings are old, the campus is spacious.

Eugene is a clean, spread-out city. Every night the Weyerhaueser paper mill pollutes the air.

Most of the older buildings on campus are brick, ivy-covered and respectable. Prince Lucien Campbell is a new nine-story building that looks like an IBM card.

Students escape by going to the beach around Florence on weekends. They also go skiing. On long weekends, students go to San Francisco. Few commuters.

Portland State University

Portland, Oregon

A big commuter school that finally woke up politically after the Kent State murders.

SERGEANT PEPPER SECTION:

10,000 students of which 1,735 are graduates. 347 from out-of-state. 200 blacks and 5 Indians.

Easy to get in—a 2.0 GPA required.

ACADEMIC BULLSHIT:

The radicals publish their own course catalog called the *Chiron*. The courses are good—some of those offered are "Human Sexuality" by Arnold Rustin, M.D., "Survival in a Social Institution: Portland State University," "Livability Criteria for a Geographical Inventory of Oregon" and "Ecological Formulae for Legislative Action." Most of these are for credit. Regular good courses include "Film History" by Andrea Steinson, "Philosophy" by Haynes, and all Sociology courses by Gary Waller. Both the Philosophy and the Sociology departments are radical. The best graduate departments are Social Work and Urban Studies.

"The Center for the Moving Image," is a student-originated curriculum concerning TV and film courses. A Free U was started but stopped when its initiators felt that this would give the school an excuse to keep the standard curriculum. Chiron studies are part credit, part noncredit, with Free U type courses. There's a Black Studies Center on campus but most of the students are white.

Tests, papers and exams, some Pass/Fail. Class attendance not required and not much interaction between students and professors. Independent study is wide open. Study abroad in Yugoslavia, Italy and Japan.

BREAD:

Tuition is $136 per quarter in-state, $425 out-of-state.

A very tight financial scene—not much available school bread. Mostly commuters who work off campus and a large night-school crowd.

There is a 14-story monstrosity called "Viking Towers" which is a privately owned dorm peopled mostly by non-students. Portland Student Services manages apartments for 500 students—rents are low but the waiting list is long. Some hips manage to find large houses and split the rent for about $40 a person—the areas are beyond that of the immediate campus.

Many students are on a limited budget and are able to scrounge by renting a house and getting food stamps. Mostly commuters who have cars although the parking problem is a real drag. Dates cost around $5—flicks and a cup of coffee. A groovy date consists of a visit to Washington Park which has a really nice cageful of giraffes.

BROTHERS AND SISTERS:

Ratio cats : chicks—about 3 : 2 (but 30% of the school is married).

Most students are straight commuter types. Guys wear chinos, windbreakers and haircuts. Chicks look like secretaries—straight dresses, nylons and "pumps." But there is a substantial minority of hips with jeans, capes and electric hair. But most females are women rather than chicks. Few couples live together and most people are going to school to get an education of the traditional type.

Portland State became very political this year after the Kent State Massacre. On May 6, 2,000 students took Smith student center. The school was closed down for two days. After it was reopened a peaceful group gathered near a first-aid tent that was still up. The mayor sent 170 tac-squad pigs in—they clubbed two beat demonstrators. Several witnesses saw a pig beating a crippled demonstrator with his own crutch. The strike continued through May. Radio Free Portland illegally broadcast a strike news hour during the occupation. SDS and the student mobe were active in the strike.

Culturally Portland State is O.K. It's on the road-tour circuit of live entertainment. There are good art galleries in town and good flicks on campus. People hang at the Student Union cafeteria. "Sam's Hofbrau" is a plastic drinking place popular with straights. The hip hangout is the "Chocolate Moose."

70% of the students have tried grass and a lot of people smoke.

SURVIVAL:

Easy in Oregon—it's such a great land trip.

BC pills available from the Portland Planned Parenthood—also an abortion referral service in town. Counseling center for students with two full-time shrinks. Draft counseling at the K house. Rodney Page is especially good.

Every survival service in town—even a People's Dental Clinic. The student newspaper is the *Vanguard*—excellent and radical undogmatic. The underground sheets are *Willamette Bridge* and *Hasheesh* (from Vancouver, Washington).

ENVIRONMENT:

Mental—People are debating about violence and revolution. The

Ecological Action Group led a good ecology workshop.

Physical—The school is in downtown Portland but it's not a slummy area—just filled up with buildings. Visual air pollution—factories in four directions. No campus—just buildings of colorless yellow that are connected by tunnels over the streets. It looks like an urban hospital complex. Building boxes involve engineering, not architecture.

Escapes include Mt. Hood for skiing and hiking in Oregon.

Reed College
Portland, Oregon

Totally 1950s-beat oriented. Students are brilliant, eccentric and molded into their own community. Three-fourths go on to graduate school.

SERGEANT PEPPER SECTION:

1,200 students of which 60 are grads. 85% from out-of-state. 50 blacks.

Very difficult to get in. High grades, about 1,400 average SAT scores. But the school takes everything into account.

ACADEMIC BULLSHIT:

Reed is one of the most unstructured colleges in the nation. No big lectures—only small conferences which include a professor and a small number of students. These conferences discuss and initiate ideas—like private tutors.

Excellent from an academic standpoint. Best courses include "The Novel of Consciousness," all the ones in Sciences (the school runs a nuclear reactor) and many in the Math department (the school has a computer center). The only graduate degrees offered are a Master of Arts in Teaching and a Master of Liberal Studies. There are no official grades until after graduation. Lots of independent study. The student : faculty ratio is 10 : 1. Very informal classes, students bring their pets, sit on the floor and rap.

The Black Studies department discourages whites from taking courses and tries to be as autonomous from Reed as possible. Courses include "Black Culture," "The Black Novel in America," "Black Writers," and "The Negro Syndrome and Black Regeneration." Very close relationships between teachers and students. Students get four weeks after Christmas to do whatever project they want. Study abroad in England and Germany. Classes may be taken at Portland Museum Art School.

BREAD:

Cost is $2,450 a year. 40% of the students get aid averaging over $1,000 a year. There is a special aid program for minority groups. Campus jobs at $1.45 an hour.

Room and board costs $935 in the dorm. No rules. Most common off-campus situation is for students to live together in a large house a few miles from campus at about $20 a head. A few students live on farms or in trailers.

Reed students live very cheaply otherwise. About five years ago they put out a low-cost cookbook suggesting horsemeat and listing other cheap foods. Inexpensive clothes and dates.

BROTHERS AND SISTERS:

Ratio cats : chicks—7 : 5.

Reed students were the original beatniks, the original "weirdos." The campus is usually associated with the lunatic fringe because there are so many brilliant eccentric students who are very much into their own thing.

Most cats have hair to their shirt collars, and beards. Blue work shirts and jeans. Chicks wear long skirts and long, long hair—occasional overalls. Everyone looks natural. Lots of living together and the social scene is nonexistent. "The only way to do it is to find a partner to last the academic year."

Reed was one of the first radical schools but the students can rarely get it together enough to get active. Intellectually stifled radicals. They demonstrated way back when Hubie was V.P. They often get arrested at induction centers. There are no military recruiters on campus. There was a tuition boycott in 1970. Half the students didn't pay tuition over the denial of tenure to nine teachers.

Reedies hang at their "Coffee Shop" on campus. It's stuffy and smells of hamburger grease but the jukebox has some wicked Chuck Berry. Over 21s go to a tavern called "Lodz's." Most Reedies group and regroup during the first few weeks of school each year.

Everyone smokes dope. It's Vietnamese, Thai or Mexican flowertops. Acid used to be really big and some people still drop on the weekends.

SURVIVAL:

Portland has all the survival services. Student health gives gynecological referrals but no BC pills. The Reed Draft Union gives draft help. Bulletin boards abound with "Wanted: Farm to Rent in the Summer" signs. Pets live clandestinely in the dorms. *The Quest* is the radical campus paper that comes out occasionally. SDS puts out a "Wall poster." Lots of people are into health foods. Some live on farms and plant gardens. A half-acre garden was planted on campus near the soccer field.

ENVIRONMENT:

Mental—Heavy intellectual conversations. People dig ecology—recently all canned-soda machines were eliminated from campus.

Physical—Portland is mild, rainy and green. Reed is surrounded by a wealthy residential neighborhood, Eastmoreland, which has nothing to offer the Reed community.

The campus is 98 acres, has large green lawns and is split into two parts by a canyon with a stream and swamp in it. The water area is a wildlife sanctuary. Air pollution is all over Portland. Campus buildings consist of two old stately buildings in Tudor-Gothic style and the old dorm block. Red brick and ivy. Oregon beaches are the most popular escapes on a rare sunny day. At the beginning of the year a whole dorm chartered a bus and went to the beach. One girl stripped and ran into the water. Reed has a ski lodge at Mt. Hood.

Southern Oregon College

Ashland, Oregon

Southern Oregon College has a two-year program in Secretarial Science.

SERGEANT PEPPER SECTION:

4,300 people, 25% out-of-state. Southern Oregon College is a state-supported liberal arts and teachers' college. 13 blacks, 5 Indians.

In-states need a 2.0 GPA or 880 combined SATs. Out-of-states need a 2.5 GPA or 950 SATs.

ACADEMIC BULLSHIT:

This is primarily a teachers' college and has a lot of crummy education courses. Southern Oregon College is the cosponsor of the Oregon Shakespeare Festival and has a good Drama department.

Favorite courses include "English Composition" by Casebeer, "Literature" with Briggs and "The History of Film." Some Pass/Fail, small classes and two black studies courses—"Black Literature" and "Black History."

205, 207, 405, and 407 are upper- and lower-division courses which may be either student- or faculty-initiated courses. The students must get faculty or departmental approval. Some courses in the past were "Theater Costume Design" and "Rhetoric and Revolution." One student did independent study on epilepsy.

Factory. No close student-faculty relationships. Some study abroad through Oregon State and the University of Oregon.

BREAD:

Tuition is $136 per quarter in-state and $359 out-of-state. There are some financial awards but they are few and far between. Lots of people are on work-study and make $1.50 an hour. Dorms cost $900 for room and board—freshmen and sophomores must live at home or in dorms. About one-third commute from home, one-third live on campus and one-third live off campus in apartments that cost $50. Many of the commuters come from Medford, about ten miles away. Cars and feet, and people dress cheaply. Students can scrounge if they want to as food commodities are available and trailers can be rented for as little as $35 a month.

BROTHERS AND SISTERS:

Ratio cats : chicks—about equal.

Most of the students are, pardon the expression, yokels. They are Middle-America, pure and simple. A few guys make a meager attempt at a hair-do. The chicks don't even do that. Lots of small-town types except for a group from Portland and California. Everyone wears jeans. About 5% are hip. There's a local dance that costs $1.25 every weekend and flicks, too. Most people go into Medford for live entertainment and bars. Dating, not much balling. Two fraternities exist but they are nonresidential.

Bars close to campus are "Omar's" and the "Black Forest"—very nondescript. In the middle of town is a coffee house called "The Pillars"—it blends in with the atmosphere of the Ashland Shakespeare Festival which happens every summer. Hips and actors hang at "The Pillars"—it has great food, chessboards, poetry readings and some music. Lithia Park is a small beautiful place to go on a nice day.

Britt Union is the principal on-campus hangout.

Quite a few smoke grass that comes in from Eugene at $15 a lid. Two students were arrested in a dormitory for hanging a b.a. (bare ass) at a pig passing by. They were expelled. Very little political activity. After Kent State, two students were arrested for carrying a sign that said "Fuck the War." 700 people showed up for a candlelight parade. There were rumors that rednecks from Medford were going to come on campus to defend the flag but they never came.

SURVIVAL:

There's a nice art gallery in Swedenborg House on campus. Student health is lousy. There's a center in Medford for birth control. Draft counseling is also done in Medford. *The Siskiyou* is cornbally and comes out once a week.

ENVIRONMENT:

Mental—People watch TV. The big ecological issue is smudging —fruit growers smudge their fruit trees during the winter—it pollutes the air.

Physical—Ashland is a town of 9,000 in the Rogue Valley amidst the Siskiyou Mountains of southern Oregon. It gets cold at night even during the summer. The country is very green, beautiful and peaceful. The campus is small and unimpressive. The older buildings have red Spanish-tile roofs—functional state-school architecture. The Britt Union has a large porch with old-folksy type chairs and a roof like an airplane hangar. Suzanne Home, a girls' dorm, is known as "Suzie Snake Pit" to its residents.

People go home to small towns like Grants Pass and Klamath Falls on vacations.

Willamette University

Salem, Oregon

A traditional Christian type school in beautiful Oregon.

SERGEANT PEPPER SECTION:

1,600 students of which 300 are law students. Two-thirds from out-of-state, 15 blacks, 2 Mexican, 1 Indian. Somewhat selective. Applications are judged individually on SATs, grades and recommendations.

ACADEMIC BULLSHIT:

English, Political Science and Math departments are best. The graduate departments are very small—Law, Music and Education.

Most popular courses include "Philosophy of Self" (an earthy sensitivity group taught by Dr. Canning) and all the interdepartmental courses such as "Faustian Man in Western Literature" and "James Joyce." The school is very grade-conscious but Canning doesn't like to give grades so he tells students to take his courses Pass/Fail.

Pass/Fail, tests, attendance required in some classes, average size 40, some rare student-originated courses. A good Free U with 25 courses like "Women's Liberation," "Stocks and Bonds," "Sex on Willamette's Campus" and basic "Rock Climbing."

There is one black studies course—"Black Culture in America and Africa."

Relationships between students and professors are very close. You have to take three or four courses with all the professors in your major. Some independent study in Art and English. In Political Science, the student can work as an intern in the state capitol across the street. Some study abroad.

BREAD:

Tuition is $1,660 per year. This private Methodist school is very wealthy—there is financial aid for anyone who needs it. Above a 3.0 GPA can get a scholarship. It's also easy to get a work-study job at $1.45 an hour.

Only a handful of students live off campus. Room and board is about $930 a year for dorms. One coed dorm with faculty living there. "This is a Christian school where Christian standards are upheld." Only this year did the students get up to 18 hours of visitation—and many students opposed this liberalization. Freshmen and sophomore girls have to be in by midnight.

Small street-person scene—nothing to do with Willamette. Some cars. Chicks have dressy clothes hidden in their closets. They wear casual dresses to class.

BROTHERS AND SISTERS:

Ratio cats : chicks—3 : 2.
Most everyone is straight. Guys have barbershop haircuts, wear

loafers and button-down shirts. Chicks wear neat type dresses. Hair spray and permanents.

Parents send their kids here so that they won't evolve. People who are hip or nonconformists are thrown out of school (three violations of the "night rules" and you're out. Activity is frat parties, flicks and sports events. Couples stand outside the dorm and neck. Bleahh!) Motels are busy during the weekend. Fraternities are strong.

The school has a deadening effect on a student's political development. Students were working on signatures for the Hatfield petition on Cambodia (the dean of women wouldn't sign it). The big issue has been open hours in the women's dorms which were recently O.K.'d.

There is a big vocal competition between the four classes each March called "Glee." A ritualistic panty raid always follows.

The school is a big Christian family. No pick-up scene. Students hang at the Student Center snack bar and at the fraternities. A group called "Concerned Students" gets liberal and leftist speakers to come to campus to talk.

SURVIVAL:

Ecologically possible, mentally unlikely. Everyone raps about basketball and ripping off panties during panty raids or motel scenes.

The school chorus tours Europe every summer. A bad Art department, one darkroom in the student center.

Sex is immoral. No BC pills or abortion referrals. Two doctors in the health service, one in the morning, one in the afternoon. Diagnosis is either pregnancy or postnasal drip.

The chaplain does draft counseling—good man. Pets prohibited. The school paper, *Willamette Collegian,* is blah. $10 for a lid—plenty available among Viet vets and high-school kids who form street scene in town. Very few heads on campus. Those that smoke are discreet. The students spend most of their time in dorms.

ENVIRONMENT:

Mental—Everyone talks about tests and grades.

Physical—The school is situated in the middle of Salem (60,000), Oregon's capital. Mild rainy climate. Countryside nearly green and beautiful all year around. Lumber and paper mills pollute the air and water. Noisy freight trains pass by the campus all the time.

The campus consists of graceful colonial style brick buildings, comfortably spread over a large city area. Most of the campus is less than 25 years old.

Most people escape to the beach in summer and to Mt. Hood (skiing) in winter.

There is a Shiloh House of new "Christians" in Salem. Last year they got a girl to drop out of school. The school warned students against it (Old Christians vs New Christians).

PENNSYLVANIA

Bryn Mawr College
Bryn Mawr, Pennsylvania

The most intellectual chicks of the sister schools.

SERGEANT PEPPER SECTION:

1,328 chicks, 31 blacks. Difficult to get in. High-school record, tests, and recommendations. The interview is important. It helps to have a relative who went here.

ACADEMIC BULLSHIT:

The two best departments are Classics and Archeology. Most courses are excellent. "History of Art" is a year-long course with each teacher in the Art department lecturing on his specialty. It has two hours of studio art work included with it each week. Mr. Lattimore's classics courses are also very popular. Mr. du Boff is the local expert on Vietnam.

Traditional academia. Pass/Fail only in freshman composition. Bad dialog or nonexistent dialog in class. Few student-originated classes. No black studies, but a few courses. Professor-student interaction in majors. Some independent study and study abroad. Cross enrollment with Haverford.

BREAD:

$2,150 per year tuition. Loans and scholarships are easy to get if you can show need. Campus jobs like library clerking and waiting table are common at $1.60 an hour.

Dorms cost $1,250 per year for room and board. Students are required to live on campus until their senior year. Some girls live in coed dorms at Haverford. Few girls live off campus.

Walking and cars for transportation.

SISTERS:

The chicks at Bryn Mawr are somewhere in the great divide between lukewarm hip and straight. They dress in either jeans and work shirts or skirts and knee socks. No freaks. Casual neat look. Not much of the comfortable grubby look.

Bryn Mawr chicks are intellectuals and not too friendly. Many of them are suffering from image conflict. The image they desire vs the image they are stuck with. Where is the real person? They don't know and most of them admit to being "neurotic." They usually date Haverford cats and there's a lot of cohabitation on the weekend.

Dates include food and a flick at Haverford or a rock concert at the "Electric Factory" in Philadelphia. Drinking is more popular than grass; some girls have smoked but don't do it regularly. Some super-straights on campus who don't drink or engage in sexual activity.

Some go to the "College Inn" or "The Hot Shoppes" to meet and greet. The campus runs a weekly flick series.

Most chicks split on the weekends.

"I don't know if we have a radical here any more. We used to." That sums up the lack of revolutionary spirit. Armchair liberals. Leafletting and canvassing in response to the Cambodia decision. The black students sat in for 45 minutes at the dean's office in 1970 to demand a black sociologist on campus. The situation was more friendly than militant and the school gave in. The few activists go off campus to participate.

SURVIVAL:

Little emphasis on the creative arts. Student health is decent, no BC pills. Psychiatric counseling on campus. No health-food stores or dealers nearby. Women's Liberation has about 40 cohesive members. They were responsible for getting a "History of Women" course started in 1970.

ENVIRONMENT:

Mental—Most chicks study a lot. Some read *Winnie the Pooh* and *Lord of the Rings*. No ecology action.

Physical—Bryn Mawr is just ten miles from Philadelphia. Winters are cold, summers hot. The campus is beautiful—greenery, trees and brooks and squirrels. Slightly medieval and rural. Gothic architecture. Each dorm looks like an English inn. The only eyesore is the dorm, Erdman Hall.

Chicks escape to Haverford or home on the weekends.

Bucknell University
Lewisburg, Pennsylvania

The campus is divided into the rich and the poor—those that can afford it and those that are on financial aid.

SERGEANT PEPPER SECTION:

2,700 students of which 200 are grads. Fairly difficult to get in. Admission is based mostly on class rank and SAT scores (average about 1,250). The personal interview is also important. Chicks tend to be in the top tenth of their class and cats in the top fifth. Transfers need a 2.5 GPA. About 65% are from out-of-state. 50 blacks.

ACADEMIC BULLSHIT:

The best departments here are Mathematics, History, Chemistry, Biology and Psychology and especially Engineering. The grad departments aren't "big time"; the only two good ones are Engineering and Psychology.

Favorite courses include Dr. Keen's abnormal psychology class, Dr. Harclerode's physiological psychology, and Dr. Wheatcroft's English classes.

The school is small and tries to create an intellectual atmosphere but it just doesn't quite make it. The faculty are much brighter than the students. No student-initiated classes and a weak Free U (square dancing was a "biggie" as was "Sin and Love"—sounds like a hot one). The professor-student relationship is very good as "They take a deep interest in students here; professors are here almost all day long." No Black Studies department and very few blacks on campus. Independent study is available to a limited extent. Psychology, Religion and a couple of other departments have a thing called "Continuous Progress" in which the curriculum is so divided that the student progresses at his own rate but he has to finish all his work before the semester is up. Seniors can do honor work in their major field. The school is on a voluntary 4-1-4 program so that those who want to can do independent study in the month of January. 25% participated in it in 1970 (some went on a cultural arts tour of the Soviet Union, others went on a business administration tour of Western Union).

Some study abroad.

BREAD:

Yearly tuition at this private school is $2,425. Financial aid is tight and they are only able to offer aid to about 25% of those who request it. Jobs are available at $1.50 an hour. Dorms cost $1,000 for room and board and an additional $75 if you stay for the January session. Apartments range from $80–$160 a month for a two-bedroom. Most people live in the dorms.

Many have cars and costly rags.

BROTHERS AND SISTERS:

Ratio cats : chicks—around 2 : 1.

"The Bucknell chick is the ideal old style college girl, polished, well-dressed and mannered!"

This campus is casual—everyone looks the same, very few colorful freaks or just plain colorful people. Students wear jeans, sneakers, frat T-shirts, Bucknell T-shirts and dresses. The guys all look like Fraternity Joes with a hangover. The fraternities are still very big and control the social life. Theta Chi is a freak frat, but most are straight.

Everybody dates. There aren't enough chicks to go around so guys keep trading them until they find one they like. Lots of dates are arranged by the fraternities (they have big spring and winter formals). Some cats go into the city and find townie chicks or go to nearby schools.

The few freaks that go here hang at friends' apartments. Fraternity kids hang at fraternities. Other hangs are "The Bison" (snack bar on campus) and "Dunkle's"—a bar in town that has a good cross section of Bucknell students.

About 50% of the students smoke, but it's still underground. Grass is fairly hard to get hold of and there's a paranoia about busts. Kids are getting into DMT and acid. Grass costs $20 an ounce.

There are few militant people on campus, most students are apathetic. Lewisburg ignores the students—no repression on campus. Most kids are more interested in social life than politics.

Every Saturday, starting in 1966, they've had a vigil for peace in front of the local post office. In 1967, panty raids were the big demonstration things. In May, 1968, Hubert Humphrey spoke at Bucknell and got an honorary degree. Only 20 students walked out saying, "You, sir, are a disgrace to your country."

In the fall of 1968, there was a sit-in over Army recruiting. 75 people had a "lay-in" in the recruiter's office. Jocks to the rescue! They put on their football spiked shoes and walked over the demonstrators. The Moratoriums garnered support and on Earth Day, 1970, students started a Lewisburg People's Park by cleaning up an area near the Susquehanna River.

The 1970 student strike polarized the campus. Humanities students canvassed, marched and went to rallies while most Engineering students went to classes. Demonstrators marched on Allenwood Prison (a prison for political prisoners convicted of not complying with the draft laws) and held a Festival of Life (most of the people were from Philadelphia but there were some people from Bucknell).

Campus pigs get their jollies by trying to catch chicks leaving guys' dorms at night. "Outer Ripple" is the intellectual organization on campus. They put out position papers on things like racism and birth control.

SURVIVAL:

Service is good at the dispensary, but no BC pills. No survival services—one Free Clinic at Geisinger Medical Center in town. No Planned Parenthood in the area. Draft counseling is done by Quaker students on campus and Dr. Richard Drinnon, a history professor, on campus. Intercollegiate sports are very big here—especially soccer, swimming and lacrosse. *The Bucknellian* has a page for sports, one for frats, one for letters and a fourth page is the front page.

ENVIRONMENT:

Mental—People don't read much outside of class.

Physical—Rainy springs and snowy winters. No air pollution to speak of—a clean country atmosphere. Some people call the architecture "Tidewater Colonial" and others call it "Harvardian"—but either way it still is brick buildings with steeples—collegiate buildings. The Library and the Chapel are very pleasing to look at.

There are a million beautiful country places to escape to, especially Red Rocks, Half Way Dam and Swinging Bridge (a suspension bridge across Buffalo Creek).

Carnegie-Mellon University

Pittsburgh, Pennsylvania

Still old Carnegie Tech in real life.

SERGEANT PEPPER SECTION:

4,912 students. 1,925 are out-of-state. About 160 minority students. Rather difficult to get in—about 1,200 combined SATs and
upper two-fifths of high-school class. Drama majors are required
to audition. Humanities applicants may send poems.

ACADEMIC BULLSHIT:

The Carnegie Institute of Technology (Engineering) recently
merged with the Mellon Research Center. In addition to these programs, the University includes a graduate school of Industrial
Administration, a division of Humanities and Social Sciences, a
College of Fine Arts and the Margaret Morrison Carnegie College
for Women. Carnegie-Mellon has the nation's finest school of
Drama.

Professor Alan Pinkus' psychology class is popular. Each major
has such stiff requirements that you don't get to select many classes.
"All I can take are engineering courses, they aren't popular but
I need them to graduate." Other top departments include Electrical
Engineering, Computer Science and Physics.

Average class size is 50, ambiguous Pass/Fail policy, not too
much class participation except in drama. A few student-originated
courses. A few courses related to ethnic groups. "C-Map" is the
name of the minority recruitment program directed mostly at
blacks. There are currently 90 black students.

Independent study is allowed as are self-determined majors. One
such major is Radio and Communication which was put together
by a student interested in broadcast work. He gets over half his
credits for working for a local radio station. Most student-professor
action is impersonal except in the Arts. Some study abroad.

BREAD:

$1,100 a semester. Heavy. More loans than scholarships, lots of
campus jobs at $1.60 an hour.

Dorms cost from $350 (without board) to $610 for room and
board per semester. Apartments are the most popular digs. But
more than one-fourth of the campus lives in dorms. About 500
belong to fraternities (sizable considering the size of the campus).
Most kids walk, some wear costly threads, but most dress in early

grub. Dates are fraternity parties for straights and rapping for hips. Plays or concerts on campus cost $1.50 per person and have good attendance. Pittsburgh is not where it's at actionwise.

BROTHERS AND SISTERS:

Ratio cats : chicks—3 : 1.

The campus is divided between Fine Arts and Humanities freaks and Engineering and Science straights. Few have the rich-hip look. Most of the chicks wear jeans, T-shirts and sandals. Everyone looks sloppy and comfortable. Few couples live together—except for the Fine Arts people who do it on weekends. The fraternity dudes date and seduce. Few chicks are liberated, most wear bras. They die just getting wind of the sexual revolution. Fraternities are very strong and can still pick and choose and do their Greek Sing.

The Carnegie-Mellon campus isn't politically active. An *ad hoc* group called the "Workshop in Revolutionary Non Violence" pops up when big issues arise. They work within the eroded channels. The administration always opens up its doors and lets everyone sit-in if they want to. Incoming freshmen seem to be more active.

Carnegie-Mellon students frequent University of Pittsburgh hangs. They also go to "The Crumbling Wall" (hip coffee shop), "Gazebo" (sandwich shop on shady side) and the "Holiday Bar" (straights).

SURVIVAL:

Bring gas mask for air pollution.

The health service is sick. "Cough syrup for V.D." Draft counseling through The Resistance or American Friends office in Pittsburgh. Carnegie-Mellon students use the Student Help Center at the University of Pittsburgh for survival services.

The Tartan is O.K. for a campus paper and the underground *Relative Truth* is mild (even though students view it as a flaming radical paper).

Drugs are light. Most kids smoke grass, frats smoke and drink. The Fine Arts kids are more into the drug scene. Score on shady side or in the dorms.

No one is into health foods yet.

Women's Liberation is embryonic.

ENVIRONMENT:

Mental—People are reading Brautigan and Vonnegut. The world situation is the gloomy topic of conversation.

Physical—Very Pittsburgh-looking (see the University of Pittsburgh). Carnegie-Mellon, unlike the University of Pittsburgh, is set apart from the community. Still has air and noise pollution. The buildings are usually semi-modern and some are covered with ivy. There's a grassy area in the middle of campus.

Not much weekend travel but otherwise same as University of Pittsburgh. 40% are commuters. Carnegie-Mellon students and University of Pittsburgh students mingle.

Chatham College
Pittsburgh, Pennsylvania

Chatham is a secluded girls' school with an emphasis on studying during the week and finding a man on the weekends.

SERGEANT PEPPER SECTION:

600 chicks. 60% out-of-state. 40 blacks. Hard to get in. High-school transcript is the most important criteria—applicants are usually in upper two-fifths of their class. SATs and ACTs required.

ACADEMIC BULLSHIT:

This is a small high-quality women's liberal arts college. There are no longer any breadth requirements here. Undergraduate departments only. The best are Psychology (experimental), Political Science (relevant) and Biology. The largest departments have about five professors. Students at Chatham can take courses at the University of Pittsburgh and Carnegie-Mellon.

Popular courses are Dr. Frank Lackner's "Abnormal Psychology" course (he relates things to sex and these broads eat it up), Dr. Morrill's "Ethics and Modern Christian Thought" and Dr. Adelman's "Cultural Anthropology."

Small stimulating classes which emphasize individual participation. Pass/Fail, small classes, a small Black Studies department.

If a class is not relevant to the needs of the students, the chicks can walk out and stay out until the professor has restructured the class. If three students come to a department and request that a class be added, it must be done.

Chatham prides itself on the excellent communication between teachers and students. They discuss, rap and group together in an informal way.

BREAD:

Tuition is $1,500 a semester for all. Chatham insures that anyone who is admitted has enough money to make it through loans, scholarships or jobs. 40% receive aid—the other chicks are rich. Many jobs.

Most students live in the dorms—they cost $620 per semester for room and board. Men are allowed to stay until 2:30 A.M. (but they stay on—and on—and on).

Chatham chicks wouldn't think of scrounging. Expensive wardrobes are wearing out. Most chicks get dates in the area but the pucker-face ones have to offer to go dutch. Flicks, drinking, smoking, going to the Pittsburgh Zoo and looking at the Westinghouse sign at night are popular forms of entertainment.

SISTERS:

Getting hipper all the time. Lukewarm hip at the moment. Jeans and T-shirts. Some dresses and rich type shirts and loafers. No hard-core freaks but the rich ones are really trying to be hip. Give them an E for effort.

A few chicks live with their boy friends; most don't but shack on the weekends. The younger chicks are more liberated. They go to the University of Pittsburgh, Carnegie-Mellon or Washington and Jefferson College to meet cats. Chatham girls are taken on dates to "Walt Harper's Attic" (bar), "Bimbo's," "Sodini's" (restaurant) and "Stolen Base" (beer joint).

Chatham has peaceful political groups—BSU, YAF and the Chatham Strike Committee. They are proud of the fact that they were the only college in the Pittsburgh area to be entirely shut down during the strike. No militancy.

SURVIVAL:

More chicks into the academic bag than the creative bag. Two regular nurses and one doctor every day for an hour. No BC pills or abortion referrals on campus but they are available in town. Student Help Center at University of Pittsburgh used. The student paper is *The Matrix,* a drag.

Drug use is moderate—60% smoke. Some drop acid—mescaline is increasing. No busts. The school is very conscious of its name and doesn't want trouble. No one is into the health-food thing. Women's Liberation is small.

ENVIRONMENT:

Mental—The chicks read *The Electric Kool-Aid Acid Test* and Richard Farina. They say they have so much required reading that they can't do pleasure reading.

Physical—For area, see University of Pittsburgh.

The campus of Chatham is gorgeous. It used to be the Mellon estate. The dorms all look like mansions, lovely trees and fields. The campus looks peaceful and inspiring. The buildings are brick and ivy or large white mansions. Chatham is one-half mile down the road from a residential area of the city.

Chatham chicks escape to their brother school, Washington and Jefferson College, on the weekends. They also go to other campuses —wherever there are rumors of dudes.

Franklin and Marshall College

Lancaster, Pennsylvania

All the cats want to grow up to be AMA conservative doctors like their AMA conservative physician fathers.

SERGEANT PEPPER SECTION:

1,816 students of which 1,148 are out-of-state. Must have good grades and good board scores.

ACADEMIC BULLSHIT:

Franklin and Marshall has a very good Science department. It's considered the best pre-med school in the East for a school that is not associated with a medical school. The Biology department is considered the best in the country. Chemistry and Biology are excellent.

The most popular faculty member is Gerald Enscoe of the English department—he's the house radical. Other popular professors are Wickstrom of the English department, Max Drake of the Sociology department, and Charlie Holtzinger of the Anthropology department.

Classes are kept small just for the purpose of having good class participation. The average size is 20. Some Pass/Fail, few student-originated classes, no Free U. Several black studies courses but taught by whites. Faculty and students are quite close and they often rap and drink together. Everyone congregates after class in the coffee shop. Some independent study and study abroad at the University of Lancaster in England.

BREAD:

$2,400 per year tuition. Tight money—not much financial aid—jobs are hard to find—wage is $1.60 an hour.

There are three popular living arrangements. Dorms cost $1,020 a year for room and board. There's a shortage of dorm space, though. The administration is discussing the possibility of moving in mobile units to take up the slack. Lots of students live in the 11 fraternity houses that cost the same as the dorms. Apartments run $50 per month per person—they are hard to find. Many rich kids—lots of cars and expensive rags.

The average cost of a date is $3—there's nothing to do in Lancaster. Fraternity parties or flicks and lots of drinking and tube watching.

BROTHERS AND SISTERS:

Ratio cats : chicks—15 : 1.

Lots of pre-professional cats who want to be conservative AMA type doctors like their dads. Most are lukewarm hip—they wear jeans, T-shirts and sandals. A few freaks garbed in faded jeans and work shirts. Lots of neat starched-shirters. Chicks dress up and wear dresses. No chick freaks. Most cats date chicks that go to other schools since there are so few chicks on campus. Two nursing schools in Lancaster provide dating fodder. Some cats even date local high-school girls or go to Goucher and Wilson for dates. Not a sexual haven by any standard.

Local hangs are the student center, "Hildy's Tavern," and Buchanen Park—where the kids lie around and rap.

The Greek system is still strong since they provide the only social life. Drugs aren't big. Not that many smoke grass and the town cops scare any would-be-users by semi-annual busts. Juice heads.

Political action is light and is done through *ad hoc* committees. Most kids are here primarily to study and get into graduate school.

The Afro-Americans are the only powerful group on campus. The only crisis so far took place in early 1970 when two popular professors were fired for letting students grade themselves. Class boycott, strike and sit-ins. The students never got the professors rehired but they did raise $12,000 to pay for one of them, Henry Mayer, to come back and teach anyway. Moderate interest in the student strike.

SURVIVAL:

Bad prognosis for males. Dating situation is very bad. Girls were admitted for the first time in 1969. The infirmary is bad—no BC pills. No draft counseling, no survival services. *The College Reporter* is decent but average.

ENVIRONMENT:

Mental—Students are studying, reading *Soul on Ice* and *One Flew Over the Cuckoo's Nest* and rapping about sex. The Environmental Control Unit is moderately into ecology.

Physical—Lancaster is 60 miles west of Philadelphia—same weather. The city is flat and suburban. Spread out, even lawns, square buildings. There's a great amount of weekend traveling to other schools.

Haverford College
Haverford, Pennsylvania

A fine, small school.

SERGEANT PEPPER SECTION:

640 students, all undergraduates. 485 out-of-state. 8% black, 1½% Puerto Rican. Only official requirement for admission is "ability to contribute to and benefit from the College." Standards, though, are high. Grades are B and up, and SATs are 1300 and up.

ACADEMIC BULLSHIT:

Academic standards are very high in every department. But Biology, Philosophy, Chemistry and English are the best departments.

Best courses are "The Impressionist Era" with Professor Pat McCarthy, "Religion and Modern Culture" with Professor Gerhard Spiegler (flicks on modern forms of religious expression and critiques of religion), "Topics in Modern Biology" (tutorials on such topics as the nature of living organisms and the theory of evolution).

Seniors have one Pass/Fail option in a course outside their major. Class participation is intense as classes are small. Students can organize courses and recruit faculty support for them. Some black studies courses in various departments. Students and professors are very close; many work closely together on research. Lots of independent study. Some study abroad, "an unusually high number go to Africa."

BREAD:

Full year tuition is $2,325. Loans and scholarships are available, but tight.

Dorms cost $1,300 for room and board; 95% live in the dorms. Some off-campus apartments which cost around $150. About 120 spaces each at Haverford and Bryn Mawr are in coed dorms, alternate floors. Lots of cars and bikes.

Expensive threads aren't necessary.

The average date costs $2.50—flicks and the pancake house.

BROTHERS AND SISTERS:

Ratio cats : chicks—15 : 1.

Most students are bright lukewarm hips. They wear shabby clothes, tend to hang together, smoke dope and talk about philosophy and art. About 10% are heavy hip, long-haired and into heavy dope. Straights are generally self-exiled, defensive and unhappy.

"Sexual activity is very hard to judge. There is certainly a lot, but not nearly enough to make most people happy or satisfied." Some cats live with Bryn Mawr chicks. "Chicks are beginning to see themselves with greater self-respect as fully human beings and not be bullied by guys."

Grass is $12–$20 a lid. Mescaline is $4 a tab.

School politics are left-liberal. "Many kids are frustrated radicals but almost all are nonviolently oriented and thus suffer from the pitiful lack of imagination and leadership now evident among nonviolent radicals. They tend to avoid politics sporadically when something good turns up such as last winter's occupation of the University of Pennsylvania." There are occasional off-campus marches and there was extensive participation in the Moratorium.

There are no on-campus demonstrations (by choice, not edict) since the campus is by policy not connected in any way to the military (Quaker tradition) and is reasonable and conciliatory on student power.

"There was SDS in 1970 but they all graduated. Some into Weathermen, some into law school. Oh well."

SURVIVAL:

Good Fine Arts department, much photography, ceramics and sculpture. The infirmary is to be avoided if possible. The student counseling center is competent, popular and overcrowded. Draft counseling is readily available at the school. Switchboard called HELP if you need it.

"Only a few kids are into health foods or vegetarianism. The only thing that I know of kids growing is dope."

ENVIRONMENT:

Mental—"Nobody reads. If forced, I'd say a few are reading Vonnegut and Marcuse. The topics of conversation are each other and ourselves."

Physical—The climate is eastern temperate—one big snowstorm a year. The campus is a lush green enclave in a quiet suburb. Lots of land—216 acres for 600 students. Buildings are small and in Quaker plain style—simple and elegant. People don't leave campus on the weekend. 95% live on campus.

Lafayette College
Easton, Pennsylvania.

Girls were finally admitted in 1970.

SERGEANT PEPPER SECTION:

1,904 males. In fall, 1970, the school went coed and admitted an unspecified number of females. 40 blacks. Fairly difficult to get in—1,300 SATs and good grades.

ACADEMIC BULLSHIT:

The best departments are Business and Engineering. The Psychology department is the most popular among students—progressive and liberal (take Professor Rogers and Professor Gallup). Professor Franks of the Music department is also very popular. The Biology department has one of the best pre-med programs in the country.

Some Pass/Fail, not much class participation and increasingly more student-originated courses. Some departments hand out cards and ask students what courses they would like offered. Students can also petition through their department to have a course offered—in 1970 courses on Vietnam and Indochina were offered in response to students' wishes. A few black studies courses are offered.

Most teachers are approachable but the students don't take the time and effort to get to know them. Independent study is very unusual—some study abroad.

BREAD:

Tuition is $2,050 a year for everyone. Loans and scholarships are tight. Campus jobs are available—the usual at $1.75 an hour. Off-campus jobs pay more and some students drive taxis and work in restaurants. Dorms cost $1,000 per year for room and board—frats about the same. Apartments can be found for $50 per person. Most students live in fraternities or dorms. Only about 10% of the students live off campus because there's nothing to do in Easton. Many kids have cars. Cheap clothes are fine and dates cost little. But Lafayette students don't scrounge—they are in general well off.

BROTHERS AND SISTERS:

1,904 cats and a few chicks.

The campus is just like the real world—strive, achieve, etc. Lafayette cats want to be executives—they are hip socially but not politically or intellectually. Fraternity parties and football games are still the big attraction—they have tried grass but aren't regular users. Lids go for $20. They wear jeans and T-shirts and sandals and have medium-long hair. Nothing very outlandish. Dates were really hard to find before it went coed and boys used to froth at the mouth for a date with a chick from Cedar Crest College or Centenary College (and if you saw those chicks). They aren't particularly liberated but do ball if it looks like marriage is in the offing. Fraternities are very strong—they control the lack of social scene—19 houses. Longhairs can get in but not in the top jock houses.

The local hangs are "The Gourd" (snack bar), "Jack's" (bar), "Beef and Ale" (a bar) and the frat houses.

There's not much political activism and what changes there are happen through accepted channels. The ABC (Association of Black Collegiates) make themselves felt even though they are a small group—they want more minority recruitment.

The big issues of 1969 were going coed and making ROTC optional—both were passed. In 1970, the two issues were Curriculum Reform (many changes were made) and the Cambodian-Kent strike, the first real show of activism. There has never been violence or police called in here.

SURVIVAL:

Except for the lack of chicks, it's possible.

No artsy-craftsy students, "they'd rather watch TV."

Student health is adequate—some shrinks are available. Draft counseling was just started in 1970. No survival services in Easton. *The Lafayette* is the school paper—everyone reads it (for lack of anything better to do). Health foods haven't hit.

ENVIRONMENT:

Mental—People are talking about their courses and reading Jerry Rubin's *Do It!* They also talk about chicks a lot. The Biology department is into ecology.

Physical—Easton is a drag. It's 60 miles from Philadelphia and Philadelphia is a drag. The fall has the only nice weather. Suburban campus on a hill overlooking the city. Two- and three-story red brick and gray concrete buildings. Pardee Hall is the ugliest building with its obnoxious color scheme (sick pink).

Most cats dig their fraternities on the weekend and don't travel—and if they do, they go to Philadelphia or Fun City or the Delaware River area.

Lehigh University
Bethlehem, Pennsylvania

The most exciting thing here is the wrestling matches—they really pack them in.

SERGEANT PEPPER SECTION:

5,000 male undergraduates, 100 females. 50% out-of-state. 39 black students. Good grades and board scores. Three achievement tests are required.

ACADEMIC BULLSHIT:

Lehigh is known for its Engineering school. The facilities and teachers are excellent. The curriculum is updated every year—best departments are Civil Engineering and Metallurgy. Bethlehem Steel gives the school lots of money and provides excellent labs for steel research. The Business school is also good. The most popular course is Dr. Richard's "Ocean Engineering"—he's one of the most prominent oceanographers around. Professor Wilson is the popular house radical. Professor Aronson is the most popular faculty member in the Business school ("he has a great sense of humor").

The "Creative Concepts" courses, open to those with a 3.0, discuss any topics of relevant interest—creative writing, Russian law, etc. Some Pass/Fail, lots of tests, not much class participation and a few student-originated courses. Several courses dealing with the Black Experience. Lots of interaction between teachers and students. Study abroad and students in Government or History can spend a semester at American University in Washington, D.C.

BREAD:

$2,300 per year. Limited financial aid and jobs. Dorms and fraternities run $1,070 a year for room and board. No dorm rules. Apartments off campus run $70 each and are shabby. Lots of off-campus jobs in factories at $2.00 an hour. Go to the Pennsylvania State Employment Agency for referrals.

Half have wheels and the rest walk or have cycles. Expensive threads aren't necessary. The average cost of a date is $0 for a fraternity party or 75¢ for campus flicks. Booze, grass and rapping.

BROTHERS AND SISTERS:

Ratio cats : chicks—50 : 1.

Students dress in comfortable threads—jeans, T-shirts and sandals. No one cares about clothes—they all look respectably grubby. No plastic-hip clothes.

The girl situation is drastic. Most cats go out with someone from their home town or date chicks from Cedar Crest College. Weekend shacking up in the dorms. Frat rats like to go into town and pick up a "Scruff" (town chick) for a one-night shot.

417

31 fraternities and they are strong—the center of everything. Frats smoke dope a lot and even longhairs get in. Hangs are the "Catacomb" (coffee house in basement of the Chapel) and the "Ale House."

Two groups are active politically—the New Committee (like the Student Mobilization Committee—informative) and the black students. The blacks have instigated black courses and gotten a black-culture-center room. Students are moderately active—they pushed for the school to be coed. Curriculum revision hassles caused the school to be shut down in April, 1970—the students wanted more of a say in things. No outside pigs ever called in.

40% use grass regularly. Mescaline is getting popular. Grass is $20 a lid and mescaline is $2.50 a hit.

SURVIVAL:

Hard with so few girls. Oh—and that archaic fraternity system is also a drag. Student health gives only sympathy. No draft counseling service on campus. The Lehigh Valley Friends, a Quaker group in the area, will give draft counseling, though. All the fraternity houses have dogs. The campus paper is the *Brown and White*—O.K. Good cartoonist.

ENVIRONMENT:

Mental—People are talking about student-inspired reforms of the school's curriculum. They are reading Hesse, *Stranger in a Strange Land* and *The Godfather*.

Physical—Bethlehem is a steel town. Obnoxious weather and environment. The campus seems beautiful in comparison with the town. Bring hiking boots—it's built on a hill. Big churchlike buildings.

Students stay around campus on weekends and import girls.

Pennsylvania State University

University Park, Pennsylvania

Still the play school of Pennsylvania.

SERGEANT PEPPER SECTION:

26,823 students, mostly Pennsylvania residents. Not hard to get in—SATs required (average of 1,100) and good grades. The main campus is supplemented by 19 commonwealth campuses and three graduate centers.

ACADEMIC BULLSHIT:

The best departments are Engineering and Agriculture. The government does a lot of Agricultural field research on Penn's 4,550-acre campus. In the Liberal Arts departments, the Speech department is said to be the best in the East (the course offerings are close to what a Free U would offer). The Biology graduate school and the Biology department are also good.

Dr. Latman of the Geology department is regarded as something a notch higher than God or Ché (your preference)—he is one of the most popular professors in the country. Students adore him. He teaches geological science and is "so fucking hilarious he's unreal." Dr. Wagner's course on ecology is also very well peopled (he's a prophet of doom) as are Dr. Phillips' speech courses.

One of the most radical faculty members is Welles Keddie, a labor management professor. He's the SDS faculty sponsor.

Some Pass/Fail, multiple-choice tests are still happening and class participation isn't particularly important. Lower division courses are large, often 300 or more. 198 and 489 are Liberal Arts courses that students can set up on any topic they want—the professor is merely an advisor. Some courses in the past have been "Study in Communal Living," "Mythology" and "Muckraking." There's no Black Studies department and only a limited number of courses are available. The Free U offers "Housing and Legal Affairs Education," "Astrology" and "Zionism." Some departments have independent study. Study abroad is possible.

BREAD:

$200 per quarter for in-state, $450 out-of-state. Lots of loans and scholarships are available. Jobs are also plentiful at $1.50 an hour.

Dorms cost $345 per quarter for room and board. Apartments run $65–$75 a month per person. Dorms make their own rules. Freshmen have to live in the dorms for a year. There are 26 sororities and 56 fraternities. Lots of communal living situations—one group is called the "Shelter"—there are 40 guys and gals there. Effective scrounging is done by students with the knack for it. Panhandling can yield a good take if you have a sweet smile. Visitors to town can go to "The Wall" on College Avenue. Cars, motorcycles and buses are all popular forms of transportation. Sorority chicks still dig expensive rags.

BROTHERS AND SISTERS:

Ratio cats : chicks—2 : 1.

This school is so large that there is an abundance of every type. The plastic-hip look with embryonic moustaches is in. Lots of dress-up girls with that well-kempt look. Cats wear jeans and a shirt. The freak population has shoulder-length hair, jean bell-bottoms and grubby shirts.

Sex is a big thing here whatever faction you're in. Freaky chicks are liberated while others are not but "on the average it's pretty hot here." What with 56 fraternities and 26 sororities, they are influential. Independents look down (or up) at the Greeks as rich snobs. It still has elements of the rah-rah school it used to be. Dorm regulations have eased making the frats less attractive. Most fraternity boys smoke grass now instead of drinking booze. Drugs are really heavy with the freaks—lids go for $20 an ounce and

acid goes for $2.00 a tab. The freaks here are into heavy dope—
you can get anything you want.

People hang at "The Hub" (Hetzel Union Building), "The
Wall" (people sit and smoke), "The Jawbone" (coffee house) and
"My O My" (bar). People rap on the lawn in the middle of
campus. You can play Frisbee or watch the dogs play there.
Other forms of entertainment include concerts and roaming in the
woods.

Most students are apolitical and apathetic. There is a small hard-
core of radical activists. They are grouped into The Coalition for
Peace (anti-war students), SDS (20 members and 300 back-up
freaks), the BSU (100 active members—separatists), and The
Workers League (4 Trotskyites). The BSU is very militant. They
have been lobbying for more recruitment of blacks (they built a
brick wall in front of the president's office to symbolize the lack
of communication between the president and the blacks.

Violent confrontation came to Penn State for the first time in
1970. First, the Military Ball was disrupted by Women's Liberation
and SDS and later Old Main was occupied. Students presented
four demands: (1) open admission of blacks; (2) ROTC off
campus; (3) disaffiliation with the Ordinance Research Lab; and
(4) support for Bobby Seale. Pigs came on campus and 29 students were arrested. There was half-hearted support for the strike.

SURVIVAL:

Yes, if you eat ice cream at the creamery.

Students are into the arts-and-crafts thing, both as vocations and
as avocations. The Ritenour Infirmary is always very busy and you
have to stand in line for hours. One pre-med student said, "If
Ritenour was the only place I could practice I'd never become a
doctor." Shrinks and BC pills are available. The Coalition for
Peace runs a Draft Counseling Center. "Help" runs a switchboard.
Pets abound. *The Collegiate* is an interesting liberal campus paper.
The Water Tunnel is the underground paper—totally political with
lots of rhetoric. The staff got arrested for putting a picture of the
naked John and Yoko in the paper. They were acquitted. The
freaks are into health foods—buy foods at "Youngberg's General
Store." Women's Liberation meets in a women's bathroom.

ACADEMIC BULLSHIT:

Mental—People are talking about being hip and reading *The
Electric Kool-Aid Acid Test* and *Stranger in a Strange Land.*
The Department of Mineral Science studies ecology problems and
the Free U has ecology courses.

Physical—University Park is three and a half hours from Philadelphia. Cold in the winter, hot in the summer. A beautiful campus
—forests and natural habitat. Acres and acres of land.

Some people split on the weekends to their homes, to the area
surrounding the school for camping and to Whipple Dam or Stone
Valley in the state park area. No one travels during the fall term
because the school is a big social action place.

University of Pennsylvania
Philadelphia, Pennsylvania

People study, go to grad school and become high-echelon professionals.

SERGEANT PEPPER SECTION:

18,769 students of which 10,884 are from out-of-state. One of the Ivy League schools—hard to get in. High grade and high SATs and good recommendations. Competition for admittance is very keen. In 1970, they had 8,000 applicants for only 1,700 places. 3.5% blacks.

ACADEMIC BULLSHIT:

Penn is academically excellent. The Wharton School of Business, the Medical school and the Life Science department are nationally known. But it's for the serious studier—not much of a creative curriculum. The students clamor for the good liberal arts courses which include art, history, "Russian History" by Professor Riasanovsky, and "Film Making." Popular anti-war professors include Phil Pochota (Sociology) and Dr. Gandhi (Economics).

Penn is really geared to the graduate schools in Business, Law and Medicine. The Anthropology department is also well known and has been responsible for many important finds in the field. An unusual department is American Civilization—it studies the American culture in detail.

Lots of tests, papers and hard work. Some Pass/Fail and not many student-originated courses (too much bureaucratic tangle).

They have been hassling over the formation of a Black Studies department for two years. At present there are just a few courses relating to Black America. The favored proposal is to allow juniors and seniors only to eventually major in Black Studies. There has been increased recruitment of minority students and the class of 1970 was 8% black. Independent study is allowed—just find a professor. Study abroad.

There's a Free U and it's really good. Courses include "Encounter Group," "Problems of Home Ownership," "Creative Cooking," "Freaky Thoughts and Weird World Views" and "Panhandling" (the basic techniques of panhandling for fun and profit combined with outlines for general seediness. Field trips to skid row.).

BREAD:

Tuition is $2,550 per year. But like the other Ivy League schools, if they let you in, they will help you. However, some students say they don't give you enough bread to survive on. Some loans, scholarships and campus jobs. The average wage is about $1.60 an hour.

Dorms cost $1,250 a year for room and board and fraternities are about the same. Neither are worth it. Most people prefer to live in apartments—the nice ones run about $75 per person, the not-so-nice ones about $50 per person. Buildings off campus are cheap, dilapidated and crumbling (and smell like cat shit).

Free campus buses—some have cars. Frats dress expensively but most dress in comfortable grubby threads.

Scrounging is nearly impossible in the Ivy League schools because of the tuition. However, you can live in a cheap ghetto pad and hitch to school to cut down on expenses. Dates are cheap—rock concerts for a fancy one. Most students get stoned, get a cup of coffee and rap. Walking around the Philadelphia Art Museum is popular. There are several used-book shops in the area.

BROTHERS AND SISTERS:

Ratio cats : chicks—2 : 1.

Penn students are serious. They are more intellectual than the Temple plodders but less intellectual than Harvard or Berkeley people. They are usually organized and energetic.

Most are hip and wear jeans, sandals, and T-shirts and have medium-length hair. There is a dress-up big-city Philadelphia clique on campus. The professional-school students wear either sport coats and jeans or loafers, button-down shirts and sweaters. There is another group of freaky-lookers—kinky frizzed hair, bell-bottoms and old shirts. You can wear anything and be in.

Lots of semi-shacking (cohabiting on weekends when parents won't find out). Most of the chicks are liberated and balling is common.

Fraternities are declining at a rapid pace.

The University is ripping down some of the houses to help them fall. About 30% of the men still belong.

Students study during the week and break loose with parties on the weekend. Hangs include "The Penn Luncheonette" or "Dirty Drug," as it's variously called, on Walnut, "Smoky Joe's" (a bar near campus), "Marco Polo's" (kids like to play the pinball machines—sandwich shop) and "The Back Bench" (a commune where people live and rap).

Politically, Penn students just "don't have it in for capitalism; we like capitalism." There have been a few protests and demonstrations and a couple of firebombings over alleged racist admissions policies, but no violent confrontations. The most powerful group is the SAAS (the Student Afro-American Society) which occasionally gives the administration a jolt. The Strike Committee did some canvassing during the days following the Cambodia decision.

SURVIVAL:

If you like to study and enjoy what the city of Philadelphia has to offer, you can survive. Penn doesn't have much of a sense of community so you have to make most of your own entertainment.

The school has adequate facilities for creative outlets—lots of kids are into photography. There's a listening room in the Music department and a Moog synthesizer.

Student health is very competent and gives BC pills. Each student is allowed ten free psychiatric counseling visits. Lots of good draft counseling as there is a strong Quaker influence in the city. Penn sponsors draft counseling in the basement of the Student Union. The HELP Switchboard is excellent—call KI 6-7766. The *Daily Pennsylvanian* is O.K. but there are two good underground papers in the area, *The Plain Dealer* and *The Distant Drummer.*

Most smoke grass—it goes for $20 a lid. Some are into acid and mescaline.

Chicks are getting into Women's Liberation. They have an office on campus and pass out abortion referrals.

ENVIRONMENT:

Mental—People study and read Tom Wolfe and Vonnegut.

Physical—Bad Philadelphia weather. It's an urban campus set back from a rather dilapidated area. Trees and grassy spots line the campus. Most buildings are brick and ivy covered.

There's a fair amount of weekend traveling—to the Jersey shore and to New York.

University of Pittsburgh

Pittsburgh, Pennsylvania

Pitt has been especially innovative in its approach to minority students. It even has one program funded by the University in which ten white and ten black students live together as an experiment in interracial living. The University lays out the bread. Good academically, bad for your lungs.

SERGEANT PEPPER SECTION:

24,186 students. 3,000 out-of-state. 638 blacks, 34 Mexican-Americans, 67 Orientals, 8 Indians. Average 1,000 SATs and upper one-fifth of high-school graduating class.

ACADEMIC BULLSHIT:

The most popular course is "Existentialism" taught by Rabbi Rubenstein. He "makes things real" and "talks in today's language." "Sex Education" is popular and taught by graduate students (how-to-do-it). This class always has to turn away hopeful students. David Montgomery of the History department and Myron Taube of the English department are popular professors. Movement leaders among professors include Montgomery, David Houston and James Holland.

The best department is Philosophy—it's rated top nationally. The Graduate School of Public and International Affairs studies the working of the community and participates in a lot of field

work. Political Science has a hip department. Some Pass/Fail,
both tests and papers. Both big and small classes. Quite a few
student-originated classes—all you need is a professor to teach
the course of your choice. Some last year were "Non Violence,"
"Revolution," and "Blues Guitar."

There is a Black Studies department called the "Department of
Black Community Educational Research and Development." It is
considered to be one of the best in America. In 1970, 70 courses
were offered—some famous professors are on the staff, including
Sonia Sanchez, Rob Penny and Curtis Porter. Blacks attend en
masse and enjoy the courses.

Minority recruitment is handled by the Black Recruitment and
Admissions office. The effectiveness of this new organization can
be judged by these figures. Blacks have increased substantially.

	1968–69	1969–70
Black	266	638
Indian	3	8
Oriental	72	67
Mexican-American	14	34

There is a great deal of independent study. All you have to
do is find a professor willing to sponsor you. Some study abroad.

BREAD:

In-state is $355 per semester, out-of-state $830.

Some loans and scholarships; many campus jobs at $1.60–$1.90
an hour. Work-study obtained through the Student Aids Office.
Dorms cost $585 per semester for room and board. Apartments
run $60 and up per person per month. Communes are about $50
per month and fraternities about $70 per month. Most students
live in dorms and apartments.

Scrounging in the Pittsburgh area is difficult due to the Dow-
Jones cost of living. Shady Side is a good area for freaks.

Most students walk or ride motorcycles. Only commuters drive.

Greeks and rich hips wear costly threads. Dates run $2–$3 for
school flicks, a bottle of wine and a walk in Schenley Park. Free
concerts at the Syria Mosque in Oakland. Flicks and dope are
popular forms of entertainment.

There's a nonprofit student-run record store called "The Free
Peoples Store" in the area.

BROTHERS AND SISTERS:

Ratio cats : chicks—1.5 : 1.

These city dwellers have the lukewarm-hip look with medium-
long hair, sideburns, old pants, work shirts and sandals. The
straights look like Sears circa 1960. The number of heavy hips
wearing jeans, boots, tie-dyed shirts and frizzed hair is ever increasing. Some are rich-hip types with expensive boots.

Subcultured community hips cohabit, straights date. Most chicks
are just getting liberated. Fraternities are still alive and into their
own thing (blackballing). Greek Week.

Most of the community is apathetic politically. You have to search to find the radical leaders. The Black Action Society is powerful but it is more of a cultural organization. There have been the usual demonstrations but the administration keeps it cool by not calling in outside pigs The Black Action Society unites the black community of Pittsburgh in many instances. The strike over Cambodia ended in violent confrontation.

Popular hangs are the "Wooden Keg" and the "Tower B" snack bar for freaks, "Wolfarth's" and the "Tuck Shop" for straights and the Shady Side—hip area around campus. Popular entertainment includes free flicks, rock concerts on Flagstaff Hill and tripping.

SURVIVAL:

Yes. Make your own ecosystem out of what you can in Pittsburgh.

Draft counseling through the RSU, The Resistance, and the Student Help Center. The Student Help Center was started because of the incompetency of student health. It is staffed by graduate students and is good! Any service can be obtained at minimal price. For mental problems, student health refers you to the Western Psychiatric Institute—the University foots your head bill. Otherwise, student health is a bad trip.

Not many creative artsy-craftsy type people.

The drug scene is pretty new around Pitt. Usage is beginning to increase, lids are $10 and tabs $2 and mescaline is $3. Score on Shady Side and Flagstaff Hill.

The *Pitt News* is another liberal rag. No fine underground paper. No health-food stores in immediate area.

GASP (Group against Smoke and Pollution) held a mildly successful environmental teach-in. They're active and are trying to put pressure on the industries in the area to curb their anti· environmental actions.

ENVIRONMENT:

Mental—People are talking about the state of the world and reading *Stranger in a Strange Land* and *The Electric Kool-Aid Acid Test.*

Physical—Ugh. You may survive but will your lungs? The campus is located in an industrial urban area. The sun almost never shines brightly because of a gray haze (compliments of the steel mills). Noise pollution too. The climate is obnoxious— muggy hot summers, biting snowy winters. Except for Schenley and Frick Parks, the University of Pittsburgh is like a big crowded cage.

Most buildings are stone boxes. They look dirty and depressing in this semi-commercial area. ·

Escapes? None near. Some go to Seven Springs Ski Resort in winter or to Raccoon Creek State Park outside of Pittsburgh. Half are commuters. Carnegie Library has a large collection of classical records that you can listen to if things get unbearable.

Swarthmore College

Swarthmore, Pennsylvania

People are into intense intellectual bags. Primary noise pollution is the sound of medium-sized mouths yapping. One of the hardest schools in the United States to get into.

SERGEANT PEPPER SECTION:

1,100 students, 80% out-of-state. Only a few grad students. 7% black.

The admissions committee has no set standards—but it's very difficult to get in. They want a diverse student body from different parts of the United States, many foreign students, various social, religious and racial groups from both public and private schools. You need high grades, SATs, achievement tests and a snow job on the dean who interviews you.

ACADEMIC BULLSHIT:

Swarthmore is known for its intellectual environment. Competition is intense. Serious academic study. Juniors and seniors can take the honors program which permits concentration on one major and two minors through small seminars and independent study. No tests till the last week of school. Not all students choose this form of study and the regular course of learning is just as good here.

Popular courses include "Philosophy—Methods of Inquiry" (offered in interdepartmental approach—each week a lecturer from a different department talks about the subject), "Modern Painting" with Professor Rhys and "Group Dynamics" with Dr. Gergen. Thompson Bradley of the Russian department is popular for his radical activities. Professor Van De Kamp in Astronomy is world famous.

Interaction is very good between students and professors, and classes are kept fairly small.

The entire freshman year is taken Pass/Fail as are the honors programs. Students can get a faculty member to sponsor them and originate courses such as the ones they did in 1970—"Mysticism" and "Radical Education." A new Black Studies department. Independent study if you want it.

BREAD:

$2,300 a year. Each student that is admitted to Swarthmore is given the financial aid he or she needs. About 35% of the students are on financial aid. Most is in the form of scholarships. Jobs are very easy to find and pay $1.40 an hour.

Almost everyone lives in the dorms. They cost $1,135 per year for room and board. Very free. A new coed dorm.

Scrounging is impossible—this school is for the rich.

Most students walk (few cars) and an expensive wardrobe is

a waste. Very inexpensive threads. Dates cost nothing. There are free movies every weekend and a couple of free dances a month. If students throw parties in their dorm rooms, the school supplies $7.50 worth of food for free.

BROTHERS AND SISTERS:

Ratio cats : chicks—about 1 : 1.

The Marxist intellectuals are the BMOC (Big Minds on Campus). Everyone is very hip. Swarthmore students are intense and serious and always ruffled up about some issue. Politics, culture, school policy—they care about it all.

Cats have very long hair and beards and wear grubby threads— torn levis and T-shirts. Chicks wear tattered jeans and T-shirts too. No one wears plastic rags—no fancy vests or costly bells. Students here can't be bothered with dressing the part, they are into the intense intellectual bag. Philosophic and political raps are rampant. An affair with a Swarthmore chick is a mental exercise.

Dating is on an informal level. People have to have good mental vibes before they can get it together. Lots of semi-living together within the dorms. In spring of 1970, one of the new faculty members found out for the first time that Mary Lyons (a boys' dorm) wasn't married housing. All year he had seen so many couples walk out in the morning that he had assumed it was married housing.

Hangs are the student center and "Green's Bar."

Some fraternities but not important.

Students aren't militant but go through regular established channels of communication. The only powerful organization is the SAASS (Swarthmore Afro-American Student Society). They led the only sit-in at the college over more black admissions and more emphasis on black studies—demands were granted. Canvassing and petitions in reaction to the Kent State murders and the Cambodia decision. Strong Quaker peace traditions here.

SURVIVAL:

If you like to discuss issues, you can survive fine. The drug scene isn't heavy. Many students smoke but aren't regular users. Lids go for $20.

Many students are musically oriented—pianos all over the place. Students jam at the student center. Student health is efficient and refers students to shrinks that work strictly for this campus— "and with our mental condition, we need them." BC pills and abortion referrals in town. Draft counseling isn't very good at the student center.

Pets run all over. *The Phoenix* is an interesting school newspaper. No one is into health foods. Women's Liberation has a core of five-ten.

ENVIRONMENT:

Mental—People are very individualistic in what they read and talk about. They do read Norman O. Brown, *Catch 22* and *The Alexandria Quartet*.

Physical—The campus is located in a lovely suburban setting (as lovely as suburbia can be) 15 miles from Philadelphia. Trees and tranquil setting. Looks semi-rural. The air is refreshingly clean. Small but airy. Stone ivy-covered buildings.

Very few split for the weekends. People go home for vacation.

Temple University
Philadelphia, Pennsylvania

City people. Get up, shave, wear a clean shirt, check your notes, ride the subway, get to class, take notes, write down assignments, grab a donut from the food machine, finish classes, go to work, go home, eat dinner, do homework, go to bed, get up, shave, wear a clean shirt, check your notes, ride the subway . . .

SERGEANT PEPPER SECTION:

32,500 students. Out-of-state, 8.6%. 14% blacks. Easy to get in. Must be in upper one-half of graduating high-school class and get a satisfactory rating on the SATs.

ACADEMIC BULLSHIT:

Mostly a commuter school. Go to your classes, go to work, go home.

People are here to get a grade so that they can get a degree so that they can get a job. Temple serves metropolitan Philadelphia and most students are middle-class job aspirants. Everyone is either pre-law, pre-med or in business school. They take courses because they are an easy A. Four teachers on the campus have full enrollment because they are such "nice guys"—they are Henry Braun (teaches advanced literature courses and is a radical), Bob Edenbaum (in the English department and does draft counseling), Bill Wisdom (the Philosophy department) and Paul Lyons (History).

Good departments include Radio and TV, Psychology, Russian History, Biology and Chemistry. The Medical school is excellent.

Grades and busy-work. Huge lectures. A grade factory. Very few student-originated courses. One is called "Youth Participation in the City."

Temple has a new Afro-Asian Institute that may turn out to be good.

Study abroad in a "Temple in Rome" program.

BREAD:

In-state is $365 per semester. Out-of-state is $815. Most people commute from home and so have to pay only tuition. Loans are feasible, scholarships very tight. Jobs aren't plentiful. Some of the normal student jobs like cafeteria workers are given to union people. Most work off campus.

Out-of-town students have to live in dorms their first year—they are $700 per semester. Many students have $60 a month apartments in the Center City area or the Germantown area.

The only way you can scrounge is to live in the ghetto—typical ghetto houses. But most students don't live there.

Transportation is the subway and the bus—a real parking problem for those that have wheels. Some kids go grub to class while the professionals and chicks on the lookout for a med student dress up. Those types do the downtown Philadelphia date for about $10. The hips get stoned and go to the Philadelphia Art Museum or to a rock concert at the "Electric Factory."

BROTHERS AND SISTERS:

Ratio cats : chicks—1.5 : 1.

Most are middle-class hip. Hair longer than short but not long enough to lose a job opportunity. People dress plain and comfortable. Quite a few dresses and skirts. More chicks dress up than cats. Few freaky types. The professional cats wear coats and ties. Most chicks are looking for their future breadwinner.

Lots of nice Jewish girls. And lots of nice Jewish boys. Dating, engagement, marriage types. Some hips live together in Germantown. Frats are dying a slow death.

Hangs are "Fronzi's" on Germantown Avenue (professional-school cats), "Joseph's" on Germantown Avenue (jocks), "Ebony Lounge" (student government people) and "Al's Snack Bar" (dorm rats).

Political action is at a minimum. The only people who attend rallies are those who are walking past to class. The Strike Committee tried to organize a strike over Cambodia. They wanted to cancel classes a day and add an extra one at the semester's end. But the students complained so much about having to stay around that the strike was canceled. There was a small memorial march over Kent State—no confrontation. In 1970, the black students and the SDS demanded that the administration stop expanding the University and ripping down neighboring houses—a few demonstrations.

SURVIVAL:

No sense of community. Students are just starting to look into the creative arts. Draft counseling at the Student Union. Very good student health service—open 24 hours a day. They give BC pills and psychiatric counseling. Most people buy crud to eat out of the food trucks. The *Temple News* is a moderate paper. *The Philadelphia Free Press* and the *Plain Dealer* are both interesting underground sheets.

Most smoke grass—$20 a lid. Mescaline goes for $3 a tab—not too popular. Hash is the most popular drug. Score all over the city.

ENVIRONMENT:

Mental—People talk about jobs. Hips read *The Electric Kool-*

Aid Acid Test and Cleaver's book. More and more students are digging ecology.

Physical—Muggy Philly weather in the summer, cold in the winter.

Temple is in the middle of downtown Philadelphia. Modern corporate structure. The ghetto is just a stone's throw away. Air pollution is terrible.

People don't split on the weekends—they study. Fairmont Park is a nice escape in the city.

Villanova University
Villanova, Pennsylvania

A Silent Majority Catholic school.

SERGEANT PEPPER SECTION:

8,410 students of which 40% are out-of-state. 200 blacks. Not hard to get in—above average grades and 1,100 SATs.

ACADEMIC BULLSHIT:

Villanova's best two fields are Engineering and Biology. But none of the students seemed very excited about any of the departments. The most popular courses are Mr. Palazzolo's "Group Dynamics" course, Father Burns' education course and Mr. Regan's "Social and Political Philosophy."

Very limited Pass/Fail, not much class participation, and no student-originated courses without a big hassle. Because it was nearly impossible to originate relevant courses, students got together and formed the Free School—like a Free U (courses are offered on J. D. Salinger, on ESP and on contemporary theater). No Black Studies department and just a few courses. No independent study and no study abroad. If you're Catholic, four semesters of theology are required.

BREAD:

Tuition is $900 per semester. Aid is very tight but campus jobs are plentiful.

Dorms cost $600 per semester for room and board. Lots of students live at home and commute or live in apartments ($75 per person). Strict rules in the dorms which the students don't dig (no visitation, no liquor, curfews). Chicks can't move off campus until they are juniors and all freshmen must live on campus. Not much scrounging—the kids are too straight and middle-class to scrounge. Most have cars and college-shop wardrobes.

BROTHERS AND SISTERS:

Ratio cats : chicks—3 : 1.

A very straight campus with a miniscule number of freaks. Chicks are conservative and look prim and proper. Very few chicks would be caught dead in a pair of levis. Cats have short hair and wear cotton pants and button-down shirts.

Frat parties are a very big date function. A coffee house in Bryn Mawr called the "Main Point," flicks and athletic events are the other types of entertainment. Some students go to the "Electric Factory" in Philadelphia.

Sexually, they're about five years behind the times. Daring is sneaking a chick into your dorm room for the night. No liberated chicks. Fraternities are still the center of the social scene. Greek Week (eek!) is a big event on campus.

Hangs include the "Pie Shoppe," snack bar on campus, the lawns, "Campus Corner" (a sandwich shop) and the "West Echo" (frat type bar).

About half the guys have smoked grass—it's the only thing that has hit the campus so far.

If you're interested in politics, don't come to Villanova. The silent urban majority.

The only significant demonstration happened in 1969. The University wanted to raise tuition without discussing it with the students. The University agreed to discuss it after a series of demonstrations, but they raised anyway. Few students got upset about the Kent-Cambodia days.

SURVIVAL:

Hard. No artsy-craftsy students or politicos. The infirmary is O.K. but no BC pills. No draft counseling or survival services.

The Villanovan is O.K. but nothing special.

No health-food freaks and no Women's Liberation.

ENVIRONMENT:

Mental—People are studying and reading *Couples* by John Updike.

Physical—Villanova is only minutes away from Philadelphia and has the same awful climate. It is a small suburban town. The campus looks just plain ugly—buildings are made of drab gray stone.

Students would like to split a lot but can't because it costs too much.

RHODE ISLAND

Brown University and Pembroke College
Providence, Rhode Island

A calm, sane place.

SERGEANT PEPPER SECTION:

3,000 cats, 1,150 chicks. Most are from out-of-state. 7% blacks. Very hard to get in. 1,300 total SATs for Brown, 1,400 for Pembroke are average. Most applicants were in the top tenth of their class.

ACADEMIC BULLSHIT:

Biology is a superior department with a great staff and good lab facilities. Engineering and Applied Math are also excellent. The school concentrates on the undergraduate education but the Math and Physics graduate schools are good.

Favorite courses include "Modern Architecture" with Jordy ("there was a capacity crowd at every one of his lectures"), "Conceptions of Man: Diversity and Coherence" with Morgan (readings include C. S. Lewis, Huxley, Camus, etc.—it's so popular you have to write a request to be considered for admission to the course), and "Human Organismal Biology" with Quevedo (it deals with aging, death and the population explosion, as well as with the usual genitalia).

The most popular professors are Dick Dannensfelser, the chaplain, William McLaughlin, History, and Roswell Johnson.

Courses are very loose and professors are open to suggestion. There's lots of take-home exams and much class participation. Students originated many courses such as "Population," "Revolution" and "Computers in Biology." There's a new Afro-American Studies department. Blacks are heavily recruited. Anyone can take independent study and study abroad is offered.

BREAD:

Tuition here is $2,600 a year—"too goddamn much." Some loans and scholarships are available and almost 45% of incoming freshmen get some sort of aid. Campus jobs at $1.75 an hour.

About half the cats and most of the chicks live in the dorms, which cost $1,300 a year for room and board. Freshman cats all have doubles in "atrocious dungeons—the favorite color is puke yellow." Pembroke's housing is better but chicks can't get singles in a coed dorm unless they're seniors. Few rules.

About 15% of Brown people live in apartments that go for $140 for a two-bedroom. Some Brown cats still live in fraternities but frats are dying fast and few people are impressed that you're a "Theta Foo Quangus."

Relatively few cars on campus—chicks have to be seniors to have them. The bus to Boston goes every half hour for $3.50 round trip, anyway. Casual dress—clothes horses don't run at this track.

BROTHERS AND SISTERS:

Ratio cats : chicks—2.5 : 1.

Most students are bright, relaxed and casually dressed. There are very few freaks. Most are relatively well-off eastern kids, articulate and courteous, who seem thoughtful and interested in everything. Hair is generally long with some moustaches. Pembroke chicks study harder and do better in school than Brown cats.

Some facts supposedly culled from a national magazine's survey: 47% of Pembroke chicks have done it, 37% have had oral-genital contact and 44% think it's cool to ball, whether in love or not. About 20% of Pembroke chicks are living with someone.

Dating is super-casual—hangs include "The Rock" (Rockefeller Library), Grad Center, "The Gate" and "Faunce House" (movies are 50¢). The drug scene is present but not heavy. Lids go for $20, acid and mescaline for $5. There's been just one bust.

Brown is a "calm campus because there's no point in getting violent." There's no flaming political activity. In 1969 there was a movement for more black admissions which included a black students' walkout. Their goal was 11% blacks and they got it.

People went to Washington for the Moratoriums. Earth Day in 1970 included many planned activities on the college green which the eco-activists left disgustingly littered. There was the whole shot for the strike—canvassing, petitioning, leafletting and "everybody was behind us." No violence.

SURVIVAL:

Modern dance is popular, but it's not an arty group. Excellent student health facilities, no BC pills but they'll refer you. All survival services are offered by "Together" in Providence.

The Brown Daily Herald is worse than a hometown newspaper.

ENVIRONMENT:

Mental—People are reading *Been Down So Long It Looks Like Up to Me* by Farina and Hesse. They are rapping about the War.

Physical—An urban campus in Providence which is a rather dull large city which culturally sucks. Both air and noise pollution. The campus consists of handsome brick buildings with newer high-rise Math-Science facilities, nice lawns and a fair amount of ivy. It's a prosperous looking place that doesn't have the idyllic opulence of Wellesley.

People escape to ski resorts and the Caribbean.

—

Rhode Island School of Design

Providence, Rhode Island

It was meant to be a school of creative arts.

SERGEANT PEPPER SECTION:

1,800 students of which 300 are grads. Most people are from out-of-state. 6% black. You have to submit a portfolio of your work to be admitted—it's purely subjective. SATs and grades are important (SATs are usually in the 1,200 range) but your portfolio is more important.

ACADEMIC BULLSHIT:

The areas of professional instruction include Architecture, Fine Arts, Industrial Design, Textiles and Art Education. Most grads are in the Master of Arts in Teaching program. The school is on the 4-1-4 system.

After the freshman year, no real courses are set up. It's almost completely independent study. Students say "Architecture and Photography are the only good departments in the whole school. Painting is atrocious and Sculpture sucks." Popular professors include Harry Callahan in Photography and Richard Merkin, a painter. On the whole, students seemed very dissatisfied with the school. Classes aren't usually well attended, "nobody cares." Some courses are student-originated like "The Use of Materials." A Free U offers "Silk Screen Workshop," "Photo Workshop" and "Drawing."

The school has two buildings in Rome, Italy, and every year about 20 people go over to study on the "European Honors Program."

BREAD:

Tuition is $2,200 a year, but figure another $1,000 for art supplies. Loans and scholarships are very tight but you can earn $3.50 an hour if you can play dinner music.

Dorms cost $1,100 a year for room and board. About 70% of the chicks live in the dorms. After their freshman year, cats have to leave the dorms as there isn't enough room. Rules are lax. Apartments run $140 for a two-bedroom place. They are usually old and fairly funky.

Bicycles and feet are big (not everyone's). There are no real dates, just a hamburger, so it's cheap.

BROTHERS AND SISTERS:

Ratio cats : chicks—1 : 1.

Most people are semi-grubby long-hairs. The dress is far out for Providence, tame by Berkeley's standards. People are hip and artsy-temperamental-casual in their outlook toward school and toward each other. Lots of people live together; chicks say many of the cats are bisexual and that they (the chicks) are sexually frustrated. But then the chicks aren't especially liberated—lots of homespun New England types.

Hangs include "Joe's Sandwich Shop" and your own room—there's really not much to do in Providence. Most people get stoned and drink wine at home. The school is 50% beer people and 50% drug people. Grass goes for $20 a lid, acid for $4 a tab.

Politics aren't happening at Ris-D. as students call it (looks like a vitamin label). For the strike, those who cared went next door to Brown to participate.

SURVIVAL:

Q. "Are students into creative arts?"
A. "No, not really."
What are they doing at a school of design?
Student facilities are adequate. BC pills at Planned Parenthood nearby. All survival services from "Together" in Providence.
People eat "Space Food Sticks" outside. "One Clear Grain" is a groovy macrobiotic-food store in Providence.

ENVIRONMENT:

Mental—Students don't talk and read that much. Ecology action in Providence has a few Ris-D people in it.
Physical—Boston type weather. Providence is an uninspiring city that seems to have given up the effort to look respectable.
Architecturally, the campus is "curiously absurd—everything is a curio." The dorms look like Holiday Inn motels. Other buildings are old and funky. The Museum of Art has lots of Impressionist stuff and a floor of Chinese sculpture.
Escapes include Boston, skiing and warm spots.

University of Rhode Island
Kingston, Rhode Island

URI is still involved in panty raids.

SERGEANT PEPPER SECTION:

10,000 students. 10% from outside of New England. About 100 blacks. In-staters need average grades and boards scores of about 1,000. Out-of-staters need higher grades and board scores.

ACADEMIC BULLSHIT:

Students complain that there is no particularly good graduate school. The best undergraduate departments are Engineering,

Oceanography, Agriculture and Fisheries. Best courses are all those in the honors program (students need a 3.0 or better), "Principles of Economics" with Roack and many anthropology courses.

Some Pass/Fail, little class participation, no black studies, and a Free U that offers "Women's Liberation." There is a Talent Development Program in operation which recruits minority students. They get special summer courses, if they need them, to prepare them for college. Independent study is available for seniors.

BREAD:

Tuition and fees are $250 in-state per semester, $800 out-of-state. Loans and scholarships are tight unless you have pull. Jobs are also tight—just a few are available at about $1.60 an hour. Some with need can get on work-study. Dorms are around $500 a semester for room and board—most freshmen live in them. No drinking is allowed (this rule isn't really enforced) and there is intervisitation. People are still living in fraternities and sororities and these cost about the same. Some upperclassmen live in apartments nearby, but most everyone either lives in dorms or frat houses.

Cars and motor bikes are it for transportation. Out-of-staters have costly threads.

BROTHERS AND SISTERS:

Ratio cats : chicks—about 2 : 1.

In-state students are usually conservative and wear drab dull threads. Out-of-staters (never the twain shall meet) wear hip threads—bells, body shirts, boots. "Out-of-state cats dress very well, keep up with fashions and are real studs." Cats wear their hair medium-long—real long hair is a rarity.

Fraternities are still strong and 40% of the 1970 freshman class went Greek. Students are still into making a big deal about student government. Most chicks are liberated. There's not much permanent shacking up but lots of one-night stands. Most kids are conservative politically.

"Students do their homework, get drunk, engage in sexual fun, and go home on weekends—Agnew would love them."

Politics as such don't exist for the majority of students. There was sporadic activity over the student strike of 1970. A course on "Revolution in the Modern World" that was to be offered in 1970 was cancelled by URI President Baum, who said the course was unbalanced because only the radical side was presented. The course was construed mainly as teaching revolution and "God and Country" politicians came out against it. Charges of violations of academic freedom rang out and finally the course was taught with the addition of a few conservative speakers.

People hang at the "Pub," "Iggy's Restaurant" and "The Beachcomber." Lots of students are into drugs, no big busts yet.

SURVIVAL:

Student health has been improving in the last few years. Draft counseling is offered, but it's poor. Most kids eat in the cafeteria. The campus paper, *Beacon,* is straight. Women's Liberation is just getting going.

ENVIRONMENT:

Mental—People are reading *Everything You've Always Wanted to Know About Sex* and are talking about what they learned from reading the book. HEED is a fairly active ecology group.

Physical—URI is a rural type campus but Rhode Island is such a small state that you're close to everything. The buildings are covered with ivy and there are lots of trees. As to climate, "We're the only college with a monsoon season."

Everybody escapes on the weekends.

SOUTH CAROLINA

Clemson University

Clemson, South Carolina

Where do Clemson students go to escape? "They go home to mom and dad and their girl. They ride around the drive-in restaurant. They ball around the dikes that overlook Lake Hartwell."

SERGEANT PEPPER SECTION:

Clemson is easy to get into—you need a combined 800 SAT score and a C average from high school. 6,500 students attend, of which 500 are graduate students. 41% are out-of-state. 1% black.

ACADEMIC BULLSHIT:

Clemson was formerly an agricultural institution so there are many good courses relating to agriculture and forestry. It's a technically-oriented campus and most of the school's money is spent on engineering and architecture courses.

"The academic freedom here is comparable to pre-Hitler Germany. This is God's country and we still burn witches and commies at the stake. It's oppression at its finest."

"Richard Fredland was everyone's favorite professor. He taught political science courses. It finally got to him in January, 1970, and he got the hell out."

No Pass/Fail. No student-initiated course. ROTC is popular.

"There is a very close relationship between students and teachers. What we around here term 'ass and nose.' "

There is one course in black history taught by a white professor. All 60 black students took it last semester. No independent study and tests are the thing. One architecture course given in Europe as far as study abroad goes.

BREAD:

In-state tuition is $298 a semester, out-of-state $598. Room and board runs approximately $870 a year. Work-study and loans and scholarships are almost nonexistent. Hardly any campus jobs. No used books. Everyone has cars and "if you want to be a leader you have to have an expensive wardrobe." Dates run about $10.

BROTHERS AND SISTERS:

Ratio cats : chicks—12 : 1.

Most students come from a conservative Baptist background and they will not tolerate nonconformity. Everyone aspires to have that fraternity look. Greeks are quite important to the 6,000 insecure students. People meet each other at the "Study Hall"— a beer parlor. Not enough hips to hang anywhere. Sports heroes are GODS (another school to be preserved for the Smithsonian). The campus paper, edited by Dick Harpootlian, is the only stimulating thing on campus.

Sexual activity, on a limited basis, is what the school does for entertainment. How can you expect a girl from Wahalla, S.C., to be liberated? A lid is $25 and very few turn on. They think "pills" mean the things you take to keep awake for exams.

Clemson students are completely straight and really into the Young Republican Club. There is no political activity other than fund raising.

SURVIVAL:

Nearly impossible. No draft counseling, no health-food stores, no easy access to drugs, no BC pills given out at the student health center ("let her get pregnant so we can stone her"). The nearest city to campus is Greenville, S.C., 30 miles away. And the nearest city to that is . . .

ENVIRONMENT:

Mental—Nobody reads, talks or breathes.

Physical—The only good thing about this school: it's located in the Blue Ridge Mountains which are lovely to look at. No air pollution. The buildings have that modern sterile look.

TENNESSEE

University of Tennessee
Knoxville, Tennessee

Not much culture in eastern Tennessee, but things may be looking up.

SERGEANT PEPPER SECTION:

23,000 students, of which 5,000 are graduates. 40% are out-of-state students. Almost no requirements for state residents—either a 2.0 GPA or an ACT score of 18. Out-of-state students not strongly encouraged.

ACADEMIC BULLSHIT:

Best departments include Journalism, English (Shakespeare classes best), Psychology, Engineering and Agriculture. Best graduate departments are Psychology (has free psychology clinic and good labs) and English. The Sociology students have their own settlement house and work in Appalachia.

Popular professors include Dr. Howard Polio (Psychology) and Dr. Richard Marius (History).

Both grades and Pass/Fail are used, no student-initiated courses and no Free U. There is a fairly close relationship between students and faculty united against the administration. Some black studies, but the blacks are boycotting them so they are being improved. Many tests except in liberal arts. No independent study, no study abroad, no smoking in class.

BREAD:

In-state tuition is $120 per quarter, out-of-state tuition is $325. School has an abundance of scholarships and loans and ample work-study. Many campus jobs at $1.75 an hour. Chicks that are straight wear costly threads. Dates run $5–$7. Not too easy to scrounge.

BROTHERS AND SISTERS:

Ratio cats : chicks—2 : 1.

The modified hip look is the most popular, expensive replicas of hippy threads (which of course makes it unhip). Cats wear— if you can dig it—suits (remember them?) to class a lot. Other cats are starting to dress hip. Only 10% of the campus is Greek and even they are ailing. Hips meet at the University Center and the Epworth Methodist Church. Straights guzzle booze at "The Place" on Friday afternoons. Chicks don't want to be liberated. They might have to think.

Lids are cheap and available on University Avenue. However, cow manure has been found in the marijuana of late (you can really smoke some shit). The most popular entertainment is parties.

A political consciousness is just beginning to dawn. In 1969, there was a walk-out of women's dorm members protesting rigid hour requirements. In January, 1970, there were demonstrations against the new University president—22 students arrested. About 40% of the students struck peacefully against the Indochina war.

SURVIVAL:

Not bad for the South.

There is a "crisis clinic" for suicides, if you can't survive. Draft counseling is done by concerned students. Student health is mediocre—sometimes gives out BC pills. Sports heroes are still popular, complete with deferential treatment accorded them. The UT *Daily Beacon* is good and straight. The underground *Up Country Revival* is interesting.

ENVIRONMENT:

Mental—People are talking about sports and reading *Airport* and Rod McKuen.

Physical—Rain, trees, grass, lush southern vegetation. Cold in winter, hot in summer. Water pollution due to big industries. One of ten top cities with dense air pollution. Campus is composed of old buildings with the traditional red brick. New buildings are made of molded concrete.

Escapes are the lakes and mountains in the area. Mostly live-ins.

Vanderbilt University
Nashville, Tennessee

One of the best southern campuses.

SERGEANT PEPPER SECTION:

12,000 students of which 6,000 are grads. Difficult to get in; you need good grades, SATs in the 1,200 range and very good recommendations. Vanderbilt University wants a national distribution, so it may be easy to get in if you are from outside the South.

ACADEMIC BULLSHIT:

This is one of the best schools in the South. There is a lot of stress on academics. It has good departments of Engineering, Nursing, Philosophy, Anthropology and English ("English is considered the best in the South here but I don't know how much that says"). Dr. John Lachs of the Philosophy department is a favorite professor.

The best graduate school is said to be Business.

Juniors and seniors can take Pass/Fail, no student-originated courses for credit; only a Free U which offers "Ethics," "Camping" and "Mechanics." Minority recruitment is increasing under student pressure. Not much student-faculty interaction.

Independent study and study abroad.

BREAD:

$1,000 a semester for this private school. Scholarships and loans are readily available as Vanderbilt is one of the best-endowed universities. Campus jobs and work-study are also available. The dorms cost $1,300 for room and board a year. "The dorm rules are just moving the Vanderbilt lady into the 20th century even though many Vanderbilt men don't seem to care for it."

Most students live in the dorms. Some cats live off campus in old apartments in the semi-slums that surround the University. Nashville has some of the lowest food prices around.

People walk or have wheels.

BROTHERS AND SISTERS:

Ratio cats : chicks—about 3 : 1.

There are many graduate students here who are straight. There is a wide diversity among undergrads from YRs to SDSers. Super-straight preppies to full-grown (and blown) freaks.

Some big-city chicks are sexually liberated while the farm chicks aren't. About one-fourth of the students belong to fraternities but they are dying.

Local hangs include the fraternities and the freshman quadrangle.

Drug use is moderate, nothing more than grass; the price is $10–$20 for a lid.

School politics is completely mixed. After Kent State there was an active demonstration against the War followed by an active demonstration for the War.

SURVIVAL:

Student health is O.K., "competent, clean and efficient and shrinks are very available." Survival services in Nashville. *The Hustler* is the school paper, a liberal rag. Some people are getting into health foods and have gardens.

ENVIRONMENT:

Mental—"No one ever reads the same book. People talk about school, the draft, sex, books, movies, and vacation spots."

Physical—Vanderbilt University is an urban campus two miles from Nashville (pop. 265,000). The climate is cold and snowy in winter, hot and humid in the summer. Both air and noise pollution exist in Nashville. Campus buildings are red brick, ivy-covered.

People escape on the weekends because "pressure is high and it's good to get away." People go home and to the beaches.

TEXAS

Stephen S. Austin State University
Nacogdoches, Texas

Peace symbols are considered "communist" by the school. Repression! One of the biggest Ku Klux Klan groups is right outside of Nacogdoches.

SERGEANT PEPPER SECTION:

8,740 students of which 321 are out-of-state. Easy to get in—about an 18 average on the ACTs.

ACADEMIC BULLSHIT:

Traditional academics.
Best departments are Sociology, Biology and Political Science. Only graduate work offered are Master's degrees (offered in Physical Education and Forestry among others).
Popular professors include Bill Stiles (Sociology), Richard Kim (Political Science), Jim Steel (Political Science—he's active in the Nacogdoches black movement), and George Mears (Sociology).
No Pass/Fail, tests and papers, no student-originated courses, no Free U, no Third World College . . . no, no, no. No to everything else.

BREAD:

Tuition is $100 per semester in-state, $250 out-of-state. Loans are easy to get if you are white and have short hair. Scholarships are very tight. Campus jobs are also tight and never given to longhairs. Everyone must live in a dorm or frat until they are 21. Girls mustn't leave the dorm barefoot and must be in by 11 P.M. on weeknights. Boys are allowed in girls' dorms for two hours a semester. The dorms cost $400 a semester. The apartments are cheap at $60 for one room. Heads try to live off campus and get welfare. Most people have cars. Dates run $10 for a flick, a hamburger and booze.

BROTHERS AND SISTERS:

Ratio cats : chicks—1 : 1.
Most are frat type conservatives. Short hair, slacks, sport shirts and loafers. Dresses and set hair for the chicks. About 25%

443

cowboy—the unenlightened-oaf type. 5% are hip with old jeans, T-shirts and long hair. Dating is the thing and people neck. At last count there were two liberated chicks. Fraternities are vital. They control student government (wow) and all the social functions. Frats hang at the "Lumberjack Drive-In," listen to Merle Haggard (Okie from Muskogee) on the radio and drink beer. The few heads dig acid, rock and balling.

Dope is available—grass goes for $12 a lid—frequent busts.

The school is apathetic politically except for a few extremists on either end of the political spectrum. However, 1,000 people did show up for the Kent State rally and there was racial trouble in May, 1970. The dean of the school has veto power over everything. The leftists are trying to take over student government and refuse to listen to any vetos. Shit may hit the fan soon in Nacogdoches, Texas.

SURVIVAL:

Bring a sheet for survival disguise.

No draft counseling, BC pills, abortion referrals, suicide prevention center or shrink. The school paper, *The Pinelog,* is a bore.

ENVIRONMENT:

Mental—Freaks are the only ones reading—Hoffman and Rubin. Straights take *Playboy.* People are into ecology and at first the dean said there could be no ecology group (it's subversive) but later rescinded when they got the support of a liberal Texas senator.

Physical—Urban. As urban as Nacogdoches is. Small rural town. Texas weather, hot in summer, cold in winter. It's very green all around, no barren land. Air pollution from the Lone Star Feed and Fertilizer Company.

The campus buildings are brick or gray stone and about four stories tall. Pine trees about.

People go home to Houston, Dallas or Austin on the weekend. School administrators talk like LBJ.

Baylor University
Waco, Texas

Baylor is Baptist. And you've heard of southern Baptists.

SERGEANT PEPPER SECTION:

Baylor University is owned and operated by the Baptist General Convention of Texas and is very denominational. However, there are a fair number of heathens. Grades must be average and students must have an ACT score of 20.

6,377 students, of which 350 are graduate students. 20 blacks and 15 Mexican-Americans.

ACADEMIC BULLSHIT:

Baylor has a Medical school in Houston and a Dental school in Dallas. Lots of Business and Education majors at the Waco campus. Two popular professors are David McHam of Journalism and Robert Packard in Physics.

There are no student-initiated courses at present but the student council is pressing for them. "The Free University was in operation last year but due to lack of interest was canceled this year." Independent study is confined to the graduate program. Not much interaction between teachers and students. Tests are still required in all courses. Students are not allowed to smoke in class. Girls must wear a dress or pants-dress—minis and shorts are not allowed.

BREAD:

Tuition is approximately $1,000 a year. Dorms run $200 a semester. An average apartment runs $120 for two people. Campus loans and scholarships are tight. Work-study and campus jobs are available at $1.45 an hour—the usual cafeteria and receptionist type jobs.

Dates run about $5 for a cat—flick and coffee.

BROTHERS AND SISTERS:

Ratio cats : chicks—1 : 1.

The students are very straight. Expensive wardrobes are necessary and chicks wear nice Sunday-school type dresses. Chicks have to wear raincoats over that P.E. outfit when going to class so as not to project the wrong image at Baylor. Cats wear dress shirts, pants, buckle shoes.

The Baylor cats dig chicks from other schools and Baylor lovelies are dateless a lot. Limited sexual activity—chicks definitely not liberated. Remember big football heroes and bouncy blond chubby cheerleaders? That's Baylor. Little grass, although it's available at $15 a lid.

Big Young Republicans Club on campus. Hanging places include church and "George's Lounge." (Cheers.)

The biggest run-in with the administration came in April, 1970, when 75 students protested against a dormitory directive requiring a student to remove a peace sign from his window. The Moratorium Day activities in 1969 drew limited attendance.

SURVIVAL:

In a church-related school? No BC pills, no draft counseling, no abortion referrals, no health-food stores.

Fair campus newspaper, *Baylor Lariat*—no underground press. Entertainment consists of parties.

ENVIRONMENT:

Mental—Everyone is reading the Bible.
Physical—Typical Texas weather, rains often and heats up con-

stantly. Lots of days over the 100° mark. There's a large lake outside of town that students frequent. Trees and pure air on campus.

University of Corpus Christi
Corpus Christi, Texas

Easy, dull and southern Baptist.

SERGEANT PEPPER SECTION:

Easy to enter—average grades and circa 16 ACT scores. No graduate school. 700 students, 30% out-of-state. 20% blacks, 20% Mexican-Americans.

ACADEMIC BULLSHIT:

What can you write about a school that considers its eight hours of Bible study its most important course? Well, there's "Latin American History," which is taught by an ex-Army colonel "who knows every bit of trivia about Latin America," and there's the Education department which loves standardized tests. There are also many field trips (?). The only good professor seems to be Dr. Henry Hildebrand who is world renowned in his field of marine biology. No student-initiated courses or Free U.

The Baptist General Convention of Texas officially prohibits smoking and dancing on campus. Students have to dress up for class and this is a source of unrest.

BREAD:

It costs $930 out-of-state and $830 in-state for the year. Dorms are $180 per semester and all freshmen must live on campus. Loans and scholarships are VERY available. (Is it worth it?) Work-study and campus jobs are also plentiful at $1.40 an hour. Flick and coffee run a cat $3.50. Cars are plentiful.

BROTHERS AND SISTERS:

Ratio cats : chicks—3 : 1.

The "northerners" bring big-city evil hippie ideals down to Texas with them—long hair and beards. The Texans are straight. Some chicks are liberated.

The "Intrascope" is a weekend coffee house operated by the Baptist Student Union—the moralistic place to meet and greet. Others hang at the "Haunted House."

The drug scene is developing—lids go for $5. Northside and Westside Corpus Christi are places to score. No political activity at all.

SURVIVAL:

There's no draft counseling, no BC pills, no abortion referrals and no cursing! A suicide prevention center exists in town and a few students have used it. The student newspaper is uncensored and interesting—*The Seabreeze*. There is a natural-food store in town, "Six Points."

ENVIRONMENT:

Mental—The student book store (?) is practically empty—only a very few texts and no other books at all. A real book store is nonexistent in Corpus Christi.

Physical—Texas subtropical type weather. Favorite escape is Padre Island National Seashore—a few miles east. Many school buildings are old World War II converted Navy barracks. UCC was formerly part of a naval air station. New buildings are sterile modern. The school is on an island ten miles from Corpus Christi. Laredo is the closest border city—143 miles west. Half live-in, half commute.

East Texas State University

Commerce, Texas

The most important topic of conversation to the majority of students is how they souped up their cars.

SERGEANT PEPPER SECTION:

8,281 students of which 389 are out-of-state. Average of 800 on combined SATs and 18 on ACT required.

ACADEMIC BULLSHIT:

Best departments include Journalism, Art and Agriculture. But most departments, even the best, are unfortunately boring academia. Ralph Voss of the English department is a very popular professor. No progressive education, no Pass/Fail, lots of tests, no student-originated classes and no Third World College.

BREAD:

Cheap. Tuition is $100 per semester in-state and $250 out-of-state. Some scholarships and loans are available. Campus jobs at $1.60 an hour are easy to find. Most students live in dormitories that cost $110 a month for room and board. Chicks have 11 P.M. curfews on weekdays, 1 A.M. on weekends. A few students live in apartments that run about $70 a month and the rest commute.

BROTHERS AND SISTERS:

Ratio cats : chicks—3 : 2.

The campus is mostly frat type conservative with the cats sporting short hair, Sta-prest slacks and loafers. A good many cowboy types also—western regalia and drawl. About 10% of the campus is embryonic hip with sideburns, jeans and work shirts. Chicks wear dresses, nylons and bras and aren't liberated. A big date consists

of a drive-in movie and a hamburger. Lots of dating. Few intimate roommate situations. Cowboys hang at the Agriculture
department and the "Sonic Drive-In."

The campus is politically conservative. The largest demonstration they ever had was 100 hips protesting the war and 400 frats
and cowboys protesting the hips. The fraternities dominate student government and are very strong.

The hips are into drugs and score around campus at $15 a lid
and $3.50 for a tab of acid. Local pigs enjoy the bust scene.

SURVIVAL:

Chances aren't too good.

Not many students are into the creative bag. Bad student health
services and no BC pills or abortion referrals. Some psychological
counseling offered on campus. The campus blah, *The East Texan,*
is a straight bore.

ENVIRONMENT:

Mental—The few existing hips are discussing the Cambodian
situation and reading Abbie Hoffman.

Physical—Wet and cold in the winter, hot in the summer. The
campus is urban, in the middle of Commerce, a town of 4,500.
Roads run through the campus and there's a lot of construction.
Main noise pollution comes from the cowboys laying scratch with
their souped-up cars.

Buildings are old red brick about one–five stories tall. The
major eyesore is the Journalism building which is a two-story
white wooden bungalow.

People go to Dallas or home for excitement.

University of Houston
Houston, Texas

This is where it is. The Conrad Hilton School for Hotel and
Restaurant Management. Besides that there is a very strong
redneck factor in Houston, both on and off campus. They blow
up things (like the new Pacifica radio station in Houston in
May, 1970).

SERGEANT PEPPER SECTION:

24,383 students of which 11% are from out-of-state. 3% black,
4% Mexican-American. Easy to get in—sliding eligibility scale.
Students in the top one-fourth of their high-school graduating
class need a combined 700 SAT score; those in the bottom one-
fourth need 1,000 SATs.

ACADEMIC BULLSHIT:

Best departments are History and Biology. Best graduate divisions are Law, Business and the pure Sciences.

Most popular professors include Dr. James McCarey (teaches "Sexology" and wrote the text book for the course—he's appeared on the Middle-America nightcap, *The Tonight Show*) and Dr. James Anderson (teaches folklore and sings folksongs to the class). The Architecture department is full of freaks who barbecue goats and eat them. They built a silo and painted it white so they could write graffiti on it.

No Pass/Fail, papers and tests, 150 students in an average class. The Experimental College is a Free U—love but no credit. It offers "Astrology," "Propaganda and the Pig Press" and "How to Level the University and Rebuild it."

Last year they had a grand-jury investigation over "Immoral and Illegal Activities Between Students and Teachers" (balling). One teacher got the shaft. Still some dating between professors and students.

Study abroad in Mexico and Europe.

BREAD:

$100 tuition in-state per semester, $250 out-of-state. Loans and scholarships are available. Campus jobs at $1.60 an hour are hard to get. Dorms cost $933 a year for room and board and aren't popular. Apartments are the most popular digs and go for about $125 for a furnished one-bedroom. Many students live at home. Lots of cars and $6–$7 for a burger and a flick. Very hard to scrounge in Houston.

BROTHERS AND SISTERS:

Ratio cats : chicks—5 : 3.

Most University of Houston students are straight and dull. Slacks, sport shirts, short blond hair for cats. Villager dresses and hair-dos for the chicks. There are also some cowboy conservatives and some frat conservatives. Lots of dating and the school still has a strong fraternity atmosphere. A few freaks who do the usual freaky things. Freaks hang at the "Family Hand" restaurant and the "Jubilee Hall" (rock concerts). Cowboys dig the "Stampede Ballroom" (they give away a free horse every week). Frats dig the "Scene West" (night club).

The campus is starting to come alive politically. The YAFs are always hassling freaks and recently burned an NLF flag. The Committee to End the War is the most active anti-war group, but can only get 1,000 at the biggest rallies.

SURVIVAL:

Texas again. A new Fine Arts building will help tap any existent creative potentials. No BC pills or abortion referrals at student health. Some counseling services. Draft counseling by the Committee to End the War, AFS and Professor Clark Reed. *The Daily Cougar* is O.K. Not a heavy drug scene. Lids go for $12, acid tabs for $4. Score in the Montrose area of town.

ENVIRONMENT:

Mental—At least Texas people are talking here. Freaks are reading Rubin and *Portnoy's Complaint*. The ecology group is called "Earth Works"—very good. They picket Houston's biggest polluters every month.

Physical—Climate is hot in the summer, cold in the winter. The University is an urban campus—large, sprawling, ugly. Air pollution. Buildings are all foiled attempts at modern architecture—cold gray stone.

People escape to the beach on the weekends.

Lamar Tech

Beaumont, Texas

"Lamar Tech is sunken in a pit of apathy."

Lamar Tech students think draft counseling refers to recruitment. "Yeah, we have a really good program here, the Navy is really active. The Army Reserve does a big business too." Holy shit—they haven't even heard of draft counseling. They also describe their main entertainment as "Loving—done in the gym parking lot." Loving is alright—but in the gym parking lot?

SERGEANT PEPPER SECTION:

Lamar Tech is "easy to get in, hard to get out." There's not much of a grade requirement and you need 700 combined on your SATs. 10,000 students go here, 1,700 of which are graduate students. Only 15% are from out-of-state. Prepare to meet Texans. 10% black.

ACADEMIC BULLSHIT:

All the good undergraduate courses sound like a drag—"Legislative Process," "Shakespeare" and "Medieval Literature." The "Old South" might by a trippy course (bring a Confederate flag). The best grad departments are Engineering and Business. Pass/Fail is used. Edward Vinson is listed as the most popular professor—teaches "Social Problems." No student-initiated courses. Their equivalent of the Free U is a religious center which features speakers. Formal relationship between teachers and students. Tests and papers, no independent study, and foreign programs in Spain, Arabia and France.

BREAD:

Lots of bread is not a necessity—cost is $85 per semester. Out-of-state is $200 per semester. Dorms cost about $950 a year for room and board. Scholarships are tight but loans are available to those who need them. Some campus jobs are available—$1.40 per hour for library work and $1.60 an hour for part-time secretaries. There are no used-book or record stores. Dates cost a lot—$10 average.

BROTHERS AND SISTERS:

Ratio cats : chicks—2 : 1.

It's straight, straight, straight here—bouffant hair-dos for the chicks and short hair for the cats. A few hip types but generally long hair is considered taboo. "There is SOME dating, the sex life is confined to the weekends and when girls can sneak away from the dorms." Jocks and fraternity guys are the popular heroes. The few hips can meet at "The Light House." Straights hang at the Student Union which has "recreation facilities." Grass is available on campus in the old dorms at $15 a lid. No revolutionaries (are there any liberals?). No Women's Liberation. The 10% blacks have made certain demands on the administration but these were denied. There has been "book store vandalism" in retaliation.

SURVIVAL:

BC pills not available on campus, nor are abortion referrals. No, you can't smoke in class, nor can you stay overnight in a chick's dorm room. No "anti-draft" counseling but lots of Navy activity. The campus paper, *The Redbird,* is O.K. Underground paper called *What's Left* supposed to be good—for that area. Student health service good.

ENVIRONMENT:

Mental—Not much cerebral stimulation since 85% of the kids go home immediately after class—it's a commuters' school. Those who can read are taking in *Groupie* and *Portnoy's Complaint.*

Physical—The area is 75% industry and badly polluted. The air smells foul. There are plenty of trees but with the pollution it may change. The students are very much into ecology and saving their greenery. The climate is warm and dry. The Gulf of Mexico is very close—everyone goes to the beach on the weekends.

Rice University

Houston, Texas

Rice did not admit blacks until 1964. In spite of that blot, the school is known nationally for its outstanding Science program.

SERGEANT PEPPER SECTION:

2,200 students, of which 600 are graduate students. Difficult to get in. Must be in top 10% of high-school class to be considered. Average combined SATs, 1350–1400. More Merit Scholars per capita than any other school. 40% from out-of-state. 23 blacks, 25 Chicanos.

ACADEMIC BULLSHIT:

Chemistry is the most famous department. Faculty is small but star-studded in chemistry-research circles. Former president Kenneth Pitzer and president-designate Norman Hackerman are both distinguished chemists. A brand new Fine Arts department, somewhat autonomous, "The Institute for the Arts." Hordes of students are transferring to Art History or Media majors. Many seminars with critics and artists. Very good, competent Engineering department.

The Chemistry and Space Science graduate departments claim to be first in the world. All of scientists/astronauts are actively part of research or faculty. The Biology graduate department is currently working with the transplant man, Dr. Michael De Bakey, to develop an artificial heart. Crossdiscipline with Mechanical Engineering department.

Popular professors for political reasons include Dr. Reed and Dr. De Bremaeker. Dr. David Nissen is a popular hairy freaky Berkeley Ph.D. in Economics.

The University is on the college system (like Yale). These colleges are composed of student membership and replace dorms and frats. These colleges sponsor different student-originated courses.

Some Pass/Fail, mostly tests and no Free U. Very good communication between professors and students. Because of the college system, most bachelor professors live with students. No Third World College. Honors students can do independent study.

BREAD:

$1,800 a year (it was free until 1965). Loans and scholarships are easily available. Campus jobs are also available at wages from $1.25 to $1.50 an hour. Room and board in the colleges is $1,100. Apartments run $145 for an air-conditioned one-bedroom (furnished) in Houston. It's impossible to scrounge in Houston—a very uptight city. Dates run from $0 to $25 depending on what you do, from drives, talking, to expensive restaurants. Most students have cars.

BROTHERS AND SISTERS:

Ratio cats : chicks—5 : 2.

"Most students appear straight, but they just don't give a damn. T-shirts, levis, sandals and tennis shoes have long been usual for all Rice students. Hair is usually shaggy but because they usually forget to get haircuts or don't bother till Christmas or Easter. Shorter than most schools, though. This is Texas, suh. A few people with the Movement. A few people dress like all their clothes came from Nieman-Marcus (because they do), but actually few people care at all.

"Dating is mostly casual. During football season it is a little more traditional. Usually the weanies find themselves a homely chick and they study together at night during the week and sleep together on weekends, or so goes the legend. Girls are easier than at most southern schools. Liberated? Well, the chicks can carry their own books."

Hips hang at the "Family Hand," a restaurant and "Jubilee Hall" (rock concerts). Cowboys hang at the "Stampede Ballroom."

They give away a free horse once a week. Hips meet at *Space City!* (underground rag) office and the University of Houston Center.

The school is apathetic politically. There have been a few run-ins with the administration. In April of 1970, Abbie Hoffman was invited to speak but the board of trustees denied him permission. He spoke anyway, without fanfare. Students occupied a building— no arrests. The only student to go to jail had desecrated "the Flag" —three other students pressed charges against him.

SURVIVAL:

Marijuana is still a mortal sin according to the pigs in this area— stiff prison penalties and lots of busts. But you can score around the Montrose area. Or you can import it yourself from Mexico— six hours away. BC pills from Planned Parenthood up the street. Student health has a good psychiatric center but Rice still has the highest rate of student and teacher suicide per year. *Space City!* is a good underground paper.

ENVIRONMENT:

Mental—People are reading Abbie Hoffman and stuff by Norman O. Brown.

Physical—The climate is hot and humid with lots of trees. Polluted Galveston beach is only 45 minutes away. Air is polluted from nearby refineries.

Architecture is Neo-Mediterranean. Gardenia bushes and lawns. Beauteous quadrangle. Escapes include the Herman Park and Zoo which is close.

Texas Southern University

Houston, Texas

SERGEANT PEPPER SECTION:

4,752 students. 99% black. Easy to get in. High-school gradua- tion and average scores. 536 out-of-state.

ACADEMIC BULLSHIT:

Best undergraduate departments are Pharmacy and Business. Law and Education are the best graduate departments.

Lots of good courses on black culture. Dr. Biggers, the well- known black artist, teaches African-oriented art. Popular professors include Ben Butler (Music) and Mable Lott (Psychology). Tradi- tional academic environment. No Pass/Fail, lots of tests, classes about 30 students, some student-originated classes ("Legal Aid" and "Social Change"). The African Studies department has out- standing teachers. Independent study for honors students.

BREAD:

In-state tuition is $100 per semester, out-of-state is $250. Loans

and scholarships are available. Campus jobs pay $1.50 an hour.
Dorms are $642 per year for room and board. 25% live on campus.
Apartments are more popular and cost $60 for a hole—$100 for
a decent one-room. No coed dorms and chicks have restrictions.
Difficult to scrounge. Most have cars. Average date is $6 for a flick
and a hamburger.

BROTHERS AND SISTERS:

Ratio cats : chicks—1 : 1.

Students are mostly lukewarm hip. Most have smoked and ball
regularly but are still into the middle-class consumer bag. They
buy costly threads and fancy cars. Short naturals. Students are just
beginning to understand that black is beautiful. A few straights and
a few heavy hips. Lots of dating but chicks aren't liberated. Fraternities are strong. 12% are married.

The only real political action (other than a riot in 67 because
of repression in the city) is the community projects started by the
Organization for Black Student Unity. On a whole, the students are
apathetic.

Good music at "The Cinder Club" and the "Latin World" for
hangs.

Lots of weed—lids go for $12. No hard drugs. Scoring through
friends.

SURVIVAL:

Hard anywhere in the South. The school has some facilities for
creative outlets. There's no draft counseling on campus but the
American Friends Service does it in Houston. Student health is in-
competent. No BC pills or abortion referrals. No hippie clinic but
the County Health Clinic treats some cases for free. The *Texas
Southern University Herald* is so-so.

ENVIRONMENT:

Mental—Students are into black consciousness. They are reading
Black Rage, Soul on Ice, and *The Autobiography of Malcolm X.*
The topic of conversation is repression.

Physical—An urban ugly campus in Houston complete with air
pollution. Plain, run-down buildings and newer plain red brick ones.
The Fairchild Building looks in danger of collapse.

Not much splitting on weekends as most of the students commute.

The white people's school is right up the street (U. of Houston).

University of Texas at Arlington

Arlington, Texas

Mostly commuters and mostly a bore.

SERGEANT PEPPER SECTION:

13,689 students of which 281 are out-of-state. Must be in top one-fourth of your high-school graduating class and have 600 average combined SATs or be in top one-half of your high-school graduating class and have 650 SATs.

ACADEMIC BULLSHIT:

The best departments are Engineering and the Pure Sciences. The most popular course is psychology by Ward Hodge ("he's easy to talk to and used to be a beatnik").

Pass/Fail is used on rare occasions. Classes range from 50–300. A few black studies courses. The Free U teaches "How to Protect Yourself from the Pigs" and the "Occult." Not much interaction between students and teachers and no independent study.

BREAD:

$125 in-state, $250 out-of-state per semester. Loans are fairly easy to get, scholarships are tight. Some campus jobs at $1.50 an hour.

The dorms cost $165 a month with food. Lots of dumb rules. "No boys allowed in girls' rooms and no girls allowed in boys' rooms." Apartments are the most popular digs and run about $120 for a one-bedroom. Lots of students live at home. Students can scrounge as panhandling is very easy in Dallas. An unbelievable amount of cars—the school looks like a parking lot.

The average date includes a flick, a hamburger and booze for about $10.

BROTHERS AND SISTERS:

Ratio cats : chicks—3 : 1.

Most are straight—short hair, shellac for the chicks, sport shirts and slacks, and Villager dresses. About 10% are lukewarm hip with sideburns and jeans. The others are cowboy conservatives and frat types. Fraternities and sororities are gaining membership. Lots of dating but hardly any living together. Freaks can meet at Lee Park on Sundays in Dallas—rock bands. The Methodist Center sponsors the "Belly of the Whale" for folk music. Straights flock to the "Pizza Inn" in Dallas. Freaks dope in Dallas—$15 a lid for weed.

The campus is apathetic politically. The strike pulled about 200, the Moratoriums about 300. Conservative on the whole.

SURVIVAL:

Difficult in Texas. Student health is O.K. No BC pills or abortion referrals, though. Draft counseling in Dallas and Ft. Worth. You can buy bust insurance which will pay bail and get you a lawyer if you get busted. Free hippie clinic in Dallas. The school newspaper is the *"Shorthorn,"* a conservative daily. The underground paper is the *Free University Press.*

ENVIRONMENT:

Mental—Freaks are reading *The Electric Kool-Aid Acid Test* and *The Book* by Alan Watts. STOP is the ecology group. They try to clean up lakes in the area.

Physical—Arlington is a suburb about 15 miles from Dallas. Cold and rainy in winter, hot and humid in summer. The campus looks like one big parking lot; buildings are one-six-story brick jobs. Few windows. ROTC building has all the windows sealed off with white cement.

Escapes include Dallas, Ft. Worth and home.

University of Texas at El Paso

El Paso, Texas

A University of Texas commuter type school. Hot dates include the sights in Juarez, Mexico. Imagine spending four years in a border town without being a pusher.

SERGEANT PEPPER SECTION:

10,045 students of which 1,282 are out-of-state. About 30% Mexican-American. Easy to get in. Combined score of 800 on SATs and top one-half of graduating class.

ACADEMIC BULLSHIT:

General academic level is mediocre.

Best undergraduate departments are Engineering and Political Science. The graduate department only offers Master's degrees.

Popular professors include Dr. Paul Grosser and Dr. Edward Leonard, both of Political Science. They are the main anti-war heroes at this Texas school.

Most classes have about 40 students in them—not much of a relationship between students and teachers. No student-originated classes, some Pass/Fail—lots of tests and shit like that.

A new Free U that offers "Bull Whipping" and "Astrology."

A student can have Black or Mexican-American Studies as an inter-departmental minor which means he takes a few ethnic courses from various departments. There is no Black Studies department per se. Study abroad in Mexico.

BREAD:

Tuition fees are $250 per year in-state, $550 out-of-state. Loans and scholarships are available. Campus jobs are very hard to find. Dorms cost $550 per semester for room and board. Most popular are apartments—$75–$80 for a one-room apartment. It's cheapest to rent a place across the border in Mexico, but then you need transportation. Students can scrounge if they live in Mexico—can make ends meet for about $40 a month. El Paso has an incredible amount of used-clothing stores. Most people have cars or cycles.

Students are comparatively poor and have neat plain clothes. The average date costs $10—a meal and a movie in either El Paso or Juarez, Mexico.

BROTHERS AND SISTERS:

Ratio cats : chicks—3 : 2.

Students are 70% straight—dresses, nylons and hair spray for chicks, sport shirts and slacks for cats. About 8% are just starting to be hip—a few moustaches. The others are fraternity type conservatives. Fair amount of dating with straights—sex among the hips. A few fraternities.

The hips hang at the "Levee" (which is on the bank of the Rio Grande and has bands). Straights hang at the "Carousel Bar" in El Paso.

Hardly any political action so far. MECHA, the Mexican-American Student Association, is trying to get a Mexican-American Studies department.

There was a peaceful march after Kent State.

SURVIVAL:

Not too many into dope—lids $10, acid $3. Lots of busts. The jail is bad news. All they feed you is chili and doughnuts.

No BC pills or abortion referrals from student health—just free psych counseling.

Draft counseling is done at the Student Methodist Center—Rush Smith is the director.

There's a suicide prevention center and a Free Clinic. The help switchboard is called "Hotline." The campus newspaper, *The Prospector,* is a bore. Expensive health-food stores.

ENVIRONMENT:

Mental—Heads are reading Hesse. Straights discuss the weather.

Physical—The climate is hot and dry in the summer, cold with a little snow in the winter. Desert and barren mountains around. The urban campus is built on mine slag. Air pollution from the copper mines and a sulphur smelting plant that stinks to high heaven.

The campus is composed of cream stucco stone buildings of varying shapes and ugly parking lots. A few lawns, no trees, much construction. Escapes include Mexico and camping near the Rio Grande. Largely a commuter school.

Texas Woman's University
Denton, Texas

The school puts out a book that is at least 100 pages long full of rules, regulations and shit, i.e., no smoking on campus; no bare feet, etc. Drinking is against the law in Denton County.

SERGEANT PEPPER SECTION:

5,325 girls, of which 683 are from out-of-state. Average grades and SATs. A lot of transfers out. 2,090 blacks.

ACADEMIC BULLSHIT:

Boring academia—mediocre quality. The best undergraduate department is Nursing. Health, physical education and recreation are all one field here. The graduate school of Social Work allows students to do community social work. No Pass/Fail, tests, big lectures, no student-originated classes, no Free U, a few ethnic studies classes. Some interaction between students and teachers—on the dating level.

BREAD:

$90 in-state and $250 out-of-state per semester. Loans and scholarships are somewhat available. Some jobs at $1.35 an hour.

Dorms cost $1,050 a year for room and board. Most students live in them. Apartments cost about $100 a month for a one-bedroom. All types of shitty dorm rules: "You can't leave the dorm through the front door if you are barefoot or wearing pants or shorts." "No boys are allowed in the rooms." No scrounging as area hates longhairs.

SISTERS:

All straight arrow. Dresses, nylons, "flats," bubble hair-dos ad nauseas. The girls date guys from a G.I. base nearby 'cause "they spend lots of money." Beer parties are the thing. Many girls have that dyke look. No liberated women.

People go to "La Salle's Drive-In" for fun. Country music is popular. Not many are into drugs.

The administration runs everything, student government has no power. A girl reporter for the school newspaper discovered that the school won't pay athletic tournament fees and the administration wouldn't let her print the story. The blacks are into making it in a white world.

SURVIVAL:

Forget it. Student health is terrible, no BC pills or suicide prevention. The *Daily Lass-o* is a bore.

ENVIRONMENT:

Mental—The few readers are reading *The Naked Ape*. Tri-Beta is the ecology group.

Physical—Uggy Texas weather. The school is in the town of Denton which has a population of 7,000. Roads running through. Modern brick buildings of two–three stories.

People escape to Dallas (?).

UTAH

Brigham Young University
Provo, Utah

One cat was almost expelled from this school because he had a quote from Eldridge Cleaver on his dorm door.

The guy who has the longest hair on this campus is the statue of Brigham Young in front of the administration building. Mormons, Mormons and more Mormons. Church parties are what's happening, take it from there. The students are all very conservative and if they play their cards right they may even grow up to be reactionaries. Instead of dividing categories into in-state and out-of-state, they divide along church member and nonmember lines.

SERGEANT PEPPER SECTION:

BYU is a Mormon school made up of 24,000 students—13,000 males and 10,500 females. There are 2,000 graduate students and 987 nonchurch members attending.

It's relatively easy to get into (but will you get out?). No average GPA and ACT scores. Transfer students need a 2.25 cum. All students must submit to Mormon beliefs that the body is a temple of God and therefore must not use alcohol, tobacco or any drugs.

ACADEMIC BULLSHIT:

BYU is known only for its graduate program in Education. Practically all of the Los Angeles area principals are working with BYU for their terminal degrees in Elementary Education. Five years ago they graduated more certified teachers than any other college in the country!

Many "Hollywood stars'" children hang in for the Music and Drama department. Zoology professor Dr. Braithewaite is a favorite for those who dig invertebrates.

There are no student-initiated courses, no Free U and no Pass/Fail—a step backward for the world of education.

No Third World College since there are only five blacks. However, there is a good Indian Studies program and many Indian students attend. Study abroad in Salzburg, Madrid and Grenoble.

BREAD:

No in-state and out-of-state tuition—in-church and out. Since the school is owned and operated by the Mormon Church, Mormon students have already paid for a good deal of their education through tithings. Members pay $240 a semester and nonmembers pay $375. No federal scholarships or NDEA programs. A few short-term loans. There are 4,000 student campus jobs, the usual. No work-study. An expensive set of threads isn't necessary and dates are cheap—$1.50 for a movie. There's a used-book store in Provo, "The Emporium." Dorms are $745 a year for room and board. Apartments run $45–$60.

BROTHERS AND SISTERS:

Ratio cats : chicks—about equal.

Student dress codes are governed by the maxim, "Wear what is appropriate," and love beads and beards aren't appropriate—neither are blouses that reveal the existence of nipples. The students are conservative (even saw one "flattop"). Chicks wear girdles. There is a small minority approaching lukewarm hip but no freaks. Dress codes say that no moustache can dip below the lip and no male's hair can cover the ears (Army regulations). The students enforce these fucked-up rules by refusing to serve you food in the cafeteria.

Dating and church parties are in, football heroes are big (give this school to the Smithsonian). There is hardly any cohabitation since most of the student houses are BYU approved. School security officers can enter any time they wish.

Straights are easy to meet anywhere on campus. The only head shop is the "Body and Soul" store. Juice is the high—little dope, only high-schoolers in Provo.

The only political clubs on campus are the Young Republicans, Young Democrats and YAF.

SDS is not allowed to speak on campus. There has never been a demonstration. The administration frowns on them. Their favorite line is, "Like it or leave it."

The Environmental Teach-In last spring was the first teach-in in the school's history. There are no radical professors as they are screened out before they are hired. President Wilkinson brought the film *Communists on Campus* to the school. ROTC is very welcome here and they even have a female program.

SURVIVAL:

It's nearly impossible to survive here. No BC pills, no abortion referrals, no sex and little grass ($10 a lid). Student health is mediocre. The draft counseling is done by Young Democrats. Dogs aren't allowed on campus and if they find one they'll slice him up in the zoology lab. One theater in town tried to show *Candy* but it was confiscated.

ENVIRONMENT:

Mental—Students are trying to inform themselves about blacks (post-Civil War). They are reading *Soul on Ice* and *Black Like Me*.

Physical—The campus has many new buildings, blocklike and square. The Karl G. Maeser Building is really nice-looking. It's an older building and sort of looks like the front of the Lincoln Memorial. There are many flat expanses of lawn but very few trees. All the buildings are rather small, the largest being six stories.

If you like seasons, the climate is nearly ideal. Escapes are ski places, mostly, also mountain climbing and hiking. A ski hang is called "Sundance" and is owned by Hollywood glossy Robert Redford who lives there.

Utah State University
Logan, Utah

Straight arrow here with the rest of Utah—hang onto your hats for a wild time at the church parties. "Anyone who is not from Logan is thought of as a foreigner and treated badly."

SERGEANT PEPPER SECTION:

Easy to get in. In-state need a 2.0 and out-of-state need a 2.2. Some people are let in with lower grades, though. ACT is a necessity. There are 8,738 students, approximately 35% out-of-state.

ACADEMIC BULLSHIT:

No one could think of the best undergraduate department but they did suggest a couple of unusual courses—"Biology 11, the Evolution of Ecology" and "Family Life"—a marriage class. The two best graduate departments are Agriculture and Natural Resources (forestry and wildlife).

There are few radical professors on campus. Sterne McMullen, who teaches in the English department and is a regional leader in the Young Socialist Alliance, and Clarence Munford, who teaches "Black History." No student-initiated courses—Pass/Fail and a Free U but "no one knew what was being offered." Most classes are big and informal. There is no Third World College but a couple of black studies courses. Both tests and papers. Study abroad in Mexico. No smoking in class.

BREAD:

In-state $142 and out-of-state $312. The price of housing is the biggest recommendation for this campus. Apartments range from a furnished kitchenette at $25 a month to a furnished two-bedroom at $65 a month. Dorms are $282 a quarter for a double room and board. Also, the Mormons have a set of dorms—all you have to do is abide by the Mormon principles—no tobacco, coffee or tea. Work-study is available but tight. Some loans, few scholarships, students' jobs hard to get but some available in the library and cafeteria at $1.45 an hour. No used-book shop and dates run $4 a shot.

BROTHERS AND SISTERS:

Ratio cats : chicks—5 : 3.

"The girls are dressed in the latest fashion—circa 1967." Straight, straight, straight. The guys wear levis, boots (cowboylike) and short hair with an occasional sideburn or two. The whole campus is composed of plain janes except for a few freaks who add color. Dating and MARRIAGE are the thing. 90% of the social activities revolve around the Mormon Church. The Greeks are very important even though the students don't like to admit it. Though the student newspaper only comes out tri-weekly, one whole page is devoted to the Greeks.

The straight hang is the "Bristol"—a bar in Logan. The "Briar" is an automat on campus and the only place you can smoke (cigarettes). Salt Lake City is the clearing house for all the dope in the entire western mountain area. Lids go for $10—but not that many kids turn on, except out-of-staters. Not many hard drugs.

The students are politically conservative and the only radicals are those from out-of-state. Young Republicans are going strong. SDS isn't allowed on campus. The BSU is growing as is the YSA.

Their most famous political event was in 1966—there was a Smoke-In—the students won a minor concession and can now smoke in one building—the Briar.

Last fall the student government tried to change the nickname of the school from the "Aggies" to the "Highlanders." The change of the name was announced at a football halftime and when the students heard it they started booing. They won their protest.

BSU has been protesting lately about Mormon racial policies but not much luck yet. Utah State participated in the October Moratorium. They are now very interested in ecology. There's a temperature inversion in the Cache Valley where the school is located and if many industries come in—bad pollution? A new heating plant is being built on campus.

Panty raids are still happening.

There is a sort of unorganized organization of freaks in the dorms called the "Jones."

Between $30,000 and $45,000 are collected in parking tickets yearly and instead of using the money for getting more parking lots the money goes into a scholarship fund (ain't that bad).

There is a lot of construction going on and there are even more plans to build a bunch of new buildings, even though enrollment has been dropping off. The administration's thinking is that the new buildings will solve their problems and attract new students. Military recruiters are in the student union and the ROTC marches through the quad and the students don't mind.

Some complaints from the freaks:

1. You can't smoke in any of the buildings (only in the Briar).
2. You can't go barefoot in the U.B. (University Building—used to be called Union Building but "union" has a bad connotation.)
3. Can't initiate classes.
4. There aren't windows in all of the classrooms.

5. Never had a student body pres that wasn't a Mormon—70% of school is LDS.

6. Sexual revolution hasn't arrived.

SURVIVAL:

Naturally, no BC pills or devices are given out at student health (Gracious!). Birth control through self-restraint, asceticism and cold showers. No Free Clinic, some help with suicide preventions at the health center. Student health is mediocre.

ENVIRONMENT:

Mental—Talk about ecology, little action. Students reading *Portnoy's Complaint* and *The Peter Principle*.

Physical—Weather is O.K.—snow in winter, not much pollution yet. All the buildings look like squares and boxes. For freaks, the big escape is Logan Canyon. Others go skiing at Jackson. Most people live off campus.

University of Utah

Salt Lake City, Utah

The chicks not only wear bras here, they wear chastity belts. People are still in their high-school cliques and it's kind of like Emmy Lou. The school is made up almost all of Utah residents. The state of Utah sucks.

SERGEANT PEPPER SECTION:

20,543 students go here and 3,300 are graduate students. Only 2,000 are from out-of-state. Requirements for admission include a 2.5 GPA from school and ACT tests (no specific score—just take the test). Transfers need a 2.0.

ACADEMIC BULLSHIT:

Engineering and Social Work are the best undergraduate departments. Dance is also very good and they have a Repertory Dance Theater. There are even a couple of hip professors here—Bruce Landesman, a Philosophy professor, who is friendly with the SDS, and Peter Appleby, a Law professor. The best grad departments are Law, Social Work and Medicine. The Medical school is the heart-transplant center for the entire intermountain area (Salt Lake City).

Pass/Fail and grades are both used. There are no student-initiated courses but there is a Free U that teaches "Human Sexuality," "Zen," "Macrobiotic Cooking" and "Winemaking" (they aren't for credit). There is a businesslike relationship between students and teachers. The school recently hired a black counselor for the blacks (66 altogether). Independent study is allowed on the honors program. Study abroad in Germany, Spain, England and Switzerland. Smoking in class is forbidden unless the prof does.

BREAD:

The University of Utah is no steal at $160 in-state and $365 out-of-state. Dorms are $1,021 for room and board for the year. It's mainly a commuter campus. Students live in apartments. The average apartment is $60 if you share. Commuters come to school and go home immediately. Most kids have cars and parking is scarce. Work-study exists but is tight. Usual campus jobs are available at about $1.60 an hour. 3,350 receive scholarships or grants. The "Cosmic Aeroplane" has used records.

BROTHERS AND SISTERS:

Ratio of cats : chicks—2 : 1.

Girls wear the longest above-the-knee skirts ever. Most are straight types, marriage bound. Some cats actually wear ties and sports jackets. There are a few local freaks—progress is possible. Dating is where it's at and virginity is still a topic of conversation. Movies are popular and rock concerts are catching on (although the Doors had their concert canceled because the owners of the arena felt that they might corrupt the morals of the intended audience). A really big date, get this, is a groovy church function. Fraternities are still alive and influential.

The few freaks there are can meet at the "Cosmic Aeroplane" plugged above. (It's been in existence two years and still hasn't made any bread.) The "Huddle" is an eating hang on campus where you can score dope. Lids go for $10 and there is a little hash. Most of the dope comes directly from Mexico. People are really into booze here. Lots of student narcs. The cafeteria is also a hip place where "depraved intellectuals and artists can discuss the symbolism of poetry."

Straights can mix (if they are able) in the general campus area and the "Crimson Commons." The kids are conservative and apathetic. The only cause that draws is pollution. Young Republicans are the swingers. Women's Lib is just starting but recently they suffered a defeat. Their candidate for the Associated Women Students was beaten by a write-in candidate—a male.

October Moratorium of last year was high spot in school's political history. 4,000 students marched downtown.

Lately there has been controversy about free speech and obscenity. The school is in the midst of defining its free speech policy, but it is being pressured by downtown reactionary business interests to keep controversial speakers off campus (Kunstler for example). There was a rally April 17 in which a speaker said, and got his audience of 150 to say, "motherfucker." The speaker happened to be the head of the black community in Salt Lake City.

The Movement may be just starting here.

SURVIVAL:

The King Family is coming to campus for two concerts on one night and is sold out. Could you survive here?

No comments about student health—they don't give out BC pills. Planned Parenthood is trying to start up for the 15th time in Salt Lake City. No free hippie clinic but a suicide prevention center in the school's Crisis Center. There is no draft counseling on campus but the Unitarian Church in the city has opened its doors as a sanctuary to draft evaders. The campus paper is the *Daily Chronicle* done by the Young Republicans. The underground paper is the *Electric News,* leftist but not Marxist. There are some health-food places.

ENVIRONMENT:

Mental—Pretty unstimulating. Those that can, are reading Hesse and *Stranger in a Strange Land.*

Physical—"One thing about Utah, it has a lot of weather, all in the same week." The four seasons make it here. Snow in winter, rain in spring, but summer and fall are lovely. None of the buildings are particularly inspiring. Utah is right after Chicago in sulphur pollution, and it's still trying to attract industry so controls are lax. Kennecotte Copper emits at least 300 tons of SO_2 a day and the air currents just don't clean up the valley.

Students go skiing or to city parks for recreation, but the parks have a 10 P.M. curfew.

VERMONT

Bennington College
Bennington, Vermont

Bennington sounds like a nearly perfect place if you have the bread. It's located in rural, wooded Vermont, the classrooms are New England style farmhouselike and there is a heavy emphasis on the arts. Although dudes are admitted, the majority of the students are most decidedly female and date Yale, Dartmouth, and Williams College refugees.

SERGEANT PEPPER SECTION:

500 students, 450 of which are chicks. All undergraduates. Most from the East. Very difficult to get in. The college takes the student's entire personality and achievements into account. Average SATs are 1,300 combined. Interest and ability in the arts is very important.

ACADEMIC AND ARTISTIC BULLSHIT:

Bennington is into the arts. It has a fantastic faculty and many opportunities for creative outlets for the students. Extracurricular activities and studies are one and the same.

Music, literature and dance are all excellent. Courses are small personal experiences. There are no specific course requirements for graduation.

Stanley Edgar Hyman teaches "Myth, Ritual and Literature" which has acquired some well-known myths of its own. All the Music courses are outstanding because they are based on composition above all else. No straight "conservatory" procedures are indulged in and the students learn theory through composition. Bennington is one of the country's foremost dance centers. Martha Graham and Jose Limon have taught there.

Harry Brant and Louis Calabro, both known composers, teach in the Music department. The teachers are almost always practicing professionals. Writers include Bernard Malamud and Nicholas Delbanco.

No grades are given, instead a fairly pervasive comment is written by the instructor about the student's individual work. There is a close relationship between faculty and students.

Many student-originated courses. Tutorials are often set up for those courses that only two–six people wish to take. If the student desires a close relationship with faculty members, it is very avail-

466

able. There are mostly projects and papers—whatever the student wants. All the work is approached in an individual way. Much innovation and creativity.

BREAD:

Heavy. Total cost for a year is $4,500. About 25% of the students receive some financial aid. All students live in the dorms which are coed houses of 30 people each. They eat in a common dining room. Campus jobs are available at about $1.25 an hour.

Bennington students are allowed a nonresident term from December 15–March 9, during which the college closes down and everybody returns to the outside world for a short time. They are supposed to take some job connected with their main academic interest but the jobs are usually whatever you can get.

BROTHERS AND SISTERS:

Ratio cats : chicks—1 : 10.

A paradise for cats. Everyone at Bennington is heavy hip intellectually. Students dress in levis, army jackets and boots. Clothes aren't a big thing as students are in paint and ceramics all day. There's a lot of relationshipping and the chicks are "extremely liberated." People are into drugs in a quiet way. The campus is not activist, more philosophical and creative.

It's isolated, and if you don't find your counterpart in good vibrations, you look around at other schools' offerings. Dartmouth, Yale and Williams men drop in often to look over new crops.

Students are advocates of nonviolent change.

SURVIVAL:

You can have peace of mind and fulfillment of body and soul here. The school takes care of you. Dorms have liberal hours and social life is good. Pills and abortion referrals are available in town. There are counselors for suicide prevention and such. Draft counseling is done by UNDO. There are no physical-education requirements. Many cultural events on campus—lectures, bands, flicks, dance concerts. The "Ginger House" in town for health foods.

ENVIRONMENT:

Mental—Much stimulation and freedom.

Physical—What an ecological delight. Bennington is "beautiful— woods, farms, clean air, animals on farms, mountains, camping, hiking and a little bit of mud in the winter." Students are away for the worst part of winter. "Lovely late spring, quite perfect here."

The buildings are all small farmhouse barn types—just simple New England style. One new Science building, modern and wood fits in fine.

Bennington is an escape in itself. "The only reason ever to leave is to see the world."

Goddard College
Plainfield, Vermont

The entire college is like a Free University. Rumor has it that Steve McQueen got kicked out for riding his motorcycle on the president's front lawn. A progressive, creative place.

SERGEANT PEPPER SECTION:

600 students—all undergraduates. No conventional admission standards. It's easy to get in—in the sense that you don't need good marks—but only 30% of all applicants are accepted. Applicants must be "creative and mature." Average SATs, 1,100. 98% out-of-state. 8% black.

ACADEMIC BULLSHIT:

The college is divided into two campuses—Northwood and Greatwood. Goddard is an experimental, progressive school. It thinks of itself as a "community of teachers and students." Courses are highly relevant and very unstructured.

There are no departments but the best concentrations are Poetry, Photography and Dance. Anything goes. Barry Goldensohn teaches a "Great Poetry Workshop" and a poetry journal is prepared. John Mahoney helps students with photography—his class did a project called the "Soul of Vermont" in 1970. Marcus Schukind and Mark Ryder teach dance.

Students can and do teach. The Bread and Puppet Theater Company makes ten foot puppets. They were the theater in residence for 1970. Students do nothing but this for a whole term—it's great!

No grades at all. There's an evaluation process at the end of the semester where students evaluate themselves and teachers comment.

Tom Arsher teaches "Issues and Texts"—it's a read-anything course—he wants people to overcome their hatred of books.

Most courses are student-initiated. The requirements are just that you get people interested, get it together and plan the course. Students and professors are one. They do everything together. "I heard of one teacher giving a math test once"—no tests. Lots of independent study. A Third World dorm and many Third World courses.

BREAD:

Tuition is $1,300 a semester. 40% of the students are on some form of financial aid. Goddard gives out $400,000 a year in scholarships—one of the highest amounts in the country.

Dorm rooms are $250 a semester. Many people live off campus on farms—which can be rented for as little as $50 per month—or communes. Living can be cheap. Grubby clothes—the local junk store, "Dude and Harry's," sells high-heeled sneakers cheap—

50¢. No dating, just rapping and watching the Bread and Puppet Theater. You don't even have to buy books—you can borrow them from the book store.

BROTHERS AND SISTERS:

Ratio cats : chicks—1 : 1.

Heavy hip. Very individualistic—people are creative and into their own thing. Dungarees and heavy work boots. Chicks are liberated—lots of cohabitation. Students are interesting people. Goddard has the Antioch type work plan—you can work or travel one quarter a year.

No hangs—people go to "May's" the local grocery store. Watch out for town greasers.

Everyone smokes—$20 a lid.

Lots of revolutionaries but not the building-burning type. There was a sit-in in spring of 1970, when Goddard students stopped cars to leaflet. Statewide Women's Liberation Conference in March, 1970. Pretty active.

SURVIVAL:

Very easy. Student health is O.K. and the doctor just learned how to fit diaphragms. BC pills from student health and from Planned Parenthood. Sporadic draft counseling.

Great newspaper, *It's Alright, Ma.* Slant—far left to flower child. Closest big cities are Barre and Montpelier.

ENVIRONMENT:

Mental—People are thinking, talking, creating. Reading *Summerhill* and Tom Wolfe.

Physical—Cold in the winter. Rural. Mountains, woods, swamps and small lakes around. All the nice buildings are natural wood. People stay here to escape society rather than go somewhere else to escape Goddard. Adult Degree Program students come in for two weeks a semester and do work independently at home the rest of the time.

University of Vermont

Burlington, Vermont

"The type of freak you find here is not a political freak, but a nature freak. That's why he's here."

SERGEANT PEPPER SECTION:

6,100 students of which 500 are grads. Though this is a state university they don't have two separate admissions standards for in- and out-of-state applicants. Entering frosh should rank in the top 40% of their class—they try to have 60% in-state and 40%

out-of-state. Average SATs are 1,100. Few minority students. Transfers need a 2.5.

ACADEMIC BULLSHIT:

The best undergraduate departments are Pre-med, Agriculture and Home Economics. The Medical school is excellent. Favorite professors include Jim Corologos, in Education, Dr. Gregg in Chemistry (he is probably the most popular here) and Dr. Felt, History. Students really dig Dr. Rollins, the dean of the College of Arts and Sciences. They describe him as tough but fair and very progressive.

Some Pass/No Pass option in many courses beginning in the sophomore year. In the College of Arts and Sciences they have an Experimental College which doesn't use grades, only Pass/No Pass.

There's a Free U with courses on "Photography," "Mysticism," "Black Studies," the "Environment," "Speed Reading" and "Auto Mechanics." For the most part professors are available and interested in the students. Practically all courses have a final. Some independent study and study abroad.

BREAD:

Tuition for two semesters is $930 in-state and $2,380 out-of-state. They have an extensive financial aid program, mostly for Vermont residents, one-third of which are on aid. Blacks can receive aid through the Martin Luther King Scholarship Fund. The largest number of jobs are allocated to the work-study program but most departments hire students through their own budgets—wages are about $1.60 an hour.

Dorms cost $1,000 a year for room and board. Most students live in them. A two-bedroom apartment with kitchen and living room for two people goes from $100–$140 a month. Houses rent for $250–$350 a month and you can load up with people and have a sort of commune. A lot of freaks have started to buy farms with a little land. Cars are the most popular form of transportation.

BROTHERS AND SISTERS:

Ratio cats : chicks—1+ : 1.

The campus is divided into straights and freaks—about one-third of the campus looks freaky. Straights wear multi-colored Ivy League shirts, slacks and loafers, straight chicks wear mini skirts and blouses. Freaks wear a lot of different things. The only uniting thing is comfort and enjoying what they are wearing—a lot of them costume, know they are costuming, and dig it. They wear mainly bell jeans, chicks go braless and wear beads and real Indian headbands.

Dating still exists in the fraternities and dorms. For a date, you go to a frat party or a flick. Freaks are more hang loose and the freaky chicks ball. Frats are changing a bit—people are dropping out of them in their sophomore year but they still get a lot of joiners. They haven't gotten into dope as heavily as most frats.

Hangs include "The Den" (snack place in the Student Center), "The Green" (a quadlike park where freaks play Frisbee), "The Tariff" (bar) and the "Red Dog" (straight bar).

In 1969 there was a lot of hard drugs but things have changed. 30% use hash and grass a lot but no hard drugs. Students estimate 70% of the students have tried it. Few busts and the administration is fairly cool.

The students lean to the left and are much more liberal than the people of Burlington, Vermont. There are always letters in the local newspaper complaining about the hippie influence at the University (how there never was any drug problem with the nice clean Vermont kids until hippie University students brought drugs in). Most kids are non-politicized (60% wanted either Nixon or Humphrey in 1968). Only about 5% are "bomb talkers" who dig civil disobedience and trashing. 10% are arch conservatives.

There are no strong political clubs here. In 1968 there was a demonstration against Dow recruiters but for the most part students felt Dow had the right to recruit. In 1968, the last panty raid was held—the cats got into the chicks' rooms and the housemothers were freaked because they couldn't find all the cats and some spent the night there. In May of 1969, 600 students demonstrated quietly against the ROTC parade. About 2,000 people (some from the town) took part in the 1969 Moratoriums. SDS talked to the local G.E. strikers as the local plant made the "mini-gun." In February of 1970, trouble erupted over the Kake Walk (the tradition of frat rats blackening their faces, putting on silk suits and having parties). Blacks objected but a spontaneous Kake Walk was held anyway—lots of threats and a couple scuffles.

Earth Day in 1970 was very big—2,500 attended exhibits.

University of Vermont students called a strike after Kent and Cambodia and 1,100 marched into downtown Burlington carrying coffins. The strike lasted for the week of finals. There were a few busts when demonstrators tried to stop induction buses—some canvassing and petitioning.

SURVIVAL:

Student health services at Watson Infirmary are poor. "If you're not sick when you go there, you will be when you leave," no BC pills or abortion referrals. Planned Parenthood in town but no other survival services. Draft counseling by the campus chaplain and at "The Loft."

Intercollegiate sports are still popular and the favorite sport in 1970 was hockey. The campus paper is *The Cynic*—campus oriented and left-wing. The *Vermont Freeman* isn't an underground paper or an establishment paper but it's left-wing and strong; the *Vermont Underground Railroad* is an underground cultural type paper.

ENVIRONMENT:

Mental—People are talking about their studies and about politics.

Physical—Vermont is cold in the winter and clear most of the year. The worst drawback is the mud. It rains and snows but there isn't an overabundance of either. Little air pollution. Some water pollution from the oil tanks on Lake Champlain. The biggest ecology problem in Vermont is stopping the land developers from cutting up the mountains and putting up houses. Vermont's natural beauty must be saved.

"The biggest problem of this university is its inability to get out of the square brick building complex." The Chapel is attractive in its Georgian style. Fleming Museum has a great marble court on the inside. Billings Center is the Student Union built by Henry R. Richardson. Its style is Richardson Romanesque and it's made of redstone—it's gorgeous on the inside and has a fireplace and a high wooden beamed ceiling.

People escape to Stowe for skiing and millions of other nature spots all over.

VIRGINIA

Sweet Briar College

Sweet Briar, Virginia

Permeated by Scarlett O'Hara types.

SERGEANT PEPPER SECTION:

800 chicks. All undergraduates. 80% out-of-state.

Fairly hard to get in. High-school grades should be over a B and combined SATs of 1,200. The school also looks at extracurricular activities, particularly of the cheerleader variety.

ACADEMIC BULLSHIT:

Three good departments (no graduate programs): Art History has a fantastic slide collection; the English department has two really good courses, "Modern Prose" and "Shakespeare"; the Biology department is good in the areas of ecology and field biology.

Craig Simpson is well liked for his course on the "Ante Bellum South"—he's one of the few young liberal professors that Sweet Briar hires each year. They usually leave after one year. Only the old well-situated women stay on to teach.

Grades are important. Juniors and seniors can take one Pass/Fail course. No Free U. The faculty is usually available and anxious to help the students in their official capacity.

No Third World College. A very homogenous upper-middle-class white Protestant student body—just four blacks.

Tests, tests, tests and busy-work. Limited independent study. A good study program abroad in France.

Students can't smoke in classrooms.

BREAD:

Lots. $3,600 per year, paid in advance, for everything. Some residents of the county who qualify academically may enter tuition free. Some full scholarships to freshmen. Few loans.

Expensive rags are a must. Students are very clothes conscious and even the grubby ones wear expensive threads. Villager dresses and Papagallo shoes. Campus jobs are available at $1.35 an hour. Many have cars.

SISTERS:

Campus types run from lukewarm hip to conservative. Most chicks are southern social types—interested in marriage rather than politics. Hair is still set. The freshmen are a little cooler and wear jeans and slacks to class. Others look down on the hips for being "sloppy."

The archaic weekend dating and mating pattern prevails. Chicks are shipped to nearby men's colleges for weekends. Much social pressure to date fraternity men. Hypocritical chicks—appear to be keepers of the Victorian codes and in reality ball. The Image is the thing. They call Women's Liberation chicks "lesbians," and say they like "being put on a pedestal by men."

Dig this. They still have "secret societies"—about ten chicks in each one. Ugh.

75% of the campus goes trick or treating to the men's campus every weekend—catch one while you can.

On campus, straights hang at the "Venditeria" (an automat) and the few hips hang at "Boxwood Tea Room."

"The Prison," a coffee house at the University of Virginia (50 miles away), attracts the miniscule amount of Sweet Briar dopers.

Lids go for $25 and must be imported from the University of Virginia.

The most active club is the Young Republicans. CURA is a small group of dedicated anti-bigotry and pro-anything liberal chicks.

The first political activity ever to erupt was a strike in reaction to Tricky Dick's Cambodia decision. 75% of the school was involved in constructive committee work—the information stage.

SURVIVAL:

Not too good in the middle of rural Virginia.

The school infirmary is staffed by one doctor, one pediatrician and two nurses. No BC pills or antibiotics given out. And nowhere nearby to get the stuff.

No pets or brown-baggers. The *Sweet Briar News* has a slight left inclination.

ENVIRONMENT:

Mental—Students are just now discussing the possible political power they have. They are reading *Gone with the Wind*.

Physical—Lovely to look at. The Shenandoah Valley region of Virginia—rolling hills, 3,000 acres, flowering trees and bushes. The campus even has its own farm and dairy.

Architecture is Georgian—red brick with white columns. A nice Chapel. Countryish place.

Most people escape to other colleges or to Washington, D.C., on the weekends. There are pastures and dells within walking distance on campus. All live-ins.

Virginia Polytechnic Institute
Blacksburg, Virginia

VPI used to be a military academy. General Westmoreland spoke at the commencement in 1969 and only 30 people objected.

SERGEANT PEPPER SECTION:

VPI has 10,056 students, of which 1,000 are grad students. 206 are out-of-state students.

It's fairly hard for a chick (down with male chauvinism!) to be accepted but easy for a cat. A cat in-state can get in with just a little over a 2.0. The average SATs are slightly over 1,000 combined. The school hopes to attract more and more out-of-state students. .05% minority.

ACADEMIC BULLSHIT:

A very academic school—good only if you dig engineering.

Engineering Mechanics and Aerospace Engineering considered tops. The Geology department has also received recognition as being excellent. (This is a great geologic setting for faults and various types of rocks.) In Engineering Mechanics, students rave about:

1. Fluid Mechanics—Involves hydrostatistics, buoyancy, hydro-dynamics, flows of fluids through pipes measuring resistance and drag, viscosity.

2. Materials Testing—Has to do with hardness tests on materials, their tensility as well as stress concentration factors.

In Aerospace Engineering, you can get high on:

1. Aerospace Structures—Has to do with making the aircraft strong enough to fly and resist pressures.

2. Aircraft and Missile Stability and Control—Has to do with static stability, rigid body dynamics in three dimensions.

3. Aerospace Vehicle Design—Elements in the design of the full spectrum of flight vehicles bringing theory into practice in designing aircraft and missiles.

In the Geology department the students dig:

1. Pleistocene Geology—Glaciers as an agent in erosion and deposition, also takes climate into consideration.

2. Geology Summer Field Course—Intensive training in modern geologic field methods, a special course.

Best grad courses in Engineering too.

Both grades and Pass/Fail are accepted. No student-initiated courses.

Popular professors include John M. Barringer, Jr., who has been mayor of Blacksburg for 20 years. He teaches "Business Administration." Dr. Paul A. Distler teaches a "Great Theater Arts" course.

Free U was canceled due to lack of interest. Most classes have under 40 students and there is a fairly close relationship between students and teachers. There's no Third World College—it's a very WASPy school. Some independent study in political science and sociology courses. Tests. Good study-abroad program in many countries.

BREAD:

In-state is $165 a quarter, out-of-state $305. Dorms run circa $280 a quarter for room and board. But in the past few years off-campus living has increased and many new apartment buildings exist in town—two-bedroom furnished apartment runs $150. Fraternities are just local.

Average cost of date for a cat is $5.00. Students can have cars—many do. Some people dress in blue jeans, others go Villager type collegiate.

Loans and scholarships and work-study are very tight. VPI does offer a "co-op" program for students in technical areas where they work for a quarter for a local industry and then go to school a quarter—it takes five years to graduate.

One book store in town sells used books.

BROTHERS AND SISTERS:

Ratio cats : chicks—8 : 1.

This school has changed radically from eight years ago when it was a military school. There are still 1,000 ROTC cadets who live in a military system but that's the only part that remains. Most of the school is straight and conservative; however, there are about 50 freaks. Chicks are straight and unliberated but not hopeless.

However—then there's the fraternity scene. These useless groups are dying out on other campuses but VPI is striving to get them. They have about 15 local ones now. And there is much student support to go national. Only one sorority. Few commuters.

Dating isn't too cool for the Tech male with those odds. There is a college of 3,000 women over one of the hills, though—Radford.

Sports heroes are a big thing.

Local hangs for the straight are the "Greek's Cellar" (rathskellar) and the "Golden Gobbler" (bar). The few radicals hang at the underground newspaper house—the *Alice* place.

One movie theater in town and one dance place. "The entertainment scene really hurts here."

Drugs aren't happening although lids are available for $10 on campus.

Most students are politically conservative (what can you expect from engineers?). Few organized political groups.

It's a very quiet campus. A couple of small student demonstrations took place in 1970. One was against the Corp of Cadets doing their drill. But possibly student activism in the future from those 50 freaks.

SURVIVAL:

BC pills are available from town doctors if you wear a wedding band. No abortion referral or other helpful info from school but information available from Washington, D.C., not too far away. One draft counselor who is more of a technical advisor on campus. No health-food stores in area. Nearest "big" city is Roanoke, 30 miles away. The *Virginia Tech Collegiate Times* is a straight college newspaper. A new underground paper, *Alice,* is emerging.

ENVIRONMENT:

Mental—People are reading *The Population Bomb*.

Physical—The campus is beautiful—located in the hills of southwest Virginia, surrounded by mountains, trees and lakes. Fall and spring are beautiful, with temperatures in the 70s—winters cold.

The architecture of all the old buildings is done in gray quarry stone in the Gothic style. New buildings aren't as attractive.

No air pollution. Major eyesore is the duck pond on campus which is polluted by sewer lines.

People go to the mountains, lakes and caves (!) to get away.

University of Virginia
Charlottesville, Virginia

Not bad, except that blue laws still exist in Virginia. You can't buy records, kites, bathing suits or liquor on Sunday.

SERGEANT PEPPER SECTION:

9,735 students of which 4,311 are out-of-state. Fairly difficult to get in. You need good grades and approximately 1,200 on your SATs.

ACADEMIC BULLSHIT:

Thomas Jefferson founded this bastion of higher learning. It's one of the best schools in the South.

Students like History and English best of the undergraduate departments. Best graduate departments include Physics, the Law school and the Medical school.

The first black course ever offered was given in the fall of 1970. It was called "Introduction to Afro-American History" and was taught by Professor Gastin. Professor Hereford's "Philosophy of Religion" and Professor Graebener's "Diplomatic History" courses are very popular.

Some Pass/Fail, not much class participation as the majority of the teachers are very traditional with only lectures and little discussion. Some student-originated courses through the Liberal Arts Seminar program. A weak Free U. More black courses are going to be added but there is no Black Studies department yet. Minority recruitment is getting heavier as there have been many demonstrations for integration. No independent study. Study abroad only through the Language department.

BREAD:

Tuition is $535 per year in-state and $1,207 out-of-state. Loans are easy to get, scholarships are tight. Jobs are easy to find at $1.50 an hour.

Dorms cost about $1,000 a year for room and board. About half the students live in them. Freshmen have to. There is 24-hour visitation and one coed dorm. Some still live in fraternities. Many students live off campus in apartments which cost about $50 per person. The best way to scrounge is to get a cottage a little way off from campus. You can rent one for $30 a person or less. Many kids have cars and cycles.

Expensive threads like a three-piece suit are necessary only at the graduate level.

"Anderson Brothers" buys and sells used books.

BROTHERS AND SISTERS:

Ratio cats : chicks—6 : 1.

Cats go down the road to find chicks—to Mary Washington, or Sweet Briar. Flicks and picnics are the most popular forms of date. People go on dinner dates to "The Gaslight" or "The Prism Coffee House." There are three big fraternity weekends a year for sports and social action. Fraternities still exert an influence on the social life on campus—there are 33 of them and about a third of the campus belongs.

Virginia is a big drinking school—of late, marijuana is big, too. About half the students have tried grass and it goes for $15 a lid. The heavier stuff is used only among the freaks. The administration is cool and there aren't many busts.

Hangs include "The Corner" and "Hardy's."

Most students dress straight casual. Some freaks have appeared but they are in the minority. Chicks are super-straight and wear dresses, nylons and delicate shoes. The chick situation should get better now that the school is coed.

University of Virginia students were apathetic and middle-of-the-road until 1969. A group called the Student Coalition began organizing around the issue of University racism. They demonstrated in favor of more black admissions, employees and faculty. There were rallies, marches and pickets, no violence and no pigs. Since then black admissions have been improving. Curriculum also became an issue which resulted in freer core requirements and student participation in faculty curriculum committees.

The Cambodian announcement radicalized many students. They

occupied the ROTC building twice and there was a "honk-in" (all the students honked their car horns on a major road near campus). Police arrested 68 people during the demonstrations. The strike referendum was overwhelmingly passed and students were active in community leafletting and canvassing.

SURVIVAL:

Survival depends on studying during the week and letting loose on the weekends.

Not much interest in creative arts. The student health service is good. The Charlottesville Draft Counseling Center counsels on campus.

The Cavalier Daily is an average liberal paper.

The Virginia Weekly is more of an alternate paper. It is put out by the graduate students and is like a radical magazine. It covered the G.E. strike and the grape boycott.

ENVIRONMENT:

Mental—People are reading Rubin and Cleaver and talking about sex. Ecology isn't really happening.

Physical—Charlottesville is a dull little city. Students go to Washington, D.C., two hours away, for action.

The campus is spacious and beautiful with lots of trees and grass. The buildings are red brick colonial. People split to the girls' schools on the weekends.

WASHINGTON

Central Washington State College
Ellensburg, Washington

Ellensburg has a great rodeo on Labor Day.

SERGEANT PEPPER SECTION:

6,811 students, mostly from California, Hawaii, Oregon and Washington; 52 blacks, 86 Indians.
Incoming students need a 2.5, transfers need a 2.0.

ACADEMIC BULLSHIT:

The Education department has an elementary school on campus and a program whereby ed credits are given for students going out to slums or rural communities, living with the people there. The major departments are Business Administration, Health and Physical Education and History.

There are several interdisciplinary seminars that last one quarter each on such subjects as "Gandhi," "Limitations of the Scientific Mind" and "Ecology." Take Wayman Ware for "Culture and Poverty" and "Poverty and Change." There's a course on dope called "Mind Altering Substances" taught by McAffee in the Health Education department. Many courses are designed as construct courses. The teacher tells you in advance which assignments will lead to various grades.

Pass/Fail, average classes of 30, some student-initiated courses (an English seminar on Bob Dylan). A Free U which offers things like "The Living Theater," "Ecology of the Kittitas Valley," "River Navigation" and "Indian Beadwork."

Some black studies. The BSU does black recruitment and sponsors a black week. Six black professors on campus. The Economic Opportunity program recruits Indians and Chicanos. There was a Pow Wow on campus in 1970. There are quite a few Indians around Ellensburg. Pretty good teacher-pupil relationships for a state school. The Honors program has independent study. Lots of group activities, field trips to the S.F. Moratorium, the state reformatory and the state mental hospital. Study abroad in Mexico City.

BREAD:

Tuition is $120 in-state and $240 out-of-state per quarter. Aid is rare. Nude modeling pays $2.50 an hour, $1.55 for modeling with clothes on. You have to cut your hair for dining-hall jobs. On-campus jobs pay $1.55. Dorms cost $840 for room and board—coed, wing by wing. Motellike dorms. Half the students live in dorms. Three infractions of the dorm rules and you are out. Lots of apartments at $70–$125 per person. Some live on farms for $30 a month, and sometimes pay nothing if they agree to fix up the place. One old farmhouse which costs $40 a month is a crash pad. Scrounging is possible if you get food stamps and live on a farm during the winter and in a tent during the summer. Lots of cars and bikes—hitching is illegal. College shop clothing.

BROTHERS AND SISTERS:

Ratio cats : chicks—2 : 1.

95% look straight—T-shirts, cut-offs and sandals and sneakers. A few have slightly shaggy hair. Heavy juice vibes. A handful of freaks with electric hair. Lots of girls have short hair touched up with phony coloring. Wholesome Middle-America people. No fraternities.

People go to flicks at the "Village Theater"—on Sundays foreign flicks are shown on campus. The Ellensburg Rodeo happens every year on Labor Day. Eating joints are the "Pizza Hut" and the "A.W." The "SWCC" is an annual event—a big drunk that goes on for about a week in the spring. Lots of bands come here on the college circuit. There's lots of dope grown in Washington around Moses Lake, "Washington Green." Natural vegetation.

Approximately 10% of the students are vets on the G.I. Bill.

Not much in the way of politics. 40 blacks sat-in in the pres-dent's office in 1969—they got a Black Studies program. The Youn-Republicans held their convention on campus in 1970, featurin-Governor Dan Evans, without incident. There was a short stri-after Kent State.

SURVIVAL:

Difficult. A new Art building, however—courses offered in glass-blowing, photography and pottery.

The campus health service was rumored to be the source of a hepatitis epidemic that almost closed down the school. It is very crowded—referrals for BC pills. Dean Wise, the dean of men, does draft counseling as does the campus Methodist minister. The bulletin board speaks of "student wanted to work on a ranch 3 hours a day," "8-week old rabbits $1.50 each," "World Prairies Children Dance Championship to be held at Calgary Stampede, $1,000 purse, open to all male Indians over 16." Crisis clinic for suicide prevention. The last dope bust was in 1967. Women's Liberation has pushed a day-care center.

ENVIRONMENT:

Mental—Those that read are reading Jerry Rubin and *Catch-22*. Avert Man's Extinction Now (AMEN) is the local ecology group —they clean up the campus.

Physical—Ellensburg is a town of 13,800 (7,000 of which are students) in the Kittitas Valley in Central Washington, just east of the Cascades. It is flat, hot, dry and dusty—snowy in the winter. The town is surrounded by farm land. No air pollution but a ditch running through campus has a very polluted creek nicknamed the "Ganges" by the students. Dreadful tales are told of what happens to anyone who falls in. There are lots of new buildings. The SUB looks like a shoebox. The gym (Nicholson Pavillon) has a series of supports on top that make it look like a grasshopper. Since other buildings identical to it have been condemned, students have little faith in this new monster's durability.

High density of low buildings with lots of cottonwood trees and gravel roads.

Escapes include "Floating the Yak" (the Yakima River nearby) in rubber tubes on hot weekends. Skiing in the Cascades. Traveling on the weekends.

Gonzaga University

Spokane, Washington

Bing Crosby went here.

SERGEANT PEPPER SECTION:

2,710 students of which 400 are grads. 66% out-of-state from California, Montana, Oregon and Idaho. 20 blacks, 8 American Indians. Easy to get in—2.5 GPA and around 1,000 SATs.

ACADEMIC BULLSHIT:

The best department is English—it has the largest graduate program and grants about eight M.A.s a year.

Take Father Conwell for "World Religions," Dr. Polek for "American Literature," and Mr. Gilmore for "The Philosophy of Man." Pass/Fail, small classes (average size 13), student-originated courses and Free U. Recruitment of Indians.

Formal relationships between professors and students.

Independent study. A special study-abroad program in Florence where students live with Italian families.

BREAD:

Tuition is $1,300 a year. Not much financial aid—some jobs at about $1.70 an hour. Students are required to live at home with relatives or on campus until they are 22. Dorms cost $880 for room and board per year. A very small percentage lives off campus. The Universal Life Church houses some people near school. Large number of cars and parking is no hassle.

Average dates cost $2 for beer.

BROTHERS AND SISTERS:

Ratio cats : chicks—1+ : 1.

Clean, naive straights. 65–70% of the students declare themselves Catholics when they get here—this requires them to take theology courses. No cohabitation—just dating.

A few hips who hang at "The Red Lion" and "The Nite Hawk Tavern" (bars). "Vis-A-Vis" is a liberal religious coffee house. "May's" is a little luncheonette across the street from campus with photos of old teams and Bing Crosby. The campus is strewn with beer bottles on Monday morning after a weekend of drinking.

Dope isn't big but is available around the corner of North and Main—near skid row so you have to avoid the winos and Christers.

Gonzaga is peaceful. It was closed down for a couple of days during the May, 1970, chaos.

SURVIVAL:

No arts and crafts.

BC pills at the Family Planning Center in Spokane. Draft counseling in the basement of the student center. No campus newspaper.

ENVIRONMENT:

Mental—People are reading Hesse and *The Prophet.* Ecology Day was a flop on campus.

Physical—Spokane is a city of 200,000 on the edge of the eastern Washington desert. The school is less than a mile from the decayed center-city of skid row. Ugly. Smog. The campus has a lot of lawns. The administration building looks like an old rectory. Seattle is 200 miles away.

High Bridge Park in the city has outdoor concerts during the weekends in nice weather.

Seattle University
Seattle, Washington

Avoid if possible.

SERGEANT PEPPER SECTION:

3,650 students, 60% of whom are Catholic. Easy to get in—about 1,000 SATs.

ACADEMIC BULLSHIT:

Run by Jesuits. Master's degrees are given in English, History, Teaching English, Engineering and Business. Business is a very large undergraduate major.

Sister Christopher teaches a course on the French Revolution—a liberal and popular professor. Rabbi Jacovovitz of the University of Washington Hillel teaches a course in "Judaic History and

Theology." The school was going to release him for budgetary reasons but a student petition got him rehired.

Pass/Fail, class participation, few student-originated courses, no Free U—black studies courses in Sociology and History departments. Teachers are like parent images.

BREAD:

$430 tuition per quarter. 50% receive some kind of financial aid. Lots of work-study and regular jobs. Room and board are $975 a year. One girls' dorm has 468 students. 40% of the students live in dorms. Lots of rules. Nearby housing is cheap but you can't live off campus till you're 21.

BROTHERS AND SISTERS:

Ratio cats : chicks—1 : 1.

Straight chicks (girls) wear dresses, guys have short hair—some shagginess and moustaches, sport shirts and slacks. One gets the feeling that there are a lot of Vietnam veterans stalking the campus. Unhip chicks are shocked when they have nude models in the art classes. People hang in the "Tabard Inn" in the Student Union. Lots of student parties with a keg. Drinking is very big and the "Castaway," the "Forum" and "The Cellar" are the preeminent college taverns. Panty raids—the raiders get 25¢ fines. Hardly anyone is into drugs.

The big political issue is over breaking of athletic ties with racist Brigham Young University. After Jackson, the blacks presented a list of demands. Sit-ins, trashings, six arrests. That is the only political action so far.

SURVIVAL:

Difficult. There's a rumor that a new Fine Arts building will be constructed sometime in the next decade.

Just a nurse for student health but the school is located on "Pine Hill"—three big hospitals nearby. No BC pills. Survival services at the University of Washington. Cafeteria with greaseburgers. *The Spectator* (campus paper) is right of center.

ENVIRONMENT:

Mental—Rather dull. 25% of the students are married.

Physical—The campus is located on a hill near downtown Seattle, in an area on the edge of urban blight. Bad smog, water and noise pollution. It covers a few city blocks—nauseatingly dull boxlike structures. Large number of commuters.

Washington State University
Pullman, Washington

Wazoo has recently had its troubles with rednecks harassing blacks.

SERGEANT PEPPER SECTION:

13,150 students of which 1,824 are out-of-state. 120 blacks, 12 Chicanos, 27 Indians.

All applicants must take the Washington Pre-College Test. In-states need a 2.5 GPA, out-of-states need 3.0. SATs must be above average.

ACADEMIC BULLSHIT:

Most noted departments are Agriculture, Animal Science, Business and the Veterinary school. The state legislature in Washington is making this the state cow school. Unusual majors are Geography, Sanitary Engineering and Forestry and Range Management.

Favorite professors include Robert Jonas in "Elementary Biology," Al Crosby, a white teacher of black studies, Pat Morgan (Political Science) and David Kovin who teaches "Black Politics." A motorcycle gang called "Up Against the Wall Motherfuckers" is mainly composed of cool teachers and grad students.

Some Pass/Fail, class participation not important. Some student-initiated courses and a Free U run by the YMCA. In 1970 "Brewing" was the favorite course.

Both a Black Studies and Chicano Studies program. Not much independent study and some study abroad.

BREAD:

$200 in-state a semester, $440 out-of-state. Some scholarships and loans but not many. Jobs are hard to find.

Room and board in the dorms is $935. No alcohol is allowed and visiting hours are 8 A.M. to midnight. There are three coed dorms. Off-campus housing is so difficult to find that some of the empty spaces in the University of Idaho dorms were given to Washington State University students. People pay $150 for an apartment for three. But most everyone lives in dorms and frats.

Cars, motorcycles and walking. "Hill's Book Store" in town has a lot of interesting dusty old editions.

BROTHERS AND SISTERS:

Ratio cats : chicks—about 2 : 1.

There is a large minority of hips, which is a surprise considering the emphasis on agriculture—but they put out an underground rag, do peace marching and wear surplus clothes—jeans, long dresses and sandals. Some wear clenched-fist sweatshirts left over from the recent strike. Most are straight and lots of farm boys go to school here—short hair and jeans.

There are 13 fraternities and 22 sororities and 26% of the undergraduate men belong as do 18% of the undergraduate women. Sports are big. Lots of dating. About 5% of the chicks are liberated.

Students hang at "Rico's" (bar) and go to hear bands in Rainey Park. There is an extensive offering of plays by the Drama department—something practically every week. On campus people hang at the "Cougar Lair." Lots of grass—little hard stuff except for acid. Pullman pigs have sicced the narcs on campus.

The BSU is the most active group politically. In the fall of 1968, they started pushing for black studies and got them in the spring of 1969. Aggies and blacks have had a couple of run-ins; four blacks were sentenced to serve time in Colfax jail for one hassle. When their trial came up, 30 blacks chanted outside the courthouse. They were arrested. In 1970 there was a whole series of racial incidents.

After Kent State, 700 students took over the administration building with 11 demands. One day of class was canceled. A strike was called by the Three Forks Coalition, led by the BSU. The strike won a victory in the sense that President Terrell announced that all finals were optional. The Black Studies department got more people and money.

SURVIVAL:

Hard for blacks, easy for Aggies.

Student health is lousy, some BC pills. Draft counseling is done by people in the K house. There are some deer penned off in one of the corners of the campus back where all the Ag Animal Science buildings are. Women's Liberation is just getting started and is working on lobbying for legalized abortion.

ENVIRONMENT:

Mental—People are talking about imperialism and black awareness. The Environmental Council is into ecology.

Physical—Pullman is an ordinary small town. The campus is on a hill above town surrounded by rolling hills of wheat fields. The buildings are red brick boxes with high-rise dorms.

Escapes are Seattle or Spokane or keggers or the Snake River (the river of no return). Sports are very big and people go away for sports weekends.

University of Washington

Seattle, Washington

Lots of changes lately, getting hipper.

SERGEANT PEPPER SECTION:

33,000 students. 553 blacks, 150 Indians, 147 Mexican-Americans. In-state requirements are a 2.5 GPA and high-school graduation. Transfers need a 2.5 GPA.

ACADEMIC BULLSHIT:

Best courses are Dr. Giovanni Costigan's history classes, Dr. Shapiro's economics courses and Dr. Chambless' "Philosophy of Religion" (he has an FM show on which he plays the top 40 and interviews unusual people). Science, Forestry and Engineering are all good departments.

Traditional academia. Pass/Fail, large classes (300 is not unusual), no student-originated programs of note. A Black Studies major with 37 interdepartmental courses. Relationships between teachers and students are abominable. Teachers are never available for conferences. Hard to swing independent study. Study abroad.

BREAD:

$144 in-state, $350 out-of-state per quarter. Not much financial aid and jobs are tight at $1.65 an hour.

Room and board in the dorms is $945—4,700 students live in them. High-rise big types. Coed wings. Many students live in houses and apartments in the university district at $50 a month rent. A few people live in houseboats but they pay extravagantly for their cramped but romantic dwellings. Scrounging is difficult—long lines for food stamps. Cars everywhere and giant parking lots.

BROTHERS AND SISTERS:

Ratio cats : chicks—1.5 : 1.

With 33,000 students, there are a lot of all types. Straights form the majority—middle-class commuters, dormies, frat rats with that college store Sta-prest shirt look. The hips are a small percentage wearing boots, jeans and work shirts. Liberated chicks are few—more Sally types. 33 fraternities and 20 sororities but are getting hip.

The "Husky Den" in the Hub has a variety of good stuff to eat including the 60¢ Huskyburger—two burger patties, cheese, pickles, Russian dressing and soggy lettuce on a bun. Off campus, eat at "Gilly's Giant Submarine," right off the Avenue. "The Blue Moon" is a heavy bar (bikers and revolutionaries). Other popular bars are "The Warehouse," "Red Robin" and the "Iron Bowl." Flicks on campus. The "Morningtown Pizza Place" is run by good people. The "Id Book Store" is happening—it has all the underground newspapers.

A very heavy drug scene on the Avenue—speed freaks dying in front of your eyes, burns, cops, busts. Lots of dope in town of all kinds. Washington Green goes for $10 a lid. Street people and hip students smoke. Most don't.

The school is becoming politically active. There were a few black-demands incidents in 1968 and 1969 and many protests against ROTC (all three branches are on campus).

The Seattle Liberation Front was formed in 1970 to deal with city-wide issues. They had a rally in February, 1970, in front of the Federal Court House—trashing and 80 arrests. Eight participants were charged with conspiracy.

After Cambodia, there were mass meetings with 15,000 in attendance. The school was closed for one day and for one day after Jackson.

SURVIVAL:

Substantial art facilities.

Student health is understaffed and shoddy. Psychological service

is swamped. Draft counseling by AFS and The Resistance off
campus. Survival services in Seattle—check the underground paper,
the *Helix*.

The cafeteria has the longest conveyor belt in the world for
trays. The Avenue looks like Telegraph Avenue—street people,
Hare Krishnas, pushers who whisper acid, panhandlers.

Food co-op called the "Puget Sound Co-op Grocery"—it costs
$5 a month to be a member.

Women's Liberation is working on a day-care center.

ENVIRONMENT:

Mental—People are talking about real politics and the Movement. The Sierra Club is doing its bit for ecology.

Physical—Seattle is a really big city—the campus is on a penin-
sula across a channel from the downtown area—lots of smog.
Buildings are collegiate Gothic—the old quad with gargoyles on
many buildings. Lots of tree-shaded lawns and new construction.

People escape to go skiing at Mt. Baker or in the Cascades.
Basically a commuting school.

Western Washington State College
Bellingham, Washington

Give credit where credit is due: WWSC won't touch classified
or military research and doesn't have ROTC.

SERGEANT PEPPER SECTION:

8,142 students. Easy to get in—2.5 GPA or rank in the upper
one-half of your graduating high-school class. Out-of-staters need
SATs, too. 125 blacks enrolled.

ACADEMIC BULLSHIT:

Two interesting programs have been initiated: a minor program
in East Asian Studies and a Language program in Brazilian
Portuguese.

Education is a big department—40% of the students are in
teacher education.

Dr. Paul Roley of the History department ("Diplomatic History
of Soviet Russia") and Dr. John Hebal of the Political Science
department ("Poverty, Minorities and Government") are the two
most popular professors.

Pass/Fail is allowed; each department has a conference course
which has many possibilities for student-originated classes. The
Free U offers "Encounter," "New Math and Old" and "Indian Religion." An Ethnic Studies college has been started—it has its own
admission scholarships. Blacks do their own recruiting and are
aiming for 10% of the freshman class of 1971. Independent study
is allowed—some people get credit for working with the Lummi
Indians across the bay. Study abroad in London and Stockholm.

In 1968, Fairhaven, a cluster college, was begun. The structure is very loose and teachers do a lot of individual work with students. All the students live in the same dorm which is floor by floor coed. The school has 150 men and 180 women so far, out of a 600 capacity. Students take a major but are not required to take the general education courses. The faculty are not divided into departments and no grades are given; 27 units of independent study are allowed. Field trips are encouraged and one group went to Greece in 1970. People write a paper about their trip. There are no lecture classes and attendance is erratic. One class in basic physiology had some 7:30 A.M. expeditions to hospitals to see open-heart surgery. Another course is called "The Politics of Norman Mailer." In 1970 there were 800 applicants for 200 places—they look for creativity rather than grades.

BREAD:

$88 per quarter in-state, $157 out-of-state. Financial aid is tight but there are lots of campus jobs (the best one is security guard at $1.85 an hour).

Room and board for the dorms is $850 (2,820 live in the dorms). Hidden Valley Village is a trailer camp for girls on campus—there are 42 trailers (four girls in each). Room and board are $950. Many large houses are available nearby—rent for a four-bedroom house is $100–$150. Two miles away is farm land in most directions. (Beware the new groups of vigilante hicks.)

In South Bellingham, which looks like a decayed inner city, freaks took over an old bank and turned it into a coffee house called "Toad Hall." This is the type of place Ken Kesey would like to hang around when he was drunk.

Students can scrounge if they grow their own food on farms. Cars and bikes are the main form of transportation.

BROTHERS AND SISTERS:

Ratio cats : chicks—1 : 1.

The straights are in the majority, wearing clean dungarees, fashionable sideburns and meager beards. Most of the people are the outdoors type: heavy boots, ski jackets and minimal concern for style. Campus water-fights are a tradition—they occur about four times in the spring semester.

There is mediocre sex activity—lot of small town morality. Keggers cost a dollar for all you can drink and "Mama Sunday's" is an on-campus Saturday night spot with 25¢ admission for live entertainment. The "Tavern" is a jock hangout and "Kulshan Tavern" near "Toad Hall" is the hippest bar in town. People often go into Seattle or Vancouver to take in a flick or a band. Rugby is a big sport. But the biggest entertainment is the great outdoors—skiing, hiking and camping.

Most of the campus is just getting into politics. In the spring of 1968, the BSU took over a hall for ten demands—it ended amicably. An uproar was caused when jocks ripped down an NFL flag in front of an SDS recruiting table in 1969. Rallies followed.

Veterans for Peace are active (there are 650 vets on campus). Vigilante groups are starting in town. There have been bomb threats directed at the school. After Kent State, there was a large rally followed by a march to the freeway. Not much revolutionary thought. People smoke dope openly on campus all over the Pacific Northwest.

SURVIVAL:

The Art department is housed in two spacious buildings with lots of studio room for all the arts. Student health is shitty— the student government created a Sex Information office with birth control and abortion assistance. Draft counseling is in an office on the lower level of Viking Union. A food co-op and a Free Clinic are in the early stages of formation. The campus paper, *Western Front,* endorses the liberal-radical anti-war coalition. *Northwest Passage* is a good non-jargonistic underground paper.

ENVIRONMENT:

Mental—People are talking counter-culture. Huxley College, the institute for fresh water studies, is very big here.

Physical—Bellingham is a city of 38,000 on the northwest coast of Washington halfway between Seattle and Vancouver. There are total wilderness areas and excellent ski areas very close. The campus is on a hillside overlooking the main area of the town. Georgia Pacific pollutes the air and water. Lots of three–four-story red brick buildings. The Fairhaven dorms look like four-story ski lodges. The school has a ski cabin on Mt. Baker.

Whitman College
Walla Walla, Washington

An excellent small liberal arts college named after Marcus Whitman, a fighting missionary who got his from the Indians.

SERGEANT PEPPER SECTION:

1,100 students, many from out-of-state. 12 blacks. It used to be supported by the Congregational Church but is now independent. Admission is very selective. Most freshmen have a 3.4 average and 1,200 on their SATs.

ACADEMIC BULLSHIT:

Undergraduate only. The best departments are Music, English and History. The school emphasizes teaching, not publishing, in tenure appointments. There is a very high percentage of Ph.D.s on the faculty and the student : faculty ratio is 13 : 1.

The most popular courses are "Social Problems" with Dr. Bowker (he concentrates on drugs and deviant sexual behavior), "Black History" with Mr. Lang (the only black studies course at

Whitman) and "American Literature." Some Pass/Fail, lots of papers, lots of small discussion classes (45 is considered a big course) and no student-originated courses.

There are very good relationships between students and teachers—personal and familylike. The largest department has 12 faculty members so you certainly get to know the people in your department well. Students and faculty have to cling together in Walla Walla—no one else is on their intellectual plane. Independent study consists of noncredit internships with politicians. No study abroad per se but it's possible to get it through other schools.

BREAD:

$1,850 for two semesters. The school is extremely well endowed and guarantees everybody aid in some form so that they can get through college. About one-third are on aid (the other two-thirds are rich). Jobs are $1.60 an hour.

Dorms cost $900 for room and board. 90% of the students live in the dorms. Until 1970, chicks weren't even allowed in the cats' lounges. The girls' and boys' dorms are on opposite sides of campus. First-semester women have curfews. A new coed dorm is opening in 1971—it will have 72 students and be coed floor by floor. Some senior men and women live off campus—houses cost $40–$80. About 30 people live in the country on farms.

Most students have bicycles but all you need is your feet—everything is close by. Flicks and parties on campus are free.

BROTHERS AND SISTERS:

Ratio cats : chicks—about 1 : 1.

The school is changing from the stereotype of the wholesome upper-middle-class kid to the hip type. Moustaches, sideburns and slightly shaggy hair are common. Chicks are beginning to let it all hang out. Cats wear jeans and Sta-prest.

Entertainment is mostly parties or sports in the Sherwood Center. Six fraternities and six sororities exist but membership is dropping. They still dominate the campus scene (by default since the Greeks and athletics are the only structured diversions from school on a Walla Walla weekend).

The Universal Life Church, next to the Student Center, is on the order of a coffee house but can't be a coffee house because of zoning. Hips hang there. The "Green Lantern" is a tavern a few blocks away from school where everyone over 21 goes. Beer costs 25¢ for a schooner.

Sexual activity is restricted by the rules—lots of chicks live in sororities. 60% of the students belong to fraternities and sororities. Very few liberated women.

There's a little political activity and no ROTC on campus. In the spring of 1968, students blocked a roadway protesting the presence of military recruiters—pigs were called in and made two arrests. The demonstrators were victorious—now recruiters have to do all their recruiting in the basement of the administration building where hardly anyone notices them.

The Moratoriums were held, and after Kent State a few Whitman students went to D.C.

About 40% of the students are regular users of dope but they keep it quiet. There are lots of busts off-campus. Lids go for $15 and most dope is available in Seattle.

SURVIVAL:

The Art department has a staff of four and is very interested in the individual. The town has one shrink whom students say no one in his right mind would go to. No BC assistance—doctors who will help anyone who is not chaste are hard to find around here. Draft counseling is done by The Resistance on campus but those who need legal aid go to Seattle. *The Pioneer,* the school newspaper, is a drag. A few are into health foods.

ENVIRONMENT:

Mental—People are talking about going to graduate school and are just starting to talk about politics. The class of 1970 made a gift contributing to an endowed chair in Ecology—the school is getting a specialist in 1971. On Earth Day, students made a park out of a parking lot and put up geodesic domes.

Physical—Walla Walla (they like it so well they named it twice) is an extremely clean city in southeast Washington surrounded by farm areas. The campus is in a pretty residential district—it's beautiful.

Buildings are dignified, quaint brick structures. A mill creek runs through campus and feeds into a pond which has goldfish and ducks. The Harper Joy Theater looks like a gigantic barn with its gray wood face. The gym, Sherwood Center, looks like a cement pioneer fort—no windows. Many big old trees give the campus a cozy feeling.

Students escape to Seattle and Portland.

WEST VIRGINIA

Morris Harvey College
Charleston, West Virginia

SERGEANT PEPPER SECTION:

1,800 full-time students attend this private school. Eligibility requirements stipulate student must be in the top three-fourths of his graduation class and have a C average. Board scores are usually about 900 combined. Undergraduate only. Out-of-state students comprise about 50% of the student body.

ACADEMIC BULLSHIT:

There are several O.K. departments—nothing unusual. The English department is enjoyed and the Business Administration school is a short-cut to a good job in accounting (eccchh). Establishment type 1950s courses. Rev. William Albright of the Sociology department and Dr. Fred G. Holloway, an English professor, are two popular instructors.

Some Pass/Fail. No student-initiated courses and no Free U. Strictly a test-oriented system, not much interaction between students and professors and no Third World courses. Even a college policy that says, "No smoking in class." Zero so far.

BREAD:

Tuition is $675 yearly in-state and $1,275 out-of-state. The college itself has few loans and scholarships to offer although there is the usual financial aid office that gives you applications for loans you can't get. Very limited work-study program. Campus jobs are few and far between and pay $1.10 an hour. Average cost of a date for a guy is $5 but if you go to a private club (remember, it's the South) it's $15. Expensive clothes aren't necessary but you must have "at least one suit to impress Union Carbide at the proverbial interview." No used-book or record shop.

BROTHERS AND SISTERS:

Ratio cats : chicks—1 : 1.

Students run the gamut from fancy to frayed—conservative to lukewarm hip. Hip types do well to stay away from Charleston where they are sometimes hassled. Sexual activity is limited, virginity is still alive. Greeks are fairly important, basketball heroes are big. The college coffee tavern is the best place to meet others on campus; off campus it's the "Checkmate" and the "Malibu," both 3.2 beer bars.

Grass is used but not that available and superexpensive. Hash and mescaline are more popular and prevalent. The drug scene is active but underground. The best place to score is the slum area of town.

The most active campus group is the ecology group. People go to two large secluded parks in the area for relaxation.

The students aren't radicalized—with the exception of a couple. The biggest demonstration was a panty raid last year. 400 male students raided the female dorms for underwear. The pigs maced everyone. Next day 50 students were suspended so 100 students staged a sit-in overnight in front of the Student Union. It ended with only three students being expelled (for a panty raid? It's downright subversive.).

SURVIVAL:

No BC pills or abortion referral at student health—the nearest clinic is in Mississippi. No anti-draft type counseling either but it is offered by a group of conscientious citizens in Charleston. No pets on campus. The *Comet* is the campus paper—it's interesting. Occasionally an underground paper, *Going to Pot,* is published. No health-food stores in the area.

ENVIRONMENT:

Mental—People are becoming aware of what's happening at Morris Harvey but the evolution will take awhile—it's still pretty parochial. Students are reading *The Population Bomb* by Ehrlich.

Physical—The college is located in the mountainous heart of Appalachia. Trees and streams are plentiful; the college is on the Kanawha River (Little Mississippi). The water around the school is polluted by chemical factories. The air is also very polluted as this is the "chemical center of the world."

The architecture is modern middle-class; all buildings are functionally obsolescent and need to be renovated often.

The best escape is Kanawha State Forest which is over a romantic winding road eight miles away. Coonskin Park (some relationship to Daniel Boone) is a park used a lot by students also.

West Virginia University
Morgantown, West Virginia

Down under with the coal mines.

SERGEANT PEPPER SECTION:

15,000 students of which 3,000 are graduate students. Easy to get in. Anyone who graduates from a West Virginia high school with a C average is eligible; nonresidents need a B average and should be in the upper quarter of their graduating class. Transfers need a 2.0. 40% are out-of-state, mostly from Pennsylvania and Ohio. About 1% minority.

ACADEMIC BULLSHIT:

This school has several very good departments. The new $3.5 million Creative Arts Center has enabled the Drama department to get a great faculty. Both the undergraduate and graduate divisions are excellent although only a few courses are open to non-majors. The Forestry department is excellent and runs a summer camp. Cheat Forest is within an hour's drive of Morgantown—much of it is owned by the University. Commerce, in the Business department, is good as is public administration in the Political Science department. The Medical school is one of the best in the South—University Hospital (one mile from campus) is the best hospital in the state.

The two most popular professors are on opposite sides of the political coin. Dr. William S. Haymond, who was head of the Philosophy department until the Kent State/Cambodia demonstrations, is now only a professor. He's a brilliant dissenter. Dr. James B. Whisker of the Political Science department is a very popular YAF advisor.

Some Pass/Fail, no student-originated courses and no Free U. Pretty good communication between teachers and students except in the College of Commerce. Independent study in graduate divisions and no organized study abroad.

BREAD:

Residents pay $140 a semester, nonresidents pay $455. Loans and scholarships are quite available for residents. Work-study is available and there are lots of campus jobs—a favorite is that of security guard. You need good character references and the pay is $2–2.50 an hour for patrolling buildings.

Most students live in the dorms which cost about $1,600 a year for room and board. Greek housing costs about $100 per month and apartments run $150.

Most students have either cars or bikes—expensive threads aren't necessary.

BROTHERS AND SISTERS:

Ratio cats : chicks—1.5 : 1.

Students are somewhere between hip and straight—lukewarm hip. Dress is straight and casual, "fashion changes take a long time to cross the West Virginia Mountains here." Cats have just started wearing bells. A few longhairs. There's a very strong Greek community. Sororities are closing, but fraternities are gaining. The 3,000 Greeks control student government.

As to dating—they are still in the pinnings stage. The few freaks are liberated but most students are Andy Hardy types. Grass is pretty popular both on campus and in the local high schools. Fraternities deal and you can score on campus. But drugs aren't always available as threatened busts keep forcing them deeply underground. People dig drinking, dancing, smoking and rapping on dates.

Hangs include "The Mountainlair" in the Student Union (freaks dig the listening lounges and straights play the games), the "Castle" (beer and coke), "The Red Cellar" (a bar that's good for pickups) and "The Last Resort" (a coffee house with peanuts and folk music).

The most active political club is the YAFs but leftist sentiment finally surfaced with the Kent State fiasco. Students marched through the draft board and the ROTC department, occupied the main city intersection and trashed the Army ROTC building. The state police tried to disperse them with gas and riot gear. After finals, people left but student leaders started to organize in the fall, 1970. The local city jail is frequented by drunks and AWOLs. The county jail hasn't had a good escape in years and, it's rumored, sometimes forgets its occupants. The facility was built in the 1880s and looks it.

SURVIVAL:

Lots of people are into creative arts and the new center has excellent facilities. Student health service is good, both BC pills and contraceptives are dispensed. Draft counseling is given by local ministers on campus. The service is highly criticized by the local population of flag-waving rednecks. The *Daily Atheneum* is a liberal campus newspaper.

ENVIRONMENT:

Mental—People are just starting to talk about politics.

Physical—There's a short winter but the Easter snow of 1970 was eight inches high! The school is surrounded by forests and coal mines. The Cheat River Lake and Park are only a five-minute drive from campus. The area offers all kinds of water recreation. An 80-acre University-owned arboretum is adjacent to campus. Air pollution from coal dust.

Campus architecture ranges from traditional to pre-World War II economy. The suburban Evansdale campus includes a new $13 million coliseum.

WISCONSIN

Beloit College
Beloit, Wisconsin

A cool place, even though John Wayne went here.

SERGEANT PEPPER SECTION:

1,777 students of which 11 are grads. 61% of the freshmen are in the top fourth of their high-school class and have SATs of about 1,200. There is no minimum cut-off point for GPA, class rank or SAT scores. Transfers need a C. 88% out-of-state.

ACADEMIC BULLSHIT:

Students like the Philosophy, Anthropology and History departments here. There are no graduate departments—just a Master of Teaching program. The Beloit Plan allows one-third of the students to be away from the campus either on vacation or doing field work if they want to. If not, students can graduate in three years by attending all three terms.

Popular professors include Dr. Summers in the Sociology department and Chuck Seguin in the Math department.

Student-initiated courses are only in place of freshman and senior English. No Pass/Fail or Free U. If the student takes the initiative, there is a possibility of a good relationship between him and a professor. A couple of black study courses called "Special Problems." Study abroad in Germany, Costa Rica, France, England, Lebanon, Denmark, Greece, Turkey, the Philippines, Japan and South Korea.

BREAD:

Tuition at this private school is $2,900 a year. Aid is tight but available. Campus jobs range from $1.30–$1.75 an hour. Dorms cost $900 a year for room and board. Most women and half of the men live in them. The most expensive furnished two-bedroom apartment goes for $130 a month—apartments can usually be had for $80 a month.

Feet and bikes are the most popular modes of transportation. Costly threads aren't important.

BROTHERS AND SISTERS:

Ratio cats : chicks—1 : 1.

Students are casual and friendly. They come with short hair and grow it longer. They wear boots and bells in the winter ("it's important that you wear the same outfit three times a week so people can get to know you"). Freshman girls go down to the Salvation Army and stock up on flannel shirts, third-term chicks get 1940s dresses and don't shave.

Dating is hang loose. Because of the Beloit Plan, you may not know everyone in your class. The school is noted for its lack of cliques—there's a real sense of open community. Sex is free; if people dig each other they ball. Cohabiting isn't frequent because the beds are too small in the dorms. A few fraternities but they are dying. Entertainment consists of parties and flicks.

Most are into grass. 50% turn on every week. Lots of grass at $15 a lid and hash is around. Some people are into tripping with mescaline and acid. Little use of hard drugs. Score in Madison.

Six years ago one of the trustees described the school as a "hot-bed of apathy." Students are into a commune cultural trip and are not that interested in politics. Most are generally leftist and hate the military-industrial complex. The most active club is the Conservation Club. People are very concerned about ecology.

In 1967, silent vigils were held against the Dow recruiters and when (in the middle of the demonstration) it was discovered that a Beloit grad invented the main ingredient of napalm, the students became very silent.

In February, 1969, blacks presented the usual demands. 100 students sat in at the Union.

In the fall of 1969, students held a birthday party for a Marine recruiter. They gave him a giant cake and decorated his car with balloons. They also staged a naval battle for him and threw water balloons at each other. The recruiter split early.

About 800 students supported the two-day strike. 450 marched into downtown Beloit and tried to get a dialog going with the town. After Kent, President Upton sent a letter to Nixon about the war, which blew many a campus mind. Upton was a conscientious objector in World War II, served as a medic and was Nixon's campaign chairman in Wisconsin in 1968. A lot of students may not like his philosophy but they admire Upton for his consistency and lack of hypocrisy—he isn't a wishy-washy liberal who screws students by trying to please everyone. He's out front and respected for this attitude.

The strike established a draft counseling service and a food co-op.

The school just got campus cops in the spring of 1970 when the school hired a security agency from Madison.

Students really dig the place.

SURVIVAL:

Very possible.

A bad infirmary—they diagnose everything by intuition. No BC pills. A Planned Parenthood in Waukegan nearby. Acid rescue open 24 hours a day.

The Beloit Anti-draft Union is run by two brothers who run the local underground paper. John Zurich, who lives in Whitney Hall, is also an excellent counselor.

The Roundtable is a fairly interesting campus paper but the *Dreadnaught* (underground) is much better.

The local health-food store is "The Scratching Chicken."

ENVIRONMENT:

Mental—People talk a lot about ecology.

Physical—"Winter is C-O-L-D, spring is short but sweet." Rain brings mud and great mud fights. Fairbanks Morse and the Beloit Corporation are the main polluters. The Rock River died of pollution.

The school was built at different times and the architecture is varied. The Field House is an airplane hangar that the school bought and brought in.

Marquette University
Milwaukee, Wisconsin

A quote from the 1970 yearbook, *Flashback* (Vol. 56, p. 22):

> Marquette housing is centered around the dormitories where students are forced to live until they are 21 or can prove they have ulcers. The women are housed in renovated hotels in most cases. Some were never renovated. The men are sheltered in 2 impressive, color-televisioned and marble-slabbed structures. Happiness is a warm apartment.

SERGEANT PEPPER SECTION:

11,721 students, of which 2,150 are grads. For entering freshmen there is no cut-off for SATs or high-school GPAs. The most important thing is your high-school GPA, though. Average SATs are 1,100. Transfers need a 2.3 after one year. 60% are out-of-state.

ACADEMIC BULLSHIT:

This is a Catholic school run by the Jesuits but anyone can apply. Catholics must take 12 hours of theology.

Students like all the pre-professional programs—Law, Dental and Medical. The departments of Engineering, Chemistry, Speech and Biology (one of the top five in the country) are all excellent. Students hate the English department.

The most popular professors are Dr. James Barrett in Biology and Albion Ross in Journalism.

Pass/Fail is available, especially for upper-division students. Some student-initiated courses and a faltering Free U. Little student-professor interaction. No Black Studies department but a few courses. Lots of tests and papers. Extensive independent study: study abroad all over.

BREAD:

Tuition is $1,660 a year. Aid is very tight but anyone who really needs it can probably get some aid. Jobs are tight and pay about $1.60 an hour. Work-study is available.

About half the chicks and 20% of the cats live in the dorms which cost $1,050 a year for room and board. Apartments are expensive and run $150 a month for a one-bedroom.

Cars are the most popular form of transportation here. Expensive threads are only happening in the sororities.

BROTHERS AND SISTERS:

Ratio cats : chicks—2 : 1.

Most students here are straight, few freaks. There is supposed to be a dress code but no one pays any attention to it. All the chicks wear bras, although many wear jeans. Social life is very hang loose, and most events are planned by Greeks. Dates are parties and flicks, and lots of people split to Chicago. A lot of the cats go down to the "Barn" (a bar) and try to score. Most chicks still want to be a virgin when they get married and most guys want a virgin for a wife. Fraternities are still pretty big and on the rise.

Local straight hangs are "The Grill," "The Ardmore" (bar), the "Avalanche" (bar the straights go to after being thrown out of the "Ardmore" for having a fake I.D.), and the "Coffeehouse." The few freaks go to "The Rhubarb"—a left-wing book store.

Dorm people are really into grass, they turn on every day, put a towel under their door and then spray with Right Guard. Grass goes for $20 an ounce and dexadrine is big around exam times. The commuters are the straight people. Score at UW at Milwaukee. The Marquette students call the people of Milwaukee "the Cretins." If you're a freak, keep out of Milwaukee's south side. The Poles live there and dislike freaks immensely. Walking there is "unsafe at any speed."

There's a very wide spread politically—a majority of the students are apathetic. Many feel the school is repressive. The YAF is big in the Law school and the John Birch Society is making a move to recruit on campus. The RSU is the umbrella group for the concerned radicals on campus.

The political history of the school started in 1968 when all the blacks on the basketball team quit the team and charged racism.

In the spring of 1969, about 70 students held an anti-ROTC sit-in at the Joan of Arc Chapel—they were busted. The Moratoriums drew about 2,000.

Violence erupted with the 1970 student strike. The Tac Squad busted people brutally when a proposed mill-in at the Marquette Interchange was being planned. There were bomb scares in the dorms and the dorm windows were trashed. The campus closed May 11 and students got certain grade options.

The campus pigs are O.K. Their main duty is to protect Marquette from outsiders, and they don't have guns. The Milwaukee pigs are vicious, illiterate monsters. They handle demonstrators by beating them.

SURVIVAL:

Student health is terrible and you have to wait years to get service. They leave the thermometer in your mouth for 20 minutes.

The "Interbang Bookstore" is run by Yippies and they find a place for you to crash. There's a food co-op on E. Kane. The Underground Switchboard is run by the Mental Health Association —it handles everything and is excellent.

Basketball is big—they have a 12,000 seat arena that is always sold out.

The Marquette Tribune is middle-of-the-road. The underground papers, *The Kaleidoscope* and *The Pitch*, are popular and interesting. There are a number of health-food stores on Michigan between 1st and 2nd Streets.

ENVIRONMENT:

Mental—People don't read much.

Physical—The climate varies. Fall is comfortable, winter is snowy, spring comes in early March and the summers are superhumid. You don't hear much about Milwaukee's air pollution. They seem to have gotten a head start on trying to solve it about seven years ago. The main polluters are Red Star Yeast, the brewers and Ambrosia Chocolate (which smells bad enough to make you throw up). The Milwaukee River is stagnant and has a lot of dead fish.

The campus is in the city and looks like any other city street. The School of Journalism uses an old apartment house and the baths still work.

Kids go to the bars to escape and are mostly commuters.

Wisconsin State University at Oshkosh

Oshkosh, Wisconsin

A national magazine called this place "a high school with ashtrays." We agree.

SERGEANT PEPPER SECTION:

9,100 students, almost everyone gets in. A Wisconsin resident should be in the upper 75% of his class and take the ACTs. If he's in the bottom quarter and gets an ACT score of 17 or above, he will be admitted on probation. A nonresident must be in the upper 40% of his class and take the ACT or be in the upper 75% but under the top 40% and get an 18 or above on the ACT. Transfers need about a 2.0. 80% out-of-state students.

ACADEMIC BULLSHIT:

"There is no such thing as a good undergraduate department here—they have mediocre and bad departments and that's about it." And the worst of the bad are Sociology and English. Many students are in Education—they hate it. The only two good departments are Art and Economics. Business on the graduate level is O.K.

The professors are terrible. Many discriminate against freaks and a lot of them went out of their way to give tests on the days of the 1970 student strike. All the good professors left but good guys J. C. Smith and Harry Phillips in the Sociology department may still be there.

No student-initiated courses and no Pass/Fail. The Free U was canceled due to lack of interest. The relationship between students and professors is terrible, no meaningful dialog at all. "The Student as Nigger." No Black Studies department and no independent study on the undergraduate level. Some study abroad.

There are no dress codes although some Speech teachers have told their students to either cut their hair or take an F.

BREAD:

Tuition in-state is $203 a semester, out-of-state is $668. Some packaged aid is available. The food service hires a lot of students at $1.50 an hour.

Half the students live in the dorms which cost $500 a semester for room and board. Apartments go for about $50 .. person when four share. Threads are cheap and people walk or hitch.

BROTHERS AND SISTERS:

Ratio cats : chicks—1 : 1.

Clothes are totally middle-class here, right out of Sears. Cats wear tight, straight, colored stretch levis. Chicks wear jeans or dresses, makeup and nylons. They are really into the girdle and stocking thing and wigs.

Dating consists of going to bars. In relationships the "game" is big. They have conventional dating habits, tit grabbing and ass grabbing. The Greeks are into screwing and have "passion pits" in the dorms where people try to get the most out of the last five minutes. There are some freaks who dig smoking and rapping.

Oshkosh used to be a big beer-freak center of the country like Madison. When Madison switched to dope, Oshkosh did too. About 75% have smoked and 25% are grass users. They had 18 busts in 1970 and there are two federal narcs in town. Lots of downer freaks too. Acid is falling off.

Fraternities still live and breathe and they are dopers.

Hangs include the snack bar in the Student Union. Freaks are near the jukebox, Greeks are in the middle and the scholars (complete with briefcases) are near the door. The faculty sits in the alcove section.

Freaks go to "Professors 3," a teen-age bar. Straight bars include "The B&B," "Andy's Library" and "End Zone."

Kids are, for the most part, politically apathetic and middle-of-the-road. All they get excited over is beer. Student Mobe is the only organization that has done anything although the YDs did build the Moratoriums and provide literature on the California grape boycott. YAFs red bait any anti-war people and give freaks' names to the pigs.

1966 was the first year of demonstrations—these were against the Wisconsin legislature raising the drinking age.

In 1968, blacks trashed Dempsey Hall in reaction to the fact that none of the demands they had presented a year before had been acted upon. Pigs came with rent-a-trucks and carted off 104 people (94 of whom were blacks). People came in to demonstrate from all over and 3,000 attended a rally. School was finally called off six days before Thanksgiving. Some students went to Madison for a Board of Regents meeting—they were successful and got an Afro-American Cultural Center and a couple of black professors. 104 people were expelled (again, 94 of whom were black). The Moratoriums were composed mainly of the freaks. There was a teach-in in March, 1970, during Anti-Draft Week.

Action became a little heavy during the Kent crisis. Students tore up Algoma Boulevard with picks and shovels (it's a safety hazard as it runs through campus). Pigs came in and the street was repaved. On May 6, a rally attracted 3,000.

If busted, freaks should watch out for Judge Sitter.

SURVIVAL:

Student health is terrible. There was a rise in the incidence of clap under the guise of "bladder infections" in 1970. BC pills only to those 21 or older. Few prescriptions. The only good part is the psychiatric counseling department.

Acid Rescue is open 24 hours.

Go to Madison (the "Miffland Street Community Co-op") for draft counseling.

It's a big thing to have a dog for status.

ENVIRONMENT:

Mental—Freaks are reading *Do It!*

Physical—It's either really cold or really hot and always humid. Paper mills cause air pollution and the Fox River has so much mercury and phosphorus in it that you can't fish.

All the buildings are boring—square or rectangular. Three city streets run through campus.

Escapes include Madison, High Cliff State Park and The Sand Pits.

University of Wisconsin
Madison, Wisconsin

The University of Wisconsin is one of the original radical thinking schools. Back in 1963 they were already holding candlelight vigils in protest against the Vietnam War when no one else had heard of it. It's the center of the midwestern underground and very heavy into political activity with the real revolutionary spirit. Demonstrations and marches daily and almost everyone is very hip. It's also the fourth biggest school in the nation with lots of variety in courses and life styles. Try to catch it for at least a year.

SERGEANT PEPPER SECTION:

35,000 students, 85% from the North Central states. In-states need to be in approximately the top 75% of their class and have SAT scores of about 1,200. Out-of-states should be in the top two-fifths of their class.

ACADEMIC BULLSHIT:

Wisconsin has a lot of really relevant courses and many radical professors. History is a good department and has a really strong student potential in the form of the History Student Association which is always organizing. "Black History" (Uya), "European Cultural History" (Mosse) and "History of East Asian Civilization since 1650." Anthropology and Sociology are good departments. "Buddhist Social Institutions" with Professor Miller has very good material. Only Quechua course in North America at Anthro department.

Many good graduate departments—History and Sociology are outstanding and have organized militant students. The most interesting department is the Educational Policy Studies. Lots of experimental courses focused on new ed policies (if you dig that stuff).

Popular professors include Edward Friedman who teaches the politics of the revolution and Ugo Camerini and Robert March who teach physics for nonmajors including such things as "Physics for Poets" and the "Physics of Color and Sound." Grades are still prevalent and only a limited Pass/Fail program. Very few student-initiated courses—faculty obviously uptight. "Progress is slow and the future is black for student-initiated classes."

There's a Free U (no credit) with courses like "The Cultural Revolution in China," "Socialist Economic Theory," which are thick to funky crafts and astrology.

Teaching assistants do 60% of the teaching and there is a good relationship between them and the students. Faculty members are distant and formal. A Black Studies department is being formed—some black courses are offered—history and music.

There's a little independent study, study abroad in France, Germany and India.

BREAD:

It costs $225 a semester for residents and $863 for out-of-state. The average two-bedroom apartment near campus runs about $150, efficiencies are $85–$100. State dorms are about $1,000 room and board per semester. Expensive private dorms with luxurious accommodations are available for those desirous of upper-class accommodations. In the Williamson Street area old three-bedroom houses can be rented for as little as $100 plus heat. There are co-ops for about $50 a space. Loans and scholarships are available. A lot of food service jobs around for $1.70 an hour. Manual labor for $2.00 an hour. Used clothes from the Rescue Mission or St. Vincent de Paul are the rule. Cheap entertainment is the rule. Lots of walking, bikes and motorcycles. "Paul's Used Book Store" is good.

BROTHERS AND SISTERS:

Ratio cats : chicks—3 : 2.

Heavy hip types mostly. The Miffland Street Tribe (radicals) are known for long hair, blue jeans, black leather jackets, flannel shirts, buckskin and fringe shirts and work shoes. The Langdon Street Greeks have neat moustaches and long sideburns. Girls still bleach their hair. People are fashionable and clean looking. Chicks also wear expensive boutique type clothes. Then there are the engineers—they suck. White socks, Sta-prest and short hair.

Most chicks are liberated and rarely suffer from the virginity crisis. "VD is commonplace here." "Virgins rarely last past the freshman year." Dating is very casual and living together is routine.

The best place to hang is in the Union. It has workshops, darkrooms, a real pool hall complete with hustlers, a music lounge, a reading lounge, a TV lounge, movies, card rooms, the Union Theater and the Union Gallery. Best of all is the "Rathskellar Cafeteria and Terrace." Local freaks gather at the "Cavernous Rat" to rap, drink delicious Union coffee and pick up on the latest revolutionary developments.

Straights hang out at the library and at "Rennebohm's Drug Store."

Constantly growing nucleus of revolutionaries, due to the continuing radicalization of the campus. The turning point in the radicalization of the Madison campus was reached when riot police were called in on October 18, 1967. A sit-in was being conducted where the Dow Chemical Company was interviewing. The police were so brutal that even people who were unsympathetic to the demonstration fought them. A large riot ensued, followed by a one-week strike by students opposed to the use of outside police on campus. Since Dow, actions have escalated, and the National Guard has been called twice. In the spring of 69 there were two big confrontations. The first was over the issue of whether or not UW should have a Black Student department. The Black Students' Union had been trying for months to get approval, but there was too much opposition from conservative faculty, the administration and the State Board of Regents. A strike was called by the BSU. The Regents got Governor Knowles to call up the Guard to keep the U open. The strike was supported by a majority of students for two weeks. As a result, some of the bureaucracy was speeded up and a Black Studies department was finally approved.

The other big event took place off campus in the Miffland-Bassett Street area, where large numbers of students live in run-down old houses. A co-op grocery has been established, and is a focal point for activity in the area. Wisconsin struck against Nixon's decision to enter Cambodia. Massive anti-war rallies continue. Women's Liberation is very active as is the Ecology Students Association.

Lids are $10–$20 and you can score most anywhere. The underground paper, *Kaleidoscope,* prints closing prices on the Madison Dope Exchange. Smack and speed are turning up a lot these days. Madison detectives think that Madison is a major distribution center.

The Tenant Union is organizing as is the Welfare Rights Association.

SURVIVAL:

Draft counseling is available at the University Center and the St. Francis Episcopal Church. The counseling is done by the American Friends Service. There is a lot of CO guidance and Canadian immigration information. The best draft advice is given by the draft-dodger students—there are many experts here.

BC pills obtained from private doctors without much trouble. Women's Liberation helps with abortion referrals. There is a suicide prevention center with a staff of professionals operated by the Dane County Mental Health Center. There is an acid number to call if you are bum tripped.

There is the "Madison Health Food Store" and the "Whole Earth Co-op Store" for natural foods.

The campus newspaper is the *Daily Cardinal,* which the conservative Regents think is sponsored by Mao. It's a very good paper. The underground paper is the *Madison Kaleidescope*—it performs a community service by printing news of bombings, strife and big busts in other parts of the country. Also printed are names of narcs and informers.

Student health is overcrowded and inefficient.

ENVIRONMENT:

Mental—Read the "Whole Earth" catalog and the *New Left Reader* to prepare.

Physical—The main campus has been blighted by overexpansion. Cheap functional concrete and glass structures continue to encroach on the remaining open spaces. The winter is gloomy and cold. The summer is hot and humid. Spring is sanity.

The original campus buildings are late 19th century midwestern brownstone. They have character. The newer buildings are ugly—especially Van Vleck. When Van Vleck was being built a member of the Classics faculty organized the Penelope Club with the goal of undoing each night what the workmen erected. This proved impractical so they began just giving the building a symbolic kick when they passed.

The best escape is a two-mile walk along lovely Lake Mendota (which suffers from pollution sickness and is taken over each year by slime) and then out on Picnic Point. Sailboats and canoes are available at the lake for water activities.

WYOMING

University of Wyoming
Laramie, Wyoming

This is Wyoming's only college—take it or leave it!

SERGEANT PEPPER SECTION:

8,419 students of which 1,270 are grads. Entering freshmen in-state just need to graduate from a Wyoming high school—out-of-state need a C average in high school and must take the ACTs. Transfers need a C. 30% are out-of-state. 75 blacks, 65 Chicanos, 16 Indians.

ACADEMIC BULLSHIT:

Students like the departments of Agriculture, Forestry (offers a good Ecology program) and Commerce and Industry best. About one-fourth of the students are in Education. In 1970, there were a lot of groovy professors but many resigned because of the school's attitude after Kent State.

Favorite professors still there are Dr. Richard Howey (Philosophy), Adrian Howey (American Literature) and Dr. Cramer (Economics—"one of the heavier people here").

There are some student-initiated courses, no Free U. Good interaction between professors and students only in the Humanities department. Even though the school is small, it is heaped in academia—lots of exams and papers. Independent study in the Humanities department and three black studies courses offered for no credit in the evening.

BREAD:

Tuition in-state is $195.25 a semester, out-of-state it is $525.25. Lots of Pharmacy and Nursing loans and scholarships but other aid is tight. Banks in Casper are better than those in Laramie for loans. Some campus jobs at $1.50 an hour.

About half the students live in dormitories, which cost $900 for room and board a year. Apartments are $115 and up for a one-bedroom place. People rent out basements and shacks for from $60–$80 a month.

Most have cars—only Greek chicks have costly threads.

BROTHERS AND SISTERS:

Ratio cats : chicks—2 : 1.

About 20% of the kids here are freaks. Anyone who has long hair is a freak and deserves a purple heart and a medal of honor—it's dangerous to be a freak here because of local vicious rednecks. Freaks wear bells, beads and loose fitting Indian shirts. Straight chicks wear "trend-setter clothes" and have such tightly plated chests that you wouldn't get to them with a hacksaw. Cowboys (who have never turned on) have a basic odor of the land on them. Straights wear Hush Puppies and carry two-toned briefcases (black and brown). Their hair is longer than flattops (because they hate the jocks) and shorter than mod (because they hate the longhairs). Jocks wear flattops and lettermen jackets and an athletic stupid grin.

Dating is immature and shallow among the straights. If you have the ability to talk you may culture shock a chick. Chicks break down into two categories—those who dig balling longhairs and those who fuck for status (a football player or a student government man at least treasurer or above). The only action is for freaks, jocks and upper-echelon Greeks.

This is one of the biggest drinking campuses around—drinking and going to big games is the entertainment. On an average date, the average guy (who has difficulty talking and getting some action) takes the following mode of action in trying to get laid: he tries to discuss ranching, irrigation and strip farming; the chick tells him how she breaks in horses; then the cat tries to get the conversation around to "Did you ever see two horses do it?" and then tries to turn the conversation around from horses to humans to him and her. Good luck.

Local hangs include "The Campus Shop" for freaks (not on campus, of course) and the Union for cowboys.

Grass is big in the Greek system—about 65% of the campus has turned on and 35% of the students are hard-core grass users. Lots of acid and mescaline—not much MDA. Score in Laramie—lots of paranoia, ranchers jump you.

Most people are in the position of suspended animation politically. Only about 20% of the campus are active—half leftists and half rightist cowboy. YRs and YDs are very active. The furthest left group is Student Government in Exile.

Political action with the 1969 Moratoriums—about 600 participated. In November, 1969, there was the "Black 14 Incident." Fourteen black football players wanted to stage a protest at a game with BYU about Brigham Young University's treatment of blacks (i.e., as soon as BYU finished a home game with a team with black players, they'd turn on their sprinklers on the field after the "niggers" were on it). The 14 blacks wanted to discuss this with their coach (who is more important than the governor of Wyoming because if the team doesn't make it the whole fucking state goes into fits of depression). He threw them off the team and they lost their athletic scholarships. The governor came down and tried to talk to the coach but nothing was worked out.

Ranchers came in and shot into the windows of black athletes' rooms. A national ACLU lawyer was brought in but nothing ever happened.

Students tried to lower the flag in memory of the Kent State students but the administration refused. A cowboy contingent guarded the flag; the highway patrol came armed. That night, students raised their own flag and a black Kent State flag at half mast. The highway patrol returned (they looked like a vigilante group and had toothpicks hanging out of their mouths) and said they had orders from the governor to take it down. Hassles ensued, the president went into hiding and the pigs finally pulled off campus. Many professors resigned after this.

Cowboys walk around campus at night and kick the shit out of any longhairs they find. Freaks should stay out of western bars in downtown Laramie and travel in pairs.

SURVIVAL:

The student health clinic is like a meat market. They have misdiagnosed recurring cases of malaria of Vietnam vets. No BC pills. No survival services. Planned Parenthood in Denver—140 miles away. Some people in the Humanities department do draft counseling.

Students are absolutely nuts about sports ("women clutch their babies and cry at touchdowns").

The Branding Iron, the school paper, is an apathetic organ. An underground paper called *The Free Lunch* is a cultural/political paper.

ENVIRONMENT:

Mental—Many disturbed.

Physical—The climate is bad—white from October to June—"it's so bad you have to breathe through your mouth because your nostrils freeze. In the summer mosquitoes make rocket runs on your body." Plenty of air pollution from the Monolith Cement Plant. The Laramie River is totally polluted.

Architecture is western-modern—fairly nice. The buildings around the quad (Prexy's Pasture) sort of look like a Pueblo village. The football stadium is new and was built instead of a new Fine Arts building. The Ag people keep up the campus.

Escapes include "Happy Jack," a recreation area, and the mountains.

More SIGNET Books for Your Reference Shelf

THE NEW AMERICAN LIBRARY, INC.,
P.O. Box 999, Bergenfield, New Jersey 07621

Other SIGNET Books You'll Want to Read